THE WHOLE SPY CATALOG

-lee lapin

Special thanks to:

Andersen Media
Brenda Crudon
"John Smith"
Peter Laufer
Mike Russell
Scott French
Bill Underwood
and, as always, a host of people who don't want to see their name here…

Publisher's Cataloging in Publication

Lapin, Lee.
    The whole spy catalog / Lee Lapin. - San Mateo, CA:
Intelligence Inc., c1995.
    p. cm.
    Includes bibliographical references and index.
    ISBN: 1-880231-10-7

    1. Private investigators--United States--Equipment and supplies
--Handbooks, manuals, etc. 2. Espionage--Equipment and supplies--
Handbooks, manuals, etc. 3. Research--Equipment and supplies--
Handbooks, manuals, etc. I. Title.

HV8093.L37 1995   363.2'89
                             QBI95-224

The Whole Spy Catalog
Copyright 1995 Lee Lapin

Additional copies of this book available from:
Intelligence Incorporated
2228 S. El Camino Real
San Mateo, CA 94403

ISBN 1-880231-10-7

CONTENTS

FOUR DAYS IN AUGUST

On August 14, the 6 citizens of Little Barstow, California, Death Valley's smallest, and traditionally, hottest town, awoke to the dreaded sound of Incoming.

Incoming Scirocco; the devil wind that always blows hot and always blows dry. As they prepared to open the town's only remaining business, a combination gas station and AM/PM Mini-Mart, left in place only to service the few tourists brave enough to take this alternate route to the Las Vegas gambling dens, or lost, they noticed something.

And it was not good.

The normally orange-hot horizon was gone; completely blotted out by what appeared to be a tidal wave of dust. As luck would have it, the only radio in town had broken two days before so they had no way of knowing that the century's worst dust storm was online and heading directly for Little Barstow.

A half an hour later, after boarding up the Mini-Mart windows, the 6 terrified residents huddled together, not for warmth but for security, the screaming 110 decibel wind hurtling pellets of sand against their world at what seemed to be barely subsonic speeds.

In an eye blink, 12-foot high sand dunes had formed on the tarmac, completely covering the two gas pumps. The building's doors were being relentlessly sealed by an angry Mother Nature.

A hellish 6 hours later the screaming faded and citizens of Little Barstow begin to dig themselves out, only to emerge into what appeared to be a post-nuclear landscape.

Madaline Murray O'Hare, the town's elderly post-mistress was the first to notice the wreckage of the two yellow school buses. Their roof lights were barely visible under the sand that buried what was left of California state route 42.

Fearing the worst, the residents dug frantically at the piles of sand with anything they could find. Shovels, tin cups, even hubcaps were employed to uncover the buses. Everyone was fearful they would find dead children stacked like cord wood.

Instead, the rescuers found an amazing mixture of very live bodies.

Impacted by the zero visibility wreck, the occupants of the two vehicles were now one group. Clutching each other for reassurance, covered with fine white grit, some weeping uncontrollably, the two very diverse groups were fast on the way to becoming a single unit.

Bus 184, containing a tour group of research librarians, on their way to Las Vegas for the annual Searching Online Conference had just driven themselves into librarian legend.

Days later, each librarian would be interviewed by the media, make the cover of Life magazine and sell her story to the Fox network for a mini-series.

On the other hand, the occupants of county school bus #63 would never make the papers, the TV news people were not allowed interviews and all speculation was neither confirmed nor denied.

Bus #63 contained 34 CIA agents heading towards a remote desert just outside of Vegas to take part in an exercise designed to hone the skills necessary to allow them to pass as indigenous Kurds.

For the next four days, Little Barstow had no electricity, no water, no air conditioning, little food (except for 6 cases of Ding Dongs that had been forgotten in a back closet and a few warm cokes – The Classic version) and was completely forgotten by the world because, unknown to them, a 6.7 earthquake had just leveled a major portion of Los Angeles tying up all available rescue efforts.

It would be days before a registration official at the Online conference would begin to raise questions about the massive no-shows.

Over the next 96 hours the librarians and the agents were completely dependent on one another's skills, not only for survival, but for morale and entertainment, such as it was.

Suspecting each day could well be their last, everyone rationed the Hostess snacks and extended the rusty water in the two toilet tanks by mixing it with a touch of warm Coke.

As so often happens in life threatening situations, The Stockholm syndrome set in – traditional suspicions were set aside, politics were forgotten and, in between the occasional liaison, each group began swapping stories and comparing methodologies.

A new, top secret, method of research (MOR) was spawned from these humble beginnings.

This book is the unedited result of those four days of infamy.

READ THIS OR I'LL COME LOOKING FOR YOU

So what the hell is THE WHOLE SPY CATALOG? Choosing the name of this book was by far the most difficult part of putting it together. I realize the term "spy" conjures up a certain image that, although it fits some sections of this sterling publication, does not fit others.

At least in the conventional sense.

My first choice would have been THE WHOLE INTELLIGENCE CATALOG, but the word intelligence is somewhat ambiguous (could it be a how-to-increase-your-IQ book for the upwardly mobile?) and, frankly, THE WHOLE SPY CATALOG has a sexier ring to it.

So, first and foremost let's define our terms – this is a book about acquiring intelligence (as defined by Dr. Adda Bozeman in Strategic Intelligence and Statecraft) "stands for the human being's inborn capacity to come to terms with life by engaging in thought, and acquiring, developing and investing knowledge." It's my personal opinion, for whatever that's worth, that one can never have too much knowledge.

But see, it's also a book about having fun – listening in on the cellular telephone call from the guy in the Mercedes next to you who is calling his wife to explain why he's going to be late to dinner and then calling his mistress to set up the evening's entertainment...

It's how to find your old college lover and see what really happened to his dream of curing world hunger, or running down the guy who owes you $28,000 from that stock scam, or checking if your new fianceé really does own those companies he claims to be CEO of.

It's about hiring a real life KGB agent to tell you what your company's competitor is doing, renting a model airplane with a built-in video camera to fly over the new neighbor's compound (you know, the one who's just moved in with the 28 wives, guns and armored vehicles) to see what's really going on...

Ms. Bozeman goes on to define strategic intelligence as that ,"which is a component of statecraft that centers on the needs of one politically unified community to have reliable information, knowledge, or 'intelligence' about other societies in its environment."

Well, Virginia, I hate to be the bearer of bad news, but we are all in one or more "politically unified groups," be they families, companies, clubs, organizations or countries. And, as we will soon see, there are amazing in-place resources to help you in your quest for either tactical or strategic intelligence.

THE WHOLE SPY CATALOG is also about understanding what the hell is happening to our political world as we know it. Where have all the spies gone?

We'll talk to CIA agents, KGB agents, out of work (and bitter), STASSI agents, look at how France and Japan are stealing our companies' secrets, and how you, I mean *you* personally, can buy a tank, locate anyone who subscribes to a magazine, find who owns the company that just bilked you out of your life savings, protect your private information, hire a satellite to take photos of any part of the earth you want a picture of, get on forums and bulletin boards that let you talk with some of the heaviest hitters in the info and/or spy biz, and have some fun.

Yeah, this book is going to break some rules: one of my favorite reviews (from an earlier book) was from, I believe, *Library Journal*. The nice, staid, realistic, librarian said, "great information, but the writer's a real smart ass."

Right ON.

I'll provide esoteric, jagged pieces that seem to fit no immediately discernible jigsaw puzzle that can suddenly and unexpectedly fall into place during those embarrassing lulls at the company Christmas party, or maybe win you $25,000 on Jeopardy.

I accept this award for my family, my wife who never gave up on me and most of all, for Lee Lapin who had the...

Well, you get the idea.

As our world changes, information, intelligence, knowledge, or at least the ability to procure it becomes more and more important. **Intelligence is the hard currency** of the decade. Although admittedly presumptuous, I would like to think of this book as the WHOLE EARTH CATALOG for the 90's.

Not only has the amount of available information increased logarithmically, access methods have exploded. Everything from on-line database searching to electronic surveillance can be, and is, used to collect and correlate intelligence in order to give people advantages in situations ranging from getting a job promotion to checking whether the spouse is making waves in someone else's waterbed.

If you don't know what is out there and how it is stored you will soon find yourself watching daytime television and responding to those ads where little old ladies say, "Functionally illiterate? Can't access databases? Trouble finding the right CD-ROM? Don't know what competitor intelligence is? Dial 1-800-555-1212 for a list of programs offered by your local library that will help bring you into the 20th century and get a better job."

Or you're going to be responding to the ones that promise a "high paying career in bartending", 'cause there just ain't going to be much left that doesn't depend on information procurement in one form or another.

Oddly enough, spies (real spies) and librarians now share many common collecting and retrieval methods. Knowledge acquisition has become dependent on planning and research skills instead of shady deals done in the smoke filled back rooms of Casbahs.

So did Gary Powers get shot down in vain?

No. But the next prisoner exchange between one of the final communist holdout regimes and us will be that of two research librarians. Not U-2 pilots. (Although, damn, we do have a new spy plane that is just amazing, I'll show you how to listen to conversations between it and the tower.)

THE WHOLE SPY CATALOG is designed to be a hands-on look at how skilled information collectors operate and *how you can do the same things*.

Let's recap here: need to find sugar production in Tahiti, your old college girlfriend (or boyfriend, let's keep this evenhanded), listen to anyone's wireless or cellular phone calls, (or protect yours) develop a complete dossier on your business competitor, hire an ex-CIA or still employed KGB agent to do it for you, get the latest data on where it's safe to travel, see what the CIA (or KGB) thinks about other countries, get a spy plane photo of an industrial complex, hire a satellite to photograph any part of the world, watch the best spy films, visit real CIA (and KGB) hangouts, see over your neighbor's fence, track down long-lost relatives or get the real info on your new fianceé who seems just a bit too good to be true, find any book, hire a convicted computer hacker to safeguard your business, get the inside info on any potential investment, protect your computer data, crack computer codes, schmooze with research librarians, communicate with experts on any subject, anywhere in the world on a real-time basis, find a 5-year-old newspaper article, join an "electronic club" hosted by the world's best private detectives, see what the real spies are doing to protect their jobs in The New World Order, buy Russian military equipment, attend a conference of surveillance experts, disappear, reappear, or just have fun reading about this stuff.

Hell, I'll even throw in books that rate the best spy films, TV shows, actors, smuggler's pubs, show where to get kits that teach your kids to create secret codes to write their friends or lift fingerprints just like the FBI does.

Then we'll talk to some of the top spies in the world (on both sides of the fence) about what they did, how they did it, and what they are going to do next.

Okay, you get the idea. I don't want to oversell it...

Now, I know some readers, and God knows, some reviewers are going to object to the portions herein that show how personal privacy is violated, but this information does exist and you better know about it.

You gotta admit, restricting Xerox machine access to high party officials didn't work too well to protect the secrets of the former Soviet Union.

THE WHOLE SPY CATALOG is designed to be both a horizontal and a vertical book. This means you should be able to use it to find where damn near any information you need is stored (the personal phone number of the under secretary of electronic import controls?) as well as how to access it, but you should also be able to pick up THE WHOLE SPY CATALOG, open to it to any page and enjoy what you are reading.

A tall order I admit, BUT it works. If you find a database, or use a program that saves time and money, protect your data more efficiently, or even use this information for purposes that could be considered a bit less than completely moral, try to think of me kindly.

Uh, just don't mention where you got the idea to any folks that wear badges or have strange bulges under their suit jackets...

—lee

HOW TO LOCATE & INVESTIGATE ANYONE

Thanks to modern technology and the propensity of minor bureaucrats to keep tabs on everyone and everything (I wonder how many children George Orwell had?) for the first time in history, it is possible for *anyone* to track down and build a background file on anyone else.

If you are a worker, investigator, skip tracer, employment screener or law enforcement worker, I trust you will find many new sources and strategies in this section.

If you're just a general snoop, I'm happy to say your decade has arrived.

The reasons for investigating someone range from wondering what your old friends are doing, whether a prospective business or martial partner is representing his assets and attitudes truthfully, to tracking down estate heirs (for a fee), adopted children or natural parents and finding deadbeats, bail skippers and those on the far side of the law.

Background investigations are almost mandatory for any sort of court action, debt collection, partnership arrangement, or business arrangement. It is not out of the question, nor unfair to do a bit of digging on would-be lovers, doctors who plan on viewing your insides, contractors who want large amounts of money up front, investment counselors, or any other person who make have significant influence over your life.

Times past, this meant employing a professional investigator. Days present, you can do most of it yourself.

Several different approaches exist for both locating and evaluating people. It's extremely possible to find out everything from a person's address and education to their credit and employment history, legal hassles they may have encountered, real property they own, licenses they've acquired, family history, and so. on, with a minimal cash outlay and some footwork on your part. Combine this with the auspices of the US postal service and you will soon know more about your target than his mother/wife and mistress combined.

Let's call this approach number one – finish this chapter, read a couple of the recommended reference materials and approach the recording agencies directly.

Cheap, kinda slow, but effective.

If your search requirements are going to be extensive, please enroll in approach number two. This will save money and time by approaching the primary data sources rather than dealing with secondary or tertiary providers.

Each step up the chain increases your efficiency but at a trade-off in cost. Even through large data providers are cheaper per inquiry, most demand a certain minimum number of inquiries per month to grant access.

Behind door number three we find a compromise method that is the best system for most people. By utilizing one or two listed information providers, you can receive hard copies of the necessary information in days, sometimes even hours, often with no additional effort on your part.

A few of these information providers will run a search strictly by FAX. Fill out the form, dial up, FAX it and wait for the return.

This may be enough in itself to answer simple questions, such as where the target is located.

By expanding on the records, combing them with some active investigative work, and making a phone call or two, you can establish a dossier worthy of the CIA, or even the IRS...

A few records, a little social engineering, approaching the right databases and/or people in the right manner, and viola!

No matter which approach you plan to utilize the basic keys to success are the same:

- Write down specifically what information you are seeking.
- Study the suggested reference materials and list exactly where your sources lie.
- Peruse the flow chart, starting as far in as the information you have on hand allows.
- Plan your strategy in advance, on paper. Online is an expensive place start asking questions.
- How are you going to approach each source, and in what order?
- Be flexible, each new record may point the next inquiry in a different direction.

PEOPLE TRACKING

APPROACH NUMBER 1

It is possible to get a wide variety of information from state and county agencies, the post office, the phone company, courts, libraries, the department of motor vehicles and a host of other public or semi-public agencies.

Many of these knowledge storehouses can be approached in person, most will take requests by mail, a few by phone and a few now offer dial-up computer access.

The trick to a successful do-it-yourself search is knowing where the data lies and what you must do to procure it. Many civil service employees, bless their little hearts, are not wont to volunteer anything, so knowing how to ask for exactly what you need is a crucial factor.

What kind of information is publicly available? Lots.

Record keeping crosses into everyone's lives and includes: entries showing where you live, how you drive, what you drive, how you vote, where you pay your water bill, what credit cards you possess, your payment record, your employer, your phone number, whether you own your house, the price of said dwelling, your neighbor's names and phone numbers, location and value of any real property you own, your bank accounts (balances and locations), criminal proceedings, civil (including small claims) court records, driving record, driver license application information, vehicles owned, tag numbers, children's names and locations, educational records, health records, insurance claims, information on your hitch (if any) in the armed forces, your income, what magazines you subscribe to, previous addresses, previous cars, previous wives or girlfriends, and wedding application data (often includes names of both parents, addresses, witnesses, blood test info, previous marriages, maiden names, and so on) to name but a few.

Divorce files are a particularly enjoyable source of entertainment for researchers, as they tend to show who filed on whom, the alleged offenses, who hit whom, who was seeing whom's best friend on the side, the verbatim contents of drunken arguments, who owned what and who ended up with what.

Tired of People's Court? Well, spend an afternoon at the county courthouse, or a few minutes online and you too can enjoy the debauchery of your friends and neighbors in living color from the comfort of your own living room.

County Clerks are one of the best sources of many civil and criminal records and will send back copies as long as the question is posed on

How to Locate and Research Anyone

Starting With One or Two Pieces of Basic Data

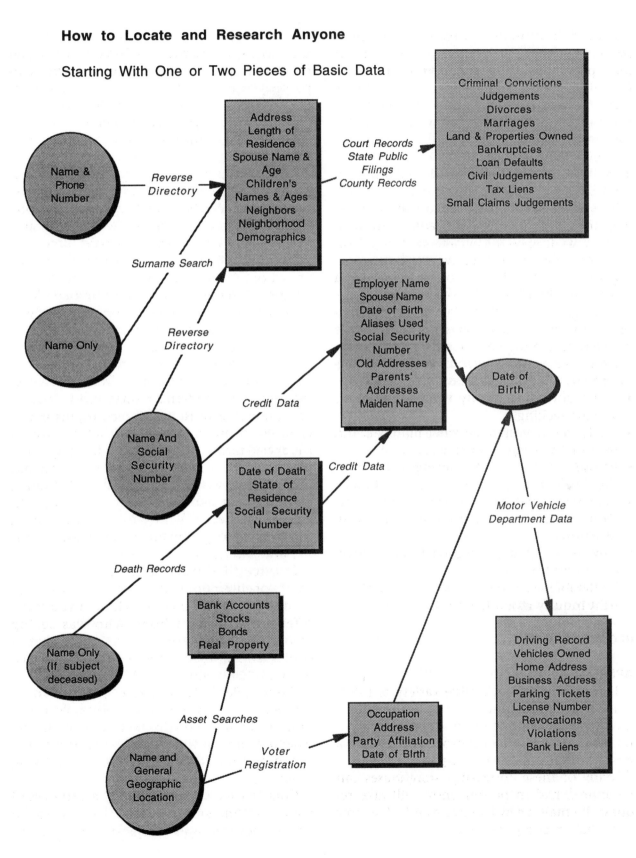

an official form and the correct amount of money enclosed.

In small towns they are often happy to do this, and in fact, may even answer their own phones. In large cities just getting through to the County Clerk's office may be an all day procedure and the person on the other end of the line would really rather be on an island basking in the sun somewhere than telling you what forms you need to get what data, and makes no bones about showing this.

Every time you contact a county clerk, ask if their office provides online access to any files. If so, your next search will be much easier.

SOURCES OF PERSONAL INFORMATION

City Information Sources

The City Clerk is an invaluable source of information and will have most of the following records on file, although in some larger cities, they may be stored in other city offices.

1. Subscribers to the city water supply and sewer hook-ups. This is an often overlooked source for locating someone's address.
2. City court records – city ordinance violations and traffic court records. These records will show a number of details, primarily who was the plaintiff, who was the defendant, disposition date, location of violation and sometimes witnesses.
3. Business licenses – issued to whom and their address, date issued, date of the renewal or the expiration and bond required and who posted it.
4. Building permits – applicant's name, address, address of construction, date of application, cost of construction, builder blueprints, and building inspector's reports on wiring, plumbing, and construction compliance.
5. Dog license – list name and address of dog owner. When dog received rabies shot and sometimes the name of the veterinarian.

6. Bicycle license – well, you never know. Ma Barker and the boys started off when they were still in grade school. The bicycle license will show the name and address, make, description, and serial number of bicycle.

County Information Sources

1. Too many researchers never use the most helpful and free, source of information around – the public library. Most public libraries will have a city directory, an all-inclusive white pages, a reverse directory that ties phone numbers to addresses, a bunch of the out-of-the-area and/or phone books, old local phone books, old newspapers, and a host of other directories.

• A good research librarian can tell you how to find the exact information you need if they don't have it on hand. In many small towns, a librarian, as well as the local postmaster, should be considered the town historian and is an ideal place to start an organic search.

2. County clerk and/or Recorder – usually located in the County Court House. The county clerk will have information on business licenses and trade names including the type of business and the address of the person filing.

• Any liens on file will be available from this source and will include the name of the lien holder, date filed, and any payment agreements.

• The Probate Index lists alphabetically under the name of the estate and provides such information as the date of filing and number of the action, which correlates to a file folder that will contain the entire record of the probate action. Probates are filed in estate settlements, insanity pleas, incompetence hearings, adoption actions or minor custody cases.

• Divorces – one of my favorite sources of information is the divorce action. Besides the complainant, the defendant, place and date of marriage (which should point you towards the marriage license), the divorce action will contain the names and ages of any children, dates of separations, community properties, grounds or charges (who hit whom), who got custody of the children, attorneys for both parties, and orders for payment of fees, costs, the plaintiff's monthly payments, his place of employment and his home address. Sometimes it will include addresses of witnesses involved in the action.

• Criminal index – an alphabetical list of any criminal cases in Superior Court which will provide the date and file number of the folder normally listed by the defendant's name.

• Criminal files – the complete file folder will show the description of the crime, what exactly the defendant was charged with, who the complainant was, testimony of all parties involved including witnesses and officers, name of the prosecuting attorney who tried the case, defense attorney's name, and a probation officer's report if one was issued. The latter comprises a complete background investigation of the defendant...

3. Police department – a veritable plethora of information including offense reports, property records, sometimes the names of persons arrested for various crimes, as well as, the name and address of persons making criminal or accident reports. The accident report will have the date, location, names and addresses of both parties, drivers' license numbers, phone number, date of birth, make of car, amount of damages, where the cars were taken to, name of the ambulance service, witnesses, owners of the vehicles, weather conditions at that time of day and insurance coverage.

• Many police reports are confidential; arrest reports are normally only released to the court, lawyers in the case, or participants in any subsequent court case. In some instances, it's possible to obtain this information by acting pro se for another person involved in the incident. Accident reports generally require you to be an involved party before the report will be released.

4. Department of Education – biographies, backgrounds, education, disciplinary actions and dates of attendance are usually available for students and teachers.

City and County Courts

5. Civil Index – is a list of all civil actions arranged alphabetically under plaintiff and defendant and usually date. Each notation will have a file folder number associated with which you can request the entire record of the action.

• Lawsuits – county clerks also have on file records of all lawsuits and judgments, who sued whom, who won, and how much they got.

• Civil files – covers a wide variety of actions including name changes, divorces, insanity hearings and liens. The information contained herein usually includes the complainant, co-complainant, defendant, cause for the complaint, description of any property involved, the answer to the complaint and the judgment rendered. In some cases a transcript will have been made of the entire court hearing which can be purchased from the court reporter.

6. Registrar of Voters – voters registration cards are public information and can be requested at the Registrar of Voter's office. Normally a $1.00 - $3.00 fee is required for the information entered on the card which will include the name of the registrant, date of his birth, his address at the time of registration, sometimes his occupation, his party affiliation,

often his social security number and state of birth.

• If possible, ask to see the original registration card. This will provide you with a handwriting sample and, on some cards, there may be an optional space for a telephone number which the subject may have filled in. If the registration has been canceled, the reasons for the cancellation either their failure to vote, a duplicate registration, an affidavit of cancellation or death, will be noted. Many registrars keep old affidavits on file so it's possible to check for back addresses of a subject who may have lived in the area.

• Voter registration material is also available on some on-line databases.

7. County Auditor – maintains a list of all county employees, as well as, records of all business conducted by the county itself.

8. County tax collector – will have legal descriptions of property, names and addresses of taxpayers and the amount of taxes paid on real and personal property, as well as, the state of tax collection in each case.

9. County assessor – has maps and often plans of property located in the county. These records normally contain the address of the owner, taxable value, size of the property, and in some cases, photos or construction plans.

10. County Recorder – probably is the main source of information available to an investigator on a county basis. The County Recorder's files will usually include: Marriage licenses containing name of bride and groom, maiden name of the bride, date of birth, place of residences, places of birth, date the license was issued, dates and places of any previous divorce.

• Marriage certificate containing date and place of marriage, names of two witnesses and their cities of residence and the judge, J.P., or clergyman who conducted the ceremony.

• Marriage Board of Health Statement contains names, addresses, ages, occupations, race of both bride and groom, number of marriages that each has participated in, and the name and birthplace of their parents.

• Marriage License Applications. The County Recorder will probably have the original application for the license which includes dates of birth, ages, signatures, handwriting samples, cities of residence, an address for at least one of the parties, dates of application, and health certificates. These can often lead to the family doctor.

• Mortgages on personal property.
• Wills.
• Judgments on real property liens.
• Notices of attachment on real property.
• Instruments describing prenuptial agreements or the property of married women in that state.
• Births and deaths.
• Bankruptcy papers.
• Certified copies of decrees and judgments of courts of records.
• Deeds, grants, transfers, and mortgages (if any) on real property.
• Releases of mortgages on real property.
• Powers of Attorney and other papers involved in real estate transactions.
• Mechanics liens
• Sometimes Armed Forces discharges.

11. Business and professional licenses usually held in City Hall or the County Court House. The license will show how long the business has been active and what they do.

12. Coroner records shows date of coroner's inquest, property that was found on the deceased and what happened to it, cause

of death, copies of any notes regarding disposition of the body, and the name of the deceased.

13. Birth certificates are normally held on the county level will give you the child's date of birth, name, sex, where he was born (hospital name or institution address), names of the parents, ages, addresses, place of their birth, occupations, race, the mother's maiden name, condition of the child, and any resulting medical treatment at the time of birth, number of other children the parents have, the attending physician, and the nature of the birth.

14. Death certificate information will include name, address, sex, age, race, birth place and date of birth, as well as, where the subject died and how long he had been in the area. Also usually include marital status, social security number, military experience, sometimes occupation, parents' names, and doctor's name and/ or cause of death.

State Information

The state maintains many branches and offices that are all potential sources. As a general rule, remember that any state agency that regulates a profession or grants a license maintains publicly available records.

Here's a brief list of departments and offices to consider. Don't rule out the use of a state directory which will provide a description of all state offices and their functions.

- Secretary of State – corporation files showing dates of incorporation, number of shares, values, and annual reports.
- Department of Natural Resources
- Department of Industrial Relations
- Department of Agriculture
- Controller – Treasurer's office
- Bureau of Professional and Vocational Standards
- Department of Motor Vehicles

- State Board of Equalization
- Public Utilities Commission
- Psychology and Medial Examiner's Boards
- Plumbers and Electrician's Examining Boards
- Passenger Safety Boards
- Registered Nurses, Practical Nurses
- Home Licensing Board
- Medical Examiners
- Engineering and Land Surveyors Boards
- Architect Boards

BACKDOOR SEARCHING

Sometimes People Tracking can be best accomplished by going around the usual pathways and taking the "back door." Examples of this would include:

Lists
- Telephone Directories, current and out of date
- Reverse directories
- Post Office, METRONET or ABBM
- School records, yearbooks and alumni directories

People Who Might Help
- Old friends (yearbook)
- Neighborhood gossip ("who do you think might know?")
- Best man/maid of honor (wedding certificate)
- Former co-workers, former roommates
- Ex-wives and in-laws
- Credit managers
- Local librarian
- Mailman
- Bill collectors
- Anybody listed on the divorce records
- Local bartender
- Ex-neighbors
- Local car repair person
- Doctors and dentists
- Professional groups
- Social groups (AA, JA, Rotarians, Lions, Elks, various other animals)

- UPS person
- Newspaper delivery boy
- Utilities company

In Print
- Newspaper morgues
- Library indexes
- Industry publications
- Company newsletters
- Subscriptions

PRETEXTING

We're about at the time we need to discuss the fine art of pretexting. This is a situation wherein the investigator needs to find a person or an asset and, well, lies about who he is or what he is doing.

There exists a fine line between getting information from a source, whether it's online, hard copy or organic and investigating (which often requires pretexting).

Information brokers are not allowed, in most areas, to investigate. Licensed private detectives, on the other hand, are allowed such privileges.

If you are doing the investigating strictly for yourself, not selling the information it is usually legal.

Got it?

Oh yeah, and every so often the FBI likes to run sting operations to see if info brokers are providing records they aren't supposed to be.

Then they arrest them.

Pretexting is the art of getting someone to tell you something they probably shouldn't. It can be done in person, in which case I suggest you study a bit about motivation and body language and do your homework on the subject.

It is more often done over the phone. In TAKE THE MONEY & STRUT, Fay Faron's book, and the PRETEXT BOOK, both discussed elsewhere, a number of interesting scenarios are detailed which may work as is, or can be modified with a little creativity on your part.

Some basics are:
- Be a good guy. You are looking for John Doe to give him something so his old friend or

neighbor will want to help. Missing heir stories are getting a little old, but everyone hates to lose those frequent flyer miles and if your target's are just about to run out and you, from Nice Guy Airlines...

- If you have an approximate area, housing complex or apartment block for instance. Bring a present, Fay has worked wonders with flowers, I've actually bought empty boxes from expensive jewelry and clothing stores "that have to signed for by the customer."

- Some investigators give themselves promotions. Calling to help return stolen property (found his driver's number etched onto the TV set, DMV seems to have incorrect address, do you have a daytime phone so we can ask him to come identify the property?)

- People like to deal with other people in the same line of work, especially at companies that do a lot low end credit sales, preferably companies that carry their own paper. If you can come up with an open account (usually from a credit report, sometimes from a dumpster dive) call up, get the billing department and claim to be from a creditor your target might deal with. If you have his furniture rental company, you be Joe's Used Jeeps). Explain that you have a customer running quite a way behind on his bill, always been good before, now you're getting the letters back marked "no forwarding address."
Could they check and see if they've got a better address or contact number?
If they ask how you got them either tell the truth, "we yanked the guy's report" or say he listed them as a reference.

- Banks a credit card companies are very reluctant to give out information. Usually the best scam here is to be the customer himself. If you want an account balance the bank will probably want your SS number, sometimes your DOB and your mother's maiden name. SS get from a credit report header, driver's license, maiden name from the marriage report of bureau of vital statistics.

Many banks will tell you if someone's check they are about to write to you (buying a stereo, car, whatever) will clear.

- If you convince a credit card company that you've misplaced your card and can give them your name, billing address, SS number you will probably be able to get "your' last months billing information.

Note they will want to close the card down at once if it is "stolen", so you are simply trying to remember the last place you might have left it, or to see if your son has "borrowed" it.

It's possible to develop a limited background sketch of a person by using only a few documents or online reports. For instance, the MVR (Motor Vehicle Record) will show all traffic violations and driving related offenses committed by the named driver as well as all identifying information provided on the basic application form. A typical MVR will show such basic personal data as full name, date of birth, address, when the license was issued or renewed, physical description, type of license and any restrictions on its use.

Some states will also list what other state's license was surrendered at the time of application. That points a researcher towards other locales.

Besides all this, the MVR gives you violations of traffic and safety laws committed by the subject while he was licensed, as well as, any suspensions or revocations.

Thanks to the insurance lobby every state has an efficient mail-in, mail-back method for processing MVR requests. Some states charge only $1.00 while others are as high as $10.00, but the average price of $3.00 is a bargain for this valuable information on your subject.

The MVR also provides a date of birth and sometimes a social security number (a number of states use the SS for the driver's license number) which, in turn opens other searches in-

cluding credit header information and criminal convictions.

The Department of Motor Vehicles will also respond to your requests directly, although you're making a large trade off in time for a little saving in money. Whether you're dealing directly with the DMV by appearing in person or mailing it to the state, or going online, or requesting information through a broker, there are a number of terms that will help you make sure you're getting exactly the information you want.

Soundex Search

Requires the name and date of birth and will get you an address (as shown on driver's licenses) for most states, exceptions here being California and Massachusetts, although Massachusetts is expected to change in the near future. This search also provides the driver's license number which is the same as the target's social security number in about 20 states.

Automated Name Index (ANI),

Provides a list of license plate tags registered to any particular owner. You can then run a:

PLATE TRACE on any vehicle's license plate number which returns (in all but two states) an address, as well as, information on the vehicle.

Another term you should be familiar with for people research is the ALPHA SEARCH. This is a computer search by name and area. It will reveal ownership of vehicles, boats, airplanes and the owner's address.

In rare cases you, as a private citizen, may have lines of access that no database provides. For instance, it's possible to receive the original application address for any post office boxholder in the United States.

If the boxholder is a business, the law says you have a right to the information by simply asking for it.

If the box belongs to an individual you must write the postmaster of the city and officially request the holder of post office box number in the state. It's generally good at this point to put in something to the effect of "pursuant to postal service regulations (administrative support manual section 352.44E and 352.44E 2), I hereby certify that the address information is necessary to affect service of a court process upon the boxholder and will be used for no other purpose."

Below that list the boxholder's name, the case name, the court in which the case is going to appear, and the case number along with whether the boxholder is to be served as a defendant or a witness. Then date the letter and sign it. A fee of $3.00 should also be included.

The interesting part about this is that legally you can skate here as long as you are an attorney or a person acting in pro se, that is, not represented by an attorney but representing yourself or someone else to serve legal papers in regard to a case.

Like magic, you're now legally entitled to this information. The second important concept here is the fact that there actually does not have to be a case filed at the time you request information, only the possibility of a case being filed. (If this is the avenue you are using for an approach, write "pending" under case name and case number.)

By submitting this information you are certifying to the postmaster that it's true. However, in my experience, no postmaster has ever called to verify any of the information. Such a call would be pointless, if he simply contacted you and asked if you were acting pro se as you would undoubtedly answer in the affirmative.

Some postmasters are scrupulous in their demands for detail and will want to know what type of litigation it is (a divorce, a civil suit, small claims court, accident, etc.). Almost all will want to know the capacity in which the boxholder is to be served.

They are less stringent about case names and courts and as far as I can ascertain from my own and friend's experiences, postmasters never actually call a court to see if a case has been filed.

Remember it could be pending...

The following data on obtaining postal forwarding addresses has been invalidated by the post of-

fice as they have discontinued the policy of selling the new address. I'm leaving it in, not for the sake of history, but in the hope that someone will have a federal judge remind the nice postal workers that the information is paid for by the public and in my humble opinion, is public property, thereby reinstating this valuable program.

It's also possible for one to access the postal forwarding address file as this is public information. If you happen to be searching for someone in a town nearby, simply drive to the main post office of the town, ask for the form for forwarding address information, fill it out, (it's usually known as a change of address request) pay your $3.00 and they'll either look it up on the spot and give you the information or mail it to you in the not too distant future.

If you're trying to find a change of address for someone out of the vicinity, write the postmaster, state and zip, and simply say "Under the Freedom of Information Act I'm requesting a change of address on the following individual. Please use the enclosed $3.00, check, or money order for this search. Thank you."

Then simply list the person's name and former address.

Mr. Band, who edited INVESTIGATOR'S GUIDE TO INFORMATION RESOURCES, also suggests you go on here and provide your own form for the friendly postmaster to make sure you get what you need. He suggests you put, "Please reply below." "Date change went into effect" and then leave a space for the postmaster to fill it out. "No change was made." "New Address." "Change for an entire family or individual," leaving space to write the records. "Names of the patron" per your records. If no change was made, "Is the patron still receiving mail?" "Thank you for your cooperation," and put in your name and address.

The post office only keeps change of address records for a limited amount of time, somewhere between six months and one year. METRONET buys the information from the postmaster general, and keeps it on file longer.

LIFE AFTER THE POST OFFICE

There is life after the post office! A company called A.B.M.S. (run by the same gentleman who has given great access to METRONET and the three main credit reporting agencies under the name Tracer's Choice) has developed an alternate method of securing Change Of Addresses for the same $3.00 you'd pay the post office.

Highlights of the new service include:
1. One address to contact instead of 50,000 post offices.
2. One day service (with an SASE) instead of the weeks/months the government seems to require.
3. FAX-in available for $1.00 extra.
4. FAX-back available for $1.00 more.
5. No more writing 2,563 $3.00 checks to various postmasters.

Down side includes:
1. Ray (the owner) will not deal with private citizens on a one-shot basis, insurance companies or attorneys. He wants individuals to go thru a PI or professional tracer.

2. You must wait at least 3 weeks after the subject moved to order the COA.
3. You must pre pay service in blocks of $25.00 or more.
4. The orders can not be run until A.B.M.S. has at least a group of 100 searches, so the more people who order this service, the more effective it will be.

If you are a pro this is a break of the first magnitude: no more post office prima donnas who "will get to that when they have a chance". No more form letters or weeks of waiting.

If you are not in the biz and need a COA <u>please</u> don't contact this service – instead go thru one of the information brokers I've listed. If they are not familiar with A.B.M.S. pass this page along to them...

If you try it yourself and miss, I would suggest you go to an information provider that deals with METRONET and ask for the same search, run online. Of course, METRONET can combine your request with their other searches known as Participatory Change of Address Searches. These include magazine subscriptions, warranty cards, and phone book information.

Another good source is ANCESTRY, P. O. Box 476, Salt Lake City, UT 84110.

"Dear Mr. Lapin,

We provide a search service called a phone search. Our database has 90 million listings of names and addresses of currently living people and is compiled by PhoneDisc USA. This database is composed of mailing lists, some voter registration lists, the Polk Directory and some authorized white pages. The cost to do a phone search is $10.00 + $1.50 shipping & handling. With this search you receive up to 250 listings of the surname you would like searched. Each additional 250 listings of the same surname is $5.00 + additional S&H. You can search the entire US or specific states. We have two forms of reports:

Mailing Labels - name & address with zip codes and line listing or name and address with NO zip codes.

Both formats include telephone numbers, if available."

ANCESTRY searches are extremely powerful if your target's surname is Sozinechin (spelled the old country way) where only a few will show up. Otherwise, you need to establish parameters like specific states or first names in order to avoid the problem of dealing with 28,000 L. Smiths. Surnames are best handled with a bit of social engineering in order to track down your "long lost cousin, Steve Spielberg".

Armed with a number of surnames, a good investigator will call a number of the people, person to person for a Stu Spielberg. As the party answers and says, "Nobody here by that name," you jump in over the operator and say, "He went to UCLA film school in 67."

With any luck you get a reply like, "Oh, you mean my cousin Steve, he lives in Beverly Hills."

CSRA, Inc. 760 Wheeling Avenue, Cambridge, OH 43725, FAX: 614-439-1354, maintains a NATIONWIDE DEATH INDEX of over 49 million deaths in the US covering the last 30 years and current to last year. This index is compiled from various government sources and is kept current with regular updates and enhancements from new sources. Searches on this Index are available to the public on both a subscription and non-subscription basis. Requests may be made by mail, phone, or FAX. The cost per search is $6.00 by mail, or $8.00 by phone or FAX with immediate turnaround.

The Social Security Administration's portion of the NATIONWIDE DEATH INDEX is also available on CD-ROM format. One CD contains the database in social security number sequence. They may be purchased individually or together as a set. The cost is $975 for each disk and $1560 for the set. The CDs are updated quarterly.

At this point let's look at a resource or two, the video tape PEOPLE TRACKING from Intelligence, Inc. is an 80 minute video seminar with Fay Faron, a rather well-known private detective ("process server to the stars") who specializes in tracking people down for one reason or another, has several books out of her own, and now has a nationally syndicated column under her detective agency name Rat Dog Dick. This tape is not padded. It is a solid 80 minutes of how to find this, what office to go to for that, how much it costs to get postal registration cards, intermediate data providers that will allow you on METRONET for less than the normal minimum, tricks for finding information and building background details as well as interesting insights from Fay herself.

The tape is shot with Fay explaining the various methods she uses to track people down and then inter-cut with addresses, sources, and the actual papers that need to be filed or the numbers that need to be called. A very valuable re-source for anyone interested in tracking someone down. PEOPLE TRACKING is for the one-time to small- time investigator who wants to combine some of his smarts and leg work along with an information provider or two and come up with the best data for the smallest price in the shortest time. VHS only, $69.95 ($5.00 shipping and handling).

INVESTIGATOR'S GUIDE TO SOURCES OF INFORMATION
GAO/OSI-88-1

INVESTIGATOR'S GUIDE TO SOURCES OF INFORMATION, United States General Accounting Office, Washington, DC, 20548. This guide is a result of a study by the Office of Special Investigations' Research and Analysis Team on how government investigators should locate data on the public. The guide contains sources such as various offices within federal, state, and local governments and lists of types of information these sources provide. Licensing and regulatory agencies at all levels of government are excellent sources for investigators.

The guide is general from the standpoint that it shows which records the tax assessor will have, the tax collector, the building inspector, the small courts, the federal courts, the federal government, the Inspector General, boards of education, and the National Credit Administration. It's a very useful beginner's manual as to who has what and also qualifies as a shelf resource for any people tracker. It does not give addresses for specific agencies nor does it tell exactly how to access the information contained within. It simply lists who is responsible for what.

SEARCHING MAGAZINE

SECRETS FOR SUCCESSFUL SEARCHING, How To Locate and Find Almost Anyone, Norma Tilman, Private Investigator, U. F. O., Inc. Post Office Box 290333, Nashville, TN, 37299. Norma is another private investigator specializing in missing persons. During her 18 year run, she has found hundreds of people who were purposely or accidentally missing for pri-

vate investigators, police officers, relatives, adoptees, or bail bondsmen. This is Norma's first attempt at putting her particular skills into book form and she's done a fine job.

To quote Norma, "After 18 years searching these records it has become apparent to me that this skill can be used by anyone. Think of it as a game. To play the game, you must know the rules, the other players, and what it takes to win. My secrets are shared with you in this book."

The examples in the book are cases that Norma has actually worked; they give the reader a nice starting point from which to find various records. Norma supplies addresses and techniques to do the searches on your own (without the services of a data provider), and breaks down important information such as who has owned property, date acquired, previous owners, value, where the tax bill goes, partners, or the address of the owners.

James Cook, a well known private detective, recently founded something called the information professional's list (ipl).

This is a free worldwide network for information professionals including PI's, staff investigators, investigative reporters, info brokers public research specialists, document retrievalists and related professionals.

The purpose of the network is to form a forum where members may share resources, ask questions, provide data on current assignments and make referrals. Membership is open to all with electronic mail, access to INTERNET or any service that will talk to INTERNET such as COMPUSERVE, DELPHI, PRODIGY etc.

For more info about this network contact James at INTERNET jcook@netcom.com or COMPUSERVE 76520,2727.

Do you need the tax assessor or the tax collector? Exactly what records can you get from the County Clerk or the equivalent? How do you logically begin your search with one piece of information and expand it outward to include all possible avenues?

Two publications by Thomas Publication come into play at this point. The first one is CHECKIN'

THE RECORD IN THE 90S, The Ultimate Guide to Background Investigations, Edmond Pankau, copyright 1990. Ed is a well known and prolific private investigator who writes books on how he does what he does. This book is published in the Thomas Publication style of loose leaf kind of strangely laid out computer pages then spiral bound in the old instant print shop binder. Ed does go through a number of the same sources we're mentioning, as well as, hitting on other record sources such as birth certificates and little tips like, "Once you find that someone you are looking for is divorced, it is a simple matter to locate the ex-spouse through their divorce record or child support payments also made at the County Clerk's office."

Some interesting ideas, but a bit dated and probably redundant if you purchase other books in this field.

PREMARITAL INVESTIGATIONS

Published by Thomas, authored by Mr. Thomas himself, PREMARITAL INVESTIGATIONS, copy-

right 1991, Thomas Publications. "This is no doubt the up-and-coming field of the 1990s. You may be concerned about a person's background, you may want to know if he's "all right," you may want to know about his drinking and drug habits, you may not trust him entirely or you may think there's something a little funny in his story."

The book is primarily a start-up kit for investigative agencies and seems to concentrate mostly on marketing your services to Nervous Nellies, rather than digging into the meat of actual investigative procedures. This may be because Mr. Thomas sells other books that do dig into the meat of investigative procedures.

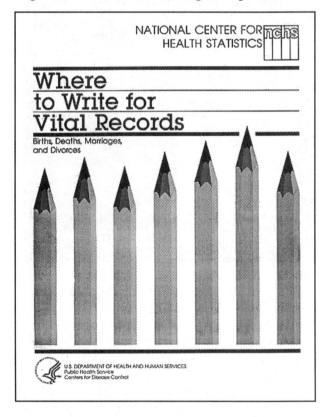

WHERE TO WRITE FOR VITAL RECORDS

For those of you searching on a real budget — you know, you skipped breakfast in order to pay your second installment on this book, you might want to go to the federal government, our old pals at the Superintendent of Documents, US Government Printing Office, Washington, DC, 20402, and try to get their publication S/N017-22-01109-03 for $1.75. Better known as WHERE TO WRITE FOR VITAL RECORDS: BIRTHS, DEATHS, MARRIAGES, AND DIVORCES. This book is strictly a list of local statistics offices, their addresses, their jurisdiction, and the estimated cost for each type of record.

INTERNATIONAL VITAL RECORDS HANDBOOK
ISBN 0-8063-1264-5

By the light of the same lantern, I *can* tell you the INTERNATIONAL VITAL RECORDS HANDBOOK By Thomas Jay Kemp, Geological Publishing Co., Inc., and available from Intelligence, Inc. ($34.95) provides not only names, and addresses of county clerks and fee estimates, but actual certificates required by every state in the union as well as US Trust Territories (American Samoa, Virgin Islands, Puerto Rico, and the Canal Zone), the Caribbean, British Isles and Europe. This book is simply reprinted application forms with addresses and funds required. You can tear out or Xerox a page, fill in the

information, staple your check for $5.00 or whatever and send it off to the address given in the book.

For anyone looking for birth certificates, marriage certificates, death certificates, and some driver licenses, passports, and other proof of identity, this book is a real bargain. It saves you not only money but time, the time necessary to write or call the county clerk (God forbid), and ask her/him to send you the forms necessary, fill them out, get the application fee, mail the whole mess back in. Although designed primarily for genealogical purposes, this book is a wonderful tool for any searcher.

INVESTIGATOR'S GUIDE TO INFORMATION RESOURCES, By A1 Data, PO Box 922169, Sylmar, CA 91392. Although not extensive in length, this book is a must for anyone in the investigative business or doing skip tracing or even adoption/genealogy tracing. It states clearly and succinctly who has what records in most states and provides samples of change of address forms and letters to approach various agencies, as well as, explaining what various databases have on file.

BEEN SUCKERED BY A SCOUNDREL ?

Now, for the first time, a private investigator risks being torn apart by other p.i.s to share the secrets professionals use to legally separate a man from his money.

TAKE THE MONEY & *STRUT!*

A Private Investigator's Guide to Collecting a Bad Debt

by Fay Faron*

*A.K.A. Rat Dog Dick. The detective who finds money like a rat dog finds rats.

TAKE THE MONEY AND STRUT ISBN 0-9620096-0-1

TAKE THE MONEY & STRUT, A Private Investigator's Guide to Collecting a Bad Debt, Creighton Morgan, by Fay Faron (AKA Rat Dog Dick). "The detective who finds money like a rat dog finds rats". Available from Zero to Sixty Publications 123 Townsend Street, Suite 220, San Francisco, CA 94107, or Intelligence, Inc. Fay happens to be a buddy, but that notwithstanding, she's also a very good private investigator, process server, and asset digger outer. Not to mention being a very funny writer. This book is an accumulation of her experiences in locating people and trying to collect on "bad debts". Her techniques are sometimes outrageous, always creative, and well worth learning. Fay has received criticism from some private detectives for her writing because "she gives away their secrets."

This book should be on the bookshelf of any serious researcher, tracker, or private detective as it covers some of the trickier types of information gathering including dealing with the electric company, getting information from banks, how to find trust funds, personal property, how to deal with the IRS as well as other record holders.

To her credit, Fay includes scenarios that didn't work out as well as she thought they would but each story is a definite learning experience.

I've never quite understood Fay's fascination with rat dogs, but other than that she's quite competent and I strongly recommend her works.

FERRARI INFORMATION BROKERS 8 Tudor Ct., Getzville, New York 14068. Besides conducting online searches FERRARI also offers a number of guides of interest including: NATIONAL INDEX TO COLLEGES, INDEX TO LICENSED PRIVATE INVESTIGATORS IN THE UNITED STATES AND CANADA, TAX ASSESSORS INDEX and THE NATIONAL GUIDE TO US GOVERNMENT RECORDS.

Let's look at a couple of other resources that are a little more generalized but can still be of great interest to people trackers. The first two are both aimed at investigative reporters but there's very little that separates good investigative reporting from the kind of researching we're interested in.

The indispensable resource for conducting any sort of background investigations is THE GUIDE TO BACKGROUND INVESTIGATIONS, A Comprehensive Source Directory for Employee Screening, published by the National Employment Screening Services in Tulsa, OK, also available from Intelligence, Inc., $124.50. This large format book of *937 pages* includes information for civil court records in each of the nation's 3,178 counties, as well as, showing which particular agency in each state holds the record you're looking for, exact access addresses and information on licensing boards and incorporation commissions, plus a complete guide to vital statistics - births, deaths, and divorces within each state.

THE GUIDE pinpoints exactly where to send your money, what to ask for, what phone number to call, how to get copies of civil records, driving records, workmen's compensation records, and criminal records.

THE GUIDE takes the reader through a suggested search strategy to utilize a plethora of information in the most efficient method possible. A city/county cross reference guide and a complete guide to all accredited colleges and universities in the US along with their vital statistics (and how to obtain a transcript on any student or ex-student) are bonuses.

THE GUIDE is the most exacting work published on information acquisition and includes all details from the address and FAX number to the exact price of any record from a felony report to a copy of a nurse's license.

One of the handiest offerings is the section that details what counties and what states have mail-in availability and which ones take a personal visit to get or confirm information.

Most states also have a central repository listed or at least an alternate state information hot line number to call to find out where the particular piece of information you're searching for is stored.

The GUIDE is published about every two years. This schedule means it is about as timely as any book can be. TGTBI allows you to conduct a background check on a specific individual, whether for employment purposes or marriage suitability.

The techniques are virtually the same.

CROSSOVER

Every so often a crossover occurs; you know; gets a Bonnie Raitt Grammy for best rock song, 52 million adults go to see what the studio considered a simpy children's movie like Home Alone, Lyle Lolvett marries what's-her-name...

Things that may or may not do well in their own niche fit in spectacularly well in another field. Such is the case with the county courthouse book, Elizabeth Petty Bently, Genealogical Publishing, 1001 N. Calvert St., Baltimore, MD 21202. $29.95.

Ms. Bentley sent out letters to 3,351 courthouses across the country asking them to verify their addresses and phone numbers, as well as, to indicate their holdings in four different record groups, i.e., land records, naturalization records, vital records and probate records. She then, politely one would hope, asked the courthouse people whom she should contact to get the best results in each category, as well as, the costs involved.

The results are correlated in this more-than-useful book which provides direct phone numbers to inside offices, avoiding the dreaded master switchboard, as well as, shows what records are available from what dates, at what price.

This was all done in the name of genealogy but sure helps when you are trying to track down a missing person, skipper, checking assets or trying to verify records...

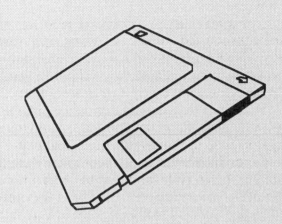

HIGH TECH BACKGROUND INVESTIGATING

One of the very, very best investigative aids, THE GUIDE TO BACKGROUND INVESTIGATIONS, has gone high tech. While the original guide is still published every couple of years, it is now also available on computer disk.

This format has a number of advantages including a substantial savings in access time (compared to the book) of 100% – 500%, the ability to be easily updated and the fact that it lives in a computer instead of occupying 6 pounds of bookshelf space.

The disk provides the same information as does the book; where and how to access criminal records, worker's compensation records, medical licensing boards, departments of education, social security number searches, academic records, vital statistics, corporations and an overview section.

The program is menu driven and allows the use of several windows at one time so you can easily switch back and forth during a search. It's "smart" enough to find complete names from partial strings and allows you to modify or include new data you run across.

Very nice idea. IBM only, from National Employment Screening Services or Intelligence Incorporated.

Information from previous employers and personal references is drying up because of the abundance of lawyers in the United States, most of whom are only too willing to file defamation of character suits on a contingency basis. So, it is important that you as a researcher understand the dangers of the direct approach and how to supplement or completely circumvent it by using this book, your telephone, and the United States post office.

BRB

There is one reference book publisher that is so damn good I'm going to be kind and give them a complete section of their very own. Most of these publications are available directly from the publisher or from Intelligence Incorporated.

BRB Publications, Inc. 4653 S. Lakeshore Suite #3, Tempe, AZ 85523, was started by a couple of gentlemen, one who ran one the largest online information providers in the country to fill gaps in investigative publications.

Their public record research library series is professionally done, nicely designed, well put together group of books that belongs on the shelf of virtually every private investigator, information provider, attorney, paralegal, researcher and snoop in the country.

Some of these books apply to people tracking, some to asset finding, some to general research, but we're going to cover them here.

Let's start with my personal favorite: THE SOURCEBOOK OF PUBLIC RECORDS PROVIDERS $29.00. 283 pages of databases, information providers national and regional public record search firms, providers of proprietry database and CD-ROM products, distributors or regional records, background screening firms and investigators who use online methodologies.

Hundreds of sources with complete descriptions of their services and how to contact them.

Now let's move on to LOCAL COURT & COUNTY RECORD RETRIEVERS $45.00, a mere 544 pages of 2,000 firms, listed on a county by county basis who physically visit records repositories on a regular basis. These are the "hands-on" folk whose job it is to search, copy, pick and record documents.

Includes a 250+ page index with 10,000+ individual county entities of record searching in a number or areas like:
- Local civil cases
- Local court criminal cases
- Bankruptcy
- UCC liens
- Marriage, divorces, birth and death records

The second half of the book provides the reader with basic information about the searcher so you can be certain of choosing the right vendor going in.

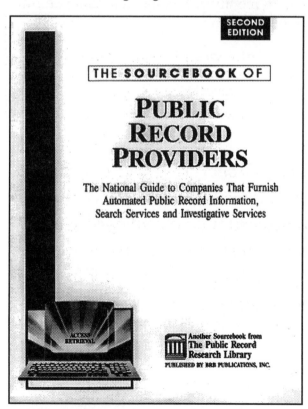

SCAN THE SOURCEBOOK OF PUBLIC RECORD
PROVIDERs ISBN 1-8879792-13-3

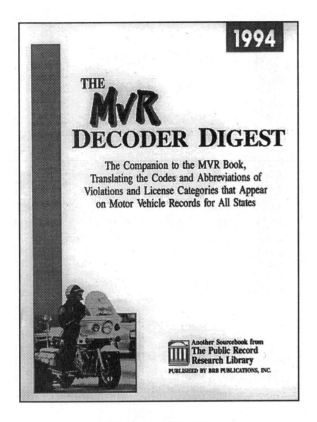

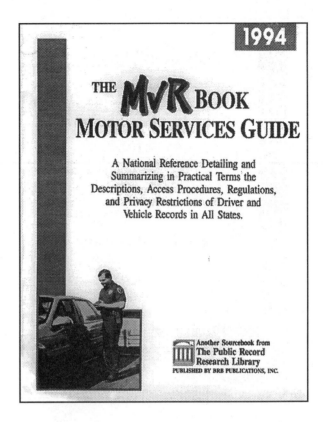

MVR DECODER DIGEST
ISBN 1-879792-15-X

THE MVR BOOK
ISBN 1-879792-14-1

How about the MVR DECODER DIGEST? $17.00. A sorta Berlitz of the DMV crowd, the DIGEST translates all those little codes and abbreviations of violations and license categories that appear on motor vehicle records for all states.

Did you know that in Vermont AFC means, "altering, forging or counterfeiting certificates?" Or how about IRM is the illumination required on motorcycles? "

Also a great guide to THE MVR BOOK $17.00, which is a national reference detailing and summarizing the descriptions, access, automation, regulations and privacy restrictions of each state's driver and vehicle records.

"*Made-up numbers: When a made number comes up on-terminal as belonging to someone else, the same number is used but at the end of the number (male/female) a "2" is placed instead of the ") or "1", if the "2" is also a duplicate, succeeding numbers are used..."

Fills in all those annoying little gaps when you run a person's DMV report and get back this fact-fillled report that you can't make heads or tale of...

THE SOURCEBOOK OF ASSET/LIEN SEARCHING
ISBN 1-879792-17-6

COUNTY COURT RECORDS
ISBN 1-879792-05-2

THE SOURCEBOOK OF ASSET/LIEN SEARCHING should legimately be in the asset searching chapter, but, what the hell. This book is a national directory of names, mailing addresses and phone numbers for all 4283 jurisdictions in the 50 states where liens are filed.

UCC searching, real property searching, corporation searching, public record and online searching. All the names addresses and sources you need to collect money from that SOB that owes you or your client.

A deal at $19.00.

INSURANCE SERVICE VENDORS $15.00. A unique directory for property and casualty insurers. Profiles the firms that provide property audits, inspections, motor vehicle recording and more.

COUNTY COURT RECORDS A directory of over 5,300 local courts detailing where you can obtain information on civil and criminal cases, probates, liens, real estate, tax vital statistic records. Includes a city-to-county cross reference guide. $33.00

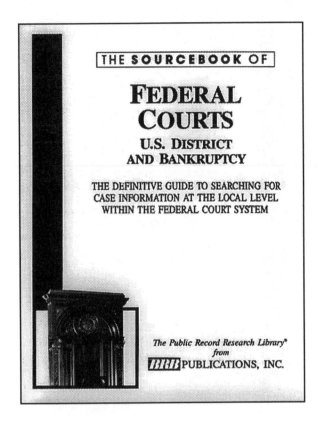

FEDERAL COURTS
ISBN 1-879792-10-9

STATE PUBLIC RECORDS
ISBN 1-879792-12-5

FEDERAL COURTS, $33.00 the ONLY search guide to more than 500 US court locations and 13 federal records centers. Location maps, explanations, record keeping systems.

STATE PUBLIC RECORDS $29.00 Accurate, comprehensive searching at the state level. Where to locate, hours of operations, names, numbers search requirements. 19 subject matters, 5,000 record center locations...

LOCUS
ISBN 1-879792-11-7

LOCUS The Ultimate Locator. 95,000 place names that accurately match ZIP codes to places and counties. Includes three cross reference indexes. $25.00.

BRB Publications updates the books *often* so every order is at up-to-date

You should be ashamed if you don't own these books.

Social engineering, the art of extracting information from people with or without their consent, is truly an art. Most people are shocked at how easily complete strangers will give out what should be personal and often embarrassing information over the telephone under the flimsiest pretenses.

Many private detectives and researchers have developed their sense of the con to the degree where they know "I'm from an attorney's office looking for John Smith. His uncle just died and left a huge inheritance," or the "Hello, I'm from the State Lottery Commission. We definitely need to contact Mr. Steven Spielberg. Do you have his address?" Works in 70% of the cases.

If you run across someone who is street smart, on the lam, or protecting someone, you'll discover that such flimsy pretenses will not do the trick and will be detrimental because they will alert the person that someone is searching for them.

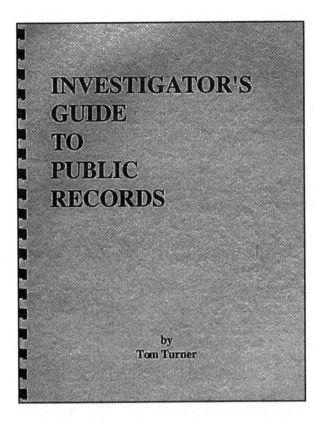

INVESTIGATORS GUIDE TO PUBLIC RECORDS

INVESTIGATORS GUIDE TO PUBLIC RECORDS Tom Turner, Tom Turner and Associates, 31341 Niguel Rd, Suite 300, Laguna Niguel, CA 92677. Although we cross with Mr. Turner in some areas (such as information providers), this inexpensive spiral bound book has a number of features such as California driver's license sequences, genealogy information resources, and a state-by-state list of the current record providing rules that's it's well worth adding to your library.

CELEBRITY SOURCES

Celebrity directory Axiom Information Resources POB 8015-T4, Ann Arbor, MI 48107, lists the addresses of over 7,000 film and television starts, authors, politicians, recording stars and other famous people.

Published every year or two, this book is simply a series of lists and will provide you a contact address for everybody from Dr. Jones Salk ("scientist") to Fess Parker ("actor").

It also includes a number of people in the biz but not as famous such as movie producers, TV executives, screenwriters, boxers and an "ex-President's son."

Well done and up to date.

CONFIDENTIAL INFORMATION SOURCES
ISBN 0-7506-9018-6

CONFIDENTIAL INFORMATION SOURCES, John Carroll is a most unusual book that takes the reader thru a guided tour of where and how damn near every record, public and private is stored.
- Employment applications
- Personnel consultants
- Acquisition of personal records from computers
- Exchange of information
- Tracking a company

- Health professionals
- National and inter-national police record depositories
- The criminal justice process, who has what
- International credit networks 5000 consumers for $400
- Bank cards and oil cards
- DMV departments and other government record systems
- Medical records and medical data banks
- Student records
- Backgrounding
- Vetting, polygraphing and voice stress analysis
- The private investigators "hot line"

Plus organizations, fair credit reporting act data, headings, language numeric code guides and much, much more.

Great book.

Available from Intelligence Incorporated $54.95 hardback.

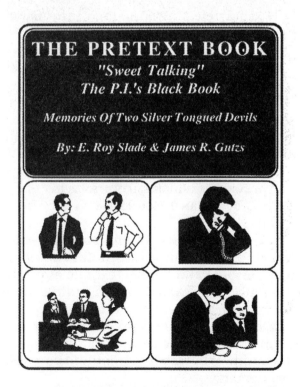

THE PRETEXT BOOK

THE PRETEXT BOOK Sweet Talking, Memories of Two Silver Tongued Devils, Roy Slade and James Gutzs, Cloak and Dagger Press, Houston, TX, available from Paladin Press. This book hypes itself as "How to become a black belt in the investigator's black art." It is basically a series of anecdotes from the lives of two very good private detectives strung together with a mild search strategy. How to ask the right person the right question, how to use misdirection to appear harmless, what words to use, tone of voice, body language, how to talk sweetly over the telephone, a number of pretexts that will work with banks to find the account number of a subject, how to talk to the apartment manager, and basically how to dig out the dirt on anybody.

"Evidence of some of the nicest little skeletons in the closet end up in the trash." This could be called a Citizen's Guide to Dumpster Diving and is just one of the many useful tips in this book that range from helping you serve a subpoena or summons to convincing a doctor or secretary to give out information he/she is definitely not allowed to disclose.

A very valuable resource for anyone who plans on tracing or simply enjoys the concept of social engineering.

PEOPLE-FINDING RESOURCES INCLUDE:

1. Phone book/directory assistance
2. Registrar of voters records
3. Department of Motor Vehicles drivers license
4. Traffic court index
5. Department of Motor Vehicles vehicle registration
6. County recorder birth, marriage, death index
7. State vital statistics birth, marriage, divorce, death
8. Post office change of address
9. County assessor (secured and unsecured property)
10. Municipal court civil index
11. Small claims court index
12. County clerk marriage license index
13. Public library's listing of fines paid
14. State Board of Equalization, resale permits
15. State Department of Real Estate, brokers and sales persons licenses
16. City clerk, building permits
17. Post office box applications
18. Superior court civil index
19. Superior court divorce index
20. Superior court criminal index
21. Superior court probate index
22. County recorder grantor/grantee
23. County clerk fictitious names index (DBA)
24. US District Court civil index
25. US District Court criminal index
26. US District Court bankruptcy court
27. US District Court naturalization court
28. US District Court tax court
29. National Personnel Records Center, former military
30. Veteran's Administration
31. State Department of Corrections
32. City or county concealed weapons permit
33. Animal regulation department, pet licenses
34. Secretary of State, limited partners
35. City business license
36. State Department of Consumer Affairs – professional licenses
37. Secretary of state UCC filing
38. Secretary of state corporate filings
39. State workers compensation appeals board
40. Securities and Exchange Commission
41. State Fair Political Practices Commission
42. Federal Aviation Administration, pilots licenses
43. Federal Aviation Administration, plane ownership
44. US Coast Guard, boat ownership

UNUSUAL SOURCES

A number of unusual and often unknown sources exist for tracing the movement of any individual. Note that many of these sources are not, ah, publicly available. They are, for the most part, available to law enforcement officers and some can be dug out by clever information brokers or clever(er) readers.

Also remember that 20+ information brokers were arrested recently in a sting conducted by the FBI for releasing forbidden information such as credit card billings.

Enough said.

The US Customs Service maintains a base called EPIC or the EL PASO INTELLIGENCE CENTER. Here every re-entry into the United States by a citizen is stored along with the entire custom declarations from filled out when crossing the border back into the states.

EPIC data is given out by FINCEN, the center that provides financial and travel history to virtually every law enforcement agency in the country.

One of the best ways to find foreign activities of an individual to scrutinize their business, personal and mobile telephone records. This will often lead to foreign business contacts, banks, attorneys and their ilk.

Credit card statements, are, of course, invaluable in tracing travel or financial transactions as they often show hotel, airline and purchases made in target areas.

If access can be gained to the subject's assistant or secretary the searcher should try for travel logs, diaries, and the Rolodex. Any telephone directories of key contacts or papers held by the secretary for the subject are also great sources.

This type of access is usually accomplished because the person involved, spurned or disgruntled has decided to roll over on the subject. It has also been gathered by threats, bribery and burglary.

The target's travel agent is usually in his Rolodex and can furnish at least three years of travel records. If this is not available an agency known as ARC or Airline Reporting Corporation in Washington, DC compiles and collates all domestic air tickets.

The International Air Transport Association (IATA) in Montreal does the same for foreign tickets issued by most major airlines.

All good hotels maintain a complete phone record for each guest, this can be procured via a friendly manager, search warrant or desk clerk made friendly by the sudden influx of some currency.

If surveillance, either personal or electronic is employed, certain days of the year are touchstones for the investigator.

- Mother's Day. Even Baby Face Nelson called his mother to wish her a happy mother's day. Check mom's phone records or tape all the calls.
- Father's Day. Ditto.
- Christmas. Check the trash for cards and letters, credit card receipts for gift purchases.
- Thanksgiving. Good day to watch mom's house.
- Valentine's Day. Check the trash for return addresses, phone or credit cards for flower deliveries.

Other resources which are a bit more general in nature, usually aimed at investigative reporters, should also be in your collection.

RAISING HELL

RAISING HELL, A Citizen's Guide to the Fine Art of Investigation, Dan Noyes, published by Mother Jones magazine and available from the Center for Investigative Reporting 530 Howard St., 2nd Floor, San Francisco, CA 94105, is a pamphlet that deals with dirt digging by employing such publications as Who's Who and Finding Facts, contacting Chambers of Commerce, and checking tax courts in Washington, DC under the Freedom of Information Act. It also has chapters on how to deal with the Securities and Exchange Commission, (the federal agency responsible for corporations offering public sales of stocks and bonds), gives a brief description of what paperwork they have to file and what you can get from it, names other books such as D & B and Moody's and tells you what to expect from correspondence with the FCC and National Labor Relations Board.

A very nice little chapter on property, *Where the Buck Lands,* teaches the reader how to ascertain exactly who owns what piece of property, what they paid for it, and how to find it. There's a nice summation and it shows where this information lives.

Remember, this is a 42 page pamphlet and is designed for reporters whose targets tend to be in the public records a bit more than yours and mine. It's handy, it's cheap and you probably ought to send for it.

THE NATIONAL LOCATOR GUIDE
ISBN 0-9620096-6-0

Creighton Morgan Publishing Group, P. O. Box 470862, San Francisco, CA 94147. Fay has put together what one would think would be the ultimate in boring books. THE NATIONAL LOCATOR GUIDE provides area codes, zip codes, and locations of 8,000 US cities and towns including maps for many parts of the country showing what town is where, what area code they fall into, what zip code prefix, if they're a city, what county they reside in, where the county seat is, the state capitol, and other helpful data.

I took Fay's book with a grain of salt in order to try it out and have since discovered it is one of the books our office uses eve*ry single day.* The first time you can't read a return address on something, there's no zip code, you need a phone number of a county seat to call for public records, you've never heard of the towns of Westmoreland or Kokomo or Kermit, reach for TNLG.

The information is cross referenced by zip codes and town names, and includes maps.

APPROACH NUMBER 2

One of the most efficient methods for gathering information on a particular subject is by using an online database. Databases are collections of information available via computer and modem. In some cases only a citation or abstract may be accessible online; sometimes a hard text copy backup service may be required for full text.

Other bases will offer the complete record to your printer for the cost of the price of the connect time and sometimes a copy charge. Large databases don't actually live on one computer but exist on a network of inter-connected computer nodes, each node specializing in a certain area of information.

Databases are fast, efficient, and cheap – pick two of the three. A number of different levels of database access exist, each designed for a different type of user. Each comes with its own restrictions, costs and availability. For our one-sided discussion let's divide all databases into one or more SuperClass(s) – those that supply information on people and those that specialize in information on things.

Examples of our first SuperClass (people) would include government public record files and commercial intelligence gathering agencies such as commercial collection agencies.

Credit agencies collect information on individuals including their full names, addresses, sometimes phone numbers, employers, and whether they pay their bills on time, as well as what transactions they have been involved in the last seven years, whether they've declared bankruptcy, and anything else that would help their customers determine if the subject is a good credit risk. Credit agencies tend to be small individual offices that deal with customers in their vicinity but virtually all belong to at least one major credit clearinghouse.

The credit system works as follows: You buy a car from a car dealer. You fill out your loan application and he immediately forwards it to the credit agency to which Joe's Sleazy Cars belongs.

The credit agency in turn accesses one of the three mother credit clearinghouses to check on your payment record and earnings history. This is a two way street: the car dealer pays a few bucks to the credit agency for a copy of your credit report and then in turn is expected to turn over any new information you provide to the credit agency in order to keep your credit history current.

The three main credit agencies in the United States are TRW, CBI (used to be called Equifax), and TransUnion. Each agency specializes in one area of the country. The boundaries often overlap so it is extremely possible you have different credit records in all three agencies. The information may be more up to date in one agency than in the others.

Credit agencies are one of the primary sources for investigators and skip tracers because they contain data input from numerous sources such as banks, loan agencies, or even health clubs that will automatically update your status, address, and employer.

There are only two minor problems with credit agency data: First, if you manage a small business you can probably join a credit agency, automatically accessing one or more of the mother agencies for a few bucks a report. The hang-up here is that these agencies have an antipathy to the word "investigator" used in any form. This is not to say that private investigators do not routinely go through credit agencies, it's just to say that they often get there under less than accurate names. Names that do not include the word "investigations."

The second minor problem is that no one can legally access someone else's entire credit report unless what they are doing falls under the auspices of the Fair Credit Reporting Act.

Basically this act says you must be actively involved in a business transaction with the consumer you are asking for the credit report on. This translates as applying for a loan, attempting to rent an apartment, sell something on time or trying to collect a judgment. Credit reports are issued with the signature of the inquiring party and are made a part of the credit record so the consumer at any time, can see who has requested credit reports on him. If there is an inquiry in the file that shouldn't be there, the target can ask one or more law enforcement agencies to prosecute the inquirer.

EQUIFAX 1600 Peachtree Street, NW, Atlanta, GA 30309 has seen the light and now offers credit records for "pre-employment" searches which include the EQUIFAX Credit Report, DMV reports and so on.

On the other hand, the data that is not classified as part of the credit report but is known as header data and usually includes the consumer's birth date, social security number and address. It can be legally obtained by anyone and leaves no footprints of the searching party. The credit header data has proven to be one of the most important means of finding people and/or beginning to build a background dossier on them.

At this point we need to mention one other major agency, METRONET Although not specifically a credit reporting agency, this database collects and distributes such handy information as listed phone numbers and addresses for all businesses and residents in the United States, postal forwarding cards, (those little green cards you fill out when you move so your Soldier of Fortune subscription will come to the new address) and warranty cards that customers send in after buying that new microwave, and also provides demographics on any particular neighborhood.

All these puzzle pieces are very useful to an investigator, or a person acting as an investigator, because they can be cross referenced with the credit union data to provide a surprising amount of information on just about anybody.

$5.00 PEOPLE TRACKERS

Okay, here's another tip that is worth the cost of this book. Hey, maybe it's worth more than the cost of this book. In fact I think it would be only fair if every time you use this information you simply tape a quarter to a nice letter and send it to me, care of Intelligence Incorporated.

You'll feel better, trust me...

METRONET, one of the best people finding organizations in the world who also happens to supply postal forwarding, subscription, warranty, white page and neighborhood information to virtual every information broker in the world, has just gone public.

Really public.

You can now access their PeopleFinder service which has addresses and telephone numbers for some 111,000,000 people and can be searched by surname, address, phone number or previous address for $0.30 a surname (up to 2500 during a one month period). Batch your queries in groups of 100+ and you get the volume discount–$0.24 per.

For other types of searches, neighbor names, phone number, electronic directory assistance, etc., figure $0.25–$0.85 each try.

These same services are resold by second party vendors, like Information America and Mead Data Central for $25.00 – $95.00 each.

So what's your point, you ask, cleverly. I know I can go on line with a computer and a modem if I do $600 of business a month, or even go through Tracer's Choice for $50.00 a month and a slightly higher per time charge?

Get this, METRONET has just started a 900# service that requires no computer, no modem, no technical help. For a mere $3.00 for the first minute and $2.00 for each additional you can access them directly.

No computers, no middlemen, just a friendly operator who will run the average search for about $5.00.

Call 900-288-3020

Quarters, remember the quarters...

Once you're practiced in the fine art of researching you can also do complete background searches that includes the above information, but will also contain other data such as assets, criminal records, real property owned, education and other valuable data. Of course, a locate-only search is easier to conduct because of its inherent simplicity, but it's surprising the amount of data about a person that comes automatically with an address locate-type search.

Many investigators and some information bureaus check in with only one of the three major credit information bureaus when they are attempting a skip trace. This is a mistake as each may have different records and one may have a hit while the others have misses on the same subject. Besides, all three credit reporting agencies often bring back different information.

Credit header searches can be run in one of two directions. Either by entering an address that is current or was within the last seven years (the length of time credit bureaus hold records) or more accurately by entering the subject's social security number.

If you don't have an SS number but do have an address that was valid at one point, lead with the address and often the search results will include the social security number that opens other possibilities for continuing the search.

Please note: TransUnion doesn't give up the SS number on an address oriented search.

Of the three credit agencies, CBI seems to provide the most information for your dollar. Besides the social security number CBI often provides the target's place of employment, date of birth (the other two only give the year of birth), often the spouse's name, and any other aliases or close social security numbers that the target might be using. Still, it's imperative that you or your representative check all three agencies and then compare the data to find which is the most recent and probably the most accurate.

It's possible to come up with several addresses on a credit header check because the person may have moved and re-entered one system and the other systems haven't yet caught up.

The United States government is the largest information collector in the world. Using your tax dollars, they will file away various bits and pieces of personal information. Much of this information is furnished upon demand; you simply have to know how and where to ask the right question.

Anyone can access large suppliers such as government agencies as long as they meet the minimum criteria which often include doing several thousand dollars a month of business with the supplier. This policy is in place to discourage tire kickers and single shot private investigators.

Several major data networks provide access to credit information, public records, court proceedings, DMV material and some asset information. These companies are set up for online use by investigators, lawyers, and researchers. Most want an initial sign-up fee and a minor monthly "maintenance" fee.

These are the key gateways for information seekers. They can be accessed directly or by going thru a smaller, value added agency.

US DATALINK 671 Bayway Drive, Baytown TX 77520, represents over 250 information banks and claims to offer the best public record retrieval in all 50 states, as well as, access to some records that are not machine readable because US DATALINK will make phone calls or actually travel to court houses to pull records if necessary. USDL has three different organizations, one dealing with personnel files, one dealing with automobiles, and one dealing with businesses. Their sign-up fee are is moderately hefty, approximately $1,000 for the user software but the online fees are very reasonable and the front end software makes searching easy.

Second is the NATIONAL CREDIT INFORMATION NETWORK (NCI), the first major vendor of credit header information. they scan 250 million credit files as well as all reverse directories, postal forwarding cards and a number of other sources.

Instant social security number traces, a toll free, 24-hour access line and good support has made NCI one of the largest data suppliers. They encourage investigators to become customers.

They are upgrading their search methods all the time and make no bones about the fact that they aim at private detectives. Ralph Thomas, a well known PI and writer of how to find 'em, get 'em, make 'em pay kinda books, uses NCI and swears by it.

NCI software and information packets are available from Intelligence, Inc. or NCI, POB 1021, Jackson, MI 49204, both of whom will also sell you the software and put you on the system with a full money-back guarantee. Sign-up fee is $695.00 for the complete access package without full credit bureau reports (you can run SS and address update searches thru credit header info, just not get the full credit report), or $795.00 for everything plus credit report availability.

The third largest is CDB INFOTECH, Box 5466, Orange, Ca 92613. CDB started off supplying information to attorneys and others in the legal field and is now welcoming private detectives and smaller information brokers to their ranks. Like USDL, their search criteria and availability increases on an almost daily basis. They offer the access to all three major credit agencies (as does NCI and USDL) as well as fictitious name statements, corporate business, automobile through tag searches, owner of automobile searches, aircraft, boat registration, and licenses, criminal and civil court records and some real property assets. CDB runs about $300 for the initial sign up. Their searches run from $5.00 for a driver's record to about $45 for business credit reports.

Most of these second approach data providers require a start-up fee and some monthly minimum, although both will be considerably less than the actual government or private data banks from which they are getting their information.

Realize you're going to need a computer, a modem, and some online practice time to become good with a particular provider. If you

CDB On Call
CDB Infotek has also added a direct call in service for members. information: on call at 800-992-7889 (FAX 714-708-1023) hooks you up directly with an experienced operator who will suggest and conduct any search without the need of a computer or a modem.

The return can be within the same hour by FAX, the same or next day using express mail or standard two day via priority mail. The per-search charge is only slightly higher than if you connect and search directly from your computer. The couple of times I've used the service, the operators had ideas I had overlooked and this more than offset the surcharge.

are a PI, legal researcher or in a position where you run a fair number of security checks, you should subscribe to one of the above agencies.

After visiting the credit reporting agencies, your next stop should be METRONET. They collect information from a variety of published sources such as the phone book, postal registration cards (which they hold for several more years than does the post office), magazine subscriptions, warranty cards, voter's registration, and other unique sources. METRONET also has a wonderful feature wherein you don't pay for many of their services if you don't get a hit; i.e., if no records show up on your particular subject, METRONET does not bill you, unlike credit agencies that bill you for every search regardless of the results.

The advantage of comparing data from METRONET with credit header data is that you can extrapolate many things not actually written in the records. For instance, it's usually possible to see when somebody moved and where they moved to METRONET will provide the head of the household, occupants of the house, and their year of birth. This tells you if the subject is living with his parents (same last name, 20 year+ difference in birth), children (if one household member is two years old and is not listed at the last address, odds are good that it is a child), if the woman is married her new name. If a couple is living together for some time and a new, 2 year old, occupant suddenly appears it's possible to draw a certain conclusion.

METRONET also provides the probability of the subject owning or renting by comparing the exact address with neighborhood demographics, how much the dwellings in the neighborhood sell for, as well as, the average income of the occupants. This information draws a picture of the neighborhood and allows the researcher to trace if the person is moving up scale or down scale, and possibly why.

METRONET often returns a phone number with the address, assuming it's listed or the subject has filled it in on a warranty or subscription card. They also show if anyone has filed a change of address card for that address in the last year or two.

Upon demand METRONET will furnish an "identity" of the building the subject lives in, whether it's a house or apartment and how many units are involved. Is it a fourplex or a 100 unit apartment building? How long have the various neighbors lived there and what are their names and telephone numbers?

All these facts help any competent researcher begin to connect the dots as to where his subject has gone, what he's doing, and how his life is proceeding. METRONET also has a lovely feature whereby they will automatically list 10 neighbors on either side of your target. The clever thing to do here is find the Widow Smith; you know, the one who's lived there 30 years and likes to sit in the back window at all hours of the day.

I guarantee she'll be able to tell you some details on your subject.

METRONET does not restrict their access except by requiring a monthly minimum. TRACER'S CHOICE, a California based information wholesaler will allow you to join METRONET with a much smaller monthly minimum, however TRACER'S does not provide online help or advice. They expect you to know how to use a computer and conduct a basic search.

If you are a legal researcher, PI, skip tracer etc. TC is a bargain. If you are just doing a search or two a week (or less) *do not* sign up with either METRONET or TC, go thru one of the information services listed in this sterling publication.

Just make certain *they* are using METRONET...

Imagine what kind of report you could draw up on a complete stranger if you could access the above information. You know, is that nice guy you met at TGIF the other night really the CEO of 7 corporations, or is he working off his parole from a rape charge?

Does that cute attorney really own her condo? What about those three children that she didn't mention plus that messy divorce and bankruptcy right after the sticky incident at McDonald's where she was head cashier...

Net worth, character, background, location, family, relationships, health matters, traffic problems, criminal-civil court contacts, educational background, can all be accessed in a matter of minutes.

In the past this type of search meant hiring a private investigator for $500-$1,000 (plus expenses) and blindly believing in the results.

Not to put down the profession, mind you. Most reports were quite good because the PI in question simply turned around and queried an information provider who accessed the very databases we are dealing with, and then sold you the report.

No more.

If you have thirty five bucks in your wallet, access to a FAX, or even a telephone, (okay, okay, or even the US mail) you can: A. locate damn near anyone, B. find out an enormous amount about their "private" lives.

All by your lonesome.

Works for lost relatives, old college boyfriends, bail bond skippers, major fugitives, dead beat husbands, heirs who don't realize favorite Uncle John died last year and left them the Leer, the ranch and Aunt Susan...

I speak from direct experience here. Having helped form and run an information provider, I can relate two quick stories that testify to the effectiveness of this route.

The firm I was helping had developed a pretty good chain-of-strategy (see the chart) for coming up with the maximum amount of info with the least outlay. Generally, this included a credit header search on all three major providers (caution – make SURE your research firm is using all three, not just TRW.), METRONET mail, subscription card, and warranty search plus a phone disc, electronic white pages search and a neighbor list of the last known address.

In difficult cases we combined this with death records, simple surname runs and sometimes DMV info.

Our record was *real* good, say about 85–90% hit rate. One customer keep coming back with different sorts of sleazy people he needed to find.

I finally asked him if he made all his friends while he was in prison. He laughed and told me he was a cop and our success ratio was far better than the FBI's...

The second little story concerns the producer of a rather well known TV show who wanted to do a story on the "miracle (or threat, who the hell knew how they were going to write it) of information providers". He scanned our highly sanitized files and charts but seemed unconvinced of the effectiveness of such a search.

Finally, I asked him to give me his address, he hemmed and hawed and said it wouldn't work 'cause he had moved a few months ago.

"Let's give it a shot anyway."

We pulled up his old address, his new address, his salary, how much he paid for the new place, pointed out that he had obviously recently separated from his girlfriend as she had moved and applied for a new credit rating (pulled her address too), asked him if he still drove the Porsche after his last three speeding tickets and then brought up a list of his old neighbors.

"Well, look, your next door neighbor Phil has lived there for 25 years. I bet I could just call him and chat him up a while. Maybe find out why your ex-girlfriend seems to have a brand new person living at her house. Ah,

seems to be a kid about a year old, maybe Phil...

"Turn the cameras off. Turn the damn cameras off. This interview is over." He shooed the crew out into the yard, "Man, that shit is dangerous! Do you know what, well, I mean, it seems, uh, you're not going to tell anyone about this are you?"

No...

So how does the average person get access to this data? Our third approach, the use of smaller information providers offers single shot access to these major databases.

Here is a list of medium to small information providers. Some can be used on a single time basis; some require minimums.

- AVERT, INC. 117 East Mountain, Fort Collins, CO 80524. FAX 303-221-1526. A large firm used by employers to check out potential applicants. Avert specializes in worker's compensation reports, DMV records, criminal histories, as well as, social service runs. Avert's prices are quite cheap and they do not seem to require a set-up fee. They do not offer the range of reports that some of the other agencies do. They prefer to work through computer but will go on an 800 number for a slightly higher rate. Avert will also check previous employer verifications by telephone for approximately $14.00 for two references.

- COURT-FAX, a division of Pooled Office Services, 225 Broadway New York, New York 10007. FAX 800-486-3628 Outside New York City. Probably the most comprehensive service for court document retrieval for the New York area.

- COURT RECORDS CONSULTANTS 17029 Devonshire St., Suite 166, Northridge, CA 91325. FAX 818-366-1985. CRC provides reasonably priced "usual" searches, credit, address update, marriage, death, person locator, etc. but, as you could surmise by their name, they specialize in court records, public filings, financial information including asset searches, and process serving. Additionally CRC will do patent and trademark searches, federal aviation, consumer public filings. UCC documents, vessels, and professional licensing (such as nurses, contractors, etc.). They require a $100.00 setup fee but have no monthly minimum. You pay only for the searches you run.

- FAX-CESS PO Drawer 429, Magnolia, MS 39652 (a division of INTEC), FAX # 601-783-2111. You can access this third-tier provider directly by faxing in the form printed in this book...

- FAXWORLD INTERNATIONAL, LTD. 330 West Maryland, Suite 106, Phoenix, AZ 85013. FAX 602-265-5016. Specializes in locate searches when you have the social security number. They claim they go through more credit bureaus than anyone else out there including some of the smaller branches such as Evict Alert, Chilton and ACS. Not particularly cheap. The average is about $50.00 a search with a $100.00 yearly membership fee.

- FERRARI, Online Information Brokers Eight Tudor Court, Getzville, NY 14068. FAX 716-689-6661. FERRARI claims to offer twice as many searches as their nearest competitor. This could be true since they offer over 150 separate and distinct searches. FERRARI is set up for computer inquiries that return text files directly to your printer or they will deal with you on a toll-free voice phone or FAX service. They also have some nice add-on fees such as FAX/rush call back Their coverage is national and they don't limit themselves to online records, as they do search out non-computer available resources.

FERRARI searches the US, Canada, and over 280 foreign countries and their searches include all the usual vital statistics: telephone number from name and address, skip trace, real property, pre-employment, civil statewide, civil county, consumer credit, date of birth identifier, federal tax liens, garbage retrieval service, (no, I'm not kidding - $475.00 plus *shipping*.)

FERRARI has maintained a very good reputation in this business and considers itself an original source for most of its searches (as opposed to simply going through another data bank and adding a value added charge) to your request.

The down side is that you need to contribute a $300.00 start-up fee plus a $25.00 connection fee.

- INTERNATIONAL RESEARCH BUREAU, INC. 1331 East Lafayette St., Suites A & B, PO Box 14189, Tallahassee, FL 32317. FAX: 904-561-1377. Especially good in the state of Florida. They provide such interesting things as a search conducted with the Florida Department of Highway, Safety, and Motor Vehicles that reports all motor vehicle accidents that an individual has been involved in from 1983 to the most recent update. This includes whether the target was the driver, passenger, or pedestrian. They also offer lots of good asset searches. Some nice background information and criminal history search, and DMV stuff in the state of Florida. They do a few nationwide searches but they are the same ones handled by everyone else.

- INFORMATION BANK OF TEXAS, INC. 111 W. 14th St., Houston, TX 77008. FAX: 713-862-6237. More limited searching agency, the Information Bank specializes in both data and offline (HUMINT) investigations within the Texas region. They provide state records, federal records, tracing, as well as video surveillance, witness statements, witness locates, liability and asset discovery.

- IRSC, INC., Information Resource Service Company 3777 N. Harbor Blvd., Fullerton, CA 92635, 800-640-4772 (California only), 800-841-1990 (outside California). One of the real major database providers around ISRC operates from their 8,000 square foot facility in Fullerton, California, with 50 employees that specialize in information resources. They use a state-of-the-art mainframe computer and will access almost all types of data from skip tracing, employment screening, consumer credit reports, to asset searches, national locates, criminal records, driver records, business databases and some special combined searches that will hit one or more of the identifiers and cross match them with other data. Prices are quite reasonable. They require a computer and a modem and work directly online with a user-friendly scenario. Most reports are ready in ten minutes. Some take 24 hours or more. One of the faster and more reasonably priced agencies in the information- providing business. They'll accept VISA and Master Card and appear to hit most of the important databases. Their initial sign-up fee is $250.00 and there's a monthly maintenance fee of $30.00.

- LOGAN REGISTRATION SERVICE P. O. Box 161644, Sacramento, CA 95816. FAX: 800-524-4111, DMV Systems Technology Specialists. Logan offers some of the cheapest DMV, Alpha, and driver's license searches available on a national basis. Prices vary depending on the time you allow for processing (they'll do overnight) and how you access them (FAX, non-urgent, mail in, mail back, phone in, mail report, or 72 hour special phone-to-phone). LRS can provide such esoteric documents as parking violations and plate renewal information. They also do the same thing on other vessels such as boats and airplanes.

- MOTOR VEHICLE RECORDS, INC. 307 Dolphin Street, Suite 4A, Baltimore, MD 21217. FAX: 301-669-8165. Specialists in driving records, vehicle registrations, title history search, tag search, vehicle I. D. search, duplicate titles, repo titles, and a number of other ancillary searches such as nationwide accident reports, witness locates, birth certificates, assets, and criminal records. They seem to be one of the

more reasonably-priced national sources for DMV and title information .

- NIGHTHAWK ENTERPRISES 5311 Miller Ave., Klamath Falls, OR 97603. One-stop source for SS number traces, employment, criminal address update and much more. Nighthawk is run by a couple who are licensed private investigators and I have personally used them for several traces and found them as good as advertised.

- QUEST & ASSOCIATES. INC. P. O. Box 23323, Pittsburgh, PA 15222. FAX: 412-563-6869. A Pennsylvania based corporation that specializes in the processing and retrieval of public records. They have active researchers available throughout Pennsylvania and provide service there cheaply and effectively. As with most info providers, they offer some national access to vehicle registrations, driving records, criminal records, federal bankruptcy, etc. Good prices.

- SOURCE INVESTIGATIVE SERVICES P. O. Box 88, Cookeville, TN 38503. FAX: 615-528-1989, offers the usual change of address, crisscross surname search, driver's license history, vehicle search, etc., but have featured no access fee, subscription fee, or minimum search. Prices are actually quite good and they have a couple of interesting searches that are not found in other bureaus such as worker's compensation claim reports and nationwide search for federal penitentiary information, as well as, county wide criminal search in most states.

- SUGARBAKER INVESTIGATIONS P. O. Box 272312, Tampa, FL 33688. FAX: 813-264-2567. Although they work for some of the largest insurance companies and law firms in the country, they also encourage private individuals in such areas as customized investigations surveillance, workman's compensation, driving records, social security records, skip locates, etc. Fees are a little bit higher than some of the more general providers but Florida the charges are very reasonable.

- SUPERBUREAU 2600 Garden Road, 224 West, P. O. Box 2246, Monterey, CA 93942. FAX: 800-4223-8915, a major information broker accessible 24 hours a day, 365 days a year. Accessible by modem or FAX. They require a subscription to their service but then make available tracking services, real property, public records, business records, motor vehicle records, workman's compensation, miscellaneous including consumer reports, data research, super searches for business and consumers, liens, telephone traces, vehicle and vessel information. Again, this is a large agency that tends to deal with attorneys or other professionals, but unlike many they branch out by offering non-detective based database research such as legal or medical research or new research along with business records. Prices are reasonable and their scope is wide.

- TRACERS CHOICE POB 5207, Buena Park, CA 90622. tc is a great resource for professional investigators. They will provide you with direct access to METRONET for (at this time) $50 a monthly minimum (METRONET wants $600 a month) plus bargain credit header searches. TRACER'S CHOICE works from FAX or MCI mail for the header searches, METRONET is accessed directly from your computer and you use their rather antiquated menu system.

YOU MUST BE A PROFESSIONAL and be able to use a computer to sign up with TC. They **do not** offer online nor customer service type help.

- VEHICLE OPERATOR SEARCHES PO Box 15334, Sacramento, CA 95851. FAX: 1-800-999-2818. Drivers searches, vehicle searches, social security searches, social locators, locator searches, surname searches, real estate searches, corporation searches, and out-of-state searches.

As one would figure, they specialize in vehicle searches including VIN numbers, plate to owner, driver's registration and soundex searches (by name and date of birth or driver's license number only). They require a $10.00 set-up fee and a $50.00 credit balance. The cost of each report is deducted from the balance. Their fees vary depending on what you want and how you want it. Mail or FAX in with mail back on a driver's license will run as little as $4.00 in California and up to $25.00 with vehicle photo history or Alpha reports (a name search for vehicles by name and address; must have full address to search) brings back a full motor vehicle report on your party including full name, address, physical description, date of birth, license status, violations and any accidents or suspension. Available in most states.

- WORLDWIDE TRACER'S SERVICE POB 6951 Corpus Christi, TX 78466. Confidential information specialists, a well-known firm that has been in existence for some time and used by many private detectives. One of the best sources for confidential information or surname type searches.

OTHER DATA PROVIDERS:
- AA CREDIT INFORMATION SERVICES 4419 Cowan Road, Suite 201A, Tucker, GA 30084.
- ATLANTIC INTERNATIONAL ASSOCIATES FAX: 207-761-0834.
- AMERICAN INFORMATION NETWORK 165 E. Southern Ave., #101, Mesa, AZ 85210.
- APSCREEN 2043 Westcliff, Newport Beach, CA 92663.
- CREDIT BUREAU REPORTS 1801 Gateway Blvd., Suite 210, Richardson, TX 75080.
- DAC SERVICES 4110 S. 100th East Avenue, #200, Tulsa, OK 74146.
- DATA CHECK P. O. Box 922169, Sylmar, CA 91392.
- DATAFAX P. O. Box 33244, Austin, TX 78764.
- DATA SEARCH - 3600 American River Drive, Sacramento, CA 95864.
- DATATRAC P. O. Box 703, Port Coquitlam, B.C., V3B 6H9. FAX 604 469-9609.

- FARMER & ASSOCIATES 16845 N. 29th Ave., Suite 1205, Phoenix AZ 85023. FAX 602-938-2688.
- INFORMATION BROKERS OF COLORADO 2888 Bluff St., Suite 152, Boulder, CO 80301.
- INTELLIGENCE NETWORK INCORPORATED P. O. Box 7227, Clearwater, FL 34617. FAX 813-448-0949.
- INTERNATIONAL RESEARCH BUREAU, INC. P. O. B. 14189, Tallahassee, FL 32317. Offers an unusual Accident Search service which is conducted with the Florida Department of Highway Safety and Motor Vehicles. Returns all accidents an individual has been involved in since 1983. Searches for the target as a driver, passenger and pedestrian. Florida only, $25.
- INTERSTATE CREDIT BUREAU 1581 N. Debra Sue, Tucson, AZ 85715.
- J. DILLION ROSS & COMPANY P. O. Box 539, Pauma Valley, CA 92061.
- MCCORD COMPANY 1915 "I" Street, Sacramento, CA 95814.
- NATIONAL CREDIT REPORTING 1211 Park Avenue, Suite 207, San Jose, CA 95126.
- NATIONAL INFORMATION RESOURCE SERVICE P. O. Box 1021, Jackson, MI 49204.
- THE SOURCE P. O. Box 88, Cookeville, TN 38503. FAX: 615-528-1986.
- SUPERIOR INVESTIGATION SERVICES 3130 Impala Dr., #201, San Jose, CA 95117. Online database access plus a licensed PI.
- UCC NETWORK 185-A Commerce Circle, Sacramento, CA 95815.

Many private detectives also offer search services, either by direct information provider access or with "enhanced" services that PI's are legally allowed to conduct.

Here are a couple of great trakcers you can use by tearing out the following forms (or, of course, Xeroxing them right from the comfort of your living room. Tracer's needs a check or money order, Nighthawk may still do credit cards – call or fax them).

TRACER'S WORLDWIDE SERVICES POB 6951, Corpus Christi, TX 78466, is one of the best known and correctly priced info brokers available. Besides the usual searches they offer a find-anyone-by-first name, find-anyone-by-first-or-last-name without/without address SS number and other delimiters.

Basically they can locate almost anyone living or dead inexpensively.

Tracer's also specializes in finding most anyone's assets: bank accounts, stocks, real estate, vehicles, boats, planes, employer.

They will do pre-employment reports, workman's comp, public & semipublic records, driving histories, UCC files, telephone information, criminal records, D & B reports, marriage & divorce records and a number of proprietary databases.

More than 600 detective agencies go thru TRACER'S to get their information.

Tracer's demands:
- No sign-up fee
- No monthly minimum
- No computers needed

In fact you can tear out, or photocopy the following form and deal with them directly.
No credit cards...

SAMPLE SEARCHES FROM TRACERS INCLUDE:

SSN Search
(Social Security Number Search)
Has been expanded to search through over a half billion social security number that have been compiled from over 10,000 credit bureaus and insurance company claims files. Needless to say, there is a duplication of individuals, except that the addresses that will be reported may be different, hence the disparity. The information reported is as follows: names used with social security number, address (up to seven), dates, and spouse (if available), 85% successful.

SSN Lite

(Social Security Number Search)
Same as above with the exception of the insurance company claims files.

Personal Identifier

Wonder who a person really is? Give us that person's name & address and we will report all or most of the following information. SSN number, spouse, former addresses, age or DOB, last known employer & former employers.

Nearby Neighbor

This search will report the following number of nearby neighbors of a given address, (5) (10) (20). Information reported name, address, telephone number.

People Tracker

This database contains over 165 million addresses with the people who reside there. Compiled from phone directories, voter registration lists, drivers licenses, graduation lists & magazine subscriptions. Searches can be made by first & last name or just by last name only. These searches are limited to city & nearby communities or by state. Usual information returned is name, address and telephone number.

People Tracker Plus

This database is essentially the same as above, but not as large. Besides searching by first & last name or by last name only, it also can search by first name only (this is good when a female has an unusual first name but has assumed their husbands last name) searches also can be made by zip code parameters for the entire USA. Information reported can include address, telephone number & date of birth (when available).

Membership

Give us the name of the club or organization your interested in and we will report to you the names of persons who are members who are listed in "Who's Who." There are over 82,000 people indexed, so if the subject of your inquiry is an accomplished person in business, sports, government, entertainment, science & technology, the arts, there's a good chance their there. Data in records also include career history, education, creative works, publications, family background, current address, political activities, religion and special achievements. Give it a try, you'll be pleasantly surprised.

Questionable Doctors

More than 10,000 doctors disciplined by States or Federal Government for Criminal Convictions, Drug Abuse, Misprescribing, Overprescribing and Substandard Care. Information Reported: Disciplinary Actions Taken.

Federal Penitentiary

This search will report if a person is currently or has been incarcerated in a federal corrections facility. Information required: Name, SSN, DOB, race/sex. Information reported: Name, DOB, conviction charge; place incarcerated, term of incarceration, release date, jurisdiction released to (if available). State prison searches are also obtainable.

California/Tax Bill

In CA we can also search the address to see what other tax bills are being sent there, this is especially good when you suspect that a person with a common name owns more than one property or has those properties in an other name. Typically returned information: name of property owner, address, assessed value, parcel number. In CA we can give a detailed report on property in most cases.

Criminal Convictions/Statewide

AR, CO, DC, FL, ***GA, ***ID, IN, **KS, KY, ME, **MI, ***MN, *MO, MT, ND, *NE, **NM, OK, *OR, PA, SC, ***VA, WI. Information required: Name, SSN, DOB, race/sex in all states. (*need home address) (need release) (***need notarized release).

PRICE LIST

Address search	$35.00/ea
Aircraft search	$20.00/ea
Business tracker	$15.00/ea
California civil $25.00/ea	$60.00/all
California death $7.00/yr	$21.50/min
California divorce $7.00/yr	$21.50/min
California marrige $7.00/yr	$21.50/min
California tax bill	$35.00/ea
Canadian tracker	$50.00/ea
Change of address	$15.00/ea
Clipping service	$25.00/mo
Competitive intelligence	cost varies
Corporations	$75.00/ea
Criminal/county	$35.00/ea
Criminal/state	$75.00/ea
Death records (national	$10.00/ea
1st name only	$50.00/ea
Directory assistanceEach bell	$10.00/ea
Drivers license history	$35.00/ea
Dun & Bradstreet Report No. 1	$75.00/ea
Report No. 2	$100.00/ea
Report No. 3	$250.00/ea
Expert search	$35.00/ea
Federal pen	$50.00/ea
Federal track	cost varies
Licence plate	$35.00/ea
Membership	$50.00/ea
Motor vehicles	$50.00/ea
Miscellaneous	cost varies
Nearby business neighbors	$15.00/ea
Nearby residence neighbors	
10 neighbors	$15.00/ea
20 neighbors	$20.00/ea
New Jersey civil, all	$100.00/ea
New York civil, all	$125.00/ea
Newspaper & magazines	cost varies
Pennsylvania civil, all	$75.00/ea
People tracker,	
per 100 names returned	$15.00/ea
People tracker plus,	
per 100 names returned	$15.00/ea
1st name only	$200.00/ea
Personal identification	$25.00/ea
Pilot	$20.00/ea
PO Box	$95.00/ea

Pre-employment	
Report No. 1	$39.00/ea
Report No. 2	$59.00/ea
Report No. 3	$125.00/ea
Probate research	cost varies
Questionnaire doctors	$75.00/ea
Real property (countywide	$35.00/ea
Real property (statewide)	cost varies
Skip tracing	$175.00/ea
SSN identifier	$10.00/ea
SSN lite	$25.00/ea
SSN search	$50.00/ea
State prison	$50.00/ea
State track	cost varies
Telephone	$10.00/ea
Texas death $7.00/yr	$21.00/min
Texas divorce $7.00/yr	$21.00/min
Texas households	$25.00/ea
Texas ID & drivers	$25.00/ea
Texas marriage $7.00/yr	$21.00/yr
Texas tags	$15.00/yr
Incomplete plate numbers	cost varies
Texas vehicles	$25.00/ea
Trash audit	$300.00/ea
Trade scan, federal	$75.00/ea
Trade scan, state	$75.00/ea
Trapline plus$15.00 per	
telephone number identified	$50.00/ea
UCC files	$50.00/ea
VIN search	$35.00/ea
Voters registration	$15.00/ea
Workmans comp	$15.00/ea
Yellow pages	$15.00/ea

ADDITIONAL CHARGES

Texas Sales Tax (Texas businesses & resident add sales tax)	7.75%
Mail back (Results are mailed back to you)	no charge
FAX back (Results FAXed back to you)	$5.00
Call back (Results verbally reported, not all searches available)	$10.00
Rush Service (Where available, not available on all searches)	$20.00
Zip ID (Searches that require a zip code you don't provide)	$5.00
County ID (Searches that require name of county you don't provide)	$5.00

AVAILABLE SEARCHES

01. Address to name & neighbors
02. Address verifier - business
03. Address verifier - consumer
04. Address to telephone - Canada
05. Address locator - utility search
06. Address locator - Credit
07. Address locator - mailing list
08. Address locator - USPOD
09. Address from name and City
10. Aircraft owner by name/registration
11. Bank assets from name & SSN
12. Bank asset search - business
13. Bank acct. verification - business
14. Bank acct. verification - individual
15. Bank asset search - individual
16. Bankruptcy records
17. Bankruptcy search - nationwide
18. Birth record search
19. Business credit report - TRW
20. Business credit -
    Canadian manufacturers
    & service companies
21. Business subsidiary search
22. Business government contract search
23. Business credit report -
    obtained archived records
24. Business credit report - info. on file
25. Business credit report -
    abbreviated summary on file
26. Business credit report -
    develop information
27. Canadian federal corporations
    & directors
28. Civil records by county
29. Civil statewide
30. College degree and attendance
    verification
31. Consumer credit report -
    CBI/TRW credit grantor's phone list
32. Consumer credit report -
    US all major credit bureaus
33. Consumer credit report - foreign
34. Consumer credit report - Canada
35. Corporation records - Canada
    nationwide search
36. Corporation records - US by state
37. Criminal identifier search
38. Criminal convictions - statewide
39. Criminal convictions - countywide
40. Criminal convictions - Canada
41. Criminal convictions -
    citywide/municipal
42. Date of birth identifier
43. Death record search - by county
44. Death record search - national
45. Divorce records by county
46. Employment search - national
47. Employment search - current employer
48. Employment search - 2 years back
49. Federal tax liens
50. Federal court records - criminal
51. Federal court records - civil
52. Foreign investigations
    & record recovery
53. Garbage retrieval service
54. Immigration research
55. Insurance casualty claim history
56. Litigation search -
    judgments/statewide
57. Litigation search - Canada
58. Litigation search - hand search/civil
59. Marriage records data
60. MVR registration search by name US
61. MVR - plate checks - Canada
62. MVR - plate checks
63. MVR - vehicle identification number
    search for title holder
64. MVR title search - NY only
65. MVR driving record from name only
66. MVR driving record from driver ID#
67. MVR driving record from name
    search from name & DOB
68. MVR driving record from name
    & DOB only
69. MVR driving record from name
    & DOB only - Canada
70. National cross reference book
71. People - trak service - monthly report
    giving address update
72. PO box trace from name and POB#
73. Police clearance for overseas
    employment
74. Pre-employment investigation

75. Probate search by county
76. Real property - national/business & Virgin Islands
77. Real property - limited national search by name
78. Real property - statewide by name
79. Real property - county search by name or address
80. Real property - county search by legal description
81. Real property - county search by
82. Security dealer background
83. Security exchange commission
84. Skip trace - nationwide from name & last known address
85. Social security - number to name
86. Social security - number to name trance enhanced

87. Social security - name to number identifier
88. State tax liens
89. Stocks & bonds search
90. Telephone trace all business using phone number
91. Telephone trace to address - consumers only
92. Telephone trace to address - name and address
93. Trade marks - Canada
94. Truck driver history
95. Uniform commercial code
96. Vital statistics - international guidebook
97. Workers comp claim records

Each state has different rules and regulations, costs, and time frames. Call for specifics.

TRACERS WORLDWIDE SERVICES

P.O. Box 6951 Corpus Christi, Tx 78466
Administration 512- 854-1892
Toll Free Customer Assistance - US and Possessions 800-233-9766
Facsimile - telecopier 512-854-0879

APPLICATION   Instruction: Please type or print legibly...complete information **must** be included.

Company, Firm or Agency Name: _____

❑ Sole proprietorship ❑ Partnership ❑ Corporation: DUNS# if listed_____

Classification:

❑ Private Investigator ❑ Law Firm ❑ Insurance Company ❑ Insurance Adjuster ❑ Corporate Legal Dept

❑ Corporate Personnel Dept ❑ Other (description) _____

Street Address:_____

Mailing Address: _____

Business Phone:{   } _____Fax Number {   } _____

State/City License # and where issued:_____Type: _____

Principal of company or officer of Corporation: {For Companies not listed in Dun & Bradstreet}

Name: _____DOB:_____SS#: _____

Home Address: _____

Home Phone: _____Title:_____

Corporate Parent/Holding Co.: _____

Address:_____

Date of Corporate Filing:_____Corp #: _____State: _____

Credit References

Name:_____

Address:_____Tel#_____

Name:_____

Address: _____Tel# _____

Banking Reference: Bank: _____Account #:_____

Branch Address: _____Phone # : _____

PLEASE PHOTOCOPY — MAIL

NIGHTHAWK ENTERPRISES AGREEMENT
5311 Miller Avenue–Klamath Falls, OR 97603 – (503) 884-7400

NIGHTHAWK ENTERPRISES 5311 Miller Ave., Klamath Falls, OR 97603, is a husband and wife team that has been supplying information for many pro's, for many years. I've used them and been very happy with the results.

They do require a $50 sign up fee, but can then be accessed directly by FAX. Fill out the agreement, send in your $50, and use them for the following searches (plus a number of others).

To subscriber: We ask for one time only start-up fee of $50. At the end of each month we will send you a statement showing your usage and ask that you remit the month's charges. There are no monthly service charges or minimums. You pay only for your request.

I AM SIGNING UP FOR NIGHTHAWK INFORMATION SERVICES BY ENCLOSING $50

FIND ENCLOSED ( ) CHECK OR ( ) MONEY ORDER

_____   _____
USER NAME   COMPANY NAME

_____   _____
TELEPHONE NUMBER   ADDRESS

_____   _____
FAX NUMBER   CITY   STATE   ZIP

INDIVIDUAL WHO PERSONALLY GUARANTEES PAYMENT OF CHARGES:

_____
NAME   TITLE

_____
RESIDENCE ADDRESS   CITY   STATE   ZIP

Above named client agrees that the information obtained through NIGHTHAWK ENTERPRISES will be used for lawful purposes only and agrees to hold NIGHTHAWK ENTERPRISES harmless for any use or misuse of this service.

Client agrees to pay all charges for searches requested and performed by NIGHTHAWK ENTERPRISES regardless of results; to pay charges in full upon monthly statements; to pay

2% monthly interest on charges that are past due; to pay reasonable attorney fees for the enforcement of this agreement. No searches will be performed for overdue accounts.

_____

SIGNATURE OF GUARANTOR   DATE

DESCRIPTION & REQUIREMENTS   **PRICE**

1. Vehicle registration by license plate/VIN number for OR.....................$ 5.00

CO, FL, IA, ID, KS, KY, MD, MS,
ND, NE, NH, NV, OK, SD, WA, TX...$10.00

AK, AL, AR, DE, IN, MA, ME, MN, MO, MT, NC, NJ, NM,
NY, OH, PA, RI, SC, TN, UT, VA, VT, WI, WV, WY...$15.00

AZ, CT, DC, IL, LA...$20.00

A search by either license plate number or by vehicle ID number. This report supplies the name & address of the registered & legal owner (in most states) and a complete description of vehicle.

Requirements: License plate number and state or vehicle ID number. In all states except CA, GA, HI.

2. Moving violations report (MVR) for OR....................................see OR DMV list.

All other states except those list below..$15.00

AL, AZ, CT, DC, LA, MA, MI, NH.. $20.00

CANADA...$25.00

Provides current information from DMV. Lists the full name, address, physical description, date of birth, license status, violations and any accidents or suspensions. No longer available for California.

Requirements: Name, driver's license number or date of birth (some states require additional information.)

3. Soundex search (MVR): Same prices as MVR (#2) except requirements.

Provides current information from DMV. Lists the full name, address, physical description, date of birth, license status, violations and any accidents or suspensions.

Requirements: Name and date of birth, or by driver's license only (in a few states.) No longer available for California.

4. Alpha search (MVR) – Same prices as MVR (#2) except requirements and report.

A search by name (and address) processed through DMV. Provides the name, address and all vehicles registered to the subject.

Requirements: Full name and address, not available for California.

5a. Social security search..$15.00

5b. Social security search (2 databases)...$20.00

5c. Social security search (5a & 5b combined search).........................$30.00

Search by social security number. Provides the current address and name of subject. This search is nationwide.

Requirements: Social security number, name (optional.)

6. National movers index...$15.00

Search by name and address. Provides current and previous addresses.

Requirements: Name and current or previous address.

7. National Locator Search..$23.00

Search available by name, address, social security number & date of birth, if available. Provides possible new addresses, sometimes DOB & SSN.

Requirements: Name (full if possible), address with zip, SSN helps.

8. Interstate consumer public filings...$25.00

Provides bankruptcies, federal court filings and any judgments against subject.

Requirements: Name and state.

9. Statewide criminal records search..$75.00

Provides only felony convictions by state.

Requirements: Name, address, SSN & DOB.

10. National business record, business record with financial abstract, business financial report.

These three searches are of the same database at different levels of information for corporations. Information on over 1.5 million corporations are available at the business record (10a) level. About half of those reports are available at the full financial report level (10c). Since we do not know at which level the information on a particular corporation exists until we access the database, specifying the request number is your way of letting us know what level of report is to be the "limit" for charges. If you request a 16c but only a 16a is available, you will be charged accordingly. We will retrieve as much information as you authorize, but only charge you for the depth of information found. Data provided:

10a. National business record...$50.00
              Cost for no record found............................$20.00

Company name, address, telephone number, SIC code, number of employees, related names (AKA's), company history, names of owners/principles, biographical info on owner/principals, detail of incorporation & stock ownership, primary lines of business, detail on parents, subsidiaries or branch locations, net sales & net worth for the past year.

10b. National business record with financial abstract..........................$75.00
              Cost for no record found............................$20.00

All information listed in 10b, Plus: total assets, total liabilities, net profit after tax, quick ratios, current ratio, return on sales, assets & net worth, percent change since last period, industry norms, industry performance rankings. (For the most current year)

10c. National business financial report...$140.00
              Cost for no record found............................$20.00

11. Vital information locator...$28.50

Provides social security number, employer, DOB, and spouse's name. This is a search of "credit header" information.

Requirements: Name and address.

12. Driver's license number locator...$45.00

Provides driver's license number.

Requirements: Name, address and DOB.

T.s.s. 330 W. Maryland, Suite 106, Phoenix, AZ 89013, requires no start -up cost and will work directly with you over your FAX machine for most searches.

Call them for current pricing and fax in the necessary info.

They will even do credit searches (for legal reasons).

INDIVIDUAL CERTIFICATION FORM

Date:_____   Direct FAX Inquiry

This form is a signed certification requesting a consumer report from the user whose name and address appear below.

_____
Name of Person Requesting Report

_____
Name of Company

_____   _____
Telephone Number   FAX Number

I certify that the credit report on the individual(s) whose name(s) appear(s) below is being requested for one of the purposes checked off by me and for no other purpose, and that I am a duly authorized representative of the company on behalf of which I request this report.

_____   _____
Consumers Name   Social Security Number

_____   _____
Spouses Name   Social Security Number

_____
Address

_____   _____   _____
City   State   Zip Code

Check one or more of the Purpose of Report

( ) In response to the order of a court having jurisdiction to issue an order.
( ) In accordance with the written instructions of the consumer to whom it relates.
( ) In connection with a credit transaction involving the consumer on whom the information is to be furnished and involving extension of credit to, or review or collection of an account of the consumer.
( ) On an individual being considered for employment, promotion or transfer to another position.
( ) On an individual who is applying for insurance.
( ) Requester has a legitimate business need for the information in connection with a business transaction involving the consumer.

I also understand that any person who knowingly and willfully obtains information on a consumer from a consumer reporting agency under false pretenses be fined not more than $5,000 or imprisoned not more than one year or both.

_____   _____
Authorized Signature   Position or Title

Consumer Release:
I certify that I am the above mentioned consumer and that I fully authorize the release of the information being requested.

_____   _____
Consumer Signature   Date

AVAILABLE SEARCHES

01. Address to name & neighbors
02. Address verifier - business
03. Address verifier - consumer
04. Address to telephone - Canada
05. Address locator - utility search
06. Address locator - Credit
07. Address locator - mailing list
08. Address locator - USPOD
09. Address from name and City
10. Aircraft owner by name/registration
11. Bank assets from name & SSN
12. Bank asset search - business
13. Bank acct. verification - business
14. Bank acct. verification - individual
15. Bank asset search - individual
16. Bankruptcy records
17. Bankruptcy search - nationwide
18. Birth record search
19. Business credit report - TRW
20. Business credit -
    Canadian manufacturers
    & service companies
21. Business subsidiary search
22. Business government contract search
23. Business credit report -
    obtained archived records
24. Business credit report - info. on file
25. Business credit report -
    abbreviated summary on file
26. Business credit report -
    develop information
27. Canadian federal corporations
    & directors
28. Civil records by county
29. Civil statewide
30. College degree and attendance
    verification
31. Consumer credit report -
    CBI/TRW credit grantor's phone list
32. Consumer credit report -
    US all major credit bureaus
33. Consumer credit report - foreign
34. Consumer credit report - Canada

35. Corporation records - Canada
    nationwide search
36. Corporation records - US by state
37. Criminal identifier search
38. Criminal convictions - statewide
39. Criminal convictions - countywide
40. Criminal convictions - Canada
41. Criminal convictions -
    citywide/municipal
42. Date of birth identifier
43. Death record search - by county
44. Death record search - national
45. Divorce records by county
46. Employment search - national
47. Employment search - current employer
48. Employment search - 2 years back
49. Federal tax liens
50. Federal court records - criminal
51. Federal court records - civil
52. Foreign investigations
    & record recovery
53. Garbage retrieval service
54. Immigration research
55. Insurance casualty claim history
56. Litigation search -
    judgments/statewide
57. Litigation search - Canada
58. Litigation search - hand search/civil
59. Marriage records data
60. MVR registration search by name US
61. MVR - plate checks - Canada
62. MVR - plate checks
63. MVR - vehicle identification number
    search for title holder
64. MVR title search - NY only
65. MVR driving record from name only
66. MVR driving record from driver ID#
67. MVR driving record from name
    search from name & DOB
68. MVR driving record from name
    & DOB only
69. MVR driving record from name
    & DOB only - Canada

AVAILABLE SEARCHES
(continued)

70. National cross reference book
71. People - trak service - monthly report giving address update
72. PO box trace from name and POB#
73. Police clearance for overseas employment
74. Pre-employment investigation
75. Probate search by county
76. Real property - national/business & Virgin Islands
77. Real property - limited national search by name
78. Real property - statewide by name
79. Real property - county search by name or address
80. Real property - county search by legal description
81. Real property - county search by
82. Security dealer background
83. Security exchange commission

84. Skip trace - nationwide from name & last known address
85. Social security - number to name
86. Social security - number to name trance enhanced
87. Social security - name to number identifier
88. State tax liens
89. Stocks & bonds search
90. Telephone trace all business using phone number
91. Telephone trace to address - consumers only
92. Telephone trace to address - name and address
93. Trade marks - Canada
94. Truck driver history
95. Uniform commercial code
96. Vital statistics - international guidebook
97. Workers comp claim records
98. Zip code ident.

Each state has different rules and regulations, costs, and time frames. Call for specifics.

ASSET TRACKING

The next logical step after finding someone, at least for most attorneys, collection agents, and skip tracers, is to locate sizeable assets. This is not as easy as it sounds. True, the IRS has a fairly good record in this field but the average person will find many road blocks when it comes to tracking down real property, bank accounts, stocks and bonds. There are a few providers, both large and small, who offer asset tracking services. Most of them also offer the more common searches we've already covered, but specialize in asset tracking.

- AMERICAN SAFE DEPOSIT BOX 330 W. Main St., Greenwood, IN 46412. One of the few companies that will locate safe deposit boxes of deceased or incompetent people. You must supply a death certificate or a letter of conservatorship issued by a probate court before they will search.

- PRENTICE HALL LEGAL & FINANCIAL SERVICES Simon & Schuster Professional Information Group 500 Central Avenue, Albany, NY 12205. FAX: 518-459-2959. Probably is the nation's largest public record information management company and they can retrieve public documents in any state including incorporation services, franchise tax searches, pending suit searches, bankruptcy searches, trademark scans, real property searches, patent searches, accident reports as well as various partnership, franchise tax, and lien services which will often come up with otherwise hidden property including stocks and bonds, airplanes, and boats.

PRENTICE HALL offers instant verbal response in a number of states and delayed hard copy response in the rest of the country. They are also going online for instant computer access.

- D.Y. JONES & ASSOCIATES, INC, is a full-service investigation company providing diverse and specific investigations to numerous law firms, banks and institutions. They offer asset investigations of varying depth, as well as, background investigations and due diligence investigations.

Their BASIC ASSET INVESTIGATION will confirm the identity of the subject, provide or verify his locations, list sources of income, banking affiliations on all types of accounts, business affiliations, Fictitious Names, partnerships, corporations, etc., plus updated and analyzed credit reports, statewide record searches (judgments, liens, default notices and bankruptcy), county records, real property search (on a statewide basis), other public records and other assets.

They also have an EXTENDED ASSET INVESTIGATION which adds stocks, bonds and mutual funds, probate records and UCC filing statements.

These records are very difficult to find elsewhere and the cost of $400 for a BASIC SEARCH and $650.00 for the extended is actually quite reasonable. JONES is a large firm with a good reputation. they have offices in Los Angeles, San Francisco, Sacramento, San Diego, Orange country (Fullerton), Riverside (California) and Ventura. Check with directory assistance for the office closest to you or contact their main office at 800-228-5112.

- INFORMATION AMERICA Online Solutions 600 W. Peachtree St. NW, Atlanta, GA 30308. IA is the "fastest growing online information service in America". For a onetime account establishing fee of $50.00, they will provide you with a user guide, and some training, and put you online in order to provide such records as state UCC and lien findings, judgments, partnership records, SEC filings, commercial lending and loan workouts which allow you to correlate information and find assets for collateral or recover funds, property transfers. They also have a program called SLEUTH which helps track moneys through a variety of corporate and commercial searches.

IA is used by attorneys to perform discovery during litigation, come up with assets and liens, identify relationships between individuals and businesses, locate businesses, etc. IA is a definite asset for anyone who wants to follow people for money through various transactions.

- VIGIL ENTERPRISES 1804 Tribute Road, Suite 210, Sacramento, CA 95815. FAX: 916-927-3389. In business since 1978, Vigil has acted as a licensed private investigative agency, business government consulting firm and consulting agency. They've been involved in such notorious cases as the tracking and recovery of assets in the Ferdinand Marcos case, the American Savings and Loan scandal, Saddleback National Bank bankruptcy fraud, etc. They specialize in corporate filings, real estate searches, asset searches, and corporate information.

- HYLIND INFOQUEST, INC. 307 Dolphin Street, Baltimore, MD 21217. A public record search and document retrieval company specializing in the ferreting out of Uniform Commercial Code and corporate records throughout the United States. They also perform federal tax lien, judgment and real property searches, as well as, the usual miscellaneous tracking type searches.

- APB 2047 Victory Blvd., Staten Island, NY 10314. FAX: 718-494-0578. A one-stop shopping center for information research and security services. They do everything from providing body guards and armed escorts to tracking assets including bank accounts, real property, and motor vehicles.

- THE BUTCHER COMPANIES 1424 W. Century Ave., Suite 106, Bismarck, ND 58501. FAX: 701-258-2637. A consortium of certified investigators and testers that do such things as drug testing and provide expert witnesses for medical cases. They also have an asset location service that will prove the true financial status of parties who may misrepresent their net worth.

As a side note, they also provide competitor intelligence services and seminars.

- DAMAR REAL ESTATE INFORMATION SERVICE 3550 W. Temple St., Los Angeles, CA 90004. Up-to-the-minute real property files for most California counties plus statewide ownership files, trustee deed database, commercial and industrial sales files, etc. DAMAR is an online database that provides instant results for California searching including specific address searches and comparable sales searches for wider area.

- TRW REDI PROPERTY DATA. One of the country's largest credit collectors is now offering real property information including ownership, parcel locating, titles, title insurance activity, area sales and analysis and tax information. This data is available on microfilm, online, even as mailing labels. Offices in Chicago, Ft. Lauderdale, New York City, Riverside (CA), Seattle. Main number 800-426-1466.

- UNISEARCH, The Boardwalk Building 525 Columbia Avenue NW, Suite 203, Olympia, WA 98501. FAX: 206-956-9504, National corporate and UCC searches including corporation dissolution, merger, reservation name, certified copy, status reports, limited partnerships, bankruptcy searches, tax liens, and property asset searches upon request.

- ACADEMY INVESTIGATIONS 29415 Avenida La Paz, #1, Cathedral City, CA 92234. FAX: 619-325-6245, specializing in attorneys, ACADEMY locates assets including bank searches, employment, real property, and comprehensive background searches.

- BANKRUPTCY DOCUMENT RETRIEVAL, INC., PO Box 45400, Laguna Beach, CA 92652. Specializes in retrieving bankruptcy documents from federal courthouses within the United States.

- CDB INFOTEK 6 Hilton Centre, Santa Ana, CA 92707. CDB is adding a real property asset investigative capability to their system. Good, so far only in California, this is a real time search which returns a wealth of information.

You can, of course, look for assets yourself by going to public record depositories, running a check through the target's bank account in order to get his bank account number (yes, all banks, by law, keep a record of their customers. No, they will probably not give it to you without a court warrant.)

You can also follow your target around for a day or so, run his DMV tags, run his house, generally figure out where he's coming from.

You can also go online – now please note that not all online services are completely up-to-date or accurate. You can miss stuff that would make a difference.

BANK HUNTING ON YOUR OWN

If you have a subpoena from a court you can force a bank to produce account information and/or of course, money.

A couple of quick tricks to help you find the bank include:
- If the target owns a business, get a friend to buy something by check.

- Watch his trash, especially towards the end of the month for statement envelopes
- Call the SOB up and tell him you're from the power company/phone company and you are about to turn his services off for non-payment of a back bill. Get the amount and account number so you can see if your "computer screwed up again."
- Call from a new bank and offer free checking plus a 9% Visa if he will transfer $2000 from his old bank. Get account #.
- Have a friend who owns a business, or store, send him a letter of apology for a recent overcharge and a check for $50. Problem here is that real scam artists know this trick and will toss it out, or worse, go down to your friend's bank and cash the check in person.

If you do find the account and have a subpoena to get the money, don't have the sheriff deliver it, place it with a private process server, call the bank on a daily basis until the money is in the account and have the server go *that day.*

The following guide is from CDB and shows, whether you use them, or do it by foot and phone, where many assets are found:

CDB INFOTEK has added a real property asset investigative service. Although limited primarily to California at the moment one can only hope this coverage will spread to other states as well.

TO LOCATE MORE ASSETS THAN EVER BEFORE...
- *Search for Ownership & Most Recent Transfer Information by Name* to uncover all real property owned by an individual or a business throughout the state of California and determine the assessed value of each parcel of property owned.

- Complete your research by reviewing information contained in *Bankruptcies, Liens & Judgments* for an individual or a business. Look for notices of default, foreclosure notices and tax liens which may have been filed against property. Or, in Los Angeles and San Francisco Counties, a *General Index* search can reveal mechanic's liens, deeds of re conveyance, quit claim deed and other property transfers.

- *Search for Ownership & Most Recent Transfer Information by Mailing Address* to determine if one or more California real property owners are receiving tax assessor bills at the same address. This search can identify real property listed under an individual's current name, a maiden name, a spouse's name, a family trust, a business, name, etc.

- Conduct follow-up searches of *Real Property Ownership & Most Recent Transfer Information by Name* using the spouse's name, business name, or any other affiliated party uncovered in your original search.

- *Search for Ownership & Most Recent Property Transfer Information by Property Address or parcel Number* to verify the owner(s) of a specific parcel of property and determine its assessed value.

- When unsure of the exact street address of a parcel of property, search a *"range" of address* which are in the same block of the property. Or, simply search by street name to uncover all property owners on a specific street.

- *Search for Refinance, Construction Loan & Seller Carry Back Information by Buyer/ Seller Name* to determine if an individual or a business has entered into a real property "non-purchase" transaction.

—Match *Refinance Information* against information obtained on a search of Owner & *Most Recent Transfer Information* to compare the original purchase and mortgage amounts with the amount refinanced. A further comparison of the average mortgage rates at the time of refinance can help determine, the approximate amount of the owner's monthly payment.

—Use *Construction Loan Information* to determine whether an individual or business is building a structure on a parcel of vacant land. Match the construction loan amount with the square footage and assessed value of the vacant land by conducting a search of *Ownership & Most Recent Transfer Information* to estimate the value of the property after construction. This important information can take up to a year or two to appear on other real property systems.

—Look for *Seller Carry Back Information* to discover when an individual or a business (seller) has an interest in the real property of another party. Even if previous searches for *Ownership & Most Recent Property Information* reflect that a subject does not own any real estate, this search can show that the individual or business is receiving "mortgage payments" as a result of carrying all or part of the buyer's real estate loan.

In Los Angeles or San Francisco Counties, conduct a *General Index* search to determine if the seller his/her interest to another party, or filed a notice of default against the buyer.

- Search for *Refinance, Construction Loan & Seller Carry Back Information by Lender Name* if an individual or business has an interest in the real property of another party. Using the address or parcel number of each identified property, conduct a search of *Ownership & Most Recent Transfer Information* to determine the value of parcel of property.

In Los Angeles or San Francisco Counties, conduct a *General Index* search to determine if the seller has assigned his/her interest to another party, or filed a notice of default against the buyer.

TO LOCATE PEOPLE & BUSINESSES BETTER THAN EVER BEFORE...

- Use the *Ownership & Most Recent Transfer Information Search by Name* to uncover all address (and possible telephone numbers) an individual or a business has filed with County Tax Assessors and Recorders throughout the state. Look for properties which list a "homeowners exemption." The owners of a property with this classification typically reside at the address. Additionally, look for mailing addresses which could reveal a residential address, business address, or the address which could reveal a residential address, business address, or the address of a relative, business partner or other affiliated party.

- Conduct a search of *Refinance Construction Loan & Seller Carry Back Information by Buyer/Seller Name* to obtain updated address information. An individual or business who recently refinanced property may have reported a new mailing address and telephone number to the County Recorder at the time of refinance. Similarly, an individual or a business obtaining a construction loan may have plans to build and occupy a residence or business on the property.

- Search for *Refinance, Construction Loan & Seller Carry Back Information by Lender Name* to obtain the address of an individual or business that has financed a real property loan for another party.

TO OBTAIN MORE BACKGROUND INFORMATION THAN EVER BEFORE...

- Search for **Real Property Ownership & Most Recent Transfer Information** to review the tax status of each parcel of property owned by an individual or a business. An individual or a business who is delinquent on property taxes may be experiencing other financial difficulties.

  A follow up search of **Bankruptcies, Liens & Judgments** will uncover additional financial derogatory information, such as tax liens, bankruptcies, civil court judgments, and notices of default and foreclosures.

- Use **Refinance, Construction Loan & Seller Carry Back Information** to determine if an individual has entered into a "non-purchase" transaction for real estate. This information can indicate that an individual or a business has the financial stability to secure new loans for real property.

Typical responses for the Real Property Asset Investigative Information System include the following information:

Ownership & Most Recent Transfer Information:

- Owner Name	- Mortgage Amount	- Owner's Mailing Address
- Owner's Phone Number	- Property Address	- Seller Name
- Assessor's Parcel #	- County of Property	- Legal Description
- Assessed Property Value	- Sale Date	- Sale Amount
- Mortgage Amount	- Lender Name	- Document Number
- Exemptions		

- Property Description (including property use description, lot size number of bedrooms, bathroom, fireplaces, parking spaces, etc.)

Refinance, Construction Loan & Seller Carry Back Information:

- Buyer/Borrower Name	- Seller Name (Seller Carry Backs only)	
- Buyer/Borrower Address	- Lender Name & Address	- Property Parcel #
- Document Number	- Document Date	- Loan Amount

Here's a nice, concise guide as to who has the information you are probably going to be looking for:

C–CDB Infotek // D–Duns Legal Search // I–Information America // L–Lexis // P–Prentice Hall Online

STATE	UCC LIENS	CORPORATE BUSINESS RECORDS	REAL PROPERTY
Alabama	D	D, C	C
Alaska	D, C, P	D, P, C	P
Arizona	D, I C	C, D, I, P	C, I, L
Arkansas	D	D, C, P	
California	C, D, I, L, P	C, D, I, L, P	C, I, L, P
Colorado	D, I, C	D, I, L, C, P	C, I, L, P
Connecticut	D	D, I, L, P, C	P
Delaware	D, I	C, D, I, L, P	C, L
Dist. of Columbia	D, I	D	C, I, L
Florida	D, I, P	D, I, P	C, I, L
Georgia	D, I	D, I, L, C, P	C, I, L
Hawaii	D, I	D	C, I, L
Idaho	D	D, I, C, P	
Illinois	D, I, L, P, C	D, I, L, P, C	I, L, P
Indiana	D	D, I, L	C
Iowa	D, P	D, I, C, P	P
Kansas	D, I	D	
Kentucky	D, I	D	C, L
Louisiana	D, I	D, I	C, L
Maine	D	D	
Maryland	D, I, L, C, P	D, I, L, C, P	I, L, C
Massachusetts	D, I, L, P, C	D, I, L, P, C	C, I, L, P
Michigan	D, I	D, I, L	C, L
Minnesota	D, I	D	L
Mississippi	D, I	D, I, C, P	C, L
Missouri	D, I, P, C	D, I, L, P, C	C, L
Montana	D	D	
Nebraska	D, C, P	D, I, C, P	
Nevada	D, I	C, D, I, L, P	C, I, L
New Hampshire	D	D, I, C, P	
New Mexico	D, I	D	C, L
New Jersey	D, I	D	C, I, L
New York	D, I, P, C	D, I, L, P, C	C, I, L
North Carolina	D, I, P	D, I	C, L
North Dakota	D	D	
Ohio	D, I	D	C, I, L
Oklahoma	D, I	D, I	C, L
Oregon	D, C, P	D, I, C, P	
Pennsylvania	D, I, L, P,	D, I, L, P	C, I, L
Rhode Island	D	D, I, C, P	P
South Carolina	D, I	D, I	C, L
South Dakota	D	D	
Tennessee	D, I	D, I, C, P	C, I, L
Texas	D, I, L P, C	C, D, I, L, P	C, L
Utah	D, I, C, P	D, I, C, P	C, L
Vermont	D	D, P, C	
Virginia	D, I	D	C, I, L
Washington	D	D, I, P, C	C, I, L
West Virginia	D	D	
Wisconsin	D, I	D, I, L, P	C
Wyoming	D	D, P, C	

And now let's go visit one of the real pro's. Tom Lawson runs a company called APSCREEN. They are, in my humble opinion, probably the best asset search firm in the world. Tom gives speeches, travels the world and finds *assets*.

Tom was nice enough to answer some of my questions and let us reprint a portion of their informative search brochure.

• APSCREEN 2043 Westcliff Drive, Third Floor, Newport Beach, CA 92660. An unusual information reporting agency that does consumer credit reporting, business reports, real property, litigation checks and several of their own combination searches including the APSCREEN general creditworthiness guide (answers the question "Would we do business with them or not?").

Business credit profile indicators, summary of individual guarantor and complete ASSET SEARCHES as well as a unique search, (as APSCREEN says, "We're famous for this one.") the ASSETPAC search which basically finds anything that can be seized, sold or dunned on any particular person.

Your best shot is to have Tom and his staff at the helm, but either way you choose to search remember some basics:

When searching for assets, one first needs to understand the nature of the pursuit, and even more importantly, the nature of the claim, by the creditor. This will direct which information will best suit the recovery, and will leave the extraneous searches for those who would be less qualified to search assets. For example, if the claim is for a $200,000 copper tubing order, forget the banks, as usually money for his so-phisticated a debtor would be transitory at best, and hard to trap in any one single, or group of accounts. This debtor has obviously accumulated enough knowledge to conduct business at a level where he can use $200,000 worth of copper tubing, and therefore the chances are good that he has amassed personal and business assets, such as real property, vehicles, and/or business property or equipment, which could be secured under an aging UCC-1.

As far as the bank searches go, EVERYONE wants the banks, because, quite simply, common sense tells any unschooled collector or attorney that the shortest distance between two points is a bank account. Oh, if procurement of this information was as easy as these potential customers think it is!

It's time to get real, here! If you were a debtor, would you leave what little money you may have left idle long enough for someone to find it, or attach it? OF COURSE NOT!!

This is why not only should you read the accompanying memo on our research into the current situation regarding Bank Account Searches, and persuade your customer that a more rounded approach (like the Homer Sleazy report, attached hereto) is smarter than limiting the budget dollars to what ends up being a highly volatile search (banks only), and which will not be guaranteed by *anyone* due to the transitory nature of this type of asset. (No firm will guarantee that money will be in an account, as it is too easily movable).

As far as first steps are concerned, and while APSCREEN *never* advises that "on line", or "database" services anything other than a cursory tool, if you have access to inexpensive/wide parameter capability databases, such as our APFILE service (this is not an on-line service, but simply the reselling of the Prentice-Hall and/or other highly proprietary and/or industry trade association databases.) Use these first, to get a "feel" for your subject.

Always run real property, always do a litigation check, always check for vehicles, always look for business ventures, and always look for tax liens and judgments. You need to balance asset information with liabilities as to get a net equity picture of the subject. They may have a $5 million home, but there could be $10 million worth of liens , judgments and/or tax liens, which rather rapidly eliminate any benefit of the asset discovery.

Run credit reports *only* if it is legal to do so, and for permissible purposes.

These are the most current credit bureau guidelines for the acquisition and dissemination of credit data. Remember one thing NEVER, NEVER, NEVER give anyone a copy of a raw credit report, PERIOD, END OF STORY!

If you are a civilian in the sense that you are a novice asset researcher, we always advise that you find an experienced asset purveyor to conduct your research for you, and that you simply resell it, as a liaison between the client and the research firm. Asset researching, like employment screening is an art and science combined, and requires that the purveyor not only be knowledgeable on a regular basis, and has long standing experience in knowing where to get what, rather than those who would have a computer, couldn't spell "asset surch" yesterday, and "am" an asset searcher today! There is a reason certain fields are specialties. It's because they need to be! Beware, as there are now literally *thousands* of little living room information purveyors who would like you to think they are the greatest asset searchers since the earth was invented.

And believe us when we tell you that we know how to purvey this avenue better than most, because we knew many specialized bases intimately, long before they were ever called Prentice-Hall, etc., you'll get better hits, for less money than the Infotek's of the world. We're a boutique, and they can't match our service attitude, they're too big!

Use them to develop at least the first steps of what will ultimately be your building blocks to better asset discovery, namely, and most importantly, in the subject identification process! (You can't search assets, unless you know what name to search!)

NOW LET'S DO AN ASSET SEARCH...

PREDICATION
It was requested of this office that an investigation be conducted to develop the current asset and liability positions of the following subject:

HOMER SLEAZY

VERIFICATION
The report contained herein is based upon the following subject data as presented by the client, and updated, enhanced, and verified (where applicable) through public and private sources:

Case No.:	0000
Date:	July 00, 0000
Name:	Homer Sleazy
Most Recent Add.on File:	0000 Meadow Road, Livermore, CA 00000
Date of Birth:	0/00/00
Social Sec. No.:	000-00-0000
Spouse:	Shirley May Sleazy

RESULTS OF INQUIRIES

REAL PROPERTY OWNERSHIP
In order to determine the extent of Real Property Ownership as enjoyed by the subject, searches were conducted of the California Statewide Real Property Ownership Indices for the 58 California Counties through 3/1/92, and updated through comparable sales registers in Los Angeles County through 1/31/94.

It was determined that Homer Sleazy is vested to one parcel of property, described as follows:

Situs Address:	0000 Meadow Road, Livermore, CA 00000
Property Type:	Single-family residence
Assessors Parcel No.:	(Los Angeles County) 0000-000-000
Vesting Date:	0/0/00
Vesting:	Shirley M. and Homer Sleazy
Lot Size:	000' x 000'
Exemptions:	Homeowners: $7,000
Assessed Valuation:	Land $00,000; Improvements $000,000

It was determined the following mortgages exist on record for the afore-referenced property:
1. Filed 00/00/00, amount: $125,000.
2. Filed 0/0/00, no amount listed
3. Filed 00/00/00, amount: $325,000.
4. Filed 0/00/00, amount: $1,350,000.
5. Filed 0/00/00, amount: $75,000.
6. Filed 0/00/00, amount: $97,000.
No other property ownership could be discovered on record for the subject.

VEHICULAR/VESSEL OWNERSHIP

Searches were conducted of the California Department of Motor Vehicles to determine the extent of vehicular and/or vessel ownership under the name Homer Sleazy, and using the address at 0000 Meadow Lane, in Livermore, CA as primary and secondary search parameters.

The following vehicles were discovered on record for Homer Sleazy:
1. 1989 Mercedes Benz, License No. 0000000
2. 1988 Toyota, License No. 0000000

Searches were then conducted of the United States Federal Aviation Administration's Aircraft Registration Indices, to determine if any aircraft and/or Pilot's License exists on record under the name Homer Sleazy (et.al).
No record was found.

A search was also conducted of the United States Coast Guard's Water craft Registration Indices to determine if any vessels appear on record as registered to Homer Sleazy (et.al).
No record was found.

BANKING INFORMATION

Confidential sources in the Banking Community indicated to this office the subject has extensive relationships with many banking institutions throughout southern California and possibly with institutions in the East (Bank of New York) through 1/31/94.

It was determined that the subject has had relationships with the following institutions within the past five years:
1. Bank of America
2. Wells Fargo Bank
3. Union Bank
4. Sanwa Bank of California
5. Warner Center Bank
6. Security Pacific National Bank
7. Independence Bank
8. World Trade Bank

We determined that depository activities specifically exist within the United Savings Bank system (where the subject has recently acquired a $1,300,000 plus mortgage, as well as the Warner Center Bank and World Trade Bank, North America).

The specific depository information pertaining to Warner Center Bank was not available, as was not the information on World Trade Bank, as these two banks do not report banking information to third parties other than the Federal Deposit Insurance Corporation.

Clearly, the United Savings Bank accounts are corresponding depository relationships, however again no specific information was available to this office upon contacting directly the institution. Previously the subject enjoyed relationships with Mission Viejo National Bank, located at 25909 Pala Place, Mission Viejo, CA 92691, and since the mortgage relationship has been terminated, so has the depository status of the subject's relationship.

It can be conclusively stated that the subject utilizes banks only for purposes of gaining additional lines of credit and then removes his money upon procurement of same, with the express intent of using the money for a short period of time until developing another relationship with another institution which will finance him at a higher level.

Clearly, the institutions listed above may have had something to do with the financing of the residence contained within Livermore and we recommend the chances are strong that this is the subject's main asset, and that which the banks make their loan recommendations upon.

FINANCIAL INFORMATION

Confidential sources in the Financial Community indicated to this office the subject is currently maintaining what appears to be a somewhat varied financial history, with the preponderance of accounts reporting current and positive accounts, however some accounts appear to show previous delinquencies and one account in particular shows a present delinquency of thirty days.

Of the 49 accounts reporting aggregate available credit limits (excluding mortgages) totaling $248,984, $86,428, or 34.71% are currently being utilized, with Bank of America reporting a $2,086 delinquency (30 days) on a $54,000 automobile loan, showing a $42,600 balance as of 11/30/93. There are previous delinquencies on record with Bank of New York (Gold Mastercharge), as well as American Express Centurion Bank and Chase Manhattan Bank revolving credit lines in the amount of $4,600, which currently show a $912 balance with these credit lines being closed by the credit grantors, as the current situation is "delinquent" and shows previous ninety day delinquency history on record.

California First Bank shows a previous thirty day delinquency on record, as does J.C. Penney, Sears, and Broadway (which appears to be thirty days past due and previously shows a sixty day delinquency).

Some mortgage information appears within the subject's report, including a $720,000 loan with California Federal Savings and Loan paid off in 1990, and a $252,000 loan (plus) paid off in February of 1990. There also exists a $1,345,371 loan with United Saving Bank, FSB, taken out in 1990 with the balance showing as of 10/31/93 and wherein a sixty day delinquency exists on a $12,341 monthly payment.

The subject previously had an account with Mission Viejo National Bank which was initiated in 1990 and paid off in 1990, and was in excess of $1,000,000 in its face amount. All-in-all, while the subject's percentages appear to be somewhat low, his credit is currently in a declining status and we recommend the chances for obtaining additional lines of credit would be somewhat limited at this time.

LIABILITIES

This office maintains a repository of the following items of public record inclusive of the thirty most populated California counties from 1985 through 1/31/94: Bankruptcies; Federal, State and Local Tax Liens; Municipal and Small Claims Actions/Judgments; Notices of Default/ Foreclosures; and Unlawful Detainer Actions (Evictions).

The following items were discovered on record as pertains the subject of this report:

1. Civil Action; Filed 0/0/00 in Beverly Hills Municipal Court, Los Angeles County; Case No. 000000000; Amount—$5,652; Listing the Plaintiff, Jiminy Broadcasting Corporation versus the Defendants, Lenny s. Potomac; Homer Sleazy, 0000 Saratoga Boulevard, Suite 220, Beaumont Spring, CA 90211, with an additional Defendant, Sleazy & Potomac Partnership.

2. Small Claims Action; Filed 0/0/00 in the Beverly Hills Municipal Court, Los Angeles County, CA; Case No. 000000; Amount—$1,887; Listing the Plaintiff, Crooked Pines Agency, Inc. versus the Defendants, Lenny Potomac; Homer Sleazy dba Sleazy and Potomac, 0000 Saratoga Boulevard, Suite 220, Beaumont Spring, CA 90211.

3. Bankruptcy Filing—Chapter 13; Filed 0/00/00 in the U.S. District Bankruptcy Court, Los Angeles, CA; File #11111; Listing the Defendants, Homer Sleazy; Shirley Sleazy, 0000 Saratoga Boulevard, Suite 220, Beaumont Sprg, CA 90211. This Bankruptcy shows assets of $100,000, with liabilities totaling $1,000,000, and was discharged on 00/00/00.

4. State Tax Lien; Filed 0/0/00 in the Los Angeles County Recorder's Office; file #11111; Amount—$48,0—16; Listing the Debtors, Homer Sleazy, Shirley Sleazy, 0000 Meadow, Livermore, CA 91436. This Tax Lien was released on 0/0/00.

5. Federal Tax Lien; Filed 0/00/00 in the Los Angeles County Recorder's Office; File No. 0000000000; Amount—$218,026; Listing the Debtors, Homer Sleazy; Shirley Sleazy, 0000 Meadow Road, Livermore, CA 91436.

6. Notice of Default; Filed 0/0/00 in the Los Angeles County Recorder's Office; File #0000; Listing the Debtors, Homer Sleazy; Shirley Sleazy, 0000 Meadow Road, Livermore, CA 91436; As regards a Trust Deed filed 00/00/00 in the amount of $125,000.

No other adverse public record items could be discovered on file for the subject.

LITIGATION

Searches were conducted of the Los Angeles County Superior Court Civil Plaintiff and Defendant Indices for any Civil Actions under the name Homer Sleazy from 1985 through 1/31/94.

Extensive litigation was discovered against the subject, which is described as follows:

1. Civil Action; Filed 00/00/00; Case #000000; Listing the Plaintiff, Homer Sleazy versus the Defendant, Mission Center Physical Therapy.

2. Civil Action; Filed 00/00/00; Case #000000; Listing the Plaintiff, Reynold O. Timms versus the Defendant, Homer Sleazy.

3. Civil Action; Filed 00/00/00; Case #000000; Listing the Plaintiff, Robert M. Walls versus the Defendant, Homer Sleazy.

4. Civil Action; Filed 00/00/00; Case #000000; Listing the Plaintiff, Christen Maritime versus the Defendant, Homer Sleazy.

5. Domestic Action; Filed 00/00/00; Case #000000; Listing the Petitioner, Shirley Sleazy versus the Respondent, Homer Sleazy.

For specific details pertaining to any of the above actions, this office stands ready to undertake said research upon further authorization.

No other litigation was discovered on record for the subject.

OFFICER/DIRECTOR

Searches were conducted of the California Secretary of State's office through 1/31/94 to determine the extent of possible corporate involvement under the name Homer Sleazy, from the Officer/Director and/or Registered Agent perspectives.

It was determined that "CALIFORNIA SLEAZE, INC." is a suspended California Corporation, originally incorporated on 10/1/83 under Corporate File #0934567, and showing a business address of 123 Memory Lane, Commerce, CA 92345.

The Registered Agent and President is listed as Homer Sleazy, 123 Memory Lane, Commerce, CA 92345, and the last Statement of Officers was filed on 12/31/92 under File #92-00000. A name change was filed on 1/5/86 from the name "Sleazy, Inc." This corporation was suspended by the Franchise Tax Board on 12/31/92 for non-payment of taxes.
No other corporate affiliations could be discovered on record for the subject.

UNIFORM COMMERCIAL CODE FILINGS
Searches were conducted f the California Secretary of State's Office Uniform Commercial Code Indices to determine the extent of UCC-1 Financing Statements on file listing Homer Sleazy as either Debtor and/or Secured Party through 1/31/94.

One UCC-1 filing was discovered on 1/2/90 under File #90-1234567; Listing the Debtor as Homer Sleazy, 0000 Meadow Road, Livermore, CA 92222; With the Secured Party showing as Bank of America, 1 Financial Plaza, Los Angeles, CA 90001.
No other UCC's were discovered on record for the subject.

FICTITIOUS BUSINESS NAMES
Searches were conducted of the Los Angeles County Clerks Fictitious Business Name Indices for any DBA recordations under the name Homer sleazy through 1/31/94.

On filing was discovered under File #90-645345; Filed 6/10/90; under the business name of "Sleazy Productions", located at 123 Memory Lane, Commerce, CA 92345.
No other DBA's were discovered on record for the subject within the afore-referenced repository.

OBSERVATIONS/RECOMMENDATIONS
Throughout the course of these inquiries, it was determined that Homer Sleazy possesses one major asset, that of the residence in the City of Livermore, and which appears to be heavily encumbered with respect to outstanding mortgages.

The subject shows a litigation history, and as well is saddled with some tremendous liabilities and State and Federal Tax Liens, which would most likely put a damper on his cash flow and cause a decline in his financial condition, which appears to be evident by virtue of the afore-referenced Financial Information section.

We recommend that Mr. Sleazy does lend himself to the possibility of additional collection effort, however, based upon the outstanding litigation on record, as well as the Tax Liens, it is advised that some form of settlement negotiation be entered into prior to the initiation of litigation.

* *

END OF REPORT
C:SLEAZY/3/3/93

ASSET COURSE

The Investigation Training Institute POB 669, Shelbourne, VT 05482, led by one Edward Burke, who spent 20 years as an IRS criminal investigator, instructed at the Federal Law Enforcement Training Center, the FBI and INTERPOL. Mr. Burke has also trained over 3,000 investigators, auditors, regulators, analyst, paralegals and attorneys. He runs seminars in asset tracing and financial investigation.

The locations of the 3 day seminars vary from city to city and run about $600 and concentrate on:
- Use of net worth to prove issues
- Identifying fraud schemes
- Conserve investigation time and cost
- Enhance litigation
- Facilitate favorable settlements
- Gain financial information sources
- Gather and use admissible records

Although designed more for professionals (including private detectives and researchers) than the average person trying to collect a debt, these are definitely hands-on seminars designed to find and identify assets.

At the moment this is pretty much the only course of its kind in the country.

IDENTIFYING AND VERIFYING ASSETS
USING ONLY AN INDIVIDUAL OR A BUSINESS NAME

Tricks for both online and organic searching. Much of this material can be found on CDB.

SEARCH TYPE AND DESCRIPTION

INFORMATION SOURCE

HELPFUL SEARCH TIPS

Real Property Search by Owner Name

Uncovers the real property holdings of an individual or a business. Typical responses include the land value, improvement value and total assessed value for each property. In addition, many searches include sale date, sale amount, and lender information.

Information source: Tax assessor records, County recorder records

Helpful search tips:
– Conduct a follow-up search by mailing address to determine if additional property is owned under other names.
– Search for judgments and liens within the county of of each property parcel.
– In California, conduct a follow-up search for Refinance, Construction Loan & Seller Carry Back Transactions.

UCC Searches

Verifies that specific assets of an individual or a business are secured by another party through a UCC filing at the state level. The name and address of each debtor is provided, which can reveal company officers, affiliations and subsidiaries.

Information source: Secretary of State or Department of State for selected state.

Helpful search tips:
– Exclude "the" when it precedes a business name when online.
– Exclude suffixes, such as "Co., Inc., Ltd., P.C.,"etc.
– Look for additional debtors, which can reveal company affiliations and subsidiaries
– Contact secured parties to determine the payment patterns of the debtor(s).
– Order a copy of the UCC1 document to obtain a collateral schedule.

Bankruptcies, Liens & Judgments

Identifies and provides derogatory financial information on individuals and businesses, including 10 years' history of bankruptcy filings, and 7 years' history of federal, state and county tax liens, and small claims, municipal and superior court judgments. Bankruptcy filings include the dollar amount of the debtor's assets and liabilities, while the amount and status of each judgment and lien is provided.

Federal Bankruptcy courts
Federal, state and county taxing authorities
County Recorder
Small Claims Court
Superior Court

– Use this search to determine the number of outstanding judgments and/or liens that are filed against an individual or a business.
– Look for additional debtors which can reveal spouses, partners, company affiliations and subsidiaries.
– Very useful to help determine whether to pursue litigation.

Judgment Docket & Lien Book

Searches Supreme Court Civil judgments, hospital liens, mechanics liens, building loans, lis pendens, sidewalk liens, and federal tax liens to provide the debtor and creditor name(s) and address(es), amount of judgment or lien, and the current status of of each debt.

Supreme Court for each county

– Use this search to determine the number of outstanding judgments and/or liens that are filed against an indivi-dual or a business.
– Look for additional debtors which can reveal spouses, partners, company affiliations and subsidiaries.
– Very useful to help determine whether to pursue litigation.

Vehicle Ownership Searches –
Alphabetic Name Index
Provides a list of all vehicles, motor-cycles, boats, trailers, recreational vehicles and other vehicles/ vessels that are registered in a a selected state. The year, make and model of each vehicle and/or vessel is provided as well as the name of the individual or business owner.

State Motor Vehicle Department

– Conduct a follow-up search by license plate number to deter-mine if a lien holder appears on the vehicle registration.

– Remember that individuals or businesses that lease vehicles will not appear as vehicle owners in this search. How-ever, a search by license plate number will reveal the name of of both lessee and lessor.

Corporation & Limited Partnership
Searches
Verifies that a business is registered as a corporation in a selected state. Many states provide information concerning the officers of the corporation as well as the original filing date, address and a history of of mergers, name changes and other transactions.

State agencies that register both both corporations and limited partner-ships (e.g., Secretary of State, Department of Business Services, etc.) for a selected state.

– Exclude "the" when it pre-cedes a business name.

– Exclude suffixes, such as "Co., Inc., Ltd., P.C.," etc.

– Look for mergers, which can reveal company affiliations and subsidiaries.

– Conduct a search by officer name to uncover multiple business affiliations.

State Board of Equalization
Searches
Provides the owner name(s) and address(es) for any business hold-ing a sales or use tax permit in a specific state. In addition, the name, address and type of business is is provided.

State Board of Equalization

–Look for "Ownership Type" which indicates whether a business is a corporation, part-nership or sole proprietorship.

– Conduct a follow-up search of of Corporations & Limited Partnerships or Fictitious Busi-ness Names to obtain a history of the business.

Fictitious Business Names

Confirms that a fictitious business name statement was filed by an individual or a business. Provides owner name(s) and address(es) and the original filing date as well as the expiration date of each filing.

County Recorder of Department of State

– Exclude "the" when it precedes a business name.
– Conduct a search by owner name to uncover all businesses owned by an individual or a corporation.

Upper Court Civil Filings

Provides the civil litigation history of an individual or a business, usually in cases involving $25,000 or more. Typical responses include the name of each plaintiff and defendant, file date, case number and type of civil filing. Many jurisdictions include information concerning family law cases and probate filings.

State courts of general jurisdiction:

Superior Court
Supreme Court
Justice Court
Court of Common Pleas
District Court

– Pull the official documents to determine the amount of any monetary award resulting from civil litigation.

Lower Court Civil Filings

Provides information about an individual or a business that has been involved in civil litigation, usually in cases involving amounts under $25,000. Typical responses include the name of each plaintiff and defendant name(s), file date and file number. Many jurisdictions also include the case type.

State courts of limited jurisdiction:

Municipal Court
Small Claims Court
City Court
Circuit Court

– Pull the official documents to determine the amount of any monetary award resulting from civil litigation.

General Index

Searches over 400 documents filed with the county recorder concerning the transfer of property. Locates properly transfers, death distribution decrees, fictitious name filings, financing statements for personal property, and much more. Provides the name of the grantor(s) and the grantee(s), the filing date, file number and the type of transaction.

County Recorder records

– Pull the official documents to determine the details of each transaction filed with the county recorder.

FAA Aircraft Ownership Searches

Searches for all aircraft owned by an individual or a business. Provides the year, make, model, and registration date of each aircraft, as well as the owner's name and address.

Federal Aviation Administration

– Contact Customer Service to verify the aircraft year, make and model to determine its approximate value.

Real Property Search by Property Address

Identifies the owner(s) of a specific parcel of property. Includes the assessed land, improvement and total property value. In addition, the sale date, sale amount and lender information is often provided.

Tax Assessor records
County Recorder Records

– Conduct an "Address Range" search if unsure of exact address or when searching for for commercial or multi-unit properties using a database like CDB or USD.

Real Property Search by Mailing Address

Uncovers real property owned by individuals and businesses who share a common mailing address. Provides the address of each parcel of property owned and the owner name(s). In addition, the assessed value of each parcel of property, sale date, sale amount, and lender name often appears.

Tax Assessor Records
County Recorder records

– Helpful for uncovering family trusts and real estate owned under a business name or other name.

Vehicle Ownership Searches – Alphabetic Name Index

Provides a list of all vehicles, motorcycles, boats, trailers, recreational vehicles and other vehicles/ vessels that are registered in a selected state. The year, make and model of each vehicle and/or vessel is provided as well as the name of the individual or busines owner.

State Motor Vehicle Department

– Conduct a follow-up search by license plate number to determine if a lien holder appears on the vehicle registration.
– Remember that individuals or businesses that lease vehicles will not appear as vehicle owners in this search. However, a search by license plate number will reveal the name of both lessee and lessor.

Neighborhood Search

Provides a demographic profile of neighborhood based on an address. The demographic profile includes median income level, average home price, homeowner probability statistics and a wealth rating which compares a neighborhood to national averages. In addition, the names, addresses, telephone numbers and lengths of residence of the occupant and up to 30 neighbors are provided.

National independent mailing lists
US Postal Service forwarding orders
Tax assessor records
Voter registration files
Telephone white pages

– Conduct a follow-up Real Property Search by Address, using an "address range" to determine the assessed value of real estate in the area.

Business Credit 1 – Market Identifier

Provides information concerning the size and profitability of a business, based on business executive reports and public record information. The legal business name and address is included along with other key facts, such as number of years in business, and possibly the names of key officers.

National Business Reporting Agency

–Look for information about company officers and principals.
–The amount of financial information available for privately-held corporations v aries.

Business Credit II – Trade Payment History

Reveals the credit history of a company by listing the types of accounts opened, the established credit and payment terms of each account, the current balance of each account and a payment history. In addition, information concerning public record filings, such as judgments, bankruptcies, tax liens and UCC financing statements is included.

National Business Credit Reporting

– Helpful for determining whether to extend credit to a company.

Consumer Credit Report

Provides an individual's credit history including a listing of all accounts, balances, payment terms, and payment history. Ten years' history of bankruptcy filings and seven years' history of judgments and liens are also included. This search is subject to the federal Fair Credit Reporting Act.

National Consumer Credit Bureau

– Can be used only with a permissible purpose under the federal Fair Credit Reporting Act.
– Obtain additional information from Customer Service for decoding credit report information.

USING AN INDIVIDUAL NAME AND/OR SOCIAL SECURITY NUMBER

SEARCH TYPE AND DESCRIPTION	INFORMATION SOURCE	HELPFUL SEARCH TIPS
Vehicle Ownership Searches – Alphabetic Name Index Provides a list of all vehicles, motorcycles, boats, trailers, recreational vehicles and other vehicles/vessels that are registered in a selected state. The year, make and model of each vehicle and/or vessel is provided as well as the name of the individual owner.	State Motor Vehicle Department	– Conduct a follow-up search by license plate number to determine if a lien holder appears on the vehicle registeration. – Remember that individuals or businesses that lease vehicles will not appear as vehicle owners in this search. However, a search by license plate number will reveal the name of both lessee and lessor.
Social Security Number Tracks Provides the name and address of each individual associated with the use of a social security number for credit purposes. Typically, a seven to ten year history of names and addresses is provided.	(up to) Three National Credit Bureaus	– Look for spouse information to conduct asset searches under a spouse's name in community property states.

HOW TO LOCATE & RESEARCH ANYONE THRU DIALOG

DIALOG Information Services, Inc., is the world's largest online "knowledge bank." Although DIALOG is the largest gateway/access provider to databases anywhere in the world, they are rarely thought of in conjunction with locating specific individuals. Most DIALOG users tend to search for business information, corporate affiliations, scientific data or general knowledge. Oddly enough, DIALOG can be a very effective source for tracking down ordinary people.

This is an important section. Please don't skip over it, don't go feed the dog; turn off the television, pay attention here...

If you subscribe to DIALOG, (and if you're an investigator or researcher of any merit, you should) this little section will show you how to effectively and cheaply search the nooks and crannies of several hundred databases for information on specific individuals.

If you do not subscribe to DIALOG, this is still a very relevant strategy because you can:

A. Often get one-time DIALOG access through private companies (perhaps where you or a friend works) or even via some of the hipper libraries around.

B. If necessary, take this section to your local information provider or researcher, and say,

"Listen pal, I want you to do exactly these steps in this order." This will save you time and money and provide the best chance of getting a hit.

C. Join DIALOG. It's well worth it if you're going to be researching any topics over the next year or so.

This section will demonstrate exact techniques for finding specific people, as well as, background information on them through DIALOG, by employing a number of different databases.

I'm going to start by describing who ends up in DIALOG files and what files they can be most logically found in, as well as, little tricks for narrowing your search parameters and limiting your online time. After that we'll take a look at a unique way to instantly, and for very little money, search most of the hundreds of files DIALOG covers in one fell swoop...

Hell, this section alone's worth the price of this book...

The major problem in utilizing a full service database supermarket like DIALOG is not a lack of data, but rather that there are literally mounds, piles, and mountains of computerized bits and bytes. An effective search strategy, pre-planned on paper (never think online) is the key to finding what you want in the shortest possible time and with the lowest number of incidental entries.

DIALOG files are stored in a number of formats. Many of the files we're interested in are full text; i.e., the entire text of the newspaper, magazine, book, or whatever, is stored in one of DIALOG'S many computers and can be retrieved article by article, entry by entry. Other files in DIALOG are simply abstracts, citations, or references to works that then must be requested from a DIALOG hard copy provider. These companies take your request online or via FAX, Xerox the entry in question and mail, FAX, or sometimes modem it back to you in fulltext format.

DIALOG, like most databases, charges you for the time spent in any search. Some individual bases also charge for printouts of the entries you have decided you wish to peruse. Some bases are individual newspapers, magazines, or company information, while other bases are collections of the most likely sources for a certain type of information. As one might suspect, these collections are the key to our type of shotgun approach.

Each database has its own charge for online time. The charges are usually quoted in dollars per hour, but any searcher worth his/her salt will be paying only in increments of that figure. AS LONG AS THE SEARCH IS CONDUCTED CORRECTLY! For example, if you are researching background information on Dan Quayle, it might be a trifle excessive to ask DIALOG to find every reference to Dan Quayle. Odds are that you'd come up with several thousand hits. Many of which would be in the context of another major subject; i.e., "Today Senator Kennedy said he'd had breakfast with Dan Quayle before going on to debate..."

The trick is to limit your search to the exact subject you're looking for without excluding any pertinent references. A higher level megasearcher, which you will be five minutes after finishing this section, takes searches to a higher astral plane by not only asking the right questions, but asking them in the right place.

One of my favorite search areas is in the news. People are often mentioned in one or more news sources even if they appear nowhere else in DIALOG. One does not have to be famous or even particularly noteworthy to appear in a newspaper, magazine, or newswire. DIALOG and several other bases keep full text files from hundreds of newspapers from around the country. If your subject has gotten married, gotten a traffic ticket, been arrested for drunken driving, given a speech at a Rotary Club, had a son who's a track star or valedictorian of his high school, bought a business, filed a fictitious name statement, or happened to wander into a man-in-the-street interview situation, he/she is in the news...

The common way to search these files is by using a free-text format, (first name(1n) last name) in one or more bases.

This format we're using means that the first name must appear within one word of the last name. You can vary this by substituting any number prior to the "n", but if you're searching for a person's name there is rarely a reason that more than one word would appear between his first and last name so the 1n format helps define our parameters to some degree. The difference between the descriptors (W) and (N) are that (W) will retrieve the words you type ONLY. The (N) will retrieve the words in any order listed in the database.

If your subject might be mentioned in a newswire, the best place to start is in the group of files known as First Release. First Release databases are four newswires that are updated every 15 minutes throughout the day. They are:

- Businesswire (File 610)
- Knight-Ridder/Tribune Business News (File 609)
- PR Newswire (File 613)
- Reuters (File 611)

To access the first file type the letter b (for begin) and then the word "first" at the question mark prompt. This will bring up the four newswire files as one group. Next we're going to ask DIALOG to search through these four files for information on the person we want. At the DIALOG question mark prompt type "s" for select.

You enter   ? bill (1n) clinton

DIALOG responds   90422   BILL
DIALOG responds   11159   CLINTON
DIALOG responds   S1
                       5857
                       BILL (1N) CLINTON

This returns us what is known as a set. DIALOG has found 90,000+ mentions of the word Bill, 111,000 mentions of the word Clinton, and 5,857 mentions of Bill Clinton. This latter grouping is automatically named S1 or set 1. Because we have such a large number of hits, we're going to try a little trick. After the DIALOG prompt type:

You enter   ? s ud=9999

DIALOG responds   S2   186   UD=9999

This i code tells DIALOG to give us information in the last update. Notice that S2, (set 2) now generated has only 186 entries. We're narrowing our search down to a manageable size in a short period of time.

Next we're going to select set 1 and set 2. DIALOG acts on this information, combines the two sets and finds only 7 instances of S1 and S2. It automatically classifies this new search as S3. Note how DIALOG searches new databases and gives you only the information that appears when the two bases overlap per your request. Think of the bases as two circles, one named Bill 1 and one named Clinton. You ask for Bill (1n) Clinton and the two circles overlap slightly. The gray area where two circles share the same data is what DIALOG returns and automatically gives a set name.

You enter   ? s s1 and s2

DIALOG responds   5857   S1
DIALOG responds   186   S2
DIALOG responds   S3   7   S1 and S2

You enter   ? s pd=920902

DIALOG responds   S4   2403   PD=930903

You enter   ? s s1 and s4

DIALOG responds   5857   S1
DIALOG responds   2403   S4
DIALOG responds   S5   34   S1 and S4

At this point a number of options open themselves; in this particular file the best choice is probably to browse all of our 7 entries. Browsing happens to be free in most DIALOG databases so we might as well make use of it. In order to browse:

You enter   ? t s3/6, k/all

This tells dialog we want to browse through set 3. The number 6 followed by k means browsing. "All" tells DIALOG that we want to browse all of set 3. So all 7 articles will now appear on screen allowing us to scan through them to see if we've done our search correctly and if it contains what we want.

I should point out here that you are accessing DIALOG through some sort of modem software, usually Microphone II, or the IBM equivalents. No matter what software you're using, be sure you have the automatic capture feature enabled. This means that everything you do is captured on your computer and put on the disk automatically so you can go back later and analyze what you did, reconstruct your strategy, or simply print out any of the references you come up with at no further charge because at this point you're going back through your own computer and using simple built-in find, locate, or search commands depending on the type of system and computer you are running.

PAPERS

PAPERS refers to all the fulltext newspapers on DIALOG, many of which are updated daily. Categories for PAPERS include:

PAPERS (All fulltext newspapers in the United States)

PAPERSCE	(Central United States)
PAPERSEU	(Europe)
PAPERSMA	(Major United States)
PAPERSNE	(Northeast United States)
PAPERSSE	(Southeast United States)
PAPERSWE	(Western United States)

You enter: ?s scott (2W)french

DIALOG responds with the following:
Processed 20 of 53 files ...
Processing
Completed processing all files
    798027 SCOTT
    562659 FRENCH
  S1   199 SCOTT (2W)FRENCH
?t s1/3/1-10
 1/3/1   (Item 1 from file: 146)
2155386

BOOK REPORT.
The Washington Post, September 26, 1993, FINAL Edition
By: David Streitfeld
Section: BOOK WORLD, p. x15
Line Count: 158   Word Count: 1746

1/3/2   (Item 2 from file: 146)
2146998
Book World Sex, Drugs and a Hard Drive.
The Washington Post, August 03, 1993, FINAL Edition
By: Louise Titchener
Section: STYLE, p. e02
Line Count: 75   Word Count: 834

1/3/3   (Item 3 from file: 146)
2144383
Books by Machine.
The Washington Post, July 17, 1993, FINAL Edition

Section: OP ED, p. a16
Line Count: 41   Word Count: 453

1/3/4   (Item 4 from file: 146)
2142322
PERFORMING ARTS - Nightwinds.
The Washington Post, July 03, 1993, FINAL Edition
By: Judy Gruber
Section: STYLE, p. d03
Line Count: 20   Word Count: 227
and on and on...

Here we want to find any reference to our subject in any of the newspapers DIALOG carries. As you can guess, searching the fulltext versions of a couple hundred of newspapers for the last several years is going to run into a little bit of time and a little bit of money. Luckily there are some innovative ways to cut this down to size.

You enter: ?s scott(1W)french
    68725 SCOTT
    278239 FRENCH
  S1   45 SCOTT(1W)FRENCH
?t s1/3/1-10

DIALOG responds with the following:
1/3/2   (Item 1 from file: 47)
14481467 DIALOG File 47: MAGAZINE INDEX   *Use Format 9 for FULL TEXT*
Byte by byte. (computer programmer writes program that writes a novel in the style of author Jacqueline Susann)
Podolsky, J.D.
People Weekly v40 p117(2) Oct 11, 1993
SOURCE FILE: MI File 47
AVAILABILITY: FULL TEXT Online LINE COUNT: 00071

1/3/3   (Item 2 from file: 47)
14074654 DIALOG File 47: MAGAZINE INDEX   *Use Format 9 for FULL TEXT*
A novel by rote and by byte. (Carol Publishing Group to publish 'Just This Once' by Scott French and a computer programmed

to help write the novel) (Brief Article)
Simson, Maria
Publishers Weekly v240 p29(1) July 5, 1993
SOURCE FILE: MI File 47
ARTICLE TYPE: Brief Article
AVAILABILITY: FULL TEXT Online LINE
COUNT: 00039

1/3/7   (Item 2 from file: 88)
14074654   DIALOG File 88: ACADEMIC
INDEX
Use Format 7 for FULL TEXT
A novel by rote and by byte. (Carol Publishing Group to publish 'Just This Once' by Scott French and a computer programmed to help write the novel) (Brief Article)
Simson, Maria
Publishers Weekly v240 n27 p29(1) July 5, 1993
 AVAILABILITY: FULL TEXT Online LINE
COUNT: 00039

Because of the style in which newspapers are written, you are fairly safe searching on a limited portion of the article. For instance:

You enter: ? s (scott or scotty) (1n)
                french/ti,lp,de

Found: 62,182 Scott
                20,681 French
                s1 - s42

We are now restricting our search to the title (ti), the lead paragraph (lp) and something called the descriptor (de) in order to make our search words more relevant.

Now DIALOG will not search the entire text of each article, but rather the title, the first paragraph and a short section which summarizes the key points in the article known as the descriptor.

Because of established newspaper style, it is extremely rare to find an article on a specific person that does not mention him in either the title or the lead paragraph.

If we miss in these locations, the descriptor

will almost surely have a reference to our subject.

This strategy is a heavy delimiter, but may still be too specific or not specific enough. If we have too many hits are returned, try:

You enter: ? s s1 and pd=920901:920902

DIALOG responds: 4736 S1
                      857   PD=920901 :
                      PD=920902
                      S2   8 S1 AND
                      PD=920901:920902

This limits the search not only to the areas we've specified but to the publications that fall between the two dates referenced. As you see, this generally produces a much more concise set to work on.

At this point we want to see if the material is relevant. Let's tell DIALOG to type set 2 in a special 3,k format. In this case I'm just telling it to type No. 1 and No. 2 rather than typing all the entries because I can usually tell from reading one or two hits, if this is the person I'm looking for and if the information is needed.

You enter: ? t s2/3,k/1-2

If enough hits don't come back, it is possible to expand the search by rerunning it and adding the delimiter "de".

This approach will also search the descriptor, a short field that summarizes each article as entered by the folks at DIALOG. This summary follows the actual article and contains a list of the key words in the article. If our hit rate is still 0, or smaller than we'd like it to be, it might be time to go back and actually search on a fulltext (read more expensive) basis. To search fulltext we'd simply type:
You enter: ? s scott (1w) french
Running this in PAPERS will bring back every single reference in any context to Mr. French.

As you can see from the different PAPERS' databases you can also limit your search geographically by selecting the correct collection. If you know your subject lives in California, don't run the entire country. Chances that he was arrested last week in Florida for jaywalking are going to be pretty slim.

If we do find what seems to be an applicable article(s) in our browse format, simply tell DIALOG to type the entire article by entering the line:

You enter: ? t s2/9/2

This tells DIALOG to print in fulltext (9 in most databases means fulltext) the second article in set 2.

If you have additional information that may pinpoint your subject, it's possible to enter it in the original search category rather than making DIALOG search the fulltext of every newspaper.

You enter: ? s scott (1n)
                      french,novel,book.

Because we're still only asking DIALOG to look at the titles, the lead paragraph and possibly the descriptor field, these additional search terms may help "open" our search strategy.

The next logical search would probably be newswires (daily). Other newswires on DIALOG besides the First Release files are also good sources of information about people. These databases are updated daily and include:

• Agence France Presse English Wire (File 614)
• AP News (File 258)
• Federal News Service (File 660)
• Japan Economic Newswire (File 612)
• Newswire ASAP (File 649)
• UPI News (Files 260, 261)

These files are accessed in the same manner as the newspapers, normally one would begin by typing the "s" for select after the DIALOG prompt:

Set	Items	Description
You enter:		? s scott (1n) french
DIALOG responds:		127470 SCOTT
		1532 FRENCH
S1		1330 SCOTT (1N) FRENCH

A slick trick to limit your returns not only is to use the subject but some other detail he's associated with, is to use what's known as an automatic proximity operator. In DIALOG this is a small "s".

We could type book (s) computer. In this case, the proximity operator requires both words to be in the same paragraph in DIALOG fulltext databases.

Now we have two bases of information that will probably intersect in some point in space. To make them intersect we're going to type:

You enter: ? s s1 (s) s2

DIALOG responds: 1330 S1
                                24294 S2
        S3   27 S1 (S) S2

This tells DIALOG to combine set 1 and set 2 with the proximity operator that requires both sets to be in the same paragraph. As it looks like we still have too many hits, let's limit it a bit further by typing:

You enter: ? s s3/1992

DIALOG responds: 27 S3
                                195128 PY=1992
        S4   18 S3/1992

Further limiting our search to items about our subject that appeared in 1992. Notice, by automatically creating our new set (S4) we have further reduced the number of hits. Now it's probably time to look and see what we've got, so we're going to type:

You enter: ?   s4/3,k/1-6

This will browse the first 6 hits of what we have come up with. If we like it, we can then print those articles or tell DIALOG to print all the hits in that set. If we don't like the results, it's time to get offline immediately, sit down with pencil and paper (remember this part of your search is free) and plan a new line of attack.

Is your subject someone of renown? Well, DIALOG can most certainly help, it contains a number of files that provide biographical data on people who have laid their footprints in the sands of time. Three files in particular:

AMERICAN MEN AND WOMEN OF SCIENCE
(FILE 236)

This directory contains approximately 120,000 names of eminent, active American and Canadian scientists in general science, physics and biology.

BIOGRAPHY MASTER INDEX (FILE 287)

This database is a master index to 630 biographical dictionaries and directories and includes over 3 million names.

MARQUIS WHO'S WHO

This file corresponds to *Who's Who in America* and contains over 75,000 names with biographical data. Top professionals in business, sports, government, the arts, entertainment, science and technology are included.

These bases are lumped together in the master index, BIOGRAPHY MASTER INDEX, (Gale Research Inc.). By using our usual search nomenclature in File 287 we will come up with any hits in these files. Normally the number of hits in this file is small enough that our various limiters and set combining tricks are not necessary. Generally one simply tells DIALOG to type the entire list.

You enter: ? t s1/3/all

This will return references to the hits showing exactly where the subject appeared and is a good preliminary measure to asking DIALOG to type the fulltext on every reference.

Now we can go into one or more of the specific bases that appears to be of interest. Let's go into File 234, MARQUIS WHO'S WHO.

You enter: ? B 234

Set Items Description
—   ———   —————————
You enter: ? e na=scott

By expanding into the NA= file, we are able to ascertain that we have the right subject. The "NA=" tells DIALOG the name should equal anything that falls within our given parameters. Often here good searchers will drop the first name and simply use an initial or use what is known as a truncation operator to include all possible variations of the subject's name. Truncation simply means you type part of the word followed by (?).

If I were to type mar (?), DIALOG would return Mary, Marie, Marquis — anything that begins with the correct three letters.

Once we have the list of possibilities, tell DIALOG to select the proper reference by typing:

You enter: ? s e4

It then places this name in a group and calls it set (or s) 1. The next step is to tell DIALOG to print out S1 in fulltext:

You enter: ? t s1/9

This same search strategy can be repeated in the other files within this database that show hits. If the number of returns is small, say one to three, it's wise to skip the NA= stage and simply ask DIALOG to print out in fulltext the references to your subject. If things become overwhelming, or you think you might have reached an end, you can save your search strategy by telling DIALOG to:

You enter: ? save temp

This will automatically save your search sets that were returned under:

You enter: ? s scott (1n) french

For a limited period of time so you can examine your strategy off-line and make any necessary repairs.

If your subject is not a complete sleaze, he may have entered into the exciting world of commerce at one time or another in his life. Conveniently DIALOG features File 526, Standard and Poor's Register – Biographical.

This database provides personal and professional data on key executives affiliated with public, private, US and non-US companies that have sales of one million dollars and over. Lets do a quick search on a businessman who we think may appear in File 526. Notice we're going to start with our old pal the name equal operator to come up with any name related to our subject. Afterward, we're going to create a set with what we believe is to be our subject and ask DIALOG to print it out in fulltext.

File 526:S & P Register-Biographical 03/92 (C) 1991 Standard & Poor's Corp **FILE526: After an individual is identified, see F527 – S & P's Register – Corporate, for company information.

Set Items Description
— —— ————

? e na=sykes, david

Ref	Items	Index-term
E1	1	NA=SYDOR, DANIEL J.
E2	1	NA=SYDOR, EDWARD J.
E3	0	*NA=SYKES, DAVID
E4	1	NA=SYKES, DAVID B.
E5	1	NA=SYKES, JOSEPH STUART
E6	1	NA=SYKES, RICHARD M.
E7	1	NA=SYKES, ROBERT F.
E8	1	NA=SYKES, ROY ARNOLD R.
E9	1	NA=SYKORA, DONALD D.
E10	1	NA=SYKORA, RICHARD J.
E11	1	NA=SYLVA, JOHN R.
E12	1	NA=SYLVEST, HAROLD MAYNARD JR.

Enter P or E for more

? s e4

    S1   1NA="SYKES, DAVID B."

? t sl/9
1/9/1
0062302
SYKES, DAVID B.
BIRTH: Austin, PA   (1918)
RESIDENCE ADDRESS:
            5600 Wisconsin Ave.
            Chevy Chase, MD 20815
UNDERGRADUATE COLLEGE:
            Penn. State Coll.   (1940)
PRIMARY COMPANY AFFILIATION:
            Sr V-P (Fin), Secy, Treas & Dir
            Giant Food Inc.
            Box 1804
            Washington, DC   20013
POSITION(S):
            Vice President-Senior

Secretary
Treasurer
Inside Director
DEPARTMENT(S):
Finance
Administration
SECONDARY AFFILIATION(S):
American Inst. of CPAs. Mem

GENERAL BUSINESS DATABASES

Use the general business files such as Trade and Industry Index (File 148), PTS Promt (File 16) or Textline (File Txtln) to find information about people in the business arena.

Pretty slick, huh...

DIALOG also has a number of general business bases. These include Trade and Industry Index (File 148), PTS Promt (File 16) and Textline. All hold information about people in the business arena.

Since these files are not necessarily grouped together in one database, DIALOG expects you to do the grouping yourself. Rather than running three or four separate searches, simply combine the files in what's known in Dialogese as a OneSearch.

SYSTEM:OS — DIALOG OneSearch
File 148:TRADE AND INDUSTRY INDEX 81-92/AUG (COPR. 1992 IAC)
**FILE148:   Weekly Alerts now available
Coming Soon:abstracts in selected records
File 16:PTS PROMT – 72–92/ September 2 (Copr. 1992 Predicasts)
**FILE016: New FULL TEXT titles added: AIDS Weekly, Cancer Weekly, FDA Enforcement Report, Health & Human Services News, Health Manager's Update.

Set	Items	Description
		? s david(1n)sykes
	129575	DAVID
	531	SYKES
S1	33	
DAVID(1N)SYKES		
? t s1/3,k/1-2 from each		

Our OneSearch automatically grouped together databases of interest and searched them on our search parameters. After that, you'll notice, we asked DIALOG to give us a sample by using the 3,k command, two examples from each database. This strategy allows us to see if information is correct and/or relevant before actually typing it out. The important thing to remember here is you can create your own OneSearch by linking together up to 40 files and having DIALOG use your search strategy in all named files. As one would suspect, it is important to have an effective search strategy at this point.

Another possibility is the MAGAZINE INDEX/ ASAP (Files 47, 647).

MAGAZINE INDEX covers general literature and is likely to have articles on your favorite celebrity or newsmaker. With today's selection of narrow band magazines, it is extremely possible that your bail jumping murderer still writes those articles for *Electronics Now.*

The normal way to search magazines is with our old standby strategy:

You enter: ? s first name (1n) last name

If your subject is so popular that too many hits appear use one of the delimiting strategies we've already covered to narrow the number to a manageable degree.

File 47:MAGAZINE INDEX 1959– MARCH 1970,1973–92/AUG (COPR. 1992 AIC)
**FILE047:   Weekly Alerts now available

Set	Items	Description
		? s sean(1n)connery
	1194	SEAN
	317	CONNERY
	238	SEAN(1N)CONNERY
		? s sl/ti,1992
	31	S1/TI
	94766	PY=1992
S2	3	S1/TI,1992
		? t s2/6/all

Once you have some hits, you can use an effective command known as Expand by typing:

You enter: ? e jn=people

This expansion command, using the "jn=" operator, retrieves all variations of a journal title.

? e jn=people

Ref	Items	Index-term
E1	3636	JN=PC–COMPUTING
E2	1858	JN=PENTHOUSE
E3	1917	*JN=PEOPLE
E4	30952	JN=PEOPLE WEEKLY
E5	13	JN=PERFORMING ARTS & ENTERTAINMENT IN CANADA
E6	388	JN=PERFORMING ARTS IN CANADA
E7	1760	JN=PERSONAL COMPUTING
E8	246	JN=PERSONNEL AND GUIDANCE JOURNAL
E9	3233	JN=PETERSEN'S PHOTOGRAPHIC MAGAZINE
E10	4265	JN=PHI DELTA KAPPA
E11	4772	JN=PHILADELPHIA MAGAZINE
E12	194	JN=PHYLON

Enter P or E for more

You can see how we have used the set searching capabilities of DIALOG to narrow down the list to the article or articles we're most interested in without printing out 200 fulltext articles at several bucks a shot.

While we're on this subject, DIALOG features an interesting database for all you groupies out there...

The Stars. Last, but of course not least, our fascination with the rich and/or famous can be satisfied on DIALOG.

MAGILL'S SURVEY OF CINEMA (File 299)
This database contains brief records on 30,000 films and comprehensive records for over 3,100 films. Actors names, the names of the characters they played and any awards they may have won or been nominated for are included.

Use the ac= term to find an actor in a film or the ar= term for the names of actors who have won awards.

2/3/1
0016981
THE UNTOUCHABLES. 1987 COLOR/BW: c
119 minutes
COUNTRY: USA
MPAA RATING: R
DIRECTOR: Brian De Palma
PRODUCER: Art Linson; released by Paramount Pictures.
                   CAST
Eliot Ness — Kevin Costner
Jimmy Malone — Sean Connery
Al Capone — Robert De Niro
Oscar Wallace — Charles Martin Smith
George Stone — Andy Garcia
Frank Nitti — Billy Drago
Mike — Richard Bradford
Payne — Jack Kehoe
George — Brad Sullivan
Ness's wife — Patricia Clarkson
SCREENPLAY BY: David Mamet; inspired by the television series of the same name.
CINEMATOGRAPHER: Stephen H. Burum
EDITOR: Jerry Greenburg and Bill Pankow
OTHER CREDITS:
ART DIRECTION, William A. Elliott,
SET DECORATION: Hal Gausman.
VISUAL CONSULTANT: Patrizia Von Brendenstein.
COSTUME DESIGN: Marilyn Vance-Straker.
MUSIC: Ennio Morricone.
         AWARD CITATIONS
AA, Winner, Best Supporting Actor, Sean Connery
AA, Nomination, Art Direction, Patirzia Von Brandenstein
AA, Nomination, Set Decoration, Hal Gausman
AA, Nomination, Costume Design, Marilyn Vance–Straker

AA, Nomination, Music (Original Score),
Ennio Morricone
GG, Winner, Best Supporting Actor,
Sean Connery
BAA, Winner, Original Score,
Ennio Morricone

ABSTRACT: Director Brian De Palma struggles unsuccessfully with writer David Mamet's screenplay and actor Kevin Costner's portrayal of Eliot Ness in this reworking of the battle between a young, incorruptible T-Man and his arch–enemy, Al Capone (Robert De Niro). Sean Connery contributes a splendid performance as Ness's mentor, Jimmy Malone.

Notice that the information returned on this includes other people who played in the movie, authors, editors, credits, consultants, citations, and occasionally well-known members of the crew.

Another interesting file on DIALOG is known as EXPERTNET (File 183)

This database contains profiles for over 100 medical experts who have signed agreements indicating a willingness to participate in medical consultation. Most are physicians in active practice or teaching. Please note that if you request format 9 for the fulltext format (the only format that displays name, address, phone number and approximate age) it is charged at $120 per record.

EXPERTNET is specific and expensive, but is a great source for finding expert witnesses. Unlike many DIALOG searches, EXPERTNET provides a nice little menu to guide you through selecting a specialty, formulating a search, and reminding you of the enormous cost of this database before you actually print anything out. When you finally are ready for a fulltext printout, simply type:

You enter: ? t s1/9/1

Format 9 includes the expert's name, address and phone number(s) and will be charged at

$120 per record. Do you wish to continue? (y/n)

So now we've seen examples of the many files that researchers, investigators, and general snoops often overlook in locating people or building a background on them. Now I'm going to show you the ultimate slick trick (UST as we call it in the trade).

There is one cost effective method of retrieving every instance of a personal name in DIALOG. This genie-in-a-bottle is known as DIALINDEX.

DIALINDEX, File 411, is a master index of all the items stored in DIALOG's non-menu driven databases. DIALINDEX can help you decide on the best databases(s) in which to begin your search. Use it with a single search statement to determine the number of relevant items in a group of databases. DIALINDEX offers preset groups of files, such as Allscience, Allbusiness, Allnews, and Papers. You may also create your personal combination of at least two databases.

Use the command Set Files ("SF") after you have begun File 411, to select the group of files whose indexes you want to search.

? B 411
? SF PAPERS

Rank Files: This command, used after you have run your search, arranges the results in a table, with the files containing the highest number of records at the top of the list. Each database is assigned an "N" reference number (i.e., N1, N2, N3), which may be used to begin a subsequent search. Use a colon to specify a range of databases (B N1:N3).

Save Temp: Use this to save your search temporarily after you have ranked your files. DIALOG assigns your saved search a serial number (i.e., TA012). You may then begin in a database(s) and execute your saved search.

? SAVE TEMP
? B N1:N4
? EXS Tnnn

Example: You want to find out which databases contain the most records on multimedia technology at Apple and Microsoft.

s roger(1n)summit
retrieves
Roger Summit
Roger K. Summit
Roger Kent Summit
Summit, Roger
Summit, Roger K.
Summit, Roger Kent
File 411:DIALINDEX (tm)
        (Copr.   DIALOG Info.Ser.Inc.)

***   DIALINDEX search results display in an abbreviated   ***
***   format unless you enter the SET DETAIL ON command.   ***

? sf all
You have 377 files in your file list.
(To see banners, use SHOW FILES command.)
? s roger(1n)summit
Your SELECT statement is:
s roger(1n)summit

Items	File	
3	1:	ERIC _ 66–92/AUG.
1	2:	INSPEC 2_69–92/9210W1
1	6:	NTIS_64–92/9209B2
8	7:	SOCIAL SCISEARCH_1972–199208W4
8	15:	ABI/INFORM_71–92/Aug Week 3
9	16:	PTS PROMT_– 72–92/September 2
1	18:	F & S INDEX _ 1980–92/AUG, WEEK 3
17	47:	MAGAZINE INDEX_1959–MARCH 1970,73–92/AUG
1	49:	PAIS INTERNATIONAL _ 76-92/AUG
10	61:	LISA _ 1969 – 1992/JUL

DIALINDEX is extremely limited in the number and details of the search terms one can use. It's best to stick to the basic's first name (1n) last name" format to retrieve all hits with the subject's name. If your subject is too popular, it's possible to restrict the search areas in DIALINDEX by the use of descriptors much as we did in PAPERS.

Notice here we've restricted the subject's name to the title, descriptor, and lead paragraph to concentrate on articles dealing with our subject and avoid incidental mentions of his name in the text of someone else's article. Not every database will use every descriptor but DIALOG will automatically exclude the non-valid search terms and use all of them when it can.

Because a large number of hits may be returned from a OneSearch, a useful command is "K" which stands for kwic, which automatically retrieves 30 words around your key words. The kwic command is used in the following manner:

You enter: ? t s2/6, k/1 from each

The kwic command gives you the flavor of the article and you still haven't paid to have anything printed. Choose the articles that you need and ask DIALOG to give you a full printout using the 9 format.

DIALINDEX 411 is probably the most cost efficient way of people or information tracking in

DIALOG. The keys are to be certain of your information before searching. Garbage in, garbage out...

As the above article was being written, DIALOG added an extremely handy feature called "Current." This feature lets the searcher define the number of years of data to be searched at the beginning of the search. It works on all newspaper and newswire files and a number of other large databases.

The "Current" feature offers five options:

Current/
Current1 (current year plus one back year)

Current2 (current year plus 2 back years)

Current3 (current year plus 3 back years)

Current4 (current year plus 4 back years)

Current5 (current year plus 5 back years)

In order to use "Current" as part of a search, you put it directly after the beginning and file number "Begin PAPERS Current2". Current will not work in DIALINDEX because file selection is not made with Begin command but rather with the s (select files command). It's an extremely handy way to limit frivolous information online costs, and establish the time parameters of your search.

GENEALOGY AND ADOPTION SEARCHES

An allied field of people-finding includes adoptees searching for their natural parents, parents searching for their adopted children, and people trying to trace their family roots or missing family members. Some of the techniques and resources cross with other material but there's also a number of specific resources designed for people in this field.

Norma Tillman, a well-known private investigator who runs an agency called U.F.O, Inc. P. O. Box 290333, Nashville, TN, 37229, specializes in locating missing persons. Norma edits and publishes a well put together publication called SEARCHING MAGAZINE, The Missing Persons Magazine. This publication aids anyone searching for a missing person including private investigators, attorneys, paralegals, law enforcement skip tracers, adoptees, birth parents, siblings or other relatives and friends.

The magazine is devoted to news and search strategies and includes a missing person's registry for people looking for one another, ads for books, magazines, conventions, and other resources for both the private investigation and missing person field. A very well done newsletter/magazine, $20.00 per year at the time of this writing.

Norma also offers a book, SECRETS FOR SUCCESSFUL SEARCHING, ($39.95), customized searches and a video tape.

SECRETS FOR SUCCESSFUL SEARCHING
ISBN 0-9634424-0-6

An example of the offbeat, very useful articles found in SEARCHING MAGAZINE is this article conveying tips for writing to law makers:

1. Spell their name correctly.
2. Use correct title and salutation:
   Dear Senator, Dear Representative.

3. Use the Honorable on the envelope and inside address.
4. Never use form letters or post cards.
5. Never send carbon copies of letters.
6. Use your full name and address.
7. Discuss only one issue per letter.
8. State purpose for writing at the beginning of the letter.
9. Give number of bill, not just the subject matter. (If you don't know the number, describe the bill).
10. Include all facts at your disposal, briefly and concisely.
11. Give suggestions for improving the situation.
12. Don't threaten, demand or apologize.
13. Limit your remarks to one page.
14. Either a hand-written or typed letter is acceptable, but be legible.
15. Thank the lawmaker.

PEOPLE SEARCHING NEWS, "Serving the Adoption Reform Movement since 1986". J. E. Carlson & Associates P. O. Box 2261, Ft. Lauderdale, FL 33335. A quarterly newsletter, $16.50, that covers legislative updates, maternity home stories, book reviews (BIRTH MOTHER TRAUMA and WAKE UP LITTLE SUSIE are two in the newsletter in front of me), videos, ads for people searching for their real parents and parents searching for their children. A bit more adoption specific than Norma's offering but is still a handy resource for people involved in people tracking.

PEOPLE SEARCHING NEWS also publishes a variety of books in the same field such as HOW TO START AND EXPAND A SEARCH and SUPPORT GROUP, Filling In The Blanks (for adoptees 10 - 14 years old on how to fill in their birth and adoptee family history), FAINT TRAILS, A Mini Search Guide for Searchers, etc.

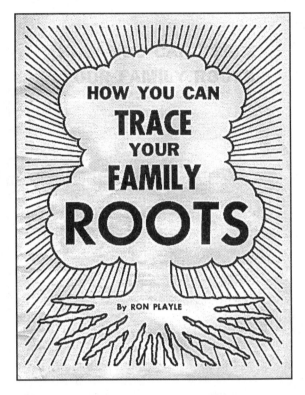

HOW YOU CAN TRACE YOUR FAMILY ROOTS

Other books include; HOW YOU CAN TRACE YOUR FAMILY ROOTS, Ron Playle, Playle Publications, Inc. P. O. Box 775, Des Moines, IA 50303. Ron has put together a slim, printed and bound book for people trying to find where they came from.

Much of the book is drawn from his own experience tracing his family back 250 years and includes some very basic information on where to research, records research, corresponding with record keepers, how to talk to your relatives, how to find vital statistics, what you can expect from county records, and the various societies that help in genealogical searching. He also sells a series of forms known as a starter kit, ($4.75), which includes pedigree charts, search calendars, group sheets, and work sheets.

THE USA SEARCH RESOURCES DIRECTORY, for Adoptees and Their Families Separated by Adoption, J. E. Carlson & Associates, a $15.00 book that is primarily of listing of agencies in every state that deals with adoptees with information on their policies for releasing information about adoptions. The book also reprints various portions of the laws applicable to each state and shows a number of support groups or other information resources in every state.

GENEALOGIST'S
address book

_____
_____
_____
_____
_____
_____
_____
_____

GENEALOGIST'S ADDRESS BOOK
ISBN 0-8063-1348-X

GENEALOGIST'S ADDRESS BOOK Genealogical Publishing Co, ($24.95) is published every two years and includes hundreds of organizations that will be of assistance to anyone involved in root searching. Organizations, special institutions publications, government agencies, societies, libraries periodicals, newspaper libraries services, bulletin boards, and databases are all covered.

When applicable the GAB provides direct phone numbers, hours of operation, contact names and search tips.

I would suggest this book for *all* people trackers...

THE GENEALOGISTS' MEDICAL AND REFERENCE GUIDE, Southern Media Ventures, Box 41695, Nashville, TN 37204. Another $15.00 book that comes in very handy if you're trying to track a person's family history and run across words you don't understand.

The Association of Professional Genealogists offers a DIRECTORY OF PROFESSIONAL GENEALOGISTS compiled by Desmond Walls Allen. It is available from the Association of Professional Genealogists, 3421 M Street, NW, Suite 236, Washington, DC 20007. Cost is $12.00 including postage and handling.

One of the best bargains in the business is a free copy of a pamphlet entitled SO YOU'RE GOING TO HIRE A PROFESSIONAL GENEALOGIST. If you'd like a copy send a long, self addressed, stamped envelope to The Association of Professional Genealogists, 3421 M Street, NW, Suite 236, Washington, DC 20007.

This pamphlet will tell you what to expect when you hire a professional genealogist. It covers such subjects as Finding a Professional, Evaluating the Professional's Qualifications, Research Costs, Defining the Researcher's Work, Evaluating Results, Resolving Differences, and Concluding the Research.

THE UNITED STATES RESEARCH GUIDES which can be obtained through The Family History Department, 35 N. West Temple Street, Salt Lake City, UT 84105, are designed to guide family history researchers through the sometimes bewildering maze of record depositories in the US.

The Church of Jesus Christ of Latter-Day Saints Family History Department has published this series of research outlines which includes outlines for the US as a whole and the District of Columbia and for each state, except for New York and New Jersey, where records are comparatively vast and complex.

Each guide discusses 26 major record types in alphabetical order with standard formatting. The headings and their arrangement are consistent with the Mormon library catalogue.

Discussed under separate headings in each outline are archives and libraries, Bible records, biographies, cemeteries, census, church records, court records, directories, emigration and immigration, gazetteers, genealogy (that is information previously gathered by others), history, land and property, maps, military records, minorities, native races, naturalization and citizenship, newspapers, obituaries, periodicals, probate records, societies, taxation, town records and vital records.

Individuals are encouraged to look at the US outline first, then the individual state outline. A helpful feature in the US outline is the records selection table. The first column is headed, "If You Need" and lists 24 items such as age, birth, date, immigration date and physical description. For a given item, the researcher looks in the second column, with the heading, "Look First In," then the third column ,"Then Search."

The outlines are available to anyone who requests them. The price is $0.75 for the US outline and $0.25 for each individual state outline. The entire set will set your budget back $12.50.

This is an extremely useful resource because the Mormon Church has the largest collection of genealogical data in the US stored in Salt Lake City. If you happen to be in that neighborhood, drop in and use their facilities.

If you don't plan a visit to SLC, you can, or attempt to, hire a researcher to deal with the files.

GENEALOGICAL PUBLISHING, INC. 1001 N. Calvert St., Baltimore, MD 21202. GPC publishes a number of meaty guides to getting records and finding people including sources not easily found anywhere else.

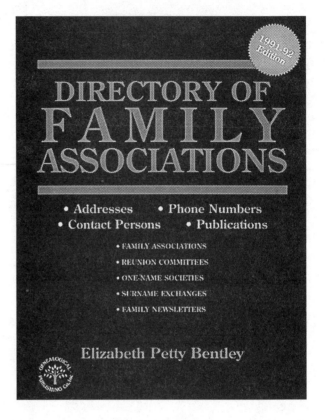

DIRECTORY OF FAMILY ASSOCIATIONS
ISBN 0-863-1319-6

Their DIRECTORY OF FAMILY ASSOCIATIONS covers addresses, phone numbers, contacts, publications of family associations, reunion committees, one-name societies, surname exchanges and family newsletters. These sources are useful for direct access to information as well as newsletters (most common family names have an association and a newsletter) to advertise for people you're trying to find.

CERA, 41 East 74th St., New York, NY 10021, a resource retailer for adoption-related issues. They also put on seminars and an annual conference with support groups, special interest groups, and Ph.D.'s who speak about things like, "The Coerced Generation; How Several Million Women Were Separated from Their Babies".

BIRTH PARENT CONNECTION, the National Maternity Home Register, Box 230643, Encinitas, CA 92023. Okay, okay, it's a bit specialized with articles like, "What Happened to the Other Woman You Knew in the Maternity Home?"

On the other hand it's only $5.00 to join and makes a nice conversation piece.

HUNTING FOR BEARS, INC., 3878 W. 3200 South, Salt Lake City, UT 84120. HUNTING FOR BEARS was started by a husband and wife newspaper publishing team. Their primary offering is something known as the SURNAME SEARCH, but they also publish BEAR TRACKS, a quarterly newsletter from the society with news of interest to genealogists, quotes from members, suggestions, success stories, queries, a "few witticisms and whatever we think our readers might like." $10.00 a year for membership in the society includes the subscription to BEAR TRACKS.

How can you lose?

Their surname searches are not, at this point, national nor are their marriage books so you need to contact them before ordering to see if your state and county is included.

"Our main concern is the SURNAME SEARCH. The total effort is concerned with marriages – we are collecting marriage records from the earliest up through 1900. They are put on computer in alphabetical order for the whole state. When you request a SURNAME SEARCH we check the index for other variations and request them all from the computer. If you want only one spelling or variation, you must request "This Spelling Only" with your order.

The index used to determine variations is available at a subsidized rate to libraries, genealogical societies, or individuals for $15.95 per volume.

Surname Searches contain up to 25 marriages per page. If one of your searches has more than 20 pages (approximately a $12 order) you have the option of searching for a particular initial or initials.

Example: you order *Williams* of Louisiana. You will receive a letter from us stating that we have 383 pages of *Williams* (9575 marriages) and informing you of your options. You determine that you are searching for a Curtis, Donald & Mary so you order and receive only the *Williams* marriages whose given names begin with "C", "D", & "M", thereby reducing your costs to an affordable amount.

CompuServe is starting a FAMILY SEARCH CENTER which will allow direct access to the huge record repository at Salt Lake City, as well as, US census data. GO ROOTS.

HOW TO LOCATE & RESEARCH ANYTHING

It is, indeed, possible to locate and research almost anything. My job is to help you accomplish this task by investing a minimum amount of time and/or money. Obviously, these two qualifications do not always correlate with each other so some decisions have to be made.

First of all, let's concentrate on the big "E" — Efficiency.

An efficient search strategy is the difference between making two phone calls and spending the better part of a week running up high priced bills. The first step is to *write down* exactly what information you are looking for, who you think might have it, and a search strategy. Let's start with the easiest method of information gathering...

ORGANIC SOURCES

The flat-out, simplest way to find any piece of information, be it the home phone number of the new director of the KGB or where to buy an M79 grenade launcher, is to ask someone who knows. Not surprisingly, most people like attention, most people like to be thought of as "experts" and most people will share what they know when asked in the correct manner.

NATIONAL DIRECTORY OF ADDRESSES AND TELEPHONE NUMBERS, Omnigraphics, Penobscot Building, Detroit, MI 48226, toll-free phone: 800-234-1340, ISBN 1-55888-771-7, $59.95 soft cover, publishes THE NATIONAL DIRECTORY OF ADDRESSES AND TELEPHONE NUMBERS on a yearly basis.

NATIONAL DIRECTORY OF ADDRESSES AND TELEPHONE NUMBERS ISBN 1-55888-140-9

This book contains phone numbers, addresses, fax numbers and toll-free numbers for America's most frequently called companies, associations, educational institutions, embassies, media, societies and travel providers, arranged alphabetically by name of organization and also in a classified yellow pages section arranged by type of business.

This large format *1,472-page book* is one of the better sixty bucks I've spent. It is flat-out the book I used most in compiling the book you are now reading. I've probably saved the price of the book in telephone information charges alone.

231,000+ listings across the country provide instant access to virtually every large or well known corporation in the United States, as well as, the headquarters and various offices of larger international firms and special sections for cities containing travel guides, hotel listings, restaurants, media events, etc. A helpful SIC INDEX is also provided for people who wish to search by the Standard Industry Codes.

Need an expert? Need a product? Need a service? Want to compare printers' prices, shellfish deliveries, electronic wholesalers, or just talk to someone at that company that was referenced in the article you read?

- Top corporations in 340 different industries
- Every four-year college and university
- Bureau of vital statistics
- Foreign embassies and consulates
- State chambers of commerce
- U. S. senators and representatives
- Major sports teams
- Zip and area code directories

The main alternative is THE ALL – IN – ONE BUSINESS CONTACT BOOK, ISBN 0-8103-7674-1, $49.95, Gale Research. This book features complete dial-up listings from 10,000 leading US companies selected from rankings such as Fortune 500, Forbes 600, Business Week Top 1,000, and Ward's Top 1,000 Private Firms. Each company is listed under as many as four product/service categories.

Most entries include a wide variety of direct-dial numbers–including main office, toll-free, fax, telex, cable, special recordings, consumer information lines and hotlines.

Find facts three ways: by alphabetical arrangement in the main text, or by geographic location or product/service listing in the two comprehensive indexes that follow.

NATIONAL FAX DIRECTORY from Gale Research, 1,990 pages, soft cover, ISBN 0-8103-7637-7,

$79.95, compiles fax numbers for US companies, organizations, government agencies and libraries.

Features more than 85,000 phone-verified entries included for the nation's leading companies, organizations and agencies, selected on the basis of size, sales, number of employees, annual billings, or industry ranking.

Two more resource directories that can put you in touch with an organic source are also published by Gale:

ENCYCLOPEDIA OF ASSOCIATIONS – National Organizations of the US, Volume 3, supplement, soft cover, ISBN 0-8103-7622-9, $285.00, published for the last 36 years, the ENCYCLOPEDIA OF ASSOCIATIONS (EA) has been the #1 source for information on active associations, organizations, clubs and other nonprofit membership groups in virtually every field of human endeavor.

This book describes more than 22,000 associations. It includes the latest information on trade and professional associations, social welfare and public affairs organizations, environmental groups, labor unions, fraternal and patriotic organizations, and religious, sports and hobby groups.

THE ART OF ASKING QUESTIONS

I once had the pleasure of working with a TV sports announcer who was detested by not only myself but most of the people he interviewed because of his obnoxious habit of thinking he knew more about anything than anyone else present. Once, after a tennis match when we had about 60 seconds to kill, he strong-armed John Macenroe who had just lost a match and said to him, "Wouldn't you say, John, that your style, even though you lost today's match, has improved noticeably over the years because, of course, you're starting to learn to control your temper in difficult situations and perhaps this has had a major impact in your playing career that I see out there never realized?"

The tennis star looked at him and said, "Yeah," then turned around and walked off leaving us with 45 seconds of rather embarrassing dead air...

The technique of organic research is an art. Most people want to talk about things, especially things they've done or been involved in. If you approach your subject in the correct manner, you'll find your responses and success rate will soar. The technique I'm giving here has been refined by several high level business researchers, a couple of good reporters and even an intelligence agent or two.

Although I'm presenting this in a business research format, the same techniques and nearly the same questions apply to personnel research as well.

There are several different approaches that one can take when looking for information but some general rules apply to all of them; the direct approach often works quite well.

"Hi, I'm Lee. I have an interest in your product. Can you tell me more about it?"

How should you pose questions? Always be friendly and unassuming. Try and build a rapport with the person ("I have an interest in"). Offer to exchange information if possible. This is especially good if you're talking with techie types and you happen to know something that some other company is doing or a new product coming on the market.

Ask open-ended questions, always show great enthusiasm, and remember to let the other person do the talking. This latter is not as easy as it sounds. The natural inclination is to jump in and add to the conversation, which tends to disrupt the flow and may cancel out what you've worked for to this point.

It's best if you don't sound like an expert. People want to educate other people. You can always ask for references to a specific product and then, instead of asking direct questions about sensitive issues, such as sales, offer something else up for comparison by saying, "I bet this is selling better than the Apple Macintosh."

Another approach is to say, "I bet you've sold hundreds of these."

The response should be, "No, no, thousands."

If this doesn't work, try to challenge the target with a statement you know is false so you can let the other person take a positive role by correcting you, "So, I understand you're going into business with Apple computers."

"No, you're probably thinking about the deal we made with IBM."

Remember, direct statements work better than questions. For best results think of what you're doing as a jigsaw puzzle. You'll get some pieces from this target and some pieces elsewhere that you must string together into a single pattern. Be flexible.

Sometimes you have to ignore conventional wisdom and take an approach that lets the target tell you what you want to know while saving face. I watched a friend of mine employ this technique to great results. He's one of the better reporters around and was trying to dig up information on a story that had just broken. He reached the principal and said, "The other side is alleging that you did thus and such. What's your story?"

The gentleman on the other end said, "I'd like to tell you, but my attorneys have advised me that I can't talk to anyone, especially reporters."

My friend said, "I understand, but if you could talk, what would you tell me?"

At this point the guy replied, "I would tell you..." and laid out every fact my friend wanted to find and that no other reporter had been able to get.

Be sure you've done your homework first so you don't ask completely useless or stupid questions that will turn the target off. Always determine first what questions you're going to ask and in what order. It's generally good to build rapport with small questions that can be safely answered and ask the most sensitive question last.

If you've done your job correctly, the target will have no problem in answering you at this point.

Try to determine possible objections and a strategy for overcoming them in advance so you're not caught short.

Many competitive intelligence business people employ slight subterfuges when calling a sensitive target. Drop a friend or acquaintance of the target's name and suggest that he said to make the call. It's better if this is true of course, and it's easy to set up: simply call someone else in the same field and ask a few questions ending with, "Who else might know that?" With any luck you'll get your target's name. Then you call the gentleman in question and say, "Bob Smith told me to call you and ask..."

If you're directly challenged and they want to know who you are, one option is to say, "My name is Lee Lapin and I'm interested in your new processor."

If you have any point of reference, use it. "My name's Lee and I saw a mention of your new stun gun in *Police Product News* and it looks to me like it's based on the Nova technology?"

Then let him reply.

It's also possible, but slightly unethical to represent yourself as a reporter or a writer for a trade publication. Everyone likes to see their name in something their colleagues and cohorts are going to read.

It's eminently possible to look up newsletters or associations for your particular field in one of the books and databases I've mentioned, call up the newsletter and say you're trying to do a freelance article on new word processors. Would they be interested if you could get an interview with the head of Intel?

At worst they'll say no. At best they'll say yes, and offer to pay your for your information but most likely you'll get an, "Of course, we'd like to take a look at it but we don't pay outside writers, or we can't pay too much."

"Hey, no problem..."

You're now a legitimate reporter for a trade publication.

One of the better guides to telephone interviewing I've seen is from HOW TO FIND INFORMATION ABOUT EXECUTIVES from Washington Researchers Publishing.

Just as important as how to talk, is whom to talk to. Organic research is a numbers game.

You will fail sometimes, other times you'll be wildly successful. Don't let the bad ones get you down.

The best strategy is to start with any known contacts, either in the target company, regulatory agency, libraries, legal departments, or your own employees. Then move on to low-level employees in the target company. This would include 800 number people, customer service people, librarians, and senior secretaries. After that try for top-level executives.

These calls are best made in the early morning when the person is alert and has not yet let the day's work become a nuisance. When you are questioning the top management level, start in the president's office and work downward. The best method of contact here is often, "good old Bob told me to call."

If you don't succeed with top management, try middle-level managers, although as a general rule you will want to avoid mid-level employees, that is, people who are in no real position of power but run one small department or consider themselves a necessary cog in the machine. These people tend to be more suspicious than either low-level or top-level management people.

Specifically, you want to talk to industry analysts and experts, customers, suppliers, insurance companies, the competitors themselves, retailers and distributors, internal sales people, any database research people who may be helping you, secretaries, the company librarian, company marketing or PR people. These folks are paid to talk...

THE DELPHI TECHNIQUE

The Delphi Method of interviewing is named after the Temple of Apollo at Delphi and is said to have been developed by Rand Corporation mathematicians Olaf Helmer and Norman Dalkey.

Specialized interviews based on Delphi Methods have become a popular forecasting technique and perhaps, the one most often subverted to serve the ends of business espionage.

These interviews deliver the single most likely guess as to what a company or industry will be doing in the future based on projections made by the best minds involved in the field at the present.

Delphi works like this:

1. Poll experts on a subject separately and in private regarding both their rational projections and their gut reaction hunches.

2. Repeat the interviews several times if possible, after the experts have had a chance to think about and reevaluate their data.

3. Break these data down to isolate a group opinion covering your area of interest. (Those being questioned may or may not know your real intent.)

4. If possible, bring those polled together to "talk out" a consensus.

The results can provide an honest and straightforward look at the future if the information gathered is shared with all of the contributors.

Those involved in business intelligence use Delphi technique in a number of ways:

They may send bogus "sales representatives" to meet with the key employees of rival firms on the pretext of "better serving prospective customers."

They may send attractive interviewers to targeted companies with a list of carefully worded questions. These interviewers may actually be the "graduate students" or "researchers" they appear to be and may not know the real objectives of the investigation.

They may send investigators to "work" trade shows and seminars. Asking loaded questions of preselected participants at a trade show or seminar can be very productive in this usually informal setting.

CONTROLS AND COUNTERMEASURES

Managers may wish to prescreen sales representatives, graduate students, reporters and others who request inside information. Ask questions before you answer any questions. This is especially true of spur-of-the-moment questions about the inner workings of your company.

"What type of information are you seeking?"

"How will the information be used?"

"Will you be recording the interview? Do I get a copy?" (Consult your attorney about the legal restrictions.)

"Do I get a copy of your article or final report?"

"Where can I contact you later?"

MEGADIRECTORIES

There are so many directories and resource guides whose very job in life is to tell *you* where to find what you need, that a super class of directories has been spawned. These megadirectories will cut hours from an average search by showing exactly, well, not where your information is found, but how to find where your information...

Some of these guides are available online, some are hard copy only and many can be found in better libraries, either public or private.

GUIDE TO REFERENCE BOOKS AND SUPPLEMENT TO THE GUIDE to reference books, both published by the American Library Association, ALA Publishing Services 50 East Huron Street, Chicago, IL 60611, is probably the most complete set of megaguides available today.

How complete is it?

The supplement alone ($76.50) contains references to 4,668 works, many of which are of interest to business or general intelligence collectors. 600 pages of sources and materials are included as well as CD–ROM and other electronic reference works.

These works are very popular with librarians and you should find both at your local library.

DIRECTORIES IN PRINT, Gale Research, 14,000 detailed entries for 4,000 different directories on a worldwide basis.

Descriptions of databases, buyer's guides, membership lists, registers, handbooks, indexes, catalogs and directories of all kinds. Covers CD-ROM's, directories, and databases for which entries are available in computer readable or online formats.

Name and address of the publisher, number of listings, scope, content, update frequency, and more. Searchable by keyword, subject or title.

Includes everything from travel related entries (accommodations, restaurants) to fellow professionals in your field. 2,187 pages, $260.00.

CONCEPTS OF INFORMATION RETRIEVAL by Miranda Pao from Libraries Unlimited, is a very scholarly work on how information, including much of the type of interest to us, is stored and how to approach it.

Sentences like, "Collateral and associative linkage of descriptors", give you some flavor of what I'm talking about.

How to create online searches, how to write a search form, semantic networks, indexes and evaluations.

A real good work.

Don't plan on a one day read on the beach.

CONCEPTS OF INFORMATION RETRIEVAL
ISBN 0-87287-405-2

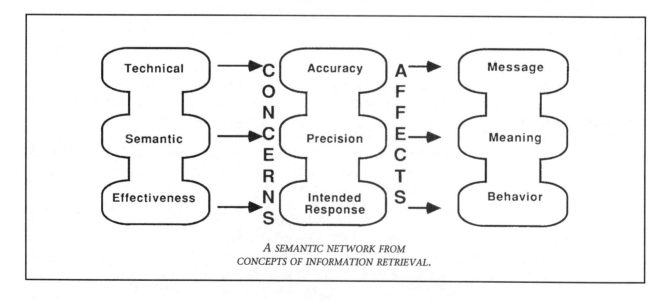

*A SEMANTIC NETWORK FROM
CONCEPTS OF INFORMATION RETRIEVAL.*

CITY AND STATE DIRECTORIES IN PRINT, 4,500 local and regional directories that cover hundreds of thousands of manufacturers, chambers of commerce, businesses, attorneys, banks, organizations, and so on and so forth. Also Gale, $145.00, 946 pages.

GALE'S DIRECTORY OF PUBLICATIONS AND BROADCAST MEDIA is a comprehensive list of 36,000 media outlets including their ad rates, circulation statistics, names of key personnel and so on.

This directory is used by virtually every ad agency and time buyer in the world and is available at most libraries.

Even if you are not in a media-related field I will tell you small town newspaper editors and reporters (and sometimes librarians) are some of the best sources of local information available. 3,379 pages, $280.00.

1000 WORLDWIDE NEWSPAPERS, Ken Albertsen, Albertsen's POB 339, Nevada City, CA 95959. Addresses of 1,000 US papers and 200 foreign. No names, not much detail. $12.00.

1000 WORLDWIDE BUSINESS DIRECTORIES, Albertsen's, no price at this time. Name sort of explains it all...

WHERE TO FIND WHAT, James Hillard, Scarecrow Books, 333 pages (hardcover) $35.00. ISBN 0-8108-2404-3. 607 subject headings are arranged alphabetically and have been selected according to the "needs of library patrons."

Everything from AIDS research to toll free number directories are listed in this free format guide. Not much in the way of evaluation of the sources, which are arranged by subject area, but all titles, publishers and other vital facts are covered.

A subjective list of what the writer considers important, this is still a nice place to begin a search, especially since most large libraries will have it in stock.

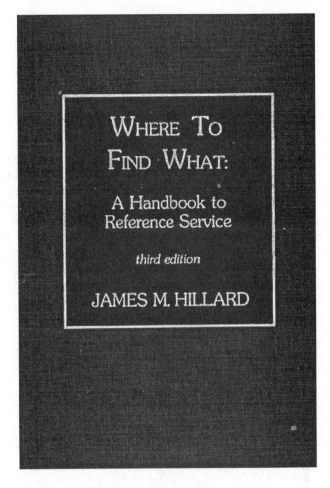

WHERE TO FIND WHAT

Academy Investigations 29415 Avenida La Paz #1, Cathedral City, CA 92234. Very inexpensive "shareware" including 4 disks entitled UNLIMITED INFORMATION which include DEMAND RESEARCH DIRECTORY, BATES DIRECTORY OF NEWSPAPERS AND LIBRARIES and MORE...

They also provide a disk of memorable quotes, Today In History, Zip Finder and a first aid tutorial. Prices are a mere $5.00 for the first disk, $2 for each additional.

REFERENCE BOOKS BULLETIN
ISBN 0-8389-3417-X

RECOMMENDED REFERENCE BOOKS
ISBN 0-87287-976-3

REFERENCE BOOKS REFERENCE is a regular section of a publication called BOOKLIST which is one of the standard reference tools designed to alert librarians to new books. Every couple of years or so the people at RFB pull out what they think are the most interesting new entries and put them together in a book called, yes, REFERENCE BOOKS BULLETIN.

Published by the ALA, this work provides articles and reviews of works in crime and criminal justice, generalities, business, economics, science, technology, management and so forth.

While some of the material, say *The Encyclopedia of Textiles,* may not be a work you would use each and every day, *The Directory of Business To Business Catalogs,* or *How To Locate Anyone Who Has Been In the Military,* just might be...

RECOMMENDED REFERENCE BOOKS FOR SMALL AND MEDIUM-SIZED LIBRARIES AND MEDIA CENTERS, Bohdan Wyan, Editor-in-Chief, Libraries Unlimited, POB 6633, Englewood, CO 80155, ISBN 0-87287-976-3.

Pretty general in nature, RRBFSAMSLAMC, besides owning what may be the longest title in America, does review some books applicable to researchers or detectives in such fields as: genealogy, research, directories, encyclopedias, handbooks and yearbooks, periodicals and serials, information science, public government, communication, science and technology.

Washington Researchers publishes a very good newsletter entitled THE INFORMATION REPORT which provides updated information on new databases and reference books.

NEWSLETTERS, PERIODICALS AND ASSOCIATIONS

Very specific information can be found in small magazines and newsletters, and the people who publish them may be one of your best organic sources. THE READER'S GUIDE TO PERIODICAL LITERATURE, carried in every library, as well as online, is the first place to look for articles on a specific topic.

You can't afford to buy the set, trust me.

ULRICH'S INTERNATIONAL PERIODICAL DIRECTORY, Bowker and Co. 121 Chanlon Road, New Providence, NJ 07094, is a little more affordable at $400 and will also be stocked by any library worth its salt.

Data on 120,000 regular and irregular serials cross indexed and priced. List includes 2,600 periodicals that are distributed free to "qualified audiences."

Online in DIALOG.

NEWSLETTERS IN PRINT, Gale Research (also on DIALOG) lists some 9,700 subscription, membership and free newsletters.

The Newsletter Clearinghouse, 44 West Market St., Rhinebeck, NY 12572, is a private company that deals with how to form, run and generally profit from publishing newsletters, they also publish HUDSON'S NEWSLETTER DIRECTORY ($118.00).

Includes 4600 subscription newsletters and tends to highlight the smaller ones that Gale may miss.

At some libraries.

OXBRIDGE DIRECTORY OF NEWSLETTERS, Oxbridge Communications Inc., 150 Fifth Ave., Suite 302, New York, NY 10011. A $345 newsletter directory that claims *over 20,000* entries, Oxbridge may be the most complete, and possibly the most expensive newsletter directory around.

Also published by Oxbridge is THE NATIONAL DIRECTORY OF MAGAZINES, a computer accessible directory of 21,000 magazines.

Remember newsletters are not only a great source of up-to-date information, they can be used to find experts as well as a nice source for a cover as a "reporter."

HUDSON'S

SUBSCRIPTION NEWSLETTER

DIRECTORY

11th Edition

. . . *Subscription Newsletters Worldwide*
■ by subject category with editors and publishers ■ by geographic location ■ suppliers to the industry ■ publications and persons indexed alphabetically ■

HUDSON'S SUBSCRIPTION NEWSLETTER
DIRECTORY ISBN 1046-8110

EXPERTS ON YOUR PAYROLL

Luckily you already have some of the sharpest people in the world working directly for you, an often overlooked resource that is as close as your telephone or typewriter. It's possible to reach out and touch a number of unique sources of advanced information on almost any subject, by simply asking your employees.

Assuming, of course, that you do pay your taxes...

Our government is literally stuffed full of people who know things you might well want to know, and most of them will help you for the price of a phone call. The trick is shifting through the levels of bureaucracy to find the correct person, or agency to whom you should direct your inquiry.

THE GOVERNMENT RESEARCH DIRECTORY Edited by Thomas Cichonski, ISBN 0-8103-7526-5, Gale Research, $390.00 is a 1,200 page, comprehensive directory of 3,700 research facilities and programs operated by the federal government.

These listings include user-oriented facilities operated by the government, cooperative programs, government agencies, bureaus, administrative offices and similar units.

THE DIRECTORY contains contact information, phone and fax numbers, details on libraries, collections, publications and more. A master index points you in the right direction with subject and geographic indexes to help fine tune your search.

Government Research Services 701 Jackson, #304, Topeka, KS 66603 publishes a newsletter ands three directories of interest to government oriented researchers:

- GOVERNMENT & POLITICS ALERT is a bimonthly newsletter that reviews books, reports, periodicals and directories on state and national government.
- DIRECTORY OF POLITICAL PERIODICALS covers 200+ journals, newsletters and newspapers that focus on the government (especially relevant in the Washington area). $45.00.
- STATE REFERENCE PUBLICATIONS is a bibliographic guide to state blue books, legislative manuals and other state reference publications. $60.00.
- THINK TANK DIRECTORY is a guide to independent and nonprofit research organizations. $85.00.

Monitor Publishing Company 104 Fifth Ave., 2nd Floor, New York, NY 10011, publishes a series of "Yellow Books" that are sort of Who's Who in a number of government and private arenas. Fer instance:

FEDERAL YELLOW BOOK 35,000 decision makers in the White House and the Executive office of the President along with federal departments and agencies and some regional offices.

Need to reach someone at the Securities and Exchange Commission, the Postal Service, National Security Council or just one of the 72 federal information centers across the country?

Names, tittles, phone numbers of significant personnel from Cabinet Members to agency staffers.

- FEDERAL REGIONAL YELLOW BOOK lists over 20,000 "key decision makers" in 8,000 regional offices of the Federal government. This list includes folks employed at independent agencies, courts, military installations and service academies across the nation (but OUTSIDE of Washington, DC).

- Three indexes organized by key words, locations and names refer to the individuals who are listed along with their titles, addresses, and phone numbers.
- STATE YELLOW BOOK does pretty much the same thing for the executive and legislative branches of each state government along with county names and seats, and some ancillary data about the areas covered. 35,000 individuals who all work for you...
- MUNICIPAL YELLOW BOOK does, well, you can probably figure that out by now, can't you? Need the fax number of a city clerk in Golden Colorado, or the registrar of voters in Cincinnati?

Names, titles, phone numbers broken down by key departments and agencies.

Monitor also has Yellow Books for corporate America, the Congress and one for associations.

Most published twice a year, subscriptions average about $165.00.

LONG DISTANCE DIRECTORY OF GOVERNMENT ADDRESSES AND PHONES, Omnigraphics, Penobscot Building, Detroit, MI 48226. $89.00. This directory features 100,000 government phone and fax numbers.

National Conference of State Legislatures, Book Order Department, 1560 Broadway, Suite 700, Denver, CO 80202 will furnish you with two useful entries:

- DIRECTORY OF LEGISLATIVE LEADERS ($25) provides the office addresses, phones, faxes districts represented, presiding officers, key staff contacts and more.
- STATE LEGISLATIVE STAFF DIRECTORY ($45) is a list of staff members who do most of the research in these offices.

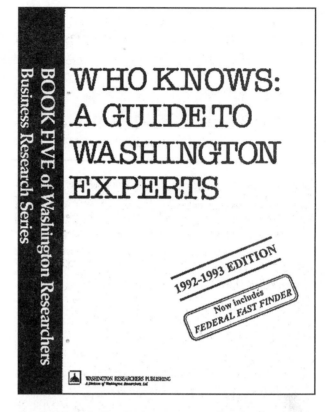

WHO KNOWS A GUIDE TO WASHINGTON EXPERTS
ISBN 1-56365-014-2

WHO KNOWS: A GUIDE TO WASHINGTON EXPERTS Washington Research Publishing, is a directly of *approachable* federal bureaucrats who have expertise on "specific topics." Arranged alphabetically by topic, this book includes a "Federal Fast Finder" which works as a shortcut for those who wish to simply contact experts by office rather than by topic.

If you are looking for a single expert on a single topic simply flip this book open to the appropriate entry. If you need several experts in order to compare or verify information you can generally go to a broader topic category and find additional entries.

Unlike most directories, WHO KNOWS does not list the head of the department (who is going to be protected by a wall of aging secretaries) but concentrates on the mid level researchers, and information providers who may actually be quite flattered to answer your question on Cartography Disaster in Geology Security, Sebacid Acid Esters (or where to get the latest data on government level scramblers, or laws governing investigators, or...).

Like all Washington Researcher's works, this book is quite useful, very reliable, user friendly and moderately expensive.

INTRODUCTION TO UNITED STATES GOVERNMENT SOURCES
ISBN 1-56308-066-4

INTRODUCTION TO UNITED STATES GOVERNMENT INFORMATION SOURCES Joe Morehead and Mary Fetzer, Libraries Unlimited, ISBN 1-56308-066-4. This book is not the kind of thing I like to read at 2 AM when I am trying to fall asleep and need some fast escapist fiction...

It is a very scholarly, detailed work that covers such topics as what the United States Government Printing Office does, examples for US Government Books, Periodicals Supplement and New Books, details on how a bill becomes law, census products, serial set classifications, what patent drawings look like, general catalogs, indexes and selected reference sources, technical report sources, statistical sources, and what various departments do for their money.

Definitely a useful publication for anyone who plans on dealing with the government on a regular basis.

INFORMATION USA, INC. POB E, Kensington, MD 20895. Operated by one Matthew Lesko, IUI offers a variety of publications that seem to be aimed at letting you use the resources of the federal government, start a business, get a grant, find an auction, or become an entrepreneur.

Lesko's newsletter entitled LESKO'S INFO-POWER NEWSLETTER (formerly The Data Informer) "shows decision makers and researches how to take advantage of unusual sources of information."

THE FEDERAL DATA BASE FINDER
ISBN 1-878346-03-2

His book THE FEDERAL DATA BASE FINDER, "identifies free databases which your computer can access." $125.00

The more affordable LESKO'S INFO-POWER book has over 10,000 sources that show you where to get "the most up to date information on any subject," for a mere $39.95.

I have not used Mr. Lesko's materials and, therefore, cannot comment one way or the other on their effectiveness.

I *can* safely say he is definitely a self promoter.

FREEDOM OF INFORMATION

The Freedom Of Information Act, passed in 1966 and strengthened in 1974 is one of the more important acts of legislation ever to clear the decks in my humble opinion.

Basically this act says anyone can request access to any records of the executive branch of the federal government and that said records must be released unless protected from mandatory disclosure by some provision of the FOIA itself or other federal law.

In practice this little law threw a number of government agencies in a bit of a turmoil; the FBI and the CIA, among others, had to create entire departments to deal with the thousands of requests that began pouring in every month.

Most agencies simply stonewalled the requests for a time by stating they did not have the personnel to deal with them for some time.

Usually time as measured in months, or years...

Finally, unrelenting pressure moved the mountain over to Mohammed's side of the street and the agencies began to comply with the spirit of the law. The FOIA now states that all agencies must reply within 10 working days except in "unusual" circumstances.

Of course this reply can be a "no", but at least you get the process moving in a limited amount of time. Many requests are still denied on the basis of being "classified material", or for a number of other reasons.

The process has a built-in appeal avenue, and one can litigate if necessary. Various organizations and senators will sometimes apply gentle pressure to the agency in question if approached in the correct manner.

The key to using the FOIA is to request the materials in the *exact* manner called for, using any and all possible names, nicknames, AKA's, limit up front the amount of money you can be charged for the search, and send it to the correct department.

Several organizations have published comprehensive manuals on the use of the FOIA. The ACLU features A STEP-BY-STEP GUIDE TO USING THE FREEDOM OF INFORMATION ACT for a mere $5.00 from The American Civil Liberties Union, Publications Department 122 Maryland Ave., NE, Washington, DC 20002.

A veritable bargain, this booklet not only tells you how to use the act, and word your letter, it even lists the FOIA addresses for a number of federal agencies.

The ACLU also offers to help you, free of charge, prepare a FOIA request.

Love those liberals...

On the other side of the coin, hell, I mean maybe on the *edge* of the coin, we find THE HANDBOOK ON HOW TO USE THE FREEDOM OF INFORMATION ACT published by the Church of Scientology 1404 N. Catalina Street, Los Angeles, CA 90027.

Talk about a bargain, this one's *free*...

You see a few years ago the government, in the form of the IRS, FBI and God only knows who else decided to crack down on the Church of Scientology for reasons I'm not going to delve into here.

The Church responded, quite admirably, I might add, by hiring lawyers and flooding the government with requests for records held on their organization and its members.

One of the better things they did to save others from reinventing the wheel, and probably to bug the bejesus out of a number of government agencies, was to publish this booklet.

Subtitled "Holding The Government Accountable For Its Actions", this very well written, very slick publication shows you how to get what you want, how to avoid pitfalls, what to expect from various agencies, sample request letters, further reading, sources of low cost or free legal advice about the FOIA, how to appeal your "no", and so on.

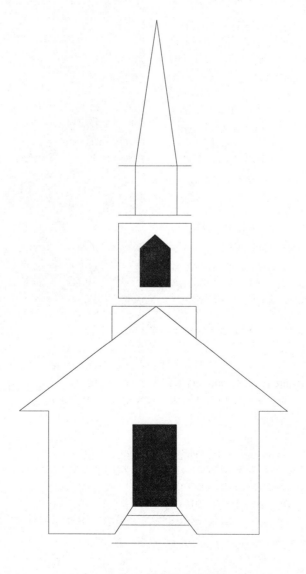

LIBRARIES

Also stocked with people already on your payroll who are just going to be more than overjoyed with answering your most difficult questions are libraries.

Well, maybe not more than overjoyed, but at least joyed...

A good research librarian can often steer you directly to the correct answer, or at least a source for the answer. At the worst he/she can start your path on the correct fork.

AMERICAN LIBRARY DIRECTORY ONLINE Gale Research on DIALOG contains update profiles of 38,000 academic, government and private libraries in the US and Canada.

An ideal starting point.

FOCUS ON THE CENTER FOR RESEARCH LIBRARIES, Center For Research Libraries 6050 S. Kenwood, Chicago, IL 60637. A newsletter that highlights what research libraries are ordering what, information on the Center's activities and so on.

RLTN, The Research Libraries Network is a online system that reflects the combined holdings of more than 100 research libraries and archival repositories. These institutions, working together as members of Research Libraries Group Inc., have created a national database of bibliographic information.

This source can be searched by anyone with an account, computer, modem and a telephone. You can either join the organization ($200 straight out, $300 with a day's training), or access them thru the INTERNET.

What's available?

Glad you asked...

- 35 million items held in both research and special libraries
- Records that describe the Library Of Congress and the GPO
- Comprehensive representation of books since 1974
- Special databases and other machine-readable files

LIBRARY OF CONGRESS. Simply stated, the largest storehouse of information on the planet earth. 500+ miles of stacks, millions and mil-

lions of book coupled with many other information storehouses makes the LOC the place where to find anything about anything.

Problems be two; it's in Washington, DC, and there are 500+ miles of stacks, millions and millions...

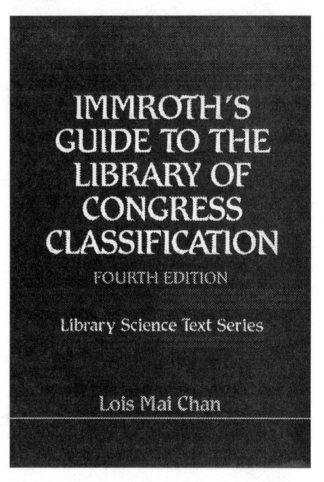

IMMROTH'S GUIDE TO THE LIBRARY OF CONGRESS CLASSIFICATION ISBN 0-87287-763-9

Second problem first – IMMROTH'S GUIDE TO THE LIBRARY OF CONGRESS CLASSIFICATION ($32.50) from Libraries Unlimited details exactly how information is stored in the Library, and how it can be found.

Although designed for librarians, this book is a find if you are planning on visiting the LOC in person or by proxy. Use it to plan your search strategy offline, so to speak.

Save time and money.

Like many libraries the LOC keeps a list of researchers who will search for you by proxy. Call and ask for their names, save the price of an airline ticket...

DIRECTORY OF SPECIAL LIBRARIES AND INFORMATION CENTERS Gale ($400) lists 30,000 sources for in-depth information on many general and some specialized fields.

Also online.

EXPERTS NOT ON YOUR PAYROLL

If you are in need of a particular database search, anything from Cuban wind surfing centers to who produces products similar to your client's, you can avoid joining and learning one or more database vendors by employing a person or firm that will do the search for you.

These people are not cheap; your average search is going to run a couple of hundred dollars, but they are good and if you are passing the fee along, well...

The
Burwell
Directory
of
Information
Brokers

Anniversary Edition   1993

10

Published by Burwell Enterprises, Inc.

BURWELL DIRECTORY OF INFORMATION BROKERS
ISBN 0-938519-08-5

The most comprehensive guide to general information brokers is probably the DIRECTORY OF INFORMATION BROKERS published by Burwell. This $59.50 book is published each year and contains complete listings for 1400 information brokers in the US and other countries.

This includes firms that specialize in market research, competitor intelligence, legal research, patent/trademark information, library document retrieval and just about anything else you could possibly require.

One of the better buys on the information highway, if you'll excuse the use of an overused cliché, the directory should be on the shelf of every information tracker.

Also available in a disc format ($150.00).

FISCAL DIRECTORY OF FEE–BASED RESEARCH SERVICES ISBN 0-8389-2161-2 ($65.00) lists 550 information brokers in 650 pages. Co-published by the Los Angeles County Library, this directory is designed as a list for consumers who have technical and special needs. It describes not only the capability of the provider to obtain known documents but also to find sources unknown to the consumer.

A diverse spectrum of services ranging from fee-based info brokers to research collections and thousands of online databases.

CONSULTANTS AND CONSULTING ORGANIZATIONS DIRECTORY, Gale, ($430) also online. Business-oriented listings of consultants in all fields.

INFORMATION INDUSTRY DIRECTORY, Gale, ($320) 4,800 listings of producers and vendors of electronic information and related sources.

SIMBA INFORMATION DIRECTORIES, 2200 Sansom St., Philadelphia, PA 19103,, checks in with their ($375) INFORMATION MARKETPLACE DIRECTORY which lists business and information suppliers.

A quick couple of brokers I have had dealings with include:

The Rugge Group 2670 Mountaingate Way, Oakland, CA 94618, 510-530-3635. Started by Sue Rugge, this organization is now run by a new manager but they continue to provide complete reports on almost any subject by searching both online databases and published literature.

Their output includes resources, contacts and a listing of sources the data was drawn from.

Information On Demand 8000 Westpark Dr., McLean, VA 22102, will provide full-text copy of any publicly available document including technical reports, government documents, journal articles, patents, theses and conference proceedings.

If you don't have a specific reference they will perform a search for you at very, very reasonable rates (say $15.00) and then deliver the copy.

IOD is one of the best and most cost effective methods of securing published information. Also available on DIALOG, BRS, ORBIT, and MCI MAIL.

Instant Information Systems provides document retrieval from any information source in the Washington, DC, area. This service provides you with "legs" that will access the Library of Congress, National Library of Medicine, US Patent Office and other information storage facilities.

They will also perform research and help with FOIA requests.

Located at 9916 Oakdale Woods Ct., Vienna, VA 22181.

Venture Economics, 1180 Raymond Boulevard, Newark, NJ 07102. Two new databases that are aimed towards the business community, specifically competitor intelligence applications. VE includes a strategic alliance database that helps track competitors involved in world strategies, follows world investment trends, and traces strategic alliance transactions between corporations.

Venture Intelligence Database analyzes venture intelligence investment patterns and finds active investments by product category. It's pretty much the only source for product and business financing information on privately held companies.

Savage Information Service, 2510 West 237th St., Suite 200, Torrance, CA 90505 is a good, general info broker.

Barbara Quint, editor of *Searcher,* one of the best known and best general researchers in the country. 932 11th Street, Suite 9, Santa Monica, CA 90403. I've used Ms. Quint for a search or two and also been turned on to other contacts by her.

Another one of the very best, and probably least expensive commercial search services available is run by People Who Should Know – research librarians.

For Your Information
FYI
County Of Los Angeles
Public Library
1-800-582-1093

FYI: FOR YOUR INFORMATION is run by the county of Los Angeles but can be used by anyone.

FYI is the professional research and information service for the County of Los Angeles Public Library. They can be reached at 800-582-1093.

Their literature claims they are "in business to help you get the information you need at a price you can afford," and the price schedule seems to bear this claim out.

FYI are specialists in researching and delivering published information in any subject area – from advertising to zoology, business profiles to biographical sketches, or patents to poetry.

One call to FYI and you gain access to one of the most comprehensive information services in the nation. Resources include over 2400 online databases, a staff of highly-trained information specialists, and a global network of research specialists at major universities, public and foreign government libraries.

FYI offers a wide range of services to meet most information needs including:

Research Services. FYI can search online databases, and print sources, contact industry experts, trade associations and government agencies to find the information you need fast. They will then provide their written Research Report summarizing findings and including copies of relevant articles, search results and other information depending on the nature of the project.

Document Delivery. Know exactly what you need, but don't know where to find it? FYI can provide you with copies of almost any journal article, newspaper article, book, report, patent, standard, or other published document anywhere in the world.

Most material can be faxed in 24 to 48 hours.

Information Tracking. FYI can monitor information as it develops. They will track news on your company or your competitors, or just keep you informed of new developments in your field.

Information Products. FYI offers a growing selection of low-cost information products, for many of their most frequently requested services. Products currently available or under development include: trademark searches, business-to-business mailing lists, a people locator service, brief business profiles, personalized business directories, neighborhood profiles, and more.

FYI WILL PROVIDE:
—Company research
—Prospect and mailing lists
—Biographical profiles and background research
—Medical literature research
—Newspaper or broadcast media research
—Product information
—Patent searches
—Import/export information
—Scientific or technical research
—Statistical or demographic information
—Legal and regulatory research
—Custom-designed marketing databases
—Court cases
—Management research
—Secondary market research
—Standards and specifications
—Business credit reports
—Industry overviews
—International business
—Public record research
—Trade mark searches
—Copies of newspaper, magazine and journal articles

...or almost any other published or publicly-available information on any subject from anywhere in the world.

DATABASES AVAILABLE THROUGH FYI
American Business Lists
More than 14 million businesses can be accessed by name, phone number, zip and SIC codes. This database is an excellent source for locating small, hard-to-find businesses, and for compiling reasonable direct mail lists.

Burrelle's Broadcast Database
Complete full-text transcripts of television and radio news broadcasts. Includes transcripts for all regularly scheduled news, news magazine (Eg. 60 Minutes), interview and public affairs programs airing on ABC, CBS, NBC, National Public Radio and the Financial News Network. Transcripts are normally available within 24 hours of air time.

Damar

Real estate information for commercial, industrial, and residential properties for 58 counties in California.

Datatimes

Full text of some 50 metropolitan newspapers in major markets across the country.

Dialog Search Services

Vendor of more than 300 business, scientific, current event, and general interest databases. Currently adding the full text of the Los Angeles Times and some 50 other major metropolitan newspapers nationwide.

Dow Jones News Retrieval

Vendor of full text business periodical and investment statistics databases including the full text of the Wall Street Journal, Barron's, and other business periodicals, and stock and mutual fund statistics for the past 30 years.

Dun's Direct Access

Direct access to marking information on more than 8 million US businesses, this database is designed for producing business lists, and for obtaining statistical data on business market segments. Data may be downloaded in a variety of different formats to suit individual needs. Also included is a "hot list" feature which helps identify companies which are new to the database, or which have recently had significant changes in operating conditions.

Epic-Oclc

National database of 21 million books, audio-visual material, maps, software and other material held at most university, public, scientific, and corporate libraries in the US and Canada and some libraries in the UK. If you ever need to track down a book or periodical but don't know where to look, this is the database to use.

HRIN

Vendor of a variety of full-text, bibliographic and statistical databases focusing on personnel issues. Some of HRIN's more unusual sources include a database of labor arbitrator biographies and decision analyses, full text of Conference Board reports, significant labor agreements, and the principal BNA Labor Law reporters.

Information America

Vendor of full-text public records and indexes for some 20 states. Information America offers a variety of different records including County Assessors real estate records, Bankruptcy Index, State Department of Corporations, Corporate and UCC Filings and much more.

Legitech

California and state legislative tracking database including the full text of current bills, and voting and contribution records for all legislators.

Lexis/Nexis

Full text of federal and state case and statutory law and ancillary legal sources. Full text of Supreme Court decisions within hours of announcement. Full text of more than 400 general and trade periodicals, newspapers and newswires.

Login

Local Government Information Network including information on local programs in counties and municipalities across the US as well as the Urban Affairs Index and Abstracts online and a federal legislative tracking database for bills affecting local government. Network also features a special electronic mail service called QUEST which allows local governments to request information directly from other cities and counties who may be researching similar issues.

Max National Planning Data Corporation

Demographic data and projections at the census tract level for the entire United States. Also includes the Prizm "Lifestyle" Clusters developed by the Claritas Corporation.

National Decisions System

Demographic data and projections at the census tract level for Los Angeles County. Can product custom reports and maps for any geographic unit including tracts, zip codes, polygons, circles or user defined areas.

Newsnet

Vendor of full text databases of some 450 newsletters covering highly specialized topics in business and technology. Also includes full Dun & Bradstreet and TRW Credit Reports on some 13 million businesses.

UCLA Orion Database

Database of the holdings of the 19 campus libraries at UCLA. Circulation information is being added to this database allowing you to determine if the book is on the shelf before you make the long trip to campus.

University of California – Melvyl

Database of the library catalogs of the 19 University of California campuses including UCLA and Berkeley. This database is still under development, but when finished, it will include all holdings at the University of California and provide gateways to other major university systems across the country.

Vu-Text

Full text of an additional 60 metropolitan newspapers in large cities across the US.

Washington Alert

Federal legislative tracking database including full text of all bills since the 99th Congress, up-to-date status information of all bills in the current session, full text of Committee Reports and the CQ weekly report, legislator voting records and biographies and much more.

FYI PRICE LIST

Research Services:

Basic Hourly Rate $65.47

ONE HOUR minimum, plus all direct costs including:

—online search costs
—document delivery costs
—phone calls
—photocopies
—delivery costs
—other incidental expenses

Most research projects cost $100 or more.

Normal turnaround on research projects is 5 working days. RUSH service is available at a rate of $98.21 per hour with a one hour minimum.

Document Delivery:

When you need copies of specific articles, reports, standards, specifications, patents or other material delivered directly to your office or home.

L. A. County Library Material $15.00
Material From Other Libraries $20.00-30.00

Cost per document includes:

—up to 15 pages of material
—includes FAX or regular mail delivery
—24-48 hour delivery for most fax requests
—cost varies depending on supplying library
—charges may be slightly higher from some institutions
—extra charge for courier delivery

Special Handling:

Documents requiring special handling including incomplete citations, extreme RUSH requests, some foreign or very obscure material requiring review or analysis will be charged at the regular research rate of $64.47 per hour, with a $15.00 minimum. You will be notified in advance if your order will require special handling.

Information Products:

In addition to basic research and document delivery services FYI offers a growing selection of relatively inexpensive, fixed-priced information productions including:

People Finder — $15.00

Find people by name in over 80 million households across the United States.

Brief Business Reports — $15.00

Basic information on most businesses in the United States including names of top personnel, line of business, number of employees, sales and more.

Trademark Searches — $65.00

Preliminary review search of Federal and State Registrations, common-law trade names, and company names to identify potentially conflicting marks and other legal problems.

Currently Under Development:
Personalized Business Directories
Entrepreneur Report
Consumer Report

FIND/SVP

625 Avenue Of The Americas, New York, NY 10011 is an organization representing over 1,000 consultants and researchers in the US and abroad. They can access 3,000 computer databases, thousands of files, books and CD-ROMS on the business community.

They specialize in answering any business question on any subject within a couple of days.

A good resource for competitive intelligence, FIND/SVP works for 1700+ companies on a retainer basis.

After reading this fine publication it may cross your mind that perhaps you could become an information broker – either for your own purposes or to make a living.

If you are on any mailing list that shows you have purchased any, I mean any, product about finding information you will be lucky enough, sooner or later, to receive a great mailer that shows how you can make hundred's of thousands of dollars in your spare time, and park your Ferrari on your yacht.

And the good news is they only want somewhere between two and ten thousand dollars to teach you "the secrets of information brokering."

Somebody who has taken this course please send me a sample of something they taught you that this book hasn't?

I'd like to see it.

And, in fact, if you did gain one morsel that I overlooked your next challenge is to take THE INFORMATION BROKER'S HANDBOOK by Sue Rugge and Alfred Glossbrenner, McGraw Hill Publishing, ISBN 0-8306-3798-2 and find a single thing, anything you got from your new $2,000 course that Sue, one of the best known and flat -out best researchers in the country didn't cover...

"CAN *YOU* MAKE A LIVING AS AN INFORMATION BROKER?

There's no way to tell for sure. But one thing is certain: you'll never even get of the ground until you have an appreciation of just what it is you're dealing with. So let's talk for a moment about the commodity we're supposedly in the business of finding, packaging, selling or otherwise "brokering." Let's talk about *information*.

In the first place, successful information brokers do not sell information. What they sell is their *expertise* in searching for information. That may seem like a subtle distinction to you right now, but it's crucial. A client who believes that what he or she is buying from you is information is likely to gauge your worth on the quantity–not the quality–of information you deliver. If you know anything about information retrieval, you know how short-sighted that is on the client's part. But if you know anything about human nature, you know that it is inevitable–if you position yourself as a seller of information.

Thus, one of the first jobs of every information broker is to educate the client about information and the "Information Age." The "Information Age" is a phrase used so frequently that it has become a cliché. In fact, it's worse than a cliché, for as tired and shopworn as even the most common cliché may be, at least everyone knows what it means.

We all know what "Closing the barn door after the horses have escaped" or "As scarce as hen's teeth" means, even though very few of us have ever owned a horse or peered into the open beak of a chicken. The Information Age is far less clear and far more nebulous. Most of the time, with Lewis Carroll's Alice, we make the words mean whatever we want them to mean at the time.

And that's the point. The Information Age may mean cable television, with more channels than ever before and round the clock up-to-the-minute news, weather, sports, and financial reports. It may mean the explosion of magazines and paperback books stuffed into stores shelves, supermarket racks, and even vending machines. It may also mean the increased use of electronics–computers, fax machines, cellular telephones, databases, and satellite dishes–in nearly every industry or profession.

There is simply no clear definition of what constitutes the Information Age. Yet the Information Age itself defines the seas we must all swim in as information professionals. The Information Age *is* today's reality.

Fortunately, while no one can agree on its details, nearly everyone would agree that the two most important characteristics of the Information Age are quantity and availability. It is those two features we will consider next, especially as they relate to the information profession and the market for information-related services."

PART I   THE INFORMATION BUSINESS
- The market for information
- What *is* an information broker?
- Pros and cons of the information business
- The crucial question: Is it for you?
- How to get started

PART II   FUNDAMENTAL TOOLS AND TECHNIQUES
- At the library: Non-electronic sources and resources
- Government information sources
- The telephone: Your most powerful tool

PART III   ELECTRONIC OPTIONS AND ALTERNATIVES
- Welcome to the electronic universe!
- How to go online
- Databases and how to search them
- Special Interest Groups (SIGs) and forums
- Bulletin Board Systems (BBSs)
- CD-ROM possibilities

PART IV   THE BUSINESS SIDE OF INFORMATION BROKERING
- Services to sell
- Projecting an image of credibility
- Marketing and sales: The missing ingredients
- Power marketing tips and techniques
- Executing the project: Ten steps to follow
- Pricing, contracts, and billing
- Office setup bonus section

How to find it, what to charge for it, how to keep your client happy, working the boards, dealing with middlemen, baud rates, e-mail, telex, FAX access tips on technique, addresses of the government information storehouses, cover letters.

This book is jammed with great information from a couple of people who pioneered the entire field.

Ron Wyatt, investigator and attorney, has complied and published THE FINDERS INTERNATIONAL NETWORK DIRECTORY (F.I.N.D.) which lists professional finder services to locate funding, missing persons and more.

Information about THE DIRECTORY contact him at 2128 Goldbrier Memphis, TN 38134.

ONLINE AND CD-ROMS

ONLINE: PREDICTING THE FUTURE

A paper prepared by Carol Tenopir at the University of Hawaii at Manoa and reprinted here with her permission.

NO, CD-ROM has not made online obsolete in case anyone is spreading rumors! "Reports of online's demise have been greatly exaggerated."

I've already tipped my hand about my talk on predicting the future of online—the demise of the online industry was not a part of it. But, changes, including some major changes, will be part of online's future. Five major forces are shaping online searching and the online industry. These forces are at work now and will continue to shape online in the future.

The five forces are:
1) Developments in telecommunications
2) Improvements in scanning and storage technologies
3) Expansion of database distribution options (here is where CD-ROM fits in as well as many others)
4) A broader user base with new needs AND
5) Changes in the dynamics of database production

I first thought about these categories for a talk I did in August 1991 at the New Zealand Computer Conference. In just one year lots of things have happened in each category—emphasizing for me the rapid pace at which change seems to be taking place and reinforcing for me that these categories cover the major forces. I will go over each in turn.

DEVELOPMENTS IN TELECOMMUNICATIONS

Computers in Libraries, Canada included a popular session about the Internet (and Meckler sponsored an entire Internet conference in Washington DC. in December 1992.) Internet clearly represents a major force in current informational telecommunications. Everywhere I go all over the world people ask me for my Internet e-mail address (sort of like FAX was a couple years ago, although they also still ask for that too.) Internet is significant for many reasons, beyond the scope of this presentation, including e-mail, electronic journals and newsletters, resource sharing, OPAC access, etc.

From the standpoint of a telecommunications development shaping the online industry, Internet can now be used to access many of the major commercial online systems like DIALOG, BRS, Orbit, Mead, EPIC, Data-Star, NLM. As such it represents an alternative to standard packet switching networks and can be (for some Internet users) less expensive than the networks. For example, if a university or company doesn't charge back each department for their Internet use, the department can access DIALOG for just $3 per hour extra telecommunications charge on the DIALOG bill.

Internet can also be faster than the networks, depending on the speed supported by your Internet connection and other local factors. For example, in my office through my direct line to the computer center, I get 9600 bps access to online systems others will be able to get up to 56k bps soon.

Many online searchers can now also search at 9600 bps through packet-switch networks and a 9600 bps modem. As telephone companies around the world continue converting to digital lines, speeds will continue to increase, soon to 56k bps and beyond.

I've heard some searchers say "I can't read that fast online and I certainly can't type that fast, so what's the point? I'll stick with my 2400 or even 1200 bps modem, thank you." Well, the point is: faster transmission will have some major impacts on the way we search and, as a result, on the information industry.

At fast speeds on connect time based systems like DIALOG it makes more sense to upload your best guess at a search strategy, download titles or another intermediate result format, logoff, and do all of your thinking and reformulating offline. Then you logon and re execute the search, downloading or offline printing all the results rather than picking and choosing. For connect based systems at fast speeds this is the most cost-effective way to search.

I HATE to search like that and end users just plain DON'T search like that. Connect time systems don't like you to search like that either because it cuts their revenues.

So faster transmission speeds are one main impetus for all connect based systems to rethink their pricing policies. Some systems like Mead and NLM changed their policies a long time ago, charging for the amount of work you ask the computer to do, the amount of information you search, and how much you retrieve. Even connect based systems added online display charges when downloading first became widespread about 10 years ago (and those charges are going UP you may have noticed.) More changes in pricing algorithms are coming, including differentials based on access speed, additional flat fee contracts, and more emphasis on the amount of information transmitted. These changes will not always benefit the searcher.

Faster transmission speeds mean more information can be transmitted faster. For the first time this will mean high quality graphics can be transmitted online in a reasonable amount of time. This means more charts, graphs, table, and pictures online. Our text-only full text online databases will soon look as outdated and old-fashioned as black and white television does to my 7 year old.

IMPROVED SCANNING AND STORAGE

A second force goes hand in hand with faster transmission of more information and more graphics. Scanners are getting less expensive and of better quality all of the time. Computer storage capacities are continuing to grow exponentially while the cost keeps coming down. Take these two things together with faster transmission speeds and you have lots more text and graphics available to users.

Some database producers have turned to scanning to add to their existing databases. (ABI/Inform and PTS Prompt for example both now have full text when they used to only be bibliographic.) Others will use scanning to do retrospective conversion of bibliographic databases, so young researchers will find out that the world didn't really begin in 1972. Look for *more* db, *larger* databases, more *retrospectively*, and a larger *variety* of electronic texts. Full text collections online, on disc and on magnetic tape to support bibliographic files will become the rule rather than the exception.

One big impact of all of this on search strategy is learning how to cope better with more and often too much information. Meager databases of many millions of records searched together with the multiple search features such as StarSearch or OneSearch we all love, quickly means information overload. Already, end users and customers of intermediaries are calling for just the *best* information. We need more quality filters to make information usable. Of course, in many ways the online librarian is a quality filter, who uses appropriately precise search techniques and reviews and cleans up search results. But databases and online systems will need to help you out more, with better controlled vocabulary indexing (nope, that's not obsolete either), other value added information that helps you measure impact or importance of articles, and better software that lets you sort things in order of likely relevance. Experienced searchers need to work with online systems and software developers before the *too much* problems gets out of hand.

EXPANSION OF DATABASE DISTRIBUTION OPTIONS

The third force on my list is the expansion of distribution options beyond traditional remote online. I've already mentioned the Internet as an alternative online system for accessing commercial databases, but also for accessing alternative databases like UnCover and hundreds of full text newsletters, journals, and books. Another obvious distribution option is shown by the widespread acceptance of CD-ROM in just a few years within the library marketplace.

CD-ROM as we know it is not and will not be the only non-online alternative—CD-I, CDTV, and Sony Data Diskman are vying for the home entertainment and education market, FM broadcast databases are offering fast updating to compete with online, and other technological advances are just around the corner. Wireless computing will be a big growth area in the late 1990s, but has hardly made a ripple yet in online.

Poised to have a big impact in the United States is the proposed National Research and Education Network (NREN). NREN is envisioned by Senator (and now, Vice-President Elect) Albert Gore as a telecommunications superhighway bringing broadband information resources to virtually everyone in the US. He likes to talk about his children getting on NREN to find picture books about dinosaurs, including text, pictures, motion, and sound. Although NREN is still only a vision on paper (with some money and support behind it), national ISDN-broadband networks in many countries can forever change the nature of online access.

If their promise is fulfilled they represent a combination of commercial and not-for-profit enterprises, a mix of text and graphics and sound, an educational, research and even en-

tertainment resource that will touch the lives of millions of people. Online may no longer be the province of just a few of us as it has been for 20 years and really still continues to be.

All of this is **WHEN** or **IF** NREN and other broadband networks reach their potential. Right now there are many years of arguments and negotiations ahead of us. The American Library Association and Information Industry Association have already squared off on their respective visions of not-for-profit vs. for-profit domination of the network. Publishers are worried about copyright violations and decreased revenues. *We Shall See*, but I hope, not just see, but be involved with realizing the potential. No matter what happens, the awareness of the power and potential of online will take great leaps forward in the next decade.

MORE AND DIFFERENT USERS

This leads to the next force, more and different users, a force that may be profound if information superhighways get build, or slightly less so if we continue to use the 4 lane highways or even 2 lane back roads available now.

Additional distribution options are already bringing more awareness among categories of people that did not search databases before. School children as young as 5 years old use CD-ROM encyclopedias and other multi-media learning tools; public library users go straight to CD-ROM indexes and databases loaded on library OPACS; college students line up to use dozens of CD-ROM databases; and students, faculty and researchers in companies access locally mounted databases from their offices or homes. The key to all of these is easy, non-scary and free (to them) access.

All of us here know that their search results are not as good as they could be or as good as we could do for them. We also know that the interfaces of many of the best online systems are too unfriendly to be suitable for most end users. The exclusive end user market is building, largely because of the efforts of libraries and librarians, but it will still take major improvements in interfaces, transparent search aids build in to the software, and lowering of costs to reach the full potential dreamed of for years by the online industry.

At the local library or company level going along with this is the continued blurring of the lines of online. In-house systems, either through OPACs. or locally mounted databases on stand along systems, or decision support systems or document-based management information systems in corporations, are being linked with external commercial database services. A one-stop shop, a workstation that allows access to all types of internal and external, bibliographic, directory and full text information has long been a dream of many of us. That dream is beginning to come true.

Don't be surprised if you are asked to be an "expert" by an expert system software designer. More designers are tapping the expertise of experienced database searchers and building it into end user software. Don't be surprised if your role as instructor continues to grow (it already has), both in person and online. When people search in their offices or dorm rooms you lose contact with them. Libraries need to rethink this contact, and build it into locally loaded databases on the OPAC. Take a lesson from the EasyNet gateway and build in an SOS feature that provides interactive online help as needed from a human librarian at the other end.

Right now momentum is building, but expect a backlash from users who want more personal contact again and those people who get tired of it al or overwhelmed and want you to do it for them. Intermediaries have more challenges ahead.

CHANGES IN THE DATABASE INDUSTRY

That brings me to the fifth and final change. Changes in the dynamics of the database industry are already occurring and will continue to shape the future of the database industry. For 20 years online was a nice little niche industry. We knew the companies involved and they knew us. Nobody made much money, but most people didn't lose much either. You've probably already noticed in the last few years this is beginning to change.

Major companies are becoming interested in electronic information industry, buyouts are becoming a common event. When this happens your favorite online system may change direction or tighten up by eliminating low profit database. (BRS and ORBIT are doing this now.) The loyalty to you is less, the emphasis on profits is more. Market fallout occurs and some of your favorite little databases may disappear.

Even many database producers would like to not be so dependent on large online systems. The biggest trend in the industry right now is tape loading. High volume users circumvent the online system or CD-ROM vendor and lease databases directly from the database producer for loading on your local system.

This is economical only for a few databases because it requires a big up front investment. Unless you are Folger's you don't want to commit tens of thousands of dollars per year and a major project effort to bring Coffeeline inhouse.

So, even though the overall numbers of databases will continue to grow, the number of dead databases each year will increase.

CHALLENGES AND OPPORTUNITIES

That is a terrible note to end on—before I finish let me swing things around to a more positive note.

All of these changes here now and coming soon mean challenges for the searcher, but also opportunities and choices. More choices in ways to access databases, more choices in pricing, more choices in hardware. The challenges come in choosing the most appropriate medium of distribution for your users, choosing the best databases (not just the cheapest), and coming up with strategies that are best for increasingly large and complex databases.

Your opportunities are also challenges I give to you for the future—the opportunity to help software developers improve software for all levels of users, the opportunity to let online systems know what types of databases are important to the larger information community, the opportunity to help database producers come up with better ways to improve the quality filter and the opportunity and challenges to keep up with a dynamic industry and help to shape its future with your considerable experience and your unique viewpoints.

–end of paper

* * * * * * * * * * * * * * * *

One of the more efficient ways to find out anything about anything is to go online; find a database, or database vendor that will track down the information you are seeking and relay it instantly.

The advantages to online searching are obvious: it's quick, you can do it from the comfort of your living room, it's usually comprehensive and accurate and it may produce material that is too new to have been published.

The backside of this miracle includes the costs of joining one or more database vendors, the frustrations (and cost) of a search that goes haywire due either to human or computer error, and the learning curve involved in using a variety of databases.

A couple of ways around this latter dilemma include becoming reasonably proficient in a couple of major vendors, say DIALOG, COMPUSERVE and CDB, or using a fairly expensive online expert to run the search for you (great if you are billing expenses to a client, rather top heavy if you are taking them out of your daughter's college funds).

A new, sorta compromise is now on the scene – front end software that helps you formulate the right question to the right database, structure the search offline (read "for free") and then automatically goes online for the minimum amount of time required to electronically ask your question(s) and retrieve the answer.

We'll get to those in a minute...

Databases hold more information than you can imagine. Dial in to the correct source and you can get newspaper records, magazine articles, dissertations, personal data, postal forwarding information, magazine subscribers, full text transcripts of the *Oprah* show, business reports, technical abstracts, newsletters online, law reviews, medical advice, competitive intelligence, the list is virtually endless and ever expanding.

The trick is knowing "whom" to ask.

TEN RULES FOR ONLINE INVESTIGATIONS
By Barbara Quint

1. Try online databases first. Searching online is expensive. Get the maximum value by letting it replace or assist time-consuming manual techniques.

2. Try full-text databases. They deliver the document and the information immediately. Though they may cost more than bibliographic index databases, they can eliminate these long trips to libraries.

3. Use bibliographic databases to locate experts for interviewing. Most large subject-oriented bibliographic databases include an institution field for the author's location at the time of writing. The citation indexes from the Institute for Scientific Information have the most complete and current coverage of scholarly publications.

4. Use the Encyclopedia of Associations (DIALOG File 114) to find groups focused on anything and everything and the Ulrich's Periodical Directory (DIALOG File 480) and Gale Directory of Publications and Broadcast Media (DIALOG File 469) to find editors of newsletters, magazines, newspapers, etc. about anything and everything. If you have time, it's cheaper to use the Encyclopedia of Associations at the library, but the library's version of Ulrich's may take too much browsing.

5. For public records information, consider specialized information services including those that combine offline access with a network of private investigators like US Datalink (6711 Bayway Drive, Baytown, TX 77520, 800-447-7421).

6. Use professional searchers whenever possible, particularly for major search services. Online searching costs too much to fool around with its tricky command software while learning on the job. Use the library's searchers or hire an information broker. If you don't trust them, supervise them better. If information you gather online is critical, e.g., part of the final story, let them double check your search strategy.

7. Ask the full question. The searcher is not your enemy or your rival. They need to know the whole question, what you need to know, why and where you plan to use the information. They can always scale the question down to accommodate your budget or deadlines, but you will lose money and data if you don't explain the whole problem.

8. When you start searching yourself, start with high-use, end-user services. Use gateways to reach supermarket search services, e.g., Telebase System's EasyNet AKA CompuServe's IQuest. If you decide to search general database services directly, watch your professional searchers. Ask for advice and tips.

9. Stay offline when the best sources are not online, e.g., government directory information. Stay offline when the cheap, adequate sources are not online, e.g., Statistical Abstract of the United States.

10. Build your own online databases of your own files. Try good full-text search software like askSam or Folio or EndNotes or Personal Bibliographic Software's ProCite.

One of the more timely ways to track database comings and goings is to subscribe to one or more newsletters that specialize in reporting on online access. Some of these newsletters are intended to promote one product line, (but may still contain useful searching tips) others are designed to keep researchers up to date on the latest developments in the database world.

SEARCHER, The Magazine For Database Professionals Learned Information, Inc. 143 Old Marlton Pike, Medford, NJ 08055. $49.50 per year. Edited by one Barbara Quint, the Willy Mays of database searching, SEARCHER is probably worth subscribing to just for the ads touting new databases.

They also feature, as one would speculate, well researched articles on database use, software, search strategy and so on. Coupling this with new book and base reviews, contact names and addresses (bases, experts, searchers), "best buys" and general advice on the entire field makes SEARCHER a necessity to anyone who needs to keep abreast of the ever-changing world of database searching.

I should also point out that Barbara is one of the best for-fee searchers in the country and you might wish to consider using her for searches that are beyond your ken.

DOCUMENT DELIVERY, Meckler 11 Ferry Lane West, Westport CT, 06880. DD used to live under another name, and was edited by Ms. Quint (see above).

She left, the name changed and it's not quite back up there with SEARCHER. Too many press releases, printer reviews, ads, too little useful info, but hey, who knows?

Good restaurants lose their cooks and eventually come back. Right?

Stay tuned.

DATABASEALERT, Knowledge Industry Publications, Inc. 701 Westchester Ave., White Plains, NY 10604. This is what the image "newsletter" should conjure up – small print, no drawings, no ads, no cute stuff.

"DBA is designed to keep users, producers and distributors of online information up-to-date on what's available and who's making it available. DBA supplements the annual DataBase Directory."

Comprehensive, and should be for $400 a year...

ACTIONLETTER, NewsNet Inc., 945 Haverford Rd., Bryn Mawr, PA 19010. $120 a year gets you the newsletter and $60 of free online time with NewsNet.

An in-house letter.

BOOKS

A number of books (you remember, the things printed on paper, covers and stuff? Well, try the local library, they may still have a few). The first one you might want to ask for is DI-RECTORY OF ONLINE AND PORTABLE DATABASES, Gale Research.

6,300 databases are described in this directory. The bulk of the bases are online, a few are available in CD-ROM or tape formats.

Each record provides names by which the base is known, what type it is, name and address of the publisher, the online service(s) offering the base, description of the content, subject, language, time span, frequency of updating and pricing.

With this material, a clever searcher can create a list of databases available through a specific vendor, compare the same database in different media, and find all databases which contain the information you are searching for.

And now the real good news – DOOAPD is available, guess where?

Online.

Look for it on ORBIT, DATASTAR and QUESTEL.

For non-QUESTEL subscribers Gale provides COMPUTER READABLE DATABASES. This publication is also available in hard copy and online through DIALOG.

CRD is presented in a more practical online format which allows the user to search using 1,000 subject terms and even provides a MAP command which will give back the descriptions of all bases available from a particular vendor.

FULLTEXT SOURCES ONLINE
ISBN 1-879258-03-X

FULLTEXT SOURCES ON LINE, Bibliodata, POB 61, Needham Heights, MA 02194. $90 per issue or $165 per year (two issues) gets you a listing of 4,000 journals, magazines, newspapers and newswires that can be found online in a fulltext format.

This information shows which publications are covered cover-to-cover and which provide selected articles only.

The listings are alphabetical, and shown along with the databases/vendors which offer them with special comments about the contents.

As the copy writers at Bibliodata say, "a subscription to fulltext sources online costs less than one online search in the wrong database."

Maybe.

NEWSPAPERS ONLINE, Bibliodata $80. 125 US and Canadian newspapers categorized by region served, electronic availability, CD-ROM availability and online specifics.

Includes names and numbers of the publisher, editors, librarians and the availability of online help.

DIAL IN AN ANNUAL GUIDE TO LIBRARY ONLINE PUBLIC ACCESS CATALOGS from Meckler $55.00. The dial-in numbers of public access catalogs from hundreds of libraries internationally. Entries include library name, address, data on special collections, network membership, Internet access, loan polices etc.

National Institute of Standards and Technology, US Department of Commerce Information and Resources Division, Gaithersburg, MD 20899, provides DATABASES AVAILABLE IN THE RESEARCH INFORMATION CENTER OF THE NATIONAL INSTITUTE OF STANDARDS AND TECHNOLOGY for a mere $6.00.

A list of online databases available from our friends in the government including bases from the Bureau of Census, GPO Monthly Catalog, National Technical Information Service, Federal Research In Progress...

ONLINE
REFERENCE
AND
INFORMATION
RETRIEVAL

Library Science Text Series

Roger C. Palmer

ONLINE REFERENCE AND INFORMATION RETRIEVAL
ISBN 0-87287-536-9

ONLINE REFERENCE AND INFORMATION RETRIEVAL Roger Palmer, Libraries Unlimited. $26.50. Many services and/or vendors publish guides to their particular universe, which is all well and good. The problem arises that very few people actually bother to explain exactly what databases are, how they are organized, how search operators work, and how to formulate searches.

ORAIR is all that and more; specific log on and log off procedures for a number of databases are included, search strategies explored, save techniques explained, and perhaps most importantly, how to set up your search on paper is detailed in full.

A highly recommended book, ORAIR just happens to draw many of its examples from dialog, BRS and other bases I've suggested.

This is an excellent guide for beginning to mid-level searchers and you will find yourself using it over and over...

Bibliodata POB 61, Needham Heights, MA 02194, publishes COMPUSERVE COMPANION: Finding Newspapers and Magazines Online ($29.95). This newly published book shows you newspapers, magazines and newspapers carried on COMPUSERVE (which, at this writing, is not as complete as DIALOG, but trying harder), and the commands you need to get to them.

COMPUSERVE is the largest on-line service in the world and is ever expanding. This guide will take you by the hand and lead you through the various necessary tricks and techniques.

Dates of coverage, lag time and subject indexes help locate exactly where what you need lives, and various "GO" commands are shown to get you there in the shortest possible time.

BOOKS AND PERIODICALS ONLINE

Finally, BOOKS AND PERIODICALS ONLINE from Library Alliance, claims to be the largest database of electronically accessible databases. $199.00 gets you 43,000 listings...

ONLINE AND CD-ROM DATABASE SEARCHING
ISBN 0-7201-2093-4

ONLINE AND CD-ROM DATABASE SEARCHING by John Cox, Mansell POB C831, Ruthford, NJ 07070, $90.00. An overview of what's involved in searching these two popular sources including search terms and addresses.

A bit frustrating, published in 1990 it lacks a number of sources and some of the information is outdated.

COMPUSERVE

COMPUSERVE, the poor man's DIALOG, offers a number of business-related databases. COMPUSERVE is not as complete nor as expensive as DIALOG, but will solve common business search problems in a matter of moments. Some bases to check are:

BIZ#FILE (GO BIZ#FILE) – Database of 10 million businesses, including addresses and phone numbers. Search by company name or by type of business, in the US or Canada.

BUSINESS DATABASE PLUS (GO BUSDATE) – Covers more than 450 regional, US and international business and trade publications. Search by word used in text for company names and trademarks.

BUSINESS DATELINE (GO BUSDATE) – Coverage of business news in the US and Canada with a strongly local emphasis. Search by subject words. Coverage includes articles from 115 regional publications from 1985 to the present.

COMPUTER DIRECTORY (GO COMPDIR) – Database oriented to computer-related products detailed information on more than 13,600 manufacturers.

D&B–CANADIAN DUN'S MARKET IDENTIFIERS (GO DBCAN) – Contains directory information on about 350,000 Canadian companies.

D&B–DUN'S MARKET IDENTIFIERS (GO DMI) – Contains directory information on more than 6.7 million US establishments, both public and private.

EUROPEAN COMPANY LIBRARY (GO EUROLIB) – Selected financial information on more than 2 million European companies. Included are D&B–EUROPEAN DUN'S MARKET IDENTIFIERS, which can be searched by company name.

EXECUTIVE NEWS SERVICE (GO ENS) – Set up a clipping file with the names you wish to check, casting as wide a net as possible. Automatic clipping will alert you to uses of the name or names in question.

D&B–DUN'S MARKET INDICATORS (GO DBINT) – Contains directory information on approximately 2.1 million public, private and government-controlled companies in 120 countries. Can be searched by both geographical location and company name.

GERMANY COMPANY LIBRARY (GO GERLIB) – By entering the company name, industry codes or geographic location, users can find directory, financial and product information for more than 48,000 companies.

MAGAZINE DATABASE PLUS (GO MAGDB) – Articles from magazines offer backup for checking unregistered trademarks and trade names. Coverage dates to Jan. 1, 1987.

NEWSGRID (GO NEWSGRID) – Functions as a daily check of names in world news. Useful backup to track common law use of trademarks and foreign names.

NEWSPAPER LIBRARY (GO NEWSLIB) – Contains selected full-text articles from 48 US newspapers.

TRADEMARK RESEARCH CENTER (GO TRADERC) – Trademarkscan-Federal, updated twice weekly, contains all active, registered trademarks and service marks filed with the US Patent and Trademark Office, plus pending applications. Also includes inactive marks from 1984 forward.

U.K. COMPANY LIBRARY (GO UKLIB) – Selected financial information on more than 1.2 million U.K. companies. Includes information from D&B–DUN'S EUROPEAN MARKET IDENTIFIERS database, which can be searched by company name.

U.K. TRADEMARK LIBRARY (GO UKTRADEMARK) – Database includes BSI Standardline database (industrial codes and standards) and British Trade Marks, a database of all registered U.K. trademarks and pending applications.

SOFTWARE

While there is no totally "automatic search" program on the market there are a couple of examples which can, and will, cut both your online time and cost to a significant degree while rummaging in either of the two most popular database vendors around.

Personal Bibliographic Software, Inc. POB 4250, Ann Arbor, MI 48106, produces three different products which help access DIALOG INFORMATION SERVICES (and a number of other vendors), get the goods and get offline.

For us, the most useful product is probably PROSEARCH; a unique disk-based program that will allow you to format a search offline by translating the Queen's English into a DIALOG readable command format.

You remember, of course, that DIALOG does not use a menu system in most databases. Specific, proprietary commands *must* be employed to get you where you want to go.

A single mistake in asking for 20 full printouts at $55 each, or getting 978 hits because you forget a delimiter can run the old DIALOG bill up to a point in the stratosphere where they will request you to hock your first-born until the check clears...

PROSEARCH parses your possibly poor pformatted request into dailogese offline (you know, *free*) then dials DIALOG, inserts the request at an electronic speed, gathers up the reply, says good-bye and hangs up.

In seconds.

You save because your search will be coded correctly, the software is most likely better at the old electronic keyboard than you are, doesn't make mistakes and gets on and off the ticker ASAP.

As if this wasn't enough, PROSEARCH also provides a disk of database blue sheets for DIALOG databases. A great touch, you can look up your subject by subject matter, file number or DIALOG grouping.

This list is updated several times a year and not only provides the latest information on available databases. PROSEARCH can save massive amounts of time otherwise spent thumb-ing through blue-colored paper. It allows one to entirely prepare a search off-line, go on short time, then review the findings at leisure.

I use and recommend PROSEARCH for anyone who plans on using DIALOG more then once or twice a year.

CD–ROMS

The next best thing to online searching is probably the use of CD–ROMS; patterned after the Compact Disc music format, these shiny little disks hold about 380 MB of storage capacity per.

This feature alone makes them ideal for investigative purposes as the sheer volume of information involved (the Oxford English Dictionary disk weighs exactly 137 pounds less than the hard copy version) allows for entire phone books, cross directories, legal libraries, etc., to be stored on one disk.

The retrieval time is better than with a diskette and the time saved over hard copy searching is formidable.

CD–ROM players are dropping in price (although still more expensive than their music player counterparts as they have to be much more accurate) and should be considered as a natural addition to most computers.

As this is written, it is not possible, or at least not economically possible, to write on a compact disk, only read from it. This is not a major problem and will probably soon change anyway.

By definition any disk, even a CD is not as current as a good online database, but many sources of information are available on disk that are not yet online and, once it's purchased, you own the information for eternity.

No more access charges...

We have already seen the various CD-based phone directories and address listings that are available on this format, what else is of interest?

Learned Information, Inc. 143 Old Marlton Pike, Medford, NJ 08055, seems to be striving to become the primary source of neat CD's as well as information about what's available. CD–ROM FINDER ISBN 0-938734-70-9 ($69.50) is a comprehensive guide to 1400+ titles about such topics as business, technology, law, and so on.

Each entry is described fully as to content, hardware requirements, publisher, and market data.

The book is indexed by product type and application; the listings include statistical information, bibliographies, abstracts and full text information.

Besides the wide variety of information available on CD's, one should remember that once a particular edition is purchased there are no (in most cases) additional fees for list rentals, mailing label printing or per-time access.

Meckler, publisher of a number of relevant magazines for information diggers, offers CD–ROM WORLD ($29.00) a newsletter/magazine that updates the CD marketplace.

Don't forget AMERICAN YELLOW PAGES ON CD–ROM, mentioned elsewhere, that gives you direct access information drawn from 5,000 yellow page directories, business directories, corporate reports, chambers of congress and state directories. (American Business Information POB 27347, Omaha, NE 68127.)

Online Press, Inc. 462 Danbury Rd., Wilton, CT 06897, publishes "the world's largest paid circulation magazine for CD–ROM publishers and users." CD–ROM PROFESSIONAL seems to be aimed at producers and publishers a bit more than users, but does give the reader a feeling for what's going on in this rapidly changing world.

They also sell a book compiled from the best articles that have appeared in the above publication. TIMELESS TIPS AND PRACTICAL ADVICE may be the best way to approach this resource.

CD–ROM DIRECTORY published by UniDisc 4401 Capitola Rd., Capitola, CA 95010, serves as a directory of available CD–ROMS.

MISCELLANEOUS DATABASES

Not too many years ago your only hope of finding criminal court records in Tallahassee, Florida, or how many lawsuits had been filed against the Izusu Trooper that your client had just rolled, or who had what products similar to your client's (or your brand new invention), or what advances were being made in the field of electronic surveillance, searching, etc., was to take half a day, drive to your local library and pray you got one of the librarians (A.) who was not affected by the cutbacks in funds, (B.) who had been to some kind of library school, (C.) seemed to give a damn.

At best this sort of strategy was hit and miss; today it is totally outmoded. It's possible, using a computer and a modem, to find nearly any fact that has appeared in published form anywhere, as well as, many facts that *haven't yet been published*. As with tracking through databases, you need to design a search strategy, know whom to ask, or how to get online and then how to format your questions for the most correct and least expensive response.

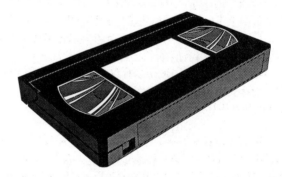

A handy resource for database queries is the video tape INVESTIGATING BY COMPUTER, Intelligence, Inc., $59.95. This tape was shot directly from a computer screen and while it lacks the drama of a *Lethal Weapon* or a *Rocky*, it crams in 40 minutes of how to get online, how to deal with computer databases, how to use menus, as well as, how to write scripts off line in order to save yourself both time and money.

The tape is designed for the beginning or intermediate searcher and concentrates primarily on personnel data such as tracking, tracing, and background building, but many of the same techniques apply, especially in the DIALOG section, for empirical information as well.

I'm going to review a variety of databases from huge supermarkets with compartmentalized subject matters to esoteric-almost bulletin boards that concentrate on one specific area of interest. Remember, you can find almost anything on a database. It's going to be a little more expensive than researching it out yourself, but will save one hell of a lot of your time and shoe leather. Many of the databases we're going to take a look at work in more than one area; i.e., information on specific people, information on groups, information on businesses, the news media, the medical field, scientific achievements, and equipment suppliers.

Don't overlook a database simply because the title does not sound like something you need for your current project. Check it out, see what they offer, and then see how they can be accessed. Many large databases have a rather expensive sign-up fee or monthly minimums, but *most* can be accessed through other vendors which in turn resell the data at a slightly higher rate on a per use basis.

As we'll see shortly, some giant database vendors like DIALOG will get you into almost anything as long as you're willing to pay...

BRS INFORMATION TECHNOLOGIES 8000 Westpark Drive, McLean, VA 22103. FAX 703-893-4632, both a database and a search service that covers many major disciplines including health, medicine, pharmacology, bio-sciences, science and technology, business and education, finance, social services and the humanities.

Their databases include current and historical information from journal articles, books, dissertations, and government reports. Many of their databases are comprehensive indexes to available literature which must then be ordered separately through a document retrieval service. Others include abstracts or the complete text of the work.

BRS provides command driven search software and a customer service department to guide you through their various bases. This is an extremely important base to anyone who will be doing any research having to do with the field of medicine, such as accident verification. It features a very nice legal resource index which references more than 960 law reviews and bar association journals, six legal newspapers, and selected monographs in government publications allowing even the non-legalized researcher to get an idea where he or his client may stand on any given problem.

One of their more interesting selections is the Knowledge Publication Database which provides descriptions of databases available online in America. This listing includes all types of databases; full text, numeric, bibliographic, directory and reference.

BRS offers a number of payment plans including one that is based on pay-as-you-go. In the latter, no prepayments or monthly minimum is necessary. The databases themselves range in hourly connect times from $61.00 to about $155.00, but an hour connect line is just about enough time to download the entire personal medical history of every resident of Detroit. If most of your billings are not in minute increments, you need to sit back and review your search strategy seriously.

DATA TIMES 14000 Quail Springs Parkway, Suite 450, Oklahoma City, OK 73134. FAX 405-755-8028. An information network which provides access to over 400 business, financial, and news sources, including the Wall Street Journal, 80 newspapers, 500 magazines, business journals and industry publications, real time business news wires, company and industry reports and 300 international sources.

They offer heavy customer support at no extra charge, including seminars and toll free customer services. DT also offers something called Passport which allows you to create a search, then they will run it through 1,000 sources to find the information you need.

DT can also be accessed through Dow Jones.

DOW JONES NEWS/RETRIEVAL, Information Services Group Dow Jones and Company, Inc. P. O. Box 300, Princeton, NJ 08543 hits 32 of the top newspapers, 22 major business publications and loads of smaller more specialized newsletters and reports such as High Tech Material Alert, Computer Security Documents, Electronic Design, Consumer Electronics, Electronic News, Video Marketing News and a host of computer-oriented information from all the standard PC Week/InfoWeek journals to CD-ROM databases.

Stock histories, federal filings, company headlines, middle East and Japanese news, the Wall Street Journal and clipping service alert that allows you to have the database automatically search for and "clip" any articles on the subject at hand.

EASYNET/TELEBASE SYSTEMS, INC., well supported access to about 1,000 databases from 12 leading search services. The EASYNET service is accessible through 15 different electronic mail and bulletin board services including COMPUSERVE where it's known as IQ Quest.

If you purchase access time directly from the parent company with a credit card, you'll reach all the Easynet access interfaces.

INFO GLOBE. Online access to text of Canadian newspapers and directory information including selected federal and provincial budget speeches and public papers.

LEXIS/NEXIS Mead Data Central, P. O. Box 933-NR, Dayton, OH 45401. LEXIS/NEXIS puts over 750 sources "at your finger tips", primarily legal, government, international, marketing, people, insurance and company information.

Expect to use NEXIS for international business information, abstracts of many news services and newspapers throughout the world, some magazines (although more general than newsletters), along with trade and industry research.

NEXIS is a specialized knowledge base dealing with trade sources that employees, newspapers, wire lines, etc. use to develop company profiles and follow legal and political changes. Information is available on transportation,

marketing, insurance, energy, consumer goods, politics, international business, computers, communications, entertainment, patents, banking, environment, sports and legal news.

LEXIS, on the other hand, is a comprehensive computer legal research service which offers access to state, federal and foreign case law, legislative services, and administrative codes, the Congressional Record and Federal Register, federal regulations, a number of specialized libraries for research and tax, corporate law, banking, communications, military law, copyright law and more.

MEDLINE/PAPER CHASE 350 Longwood Avenue, Boston, MA 02115, produced by the National Library of Medicine, contains over seven million references to biomedical journal articles with about 8,000 new references added weekly. These are of interest to anyone in the medical field, sometimes to researchers and private detectives in investigating cases involving that inexact science, medicine.

PAPERCHASE does not charge a sign-up fee nor a monthly minimum and they're open 24 hours a day, 365 days a year. They will provide a free demonstration disk and reference manual guide when you sign up. PC claims their average search cost is $5.46.

NEWSNET INC. 945 Haverford Road, Bryn Mawr, PA 19019. NEWSNET, as the name implies, is one of the largest collectors and disseminators of newspapers, news wires, technological reports and corporate reports. This includes everything from the AP Datastream News wire to Catholic News Service.

A few things that can be found on NEWSNET including Freedom of Information Reports, Travel and Tourism, Research and Development, and the latest news from the communications industry including cellular sales, marketing and data channels.

ORBIT SEARCH SERVICE 800 Westpark Drive, McLean, VA 22102, FAX 703-893-0490. ORBIT states their primary objective is to provide the immediate, accurate and uncompromising access to the world's technical information resources. They've brought together over 100 different databases in the fields of patent information, chemistry, material science, and related disciplines, and a lot of databases which are simply not available from any other source.

ORBIT has some interesting bases such as American Men and Women of Science, Claims which lets you through to two million patents, and Microsearch which provides coverage to more than 50,000 reviews from micro computer related literature, specifically the availability of applications, compatibility and comparisons of hardware and software products.

Subscriptions cost between $150.00 and $500.00, depending on what you want in the way of handbooks and training.

RADIO SUISSE/D.S. MARKETING INC. 485 Devon Park Drive, Suite 110, Wayne, PA 19087, 800-221-7754. One of the largest and most useful international databases is provided by RADIO SUISSE and marketed in the US by DATA-STAR MARKETING. DATA-STAR is Europe's leading online database covering over 250 bases with worldwide coverage. They specialize in handling information about the continent including business news, health care, pharmaceutical technology and Biomed. It is a gateway to several other German services and provides a nice bulletin board section where anyone can run a bulletin board asking anything about anything.

One of the most useful databases onboard is FORS, Forensic Science Database, which allows anyone with a computer and the sign-up fee to study the latest in forensic science techniques.

UMI, UNIVERSITY MICROFILMS INTERNATIONAL, 300 North Zeeb Road, Ann Arbor, MI 48106, owned by Bell & Howell, is the world's largest collection of dissertation abstracts online. Instant access is provided to research results from thousands of papers in the fields of science, technology, business, engineering, the arts and humanities.

More than 475 universities contribute to this database which contains 9,000 titles with about 2,500 new abstracts added monthly. This is a wonderful service if you're looking for cutting edge theories or technology, because dissertations have not yet been made into books.

UMI has a sister company called DAYTRIX DIRECT. While UMI needs to be accessed online UMI will perform a comprehensive computer search of master's theses and dissertations dating back to 1861, if you simply write to their service, DAYTRIX DIRECT.

The cost of any search is just $20.00, regardless of the number of citations retrieved.

VU/TEXT INFORMATION SERVICES, INC. 325 Chestnut St., Suite 1300, Philadelphia, PA 19106, can be reached through EASYNET and now for the first time through DIALOG. VU/TEXT consists of the Knight Ridder newspaper group.

VU/TEXT is similar to Dialog in many respects although they offer access to more local papers.

WESTLAW, West Publishing Company, 50 W. Kellogg Blvd., St. Paul, MN 55164. Westlaw is the nation's oldest and largest legal publisher. They now have a database which is in itself a collection of different legal databases and supplies full text access to various topics including bankruptcy, energy, and patents.

WESTLAW puts over 200 legal magazines directly online and will help customers formulate search queries until the correct articles are found.

INTERNET

Imagine for a minute, if you will, that a vast network of computers was tied together by phone lines crisscrossing the globe. Imagine that you could access thousands, or even millions of computers and computer users in every state in the union, most countries of the world, instantly and access huge amounts of expert inormation on damn near any subject you wanted.

Oh yes, now imagine that it's free...

Welcome to the INTERNET. The INTERNET was "born" 20 some-odd years ago as a child of the US Defense Department and was known as the ARPAnet. ARPAnet was an experimental network designed to support military research and connected the Defense Department to universities, military proving grounds, weapons laboratories, and IBM launch sites across the United States.

ARPAnet was designed to function in case of a national disaster (you might want to think about what our old friends the Russians were doing 20 years ago), even if the civilian phone systems were destroyed or down. Instead of depending on a central source, ARPAnet depended on each host computer to have the minimum required information to contact other computers. In order to send a message on ARPAnet, a computer put its data in an envelope called a packet and addressed the packet correctly in computerese. The communicating computers – not the network itself – were responsible for insuring the communication was accomplished. This meant that every computer on the network could talk on an equal level with any other computer. If the eastern seaboard was destroyed by a tsunami, the network would remain "intact."

Like a worm, if you cut off a segment of the ARPAnet it did not destroy the organism, in fact it would soon grow another segment to replace the missing one.

ARPAnet was a favorite playground for phone phreaks and early computer hackers because of its interesting architecture and, of course, the people it served.

Gradually ARPAnet disappeared to be replaced by INTERNET, founded on the same principles. INTERNET developers began to put their packet software on every conceivable type of computer, making it one of the only practical methods for communication between computers of different manufacturers with different operating systems. Many of the early users, that is, government departments and universities, stayed on INTERNET using the old ARPAnet package technology. INTERNET changed ARPAnet's connecting technology somewhat by creating regional networks in each area of the country; schools would be connected to their nearest neighbor, corporations to the nearest corporation, etc. Each chain was then connected to a super computer center at one point, then the centers were connected together. Within this configuration, any computer can eventually communicate with any other one by forwarding its packet of conversation through its neighbors. This turns out to be much cheaper than most dial-up access services. In many cases you can communicate with someone in Germany without paying any long distance charges.

When INTERNET began, access was limited to researchers, computer scientist, government employees and government contractors. This changed a number of years ago when the National Science Foundation, an agency of the US Government, created the five super computer centers and began encouraging universal access by funding campus programs with the stipulation that that college could show a plan to spread the access around. Immediately everyone attending a four-year college became a potential INTERNET user.

The system is still growing in leaps and bounds. From its initial founding in the early 1980s. INTERNET has increased over *1,000 times..* Each year about one million people worldwide use INTERNET daily and information traffic has risen by 11% each month. As this is written, INTERNET has well over one million users and, because of some developments we'll see in a moment, this figure is about to become logarithmic.

INTERNET is the largest computer network in the entire world. So now for the conundrum; there really is no such thing as INTERNET, at least in the conventional sense.

If you join CompuServe, the nice folks at CompuServe headquarters in Ohio are only too happy to remove a few bucks from your bank account each month to pay for the maintenance of their system. INTERNET, per se, has no central office, owns no computers, and really has no employees. The philosophy behind INTERNET is that each user, or data provider, is responsible for his portion of the network. There is no president, no CEO, no vice president, not even a Pope or dictator.

INTERNET does have a council of elders that offers opinions about how things should work and allows you to take part or not as you wish. The ultimate authority for the directions INTERNET takes rests with the Society or ISOC. This is a voluntary organization whose purpose is to promote global information exchange through INTERNET technology. It appoints a council of elders who take responsibility for the technical management and direction of the INTERNET.

INTERNET is a voluntary organization. If a network or university or corporation accepts the teachings of INTERNET, is connected to it, considers itself part of the network, then it is. In extreme cases, networks can be kicked off the INTERNET if they seem to be doing damage to the INTERNET itself, but there is no set organization with system operators, managers, customer relations, or paid help.

INTERNET does not charge anybody anything. Instead everyone pays their part as they go. NASA pays for the NASA Science INTERNET, the Library of Congress pays for the Library of Congress network on INTERNET. INTERNET simply connects all these networks together by standardized access protocol and providing portals for users to reach one or more of its networks.

INTERNET invalidates Groucho Marx's favorite comment, "I wouldn't want to be a member of any club that would have people like me as members."

The upside of this existentialist mindset , I think, therefore I am a part of it, philosophy is that access is virtually unlimited and, in many cases, absolutely free. The downside is that there is no central body massaging the software engine, no central MegaCompany Inc., updating protocols and constantly working to simplify user access.

INTERNET can be a bit of a bitch to use.

There are no menus on INTERNET. There are no nicely standardized helpers to make the network user friendly.

This is not your father's CompuServe...

In the early days of INTERNET, you pretty much had to have a good grasp of computer abilities and hopefully, the UNIX operating system in order to navigate around INTERNET. In those days, the best and, in fact, the only way to learn about INTERNET was by asking INTERNET. This is not to say there are not specific areas of interest.

There are.

INTERNET has lists for library administrators, romance readers, bird watchers, Russia watchers, engineers, techies, weapons designers, computer whizzes and thousands more. There's no cute monthly newsletter, so one network on

INTERNET is simply a list that announces the creation of new lists.

WHAT'S IN IT FOR ME?

INTERNET consists of three kinds of resources: files, services, and messaging. Normally, to use a computer on the INTERNET, one would have to master TELENET and FTP or File Transfer Protocol. The former is the actual logon procedure to reach the more remote computer from your host computer or service, the second allows you to download information of interest.

INTERNET offers two types of data sources. The first is files which can be found in downloaded FTP protocol. The problem is, that unlike CompuServe, INTERNET has no front menu. You can't just log on and dive into the service. You need to connect through an access point, learn the commands of the particular service you are seeking, then decide what you need and how to find it. There are literally thousands of network sites that allow "anonymous FTP"; in simple words, FTP says to another computer, "Let me in, check your directories and make a very quick transfer of any files to my mainframe or server." "Anonymous FTP" can access the file's archives without an account.

Luckily, several new tools are appearing on the INTERNET horizon as the user base expands from government researchers toward general public access. One of the most interesting tools was created at McGill University and is called Archie. Archie periodically searches the index files of many anonymous sites and compiles a master list. Several networks around the world receive copies of this new master list automatically. Archie currently tracks over three million files at two thousand archive sites.

Once you're connected to a site, enter a keyword and Archie will search the index for any files or directories that contain the word or substring in their titles. The UNIX operating system that works with Archie does not limit file names to eight letter maximums, allowing the user to expand the file into a long string, increasing the chances of a hit.

Archie tells you what files and directories match your search word and where they're located. It's up to you to perform the FTP necessary to get to the service and the file. Most files can be downloaded by simply registering on the host computer as "anonymous," "visitor," or possibly "guest." If these don't work, you can always call the system operator, ask how to register in order to download files.

An even hipper tool has been developed by the University of Minnesota and became a standard INTERNET utility. Gopher, named both because it's the university mascot and it will "go for" what you want, saves you from having to work with FTPs or TELENETS. Gopher checks its indexes for your area of concern, lists what it finds, then sends you to the site to access the information you want. Gophers are the closest thing to a front-end that INTERNET provides.

Gopher will list menu choices and then submenu choices following the thread of your request for all the services it knows about on the INTERNET.

Unlike Archie, Gopher is not copied everywhere. Each particular Gopher in each particular network may utilize its own setup protocols. What you need may exist but may not appear on your Gopher menus, as there are several hundred Gophers living out there on the network.

What to do? What to do?

Veronica (no, I'm not making these names up), an acronym for Very Easy Rodent Oriented Netwide Index Computerized Archives, will help you use the various Gophers. It takes your keywords and automatically searches Gophers to make up custom menus, which are then used for automatic TELENET or FTP transfers. Veronica was developed at the University of Nevada and still lives there, although many other networks are starting to adapt it as a standard tool.

One can always find the latest developments on the Archies, Gophers, and Veronicas, of the world by going on INTERNET and contacting the management or development teams through E-mail (which we'll get to in a moment) or joining discussion groups on these tools.

What kind of information can you find on INTERNET? Well, to start with how about several hundred college library catalogs and databases (all accessible without charge)? Or direct access to the largest depository of information on the face of the earth – the Library of Congress?

- The Reader's Guide to Periodical Literature.
- Meckler's Electronic Publishing Service, which makes a number of the Meckler journals and books online plus hard copy ordering information.
- The Washington Law Library.
- An index to US Government program abstracts.
- The CIA World Map.
- Federal Information Exchange.
- State Department of Travel Advisories.
- Network information on a number of different networks.
- Various engineering group documents.
- Computer security files.
- The CIA World Fact Book.
- The NNSC Internet Resource Guide which is operated by the NSF Network Service Center which lists all the services they know of on the INTERNET and provides access information.
- Scientific database bulletin boards.
- The Electronic Frontier Foundation.
- Soviet archives.
- The King James Bible.

It's virtually impossible to list the thousands and thousands of available bulletin boards, forums, and libraries of information as they change extremely rapidly. For access your best bet is to start off with a couple of books reviewed below, especially the WHOLE INTERNET, get on INTERNET itself, and inquire as to what's available.

INTERNET'S second major strength is Organic Experts. With *one hundred million* users, INTERNET is the largest resource pool for experts on almost any subject. Remember, ARPAnet/ INTERNET started as a network for scientists, researchers, and missile launchers and has ex-

panded into the university and commercial communities.

What good are these experts to you? Looking for a CD-ROM on a particular subject? Send one query and "ask" the three thousand folks on the public access computer systems list for advice. In a few hours you'll have personal testimonies on the pros and cons of any disk in the subject area you're looking for.

There are also many discussion groups that one can join, participate in, or simply monitor. Mail that is sent to any group address is distributed to all "members." It's kinda like a round robin discussion, only not in real time.

In some sections of the INTERNET, these groups are known as mailing lists, discussion groups, reflectors, aliases, or listservers, depending on where they're located and how they're driven. Subscriptions are free. It's also possible, of course, to start your own user group or discussion group and take advantage of the thousands of people probably interested in the same subject matter that you are.

ELECTRONIC MAIL

In order to use INTERNET and many other services, you need what is known as an electronic mailbox. This phantom box lives in the network you are a subscriber to, is identified with your name, followed by some protocol information, or just a number depending on which "postal" service you are subscribing to. Electronic mail is extremely handy and even if you don't use INTERNET, I would suggest you join a service that will provide you an electronic mailbox.

Your box allows you to receive mail from anyone who can reach the service and has your address, at any time, day or night. You can retrieve mail at your leisure, copy it, download it, leave it in the box, or delete it. Most services that will get you to INTERNET provide electronic mailboxes. If you want a general box, I would suggest MCI mail or THE WELL.

FINDING PEOPLE ON THE INTERNET

The INTERNET is a vast and mysterious place. Over a million computers and a hundred million users are connected in this network. With an electronic mail address in hand, you can send electronic notes, love letters, or secret messages to your associates, friends, and enemies.

The problem is locating them.

With so many computer systems and users in the world, it is impossible to maintain a phone book of the INTERNET. The problem is compounded because people – especially students – come and go from the net all the time.

However, it is possible to find specific people on the net. Programs exist which, given some amount of information about your target, can track down his or her e-mail address. The more information you know about your target – name, place of business or school, and so on – the higher your hit rate will be.

To be listed in any of these services, you need to have an account on the INTERNET and, to some extent, you must want to be found.

Here are four INTERNET tools that can help you find someone. Each particular tool may list people not included in one of the others, so it's best to try all four if you're a serious searcher.

A. Finger

UNIX, VMS, and some other systems support a command called "finger." Finger can provide basic information about a user on a given computer. It usually allows searches by first name, last name or log on name. To list users named Steve on your local system, "finger Steve" should produce a list of everyone whose name or log-on contains "Steve." Finger may return information including the user's real name, log-on, and a phone number and any other personal information, if these are supplied.

Finger's power grows when used in conjunction with other programs.

B. Netfind

Netfind is a "white pages" that uses a number of sources to find electronic mail addresses. Netfind can locate users at thousands of sites worldwide. The majority of the domains it can access are educational institutions, so this service is very good for locating students. Netfind can also access a vast number of commercial, military, government, and other organizational computers.

Netfind can be used either as a client program running on your local computer, or accessed by TELENETing to one of several public servers.

To use Netfind, TELENET to any Netfind server and list the target's name plus his place of business or school. Servers are limited to a certain number of searches at any given time, so you may be denied access. If so, try again later or choose a different server.

Netfind displays a menu of selections. To search for a specific person, enter "2" (search). You'll then be asked to "enter person and keys." Enter one word for the name, followed by one or more words defining where to look. This is a bit more complicated than it sounds but netfind protocol information is available online from INTERNET itself. Basically it will search through a number of remote networks, querying each computer that might have an account name (in our case, Steve) and provide you with potential matches.

C. Knowbot Information Service

The Knowbot Information Service (KIS) is another "white pages" service that performs a very broad name search, checking MCI Mail, the X500 White Pages Pilot Project, WHOIS servers at various organizations, and the UNIX "finger" command. It can be used either as a client program resident on your local machine, through e-mail, or by TELENETing to a public server.

KIS uses subprograms called "Knowbots" to search for information. Each Knowbot looks for specific information from a site, and reports back to the main program with the results.

In the body of your mail message to netaddress, simply list the names of the people you are looking for, one per line. Sending "Johnson" will search the default list of directory servers for user "Johnson". Since KIS checks a predefined set of services, you do not need to supply an organization name to check for.

KIS also includes commands for narrowing your search and searching for an organization. For more help, put "?" or "man" in the body of your mail message.

D. Usenet Search

A final person searcher is the Usenet search. This service compares a search request to a database of people who have recently posted messages to the Usenet. (The Usenet is a worldwide bulletin board of sorts, where people send public messages on every imaginable topic.)

This search, obviously, can only find people who have recently sent a message to the Usenet. If you think your associate is a regular poster to the Usenet, you might want to try this. You use the Usenet search by sending electronic mail to a server that possesses your query ad replies by e-mail. The advantage to a Usenet search is that you do not have to have any other information except the person's name to make the search effective.

A good source book is, !%@: a DIRECTORY OF ELECTRONIC MAIL ADDRESSING AND NETWORKS by Donnalyn Frey and Rick Adams, ISBN 0-937175-15-3, published by O'Reilly. (Current edition published in January 1991; $27.00 cover price.).

One of the handiest tools to access INTERNET is called TELENET. This feature lets you virtually teleport anywhere on the network and use resources located physically at that computer. Moreover, some computers and networks have gateways to other networks that have gateways to...

You get the idea.

How can you be in two places at once? Actually, it's fairly easy. You should master the TELENET concept when you first start studying INTERNET.

ELECTRONIC NEWSLETTERS

Subscribing to discussion groups or lists with abandon will not only clog your mail but will soon deprive you of any social life outside of the network. There are a growing number of electronic journals and serials that can be subscribed to through INTERNET which will be automatically electronically mailed to your box when they come out. A few of the interesting selections for researchers would include:

- ALCTS NETWORK NEWS: sponsored by the American Library Association's Association for Library Collections and Technical Services, this newsletter provides various ALA news, etc. and other items of interest to librarians.
- CURRENT CITES: bibliography of current journal articles relating to computers, networks, information issues and technology.
- EFFECTOR ONLINE: the online newsletter of the Electronic Frontier Foundation. All the hot net issues are covered here: Privacy, freedom, First Amendment rights. Join EFF to be added to the mailing list or use the File Transfer Protocol (FTP, explained elsewhere) to get the files yourself from the EFF org.
- HOT OFF THE TREE (HOTT): provides excerpts and abstracts of articles about information technology.
- NETNEWS: an irreverent compendium of tidbits, resources, and net facts that is a must for true INTERNET users.
- PUBLIC-ACCESS COMPUTER SYSTEMS NEWS and THE PUBLIC-ACCESS COMPUTER SYSTEMS REVIEW: sent automatically to PACS-I subscribers. For a list of back issue files, send the following message to listser@uhupvmi: INDEX PACS-1. To obtain a comprehensive list of electronic serials on all topics.

So you're convinced. INTERNET is great! It's wonderful! How do you get hooked up? If you're a student or have access to a university, try to become an INTERNET subscriber through them. If you have contacts at a major corporation that may have INTERNET, ask if you can be put on the system. Lastly, some libraries are beginning to subscribe to INTERNET and you may be able to access it on an occasional basis through your branch.

Ah, the good news is INTERNET has just sprung into the public domain. Access is now available through a number of other services, one of which should be right for you.

The California Education and Research Federation (CERFnet) has announced DIAL N'CERF USA. It allows educators, scientists, corporations and individuals access to the INTERNET from anywhere in the continental US. A toll-free number 800/7CERFNET, provides subscribers with the capability to log-in to remote machines, transfer files, and send and receive electronic mail as if they had a standard, dedicated connection. The cost of this toll-free connection is $20 a month with a $10 per hour usage fee and setup charge of $50.

For more information contact CERFNET, California Education and Research Federation, c/o San Diego Supercomputer Center, Box 85608, San Diego, CA 92186-9784.

Performance Systems International (PSI) offers several permutations of network connectivity, including low end e-mail only accounts, dial-up host connectivity on demand, and dedicated connections. Costs are competitive and performance is reliable. PSHLink, E-mail, and delayed FTP is $19 a month for 2,400 baud or lower service, $29 per month for 9,600 baud service. GDS (Global Dialup Service) includes TELENET, rlogins (remote log-ins) at $39 a month for 2,400 baud, twenty-four hour access. Host DCS (Dialup Connection Service), at about $2,000 per year includes a full suite of INTERNET activities (mail, news, FTP, TELENET). PSI has POPs (Points of Presence) in over forty US cities. For more information contact Performance Systems International, Inc., 11800 Sunrise Valley Dr., Suite 1100, Reston, VA 22091.

More and more public databases are offering access including THE WELL 27 Gate Five Road, Sausalito, CA 94965, access through X,25 and direct dial-up. THE WELL is also a very handy

resource for electronic mail, discussion groups, and accessing techie experts.

PORTAL in Cupertino, CA (408-973-9111), provides $20 a month INTERNET access plus dial-up lines through Timenet.

GENIE has just added access to their database for the same $20 a month and a host of other more specialized bases and networks act as gateways to INTERNET.

• ANS (Advanced Networks and Services) 2901 Hubbard Road, Ann Arbor, MI 48105, worldwide, dedicated.
• CLASS (Cooperative Library Agency for Systems and Services) 1415 Koll Circle, Suite 101, San Jose, CA 95112-4698, national, dial-up.
• PSI (Performance Systems International) 1180 Sunrise Valley Drive, Suite 1100, Reston, VA 22091, worldwide, access through both dedicated and dial-up lines.

Try libraries and universities first for free acess and the contact one of the above-named services to find out who offers the most economical package for your area of the country. Don't forget to count your phone charges to access the gateway.

INTERNET is so good that East German crackers have searched through systems connected to INTERNET for any information on such matters as strategic defense initiative, missiles and nuclear weaponry. (See the book The Cuckoo's Egg).

Dutch hackers pierced some of the operation Desert Shield-Desert Storm information, the Soviets had apparently been in INTERNET and it's believed that hackers in the employ of Bagdad tried to use the INTERNET to find intelligence reports on our forces during Desert Storm.

Recently the Japanese have been accused of accessing proprietary data from the INTERNET using supercomputers, known networks, and artificial intelligence to "borrow" technical secrets from both the government and leading US industries.

INTERNET RESOURCES

THE WHOLE INTERNET USER'S GUIDE & CATALOG, Ed Krol, O'Reilly & Associates, Inc. 103 Morris St., Suite A, Sebastopol, CA 95472. This publication is one of the better jobs I've ever seen on covering a complex situation in laymen's language. Mr. Krol does a marvelous job of describing what the INTERNET is, how to use it, how to make it user friendly, how to get connected, where to look for certain facts and experts, and explicit instructions for using the various tools such as Archie, Veronica, and Gopher, generally a complete treatise on the INTERNET.

Let's take a look at a quote from an INTERNET user who found his life significantly changed by the whole INTERNET, "To all stumblers from an ex-stumbler. I recommend, from personal use, the introduction to INTERNET titled "THE WHOLE INTERNET." It is published by O'Reilly & Associates. It tells you everything you might ever want to know, and in simple language-how to get started, tie into local accesses, downloading, etc. At a cost, including shipping, of under $30, it is worth every penny."

A self fulfilling prophecy, Ed compiled this entire book without leaving his living room using the INTERNET.

DIRECTORY OF DIRECTORIES ON THE INTERNET, Gregory B. Newby, Meckler 11 Ferry Lane West, Westport, CT 06880, $29.50. The INTERNET is the basis for a global communication system with thousands of discrete discussion groups and information resources. This guide helps in navigating the INTERNET'S maze of data and helps people from all professions find resources of interest to them.

EXPLORING THE INTERNET: A TECHNICAL TRAVELOGUE, Carl Malamud, Prentice-Hall, $26.95. Mr. Malamud specializes in writing about networks. We all have to specialize in something, I guess. He recently took a trip to Europe to talk to people on the continent about INTERNET and see what they use it for. The primary plot of this book concerns his interviews with those people interspersed with comments on the eating habits of the French.

THE INTERNET COMPANION: A BEGINNER'S GUIDE TO GLOBAL NETWORKING, Tracy LaQuey with Jeanne Ryer, Addison-Westley, $10.95. This book concentrates on what you can use the network for, which is a welcome change from the excessive concentration on specific networking services often found in network books. It does emphasize the most common INTERNET applications—TELENET, FTP, and e-mail—but with examples of what they can be used for, not just bare statements of their technical capabilities. The general organization of the book is according to broad topics such as communicating with people and getting connected, as it should be.

THE INTERNET COMPANION scores many interesting points that you need to be an effective INTERNET megauser and use some of the more interesting tools on INTERNET.

A nice companion to the WHOLE INTERNET, but if I had to choose just one it would be the former.

INTERNET itself is one of the best guides of how to use the INTERNET. Here are a few online guides that I've found handy.

DELPHI is one of the first online services to offer direct access to the INTERNET. They will get you thru to all areas of the service including the bulletin boards, newsletters and so on and even offer live online assistants, as well as, help files and books to get you started.

You can try DELPHI by dialing (via modem) 1-800-365-4636, hit return a few times and then type MND43 for your password,

This will give you a free 5 hour trial.

Digital Data Express 1072 S. Saratoga Road, Suite #406, San Jose, CA 95129, offers a 70 minute video tape ($9.95 + $5.00 shipping) which is designed to teach the use of INTERNET, it's various servers such as Gopher, Veronica, Finger, USENET and more.

With your tape you get 5 hours of free INTERNET time and a subscription to INTERNET WORLD MAGAZINE.

THE INTERNET YELLOW PAGES ISBN 0-07-882023-5, published by Quality Books ($27.95)

gives you 447 pages of thousands of INTERNET resources from the world over.

THE INTERNET COMPLETE REFERENCE ISBN 0-07-881980-6, $29.95, also from Quality Books is a new 817 page guide to using internet. Your $30 also buys you a month of free INTERNET access.

Both books available at computer book stores or by dialing 1-800-822-0158.

And now for what you've all really been waiting for – Internet Business Pleasure and News provides a 24 hour a day adult BBS where "erotic singles and couples meet."

You knew it had to happen.

WINGOPHER NOTIS Systems Evanston, IL 60201, provides a graphic front end interface for INTERNET. For $129 you get set up with everything you need (including 30 free minutes of connect time) to use INTERNET with a minimum of hassle.

WINGOPHER provides you with a graphical interface that uses pull-down menus and point-and-click functionality for easy Internet navigation. Using the Gopher protocol, WINGOPHER supports Archie, Veronica, and WAIS searching FTP transactions and Telnet sessions are supported, as well as any Windows sound or video viewer. An image viewer and text viewer are included with WINGOPHER.

COMMERCIAL USER'S GUIDE TO THE INTERNET Thompson Publishing Group POB 26185, Tampa, FL 33633. The other end of the INTERNET guides, this book concentrates entirely on using the network for business.

Well, I'll bet some of those executives occasionally look up the old sexual forum, but that's not here nor there.

This book does have a different viewpoint and additional information from your standard get-started-on-the-INTERNET books. It also costs a bit more than most of those books – $400.

Chapter titles include:
Section One: Guidance
1. Using the Internet for Business
2. Connecting to the Internet
3. Primer to navigating the Internet
4. Data security solutions
5. Internet E-mail for commercial uses
6. Promoting products/services on the Internet
7. Providing customer support on the Internet
8. Selling information on the Internet
9. Using Internet for market research
10. Other commercial uses of the Internet

Section Two: Directories & Listings
1. Business sources on the Internet
2. Commercial access providers
3. Internet storefronts and distribution sites
4. Internet consultants and business services
5. Business data resources on the Internet

BOOKS

Regardless of the on-rush of the information super highway, most of the world's information still, and probably will for some time, live between the covers of one or more books.

Last year there were over *60,000* books published in this country alone. Many by small or self-publishers.

I've tried to provide enough information to allow you to procure most of the publications I've mentioned. If the book is from a small, or very specialized publisher I've tried to list the address and/or other ordering information.

If you are ordering a book by mail order, plan on including something for shipping and handling. The average charge probably works out to about $5.00 for a book or two. If you order more, you may pay more, if you send less the publication may be shipped in a manner that is slower than you desire.

If you include too much for shipping and handling, the publisher should refund the difference.

Some publishers will provide catalogs free of charge, some want anywhere from $3-$30 for their offering. *Do not* send Xeroxed cards or labels that are obviously generic in origin, requesting catalogs.

Write on a letterhead if you have one, if not, at least type the request. Sloppily written sloppily worded requests are a lot less likely to be considered serious customers.

It does cost a publisher, especially a small one several dollars to fill a catalog request when you consider designing, typesetting, printing, postage and handling costs. It is not rude for companies to expect to break even on requests.

Large (and some small) publishers can be located with a minor amount of research, the easiest method probably being to simply ask your local librarian to see a copy of LMP (Literary Market Place). Therein you'll find a brief rundown on each publisher including what types of books they do, number of books outputted per year, address and contact information.

The International Standard Book Number (ISBN) is a specific number assigned to each publisher and in turn, to each book. This number will help you find or order any book that subscribes to the ISBN (99+%) system.

If the book is in print (look in BOOKS IN PRINT and PAPERBACK BOOKS IN PRINT at bookstores and libraries), you can order directly from a bookstore or from the publisher. It is usually smarter to order through a retailer if possible – if the book is stocked by a major distributor or wholesaler, the store will get it faster than you probably would by ordering direct.

If the book is not in print and you cannot find the publisher, go to a rare and/or out of print dealer (in the Yellow Pages or classified section of many magazines) and let them search for you.

SPECIFIC SOURCES

In no particular order, some of my personal favorites – mostly companies I've made reference to in this lovely work, are as follows:

Paladin Press, Box 1307 Boulder, CO 80306. Started by one of the gentlemen who founded Soldier of Fortune magazine many years ago, this excellent publisher has grown from a out-of-the-garage operation (called Panther Press in those days) to a full fledged, fully respected publisher of books on surveillance, investigations, weapons, martial arts, ID's, detective reference manuals, explosives, lock picking, bounty hunting and a host of other interesting fields.

They have recently expanded into videos and stock some very unusual selections in this media also.

Paladin has a reputation for no bullshit, customer satisfaction and cutting edge materials. They issue a new catalog about every 60 days and I strongly suggest you get on their mailing list.

Loompanics Unlimited POB 1197 Port Townsend, WA 98368. I'm not going to go into how this company got its name, trust me it was funny at one point. They too have expanded over the years from a two-book publisher to a large warehouse operation offering some of the most unusual books around.
Catalog as of this writing $3.00.

Delta Manuals POB 1751 El Dorado, AR 71731 publishes over 1,000 government manuals on survival, firearms, aviation, electronics, history and more. Catalog $2.00 at this point in time.

Butterworth Heinemann 80 Montvale Ave., Stoneham, MA 02180. A well established publisher of original books on security, investigations, and security management. Their books are high quality, hard cover treatises on physical security, computer security, law, and other topics of interest.

Learned information, Inc., 143 Old Mariton Pike Medford, NJ 08055 produces works on library and information science, online and CD-ROM databases and such necessary fields as naval architecture.

DIANE Publishing Co., 600 Upland Ave., Upland, PA 19015 features a number of different catalogs having to do with law and justice, security and so on. The name is an acronym for Defense Information Access NEtwork and their bit in life is to gather up a percentage of all the cool reports, research studies and books that have been produced with your money, that you never got a chance to see before they disappeared into some faceless warehouse chocked full of government sponsored projects.

They combine these taxpayer sponsored reports with offerings from small publishers, nonprofit groups and "police authors" into a really good selection of reasonably priced materials you will never see at Crown Books.

Calibre Press 666 Dundee Rd, #1607, Northbrook, IL 60062. Twice yearly catalogs of about 50 titles of interest of law enforcement, PI's, EMT's and correctional personnel.

Brassey's (US), Inc., 8000 Westpark Drive, First Floor (where else?), McLean, VA 22102. Although you should order from Macmillan Distribution Center, 100 Front St., Bo 500 Riverside, NJ 08075. Very scholarly, very well done books on law enforcement/intelligence issues, as well as, such major projects as the INTERNATIONAL MILITARY AND DEFENSE ENCYCLOPEDIA, a six volume set that may be the most comprehensive reference work ever published in this field.

Quanta Press 1313 Fifth Street SE, Suite 208C Minneapolis, MN 55414. A publisher of compact discs (CD-ROM's) including the CIA and KGB WORLD FACTBOOKS, the AIRCRAFT ENCYCLOPEDIA and, of course, ABOUT COWS.

Libraries Unlimited POB 6633 Englewood, CO 80155, includes library science, information retrieval sources, research guides, etc.

UMI Dissertation Services, Inc., University Microfilms Inc., 300 North Zeeb Road Ann Arbor MI 48106. A number of different catalogs of books that never were – thesis produced by young people who are still invigorated with the writing process.
Subject catalogs make good reading, also online with DIALOG.
UMI also offers a Xeroxing service for books that have gone out of print.

PAIS (Public Affairs Information Service) 521 West 43 St. New York, NY 10036. "PRINT, ELECTRONIC AND OPTICAL BIBLIOGRAPHIC INDEXES TO NATIONAL AND INTERNATIONAL ECONOMIC, POLITICAL AND SOCIAL ISSUES"

And you thought I used run-on sentences... 300,000 indexed items, 8,000 main headings, also on CD-ROM and DIALOG.

Catalog $2.50, special searches on demand.

Intelligence Incorporated 2228 S. El Camino Real San Mateo, CA 94403. Yes, our catalog is on the expensive side, but we try to stock the very best in not only books but equipment of interest to investigators, spies, and people with inquiring minds. Includes information that should be of use even if you don't buy anything from us.

Catalog $15.00.

BookQuest/SerialsQuest 15 Southwest Park, Westwood, MA 02090 claims 1400 participants including 500 of the nation's out-of-print and used dealers and 500 libraries.

Find damn near anything. $100 set-up fee about $40 an hour. If you need one-time access find a library or info broker that subscribes. INTELLIGENCE BOOKDEALERS FOR IN-PRINT US AND FOREIGN TITLES.

Cloak and Dagger Books ("World's Largest Dealer in Out of Print Espionage Books") 9 Eastman Avenue Bedford, NH 03110.

How can I follow that act?

Non-fiction titles concerned with espionage, military intelligence, codes, guerrilla warfare, terrorism and such. Even Colonel Bowen says, "the best stock of used books on the subject of Intelligence in the country."

Francis Scott Key Book Shop, 1400 28th Street NW, Washington DC 20007. Vivian Brown or Jennifer Herman. A tiny shop, but they truly shine at special orders. Fast.

Olsson's Books, 1239 Wisconsin Ave. NW, Washington, DC 20007. Attn: Victor Gaberman.

General store with many intelligence oriented offerings. They do mail order on both domestic and foreign orders. Large, bustling, with many titles on display.

Sidney Kramer Books, 1825 I Street NW, Washington, DC. Attn: Mark Cozy. Beautiful mid-town store chocked full of foreign policy titles.

Reiter's Scientific & Professional Books, 2021 K Street NW, Washington, DC 20006. Reference and Technical book heaven.

Of course, the real grandfather of all intelligence bookstores was founded by Elizabeth Bancroft, publisher of SURVEILLANT.

The NATIONAL INTELLIGENCE BOOK CENTER, was "hidden" on the sixth floor of a downtown Washington office building and was truly a bookstore for spies, where you could learn how to change your identity, look inside the KGB or get some self-help guidance on becoming an agent.

The store was a Washington "secret" with customers coming primarily from word of mouth. If you didn't know it was there, you really shouldn't be a customer...

Access was controlled by a high-tech security door. Phone calls placed on hold were treated to tape-recorded readings from famous spy tales. The store was open to the public only three days a week, and visitors had to check all packages in lockers before entering.

Ms. Bancroft, has steadfastly refused to name her customers, but word has it that they included famous authors, literary editors, doctors, lawyers and, of course, government officials from the United States and abroad.

Names like William Casey, Jackie Onassis and Norman Mailer have been included as customers in articles about the store.

The store is no more, SURVEILLANT is now the official catalog of the NIBC and the books are offered via mail order only.

GOVERNMENT DOCUMENTS: FREE COPIES

Capitol Switchboard for Information: 202-224-3121.

House Resolutions (for copies at no charge): 202-225-3456

Senate Bills (for copies at no charge): write Senate Document Room, Hart Office Building, Room B04, Washington, DC 20510.

Legislative Status Office (to obtain status of bills): 202-225-1772.

GOVERNMENT DOCUMENTS: TO PURCHASE COPIES

Bernan Government Sources (obtains most government documents for a small add-on fee), 4611-F Assembly Dr., Lanham, MD 20706.

CIA Maps and Publications Released to the Public office of Public and Agency Information Washington, DC 20505. More maps than publications. Useful stuff like ESTIMATED SOVIET DEFENSES SPENDING IN RUBLES 1970-1975.

Hey, we pay these guy's salaries...Write your Congressman.

NTIS National Technical Information Service Springfield, VA 22161. This is the official publishing arm of the US Department of Commerce and makes available some *30,000* government research results, business information studies and engineering solutions each week.

Databases, books, reviews, newsletters – a plethora of information where you can find government inventions available for licensing, test results of new weapons and even the latest surveillance toys.

US Government Book catalogs are available from the Superintendent of Documents POB 37000 Washington, DC 20013. Free catalog. Cheap good stuff that is reprinted by many other publishers for many times the price...

OUT-OF-PRINT INTELLIGENCE BOOK DEALERS

Cloak & Dagger Books, 9 Eastman Avenue, Bedford, NH 03102. Attn: Dan D. Halpin, Jr. Catalog available, handles want-lists.

Elm Spy Books, P. O. Box 9753, Arnold, MD 21012. Attn: Emil Levine. All intelligence titles; catalog available.

The President's Box, P. O. Box 1255, Washington, DC 20013. Specializes in assassinations and conspiracy theories. Catalog available.

The Last Hurrah Bookshop, 937 Memorial Avenue, Williamsport, PA 17701. Specialists on political assassinations, conspiracies and matters relating to the Kennedy family.

The Military Bookman, 29 East 93rd Street, New York, NY 10128. Primarily military but they often list 40 or 50 intelligence titles in their catalogs.

Q M Dabney & Co., 11910 Parklawn Dr., Rockville, MD. Military and intelligence titles.

Many of the above titles courtesy of SURVEILLANT.

Just to show you I'm not espousing any political viewpoints here, you might want to also visit "THE REVOLUTION BOOKS NETWORK."

Bookstores:
NY 13 East 16th St.
New York, NY 10003
MA 38 JFK St.
Cambridge, MA 02138
DC 1815 Adams Mill Rd., NW
Washington, DC 20009
OH 2804 Mayfield Rd.
Cleveland Heights, OH 44118
CA 2425C Channing Way
Berkeley, CA 94704
Libros Revolution
312 W. 8th St.
Los Angeles, CA 90014
WA 5519A University Way NE
Seattle, WA 98105
HI 2567 S. King Street
Honolulu, HI 96828

These bookstores are controlled by the Revolutionary Communist Party.

STAR WARS
SPY SATELLITES GO COMMERCIAL

Since the late 1950s many governments have used satellites to monitor enemies, potential enemies, allies, and in many cases, their own citizens, through a variety of electronic and photographic means. Military satellites were shown off during the Desert Shield – Desert Storm conflict where, through the graces of CNN, one could see actual Scud missile launches in real time and then follow the computer enhanced trajectory of the bird into the impact site in Kuwait or Israel.

Experts disagree on the most important facet of military satellites: that is, their resolution imagery distance translated into the Queen's English that means the size of objects they can see and correctly reproduce (with or without computer enhancement) from their orbit. In the United States the CIA and NSA have the most sophisticated satellite capabilities. 10 years ago one "highly placed source" in NSA when asked if the satellites could read license plates from their orbit answered "license plates, we can tell the sex of a cat walking down the street."

Perhaps this was a touch of disinformation or just bragging on the part of some unheralded technician, the fact is he was probably telling just about the truth. Picture the obvious ramifications of satellites that can detect very small objects on earth coupled with powerful night vision Starlight scopes and thermal imaging devices. A rather unusual scenario begins to develop where government officials can almost see (and, of course, if electronic emissions are involved, also hear) action any where in the world in real time.

The first effective spy satellites photographed their images by using long lenses and high grain film. Rolls of such film were ejected from the satellite, snatched in midair by specially equipped air force planes as they re-entered the atmosphere. The film was rushed to the developing lab and to the key of all satellite interpretation, the photo reconnaissance guys who were the ones who go on record saying that the cat was indeed male...

Although the use of satellites seems a bit far from an option most readers would consider as a viable means of surveillance or simply curiosity solving, you will be happy to know that the "end" of the Cold War has brought about an enormous unemployment scare frenzy in the satellite imagery business which has resulted in not one, but many governments, companies, and commercial branches of spy agencies that are willing to serve up an enormous amount of graphic information on almost any spot on the entire planet.

Think I'm kidding? France will not only sell you facts on file but for the right price they will move one of their high-level military graphic satellites to position at any time you want to take pictures of anything you want on the ground. Not to be outdone a Canadian corporation known as SPOT will provide photographs and/or radar images from Russian satellites (and for you very discriminating customers near infrared imagery which pierces both night and cloud cover). The NASA United States entry will sell graphics on file or try and get what you need.

A number of inexpensive commercial computer programs allow enhancement of satellite-generated photographs and there are even clubs with electronic bulletin boards available to "amateur satellite users."

Ah, we're getting a little ahead of the story here. Let's start at the beginning...

SATELLITE SURVEILLANCE, Harold Hough, Loompanics Unlimited, ISBN 1-55950-077-8. A helpful beginner's text on the possibilities of satellite images, this book is a detailed work on what satellites are capable of, which satellites are in orbit, and what they were designed to keep track of,  the difference between military and commercial satellites, the amounts of light needed for a certain resolution, what radar does, whether you should order color or black and white, the effects of CCD's, thermal imaging, etc.

SATELLITE SURVEILLANCE lists a number of satellites whose output is commercially lavailable as well as how to access this information and touches on how to hide various activities from the prying eyes of this new breed of satellites.

I recommend this book because it shows how satellites are used commercially by TV stations and people employed in the areas of mapping, land and water navigation, tax assessment, zoning and use planning, building roads, bridges and dams, investing in commodities, oil and gold exploration, pollution control, controlling forest fires, crop damage assessment, pest control and much more. SATELLITE SURVEILLANCE is the primer of the new do-it-yourself aerial age.

EARTH DATA AND NEW WEAPONS, J.L. Larson and George A. Pelletiere, National Defense University, sold by the U. S. Government Printing Office, Superintendent of Documents, Washington, DC 20402. Although designed for an obvious specific purpose, the acquisition and con-  version of data for modern aircraft missiles and artillery, this book also offers a very technical look at satellite collection under the general aegis of the Department of Defense with the Defense Mapping Agency taking a leading role. The authors have managed to put together a very controversial book and make no apologies for the fact that they are trying to improve weapons delivery systems; but in doing so they break down the capabilities of agencies from the 9,000- employee Defense Mapping Agency to small intelligence groups, and quite concisely show how information is then processed and standardized into a format that can be used in various weapons or observation systems.

The book goes into the intricacies of various advanced cruise missiles, joint-attack radar systems, NAVSTAR global positioning system, precision location strike systems, etc. While not designed to touch the investigative audience, EARTH DATA is an interesting work on clarifying exactly what satellites do to map and photograph in fixed location on the earth's surface.

NASA PHOTOGRAPHY INDEX, Public Affairs Division, Washington, DC 20546. NASA sells, rather inexpensively I might add, very dramatic pictures of their various shuttle craft, launch vehicles, and satellite operation. This book is an index of photographs available from NASA either in color 4" x 5" transparencies or in black and white 8" x 10" glossies. They're free to the information media and can be purchased by anybody else through various photographic contractors listed in the book on a non-copyrighted basis.

The pictures are exciting, suitable for framing, and not sold in many stores. Photographs are available from all major and minor launches which include manned lunar missions, closeups of the moons of Jupiter, more detail than you could possibly want on various craters as well as various cities in the United States photographed from the Skylab, Pioneer, Viking, Orbiter, Aviation and Space Shuttle launches. A fun book with some neat stuff in it. See your neighborhood from 120 miles up! Not really the Bible of investigative satellite imagery.

The United States Department Of The Interior Geological Survey, Eros Data Center, Sioux

Falls, SD 57198. Film, negative and paper aerial and satellite photographs of many areas of the world and most U.S. metropolitan area districts. The photographs that have been chosen are of high quality and are under minimum cloud cover. The predominant scale of pre-selected photographs is 1:58,000, which means one inch equals .09 miles. The majority of the photographs are color infrared, some are natural color, and many large areas cannot be covered in one photograph but must be put together in a mosaic from various sources.

Eros Data Center also coordinates the NAPP or National Aerial Photography Program which offers many normal and infrared photographs taken from an altitude of 40,000 feet during the last five years. USDI materials are generally useful for long range planning, mapping, predicting commodity outputs or finding exact global locations. They are not good enough for normal surveillance applications. Information or assistance on this matter may also be obtained from the following U.S. Geological Survey Earth Science Information Center offices:

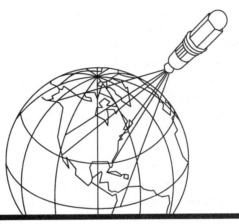

Reston – ESIC
U. S. Geological Survey
507 National Center
Reston, VA 22092

Rolla – ESIC
MS 231
1400 Independence Rd.
Rolla, MO 65401

Stennis Space Center – ESIC
Building 3101
Stennis Space Center, MS 39529

Anchorage – ESIC
Room 101
4230 University Drive
Anchorage, AK 99508

Denver – ESIC
169 Federal Building
1961 Stout Street
Denver, CO 80294

Menlo Park – ESIC
Building 3, MS 532
345 Middlefield Rd.
Menlo Park, CA 94025

World Image, 6348 W. 95th St., Suite 104, Oaklawn, IL 60543. Uses over 160 sources to get their customers photos or maps they want. Rather than printing what would amount to an 900-page catalog that would list every photo and map available, they offer one-to-one personalized service from which you can custom order their products to your own satisfaction.

World Image provides photographs of excellent detail taken from about 20,000 feet. Each photograph covers an area of about 20 square miles. Black and white, color or infrared are available. The best available scale on this is about 1 to 10,000. They offer high altitude (our old friend 40,000 feet) and various satellite and space photos. In addition they carry topographic maps, foreign travel, road and wall maps, old maps, geologic maps, and other paraphernalia of interest to anybody mapping anywhere in the world. The photos are vivid and striking but probably a bit general for specific surveillance purposes.

Don't worry, we're getting there ...

Spot Image Corporation, 1897 Preston White Drive, Reston, VA 22091. Was created as the world's first commercial remote sensing system providing, at least at that time, the most detailed unclassified image available. They put up their own satellites and distributed their products throughout the U. S. and the world and have recently signed contracts with our pals the Russians to distribute some of their high-resolution satellite image products from their Sojuzkarkta satellites. Spot provides geocoded ortho- corrected imagery for a " world of applications."

Spot images can be laid directly upon U. S. geological maps to show, through color coding, various different types of land such as wetland, forest, etc. Their resolution of approximately 10 meters (originally designed for assessment of bomb damage following a conflict) shows individual buildings which can be computer-enhanced to the point where they become extremely viable in such fields as commercial and business intelligence. In quickspeak 10-meter image capability allows one to look behind the fences and see if a competitor is building new buildings, what sort of large equipment is being trucked or railroaded in, if oil tanks are going up, where secure areas are being created, etc.

Spot provides imagery of any location in the world, large area coverage and an archive of millions of worldwide scenes giving you a historical perspective on what may be an area you or your company may be interesting in seeing. They also offer—and this is so reassuring—frequent revisit capability.

Now that Spot has signed up the Russians, they can actually offer five-meter resolution on many parts of the world as well as that great Russian product the Almaz Synthetic Aperture Radar that relies on the illumination of the earth with microwave which is then reflected back to the satellite sensors to create an image of the earth's characteristics. Radar, of course, offers year-round imaging of cloud covered or night hidden areas.

O.K., now for my favorite. Something that bills itself as "The Leading Edge Investigative Imaging Tool," satellite and aerial surveillance offered by PSYTEP Corporation, distributed in North America by J. W. Wood and Associates, 4950 W. Dickman Rd., Suite B - 4, Battle Creek, MI 49105.

PSYTEP offers satellite images based on a 10 meter original that is re-sampled and computer enhanced down to a two meter resolution photograph. Let's let the nice folks at PSYTEP tell us what they think this means.

"EXAMPLE: A crime was committed on any date between 1964-present anywhere in the world.

"You call us with this information. Our technicians will search in excess of 60 databases worldwide to ascertain if there was a satellite image, aerial, or space photograph taken within your date/time window at your specific location. If there was, through re-sampling data and imaging technology we can provide you with a photograph of the crime scene area as seen from above with clear resolution to two meters.

Spy satellite (notenhanced) photo of the Santa Ana race track

"This investigative tool is being used for current crime scenes, satellite surveillance, and historical crimes that remain unsolved."

In practical terms this means you can find out if there was a van parked in front of your company warehouse at a quarter to midnight on the night all your computer equipment was stolen or perhaps just a series of employees' cars, whether your competitors are putting in heavy telephone switching equipment in order to handle an increase in expected volume of their calls, what kind of heavy equipment they are installing, how many buildings and what size they are constructing or perhaps even if there was a car parked in front of your girlfriend's house last Tuesday evening when she said she was alone and just too tired to answer the phone...

Better Living through electronics...

AN ALTERNATIVE TO PSYTEP IS

The Research Source, Inc., 226 W. Park Place, Suite 5, Newark, DE 19711. They specialize in existing aerial photos of US plant sites.

In proof that this is just the beginning of the trend, World View Imaging Corporation, a Livermore, California company that worked on Star Wars antimissile defenses has discovered it might be possible to keep their employees in groceries by launching commercial satellites with almost military resolution. They expect to launch their first three-meter resolution satellite very soon.

Lockheed Missiles and Space Company, Sunnyvale, California, a long time manufacturer of satellites for the military, estimates that if they were to go commercial with one-meter resolution satellites, they could preserve 700 jobs and perhaps create 30,000 spin-off jobs.

Lockheed has applied to the U. S. Commerce Department for a license to operate a space satellite that could distinguish objects just one meter long (this is without enhancement), a

figure that is 10 times more precise than other commercial satellites although far short of the resolution of military satellites. There's no doubt that this blooming industry is going in the direction of better resolution, cheaper images and wider acceptance.

It won't be long until one will be able to order satellite images of anyplace in the world that can distinguish objects 6" long and perhaps less—like license plate numbers.

Imagine the fun when you can get an aerial satellite photograph of your neighbor sunbathing in his/her backyard.

Imagine the fun when you can actually get an aerial satellite photograph of that wild party at the mansion up the hill last Tuesday, or your neighbor sunbathing in his/her backyard three days ago, or see inside a "closed" practice session of a major league football team, or track that shows fast a particular horse's speed.

Already the Russian government is releasing satellite images from the archives of the Soviet military through Central Trading Systems of Arlington, Texas, and a company in San Diego, Space Liaison International Corporation already has plans to sell two meter resolution data from other Russian satellites. As one would expect, U. S. companies are unhappy with this development since they are still prevented from releasing the latest in military spec photographic surveillance unlike their former friends and foes across the pond.

It is also possible to join various groups who deal with satellite imaging such as the Dallas Remote Imaging Group, P. O. Box 117088, Carrollton, Texas 75011, which puts out THE JOURNAL OF ENVIRONMENTAL SATELLITE AMATEUR USERS GROUP as well as operating a bulletin board which is "the premier source of information on satellite tracking, satellite imagery, telemetry analysis, tracking programs, satellite data bases, NASA space communications, etc."

One should realize the folks at the Dallas group and other groups like them are a bit more

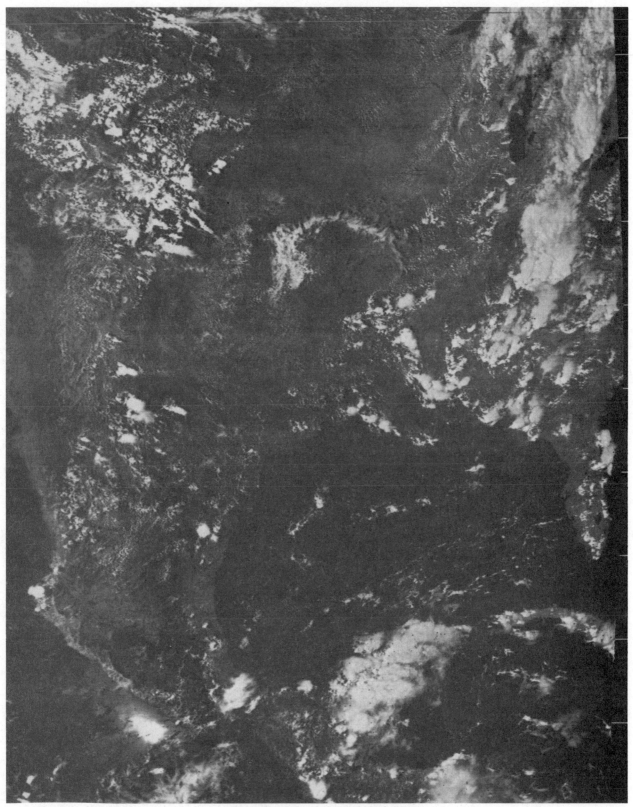

Direct down loaded weather photo

concerned with weather satellite images and NSA tracking than they are surveillance satellites. Still, the journal is written in a scholarly fashion with many good pictures and advertisements for the latest products that allow you to downlink satellite images from various birds.

RPV

Suppose you're the Shah of Emir or in our case, Secretary of Defense, and one of your neighbors has the gall to build a high fence all the way around his country, making it difficult for you to conduct normal surveillance.

What to do? What to do?

Well, if you have unlimited funds you can hire an SR71, pay France to move a satellite or you can take the poor man's view, no pun intended.

Aerovironment Inc., Monrovia, California, is an unusual company known for several things including the fact that one of their founders was the first person to fly a human-

The POINTER in pre-launch condition

powered vehicle over the English Channel. AV took the design and produced a unique line of products known as RPVs or UAVs, the first standing for Remote Piloted Vehicles, the latter for Unmanned Aerial Vehicles.

Since Alexander the Great, field commanders have understood the advantage of taking the high ground. Starting with the Civil War and continuing through portions of the Second World War, observation balloons have been deployed to spot where the enemy was, where their artillery livesd and what they were doing behind their fence.

Balloons have fallen into disuse (with the exception of the DEA) and are being replaced by some wonderful toys made by people like Aerovironment. Their primary product is a 9' wingspan Kevlar composite airplane/glider that runs on batteries.

This unit, known as the POINTER, or AV POINTER, can be hand launched by a soldier in the field after being transported in two back-packs. It will fly for approximately one hour guided by a remote control "pilot." The unit contains a video camera and/or night vision and thermal imaging equipment. The POINTER flies extremely slowly and *extremely* quietly. It was flown at altitudes as low as 50' in recent engagements, directly over columns of marching men *who never saw it.*

The POINTER transmits detailed pictures of exactly what your enemy (or your neighbor) is doing at any particular time. The signal is in real time so it can be recorded on the ground and viewed as the action unfolds.

The POINTER is very stealthy, no hot spots to attract IR sensitive missiles and almost radar proof. It is also cheap, and thereby expendable – no pilots bite the dust if a POINTER does go down.

POINTERS were used extensively in the Gulf War, giving our side a huge advantage by tracking where the enemy was and what his move-

Ground controlers "flying" the POINTER

ments were with very little risk of personnel loss or detection.

Proficiency with the POINTER takes 8–10 flights although some people can do it in two or three. It is guided by its internal camera and the "pilot" on the ground. The POINTER can go anywhere (within range) to provide an instant look at troop movements, supplies, or any other activity of interest.

Israel was the first country to use RPVs to support their ground forces. Since that time POINTERS have been employed by the Navy, the Marine Corps, and in some cases, the Army.

What a wonderful idea, right out of James Bond! Something that looks like a hobby shop toy, but is quite lethal.

Larger versions of the POINTER can be used as laser designators; i.e., they can fly over enemy strongholds, pinpointing them with an infrared laser in order to guide missiles and Pave type smart bombs onto the target.

What a marvelous concept and you thought those video games your thirteen-year-old spends every afternoon at the mall feeding your hard earned quarters into were without merit. Now he can attend West Point on that special RPV scholarship.

What good does this concept do you? Remember that your neighbor (or some other insensitive SOB) has found enough unmitigated gall to build a high fence around his house preventing visual, and perhaps audio surveillance?

Guess what? An engineer with the same perverted sense of humor that I was gifted with has come up with a civilian version of the POINTER.

SUPERCIRCUITS offers a selection of model airplanes, model helicopters, and even cute little four-wheel drive Jeeps, (you know, the same toys you use to drive your dog crazy) that really work as remote surveillance providers.

SC loads the mini-planes, boats and cars with a tiny video camera and transmitter in order to send back crystal clear pictures of neo-Nazi training programs or the neighbor's wife sunbathing nude at the pool.

SC (surveillance people and PIs also take note here, please) sells some of the cheapest video board cameras (Chinnon) and video transmitters available. They are designed to be mounted on one or more of the Supercircuits platforms where, like their big cousin the POINTER, they can fly over or drive into almost any target.

Who would believe it? Even if spotted by an alert security guard the units are likely to go unreported...

"Ah, did anybody else see that?"

"See what? Well, you know, it was this little Dodge Ram Truck, about a foot long, see, and it came over the embankment and I think there might have been a little camera on it and then it disappeared out the rear drive.

"Flying saucers? No, I really don't think I believe in them. Another Margarita? Sure, I guess I need one.

"In the sixties? Well you know, I did some drugs, I mean everybody was, see but no flashbacks, no I'm pretty sure about that, ah see it was this little truck...

"Never mind. Pass the salt, would you?"

I know this sounds like some weird TV pilot. – Star Trek meets Radio Shack, but these things actually represent a quite sophisticated niche in video surveillance.

Supercircuits provides complete kits, you provide a little time and skill. The low-priced video cameras can be removed from the helicopter and used in regular surveillance applications.

A Supercircuits/Toys R Us combination that "allows you to see and hear anything on your property from the comfort of your living room."

The camera choices include a board mounted unit with six infrared LEDs on board that can be placed above a door, hidden inside a teddy bear or stereo speaker and will provide illumination in a completely dark room.

For the ultimate expression in remote piloted vehicles we need to look at a company called DBA Systems, Inc., 8049 Monetary Drive, Suite D-7, Riviera Beach, FL 33404. Here we find airplanes, gliders, four-by-fours, and even a boat that can be remotely guided to a target.

On arrival it transmits the same high quality video, infrared or thermal target views back to its handler. The boat is very fast, very hard to find, difficult to shoot, and, let's face it, far more expendable than a live agent.

So sit back in the comfort of your favorite chair, turn the TV on, dial up the correct frequency and see what is happening in the real world.

Hey, people enjoy reality-based TV programs, somebody reads all those National Enquirers, and God forbid, once or twice in your life you may have closed the venetian blinds and watched that cute girl (okay, okay, *woman,* no letters please) get ready for bed.

This concept of real time remote video is far more realistic. View the action anywhere from a safe distance, tape it, analyze it and peruse it at your leisure without being seen.

Besides the damn things are a ball...

If you plan to do your own aerial photography, order a brochure entitled OBLIQUE AERIAL PHOTOGRAPHY from The Eastman Kodak Company, Rochester, NY 14650. Lots of good tips about what type of film to use, shutter speeds, filters, dealing with clouds, solar altitude, as well as choosing both the correct camera and airplane for best results.

The brochure is ridiculously inexpensive—something like $0.75—and even provides a phone number for tech support if additional questions arise.

For the ultimate in personal viewing you want to contact Istec Inc., 1810 Highway 6 North, Hamilton, Ontario, Canada L9J 1H2. They are an OEM supplier of the WESCAM surveillance system which can be gyrostabilized for use on aircraft. Sensing elements include optical, low light and thermal and magnification can be as high as *220X*. A radio link is supplied for real time viewing.

Have your very own spy satellite. Have the ability to see anything, anywhere. *Have lots of money handy before you call...*

INTELLIGENCE

SPIES 'R US
WHAT IF THEY GAVE A COLD WAR AND YOU LOST?

This section has it's roots in several sources – the primary one being a meeting for true super spies recently convened in Sofia, Bulgaria. Just being there made me feel like I was part of history that may never be repeated.

On a broader basis it explains what is happening with the "real" spies: who's going where? What's happened to the profession? What happens now?

Read on...

Imagine for a moment that you're James Bond and one day Miss Moneypenny wakes you with the sad news that England has surrendered to SPECTRE and, unfortunately Her Majesty couldn't afford your gold watch.

Good luck on your new career.

What do you do? Apply at the local grade school for the crossing guard job? Hire out to shake door knobs? Maybe you call a meeting with all your colleagues and, what the hell, your old enemies, to "redefine your goals".

I.e., find some new bad guys before it's too late...

John La Carre', the spy's writer says, "When the day comes that there are no more enemies the world, the governments will invent some for us."

Hmmmm...

I hate flying in Soviet aircraft. Hey, what do I know, maybe MIG's are wonderful planes, but this is my second time in a TU-154, a third world Xerox copy of a 727, and even with a shining new Glasnost paint job and some new upholstery I don't like the beast. It feels flimsy, the seats are rickety and the cabin feels like it is held together only by the fresh paint.

In fact I distinctly feel the need for a quick drink but some fool has thoughtlessly misplaced the stewardess call button and there's not an angel of mercy in sight...

Finally, we land in lovely Bulgaria where something called The Center for Democracy has invited me to Sofia. This Washington think tank has somehow convinced spies from the KGB and all the former Soviet bloc Eastern European countries to gather for a conference called "The Proper Role of an Intelligence Agency in a Democracy." The guest list is impressive: former CIA chief William Colby, the President of Bulgaria, and piles of spies ranging from 40 year KGB veterans to brand new recruits of the emerging Albanian government.

Lovely Bulgaria is recovering form 40 years of communist dictatorship. The long lines of miserable Bulgarians waiting in the streets for basic foodstuffs in the street that a friend of mine described after his visit last year, are gone. Shop windows have clothing and meat proudly displayed. Fresh cucumbers, oranges, fruit juices and espresso are all available. Life is still a struggle for most Bulgarians but they no longer seem to be starving or freezing.

I expect part of the trip's excitement to come from my day to day living arrangements – given the choice of a room at the local Sheridan ($187 a night), the only hotel around, and going through the Bulgarian tourist agency who, for the princely sum of 4 bucks a night in hard currency, will give me the key to a local's house and call and tell the landlord that a crazy writer from California is going to drop in for a few days.

Well, hopefully they'll call because I don't speak a work of, of, ah, whatever they speak in Sofia and I don't relish the thought of explaining to the local authorities what I am doing in some woman's house at one in the morning.

After examining my finances carefully, I opt for the latter choice. Maybe they have room service.

The conference itself begins well – although much of the country is crumbling, we participants in the spy jamboree are insulated from life on the streets of Sofia as we are whisked around in black Russian-built sedans by leather jacketed Bulgarian agents with grim faces racing through the streets without much regard for local traffic rules or local cops.

The conference opens at the Boyana Government Residence at the foot of Mount Riga. Boyana is like a Hyatt Regency that has been closed to the public, a cavernous marble and glass resort that caters only to official guests. It's devoid of signs or any indication of normal hotel commerce, just filled with meeting halls, restaurants, and bedrooms. There is one store in the complex, offering an illogical selection of trinkets, and exceptionally well-stocked with Bulgarian made trench coats. A special run for the spy gathering? The clerk didn't say, but I bought a stylish double-breasted model in navy blue for a bargain twenty-two dollars.

We assemble for the opening session, dozens of spies, a handful of journalists, and a sprinkling of politicians. Bulgarian President Zhelyu Zhelev appears for the official welcome. A dead ringer for Mel Brooks, Zhelev runs down the stock list of troubles that face the post Cold War world: nationalist passions, religious feuds, narco trafficking, illicit arms sales, and illegal export of capital. "These global problems," he told the attentive spies, "can be solved and the people gathered here – the specialized intelligence services – are particularly qualified" for the challenge.

Yes, this concept seems to have struck a responsive chord in the audience. Well hell, let's stop following each other around and get those no good SOB's that are laundering money and generally terrorizing the population. Hey, William's' dad has a barn, I've got some costumes, George has a gun, let's put on a show...

But the program is only half the fun – the participants are themselves a trip.

One of my favorites is KGB General Vadim Kirpichenko. No REMF here, Vadim has been out in the streets doing things to the bad guys – well, us in this case, but all that is all in the past. We've got more important fish to fry now.

Kirpichenko personifies the Russian bear. He is big, he is bold, and I'm not sure I'd want to have an overly serious discussion with him on a subject we couldn't agree on. Which is why I"m a little nonplused when he asks me for my card "in case I don't like what you write about me". He also tells me one of his proudest moments was when he was killed off in a book by a popular British writer of spy fiction.

Some of the big KGB agent's best moments come not at the conference itself but at the nightly cocktail parties where he holds court and seems to enjoy the attention a 40 year KGB veteran would expect to attract at a spy convention.

"So what are the KGB going to do for a living now that we're all such good buddies?" I ask him. Well, it turns out one thing they're going to do is sell their stories to "interested parties" via the new Foreign Intelligence Veterans Association, a group of KGB officers that's banded together to market their wares in the West. I'm not 100% sure I understand this concept. The Soviet Union, or ex-SV's, top generals in the committee for state security are going to market their histories to Hollywood? Is that what he means?

"It's not the selling of secrets," he tells me emphatically when I ask if this offer includes classified Soviet material that might be of interest to American TV because the old KGB agents need to supplement their meager ruble salaries. Not true, insists Kirpichenko, he and his colleagues are only interested in selling their memoirs. "Of course, a control system must exist, those memoirs should not divulge state secrets." The KGB leadership will decide what is okay to write.

He downs another bite of hors d'oeuvre, another slug of vodka and muses about his own autobiography "I think it would be possible to tell a lot of interesting and useful stories. I want to show that people of high intellect work in Russian intelligence, that the work is clean without any force pressing." He apologizes for his English, adequate, and prefers to speak through an interpreter. He's proud of his facility with French and Arabic, and mocks American diplomats ("diplomat" being of course spy jargon for another spy) for being too lazy to learn foreign languages.

The KGB is going to sell their material to Hollywood. Good lord, the system seems to be working after all. Why didn't someone think of this in WWII?

Kirpichenko (and later William Colby) makes an effort to differentiate between spying and simple intelligence gathering. The legend of the James Bond agent is not debunked, just de-emphasized. "Usually agents give concrete details, but not the general picture," the experienced Russian explained. "Agents cannot give a complete picture, only a group of analysts can do that, work that is ten times more valuable than an agent's."

KGB good guy Kirpichenko

The parties went well, in fact the KGB flared only when Kirpichenko was asked about KGB agents who sold out the Soviet Union and worked as double agents. "A traitor is a traitor in all cases," he said with disgust. It mattered not at all to him that Russia and America are no longer adversaries. "It was money," he spat out his assessment of what motivated the turn-coats, "not like cooperation for an idea. These people did not own the intelligence. They ran from their children and parents. They ran from their wives with their lovers. That was an immoral act. The cases of cooperation for an ideal, there were very few cases like that."

Ah, not that he was above recruiting for his own service. He turned to me with his winning smile. "For example, if I offer you a deal. It is your free will to cooperate. It is not known to the authorities. This is normal, cooperation of a citizen with foreign intelligence."

Cold war or not, some habits apparently die hard.

My very favorite spy, however, is Irakli Kocollari, the new president of the Albanian Intelligence Committee. Kocollari is a young fellow with an easy smile who is a prime example of the crunch in the spy vs. spy business. He drove to the conference from Tirana in his new Fiat, dodging a war along the way. You see, the poor Albanian government had no leks in the budget to send him on an airplane.

Still he seems quite excited about the whole idea of the conference, mixing with the big guys, listening to war stories, parking his new Fiat at the curb in front of some of the toughest guys in the world.

This attitude will wear somewhat thin three days later when some enterprising Bulgarian, eager to try his hand at this new concept of capitalism, steals this very Fiat from under the noses of our machine gun toting guards and Kocollari is forced to call his embassy and plead for airfare to return home, bit I'm getting ahead of the story.

The Intelligence Committee is a new organization, replacing the dreaded Sigurimi secret

Irakli Kocllari

police of the old Communist regime. "Sigurimi was on the front line of the fight against citizens," Kocollari explains why the old force was completely disbanded, the years of Communist schooling still creeping into his phraseology. "Since it was part of the State structure, Sigurimi played its own role defending the dictatorial clique, it was a tool in the hands of the party-state to safeguard the Party's life and interest," he is disgusted as he talks about his predecessor. "It was a censor of free thought, free speech, and free actions."

But what Kocollari really likes to talk about is American literature. He loves Jack London's stories and Walt Whitman is his favorite poet. A literate spy, my kind of guy...

The US sent it's regards that the current CIA director was too busy to attend, but did send William Colby, ex-agency director who turned out to be the star of the conference.

Colby also takes a part at the cocktail parties. One of his best raps is explaining the difference between intelligence gathering and spying. "Be-

fore you spy," Colby tells an attentive Bulgarian agent at the American ambassador's party, ask yourself three questions:

Is what you are trying to learn really important, what are risks of exposure, and what will the likely effect be when you are exposed because you eventually will be. "For example," he summed it all up, "I would never spy on Canada. They are too good of a friend. If you want to know something about Canada, just ask a Canadian."

The Bulgarian loved the lesson, but he was worried about his own professional value now that the Cold War was officially declared over. "But we do still have enemies," he implored Colby, "terrorists and drug lords."

Colby responded with caution, "You must know how important the threat is before you spy."

At this point the Bulgarian was almost pleading his case. It was an odd exchange to witness, the three of us in the Ambassador's residence, sharing gin and smoked salmon, and the Bulgarian worrying about his gig. Finally, he burst out with his final question, "There is still a justification for us to exist, isn't there? I mean the terrorists and the drug lords."

"Absolutely," Colby poured on the charm, "but you don't need thousands of people. If you're a regional country, you just need to look at your border."

The former bad guy Bulgarian was soaking it all up and nodding. "We are in a state of shock," he explained. "We are ready to talk." He was obviously enthralled with the idea of meeting Colby. "You are the greatest!" he announced.

Colby just smiled, after all his side won this particular war.

Oddly enough one of the major problems that faces the new world spies is what to do with all that secret stuff collected by the old world spies. Of course, democracy is wonderful, but there should still be some way to keep all those *secrets* compiled by the past regime...

Alfred Einweg came to the conference representing Germany. He holds the government

Colby (right) addresses former enemies

title of Data Protection Commissioner. His job supposedly is designed to ensure that German citizens enjoy fair access to the former East German secret police – the Stasi – files, files just opened to the public. Now remember that the Stasi were rumored to be some of the most ruthless and effective spies in the biz.

Einweg holds himself sternly as he walks and talks. His face is molded into a frown, a monocle would not look out of place, but when he speaks about the files there is no hint of Prussian militarism. Instead he worries about rights and ruined lives. "In principle, " Einweg explains, "all Germans now have the right to inspect their files. But," and he laughs, "the intelligence services can have an overriding interest."

That overriding interest means the files stay sealed unless various safeguards, Einweg himself being the last, are overridden, so don't make big plans for that visit to your personal file... Democracy or not.

He soberly talks about the husband who learned from his file that his wife was a Stasi informant, about destroyed careers and suicides because on Stasi records made public. More than one of the "soldiers" who shot fellow Germans when they tried to cross the wall have run with their tails between their legs, to Moscow.

Moscow is talking (as this is written) about turning them over.

As Data Protection Commissioner, Einweg acts as a go-between. When a German wants to see his file and the government says the file must remain closed, Einweg can take a look at the paperwork and then report back to the frustrated citizen. "I cannot say what is in the files. I can only tell them, 'your rights were violated or your rights were not violated.'"

Since Germany "opened" the Stasi files, other former Communist states are watching the results before making their own decisions. Alfred Einweg sees several contradictions in the mechanism Germany set up for dealing with requests to see the records.

"If a citizen wants information, he must say why," Einweg shakes his head. "So I think this is unfair, because then a citizen must give information to the Secret Service and still might not get access to the information that is being kept." And Einweg isn't convinced the Stasi is the only bad guy in Germany." "If the Stasi files are opened," he asks, "why not open the files of the West German Secret Service?"

An interesting question...

"There have been spectacular disclosures," he marvels. "People were secretly spied on, telephones were tapped, audio and video monitors were placed in flats and offices."

What he doesn't mention is that former Stasi members, finding themselves in the unemployment line, have run ads in German newspapers to the effect of, "Under surveillance? Phones tapped? Hire us, we can find the bugs for you, after all we put them there in the first place."

I particularly enjoy this example of impromptu capitalism. Hey, why not? *We* put them there...

The Bulgarian hosts are not rushing to follow the German model. Their secret police files are still sealed as their new parliament debates the pros and cons of making the spy dossiers public. Not that there's any question that Bulgarian spies pulled off some of the Cold War's dirtiest deals.

Security camera watches spy conference

Bulgarians used the poisoned umbrella trick to take out an enemy in London, they're still suspected of involvement in shooting the Pope. As the new Bulgarian Interior Minister Yordon Sokolov told his assembled colleagues, "The Bulgarian intelligence services are accountable for hiding, and even helping, corruption of power in the past."

Yet there's been no wholesale housecleaning of the Bulgarian CIA. "There is a danger that has not been overcome," Sokolov acknowledged. "We think it still exists right now."

Some, like the unsmiling, beady-eyed little Rumanian representative, Dumitru Cristea, do not seem to agree with this new philosophy of "files are public records".

"An intelligence officer," he said, "needs to reach a state of pure actuality of a Solomon. We have totally solved the problem of files regarding those who suffered under the Securitate. We intend to destroy all files except those with a political value."

Bulgaria's top spy, Major General Brigo Asparuhov agreed, but in a more publicly acceptable fashion. "I wouldn't like to reveal the files to anyone who wishes to have a look at them. This is unacceptable. I don't think it is proper to open the files. Why should we cause new tragedies? We should close this page of history and open the next page." He recommended burning the worrisome material. Clearly, his dominant concern was that his agents would suffer if the files were made public because he emotionally added, "The dossiers should not cause more tragedy for this nation. Those who work for the intelligence services are a source of national pride!"

However after chatting with some of his comrades during a break in the proceedings and he amended his comments saying before the files are destroyed, victims should be able to read their own dossiers.

There is no cut and dried solution to the files question for the spies. "We're drafting laws about data storage," says Hungarian National Security Service deputy director Istvan Chladesk, but he is not real specific as to what those laws will consist of.

The chief of the Polish Office for State Protection, Piotr Naimski worries out loud about the possibilities of blackmail if the files are opened wide. "In our buildings there is some knowledge preserved there in the achieves," he put it tactfully. "We have to solve the problem in the near future." He doesn't suggest how this will be accomplished.

Ah, but enough of this pontification: what of the real problem at hand – what exactly are these super spies planning on doing with their lives in the new world order? As Colby pointed out, at one time or another, various agents sitting around the long table had locked each other up in prison and sent assassins out to terminate each other with, as they say, extreme prejudice.

One after another of the representatives of spy agencies rose to speak to the gathering about that very problem. They all agreed, in these public sessions, that they should be working together against the common threats of terrorism, narcotics traffickers, and money laundering. It was only during the coffee breaks, dinners, and the cocktail parties that even these professional spies allowed their lips to loosen up a bit.

During one of the mixers, a robust old Bulgarian leaned over to our ex-CIA director with a wry smile. "Mr. Colby," he said slowly, "I have to tell you, in 1948 I was thrown in prison charged with being an American spy."

The Bulgarian is Ruen Krumov. He's 78 years old now and has come to terms with his false imprisonment. "They wanted in '48 that I confess I was an agent," he says about those dark Cold War days when Stalinism ruled Bulgaria. He was interrogated nonstop for 15 days and nights, told repeatedly that he must confess to being an American agent. "I confessed nothing, but I spent five years in prison."

The first fact that becomes apparent is that many old Communist spies have managed simply to announce that their affiliation changed to democracy, and stayed on the job. None of the countries that overthrew their dictators as the Iron Curtain ripped open decide to do away with secret services, in spite of all the alleged abuses perpetrated by those same spies – internally and internationally – during the Communist years. They have just cut their budgets, trimmed here, cut a little there…

Major General Brigo Asparuhov, Bulgaria's top spy, rationalizes his current force, many of them holdovers from the Communist dictatorship days. "It doesn't serve Bulgaria's interest to fire them," he says he only got rid of those agents who couldn't change with the times. Those he kept on the payroll "are intelligent people, capable of changing their attitudes."

Quickly, one might add. Quickly.

The other agents have brought along carefully thought out lists of "why were are still needed". They seem to read about the same – gotta stop those darn narcotics traffickers (oh, yeah, the KGB is going to stop crack sales, I have a little trouble with this one), corner and control the terrorists (some of whom were, until recently, supported by these very same people – find 'em? Hey, why not, *we put them there*), fight industrial espionage and generally make the world a better place for mankind.

Well, except the USA.

We have not made any cuts in our intelligence budget, citing the problems in the middle East, wars that are and are likely to break out in the former communist countries when minor generals are given the keys to the armory, as well as the real possibility of those spies who were fired from the above agencies may now be at their most dangerous as they wander now, unattached to any organization, working as freelancers for whomever has the hard cash to pay them.

In fact the intelligence moneys just went up under President Clinton. He has cited the need to replace our old spy satellites as the main reason for the added budget.

And the spying, of course, continues. On the last day of the conference, four Russian "diplomats" are expelled from Belgium, charged with espionage.

Krumov, the man who spent five years in a communist prison because they thought he might be an American spy supports this view. He is now a journalist. He's writing, not only because he's motivated to report the news, but also to augment his meager pension. He brings home 500 leva a month in retirement benefits, plus 50 more for his military service during the war. It comes to a little over 25 dollars a month, barely enough for groceries. He's covering the spy convention with cynicism, watching skeptically as the agents and intelligence officers claim to be preparing to work together. "I don't believe that they are friends," he says in slow, measured tones of disgust. "It's not possible that there can be eternal friendship among all these spies. It's only a facade. They still spy on each other."

Bottom line? I mean how does this affect you and me? Especially me – after all I pay the rent, some months at least, by writing about intelligence collection and spying. Am I out of work, on the streets, about to be homeless?

Well no, not exactly At the moment I am corresponding with the KGB, trying to convince them I should be one of the first journalists to come to Russia in order to study counter intelligence at their "university" where they have just announced they will be more than happy to take any Westerners with the hard cash to pay their "tuition."

Study with the KGB? What would James Bond think? What will spy novelists write about? Where have the bad guys gone?

And why am I not totally convinced that having all these professional spies looking for a paying gig and being buddy - buddy with each other the very best idea for civilization as we know it?

Well I guess I'm just a cynic and by the time this article appears all the drug trafficking, terrorism and private espionage will have been brought to a screeching halt by the new old spies...

Hallelujah!

WHAT ARE THEY DOING NOW?

KGB – Formed an organization in order to sell "true stories" to writers and filmmakers, and hired a Hollywood agent to represent them, opened doors the Lubyanka (KGB headquarters and prison) to any tourist with $25, contacted BBD & O, one of the largest ad agencies in the US to "give them a new look", canned a few agents, offering to teach "counter-espionage" to "western businessman" for a fee and have made numerous BIG sales to both Hollywood and producers from other countries. Now have their own PR branch (can be reached by calling Moscow 921 0762, ask for Andrei Oligov, director) and have opened a spy-for-hire section for any business that wants to use the KGB for "competitor research". As General Vladimir Kryuchkov, KGB chief said, "Monitoring business rivals should be right up the KGB's street."

The real worries, according to US intelligence sources are that they have increased their funding for their international operations and are specializing in industrial espionage and that some agents rumored to be selling their expertise to Arabic nations.

Stasi – Most fired outright, (figure varies, around 40,000!). Some offering private "counter intelligence" services, a few officers overseeing a mountain of files. Still there is a fair chance that many deep cover Stasi are still meeting and operating, to prevent the successful switch to a market economy according to Hans-Gerhard Lange a West German Intelligence spokesman.

Others – Most other ex-communist agencies fighting to keep alive after budget cuts.

France – You remember our pals, the French? They have, according to CIA director Robert Gates, "been caught spying on and stealing technology from several US companies including IBM and Texas Instruments." NBC reported the French intelligence service has put agents on French Air flights to the US disguised as stewards and stewardesses and routinely bugs the seats of Americans flying on their airline.

There are reports from "reputable sources" that the French routinely search the hotel rooms of *all* American businessmen of any note.

CIA – Ex DCI Stansfield Turner suggests the budget should be increased because we need to concentrate on the Gulf States, terrorist organizations, and "imagine what help it would be in international trade negotiations to know precisely what the other side is doing." The United States does not want to be surprised by such worldwide developments such as, "technological breakthroughs... Or unfair economic practices." He also suggests that we need to watch the former Soviet nuclear arsenal closely.

The personnel chiefs of several Western intelligence services admit they are turning down applications by the *hundreds* from employed Eastern spies. Where are they going after the-don't-call-us-we'll-call-you message?

Welcome to Iran, Iraq, Saudi Arabia, Ivan, you're gonna love it here...

One of the later replacements, DCI Richard Kerr flatly denies that the CIA is getting into industrial espionage. No one however, denies that the CIA has shifted it's recruiting strategies and is now concentrating on "businessmen, scientists and linguists."

PS. My hostess at the $4.00-a-night home-turned-into-hotel asked me, in carefully prepared English, to be sure and invite any of my "friends from California" that were sure to be soon flocking to the new paradise of Sofia, to stay at her house.

Consider yourself invited.

The Sheraton hotel with its own private, scrambled satellite uplink that costs $10 a minute to get a (the only) secure message out of Bulgaria without the government listening in. Guarded by an armed guard 24 hours a day. Used by businessmen, journalists, and low budget spies...

"Now the reason the enlightened prince and the wise general conquer the enemy whenever they move and their achievements surpass those of ordinary men is foreknowledge.

What is called foreknowledge cannot be elicited from spirits, nor from the gods, nor by analogy with past events, nor from calculations. It must be obtained from men who know the enemy situation (directly, i.e., men with access to the enemy camp)."

– Sun Tzu, THE ART OF WAR, sixth century, BC.

A LOOK AT THE INTELLIGENCE COMMUNITY TODAY

What Is Intelligence?

Spy novels, Hollywood movies, and sensational headlines have given us a distorted view of the profession. "Stripped of its James Bond/Rogue Elephant mystique, *intelligence is a dedicated information support service for (government) policy makers.* The business of intelligence is really the processing of information. For a more useful image of intelligence, picture a think tank or a news room rather than James Bond. Like a research institute, intelligence employs vast numbers of experts, including many PhDs, and like a think tank or the media, it produces information and analysis. Unlike those others, however, intelligence serves up tailored products to a restricted clientele... Intelligence is a policy support rather than a policy making function." From INTELLIGENCE WHAT IT IS AND HOW TO USE IT by John Macartney, number seven in a series of booklets from the Intelligence Profession Series published by The Association of Former Intelligence Officers, 6723 Whittier Ave., #303A, McLean, VA 22101.

AFIO has no affiliation with the US government; it was formed in 1975 by former intelligence personnel. Its purpose is "to promote public understanding of, and support for, a strong and responsible national intelligence establishment."

Their publications deal with the real world of intelligence gathering and inside views of the CIA and KGB. Interesting writing by those who actually did it, much of the techniques, flow charts and so on could easily be applied to private intelligence gathering as well as government sponsored efforts.

Intelligence can be divided into covert and overt as well as HUMINT or ELINT by the methodology involved in its collection. The trend today is slightly away from the exotic means of electronic collection including satellites, SR-70's and Aurora stealth planes towards human on-site collection methods for several reasons. They include the shift towards economic intelligence collection as well as the failure of electronic systems to perform up to par in several recent conflicts.

SURVEILLANT Acquisitions and Commentary for Intelligence and Security Professionals, a bimonthly publication of the National Intelligence Book Center, 2020 Pennsylvania Ave. NW Suite 165, Washington, D.C. 20006, is an *outstanding* newsletter that anyone involved in intelligence, security, or detective work should, in my humble opinion, subscribe to.

SURVEILLANT spends the first few pages of each issue reporting on the latest news in espionage and intelligence complied by some of the top writers and editors in the field. The next 30+ pages are reviews of new books, videos and other sources of information.

SURVEILLANT includes detailed reviews of books on military history, intelligence gathering, security, codes and cryptograms, covert action the FBI, CIA, KGB, weapons, industrial espionage and info gathering in general.

A very professional looking at all sides of intelligence and information acquisition including many things that just don't appear elsewhere, SURVEILLANT is both informative and an interesting read.

MAD ABOUT YOU

MAD SPY VS SPY THE UPDATED FILES Warner Books, ISBN 0-446-36201-8. Surely you grew up reading Mad Magazine and just as surely you followed the adventures of the black suited and the white suited spies as they blundered through 20 years of the cold war.

Maybe your subscription has elapsed, maybe you've missed a few episodes? Well here they are in book form...

INTELLIGENCE AGENCIES

Has the idea of covert intelligence loosened up a bit with the winding down of the cold war? Well, you can, for instance, take classes from former/current intelligence agents, subscribe to a number of interesting journals or even join an organization, nee' *club for* folks involved in or interested in, the work of intelligence agencies.

The SOCIETY FOR YOUNG INTELLIGENCE PROFESSIONALS is opening chapters in a number of cities and is designed as a "place where YIP's can get together to form networks, socialize and further their intelligence contacts."

I like this; a sort of health club for intelligence professionals without any machines. SYIP sponsors "a wide variety of activities on a monthly basis," including discussions, roundtables, speakers and "social events."

SYIP draws its membership form "dozens of government agencies, congressional committees, military commands, civilian corporations and major universities." Although the society will accept members from any age group, they point out that most activities are oriented towards professional men and women in their twenties and thirties.

SYIP features two newsletters, THE DIRECTOR'S COMMUNIQUE and THE SYIP JOURNAL, the latter containing articles of interest on such subjects as counterintelligence, security, and intelligence gathering. Both publications come with your $25 yearly membership fee.

How successful is the concept of what sounds like a combination intelligence dating service and resource center? Currently, they claim a membership in the "low hundreds" with chapters in both the US and Europe, but seem to be on the rise due to activities like a recent "social affair" held at *The Spy Club,* a trendy Washington dance club.

The invitation opened the door to all current members, friends or interested parties.

With the exception of former KGB or GRU employees...

One only wonders how long before an infuriated, lonely, former KGB agent convinces the ACLU to file a discrimination lawsuit.

The SYIP folks can be reached at: National Sec Forum, POB 2298, George Town University, Washington, D.C. 20057.

THE CIA

With the demise of the cold war, the CIA is undergoing changes in its hierarchy much as did/is the KGB. Although the CIA's changes may not be quite as overt, they are, nonetheless, significant for the world's richest spy agency.

The CIA evolved from the OSS headed by the late "wild" Bill Donovan. The CIA arose Phoenix-like from the carcass of the dead OSS in order to combat the newest threat to the free world (read Communism.)

The CIA began with HUMINT Intelligence relying on the efforts of human agents both in friendly environments and behind the iron curtain for its intelligence and analysis.

Over the last 20 years the CIA has shifted its collection and follow-up focus to the use of electronic intelligence gathering. Starting with the infamous U2 planes, the CIA discovered that 1. The United States has a huge advantage in technological resources and 2. Electronic "spies" rarely lied, defected or otherwise embarrassed their human handlers.

As satellites gradually took over the responsibilities of high flying aircraft, and electronic methods of data collection became more sophisticated, the CIA, with the NSA, undoubtedly was the world's best equipped and most electronically-oriented spy agency.

There is no denying the effectiveness of satellites that read lips from a geo-polar orbit, or intercept the cellular calls of Kremlin officials riding in their Zil limousines deep in the heart of the Soviet Union, coupled with night scopes, exotic telephone taping devices and frequency hopping radios. It's no surprise that the largest part of the CIA's budget is for techno toys.

This is changing. The 1980s, Desert Storm, and a number of other intelligence based-operations have pointed out that electronic intelligence provides extremely good intelligence support in the correct environmental conditions but leaves gaps in coverage as well as costing a veritable fortune. The pendulum is swinging in the other direction.

Facing the prospect of large budget cuts with the collapse of the Primary Enemy, the CIA has undergone recent shifts in both targeting and methods of collection. Virtually every CIA and DIA bureaucrat has pointed out that the end of the cold war did not end the need for intelligence collection, simply shifted the primary target from the Soviet Union to the Middle East and even to such "friendly" competitors as Japan and France. The "new" CIA is in fact shifting it's focus from electronic intelligence collection back to the tried and true methods of human, hands-on, collection.

Advocates of electronic intelligence point out the numerous recent failures of human collection operations including the fact that almost all of our recruited Cuban and East German "agents" were found to be doubles actually working for the other side. A lack of strong quality control and vigorous counterintelligence scrutiny has often been the bane of US clandestine human intelligence.

Advocates of human collection (HUMINT) are quick to point out the failures of electronic intelligence gathering during Desert Storm when our best satellites, surveillance planes, and thermal viewers failed to find Iraq's chemical weapons and most importantly, their immense nuclear program.

Some say these efforts demonstrate the error of relying too heavily on gadgets. We seriously underestimated the Iraqi nuclear program until the human, on-site inspectors uncovered the plethora of uranium and enriching machines. We had no idea of how close Iraq had come to producing its own version of Hiroshima, probably in downtown Tel-Aviv.

While maintaining healthy budget requests for aging satellites, development of the new super secret Aurora spy plane and other sophisticated Silicon-based collection methods, for the first time in 20 years the bulk of the CIA's "black budget" is the training and implementation of upgraded human intelligence efforts.

The CIA has begun improving the quality of human collection including programs to test our spies and agents and to scrutinize clandestine HUMINT operations and hold program managers accountable. Analytical and technical experts are developing strategic targeting in working with new techniques that supposedly will produce high quality, human-based intelligence. These upgraded efforts require upgraded funds leaving the CIA as well as or better funded than it was in the days of the cold war.

The other side of the new intelligence regime is the question of economic and business intelligence collection. Imagine what help it would be in international trade negotiations to know precisely what the other side is employing. Information is power, and today there's more opportunity to obtain good information than ever before. The United States has more capability to accomplish this than any other nation, although we face the reluctant approval of those who would agree with Mr. Churchill, "gentlemen do not read other gentlemen's mail."

A number of politicians and authors have called for better economic intelligence because the United States does not want to be surprised by worldwide developments such as technological breakthroughs, new strategies, or sudden shortages of raw materials.

Physicist Edward Teller, father of the H-bomb, has said the US can easily construct an electronic satellite-based system that would detect any significant activity on the surface of the earth, day or night, under clouds or jungle cover and with such frequency as to make "deliberate evasion" difficult. He also estimates this system would cost 5 billion to purchase and 1 billion a year to operate. A number of economic analysts have suggested that it would cost twice that and still be a bargain, but no one in the know disputes that it could be done.

On the other hand, human intelligence collection is cheap. Well trained economic collectors can produce the same or better raw data for an analyst at far less the cost of a spy satellite.

Not everyone agrees on exactly how far the US Government should go to provide intelligence data to specific US corporations, but there is no question that "friendly" countries are shifting the emphasis of their intelligence services to act against US businesses.

Along with the shift towards economic intelligence, the new world order demands a constant input of political intelligence from third world countries such as Iran, Libya, Panama, Granada, and Kuwait.

Some spy wags also point out that the newly divided ex-Soviet nuclear forces will demand more attention than ever. What general is establishing his own retirement plan in Libya?

Electronic intelligence provides raw fodder for photo analysts, audio engineers and now artificially-based intelligence computers. Human intelligence can actually be in touch with the peasants in the bazaars who are generating followers for the next holy war against Israel or the United States.

Human intelligence can sample attitudes; electronic intelligence provides proof of strategic actions, often when it is too late to avoid a military or economic response.

One of the CIA's problems has been that it does not require its case officers to operate under the handicap of maintaining a good cover. The US Government traditionally has not asked American espionage personnel to make the sacrifices that the Soviet bloc asked of its agents.

Many Soviet agents have left their homes behind, buried into foreign societies, adapted, and engaged in mundane business activities for years before commencing espionage operations.

Americans, on the other hand, are not usually as responsive to joining Soviet society and working as a shoemaker for 10 years before being called on to act as an in-place spy. Washington has also been a bit shy about exposing American agents and case officers to the punishment of exposure without the protection of diplomatic status.

The CIA also suffers from the fact that many US diplomatic and business agencies do not approve of the CIA's clandestine people passing themselves off as employees and often cause problems that can lead to the agent's exposure. The CIA has traditionally placed agents in every overseas embassy (as have our enemies) but our case officers tend to be easily identified because of the recurring roles they play and the perks they expect.

During the 50s, the heyday of human intelligence, the CIA had its own officers club overseas that many agents belonged to. As one would presume, this made their identification somewhat easier than their KGB counterparts who worked as maids, travel agents, and low level diplomats.

The DCI or Director of Central Intelligence is the person in charge of intelligence collection for the CIA and has full operational control over all forces assigned to him. The Departments of Army, Navy and Air Force are responsible for providing support to the DCI and for obtaining and sometimes training the necessary people.

The DCI is a sort of unified commander who operates intelligence collection assets of the country hour by hour every day. His most important assets are probably the NSA and the SRA both of whom fall under the military command structure. It is more convenient for budgetary and security reasons to have the military send up satellites and man listening posts on aircraft, ships and military bases. But this will prove to be an impossibility if we shift priorities to economics and politics and mechanisms must be put in place to support this new role.

The CIA has been shifting its emphasis since Robert Gates began delivering speeches highlighting that foreign intelligence agencies are trying to steal our technology. In one speech he pointed out that the French government was caught spying on IBM and Texas Instruments for their own state-owned company Groupe Bull.

To quote Mr. Gates directly, "We have found cases of moles being planted in high tech companies, US businessmen abroad being subject to bugging, room searches and the like."

A number of senators including the chairman of the Committee on Intelligence have asked that we explore whether commercially useful information picked up by the CIA could be "sanitized" and funneled thru the State Department or the Department Of Commerce to US companies. As you would suspect, most US businessmen are in favor of this free help, which would, according to ex-president Bush, fall into the categories of analyzing foreign economics and providing data to US policy makers and trade negotiators, moderating trends in technology that could affect national security and protecting US businesses from foreign intelligence agency spies.

More tangible proof that the CIA is switching its priorities from snooping on the Soviet military to foreign businesses is that although the CIA has always employed a legion of economists to analyze business and financial trends there has been a recent reallocation of the CIA resources in the 3.2 billion dollar budget to downsizing the role of US spy satellites and deploying more economic intelligence agents. The CIA actively admits that it is now recruiting economists, linguists, scientists, and business experts instead of Russian-speaking Skull and Bones members.

Former trade negotiator Michael B. Smith says, "Other countries have active intelligence programs directed against our companies to give their companies a leg up. We ought to emulate them."

One intelligence source was recently quoted as saying, "We still want spies like the ones you read about in a John Le Carre novel but now George Smiley will have to speak Japanese."

Remember it takes the CIA about two years to build an officer's cover so we should just now be seeing some output from the shift to the "fruits of HUMINT"' as the program is privately called.

SO YOU WANNA BE A SPY?

Traditionally the CIA viewed the ideal candidate as a Yale-graduated WASP. These agents still make up the old boy network within the CIA. Who do recruiters want now?

Well, the hottest thing at the CIA is the chance to snare a young Mormon. No, I'm not kidding. Mormons tend to have squeaky clean backgrounds and thanks to their work as third world missionaries, they often have one of the skills the CIA desperately needs these days, knowledge of a foreign language. Skilled linguists, along with business execs and scientists are replacing the backbone as a new generation of covert operatives that the CIA is sending out into a world where the Soviet Union is no longer the Big Enemy.

So you want to give up working in dad's drugstore and become a full fledged spy? You're in luck, pal. The CIA now has a job line you can call and request a brochure emphasizing careers with America's secret spy agency. Said careers include jobs as intelligence analysts, economists, and linguists. The slickly produced pamphlet will show pay scales you can expect, perks of the job, and even the CIA's scholastic reward program.

This latter program actually provides scholarships to apprentice CIA agents, usually in the last years of high school or early college. These perspective employees are given schooling in return for a couple years of work with the agency upon graduation. Think of it as a ROTC scholarship.

You go to school, you work as a spy for a while...

Successful employees can, of course, expect a longer term contract with the CIA.

Four programs currently make up the CIA's contribution to higher studies:

- Undergraduate Scholar Program. Requires enrollment in 4 or 5 year college program with 90 days on the job during the summer and some holiday breaks.
- Undergraduate Student Trainee Program. Similar to above but requires full time work on alternating semester of quarter basis for a minimum of 3 or 4 periods before graduation.
- Minority Undergraduate Studies Program. Unlike above you need to have completed one or two years of college prior to applying. Work is on the 90 day in the summer plan.
- Graduate Studies Program. You must be committed to attending graduate school after a summer internship with the Agency.

All the above programs pay a salary, and offers some sort of tuition assistance possibility plus your transportation and housing while in Washington. Successful candidates also accrue annual leave and can enroll in various health and life insurance plans on the same basis as full time agents.

The Agency requires a grade point maintenance and, of course, a polygraph exam before awarding any moneys.

Applicable majors, which vary depending on current Agency needs include:

Accounting and finance
Business Administration
Cartography/Geography
Computer Science
Economics
Engineering
Graphic Design
Hard Sciences
International Studies
Languages
Mathematics
Photo Sciences
Political Science
Printing/Photography
No Writers. How come nobody wants writers?

At any rate, you can get further information and applications for CIA scholarships and regular employment by contacting:
CIA Employment Center
POB 1255
Pittsburg, PA 15230.

The agency maintains a number of local personnel centers, but the main job line is found at 412-281-4009.

I should also point out that the CIA "neither confirms or denies" that their officers who teach at various colleges including the University of Miami, Boston University and the Rochester Institute of Technology also act as talent spotters, suggesting candidates for recruitment.

So-called "spotters", professors who are also rumored to be on the agency's payroll exist at other campuses to locate potential applicants.

A very pleasant and well produced brochure (probably why that "graphic arts category is there) detailing some of the agency's functions

and job categories can be had by contacting:
Central Intelligence Agency
Office of Public And Agency Information
Washington, D.C. 20505

On of the available publications, FACTBOOK ON INTELLIGENCE offers some depth on what the various departments and directors are responsible for.

There are even books designed to give prospective agents a leg up on the competition. CAREERS IN SECRET OPERATIONS, David Atlee Phillips, Stone Trail Press, Box 17320, Betheseda, MD 20817. Written by a former senior CIA operative who's now a newspaper editor, Mr. Phillips knows his stuff and gives a summation of how to become a federal intelligence officer in a variety of government agencies including the CIA.

The guide is more than a summary of job descriptions and application procedures. Mr. Phillips covers the ethics and morality of secret operations as well as the dilemmas they raise in a free and open society. He discusses affirmative action programs, clandestine careers, and opportunities for those without college degrees as well as the jargon of the intelligence agent.

Pleasant reading even if you're not looking to be the next DCI.

If you visit any bookstore you'll find books on how to take the SAT, ACT, LSAT, and MCAT for budding lawyers, doctors and scholars. It was only a matter of time until someone got around to the CIA.

Our old friend, John Quirk, a recognized authority on international intelligence agencies, has put out *the* definitive study guide for launching a CIA career. This is especially important as the agency receives more than 200,000 unsolicited job applications each year. In order to meet this competitive challenge and come out ahead, you need "top scores" on the entrance exam.

It is safe to say there is no other book quite like this in print. In John's book you'll find detailed information on application proce-dures, a complete model of the CIA entrance examination with example answers, a CIA glossary, an intelligence knowledge review, a thorough description of many CIA positions, as well as a brief history of the CIA and an overview of the intelligence community.

The forward to this book is written by William E. Colby, who should be familiar to anyone planning a career in the CIA. Mr. Quark has done an admirable job of telling us what the CIA really does, its internal organization, job titles arranged by category, how to apply for CIA positions, what the exams consist of, points to remember, job requirements, what it's like to work for the CIA, and even how and when to apply as well as what to expect from both the written and oral portions of the test.

The second part is a full length sample examination with questions from various CIA tests. The questions are a bit different than their average SAT cousins. Number 28 asks, "Would you be able to betray the trust of someone who has supplied you with valuable information if doing so was in the best interest of your country?"

Ahh, let's see – according to the guide the answer should be "although highly unlikely, you should be prepared to serve the best interests of your country."

Okay, I can live with that...

After an initial interview CIA applicants face the aptitude test, as well as a 17-page personal history statement, an extensive background check, and a series of medical and psychological tests including the dreaded polygraph.

John's book also summarizes the most asked questions about the CIA chronology, institutions offering intelligence courses and careers in other intelligence agencies, for those of you that just don't appeal to the CIA.

CIA ENTRANCE EXAMINATION is an Arco book published by Simon and Schuster, New York, New York. ISBN 0-13-133851-X. $14.95.

John is also working on another guide to the Drug Enforcement Administration exam.

Not to be outdone, the United States Army

Intelligence and Security Command (INSCOM) is also happy to have your interest in employment with their agency. INSCOM is one of the few agencies that employs civilians along with military personnel.

If you are interested in a career rubbing shoulders with army spies, contact:

Civilian Personnel Office
Recruitment and Placement
Attention: ANFB-CPF
Sharon Kennedy
U. S. Army Fort Belvoir
Ft. Belvoir, Virginia 22060

The civilian personnel office at Fort Belvoir is a one-stop information center that can give you information on vacancies available in these areas and will be happy to send you information on applying for one of the many interesting careers in army intelligence. Phone number for the center is 703-780-4682.

The US Army Intelligence and Security Command requires all personnel to secure and maintain a top secret security clearance. This process takes approximately six to nine months.

While the work is subject to the usual hiring freezes, budget cuts and bureaucratic shifts, the beautifully produced brochure called A WORLD OF CAREERS, is great reading and provides career decision information in fields you may have never considered before such as ammunition management, ammunition surveillance, quality assurance, intelligence or just serving as a librarian.

Foreign assignments are possible and you can expect military leave with full pay for annual reserve training with liberal retirement plans and optional "survival benefits."

INSCOM promises a high degree of job security resulting from a system of nationwide placement rights if it becomes necessary to "realign the work force" as well as the opportunity for overseas environment and two and a half to five weeks paid vacation annually depending on length of service.

Join the army, see the world.

WILL WORK FOR FOOD

Career Transition Division POB 9704, Arlington, VA 22209 is a CIA talent bank that "facilitates the transition of those leaving the CIA service". They operate as a head hunting agency, matching employers needs with the qualifications of the candidates.

All requests are confidential and you can expect to find such professionals as:

Telecommunications Specialists
Computer Programmers
Analysts
Security Professionals
Linguists with hard-to-find language skills
Logisticians
Graphic artists
Operations officers

The service is free to all concerned.

DATABASES

There are a couple of extremely efficient tools for compiling information on the CIA or even intelligence in general. The first, sold by Public Information Research, Box 5199, Arlington, Virginia 22005, offers a bargain $49.00 database (IBM format) that provides 98,000 citations covering more than 275 intelligence-related books and periodicals. Topics covered include the international intelligence community, political elites, Latin America, U.S foreign policy, big business, and assassination theories.

Now known as NAMEBASE this product was once called SPYBASE and has been praised by everything from the *Whole Earth Review* to the *New York Times* as a source for intelligence topics. The program permits quick searching on key words with most responses containing the author, title, publication date and page number of each reference, allowing the user to request specific copies of citations from the book mentioned or from public information research itself which also offers a photocopy/fax service of every source listed in the database.

Another choice is CIABASE, an IBM and Macintosh compatible computerized database strictly on the CIA and includes a mass of information. More than 5.5 MB of information from 400 sources are categorized by subject in thousands of annotated entries.

CIABASE is searchable by a single key word, word combination, date or country. CIABASE is packaged on three disks with their own built-in stuffer to allow maximum information density. CIABASE is compiled by an ex-CIA agent and is an intriguing source of information on this secret agency. CIABASE is $99.00 from CIABASE, Box 5022, Herndon, Virginia 22070.

I highly recommend this as a research tool or just for intelligence browsing.

A JOINT EFFORT

KGB/CIA WORLD FACTBOOK by the Central Intelligence Agency, Tiger Software 800 Douglas Entrance, Executive Tower, 7th floor, Coral Gables, FL 33134. A computerized edition of the CIA World Factbook combined with the KGB version.

Government statistics, political evaluations, industrial information, travel schedules, trade data, and so on from the world's two largest information gatherers.

See the world from two different points of view.

THE FBI

Although not technically a spy agency, the Federal Bureau of Investigation is responsible for catching spies operating within the United States and its territories.

It would be hard to deny the FBI has made some giant steps forward since the days when every agent was an attorney and required to wear black shoes and white socks.

On the other hand certain recent, "developments" such as the various biographies of Mr. Hoover have left less than a pleasant pall on the Agency. So, without actually hiring BBD&O to spruce up it's image, the department has gone through a small Glasnost period of it's own.

For the first time in history anyone (anyone with fourteen bucks, that is) can subscribe to the FBI's inhouse newsletter – FBI LAW ENFORCEMENT BULLETIN. Order direct from our old friend the Superintendent of documents, Government Printing Office, Washington, D.C. 20402. Ask for list ID FBIEB.

Not exactly PEOPLE MAGAZINE, FLIEB is a slick, magazine formatted semi-technical newsletter covering what ever is on the FBI's collective mind. Recent issues included details of the new laser radar device under devolpement by a national labratory (LIAR), how use video to anaylze stress in a subject, current supreme court cases affecting the agency, and book reviews.

Really a nicely done publication with useful information for investigators, legal types and clever criminals.

Besides it looks so neat on the coffee table...

FBI FILES

UNLOCKING THE FILES OF THE FBI: A Guide To Its Records and Classification System. Gerald Haines and David Langbart, Scholarly Resources Inc., 104 Greenhill Ave., Wilmington, DE 19805. A comprehensive guide to the types of documents the FBI has on file, where they are located and how to access them.

A complete description of each of the 277 different classifications the bureau uses to organize its records, how much material is stored in each section and a complete guide to accessing the files is included.

U.S. Department of Justice
Federal Bureau of Investigation

Conducting Research in FBI Records

Research Unit
Office of Public Affairs
Federal Bureau of Investigation

Seventh Edition

CONDUCTING RESEARCH IN FBI RECORDS, Research Unit, Department Of Public Affairs, US Department Of Justice, Federal Bureau of Investigation, Washington, D.C. 20535.

After spending many, many hours and dollars complying with, fighting, sanatizing and generally cussing the flood of requests for information opened by the Freedom Of Information Act, the FBI seems to have decided it's time for the Willow to bend in the proverbial wind.

This publication details exactly what information will be released and how to approach the FBI with a request for any records. A list of central records system classifications helps narrow your choices as well as suggest new categories for late night reading (number 31, for instance covers anything to do with the White Slave Act and 65 deals with espionage).

In fact the agency has gotten so many requests for certain files that it has grouped them together in an appendix or two and offered them to the public. Some selections are tantalizing to say the least. For instance you can order:

—All 5 files on Ma Barker
—The 46 crucial files assembled on Lucille Ball
—6 selections on the East Coast Homophile Organization
—10,984 entries on the Weather Underground (including the SDS)
—144 inside looks at the Duke and Duchess of Windsor
—*221,999* files on the assassination of JFK
—Or my personal favorite: 9,164 "interesting cases"

In fact, the first person who tries to sell a book by just binding together the interesting cases into one.... Never mind, never mind.

Forget I said that.

THE KGB

A statue bites the dust in Red Square

The Lubyanka

In December of 1917 Lenin founded the Cheka, short for the All Russian Extraordinary Commission for Combating Counterrevolution, Speculation, Sabotage, and Misconduct in Office. As shown by its name the KGB's precursor was given fairly broad powers with the emphasis on economic watchdogging. Along with removing their political opponents, the Bolsheviks, this early KGB was thrown into action against speculators, profiteers, strike organizers, and other would-be saboteurs/capitalists.

When Stalin came to power he renamed the Cheka the NKVD, and shifted the emphasis to anti-sabotage and espionage.

It's hard for westerners to understand the immensely important role of the KGB in the Soviet system. KGB was the equivalent of the CIA, the FBI, and perhaps the Pentagon combined. The KGB employed approximately a half million people in various "directorates" or divisions who handled intelligence, counterintelligence, domestic security, protection of its borders and electronic eavesdropping.

"For 74 years the KGB was more than a spy agency. In American terms it was the CIA, the Federal Bureau of Investigation, the National Security Agency, the Border Patrol, and other intelligence units all rolled into one. To the Soviet people it was the jackboot on the stairs, the instrument of terror that could, in an instant, pluck people from the safety of their homes and send them to some Siberian gulag. The KGB, especially under Stalin, was truly the ministry of fear."–Author David Wise, "Closing Down the KGB", *New York Times Magazine*, November 24, 1991.

Even these impressive figures don't summarize the scope of the KGB. A retired KGB Colonel, Yaroslab Karpovich, admitted that each good agent ran 8 – 10 informers, which means that the Soviet total of informers alone would be approximately 2.9 million people with the half million regular KGB employees.

The KGB arrested 19 million citizens of whom 7 million were shot or died in the gulags in the worst years of terror under the former Soviet leaders. A number of KGB defectors have pointed out over the years that virtually all Russian diplomats had at least some sort of tie with the KGB if they weren't actual agents in place. The GRU, on the other hand, tended to put its agents to work as Aeroflot employees.

Join Aeroflot, join the GRU and see the world...

The KGB was without a doubt the largest secret police and espionage organization in the world. It has/had its own armor, artillery and naval vessels, as well as 300,000 troops directly under its command. The KGB had a major influence in, if not actually running Tass, the Soviet equivalent of United Press, and handled the bugging and general surveillance of all outside visitors to the Soviet Union. Even the most illiterate tourist could figure out his "tour guide" was employed by the KGB.

Recent KGB defectors have admitted that one of the primary, if not the primary target of the KGB was, of course, America. One defector, code named Mikhail, says agents spent their time searching for local officials who might pass on tidbits they had acquired from their contacts with the US.

"There's no way for me to overemphasize the importance of the KGB battling the CIA in those years," he says. "The whole life of the service was directed towards this end - harming the US, checking its policy and getting information on it, penetrating its structure, and discrediting it. The US, was known inside the KGB as GP, Russian initials for Main Enemy.

China, the next biggest concern, was known as GP2."

THE KGB TODAY

What's happened to the KGB in the last few years? A number of interesting things, depending on who you talk to and more importantly, who you believe. The Soviet Union's last KGB's spy master, Leonid Shebarshin, says that the KGB lost not only the cold war but more importantly the war of secrets. Mr. Shebarshin, head of overseas intelligence for more than two years until he was sacked by former President Mikhail Gorbachov, claims he regretted the cost of the cold war, and that the KGB was betrayed by many defectors. The agency simply could not keep up with the well-funded services of their competitors.

For particular mention he singles out the German services including West Germany's BND and admits the French were pretty good, too. However, "the United States' CIA deserves special mention; enormous money, enormous scope, enormous drive – that brings results."

Notably excluded from his praise was the British Secret Service that has provided Soviet intelligence with some of its best double agents. Spies such as George Blake, Kim Philby, Guy Burgess, and Donald Maclean that not only damaged British security but also some of its closest allies in the 50's and 60's.

There's little doubt that the KGB suffered under the era of Glasnost and Perestroika. After the KBG-backed coup to overthrow Gorbachov failed, the KGB suffered enormous losses in both scope and manpower. The Russian leaders decided the KGB as it existed, had to be abolished. The new organization should deal only with intelligence and counterintelligence, not border security, executive protection, government communication, and bugging of dissidents.

Immediately thereafter, large hunks of the KGB empire were lopped off. It lost 240,00 border guards, several military divisions, and 85,000 troops.

Public statements said the new KGB was shooting for a staff of 35,000–45,000 personnel.

There are rumors that the "new KGB," the Agency for Federal Security, is quietly rebuilding its strength and finding new roles, or in some cases reopening old roles, for its existence. Some western analysts felt the KGB had completely collapsed when a flurry of secret KGB files began appearing on the world marketplace. A KGB colonel actually toured the United States peddling files including some top secret files on Philby and other traitors, although several people to whom the files were offered said the asking prices were too steep.

In a series of interviews with the Russian press after Bakatin was fired, he warned that the KGB had really not changed that much and the organization had not gone through much "ideological Perestroika" since the coup.

"I don't consider that our special services have lost the danger for our citizens," he said, referring to the KGB.

Ironically, Bakatin did provide one of the real leaks from the KGB files: he handed over plans of bugging devices planted in the new US Embassy building in Moscow.

One "new" direction that the KGB is obviously taking is summarized by Yebgeny Primakov, who became head of the Soviet foreign intelligence after the failed coup attempt. His new and improved agency will focus on economic intelligence gathering (ah, some people have substituted the word "stealing" here) rather than military and political information that they sought in earlier days.

In November, 1991, the Supreme Soviet voted to have the KGB Six Directorate establish a Center for Combating Economic Sabotage. This was followed by a January 26 presidential decree that permits both KGB and Interior Ministry agents to "enter without hindrance the premises" of any organization engaged in economic activity. The agents are free to carry out unlimited searches, to seize "samples" of goods for quality control, to read bookkeeping ledgers, and to require from management and staff "written explanations relating to the activities under scrutiny."

One should note that foreign firms are not exempted from these provisions.

In contemporary Soviet slang the term "sabo-

tage" is used loosely to describe a variety of economic crimes, including speculation, hoarding, and the delaying of goods from the factory or farm to market.

Surprisingly, these lofty goals almost mimic the original directions of Lenin when he founded the Cheka, long before Felix Dzerinsky changed it into the more modern KGB.

So in one respect the KGB, or rather the Russian Ministry of Security and Interior Affairs, as it's now known, seems to have come full circle from the days of its inception. However, that's not the entire story of the KGB. There have been a number of changes, crooks and quirks, in the strange saga of the largest intelligence agency in the world. Some, no one in his right mind would have predicted a few short years ago.

Admittedly a number of these changes have come because of the sudden influx of out-of-work spies (one wonders how long unemployment lasts in Russia these days). Some of them who have moved on to work with their former allies such as Bulgaria and probably Iran and Iraq and may have taken a few little things, say an atom bomb or two, along with them. Other agents, both still actively employed by the new ministry as well as some creative unemployed workers, anxious to try their hands at the new capitalism, have done some astonishing things:

- KGB Major Andrei Oligov revealed recently in a television interview that the KGB wants to sell information of an "economic character" to companies engaged in foreign trade, (we call that industrial espionage). He also volunteered such services as checking on the credit worthiness of foreign partners and providing market information for new state firms, joint ventures, cooperatives, and, frankly, anyone else with the cash to pay for it.

Spying on business rivals should, after all, be something the KGB should do rather well having spent its entire existence spying on one thing or another. The speculation is that this new Dun and Bradstreet of the Far East is also in it to help flog up the KGB's dwindling cash resources.

Major Oligov pointed out that all contracts so far included "gentlemen's agreements."

This makes me feel better; how about you?

If you are interested in hiring the KGB to be your competitive intelligence experts, write them at: The KGB, 2 Vzerdhinsky Street, Moscow, or call them at Moscow 9210762.

You might want to ask for Andrei...

- The KGB has also announced they are going to back a publishing program during the 1990s. Versiya is a newspaper that is "designed to familiarize readers with various aspects of KGB activity and to discuss the problems and changes in its work."

To encourage readers, they are offering prizes. To whit, 500 rubles for slogans that are chosen for encouraging workers to cooperate with law enforcement, and a grand prize of 1500 rubles for "finding a missing person."

Find them? Hell, why not? After all, we put them there...

- Like the FBI, the KGB is allowing the public to subscribe to its in-house, up to now secret journal, Rabochaya Tirbuna. The 10-page journal roughly translated as USSR KGB Digest, had its first "general public" edition on the 45th anniversary of the end of World War II. It now appears on a regular basis.

Most of the articles seem to be based on files from the KGB archives and are intended to show the "exceptional devotion to the motherland and high patriotism of the KGB during World War II."

- The KGB, for the first time in history, has opened the doors of Lubyanka, their headquarters and infamous prison where, according to the very people who ran it, one million people have died and three million others have been "interrogated."

The Lubyanka now has a museum with a number of spy toys and tools such as camera watches and knives hidden in various things, and provides tour guides who are under orders to tell tourists as many "spy stories" as they'd like to hear.

The KGB, and the Russian military has also turned to selling long sought after materiel to both the US government and private US firms. Reports from a well-placed source indicate that a number of C5 cargo planes landed in a protected area at Dulles Airport in the not too distant past, stuffed to the gills with the latest in Russian tanks, anti-tank missiles, and other exotic weaponry. Russian night vision devices are now widely available in the United States from a number of different suppliers. The KGB has also offered access to certain top secret files such as those dealing with American POWs interrogated by the KGB during the Vietnam War and the aforementioned plans to bug the US Embassy in Moscow.

- Taking a direct lesson from the United States, the KGB has installed a kind of FOIA Section. Known as the Public Affairs and Press Bureau, it will handle requests submitted in writing, by letter or by fax on an individual basis. The concept here is to make files available to private citizens or organizations that were spied upon by the KGB.

One should point out that each request is forwarded to the proper agency for action. Like the original FOIA requests in the US, the bureaucracy refuses to give an estimate of response time and points out there are many variables that can't be foreseen, making the satisfaction quotient a little less than it should be. For further information contact the chief of the Press Bureau, Yuri Kobaladze, Kolpachny, Pereuloka, 11 Moscow, Russia, or give them a call at Moscow 923-6213, Fax 923-8191.

- As things get even more bizarre, the KGB Foreign Intelligence Veterans Association, a group formed to help KGB agents sell stories to Hollywood and book publishers, has signed an exclusive multimedia pact with a major Hollywood agent, Entertainment and Communications Holding Organization (ECHO) of West Hollywood. The KGB spies are promising "astounding new material that will shatter myths and create new controversies". The agents have said there are plans in the works to develop movies, TV miniseries and publishing projects from the unholy alliance.

Some of the inside stories up for sale include the assassination of Leon Trotsky, how the KGB actually ran Britain's five Cambridge "apostles", and tales of how it handled some famous American double agents like Kim Philby.

Anatoly Privalov, Deputy Chairman of the Foreign Intelligence Veterans Association, claims they have 500 members who are now ready to sell their best secrets to the highest bidder after refusing offers from the CIA.

Many veterans are suffering financial hardship and the Association plans to open a club where they can have a beer or even drink whiskey, "like the CIA."

The concept seems to be working. Two well known TV producers are already suing each other over the "exclusive" TV rights based on the KGB files on such subjects as the Cuban Missile Crisis and various cold war spy tales. Robert Halmi, Sr., the TV producer who paid a record nine million dollars for the television rights to Scarlet, the sequel to *Gone With the Wind,* announced he had signed an exclusive agreement with the KGB to produce a CBS television series based on the material from its archives. He claims the files will "set America on its collective ear."

RHI, another production firm underwritten by 20th Century Fox, also claims exclusive rights based on six months of 75 trips to Moscow for some of the same stories.

The problem seems to be the production companies are dealing with different agencies and, much as in normal Hollywood affairs, nobody is sure who actually has the rights to what. The group also has sold a number of books to Crown Publishing and Yale University Press as well as French, and reportedly, English publishing companies.

- In what may be the most astounding deviation from the normal shroud of secrecy, the KGB has formed its own public relations department with our old pal Andrei Oligob as the head or, at least, the head flak.

Mr. Oligob says, "Times have changed and we are assuming new roles under new conditions."

It is true the KGB does have a slight public relations problem at home where they carried out Stalin's orders to murder millions of Soviet citizens and pioneered new methods of torture and assassination.

In fact, the Public Relations Department (KGB) went so far as to pay $56,000 (reportedly) to BBD&O Worldwide, one of the largest advertising and public relations agencies in the world. The concept was to provide advertisements and press releases, smoothing the KGB's image and "disassociating it from its embarrassing history of repression and lawlessness."

Give the KGB a more friendly image.

BBD&O, after the initial workup, was ready to present the KGB with a complete budget and marketing plan for a complete facial makeover when some wags in the Los Angeles BBD&O office after, one would assume, a three martini lunch, began circulating their own versions of what the KGB ad campaign should look like.

The ideas put forth included "this Scud's for you", and "a kinder guy named Boris, how long are you going to hold that over our heads, we like to spy and it shows." And one of my personal favorites, an ad showing the Lubyanka, "last year, an unspeakable dungeon. This year a world class wine cellar."

The KGB canceled its contract shortly after the phony ads began appearing.

This department of the KGB did, however, recently host the first MISS KGB contest. Besides the traditional beauty judging the women competed in "cooking, shooting, dancing, karate and applying makeup."

I'd like to see those folks at the Miss America thing follow these guys into the 20th century.

• A classified ad recently appeared in The International Herald Tribune reading, "former KGB agent seeks employment in similar field. Tel Paris 1-…

KGB BOOKS

KGB, The Inside story, Christopher Andrew and Oleg Gordievsky, Harper Collins, $29.95. This book is a combination of the memories and files of Oleg Gordievsky, a KGB officer who, after working many years undercover for British Intelligence, defected to the West in 1985. Mr. Andrews researched into various archives and files.

This book is being criticized by some historians as primarily a rehash of already known events from World War II onward, but for those who do not consider themselves espionage historians, it is an interesting, well documented look into the world's largest spy agency especially with regard to the use of double agents and recruitments in the United States and Britain. A number of anecdotes demonstrate or raise questions about General Eisenhower and Winston Churchill's acts during the closing years of World War II.

The most shocking revelation in this book is that Harry Hopkins, Franklin D. Roosevelt's closest wartime aide, was a Soviet Agent, even if an "unwitting one", which raised dark questions and created quite a sensation when the book was first published.

The notoriety died fairly quickly as a number of historians and investigative reporters came out to say the accusations were circumstantial at best and not proved in the text.

Whether true or not, the book itself is a fascinating and well documented look at the inside exploits of an agency that has never opened itself to much coverage.

KGB: MASTERS OF THE SOVIET UNION, PETER DERRIABIN AND T. H. BAGLEY, Hippocrene. Derriabin was a Russian agent who defected to the West in 1954 and collaborated with political scientist Bagley in a rather chilling expose that shows the ruthless infrastructure and workings of the Soviet power.

The primary point of this book seems to be that the Soviet Communist Party never exercised control over the KGB (the way it was seen in the West), rather the KGB dominated the highest echelons of party membership and bureaucracy.

The authors literally take the reader inside KGB headquarters in order to demonstrate how agency spread its long arm into offices, farms, factories, collectives and local police. This book is well documented with references to materials from both Soviet and US sources.

One of the things that never ceases to amaze me is how government documents cannot be copyrighted, after all we pay for their production. A good example is when a disgruntled SR-71 pilot, or perhaps mechanic, "borrowed" a copy of the flight instruction manual and then sold it to a publisher.

Remember this plane was one of the most closely held secrets of the 60's and 70's, now you can buy the instruction book...

More recently a member, or former member of the KGB walked off with a couple of training manuals, sold them to Jim Shortt (director of the International Bodyguard Association), who passed it on to Paladin Press.

KGB ALPHA TEAM TRAINING MANUAL HOW THE SOVIETS TRAINED FOR PERSONAL COMBAT, ASSASSINATION, AND SUBVERSION. Paladin Press. No author...

This book deciphers the relationship between the KGB, GRU, MVD and other "special groups", shows who is taking over the duties of the KGB today, training methods, special programs, weapons handling, and killing techniques.

A few pages are missing from the original transcript (too sensitive?) but the rest of the book is a hands-on guide for training, fighting, attacking an enemy in position, close combat, withdrawing your wounded, slitting throats and other necessary skills.

Much of the manual seems to have been borrowed from an earlier Spetsnaz training publication, and many of the techniques parallel our own Special Forces Techniques, but this is the world's first Western translation of an important work.

SOVIET NOMENLATURA ISBN 0-88702-030-5

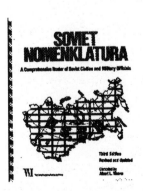

SOVIET NOMENKLATURA: A Comprehensive Roster of Soviet Civilian and Military Officials, Washington Institute Press, Suite 300, 1015 18th St. NW, Washington, DC 20036. For years the publishers of Who's Who have made a very good living from compiling names and short biographies of the movers and shakers in the United States broken down into various geographical locations and professional groups. I've always suspected Who's Who sells most of its press run to the people included in the book itself, "here, oh geez, I just happen to have a copy of Who's Who in Plumbing sitting here on the coffee table.

Have I shown you my entry?"

Albert L. Weeks has produced the Who's Who of Russia. Information contained herein came from the Washington Institute, an independent non-profit and education research organization which examines current and upcoming issues with particular attention to "ethical implications."

Mr. Weeks is known as an authority on Soviet politics and is a former political analyst for the United States Department of State. He taught at Columbia and New York Universities and is the author of a number of books on Soviet international affairs. He obviously decided that a guide to who controls what in the ex-Soviet Union and new Russia from the Soviet Space Program to the Cultural Fund, not to mention most high ranking military and KGB officers, was a necessity for anyone who watches CNN on a regular basis or reads spy novels.

There's not much style in this book. It's strictly a biographical listing of names, birthdates, and offices held. Some of the entries are a bit esoteric such as "Gellert, Natalya V. (1953-) tractor driver". This book would be very useful if you were writing about Russia or feel the need to hire a KGB agent or Russian tractor driver.

ALL MOSCOW INFORMATION YEARBOOK Shapolsky Publishing (Moscow-New York) ($161.95) ISBN 5-7110-0004-7. 782 pages of businesses, services, government and party offices and institutions in Moscow.

Street maps, photos and phone numbers. Arranged in alphabetical order.

The Cyrillic alphabet...

YELLOW PAGES MOSCOW an English language phone directory of 27,000+ addresses phone and fax numbers. $45 plus $4.50 shipping from Marvol USA, 1925 Century Park East, 10th floor, Los Angeles, CA 90099.

THE ULTIMATE FIRE SALE

The following article was written, at my request, by a well known network journalist who spent several years in Russia during, and after the breakup of the Soviet Union.

"John" had called me to discuss his luck at finding a three room apartment for a bit less than $80 (in American currency) a month in one of Moscow's more fashionable districts as well as his growing concern at just exactly what else was available for anyone with "hard" money.

Getting a piece of the peace dividend is easy to do in Russia these days. A quick visit to a local sidewalk kiosk or to the myriad flea markets is likely to present the casual shopper with unlimited opportunities to purchase previously restricted military and espionage technological goods on the relatively open market.

The kiosks in Moscow are growing in numbers daily, and aside from the ubiquitous bootleg liquor – bottled and mislabeled in Poland – these kiosks stock a large variety of goods and are the best way to gauge what is generally available. As early as December 1991, even before the formal dissolution of the Soviet Union, night vision binoculars were available at kiosks bunched across the street from the Kiev railway station. The field glasses with the distinctive green glow could be had for as little as the ruble equivalent of US $80. Night vision goggles attached to a tank driver's helmet, the kind that flip down,

were at the Oktyabarskaya metro station kiosks in May and sold for $110. These are just a couple of examples of the thousands of items suddenly available now that ownership of goods is no longer clearly defined and authority is decidedly weakened.

Interested in finding out who is calling you before you pick up the phone? An entrepreneurial former Lithuanian KGB man has modified imported telephones with a red L.E.D. readout on the phone's face that displays the number of the caller and is coded to tell you if the call is being made from a public, private, or official phone. Call screening was always a favorite phone accessory of the Soviet secret services and now it's popularly available in kiosks for as little as $30. The drawback is that this feature only works in the former Soviet Union. The Lithuanian phone also stores all numbers of phone calls that have come in and stores outgoing call numbers as well...

No need to miss that all-important mole call if you happen to be in the bathroom or sleeping off a vodka hangover.

Low-tech items such as radio tank helmets, military chronograph watches, cosmonaut flight suits, leather field map cases, Afghanistan war desert fatigues and desert caps, multipower monocular and binocular sets with handsome carrying cases, and any number of dual-purpose camping/warring items are available either at department stores (such as TSVUM on Novy Arbat Street - formerly Kalininsky Prospect) or on the streets of the Old Arbat, where young, hustling entrepreneurs will cull from their stock on hand or special order (by calling their friends' friends and paying appropriate bribes) for you. Prices vary from sucker to sucker, but the rule to remember is that nearly everything is for sale and available.

Everything indeed means everything, and therein lies a problem. Not only are foreigners and locals buying up the fun stuff, they are also picking-up items that might or should be regulated or controlled. Plutonium, for example, which is not only being sold to high bidders, but is occasionally also being delivered like pizzas (a recent shipment out of the ex-USSR was intercepted at an Austrian border before the transaction was completed. The hot items were improperly stored for transport and were kept in the trunk of the delivering automobile).

Two nuclear warheads are said to have made their way to Iran from Kazakhstan and there is a brisk trade in Red Mercury between Middle East arms purchasing representatives and ex-Soviets, as well as Eastern Europeans. Red Mercury may turn out to be a red herring of a product, but many claim that it is a low-tech necessary component used in detonating of the nuclear fissionable material used in bombs. If it's a US or Israeli hoax, as some claim, to flush out arms merchants and potential terrorists, then it is a profitable one since an ounce of the reddish liquid metal can command around US $150,000. If the stuff is for real, then there is plenty of the easily transportable, potentially lethal product floating around uncontrolled.

But it isn't merely the goods of mass destruction that are on the market. A good used AK-47 is an easy item to pick-up. Even American-made weapons used in the Afghan war are available in the former southern republics. Stinger missiles are available to the highest bidder and pricing starts around $60-$70,000 for the sophisticated airship sinker. It is a bit dangerous to go straight to the source of these rockets' ownership since Mujahedin leaders are known to be openly

hostile towards non-Muslim westerners, but there are plenty of middlemen in both the western parts of Pakistan or near the border regions of Uzbekistan.

Tashkent is a good place to start.

Of course, getting to and out of Russia is still a bit of a hassle, expense, and official inconvenience. But you can cut the travel and get the goods by visiting some of the Soviet shopping and defense outlets still remaining in occupied territories. For low-tech goods, choose from any of the Eastern and Central European countries where the troops have left: watches, uniforms, banners, small handguns, knifes, and other bric-a-brac. Poland, Czechoslovakia, and Hungary offer the convenience of shopping in what can also be considered a tourist-friendly environment. Since many of the sales of goods in these countries is monopolized by a Russian or Ukrainian dominated Mafia, they, too, will be able to special order, but you need to allow between 4 and 8 weeks for reliable delivery. And all payment is made in cash with a very strict no-refund policy. It's also wise to make any large or expensive purchases in the company of big friends.

East Germany still has Soviet/Commonwealth bases which should be considered factory-direct outlets.

It isn't just the goods produced during the cold war that are for sale – the cold warriors themselves can be picked up for a song. A bankrupt ideology and tightening resources strain the justification for loyalty. Even those who remain fiercely loyal to their organization or bureaucracy have been asked to change allegiance from the Soviet Union's central authority to the individual republics' newly established military or intelligence groups. Not the best way to maintain morale. Add to this the one commodity that can still command a high price – intelligence – and a bunch of clock punchers who are losing their relative privileges and you have the all the preconditions required in finding secrets for sale.

Some people do it in a semi-legitimate fashion, as with Igor Prelin's group of retired KGB officials who offer, for a fee, to get you the journalistically appropriate information that western news organizations so desperately seek. A recent offer to an American television network offered to find an American defector who was kept in a Russian prison. The price? $10,000.

The network declined, partly because of ethical problems, mainly because the price was too high. The group tries to get around the ethical problems that western news media might have by having formed its own media section, whereby they can use television cameras of their own to record the interesting material, then sell the footage for whatever the market will bear. Fewer established ethical problems with purchasing footage.

Prelin's organization also helped bring forward Oleg Nechiporenko, the KGB man who Oleg Kalugin accused of having interrogated American soldiers in Vietnam long after the war was declared over. Nechiporenko denied Kalugin's accusations, but did go on to tease the American public by saying that he had exclusive information concerning Lee Harvey Oswald. It turned out that Nechiporenko was one of the three Soviet embassy officials in Mexico who had contact with Oswald just prior to the Kennedy assassination. Nechiporenko has since sold the film and book rights to the story through a Hollywood agency.

Not all secrets are for sale. Some are being given away. To the United States, for instance, as when the interim head of the KGB, Bakatin, gave Ambassador Robert Strauss plans showing where and what type of listening devices had been installed throughout the new compound of the US embassy. Bakatin's move was highly publicized and is still gravely criticized, but he has yet to be taken to task for actions many consider seditioUS

Many of these individuals operated out of the Lubyanka headquarters of the KGB.

Lubyanka is a huge city block full of a building with infamous cellars wherein beatings and interrogations are alleged to have taken place. The square onto which Lubyanka faces used to be called Dzerzhinsky, named after the Polish aristocrat "Iron Felix," who established the Soviet secret service. The huge statue of Iron Felix that stood on a pedestal in the middle of the square came down immediately after the failed coup of August 1991. Cranes came to lift the enormous statue away and it was eventually placed in the back gardens of the Central House of Artists, across from Gorky Park, where he joined other Soviet statues that had been toppled.

Despite the user-friendly look of the square today (across from the country's largest toy store, "Detsky Mir" - or "Children's World"), Lubyanka is still feared and the sidewalk that runs in front of it is nearly always vacant, passersby going out of their way not to walk in front of it, such is the power and the fear that the KGB had developed.

KGB headquarters has attempted to open up a bit, however. For $35, tourists can take a limited guided tour through the building, with a small exhibit of their museum included. No earth shattering surprises here, and the exhibit tends to dwell on the glories of the traditional work of law enforcement: the success of border patrolling activities, the fight against narcotics and terrorism, devices and methods of tracking down criminals, etc. It's a bit like walking through reruns of "The FBI" with Efraim Zimbalist, Jr. No insight into the midnight knocks, the methods of torture, of eavesdropping techniques or successes. All the clandestine stuff remains so – unless you just happen to meet a former KGB agent (they are plentiful, with an estimate that nearly one-in-three Soviets had at one point or another collaborated). A fortuitous meeting lubricated with the right amount of alcohol (vodka being the preference) and stoked with cigarettes and the stories begin to ooze.

What a loose-lipped agent will say is that despite the current chaos, things at the agency are still tight. That pictures of Iron Felix and Lenin still hang in Lubyanka and that the leadership is still committed to doing a world class job of espionage. The charge of the agency may be a bit different today, with more emphasis on industrial espionage in the west than ever before, but that the basic goal of the agency remains the same.

The politics, economy, and the people are all going through a great transition. When the shakeout comes, and most expect one in a few years at best, there will be another period of defection, opportunity, and short-term chaos. Those who see clearly when the dust is flying are usually clear-sighted enough to disappear when the dust settles.

—*"John Smith" for Lee Lapin*

INTELLIGENCE LITERATURE

The largest collection of intelligence books, literature and printed paraphernalia on the business of intelligence is located at the CIA headquarters in Langley, Virginia.

The bad news is you ain't going to get in to see it unless you gotta uncle who's a station chief.

The second largest collection is probably that owned by one Walter Pforzheimer.

This is a private collection and again don't plan on perusing it unless you happen to be a personal friend of Mr. Pforzheimer's.

The third largest collection, at least in the US, and very probably the world is the Russell J. Bowen collection which is physically housed at Lauinger Library, Georgetown University, Washington. DC.

This collection, amassed and donated by Mr. Bowen, includes some 15,000 titles and is available to the public, although access is becoming slightly more restricted due to thefts from the collection.

Mr. Bowen himself worked as a psychological warfare officer prior to WWII, ran the first news service in post war Germany, spent 35 years as a strategic intelligence analyst with several MOS's including Intelligence Staff Officer and Area Intelligence Officer. He was first executive officer and then commander of the 421st Strategic Intelligence Detachment, went back to school and re-emerged to work on a number of intelligence projects relating to the USSR and the middle east as well as working at a number of other intelligence-oriented jobs and posts over the years.

He ended up at the Defense Intelligence Agency and then went to the CIA. Mr. Bowen, not your typical under-achiever, also got his degree in chemical engineering and worked with guided missiles, chemical weapons and biological warfare, to name just a few areas. He owns dozens of patents and was a member of a host of scientific and professional associations.

Mr. Bowen also had several hobbies (when did the man sleep?) including book collecting. After witnessing the horrors of Buchenwald he sought to understand how a society could permit such events and began to collect books on Nazi and Soviet society. He later expanded this to include books on intelligence, covert action, and espionage.

Mr. Bowen died shortly before this book was written but his legacy lives on. The joy of the Bowen collection is that you don't have to visit Washington to benefit by it. The National Intelligence Book Center markets an electronic database of the BOWEN COLLECTION.

This database lives on IBM discs in a special hi-speed compressed format that automatically expands on use. The database is a researcher's dream because one can look up more than 8 thousand (soon to include the entire collection) books by using thousands of key words.

These key words have boolean operators such as AND and OR, allowing you to type in CIA and Casey to get books that deal with both subjects. The OR operator expands the search to bring up books that deal with either subject.

Half of the entries contain brief outlines of the books with a listing of hundreds of names and references mentioned in the text but not always in the index of the book in question.

The database is divided into the subgroups intelligence, which includes all aspects of collection, processing, analysis and miscellany, security which encompasses counterintelligence, counterespionage, deception and state security, covert activities, covert action, guerrilla warfare, international terrorism, secret weapons programs, international intrigue, escape and evasion, special operations and special forces.

Lastly are the interdisciplinary reference texts which includes indexes, bibliographies and anthologies.

The base is user friendly and allows the user to isolate works of interest or simply browse for entertainment and educational purposes. $400.

The National Institute of Justice offers a CD-ROM database (IBM) which boasts the same amount of information as *1,000* floppy dics with citations and abstracts of more than 118,000 books, reports, journal articles, grants, government documents, programs and descriptions and evaluations.

This $295 disc is available by calling 800-851-3420 and includes numerous references to computer security, espionage, and intelligence. Most of the documents referenced are available thru inter-library loan programs.

Intelligence, like most other professions, comes complete with its own language. In fact, the intelligence community, due to the need for secrecy as well as the necessity of concisely expressing a wide range of unusual activities, probably utilizes more jargon than any other profession.

The National Intelligence Book Center now offers a digital dictionary authored by Leo D. Carl of over*16,000* intelligence and related terms with full definitions. This massive undertaking represents the most comprehensive listing of intelligence technology ever assembled.

Mr. Carl worked with Air Force Intelligence and the CIA to produce several in-house dictionaries and now brings his expertise to the general arena. IBM based, $499.95.

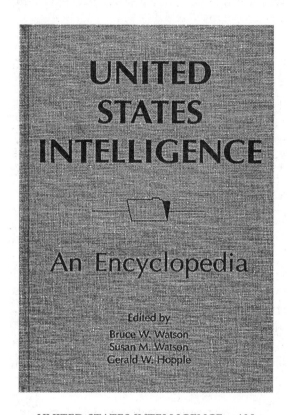

UNITED STATES INTELLIGENCE – AN ENCYCLOPEDIA ISBN 0-8240-3713-8

For those of us not IBM equipped, or who simply prefer books to CRT's, a second choice would be UNITED STATES INTELLIGENCE – AN ENCYCLOPEDIA, edited by Watson, Watson and Hopple, Garland Publishing, NYC, approximately $100.

USI is a hardcover, 792 page explanation of nomenclature, organizations, activities, happenings and Washingtonspeak. From HUMINT to RADINT (radiation intelligence) this work dissects the world of intelligence collection in layman's terms.

Besides breaking down the terms of the clandestine empire, USI provides thumbnail sketches of "names" on both sides of the ex-curtain. One can pick up this fascinating work, open it to any page and lose an hour in pure learning.

Very complete and very readable, USI should be a required handbook for anyone who follows intelligence activities or wants to decipher the *Washington Post*.

ber of sources, some of which were classified until the recent past. Was Paul Revere the head of a secret spy ring? How did William Casey rise to power in the CIA? What is a "walk-in?"

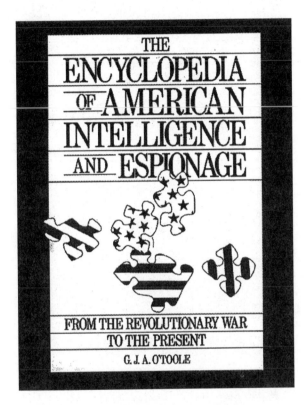

THE ENCYCLOPEDIA OF AMERICAN
INTELLIGENCE ESPIONAGE ISBN 0-8160-1001-0

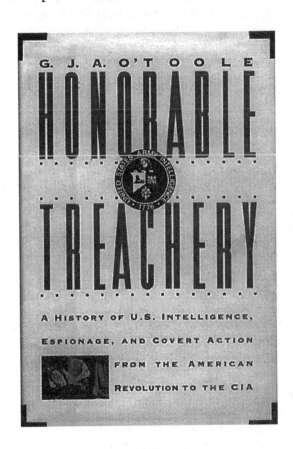

HONORABLE TREACHERY ISBN 0-87113-506-X

An ex-CIA agent, who points out that his "brief service" in no way contributes to his writing, G.J.G. O'Toole complied THE ENCYCLOPEDIA OF AMERICAN INTELLIGENCE AND ESPIONAGE, Facts on File. This large-format work offers a more in-depth look at the people and operations that have shaped U. S. intelligence from the 1700's to modern times. Insightful and well-researched, this encyclopedia shows the inside scoop on everything from civil war ops, the true story of the Cuban missile crisis, to modern Russian disinformation campaigns.

Kind of a *Who's Who* of the spy biz, EOAI has obviously been put together from a num-

Mr. O'Toole has also authored HONORABLE TREACHERY, A HISTORY OF US INTELLIGENCE, ESPIONAGE, AND COVERT ACTION FROM THE AMERICAN REVOLUTION TO THE CIA, Altantic Monthly Press, 19 Union Square West, NYC 10003. Softcover only $15.00, 1993.

Chapters, not just entries, on every important intelligence operation from General Washington to Vietnam. Kaiser Wilhelm II's plans for invading the United States, the super secret agency that helped end World War I, the transformation of the CIA, the failures, the successes.

This book should appeal to all spy buffs as well as to students of history.

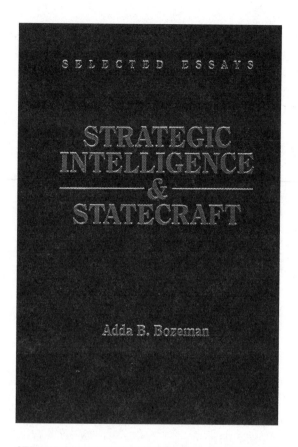

STRATEGIC INTELLIGENCE AND STATECRAFT
ISBN 0-02-881009-0

STRATEGIC INTELLIGENCE AND STATECRAFT, Adda Bozeman, Brassey's, U. S., 1992, 260 pages, hardcover. Selected essays from the people who suggest the policies adopted by our (and maybe other) government(s).

A bit drier and more scholarly, STAS diligently breaks down the major policies of political warfare and world conflicts from an intelligence viewpoint.

documents

A Shocking Collection of
Memoranda, Letters and Telexes
from the Secret Files of the
American Intelligence Community.

Christy Macy and Susan Kaplan

DOCUMENTS A SHOCKING COLLECTION OF MEMORANDA, LETTERS AND TELEXES FROM THE SECRET FILES OF THE AMERICAN INTELLIGENCE COMMUNITY ISBN 0-1400-4993-2

DOCUMENTS A SHOCKING COLLECTION OF MEMORANDA, LETTERS, AND TELEXES FROM THE SECRET FILES OF THE AMERICAN INTELLIGENCE COMMUNITY. Christy Macy and Susan Kaplan, Penguin Books, 1980. My kind of book – simply write a few hundred FOIA letters on the old word processor to the CIA, FBI, DIA, choose the juiciest answers and publish them as a book.

Well, not a completely fair evaluation as many of the files are introduced or contain footnotes setting the scene, but the bulk of the book is simple reprints focusing on how the Feds (often the FBI) lied, cheated and stole, particularly during the sixties and seventies.

The lean is obviously left, but there are some interesting files if you were involved with the woman's movement, campus unrest, desegregation, or any other activity that came under agency influence.

J. EDGAR HOOVER THE MAN AND THE SECRETS
ISBN 0-452-26904-0

Curt Gentry, a Plume Book (Penguin Group), $15.00 ISBN 0-452-26904-0. Mr. Gentry, probably best known for HELTER SKELTER: The True Story of the Manson Murders, has turned his considerable talents to chronicling a man who just may have been the most powerful figure in recent American history.

To the public he was a hero, Mr. G-Man, invincible,. on a par with Batman and Elliot Ness, but to politicians and Washington insiders he was an untouchable ogre who had something on everybody...

During the Hoover era it can be argued that America actually had a Gestapo – a government agency that ignored the laws and powers of arrest to bring down anyone the agency considered of questionable moral character.

My favorite personal remembrance is when Bobby Kennedy was elected to Attorney General stating that the first thing he was going to do was fire that Son of a Bitch Hoover.

After a short meeting Mr. Kennedy came out with a statement to the effect that "he's not such a bad guy after all, and he's doing a great job."

Uh-Huh.

This book details the paranoid man who intimidated (and blackmailed) every President from FDR to Nixon, influenced the Supreme Court, sabotaged the Warren Commission's investigation of the JFK shooting, changed the course of American history and wore dresses...

The FBI still hasn't totally recovered from the man's influence, still trying to live down the what may have been the darkest period in US government.

Power corrupts.

Curt has presented the material in a 846 page large format book based on hundreds of interviews and 100,000 pages of classified documents (and you thought you abused the FOIA process) and is a gripping read that will keep you up at night.

SILENT WARFARE
ISBN 0-08-040566-5

He also has a number of things to say about the role of secret intelligence agencies of democracies and the rest of the government.

Mr. Shulsky is a Senior Fellow at the National Strategy Information Center in Washington. He served as Director of Strategic Arms Control Policy in the Pentagon. This is, obviously, a book written from real experience describing the details of the real spy business. There are no little references to, "sorry, I can't go into that" or "this is a little bit too complicated for you to understand."

Instead he tells the down-and-out broad based facts of both the operations and the equipment involved in intelligence as well as theorizing the roles of intelligence in both open and closed societies.

An excellent beginner's text as well as a reference book for authors, researchers, and simply those interested in the thinking process of professional intelligence agencies.

SILENT WARFARE – Understanding the World of Intelligence, Abram Shulsky, Brassey's US, 8000 Westpark Drive, First Floor, McLean, VA 22102. Copyright 1991, $19.95. Unlike most spy books or covert manuals that are designed either for complete agency buffs or for simple, casual fans of John LE Carre, SILENT WARFARE tries to bridge the gaps so both groups gain some understanding of topics such as covert action, collection analysis, counter intelligence and the organization involved in the organizations involved.

THE READERS GUIDE TO INTELLIGENCE
PERIODICALS ISBN 1-87892-00-5

THE READER'S GUIDE TO INTELLIGENCE PERIODICALS, Hayden Peake, NIBC Press, National Intelligence Book Center, 2020 Pennsylvania Ave. NW, Washington, DC 20006, copyright 1992. With a foreword by our old friend, Walter Pforzheimer, this book is *the most* complete guide to newsletters, magazines, and virtually any hard-copy periodicals that have to do with the intelligence business. The READER'S GUIDE includes academic works, government bulletins, Soviet newsletters that are now available in the West, Soviet analysts, as well as those periodicals which take the more liberal line of let's throw the CIA into the ocean, such as STATE WATCH.

Periodicals are divided into various groups including intelligence periodicals, political warfare, limited distribution and intelligence, etc.

The foreword covers the rather short history of intelligence periodicals beginning with World War II veterans, who, as they began to retire, formed alumni associations like the Association of Former Intelligence Officers and the Central Intelligence Retirees Association. These groups complemented existing associations of former counter intelligence and communications intelligence officers. In nearly all cases they gave birth to house organs which carry both historical articles on certain phases of intelligence plus chapter notes on their present-day activities. Perhaps more importantly, these newsletters carry references to reviews of recent books and works on intelligence so the readership can be kept aware of current works in their profession, good, bad or indifferent.

The interest in intelligence matters has blossomed in the last few years and consequently there are now approximately *150 intelligence* publications from the well known to the obscure.

How does one decide which newsletters are applicable to a private detective and intelligence buff, an industrial spy or someone who plans to cheat on their spouse?

Welcome to THE READER'S GUIDE TO INTELLIGENCE PERIODICALS...

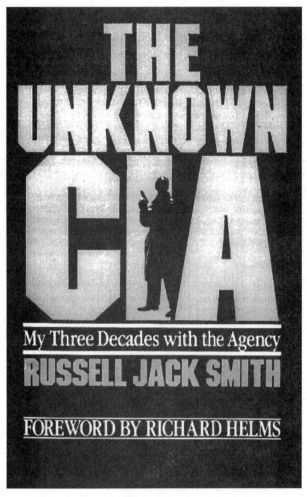

THE UNKNOWN CIA ISBN 0425-13136-X

THE UNKNOWN CIA, My Three Decades with the Agency, Russell Jack Smith, Berkley Books, 200 Madison Avenue, New York, NY 10016 paperback 1992, $4.99.

Mr. Smith was former Deputy Director for Intelligence with the CIA and spent 30 years with this clandestine organization. What makes his story different, and important is that he does not highlight "sexy" operations that virtually all the other CIA-oriented books concentrate on.

Rather Mr. Smith, with a background in historical research and university teaching, worked in the much larger (and many would say more important) divisions of the CIA, analyzing raw intelligence and providing reports and recommendations to the President, the State Department and various other government agencies.

Mr. Smith admits that many operatives look upon analysts as walking leaks, tending to distrust them. He also points out that the CIA when organized in 1947 was not designed to commit espionage or promote covert action. These ancillary activities were added later to the CIA charter.

The central task of the CIA from 1947 to this day remains that of one of centralization – to assemble in one place (Langley, Virginia) all the foreign intelligence gathered by the many arms of the US Government with missions and facilities overseas. This is what the *Central* in the Central Intelligence Agency refers to. The derring-do, the cloak-and-dagger, were tacked on later when the cold war began to intensify.

Mr. Smith feels it is one of life's ironies that the CIA's secret, most clandestine activities have been highly publicized, while its reporting and analytical chores have been kept a virtual secret.

Done in the first person, this insightful publication covers Mr. Smith's contacts with various Presidents, Secretaries of State, and military personnel during the years he analyzed and helped shape response mechanisms to world crises. This book is an even-handed look at the importance of intelligence interpretation, rather than intelligence gathering. It delves into such esoteric areas as how to convey intelligence; words have different shades of meaning and connotations for most people depend their upbringing, their environment, and what part of the country they come from and the service they work for.

A good read, a good book, and a good look at operations that constitute probably 80% of all intelligence work — analysis, interpretation, and communication.

THE CENTRAL INTELLIGENCE AGENCY, A PHOTO-GRAPHIC HISTORY, FOREIGN Intelligence Press, 42 Boston Post Road, Guilford, CT 06437, $39.00 hardback, 8 1/2 by 11 inches, 256 pages in color. ISBN 0-89568-500-0. Assembled by John Quirk with consultants David Phillips, Dr. Ray Cline, Walter Pforzheiner, and various spy advisors.

An excellent work showing how the CIA really gathers its information. Includes a history of intelligence starting with William Donovan's mysterious travels before World War II, the early cold war years, the emphasis on technology, human intelligence, and the alleged abuses the agency was accused of during the 1970s. Much of this is from recently declassified information and has not been seen by the public.

This book includes some of the first published interviews with William Colby, Admiral Stansfield Turner, David Atlee Phillips, a number of foreign station chiefs of the OSS and the CIA, and a few scattered DIA members.

A photo section contains hundreds of unpublished photographs of personalities, buildings, and operations and contains the first detailed organizational information of how the CIA functions abroad.

Special features include a Who's Who of the CIA, the KGB watchdogs, science and technology in the CIA today.

A MUST READ for CIA fans.

THE INVISIBLE WAR BETWEEN THE KGB AND THE CIA, Edward J. Epstein, Simon and Schuster, 1995 Mr. Epstein spent 20 years as chief of the CIA's counterintelligence staff. Until his forced retirement in 1974, he had the intelligence services of the west tied up in knots trying to prove that the chief instrument of the Soviet Union/ KGB was deception on a grand scale. His contention is that this was a twin effort to penetrate and then hopefully control western intelligence services as well as to divide and disarm the west politically through agents with influence and disinformation.

An interesting/suggestive work which should convince you that the Soviets were never, in fact, the good guys.

Assuming you need convincing. Interesting insights to both Soviet and American thinking during the high years of the cold war as well as the role of intelligence agencies in warfare.

Epstein implies that the post Gorbachov era is not as squeaky clean vis-a-vis operations as we would like to think.

Mr. Epstein answers historical questions with a chain of evidence based on intelligence cases. The book stands or falls on these cases.

INSIDE THE CIA ISBN 0-671-73457-1

INSIDE THE CIA, Viewing the Secrets of the World's Most Powerful Spy Agency, Ronald Kessler. A five-part book on the CIA in modern days, Kessler provides one section on each of the four CIA directorates and a fifth devoted to the office of the DCI. Mr. Kessler researched the information for this book through interviews of former and serving officers including some on-site at the CIA headquarters in Langley, Virginia.

The focus of this book is the late 80s and early 90s as evaluated by Mr. Kessler. Some of the cases and stories are famous, some are a trifle outdated, but his descriptions of purpose and functioning for each directorate as well as a very interesting chapter on what happens to new employees as they begin the career training program.

All in all, a good starting point for CIA buffs as well as those who don't have the time to read heavier works.

Some CIA followers dispute certain points in this book, and feel the conclusions are based on less than solid ground.

ECLIPSE. THE LAST DAYS OF THE CIA, Mark Perry, Morrow, $25.00, hardback. Mr. Perry makes use of classified material obtained "from a source inside the executive branch" to look at the internal debate over CIA policy and leadership after the death of William Casey in 1987 and the swearing in of Robert Gates in 1991.

Perry traces the quick rise of Robert Gates and the circumstances of his controversial nomination by President Bush. He also details some unusual operations including a joint CIA-PLO attack on mid-East terrorists, takes a look inside the national collection division and touches on how the CIA is attempting to expand its business contacts in order to recruit American and international businessmen for the new CIA agents.

This book is unusual in that information does appear to be quite "inside" and many of the covert operations and personalities have not been detailed elsewhere.

DARK GENIUS. A CHILD PRODIGY IN THE SHADOW OF THE CIA, Knightsbridge Publishing, 442 pages, $22.95, hardback, is the story of a secret company that was apparently connected with or formed by the Central Intelligence Agency to manufacture numerous assassination devices of a "highly unusual nature."

According to the book the inventor eventually went underground after a death threat and now claims that various conspiracies funneled some of his work through international drug traffickers and arm merchants.

A couple of other books that should be indulged by any serious CIA scholar are THE AGENCY, THE RISE AND DECLINE OF THE CIA, Simon and Schuster, 1987 and IN THE CIA LIFE, TEN THOUSAND DAYS WITH THE AGENCY, Foreign Intelligence Press, 1990, which details what day by day work is like inside the world's most secret spy agency.

DEADLY DECEITS ISBN 0-941781-06-2

DEADLY DECEITS, My 25 years in the CIA, Ralph W. McGehee, Sheridan Square Press, 145 W. 44th St., New York, NY 10012, 1983. Mr. McGehee also spent almost three decades in the CIA from the 50's through the 70's taking part in such operations as Vietnam (where he was in charge of the Vietnamese special police force), and domestic programs designed to keep tabs on leftist individuals within the anti-Vietnam cadre. DEADLY DECEITS is biased in its coverage and does not attempt to pretend otherwise.

Mr. McGehee seems to have spent most of his 25 years in the CIA making notes so he could become a government whistle blower after he got his pension.

One has to wonder how well he ran the operations he was assigned to while considering what the ACLU would do with his copious notes, or where the book contract was coming from.

Mr. McGehee's final admonition is that the CIA should be torn down and destroyed because it can not possibly be salvaged in the condition it's in now.

One should note that this was written before we won the cold war...

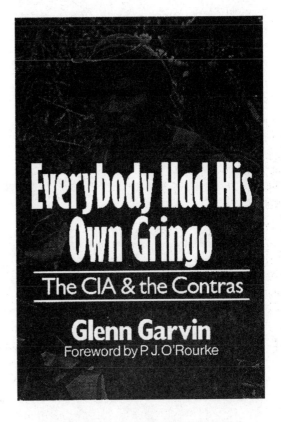

EVERBODY HAD HIS OWN GRINGO
ISBN 0-08-040562-2

Another book which is definitely not entirely pro CIA but is a more interesting read is EVERYBODY HAD HIS OWN GRINGO, The CIA and The Contras, Glenn Garvin, Brassey's USA, C/0 Macmillan Publishing, 100 Front St., Box 500, Riverside, NJ 08075.

Although not specifically a book on the CIA, Garvin's story of the Contras is rife with villains and general fuck-ups, although a bit short on heroes. He gives terse portraits of Contra battlefield commanders who got their military tactics from the Iraqi Air Force and their human rights briefing from 2 Live Crew.

This book focuses on the Contras themselves, members of the populace who took up arms in order to win their ideas. As one might suspect the Contras come out to be the good guys in this book. Small elfin-like people, who, although hunted by the largest armies of democracy, managed to prevail and gain some recognition in the turgid political waters of Nicaragua.

The writing is lively and vaguely reminiscent of Hunter Thompson, although the journalism seems to be more than 75% accurate. This book is of interest to the spy crowd because it details an operation the CIA was theoretically in charge of but seemed to have very little control over due to the inability of the Yale-educated CIA agents to pass themselves off as Nicaraguan peasants.

A problem that has arisen in other world theaters.

SPIES AMONG US ISBN 0-531-10600-4

SPIES AMONG US, The Truth About Modern Espionage, Herma Silverstein, Franklin Watts Company, 5450 N. Cumberland Ave., Chicago, IL 60656, 1988, Hardback.

SPIES attempts to be the definitive volume to bring the truth behind the perennial games of espionage and intrigue. It asks what's behind the shadowy cloak-and-dagger world of spy vs. spy that is stereotyped in movies and TV. What are the real kinds of information that modern states require for national security? And above all why have people since the beginnings of organized government decided that spying is a tempting and perhaps satisfying way of life?

Ms. Silverstein poses these questions and attempts to answer them by selecting modern well-documented cases of espionage and counterespionage on both sides of the iron curtain, following the characters involved. The book also produces a somewhat sketchy history of the CIA and parallel origins of the KGB. One of the better sections is a good analysis of atomic espionage in the cold war period, centered on the Rosenberg case.

The entire tapestry is woven together with headlines including the Iran Contra scandals, the Walker family espionage ring, and the Clayton Loantree-Moscow embassy buggings.

Ms. Silverstein is the author of a number of books for young readers and this book is a nice quick read that doesn't reveal too much inside information.

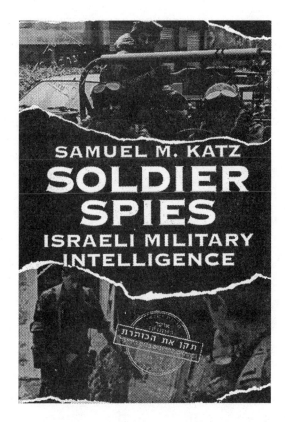

SOLDIER SPIES ISBN 0-89141-357-X

On the other end of the scale is SOLDIER SPIES, Israeli Military Intelligence, Samuel M. Katz, Presidio Press, 505 B San Marin Drive, Suite 300, Novato, CA 94945. Mr. Katz has penetrated the inner workings of what many, myself included, feel is, if not the world's best intelligence agency, certainly the most efficient. Israel has been protected by the MOSSAD (foreign espionage service) and SHIN BET which has achieved international respect with their anti-terrorist and military support operations. A number of analysts have concluded that MOSSAD operates with one of the smallest intelligence budgets of a modern country but achieves some of the best results.

Why is that?

A number of reasons come to mind including the old saying that nine times out of ten when a wolf chases a rabbit the rabbit wins because he's running for his life while the wolf is only running for his dinner. Israel cannot afford to lose a war, or become immersed in terrorist attacks that would cripple its resolve to win, when it's surrounded by an enemy-to-friend ratio of at least ten to one and countless tons of Soviet weaponry still in its packing crates.

Israeli intelligence is not a new service – their agents operated against Hitler. They were very active in the struggle for Israeli independence, protected and supported the military in the major Israeli wars, and still work today in the fight against Israel's enemies in the Middle East.

MOSSAD's covert operations include the most advanced electronic and aero monitoring equipment coupled with some of the ballsyest and best trained agents who make daring reconnaissance forays deep into enemy territory. Very few intelligence writers would argue that MOSSAD and SHIN BET are commanded by some of the best minds in the business.

Mr. Katz has drawn on official histories, war records, recently declassified documents and interviews with former and present intelligence officers to compile this book on Israel's military intelligence.

I can personally relate to MOSSAD in an offbeat fashion but with nothing but admiration for their techniques. I have met a number of MOSSAD agents in various courses, seminars, and training facilities at various times in my life and have found them to be a very close-knit, well-disciplined group who do not mix or drink with "the boys". This "stick with the people you know" attitude makes it a bit difficult to learn much about this top-secret organization.

A number of years ago I had written a book, when, unbeknownst to me, the FBI decided they would like to have a small informal book review session with me over the contents. At the time I was living with a roommate, taking the normal security precautions, phone listed in someone else's name, utility bills in a fictional name, real mail going to a mail drop that was visited only when necessary. The FBI searched for some time in vain to arrange our little chat.

One night I received a phone call. It was obviously long distance and the speaker spoke in a thick accent that I soon realized was Israeli. The gentleman wanted to know if he could order two copies of my latest book and assured me MOSSAD was good for the money and would send a check upon the book's arrival.

By this time I was both awake enough and shaken up enough to inquire exactly how they had gotten my phone number. The guy on the other end of the line laughed and said, "that's our business." I assured him the books would be on the way at the first light of dawn, gratis.

They were...

One should bear in mind that the Israeli intelligence community enjoys some unique opportunities such as their network of "sayanim", Jews, around the world, who work part time for Mossad.

It is estimated that 2,000 such unpaid helpers provide active support to Israeli agents such as renting apartments, providing funds, treating wounds and other services to maintain an agent or his cover.

After you read some of the exploits of the soldier spies during the 1967 six day war, the extreme preparedness and efficiency of their services in carrying out SIGINY/ELINT/PHOTINT against Egypt, Jordan, Syria, Iraq, Iran, etc. (and one must point out MOSSAD has never had too many scruples about spying on their so-called friends – the United States, Britain and France), one can not help but be impressed with their complete professionalism.

This book is extremely well documented and shows the interior operations of specialized branches of MOSSAD and SHIN BET as well as detailing recruitment and inducement proposals to secure or turn agents. It's fairly complete on military hardware and intelligence-gathering equipment, and best of all, is a very interesting read.

It's hard to read SOLDIER SPIES without coming away with a much better grasp of intelligence operations in general, what they mean to any particular country and exactly how good the Israelis are at this particular avocation.

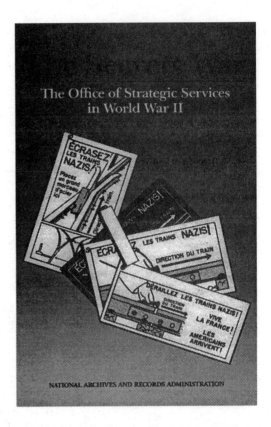

THE SECRETS WAR ISBN 0-911333-91-6

THE SECRETS WAR, The Office of Strategic Services in World War II, edited by George C. Chalou, National Archives and Records Administration, Marketing and Fulfillment Branch, Washington, DC 20408, $25.00, hard cover only.

This book is actually a series of papers published for the National Archives and Records Administration by the National Archives Trust Fund Board. The papers in this book came from a conference put on by the National Archives that was 50 years in the making.

It began on July 11, 1941, when President FDR appointed William J. Donovan to be coordinator of information, a year later establishing the Office of Strategic Services (OSS). It allows readers "to participate in the conference by enjoying the outstanding collection of presentations published in this volume." National Archives goes on to say they are publishing these papers so a wider audience can appreciate the contributions of this wartime intelligence organization.

The OSS was one of the first solutions to an intelligence crisis. Without timely and accurate information no country could hope to comprehend, let alone cope with, the worsening world situation in 1941.

The OSS records printed here are quite complete because the OSS was only in service under that name for approximately four years. These papers reveal information, most of it previously classified or otherwise unavailable, about virtually every aspect of the Second World War as well as giving the reader an advantage in understanding the administration and development of a country's top agency. As one would expect this book is highly detailed, written by the people who were there – the researchers and historians from the government (and the CIA) in charge of tracking the OSS, its missions, and its contribution to the allied war effort.

THE SECRETS WAR may be a bit technical and heavily footnoted for 23-year-old readers who have only a passing interest in intelligence, but to anyone who is interested in World War II in any fashion, it makes a nice behind the scenes diary of why our government did what they did as well as how the first well-organized national intelligence agency set up its bureaucracy and kept it running.

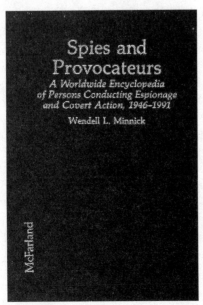

SPIES AND PROVOCATEURS, A Worldwide Encyclopedia of Persons Conducting Espionage with Covert Action 1946-1991, Wendell L. Minnick, McFarland & Co., 1992, $45.00 hard cover. Mr. Minnick is a writer specializing in intelligence and has been published in such publications as *Military Intelligence, Journal of Political and Military Sociology,* and *Army.* This book details the lives, general background, and exact activity and its consequences of over 725 agents of espionage and covert action including assassination, sabotage, political core, and intelligence gathering. The work begins with one Sirioj Husien Abdoolcader (a British clerk who was working for the KGB) to Antoly Pavlovick Zotov, a Soviet naval attaché who was expelled for spying.

Mr. Minnick differentiates between agents motivated by conviction, duty and tradition as opposed to those recruited for a foreign government who are motivated by blackmail, or more often by easy money. Admittedly this volume details more western agents and personalities than their eastern counterparts due to the fact that western-style democracies encourage freedom of the press and open debate on national policy issues, making the research a bit easier.

Mr. Minnick assures us he is going to publish a more complete volume on eastern intelligence agents in the near future as the lack of the iron curtain is suddenly making *that* research a bit easier.

SPIES AND PROVATEURS is like one of those books you are forced to read for a book report and then discover you recognize some of the names and really enjoy their biographies. One can also pick out patterns and applications employed by each particular spy agency by in their techniques of recruitment. The book also includes a chronology of significant happenings in the intelligence community since 1946 and an extensive bibliography.

SPIES AND PROVOCATEURS ISBN 0-89950-746-8

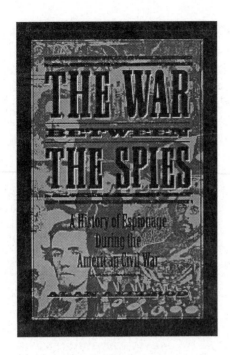

THE WAR BETWEEN THE SPIES
ISBN 0-87113-482-9

THE WAR BETWEEN THE SPIES, A History of Espionage During the American Civil War, Allen Axelrod, Atlantic Monthly Press, 19 Union Square West, New York, NY 10003, hard cover, $23.00. The first comprehensive history of Civil War espionage and counterespionage ever published. This is a compelling narrative history focusing on one of the most popular times in all American history. The book is meticulously researched and written with a flair.

Historian Axelrod weaves a story filled with treachery, heroism, and suspense but also with some comedy, as espionage during this conflict was primarily by amateur agents. These agents were often poorly trained or untrained ordinary citizens pressed into missions of espionage that were often vague in purpose.

Some of the stories included are those of Allen Lloyd, a traveling businessman who came to Abraham Lincoln for a pass so he could continue to conduct business in the South. Mr. Lincoln sagely agreed on the condition Mr. Lloyd would become a spy. This transpired and with his wife and maid in tow, he spied successfully for years.

Or how about Allan J. Pinkerton, the inventor of the private detective business? He defended president-elect Lincoln from would-be assassins and worked in counterespionage in Washington and was the main man in charge of Union spy activities.

David O. Dodd, a 17-year-old boy from Little Rock, Arkansas, volunteered as a Confederate courier, was captured, tried and wrote a letter to his parents and sister beginning, "I was arrested as a spy and tried and sentenced to be hung today at 3:00 o'clock". Or S. Edmonds, a Union battlefield nurse who put Mata Hara to shame when she disguised herself as a black man to penetrate behind Confederate lines.

This book has a very nice index and a few photos of the characters involved in the genesis of American spying. THE WAR BETWEEN THE SPIES is fun although not particularly instructional reading for anyone interested in the business of spying.

THE SPY OF THE REBELLION
ISBN 0-8032-3686-7

THE SPY OF THE REBELLION, Allan Pinkerton, University of Nebraska Press, Lincoln, NB, 1989. Here's the aforementioned Mr. Pinkerton, founder of the United States espionage and counterespionage industry, telling the story in his own words. This is a narrative history wherein he describes thwarting assassination plots against Lincoln in 1861 and his exploits as an operative during the crucial years of the war. Allan Pinkerton, (using the pseudonym Major E. J. Allan), headed an espionage organization that fed information about the Confederate Army to Major George B. McClellan.

Some of the best reading is the entertaining antidotes about how Mr. Pinkerton recruited and managed his agents. This book was originally published in 1883 but is still a fast-paced story full of narrow escapes, violent episodes and various schemes in candid conversations with the most powerful people of the time.

Modern intelligence or investigative agents will find the business has not changed that much in the last 135 years. People are still people, spies are still spies, and recruiting, alas, is still recruiting.

A good read for history buffs. A great coffee table book for any private detective.

Two other books of note are about to be (or will have been by the time you read this) released by Pocket Books. Written by *Washington Post* journalist Ronald Kessler, THE FBI: INSIDE THE MOST POWERFUL LAW ENFORCEMENT AGENCY IN THE WORLD examines the institution both before and after Mr. Hoover's reign concentrating primarily on the criminal law enforcement duties including the laboratories, training, Quantico courses, infighting and some of the late, ah, personnel problems.

Based on his research as well as numerous interviews Mr. kessler conducted for the*Post,* this book is expected to be a major work.

INSIDE THE CIA: Revealing the Secrets of the World's Most Powerful Spy Agency. Mr. Kessler does stick with a title when he has a winner, doesn't he?

A day-by-day how-to manual on joining, working for, training, and operations of the CIA.

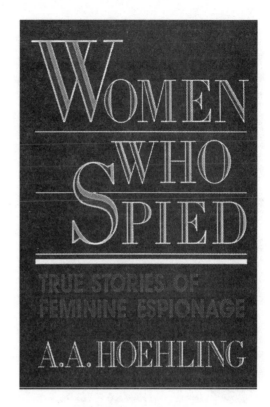

WOMEN WHO SPIED
ISBN 0-8191-8486-1

WOMEN WHO SPIED A.A. Hoehling, a Madison book, $14.95, paperback. Ms. Hoehling recounts a number of dramatic episodes of espionage by the fairer sex from Lydia Darragh, who, in 1777 alerted General Washington to Redcoat plans for a surprise attack on Valley Forge to Milada Horkova who was executed by the commies for being the leader of the resistance in Czechoslovakia.

11 stories of professional female spies that changed the course of history told in a fashion that reads like a Tom Clancy novel.

ESTIMATIVE INTELLIGENCE
ISBN 0-8191-8604

ESTIMATIVE INTELLIGENCE The Purposes and Problems of National Intelligence Estimating. Harold Ford, Defense Intelligence Center, University Press of America 4720 Boston Way, Lanham, MD 20706. Mr. Ford traces the evolution of national intelligence estimating from the days before Pearl Harbor to the post cold war era.

Ford covers such topics as the purpose of national intelligence estimating, the system at work before, during and after the Korean war, the present system of national estimating, the National Intelligence Council and tomorrow's needs.

SPY TV

The Defense Intelligence Agency (DIA) is now operating a television "network" called the All-Source Television Network. The agents were so impressed with CNN's coverage of various global happenings they have modeled their own network on the same format. The DIA network operates five days a week from 6:45 AM till 5 PM.

The programs are beamed to about 1000 intelligence and defense officers in the Pentagon and other military commands. The program is allied with the Joint Worldwide Intelligence Communications System which is able to set up transmissions to other sites.

The CIA and the State Department have been invited to join up, while DCI has announced they are going to begin a similar network for government policy makers.

The most popular show on the net is a 45-minute "Global Update" shown twice a day. The questions and interviews reflect items of interest to Pentagon leaders. Some of the show is done live by using a still photo of the subject and having him respond to the interviewer via a secure phone line.

One can only hope declassified reruns will soon make Nick-at-Night.

SPY VIDEOS

SPIES, a non-fiction television series, is now available from Columbia House Video Library, 1400 N. Fruitridge Ave., Terre Haute, IN 47811. Each episode deals with one area of intelligence or covert actions including never before seen footage combined with new interviews to unfold some of the more interesting events in world history.

How JFK really dealt with the missile crisis, how the Russians stole the A-bomb secrets, why the North Vietnamese knew of our air targets in advance, the accounts of Committee X – the operation mounted by Israel to retaliate against the terrorists who assassinated their athletes at the '72 Olympic games and so on.

The collection is quite well down, not fluff, and should be as interesting to spy buffs as the show WINGS is to aviation freaks. SPIES owes some of its authenticity to H. Keith Melton, who served the series as a consultant.

CIA: THE SECRET FILES, produced by the BBC in association with NRK, Prime Time Television and the Arts and Entertainment Network.

This series was put together by John Molloy based on work by John Ranelagh. It is available from the New Video Group, 419 Park Avenue South, New York, NY 10016, as well as from Arts and Entertainment Home Video, Post Box 2284, South Burlington, VT 05407. The entire series consists of four cassettes in VHS at $59.95 per set.

CIA, THE SECRET FILES exposes some of the unwritten rules that govern this huge spy organization by drawing its materials from interviews with past CIA directors as well as some dissidents who have come in from the cold. This tape discusses the secret wars, coups, planned assassinations, and of course, successful assassinations performed by the CIA.

The first tape, HIGH TECH – LOW CUNNING, is a look at the technology of information gathering. The second tape, PHOENIX RISING, examines the agency's involvement in the Vietnam War.

Number three, EXECUTIVE ACTION, is a review of the CIA's growth into a national weapon. Tape four, MOVING TARGETS, looks at the future of the CIA in the new world order.

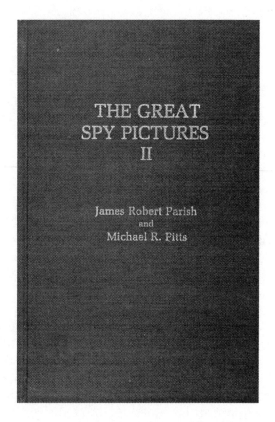

THE GREAT SPY PICTURES II
ISBN 0-8108-1913-9

SPY ENTERTAINMENT

To fill those long nights when there is no meeting of the young intelligence agents you could consider THE GREAT SPY PICTURES II James Robert Parish and Michael R. Pitts, The Scarecrow Press, Inc. ISBN 0-8108-1913-9.

First published in 1974 this new and improved version is slightly undernamed – not only does it list the "great" spy films from A-Z, it also covers the genre in the radio and TV and provides a selected bibliography of spy novels.

Next time you need to settle a bet about who played Chief Kelly (Dana Andrews) in The Cobra, or answer the perennial office Christmas party inquiry, "what spy picture stared Jackie Gleason?" (Don't Drink the Water –1968), you are going to be prepared.

TGSPII provides plot summaries, cast and production details, box office ratings, reviews and critical opinion on every bloody spy film from Dr. Goldfoot And The Girl Bombs, to the James Bond series.

Armed with this guide and set loose in a good video store a spy, or spy buff could entertain himself until the cold war heats up again.

ENCYCLOPEDIA OF AMERICAN SPY FILMS
ISBN 0-8240-5533-0

ENCYCLOPEDIA OF AMERICAN SPY FILMS Larry Langman and David Ebner, Garland Publishing "What a charming evening we might have had if you had not been a spy and I a traitor.

Then we might never have met."

With this quote from the 1931 film, Dishonored, the most complete work on American Spy films begins its journey through 1,000 films produced from the silent film days to the late 1980s.

Each alphabetical entry includes release date, releasing company, director, screenwriter and five or more major players. This 440 page work also lists spy serials, spy films that have been nominated for, and/or, won awards, and cross indexes films about political assassinations and those about specific wars.

The entries are more detailed and a touch more complete than GREAT SPY FILMS because of the concentration on American productions rather than attempting to cover the entire world.

The listings are highlighted by historical references to the real life operations (or agents) the films are based on as well as a look at the prevailing winds that "caused" a number of films including the anti-Japanese wave that went into production shortly after December 7th, 1941.

The writing is even-handed and the reviews comprehensive. I enjoy this book both because of the memories it brings of those films I watched every Saturday afternoon at the local movie theater, as well as for the interesting reviews and ancillary facts about the profession.

SPY FICTION ISBN 0-7146-3411-5

SPY FICTION, SPY FILMS, AND REAL INTELLIGENCE Edited by Wesley K. Wark available from Frank Cass International Specialized Book Services, 5602 NE Hassalo Street, Portland, Or 97213. $25.00.

Remember Three Days of The Condor? Where the bad guys came in a shot up a whole gaggle of researchers who's sole job was to read popular books to find ideas that could be used by real (read CIA) spy agencies.

After all writer's are supposed to have a certain degree of creativity, some spy novelists have actually been real life spies and every idea has to be born somewhere.

Right?

Mr. Wark edits the journal *Intelligence and National Security* and is in a position to explore the history of spy fiction and spy films and investigate the significance of the ideas they contain.

Insights into the development of British spy fiction, the early history of American spy novels, and a few cases of terrorism and Irish politics.

Not light reading, this interesting work points out the similarities between images and methodology of the 'real" world of espionage and the "fictional" version and will, at the very least, provide you with a new view of spy books and movies.

"One striking aspect of the relation between fiction and reality evident in some of Graham Greene's novels their prescient, perhaps even their prophetic quality. Thus, in *The Quiet American* published in 1955, Green accurately anticipated the American intention to intervene on a massive scale in Vietnam to prevent the Vietminh from consolidating their rule over a united country. The author attributed his own clairvoyance on this issue to the personal experience of Vietnam that he had gained during lengthy visits there in the early 50's....

Yet Green was not the only Western observer to visit there... and yet few, if any, of these 'quiet' Americans ... proved capable of comprehending the local political scene with as much perspicacity at Green displayed in a short passage in his novel:

"This was a land of rebellious barons. It was like Europe in the Middle Ages. But what were the Americans doing here? Columbus had not yet discovered their country."

UNDERCOVER WASHINGTON ISBN 0-939009-60-9

UNDERCOVER WASHINGTON Pamela Kessler, EPM Publications Inc., 1003 Turkey Run Road, McLean VA 22101. $9.95. "Touring the sites where famous spies lived, worked and loved."

Find yourself on the Eastern Seaboard with an afternoon to kill? How about lunch at La Nicoise, a small French restaurant in upper Georgetown where James Jesus Angleton, the CIA's powerful chief of counterintelligence ate lunch every day (table 41, at the rear of the establishment, next to the mirror with a perfect view of the room and the front door) around 12:30.

Be sure to start with an I.W Harper bourbon ("not too many cubes", shades of James Bond "stirred not shaken") raw oysters and shad, scampi or calf's liver.

Tip exactly 15%.

Walk off your lunch in the gardens of Dumbarton Oaks where Jonathan Jay Pollard met his Israeli handler and turned over classified documents.

Visit "Wild Bill" Donovan's Georgetown mansion where the concept of America's secret service was born, carry a copy of *Life magazine* into the Georgetown pharmacy where Elizabeth Bentley, the "Red Spy Queen" met with her Soviet handlers in order to turn over state secrets before turning on the communists and inviting the FBI to the pharmacy meets, visit old embassy sites, see safe houses, visit Kim Philby's residence or just drop by "Sigint City" home of the NSA.

Recreate great spy times by lying, cheating, spying, conniving, seducing, cheating and betraying in the exact same locations the pros did (do?). Listen to the ghosts tell their stories, discover secret places on the Mall where sleuths broke ciphers, examine the telephone poles that John Walker used as drop sites.

A fun read, and a great list of first date suggestions – what could be more romantic than suggesting a liaison where lovers passed on nuclear secrets?

70 museums, mansions, bars, bookstores, libraries, hotels and graveyards where it all happened. Complete with maps and photos, not to mention recipes for some of the dishes (Spycatcher's Scampi) eaten by ravenous traitors.

A kick.

Although not exactly spy related, BOGIE'S MYSTERY TOURS, 328 W 86th street, suite 4A, New York, NY 10024 offers a unique access to "mystery events." BOGIE'S features specifically tailored, analytical whodunits where participants actively work in teams of two or more to solve a crime. This is done by interrogating suspects (portrayed by professional actors) and searching for clues.

Well known mystery authors play the suspects, give talks and sign their books during weekend long events. During these, as well as during the shorter, dinner length scenarios, participants are often transported back to an earlier era and costumes are encouraged.

The programs range from the 3 1/2 hour dinner or party version to 7 day/6 night packages which can involve as many as 500 people. Prizes are awarded for the best sleuthing.

Prices vary but are actually quite reasonable. One recent weekend event came in at $285 including a hotel room, dinner, breakfast, cocktail party and dance. BOGIE'S offers open events at different locations around the county or will tailor make a mystery for you and yours.

I admit this entry might be mis-filed, but I think it would appeal to those spies who need a break from their normal routine. Maybe you work in administration, or records and dream of being a field agent, or better yet flying an F-16 over hostile territory shooting down Floggers and Foxbats.

A number of companies offer mock aerial combat where you "fly" a WW II based aircraft (usually a P-51 or equivalent) with a flight instructor and dogfight another pane containing an instructor and/or a friend.

No real guns of course, but gun cameras record the action so you can thrill your friends and neighbors over and over again by making them watch the video of you as the Red Baron over and over and over...

The least expensive, prop-based fighter experience I've found is located at the half Moon Bay (California) airport.

Figure about $400 for ground school and a good dogfight.

Now, for the real adventure seekers you can do the same thing in a *MIG-29 at Mach 2.3, 15.5 miles above Russia,* fighting a real fighter pilot, who, just a few years ago, would have had the gun cameras loaded with something besides video tape.

The operators call it "the ultimate high" and stress that it is completely legal. They'll even throw in pressure chamber and centrifuge training at no extra cost.

Figure a bit over $15K for your black-above-and-blue-below experience, plus some incidentals like $95 for a day's meals, $350 to own your very own Russian flight helmet, a bit more for the flight suit and $195 rate for the Zil limousine from Moscow to your point of departure.

If the price tag is just a hair out over budget you can shave a few thou off by settling for a MIG-25 or Su-27 or even that old Afghani favorite, the Hind Mil-24 attack helicopter.

On the other hand, if you've just won the lottery you might want to consider "the ultimate flight program" for a mere $50,000.

Contact:
High-Performance Flying Holidays
2206 Jo-An Drive, Suite 1
Sarasota, FL 34231

TEACHING INTELLIGENCE

A number of institutions, both public and private, offer courses in the arts of intelligence collection, surveillance, and tradecraft. The largest private group is probably FOREIGN INTELLIGENCE PRESS, 42 Boston Post Rd., Guilford, CT 06437. FIP consists of former FBI and CIA officers. Some of the courses they offer are:
• The history of intelligence
• Careers in intelligence
• How to be an intelligence officer
• Counterintelligence
• Tradecraft

Many institutions of higher learning teach courses in one or more aspects of intelligence work. Yale offers National Security Issues: Communications, Command Control and Intelligence. Willammetee College of Law produces International Dispute Resolution, covering some intelligence related issues; Johns Hopkins University, Problems in Intelligence. Georgetown U sports a number of courses from the Origins and Development of the CIA to Soviet Intelligence and Security Services.

TEACHING INTELLIGENCE
IN THE MID - 1990s

*A Survey of College
and University Courses on
the Subject of Intelligence*

NISC

National Intelligence Study Center

TEACHING INTELLIGENCE ISBN 0-938450-02-6

TEACHING INTELLIGENCE IN THE MID-1990s National Intelligence Study Center, Judith M. Fontaine, 1800 K St. NW, Suite 1102, Washington DC. 20006, is a book dedicated to openness and understanding of the intelligence community. The author surveyed colleges and universities to come up with this comprehensive guidebook to understanding courses, projects and programs which "facilitate whatever tasks are necessary to lay the foundation for a better understanding of the importance of good intelligence in a democracy."

The book covers courses, titles, descriptions and syllabi on virtually every intelligence class taught in North America.

And now for the piece de resistance – the first program in the world (outside of the government) designed for the training of intelligence analysts is offered by Mercyhurst College, a fully accredited liberal arts institution located in Erie, Pennsylvania.

Mercyhurst offers a four-year program designed for the training of intelligence analysts. Students are prepared to work as professionals in the fields or national security, law enforcement and private enterprise.

"By deriving assessments from collected and correlated intelligence data, intelligence analysts play a vital role in national security and criminal investigation activities such as drug trafficking, organized crime, terrorism and white collar crime."

The Research/Intelligence Analyst Program is the first open spy school. Although it is too early to offer grad placement figures, Mercyhurst claims it's graduates can expect salaries "in league with lawyers or doctors."

The program is open to traditional students as well as those older folks seeking a career change. It could be the perfect re-entry vehicle for bored housewives, the kids are off to college, the old man is never home...

This is a nice concept – true training for the non Skull-and-Bones crowd. My only fear is that soon you'll be up some Saturday night at 2 AM, your body refusing to put down that caffeine (oh, please, everything else is so passé') high and some average-looking ex-ambulance chaser with dripping gold chains and a thin red line around his nostrils will appear, unwanted, across the full 24 inches of your new Sony...

"Hi, I used to have a boring, nine to five job working in the mail room of a large, sleazy firm of lawyers. My life was going nowhere. "Bill more hours," they'd yell at me. '"You're not doing your part!"

I went to bartending school, (met interesting people), I went to a computer repair institute, (met interesting machines) but nothing worked until a friend, who just happened to be a CIA station chief, showed me the exciting world of intelligence analysis." (Turn to face camera) "yes, now my life is full and exciting. I meet with people who have many names, and no job descriptions. I have four passports myself, and I get paid to read any book I want, on 'company' time."

"When I meet good-looking women in bars, I simply smile and ask them if they want to come up to my place and watch *Three Days of the Condor* on my VCR.

"You can share my good fortune, while keeping your day job. Just contact the RIA Program at Mercyhurst College, Erie PA, 16546!"

Okay, so I'm a little paranoid. All writers, by definition, are weird. So what?

SPY MAKING

Besides the obvious jokes about where do little spies come from, this is a legitimate concern in the intelligence community. In the good old days (not so far removed as one would think) spies were recruited from a certain stratum of society: college students with aptitude (including those dripping with ivy leaves who belonged to cloistered clubs), ex-OSS officers, would-be ambassadors and army intel graduates.

Well cheer up bunky, if you never had the necessary exposure a couple of things are working in your direction – the aim of both internal and external spying has changed dramatically. Real life courses taught by former or sometimes active agents are available to interested parties (gee, I wonder if anyone ever gets recruited from this fertile ground?)

Hell, the CIA has a job line...

MAKING SPIES ISBN 0-87364-393-3

MAKING SPIES, A TALENT SPOTTER'S HANDBOOK, Cooper/Redlinger, Paladin Press, offers answers to the universal questions of how are bright, loyal, committed people recruited? How are they trained so they not only do their jobs, but remain steadfastly committed to the goals and ideals of the organization?

Depending on whom you talk to, spying is either the worlds first, second, or third oldest profession – soldiers, prostitutes and spies each vie for the honor of a *Jeopardy* category all to themselves.

Many politicians, generals and managers have commented on the importance of spies: one spy can be worth 10,000 soldiers, salesmen or mid level management personnel.

MS is a well thought out, well-documented book on the essentials of the trade. Spies, after all, must be made, they are not born. The authors have produced a rather unique study of finding prospective agents, refining them into professionals and then running them.

Although the concept seems a bit ethereal: "learn a new, high paying job", the execution is a cross between scholarship and effective ideas that can be applied to anyone who runs a detective agency, is interested in starting and maintaining a competitive intelligence division or simply wants to apply tried and true techniques to employee management.

MS quotes from numerous sources and draws parallels between the challenges of executive headhunting and gray-level recruiting. Good for potential Rosenthals, or hip personnel managers.

David Atlee Phillips, a former CIA operative and newspaper editor takes a more hands-on approach to spy employment with CAREERS IN SECRET OPERATIONS, Stone Trail Press, Box 17320, Bethesda, MD 20817.

This book is a summary of job descriptions and application procedures for those of us who feel that the Feds are, indeed, the guys in the white hats.

CISO touches on affirmative action programs, clandestine careers and even opportunities for those reentry folks who never quite made that long trip down the college program.

NEWSLETTERS AND MAGAZINES

AMERICAN JAILS, 1000 Day Road, Suite 100, Hagerstown, MD 21740. Subscription included in $25.00 membership fee. AMERICAN JAILS is the magazine of the American Jail Association, a very slickly produced effort dealing with, well, what you would think it would deal with, jails...

AMERICAN JAILS

Such poignant questions as "Are you concerned about making your jail suicide and lawsuit resistant, health care, efficiency and costs, personnel problems, or perhaps you're just worried about mentally ill inmates?" Whatever your correctional interests, from working in the correctional field to attending AJA conferences or reading about the latest in balancing institutional and community needs, the AJA is for you.

Actually, I'm including this because a certain percentage of you people are going to run out and take some of the techniques and equipment I've given you here and do less than scrupulous things with them. I just know it.

Perhaps you might want to start easing into the next phase of your life by subscribing to AMERICAN JAILS...

BACK CHANNELS, A Quarterly Publication of Historical & Modern Espionage, Assassinations & Conspiracies, Kross Publications & Research Services, P. O. Box 9, Franklin Park, N. J. 06823. One year subscription, $18.00. Sample copy, $5.00.

What do stressed-out spies read for entertainment and to keep up on the ever changing world of espionage? BACK CHANNELS, a magazine which covers espionage and allied fields from a historical viewpoint (John Wilkes Booth, Pearl Harbor, Who Sank the Maine) plus modern news of what spy agencies are doing what, which Medellin drug cartel heavies have been arrested this month, new theories and programs on codes and modern intelligence, along with book reviews on non-fiction and fiction books.

BACK CHANNELS is presented in a magazine format, and although not quite as slick as the full color association newsletters, is extremely well edited and a good read.

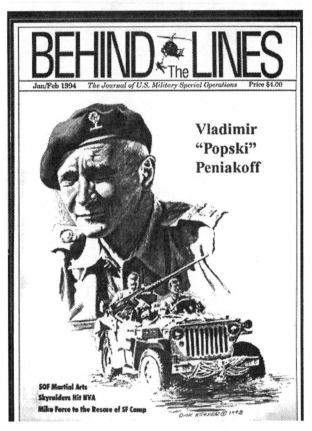

BEHIND THE LINES

BEHIND THE LINES, The Journal of US Military Special Operations, PO Box 456, Festus, MO 63028. Bi-monthly subscription $24.00. The USA Today of the Soldier of Fortune crowd, BEHIND THE LINES started out as a large newspaper-type format. It's now metamorphosed into a 65 plus page magazine. The articles are the real stuff by people who went on various operations or participated in semi-clandestine battles. One can find articles on the taking of Hill 510 (Thuong Duc River Valley, Vietnam) to reviews of the Glock 9

mm pistol and its applicability to Special Ops, articles on Randall knives, letters from various military and ex-military personnel, and some interesting ads.

BEHIND THE LINES is an interesting way to keep up on both the latest goings on of special forces, as well as, new products and offerings of interest to Soldiers of Fortune or would-bees all over the world.

BUSINESS ESPIONAGE REPORT (THE), The Business Espionage Controls and Countermeasures Association, P. O. Box 55582, Seattle, WA 98155-0582. The official newsletter of BECCA deals with anything in the fields of business espionage and competitor intelligence. It is actually published by the Questor Group ($96.00 a year).

The TBER contains short articles and informational pieces, no advertising, but many sources the reader can use to obtain further information. Some of the subjects in the recent past include:

- Professional Sweeps Find More Bugs
- Modular Wire Systems Make Computers More Vulnerable
- "Special Computer Searches" Need Special Supervision
- New Tool Against Commercial Bribery
- BECCA Survey Sheds New Light On Causes Of Business Espionage
- Laser Bugs, Hot topic Or Hype
- The Paper Trail (Internal Directories)
- Spy Entrepreneurs (Target Victim's Best Customers)
- Customized Controls And Countermeasures For Managers
- Spies And Private Lives (A Regular Feature)
- Controls And Countermeasures – Trends
- Checking Up On Mr./Ms. Wonderful
- Intellectual Audits
- "E" Stands For "Examined, Exposed" (Electronic Mail)
- Baby-Com Update
- Intentions Are Number One Target Of Spies
- Treasure Hunt (Courtroom Business Espionage)

- Fake ID And Other Documents Now Easier With Scanners
- Good Book, And It's Free (From The US. Department of Justice)
- Electronic Debugging – Are You Getting Your Money's Worth?
- Parking-Lot Spies

A unique association, a unique newsletter, that touches on electronic surveillance and various overt/covert activities conducted by those of us who think the term spy is only half a word. I don't care if you get that one.

COMMUNICATOR (THE), Ross Engineering 504 Shaw Rd., #222, Sterling, VA 20166. Edited by James Ross, the same gentleman who puts on Surveillance Expo, this monthly newsletter keeps tabs on upcoming expos and acts as an informal catalog for Mr. Ross' selection of products, as well as, some other countermeasures gear and resources.

Jim has been around this field for a number of years now and does a good job of covering the surveillance/counter/information security fields.

COMPETITIVE INTELLIGENCER

COMPETITIVE INTELLIGENCER, Newsletter of the Society of Competitor Intelligence Professionals, 8375 Leesburg Pike, #428, Vienna, VA 22180. A serious, hands-on newsletter for legal spies, or as they prefer to call themselves, competitive intelligence specialists. This newsletter is the official organ of the association and each issue provides a number of articles, papers, and applications of competitor intelligence acquisition and denial. Book reviews, ads, pictures of the nice folk who attend the various receptions and seminars, plus serious techniques, make this probably the best newsletter in its field.

The following excerpt is from a recent article entitled "Intelligence Analysis: the Process of Making Information Actionable."

Analysis is the brain of a modern business system.

A properly designed and organized intelligence system provides the organizational framework for producing actionable information, i.e., intelligence. There are several basic steps necessary to make the information, which the system collects, actionable:

1. *Ensure that you are collecting the right information, i.e., information concerning **significant external** trends. Some form of collection-priorities system is necessary to focus all the corporation's potential intelligence reporters on the few topics of current interest to senior management.*

2. *The **intelligence information** must come from rather unique sources, usually human source reporting or analytically screened published materials. In addition, intelligence analysis of publicly available information can often provide totally "new insights" to readily available information.*

3. *Identification and analysis of the **direct impact** of a reported external event upon your company is at the heart of the intelligence process. Making the linkage between the external development and its potential impact on your company is the critical step. The intelligence analyst usually performs this function.*

4. Assessment of the implications for your company is a very important analytical task. Implications analysis should include an evaluation of the external event's potential impact on your company's position, its performance, or its plans.

*5. Assessing the impact on your company's position, performance, or plans should include the **identification of possible counteractions** or if the external event is one that has been assessed as likely to happen in the future, identification of possible **preemptive actions** that your company can take. The intelligence analysts should include in the report those possible actions that are both appropriate and realistic."*

COUNCILLOR official publication of the Council of International Investigators, Inc. POB 266, Palmer, MA 01069, covers council activities, member news and articles of professional interest. Free with membership which is limited to licensed investigators as well as meet some time-in-job considerations.

A well-known and highly respected organization. I'd join except for clause (b) of the membership application, "(shall be of high moral character").

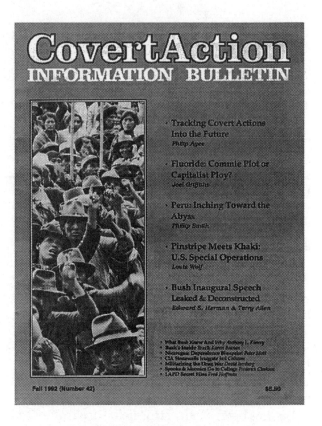

COVERT ACTION INFORMATION BULLETIN

COVERT ACTION INFORMATION BULLETIN 1500 Massachusetts Ave., NW, #732, Washington, DC 20005, published quarterly, $19.00 a year. The best way to summarize the flavor of COA is probably to quote a recent article. "Baker and Bush went around the world, gun in one hand and a begging bowl in the other, and ended up making a profit. This is cold, mercenary imperialism and war profiteering."

Perhaps a bit to the left of some of my more fervent readers, COA nevertheless provides an alternative view of many mainstream press stories, especially those which have to do with national security, the CIA, and the "religious Right." Written by professional investigative reporters, this magazine does stop and make you think.

CRYPTOLOG, Naval Cryptologic Veterans Association 593 Clarmar Drive NE, Salem, OR 97301.

"NCVA is a fraternal group of retired and active duty Communications Intelligence experts.

CRYPTOLOG is the organ of the organization, and is not normally given distribution outside of the membership. In the unlikely event someone wishes to do so, subscriptions are obtainable on an individual basis for $15 a year.

Those who wish to subscribe must advise us their reasons for wishing to subscribe. CRYPTOLOG is printed quarterly, and usually there is at least one and sometimes two extra special editions a year.

This is not cast in stone.

All stories in CRYPTOLOG have been given security clearance by appropriate authority."

Organizational coverage concentrating on who's doing what to whom in the cryptologic world and a few interesting stories and tidbits of news as well as a few reviews and sources.

CRYPTOLOG is not a hands-on code breaking publication, but rather a general overview of this side of intelligence.

P.S. They will not mail CRYPTOLOG copies to blind box numbers or drops.

CRIMINAL ORGANIZATIONS, published by The International Association for the Study of Organized Crime, Department of Criminal Justice, C. W. Post Campus, Long Island University, Brookville, NY 11548, the official newsletter of the IASOC and is free to anyone paying the annual $20.00 association dues.

Papers, articles, and stories about organized crime in the United States (read Mafia) and even in the Soviet Union. Fairly slim customer base, but perhaps if your surname is Gotti, you should think about subscribing...

COVERT INTEL LETTER, Horizone Box 67, St. Charles, MO 63302, 12 issues are $14.00. Beginning with the lead paragraph "your eyes only, not for quotation or reproduction," COVERT INTEL LETTER is a typed, stapled newsletter published by one "Walt."

This is a compendium of high tech weaponry, purchases, and sales, what countries are back in the drug business, who predicts what country will attack its neighbor in the near future, how the former USSR is doing, an occa-

sional book review coverage of various conventions such as SOF, and reports on opportunities for those of you interested in working as a mercenary.

CURRENT NEWS Room 4C881, The Pentagon, Washington, DC 20330-1024. "This publication is prepared by American Forces Information Service (AFIS-OASD-PA) to bring to the attention of key personnel news items of interest to them in their official capacities. It is not intended to substitute for newspapers and periodicals as a means of keeping informed about the meaning and impact of news developments. Use of these articles does not reflect official endorsement. Further reproduction for private use or gain is subject to original copyright restrictions." (Subscription price?)

CURRENT NEWS is the outcome of someone who has the job I want.

Our unknown editor gets to sit in a small room in The Pentagon and cut articles out of everything from USA TODAY to GOVERNMENT COMPUTER NEWS that may be of interest to people in the field of, ah, well, information gathering.

Two editions a year are devoted to spying. This year's features 67 pages of news on the KGB, the CIA, hackers, electronic eavesdropping, data security, and various security breaches.

Remember, these are simply articles taken from other publications and reprinted in full. The problem is I'm not 100% sure who they'll let subscribe, although they were certainly nice enough to furnish me with several samples.

Articles in a recent "special edition" included:
- C.I.A. Sidelines its Gulf Cassandra (New York Times)
- Dirty Little Secrets: Military Information You're not Supposed to Know (Sea Power)
- Conspiracy Itself – KGB: The Inside Story (Commentary)
- Miller Gets 20-year Term for Spying (Los Angles Times)
- US Has 9 Spy Satellites Watching Iraq (St.

Louis Post-Dispatch)
- KGB Bugs Found Above Yeltsin's Office (Washington Times)
- Furtively Infecting the Enemy's Mainframe with an Equally Furtive Sickness (German Tribune)
- Appeasement of Iraq Made Me a Spy (Wall Street Journal)
- Although Impressive, Reconnaissance Can't Get Answers Overnight
- (Atlanta Journal and Constitution)

CRYPTOLOGIA, A Quarterly Journal Devoted to Cryptology, Rose-Hulman Institute of Technology, Terra Haute, IN 47803, $34.00 per year, back issues at $9.00 each. Hands on? You want hands on serious information on every type of code from book codes to the latest in DES crypto systems?

Welcome to the bible.

Articles like:
- Verifying User Identity at the Point-of-Access
- Origins of Russian Navy Intelligence
- Key-Search Attack on Maclaren-Marsaglia Systems
- Vowel Identification: An Old (But Good) Algorithm
- Security of Ultra Dexter and Rabid Intelligence War Department

How serious are the articles? "Cryptanalysis of a Two Round Version of DES Using Index Implications":

Hoping to find a weakness in the full 16-round DES algorithm {1}, a version of the algorithm restricted to two rounds is investigated. Hellman et al. {2} concluded that such a 2-round key search requires approximately $65536*\log_2(65536) = 1.05 \times 10^6$ operations.

This paper presents a method which requires approximately 40,000 operations per key and produces all possible keys which transform known plaintext to the goal ciphertext.

Two-Round DES

The DES algorithm, when restricted to two rounds, can be found in Figure...

In a known plaintext attack, all vectors in the boxes are known. LO, RO, L1, and L2, R2, R1, are determined directly from the plaintext and ciphertext respectively. Since f (RO, K1) = LO R2, the outputs of the S boxes of both Round 1 and Round 2 are known. For a particular S box output, there are four possible input states because each S box has a 6-bit input but only a 4-bit output. The four possible key inputs can easily be found by xor'ing each of the four possible input states with the appropriate bits from E(RO) or E(R1) where E is the expansion function of the algorithm. One would think, therefore, that the search space would be $4^8 = 65536$. Initially, this is what was proposed - ordering the 65536 possible inputs to Round 1, ordering the 65536 possible inputs to Round 2, and looking for matches {2}. However, index implications from Round 1 to Round 2 greatly restrict this search space."

CYBERTEK POB 64, Brewster, NY 10509. For educational purposes only, this "in-house" newsletter of the Cyberpunk generation ("helping people control the lightning") runs a mishmash of electronic schematics, herbal cures, phone phreak tips, surveillance ideas, caller ID info, credit card scams and other useful information.

Sorta a Hints From Heloise for the 20th century.

THE DEFENSE INTELLIGENCE JOURNAL (DIJ). To subscribe first you must join the Defense Intelligence College Foundation, a private non-profit organization established to support the activities of the Defense Intelligence College. This will cost $35.00 and you become a Foundation member which gives you a subscription to the journal. The second method omits Foundation membership and provides a subscription for $25.00 per volume. Either method should go to DEFENSE INTELLIGENCE JOURNAL 1750 30th Street, Suite 441, Boulder, CO 80301.

The objective of the journal, as set out by its co-editors, Robert O. Slater & Mark Weisenbloom, of the Defense Intelligence College, "is to provide a vehicle for defining the

Defense Intelligence Community and enhancing the professionalism of its extraordinarily talented experts. It is designed to promote an intellectual and open debate on the important issues confronting national security and their implications for defense intelligence."

THE DETECTIVE a true bargain, invest five bucks with the US government (specifically the Superintendent of Documents, US Government Printing Office, Washington, DC. 20402) and you'll receive a quarterly magazine published by the Army CICD.

Investigation procedures, equipment reviews crime analysis and other topics of interest.

Ask for "THE DETECTIVE {DET}".

THE EAGLE POB 6303, Corpus Christi, TX 78466. Official journal of the International Security and Detective Alliance. A bargain at $10 per year, THE EAGLE combines classified ads with product reviews, operational tips and items-of-interest to detectives and security folk.

They also market their own line of surveillance and investigative books and reports as well as a couple of home study courses on procedures for private investigators and passing the various state licensing boards.

EXPAT WORLD, "The Newsletter Of International Living" PO Box 1341, Raffles City, Singapore 9117, US $48.00 for 1 year. The "EXPAT WORLD is an organization of INPOPRENEURS, a compound of Information and Entrepreneur. We gather, organize, customize, computerize and publicize information important to the special lifestyle of expatriates and other internationally thinking people and organizations. We sift through hundreds of sources each month to find information that is of interest to our market and save the individual and company alike both time and money. Individuals, small businesses, large corporations and government agencies all use our service."

Need a mail drop in Singapore? Need an agent to purchase Guatemalan property ("a cash buyers paradise"), secret retirement locations, overseas investment services, news on the IRS and expatriates, reports and reviews of how to live abroad, make money, get new ID, and, of course, those ubiquitous full-age ads that say "don't let life pass you by, sweet and sincere ladies are waiting to meet YOU!" These blurbs tend to feature young Singapore lasses desperately trying to look like Vanna White, or wearing one-piece, 1950s style bathing suits.

If you're actually thinking of living life temporarily, or permanently out of the United States or perhaps at one point your business will require this for a time, EXPAT WORLD is a nice way to keep up with what is going on.

THE FINANCIAL PRIVACY REPORT

THE FINANCIAL PRIVACY REPORT PO Box 1277, Burnsville, MN 55337, subscription one year $156.00, sample issue $15.00. FPR has been around a number of years specializing in articles like "7 simple low-cost strategies you can use immediately to shield your assets from lawsuits," along with many tips about dealing with the IRS (or avoiding them all together), legalities of owning gold, how to shop for various insurance, what banks in the world have rolled over and are now turning their customers to one or more agencies of the US government, basically where and how to protect yourself from what the author considers financial improprieties often perpetrated by the government.

FINANCIAL PRIVACY REPORT has a number of very good tips and techniques. My only complaint is the editorial stance is the usual one of expect them to come lock up your savings account, suspend trading of stocks and bonds, declare martial law and take away your wife next month. Subscribe for more details.

FOREIGN INTELLIGENCE LITERARY SCENE, A Bi-monthly Newsletter/Book Review 1800 K Street, NW, Suite 1102, Washington, DC 20096. A newsletter dealing with international intelligence and security. FILS is published by some of the best minds in the American intelligence community (including the late Walter Pforzheimer) and comes to us through the National Intelligence Study Center, which right off the bat should tell you the quality of this periodical is extremely high.

I don't know what I can add to the title and sub-title. They tell you what you can expect to find in each issue of FILS. Let me just say if you're interested in seeing what goes on in the world of intelligence publishing, this is the only realistic entry in its field.

FOR YOUR EYES ONLY, An Open Intelligence Summary of Current Military Affairs, Tiger Publications PO Box 8759, Amarillo, Texas 79114-8759, subscriptions $60.00 a year. A small print, hard newsletter on what's going on, militarily speaking in both the free and less than free world.

No long articles, heavy editorials, or prologizing, just short, accurate news summaries like the following:

Libya and the Lockerbee Bombing:
The Libyan parliament, the General People's Congress, voted on 18 November to accept a trial abroad for the two accused terrorists thought to be involved in the bombing of Pan Am 103 over Lockerbie, Scotland, and the French airliner in Niger. Libya called France, Britain, and the US to "promptly agree on a venue" (in a neutral country) for the trial and to lift the sanctions. All three rejected the idea of a trial in a neutral country and threatened tighter sanctions if the men were not turned over – UPI

M136 Lightweight Multipurpose Weapon (AT-4):
The US Army selected the Swedish Bofors AT-4 anti-tank weapon to replace the M72 LAW after the failure of the Viper anti-tank rocket. While no one-man disposable anti-armor weapon can penetrate the front armor of the latest tanks, the AT-4 can penetrate the side, rear, and top armor of all tanks and can destroy older tanks and lighter armored vehicles.

Advanced Missile Programs:
AGM-130: The US Air Force accepted the first production AGM-130 2,000-pound powered stand-off bombs on 16 Nov.–Rockwell ACM: The Air Force has reduced the Advanced Cruise Missile purchase from 640 missiles to 460 to save money, but averaging development costs over fewer missiles increases the cost of each 61%.–AW&ST, 23 Nov.

TSSAM:
The US Tri-Service Stand-Off Attack Missile will be delayed two years, and planned purchases will be cut from 7,450 to about 4,000 as a cost-cutting move.–JDW, 21 Nov 92.

Coup in Venezuela:

Dissident soldiers seized three television stations in Caracas in the pre-dawn hours of 27 Nov and broadcast a call for the people to overthrow President Carlos Andres Perez. Perez is unpopular due to his economic austerity measures and the widespread belief that his government officials are corrupt.

FUGITIVE, Searching for America's Outlaws PO Box 597785, Chicago, IL 60659-7785, subscription rate $9.95 at this time. The magazine for those of you who can't get enough of AMERICA'S MOST WANTED, FUGITIVE combines article titles like "Killer Claims to Be Cop, Slays Two in Rest Area, Pit Bull Attack, Gang Banger's New Weapon, Serial Rapist Terrorizes Community 25 Women Raped in Two-Year Period.".

Plus hangable wanted posters and missing child articles.

The NATIONAL ENQUIRER-type format (including the ads for instant relief from foot pain) belay the fairly interesting and serious nature of this newsletter.

FULL DISCLOSURE POB 67, Lowell, MI 49331. Started by one Glen Roberts, FD began life, rather timidly as a tax revolt newsletter, only to metamorphosize as a very interesting newspaper that focuses on electronic surveillance, privacy, cordless phone interception, new products and so on. Good buy at $29.95.

THE GOLDEN SPHINX, The Voice of Intelligence, published by The National Counter Intelligence Corps Association 4381 Brauton Rd., Columbus, OH 43220. A scholarly and close held letter that has just opened its membership policy, at least to some degree.

It is the official newsletter of the NCICA (National Counter Intelligence Corps Association), formed by ex-special agents of the US Army Military Intelligence's Counter Intelligence Corps in 1947. At present the publication is not available to non members on any basis. Perhaps this may be changed in the future.

The CIP (Corps of Intelligence Police) came into being during World War I, in order to protect our armed forces from enemy espionage and sabotage, etc. In January 1942, the CIP changed its designation to CIC (Counter Intelligence Corps). At that time, its requirements for joining were strict: college education, preferable in law, an officer's IQ (at least 110 minimum), at least 25 years of age, plus some working capability in at least one foreign language. Exceptions were made as the war progressed, such as younger men with needed foreign language skills (Henry Kissinger, for instance) were brought in; also, skilled investigators such as detectives, reporters (William Attwood, for instance), etc. provided they met the IQ requirement.

Membership in the NCICA is not limited exclusively to former and present counter intelligence agents of the US Army; also eligible are those who served in SIMILAR work in other services of the US Government, provided they pass a stiff examination of their credentials. Thus, agents and former agents in the US Air Force's OSI and in the Navy's ONI are eligible, and some do belong. Former CIA and FBI and other agencies agents who performed work similar to CIC's are also eligible for membership, as are those doing CI work in today's Army. And every year those who, regardless of the above requirements, selected individuals who have made outstanding contributions (Ian Sayer & Douglas Botting, British authors of AMERICA'S SECRET ARMY) are made honorary members of NCICA.

Membership dues at present are $10 yearly, which entitles the member to receive the quarterly issues of the newsletters. Lifetime membership is $150.

The newsletter itself is a combination of historical inside information, as well as, membership news, convention highlights, etc.

I grant you the focus is a bit narrow here, but if you enjoy this sort of thing, a great newsletter.

Sometime ago I received a letter from the editor who had goals to open the membership to a greater audience.

"I plan to seek permission from our Board of Directors to allow anyone who desires, to subscribe for an annual fee about 50% higher than our annual dues of $10. Most of what CIC accomplished in its mission has now been declassified, as witness the recent definitive history, AMERICA'S SECRET ARMY. Hence there is no further need for us to keep our own existence secret any longer."

Whether THE GOLDEN SPHINX has completely opened its subscription qualifications, is unclear at this time.

INFORMATION GATHERER NEWSLETTER a private journal "devoted exclusively to topics of interest to information professionals (i.e., investigators, information brokers, records researchers, intelligence analysts, librarians and related fields). It is circulated throughout the Internet and various public sector commercial networks including CompuServe, Delphi, Prodigy etc.

Worldwide Consultants will deliver this letter via electronic mail, FAX or hard copy. Good articles, reviews of new books, sources for associations, criss-cross directories, phone numbers of searchers and sources.

Seems like a very useful tool at $20 annually.

THE HOT MICX POB 1534 Chandler, AZ 85244. Is a free newsletter to anyone seriously involved in the fields of surveillance and counter surveillance. Published by one Tim Johnson, this letter is a mix of new techniques, tips, tests and upcoming seminars.

If you have a serious interest please write him mentioning this book. Don't bother him just to get another piece of mail in the old box every month...

INTERCEPTS 6303 Cornell, Amarillo, TX 79109. Much good inside information on secret military projects such as the "super secret" Aurora stealth SR-70 replacement. Listings include where the plane can been seen, scanner frequencies to overhear it talking to the tower, and some great, great inside information.

Secret Stealth Facility in California?

Many recent sightings of secret stealth aircraft flying over the Tehachapi mountains, 90 miles north of Los Angeles may be doing so in conjunction with a top-secret facility known as Tejon Ranch, A Northrop aviation facility. The facilities at Tehachapi are located on a hill overlooking the Antelope valley. It is from this valley that California residents have been reporting numerous sightings of strange flying objects that could be secret stealth aircraft conducting tests in association with the Northrup facility. According to Northrop spokesman, the facility known by those who work there as "The Anthill" is used to measure the radar cross sections of aircraft. This possibly explains why stealth aircraft have been seen in large numbers flying over the area. Security around the facility is tight and is guarded closely to keep the curious at bay. In recent months the facility has attracted the attention of UFO groups who say that the facility is a secret communications center used to communicate with extraterrestrials. Many in the UFO community believe that the sightings in antelope valley are UFOs and not stealth aircraft.

IPEC NEWS

IPEC NEWS 305 Ballards Lane, London, N1P 8NP, England, is "a service news publication to help police and law enforcement keep up with developments in equipment, vehicles, services and occupational problems on a world-wide basis."

A collection of product reviews and paid ads for surveillance and tactical equipment, my gut feeling is you get it free if you write on a letterhead.

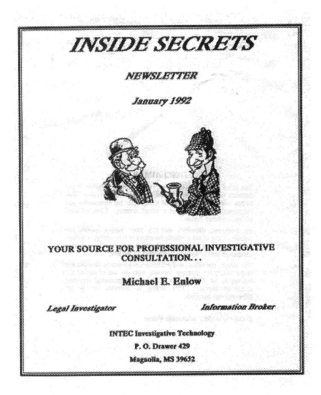

INSIDE SECRETS NEWSLETTER

INSIDE SECRETS NEWSLETTER INTEC Investigative Technology PO Drawer 429, Magnolia, MS 399652. Edited by Mike Enlow a well-known pioneer in the fields of investigative technology and information digging, ISN offers hands-on advice in these fields.

Mike prides himself on the use of inspiration instead of perspiration and offers tips to shorten your time involvement in most investigations, new ideas for electronic surveillance gear and actual investigative and surveillance techniques.

INTELLIGENCE SOLUTIONS NEWSLETTER 7035 Highway 6 South, Suite 120, Houston, TX 77083. $20 a year, monthly newsletter that deals with all aspects of surveillance, intelligence and investigations. Inside stories from the field, equipment and book reviews, helpful tips, addresses.

INTELLIGENCE STUDIES NEWSLETTER, published by The Intelligence Studies Section of the International Studies Association, Sarah Lawrence College, c/o Department of History, Bronxville, NY 10708, designed for members of the ISS, this newsletter highlights college seminars, summer security studies programs, conventions, and papers of interest to the intelligence community.

LAW ENFORCEMENT TECHNOLOGY 445 Broad Hollow Road, Melville, NY 11747. *Free to qualified professionals.* Other, simpler folk need to cough up $60 per year. Try to be a qualified professional. A good, slick magazine with articles like, "Cutting Cocaine Lines Short", or "Community Policing On Horseback", LETN also carries ads and product reviews for new items of interest to cops and security people.

LAW ENFORCEMENT PRODUCT NEWS 100 Garfield St., Denver CO 80206. $20 per year for a large format, glossy magazine/newsletter that runs display ads for products aimed at the security and law enforcement fields.

LEGAL INVESTIGATOR (THE) 3304 Crescent Drive, Des Moines, IA 50312, is the official publication of the National Association of Legal Investigators and can be gotten by joining said organization (assuming you have the qualifications) or by subscribing as a non-member for $35.00

MILITARY INTELLIGENCE, Military Intelligence Professional Bulletin, an authorized publication of the Department of the Army, US Army Intelligence Center and Fort Huachuca, Fort Huachuca, AZ, is published quarterly under provisions of AR 25-30 and the TRADOC Professional Bulletin Policy Letter. Personal subscriptions are a bargain at *$6.50 per year*.

If you like SOLDIER OF FORTUNE, but you want something a little meatier, have I got a deal for you...

R&S PLANNING: CORNERSTONE TO SUCCESS ON THE BATTLEFIELD
What Is R&S and Why Do We Do It?

Reconnaissance and surveillance are defined in FM 101-5-1, Operational Terms and Symbols:

• Reconnaissance is a mission undertaken to obtain information by visual observation or other detection methods, about the activities and resources of an enemy or potential enemy, or about meteorologic, hydrographic, or geographic characteristics of a particular area.

• Surveillance is a systematic observation of airspace or surface area by visual, aural, electronic, photographic, or other means.

How does R&S relate to IPB and situation templates? R&S is conducted to gather information about the enemy which will confirm, adjust, or deny a given template. How does R&S relate to the commander? It provides him the information about an enemy's capabilities and intentions that enables him to gain or retain the battlefield initiative.

For the purposes of this discussion, R&S planning equals collection planning or collection management. Although the level of detail is different (R&S is conducted at brigade and lower and collection management at division and higher), the same principles apply to both.

Paul Revere's ride from Boston to Lexington to warn the militia of advancing British troops is an example of a simple and effective R&S plan.

MONITORING TIMES

MONITORING TIMES published by Bob Grove and the folks at Grove Enterprises POB 98, Brasstown, NC 28902, MT has come into its own as a useful publication for anyone interested in monitoring the airwaves or communication security. $21.95 a year.

THE MOUSE MONITOR, The International Journal of Rodent Control, Scope International 62 Murray Road, Waterlooville, Haants, PO8 9JL, UK.

This rather strange publication has nothing to do with rodents in any form except those that wear badges, work for the IRS or the Customs Service. In Dr. Hill's words, THE MOUSE MONITOR is for bureau **rat** control. The report is sent to customers of Dr. Hill and contains articles on the latest countries that will sell you passports, various reports including the tax haven report, the passport report, the free car report, the Lloyd's report, the Monaco report, the Swiss report, the FBI dossier, etc.

MOUSE MONITOR does have some very valid news on laws passed by different countries about bank secrecy, money transfer, visas and obtaining residence, as well as, legitimate sources to purchase passports from a number of countries that would like to have you for a citizen. For a small fee, of course...

Besides the articles of interest, every issue seems to carry a number of suggestions that roughly fall under the heading of *Sex Havens*. Havens appear to be places where Dr. Hill and staff have investigated the local sexual scene including availability, price, and how much they like Americans.

THE MOUSE MONITOR also contains about four pages of classified ads, samples of which are:

LEGAL 2ND PASSPORT with ID card/driving license, good for visa-free travel to whole world is Just $12,000. For details contact: ICINTL PO Box 108, Chakwal-4880, Pakistan.

CARIBBEAN PASSPORT $5,000. Free details from: Miguel Guerrero, Simferopolsky Bulvar 16, korpus 3, KV21, Moscow 113452, Russia. FAX: 7-095-08875.

CHANGING YOUR IDENTITY? Experience consultant offers discreet confidential consultancy in all matters of identity change, passports (banking and travel) and finance. Full details from: Nicholas Bradbury, 101B Kings Cross Road, London WCIX 9LP.

LEGAL AFRICAN PASSPORT good for banking and travel, £4,000. Free details from David Milton, Suite 1, 281 City Road, London ECIV ILA, UK.

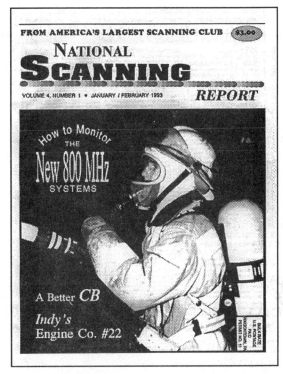

NATIONAL SCANNING REPORT

NATIONAL SCANNING REPORT, Box 360, Wagontown, PA 19376, bi-monthly report for hard-core scanner users. NATIONAL SCANNING REPORT reviews new equipment and books in the scanning field, as well as, publishes three or four feature articles about monitoring little known bands such as the DEA, the Border Patrol, Federal Aircraft areas, etc.

The report does carry advertisements and lists frequencies.

NIMITZ NEWS, Newsletter of the Admiral Nimitz Foundation PO Box 777, Fredericksburg, Texas, 78624.

America's liberty has never been so openly threatened as it was on that "day of infamy", December 7th, 1941. The ensuing war in the Pacific came to involve over two and a half million American men and women, and thousands of ships and planes. Although from different backgrounds, locations and even different branches of the service, all were under the command of Fleet Admiral Chester W. Nimitz, Commander-in-Chief, Pacific Fleet.

The history of the Pacific War is told in Admiral Nimitz's hometown, Fredericksburg, Texas, at the Admiral Nimitz Museum of the Pacific War. This museum is the only one in the world solely dedicated to telling the story of the war in the Pacific. It has been created to preserve and protect the personal memories of the men and women who served and to provide an historical perspective of the events that led to the final victory.

The Admiral Nimitz Foundation is a nonprofit, tax exempt organization whose sole purpose is to support the Nimitz Museum in accomplishing its mission. This it has done with great pride for over 25 years. It strives to achieve the museum's motto: "We inspire our youth by honoring our heroes."

For $20.00 one can become a member and receive the NIMITZ NEWSLETTER which has articles on various reunions, survivor's deaths (I know that sounds strange, doesn't it?) and other news for people who want to relive Dec. 7, 1941.

NORTH CAROLINA INVESTIGATOR is the official publication of the North Carolina Association of Private Investigators. Many states have a similar organization to promote cooperation among local PI's but this particular newsletter is one of the best I've seen covering not only association events, but technical matters and investigative procedures.

NUTS AND VOLTS MAGAZINE 430 Princeland Ct., Corona, CA 91719. N&V started life as a moderate, Computer Shopper/Hemmings type rag with classified ads (and no articles) for the folks who wait anxiously for each issue of Popular Electronics. In the early days we tried to advertise in them only to be told, "we don't want to encourage hackers or people involved in surveillance... One day the publisher woke up to an epiphany and realized where the bread was buttered, if you don't mind me mixing a metaphor, and now N&V carries great articles on cellular hacking, scanning, computer cracking and surveillance.

The ads alone are worth the $34 (first class) subscription price.

PI MAGAZINE

PI MAGAZINE 755 Bronx, Toledo, OH 43609. A relatively new quarterly publication aimed at private investigators and people who like reading about them, PIM touches on surveillance and investigative work as well as providing interviews with notables in this field, reviewing books and some actual entertainment.

POLICE AND SECURITY NEWS POB 330, Kulpsville, PA 19443. An *excellent* buy at $12 per year P&SN is a large format, newsprint monthly with articles and ads of interest to all security, all enforcement and surveillance types.

The ads alone are worth the price of this unique publication which combines the worlds of security and investigation.

POLITICAL WARFARE

POLITICAL WARFARE, Intelligence, Active Measures, and Terrorism Report, is published by the Institute for International Studies, 1815 H Street, NW, Suite 600, Washington, DC 20096.

A typeset 20-page newsletter on slick paper with detailed pictures, POLITICAL WARFARE covers the world from the standpoint of political and intelligence affairs. A large map is printed, centerfold style, showing the world divided into free states, related territories, partly free states and their related territories. Entire countries are reviewed as to their mood, political swings and applicability to tourism from a Yankee standpoint.

PRIVACY NEWSLETTER, Expat World Box 1341, Raffles City, Singapore, is designed to give the read continuous monthly information on a variety of subjects regarding secrecy, privacy and confidentiality and how to protect, preserve and expand his assets and develop tax-free income opportunities. This kind of monthly information is not available from any one source. Regular price US $120/yr, but new subscribers only — $49/yr.

PRIVACY AND SECURITY 2001 is another letter edited by Mr. Ross. This one is a bit more on the meaty side offering articles about new technological threats, as well as, less physical threats such as telecom fraud, and editorial opinions about major news stories that Mr. Ross feels are being manipulated by the major news media.

REAL CRIME BOOK DIGEST 1029 West Wilson Ave., Chicago, IL 60640, is published six times per year for a bargain $10.00 per year subscription fee, with each issue containing hundreds of up-to-date book reviews covering new titles and previously published non-fiction crime books.

Murder ... rape ... robbery ... espionage ... terrorism ... kidnapping ... child abuse ... burglary ... carjacking ... internal ... theft ... organized ... crime ... drive-by shootings ... credit card fraud ... auto theft ... insurance fraud ... hate crimes ... drug smuggling ... piracy ... assassination ... forgery ... arson ... counterfeiting ... stock market ... manipulation ... bank ... fraud ... tax ... fraud ... war-crimes ... white slavery ... larceny ... embezzlement ... unsolved mysteries — the list goes on and on and on!

With tens of thousands of new books published every year – many from small, little-known publishers and university presses – only a relatively few of the books on crime ever get mentioned in the book review columns of newspapers and magazines. And you can't count on bookstores or libraries to carry much of a selection, either, unless it's a best-seller."

REAL CRIME BOOK DIGEST aims their editorial content at "mystery writers, law enforcement officers, judges, criminal attorneys, crime reporters, criminologists, prosecutors, private detectives, librarians, tabloid journalists, armchair detectives, and everyone else interested in real-life criminal activities of all types...

From the LIZZIE BORDEN SOURCEBOOK to WHY LA HAPPENED, Implications Of The '92 Rebellion, this newsletter brings you up to date on any and everything to do with crime.

SECURITY 44 Cook St., Denver, CO 80206. Alarm dealer oriented, carries some products and press of interest.

SECURITY INSIDER REPORT

SECURITY INSIDER REPORT news on encryption, Tempest concerns, hackers, stories of interesting busts and "news, reviews and opinions" from the editor. Oriented towards electronics (cellular phones, computers, software, some surveillance) this is not a hands-on "build it" letter but does offer access to new and inter-

esting sources and products. $99 a year from 11567 Grove St., N. Seminole, FL 34642.

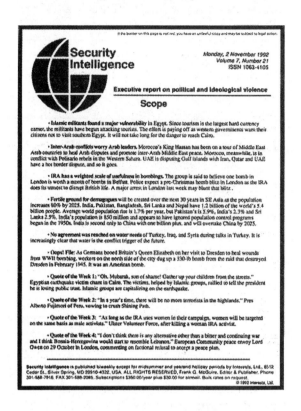

SECURITY INTELLIGENCE

SECURITY INTELLIGENCE, published by Interests, Ltd. 8512 Cedar St., Silver Spring, MD 20910-4322, a very serious newsletter on political and ideological violence ("if the border on this page is not red, you have an unlawful copy and may be subject to legal action"), chocked full of small information nuggets such as:

"American Airlines has become the latest convert to the High-Tech Checkpoint (HTC), installing the system at its Nashville terminal. The concept, developed by the Cleveland-based security firm, ITS, includes cameras, video monitors and radio communications systems for staff. The basic idea of the HTC is to make security a conspicuous feature to enhance its deterrent value, while simultaneously removing its reputation as a bottleneck. A number of airlines have installed the system. AA has 140 daily departures from Nashville, ITS says it is the largest provider of aviation security staff in the US.

Gangs in the US are learning that three members in a car, for drug trafficking or other activity, gives a great advantage in overpowering and disarming a police officer during a traffic stop. Some have been seen training in tactics, including how to destroy video surveillance gear in a police car.

A Moslem in a western US state was recently being interviewed. He refused to answer any questions, even though he was not a suspect in the case. When asked him to swear he was telling the truth, he produced a copy of the Koran. Interviewer said that was not acceptable and insisted he use a bible. A later review by the agency disclosed that it had conducted training sessions in cultural sensitivity so officers could better handle hostage situations or anything else involving minority groups. The officer had elected not to attend the optional training and never got his information."

Not aimed at the armchair follower, SECURITY INTELLIGENCE will set you back $350.00 a year.

SECURITY LETTER 166 East 96th St., New York, NY 10128. Published for the last 24 years is probably the leading executive news service of the security field. They also publish THE SECURITY LETTER SOURCE BOOK which lists thousands of security oriented organizations.

SECURITY MANAGEMENT

SECURITY MANAGEMENT 1655 N. Fort Myer Dr., Suite 1200, Arlington, VA 22209. A very professional magazine on all aspect of security including surveillance and communications. The official mag of the Association of Industrial Security. Product releases, good articles, occasional book reviews.

SECURITY TECHNOLOGY NEWS 1201 Seven Locks Road, Potomac, MD 20854. An 8 pages newsletter that deals with breaking stories about Smart Credit cards, new legislation on communication technology. and some new product reviews. $495 per year. Yes, $495.

SECRECY & GOVERNMENT BULLETIN, Federation of American Scientists, 307 Massachusetts Avenue, NE, Washington, DC 20002. The newsletter published "to challenge excessive government secrecy and to promote public oversight and free exchange in science, technology, defense, and intelligence."

The Federation of American Scientists was begun by four scientists who helped build the first atomic bomb and only afterwards decided that an unlimited nuclear arms race might not be the best thing for the world or for science as a whole. The Federation consists of 5,000 members, most of whom are natural or social scientists, engineers, lawyers and doctors.

As expected, the viewpoint is a bit to the left of other journals we've covered. The interesting point is you can pull lots of inside data on intelligence and security from the pages of this letter.

"A secret spy plane, sometimes called "Aurora," has been repeatedly described in the trade press, especially AVIATION WEEK & SPACE TECHNOLOGY, and recently in an article by Bill Sweetman in JANE'S DEFENSE WEEKLY (12/12/92, pp. 14-16).

The JANE'S article prompted further coverage in the WASHINGTON POST (12/12/92) and elsewhere.

The evidence supporting the existence of something like Aurora, a classified follow-on to the SR71 "Blackbird," is surprisingly diverse, though hardly conclusive. At the same time, the evidence against its existence, derived from budget data, official pronouncements, and related policy decisions can not easily be dismissed. (This evidence is compiled and evaluated in an updated, August 1992 version of the FAS report "Mystery Aircraft.") Most recently, Air Force Secretary Donald B. Rice insisted vigorously that no such secret program exists within the Air Force or anywhere else (WASHINGTON POST, 12/27/92, p. C6).

If it were true, as reported, that a classified hypersonic aircraft is in operational service, the deepest significance of this fact would not be the existence of the aircraft, but rather the magnitude and audacity of the deception that has been perpetrated to conceal it."

Membership in the society is $25.00 a year or if you choose not to be a member, you can still subscribe for the same price.

Very well written articles on a gray area; that is countries that are in between friend and foe and heading in one direction or the other, various terrorist groups and exactly what they're doing around the world, articles about the KGB, the FBI, and the CIA and book reviews on related subjects.

"Soviet sources now confirm that the Soviet Communist Party secretly gave millions of dollars every year in direct and indirect aid to the supposedly independent communist parties in the West. The Soviet government continued to fund the program at least through 1989, even while its leaders were claiming hardship and seeking Western economic aid.

The top three recipients of the direct handouts in 1989 were the communist parties of the United States ($2 million), France ($2 million), and Finland ($1.8 million), according to one published document, said to be a fragment of an International Department ledger. Although details of both funding channels are still emerging, it appears that Moscow was giving the US Communist Party its direct annual allocation of $2 million until 1990. Where there was more than one communist party in a country, aid was usually given to the party having the 'most orthodox positions'."

SLEUTH TIMES, "I play the game for the game's own sake." – S.H., published by McGuffin Productions 51 Main Street, Box 419000, Isleton, CA 95641, subscriptions $10.00 a year.

Reviews, items, books, and games having to do with detectives and their counterparts in the days of Sherlock Holmes. In fact, a large portion of each newsletter is devoted to our old pal, Sherlock and the Baker Street Irregulars. If you have never been a Holmes fan, the amount of interest in this phenomena will shock you.

With articles like:
- How to Live on £800 a Year, Standards of Living in Victorian London
- Does "Raffles" Exist?
- The Gentleman Burglar and Sherlock Holmes

This newsletter should be of interest to game players, Holmes freaks, and detectives with a historical slant.

SIGNAL Official Mag of the Armed Forces Communications and Electronics Association, SIGNAL sports news of its members, much like a company newsletter, fantastic ads for the latest cruise missiles, hi-tech software imaging programs, and equipment reviews. Not exactly a hands-on surveillance publication, but quite interesting. $60 a year to non-members. 4400 Fair Lakes Ct., Fairfax, VA 22033.

SOLDIERS, The Official US Army Magazine, published monthly, Cameron Station, Alexandria, VA 22304-5050. Individual subscriptions are available through the Superintendent of Documents, US Government Printing Office, Washington, DC 20402, designed primarily to keep soldiers and ex-soldiers in touch, and one would presume, to raise morale, this is actually a very interesting publication with articles on very special forces operations.

"If asked to name a state on the front line of America's war on drugs, it's a fair bet that most people wouldn't say Maine. Somehow, this beautiful and of vast forests and rugged coastlines doesn't seem to fit the profile: It's too quaint, some would say; the people are too levelheaded and laid back, others would argue; it's just too far north, still others would suggest...

But they would be wrong. For though the battle against drugs in Maine is certainly not the sort of all-out effort being waged by states like Florida and California, the struggle is no less real and no less important. It's a two-front war – fought on the state's borders as well as across its interior – and it is a fight in which the soldiers of the Maine Army National Guard are playing an increasingly important role.

Those baffled by the state's participation in the counter drug effort need only look at a map. Hundreds of small bays, inlets and islands dot Maine's jagged 1,000-mile coastline, and the 616-mile border with Canada – the longest international border of any state in the Union except Texas – is crisscrossed by hundreds of trails and unmapped roads. Moreover, the state's 1.7 million acres of sparsely populated forested land are ideal for marijuana cultivation."

SOVIET ANALYST, An Intelligence Commentary, published by World Reports Limited 108 Horseferry Road, London SW1P 2EF, United Kingdom, or Suite 1209, 280 Madison Avenue, New York, NY 10016-0802.

"SOVIET ANALYST IS aware that its realistic interpretations off contemporary Soviet/Russian behavior may be less than welcome in certain circles. But this suggests that it is having the desired effect. Because we take fully into account the fact that, as Mr. Dick Cheney, the US Secretary of Defense, noted last year, the KGB and the GRU remain in place, and have in fact greatly extended their operations despite diversionary talk of their reorganization and abolition, our investigations can yield insights which may fly in the face of 'the party line.' Those who may prefer the 'Politically Correct' comforts of fashion, are welcome to their illusions. SOVIET ANALYST is for observers who are disillusioned with and alarmed at contemporary attitudes about the 'former' USSR."

SURVEILLANT

SURVEILLANT, Acquisitions and Commentary For Intelligence And Security Professionals, a bi-monthly publication of the National Intelligence Book Center, 2020 Pennsylvania Ave. NE, Suite 165, Washington, DC. 20006 is an *outstanding* newsletter that anyone involved in intelligence, security or detective work should, in my humble opinion, subscribe to.

SURVEILLANT spends the first few pages of each issue reporting on the latest breaking news in espionage and intelligence complied by some of the top writers and editors in the field. The next 30+ pages review new books, videos and other sources of information.

SURVEILLANT includes detailed reviews of books on military history, intelligence gathering, security, codes and cryptograms, covert action the FBI, CIA, KGB weapons, industrial espionage and info gathering in general.

A very professional look at all sides of intelligence and information acquisition including many things that just don't appear elsewhere, SURVEILLANT is both informative and an interesting read.

TOP SECRET International Group 5139 S. Clarendon Ave., Detroit, MI 48204. Bi-monthly electronic or hard copy newsletter who's goal is to "provide news and information on topics related to terrorism, espionage, data security, surveillance countermeasures, threat assessment and executive protection." $50 per year. Looks like a great idea.

Available in both hard copy and electronic formats.

2008 John S. Wilson, a well known designer of electronic equipment published (note the use of the past tense) newsletters which featured his plans for transmitters, receivers, long range microphones, remote transmitters, car trackers and so on.

The schematics included building instructions and part sources. Most of the units were designed to be constructed for $25-$75. He stopped publishing the newsletter due to some personal considerations and sold the rights to his daughter (DBA Singletary Publishing) who packaged them in both law enforcement and non-law enforcement booklets and resold them at significantly higher prices.

Ms. Singletary, in turn, sold the plans to Mike Enlow who has bound them as a book and makes them available from his company, Intec Investigative Technology PO Drawer 429, Magnolia, MS 39652.

2600 "THE HACKER NEWSLETTER"

2600 "The Hacker Newsletter" POB 752 Middle Island, NY 11953. Run by those nice folks (and their kids) who brought you TAP in the '60's, this is the real thing. Computer, phone and communications hacking. Articles, ads, tips, phone numbers, meetings of similar minds. Subscribe...$21.00.

Dick O'Connell, Publisher, Washington Crime News Services, 3918 Prosperity Ave. Suite 318, Fairfax, VA 22031-3334. This is a special category, so rather than repeat myself 83 times, I'm going to group a series of newsletters all published by the same publisher, that may be of interest to people in our profession.

CORPORATE SECURITY DIGEST, $147.50 per year. Targeted towards professional security administrators in a corporate setting, CSD provides comprehensive coverage of security headaches including electronic surveillance, computer cracking, and security investigations.

CORRECTIONS DIGEST, $124.75 per year. "The only independent news service for the corrections professional." Articles like Tuberculosis Outbreak at San Quentin and Inquiry Stepped Up in Georgia Women's Prison Sex Case." The audience for this particular newsletter is probably fairly limited.

CRIMINAL JUSTICE DIGEST, $70.00 per year. Covers job stress, laws, and items of interest to justice administrators.

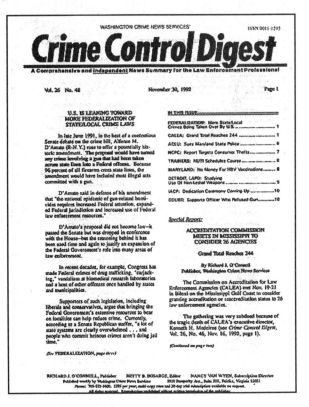

CRIME CONTROL DIGEST

CRIME CONTROL DIGEST, $147.50 per year, a comprehensive and independent news summary for the law enforcement professional.

CRIME VICTIMS DIGEST, $55.00 per year. This newsletter is actually more targeted at the police officer or person in charge of victim compensation than it is for actual people who have been mugged. New laws and new policies that affect people dealing with victims of crime.

COMMUNITY CRIME PREVENTION DIGEST, $55.00 per year, "a monthly summary of significant news of community anti-crime programs."

JUVENILE JUSTICE DIGEST, $87.50 per year, "An independent summary of significant news events in the field of juvenile delinquency prevention."

NARCOTICS CONTROL DIGEST, $124.75 per year. News of fugitives, drug testing, asset seizures, the border patrol and who's doing what to control the drug flow in this country.

NARCOTICS DEMAND REDUCTION DIGEST, $100.00 per year, "Prevention – Education – Treatment – Rehabilitation."

ORGANIZED CRIME DIGEST, $124.75 per year, "An independent news summary of organized crime activities," for law enforcement and investigative professionals. Professionals who demanded an accurate, timely and complete information news source they could depend on – bringing them the latest in court decisions, trends, tactics, legislation, training, seminars, conferences.

TRAINING AIDS DIGEST, $75.00 per year. Just what it says it is – a listing of upcoming training and seminars from the Institute for aerobatics research to street survival seminar.

Also includes tips on training for specific scenarios.

SPY WEAPONS

Over the years spies and spy agencies have developed some of the most unique "special purpose" weapons imaginable. Take the KGB umbrella with the poison tip, or a few years ago when an unusually high number of our guys seemed to be dying of heart attack for no obvious reason.

Finally a forensics expert noticed tiny slivers of glass in the collar of the one of the victims. From this it was deduced that the KGB was putting Prussic acid (cyanide) in small glass capsules which were then loaded into a pressurized "pen."

When activated the capsule was broken and the acid shot into the face of the victim, often from the inside of a rolled up newspaper. The killer took an antidote (photographer's hypo) for several days in advance of the big event, held his breath, blasted the target and just walked away.

On the other hand the CIA, according to at least one gentleman who worked directly for them designing such toys, is directly responsible for the invention of the felt tip pen.

See, the agency needed a way to silently kill certain targets in public places without attracting unwanted attention. Our friend came up with a mixture of deadly snake venom and DMSO (the latter being a chemical which has the ability to pass through skin and muscle tissue taking other chemicals with it).

Place some DMSO mixed with lemon juice on a finger tip and 30 seconds later you will taste the lemon.

Put some DMSO mixed with a three-step, paralyzing venom, apply it to exposed skin and about 5 seconds later you ain't gonna taste anything...

So how to get from a safe container onto the intended target?

The answer was to place the liquid in a pen and then replace the hard tip of the pen with a small felt wick that would deposit a drop of the contents when "accidentally" touched against your airplane seat mate.

"Stewardess, stewardess, I think there's something wrong here."

Add ink to the mixture and damn thing actually wrote...

The best source(s) for details on spy weapons are three books all written by one H. Keith Melton.

Mr. Melton is without a doubt *the* authority on special purpose weapons. There is some speculation as to exactly how he has gained access to some of this interesting, but undoubtedly, classified material.

I would speculate he has a friend or two in the Company, and when I spoke with him, he admitted that some things he could not get the good guys to admit existed, the KGB was happy to show him examples they had taken from captured CIA agents...

Hey, get it where you can.

OSS SPECIAL WEAPONS & EQUIPMENT Spy Devices Of WWII ISBN 0-8069-8239-X published by Sterling Publishing Company, Inc., 387 Park Ave. South, New York, NY 10016, $10.95.

Forward by one William Colby this is a look at the rare "mail order' catalog published by the OSS in 1944, of specialized equipment available to the secret agent. These items, from one-man submarines to gloves that shot bullets, fountain pens that shoot darts, H capsules that will automatically ignite two hours after being dropped into a gas tank, dog drags which discouraged blood hounds (or German Shepherds) from tracking their quarry and devices to blow up passing trains.

You can see the roots of many of today's modern special weapons (some of which are on the market) in this very interesting work along with a confidential equipment list for a guerrilla force of 3,000 men, photos of OSS insignia, ID cards and so on.

Besides being a hell of a read, including stories of Australian coast watchers, "famous" escape raids, and sabotage operations, many of the procedures are still valid today.

The book itself is a "coffee table" design, i.e., laid out well and attractive enough to leave around when the in-laws visit. It is the type of book one can pick up, open to any section, and lose about two hours of your life...

CLANDESTINE WARFARE
ISBN 0-7137-1822-6

CIA SPECIAL WEAPONS AND EQUIPMENT
ISBN 0-8069-8733-2

CLANDESTINE WARFARE Weapons and Equipment of the SOE and OSS distributed by Sterling Press. Joined by James Ladd, Mr. Melton has written a comprehensive history of both the British Special Operation Executive (SOE) and the American Office of Strategic Services (OSS).

Much more than a just a book on weapons, this is a study of some of the most important operations of both these elite groups, as well as the design, purpose and use of the weapons and special equipment required for their success.

A great diversity of ops is covered from assassination, elimination and sabotage to escape and evasion, radio work and even military and industrial intelligence collection.

CIA SPECIAL WEAPONS AND EQUIPMENT Spy Devices of the Cold War. Sterling $10.95. Some of the most ingenious spy toys were developed during "peace," rather than during periods of active fighting.

You will find everything from exploding flour to a rubber airplane that can be assembled one man in under six minutes, all types of surveillance cameras, plus the professional versions of many of the electronic surveillance units you'll find in this very book.

Some nice stuff on codes, including the use of one-time pads, burst communications, infrared flash photography, lock pick kits and field casting techniques.

All fully documented with photographs and how-to-use drawings.

"The Camouflaged Weapon, 22 caliber is pre-loaded for a single shot and may not be reloaded in the field. It has the same appearance as a standard European king-sized cigarette. When concealed in a pack of cigarettes it is indistinguishable."

CIA CATALOG OF CLANDESTINE WEAPONS
TOOLS, AND GADGETS
ISBN 0-87364-576-6

CIA CATALOG OF CLANDESTINE WEAPONS TOOLS, AND GADGETS John Minnery. Paladin Press. Saw blades in eyeglasses, on belt buckles and buttons, itching powder dispensers (!?), mini-guns, stashed daggers and so on.

Not as complete as the above selections, but a nice starting point. Mr. Minnery used to be known as "Dr. Death" because of some of his earlier books, especially the "How To Kill" series.

He became rather well known when he turned a gentleman who had tried to hire him to kill his wife over to the authorities.

He later got a nice mention when he committed suicide.

No, I don't know how.

Paladin Press also has a video tape on the manufacture of homemade C-4 for those situations when the local hardware store is closed and your local explosives supplier has thoughtlessly taken a vacation in Club Fed.

While the resulting product is not technically PETN or RDX based C-4, it is a moldable plastic explosive that works quite well.

FEDERAL BOMB INTELLIGENCE US Government Guide to Terrorist Explosives ISBN 0-87364-613-4, also from Paladin is a reprint of an official guide to some of the latest terrorist explosive units including their method of operation, working schematics and photos where available.

Not exactly WAR AND PEACE but if you're into this sort of thing, it's a must read.

Picture this, you and your team are called away for a sudden, clandestine mission in a small but important Latin American country. You gather up your gear only to realize some stupid SOB has shot the last Stinger Missile and not replaced it.

You have neither the time, nor the $75,000 to run out and replace it. What to do? What to do?

BACKYARD ROCKETRY
ISBN 0-87364-690-8

BACKYARD ROCKETRY Converting Model Rockets Into Explosive Missiles by Bic Farrell, Paladin Press. When I was a kid the name Estes was hallowed.

Named after the small town in Colorado where they lived and worked, this company sold kits that allowed semi-juvenile delinquents to put together these amazing rockets.

Powered by real rocket engines, the large models would actually travel several thousand feet straight up, in the blink of an eye.

What a rush!

The idea was that you could mount a small a camera on them and get a photo of the neighborhood, or a little radio transmitter, or even a mouse. The rocket was designed to float back to earth after a firecracker sized explosive charge expelled a parachute.

As you can probably guess, I spent most of my time with this these "toys" trying to top them with cherry bombs, M-80's and homemade bombs.

Yes, I still have all my fingers, although at least one of my friends can no longer make that claim...

BACKYARD ROCKETRY takes this idea and turns it into a science. As the book says, "Don't settle for those lame model rocket kits available from the hobby shop. By modifying and adapting the engines and the rockets it's possible to create short and medium range surface-to-surface and surface-to-air missiles for some *serious* fun!"

"Everything you need to know is here, principles of operation, safety precautions, improvised warhead and missile designs."

I've also discovered this book is a real conversation starter when read on airplanes or just left lying around the airport waiting lounge.

Defense Systems Group has found a nice elderly German engineer who will duplicate 3 of the original OSS type watches. The first has a 1 1/12" switchblade which pops out and the touch of the stem, the second produces a garrote and the third simply provides a nice hiding place for folded hundred dollar bills, pills, or other small objects of interest.

The watches, which resemble Rolexes in design actually work quite well. I wear one. $300-$600 price range.

CHILDREN

It's never too early. If a kid shows any inclination or aptitude towards the spying game, there are a few things on the market you can get to encourage his interest in this honorable career.

The first one is sort of a test, in fact there might be something you wanna read just to make sure of your feelings before you actually get into this field. It's called LET'S TALK ABOUT SNOOPING by Joy Wilt Berry, Published by Peter Pan Industries, 145 Korman St., Newark, NJ 07105, ISBN 0-88149-012-1. This book contains a number of basic rules and regulations for people who might wish to violate another's privacy.

"It is important to *respect other people's privacy*.

It is OK for people to have thoughts and feelings that they keep to themselves.

Do not try to get people to share the thoughts and feelings that they may not want to share."

"Do not get into another person's dresser drawers, cupboards, or closets without permission"

"Do not go into someones' room without asking. If the door to a room is closed, knock on it and wait to be invited before you go in."

Basically, this book lays it all out in plain English, i.e., don't spy on other people, don't watch other people without their knowing it, don't listen to people when their on the telephone, for God sakes don't ever their private possessions or drawers. Basically, the old Winston Churchill attitude of "gentlemen don't read other gentlemen's mail."

THE YOUNG DETECTIVE'S HANDBOOK Learn How To Be A Super Sleuth by William Vivian Butler, Joy Street Books published by Little, Brown and Company, ISBN 0-316-11889-3. This book teaches kids, hell, this book would teach half my friends actually, how to do such practical exercises as send secret messages, lift fingerprints, create disguises, fill out reports, make and break codes, starting your investigation, how alibis are used, tape recorders, cameras, "modern detection equipment," locks and padlocks. It even includes a test case for you to solve at the end of the book.

Mr. Butler suggest you form a detective club to get-together with your friends and do such things as, have a disguise party. Now, note that he says this is nothing like a costume party, its not supposed to be outlandish, the idea is to have a serious contest to see which boy or girl can assume for the evening, a personality, most unlike their own. Or you can do such things as have deduction contests. Hey I gotta tell ya, some of this stuff is pretty hip, take for instance, the deduction game:

Deduction Game

"To start the game, you divide the club into two teams, A and B."

"You pass the objects, in turn, first to one team and then the other. (Obviously, if Team A gets first look at one object, then B should have first look at the next.)"

"Each team then has *three minutes to deduce all it can about the owner of the object from the things which it contains.*"

"Someone has to act as chairman and timekeeper, and sit between the teams with a stopwatch and a gong. Someone else should also be on hand to run out to telephone the objects' owners to confirm deductions if and when required."

"At the end of the three minutes, each team is allowed to make either definite statement scores guesses about the object's owner. A definite statement scores 2 points if it turns out to be correct, but loses 2 points if wrong. A guess scores or loses only 1 point. Team B is obviously not allowed to repeat any of Team A's deductions, but they can turn one of Team A's guesses into a definite statement, if they have found new evidence which proves the point."

Here's an example of how the game works.

"Let's say that the first object handed to Team A is an old blue rain slicker, obviously a child's. The first thing the team must decide is whether it's a boy's slicker or a girl's. That's easy, of course; boy's coats button left over right, and girl's coats right over left. This slicker is found to be a boy's."

"Next the team must look at it and try to guess the age of the boy. It seems to be about the right size for a ten-to twelve-year-old."

"But wait. In the left-hand pocket of the slicker, there is a foreign coin – an English 2p piece. This could mean either:
  (a) The boy has recently been to England, or
  (b) Someone gave him the coin."

"There are two other things in the left-hand pocket: a torn ticket to a Red Sox game and a small quantity of what looks like beach sand."

"Now the price on the Red Sox ticket is 75¢. Someone says that it's been years since a ticket to a major ball game cost as little as that. No one knows how many years, but it looks as if the boy who owned the slicker is much older than ten to twelve now!"

"Before time runs out, somebody thinks of looking to see if there's a label inside the slicker itself. They find the name of the store at which it was bought – Macy's. This means that the boy probably lived in New York. Suddenly the team strikes gold; they find a name tag, ROGER RIVERS."

Just then the gong goes. Team A's three minutes are over. They decide that they have deduced eight things. Here they are, with the possible point gained, if the deductions prove to be correct.

1. The slicker belongs to a boy. (Definite statement: 2)
2. He was, at the time he wore it, ten to twelve years old. (Definite statement: 2)
3. he may now be sixteen to eighteen. (Guess: 1)
4. He had been on a beach. (Guess: 1)
5. He had also been to England. (Guess: 1)
6. He is a baseball fan. (Definite statement: 2)
7. He lived in New York. (Definite statement: 2)
8. His name is Roger Rivers. (Definite Statement: 2)"

Really a good book, highly recommended.

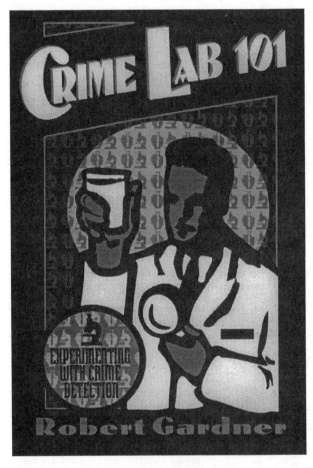

CRIME LAB 101
ISBN 0-8027-8158-6, ISBN 0-8027-8159-4

CRIME LAB 101 Experimenting With Crime Detection by Robert Gardner, Walker Publishing Company, Inc., This book is definitely beyond about half my friends. Do you know how to classify fingerprints? Using the Standard FBI

Sub-categories? Can you tell the density of glass by simple experiments? Or perhaps, read lip prints taken at the scene of the crime? Do you know how DNA testing works, or how blood samples are classified?

The book goes on to show how typewriters are used as evidence. ^It encourages deductive reasoning and sharpens one's observation skills. A number of good experiments, I mean some that you could use, are presented, for instance, do you know how to tell if a certain pen wrote a certain letter?

"To see what a chromatography test is, first collect several different felt-tip and ballpoint pens that all have black ink. Then cut some strips about one inch wide and six inches long from coffee filters or white blotting paper. About an inch from one end of the strip, draw a narrow line with one of the pens. On separate strips of coffee filter or blotter paper, draw similar lines with each of the black pens you have collected. In Figure 18a, you see the strips with the lines marked on them suspended by strips of tape from a long strip or rod. The tips of the lower ends of the strips, below where the black lines have been drawn, should just touch the surface of the water in a wide container. Notice how water moves up each of the strips. What happens when the water reaches the ink?"

"Leave the strips for an hour or so. If the air is very dry, the water may not carry the dyes in the ink far enough to separate them. If that is the case, support the strips in a tall bottle or jar. By covering the top with aluminum foil, you'll reduce the evaporation rate. Water will then travel farther up the paper strip."

This procedure will tell you if two inks are the same.

WHO DUNNIT?
ISBN 0-590-44717-3.

WHO DUNNIT? How To Be a Detective in Ten Easy Lessons. by Marvin Miller, Published by Scholastic Inc., 730 Broadway, New York, NY 10003.. Another book designed for kids as well as a number of test cases to see if you have actually learned the lesson.

"A detective sometimes needs to disguise his or her voice when speaking on the telephone. A good way to do this is to talk with a pencil between your teeth. (It takes practice to do it well!)" And you never know when may have to fool somebody, or how bout a detective tip: " If you want to walk up a flight of creaky stairs without making any noise, follow these directions. First, take off your shoes. Then, walk on the outside tip of the steps the stairs will squeak the least that way."

Besides these little helpful gems, the book is full of mystery riddles and crimes for you to solve. I'm not going to detail the entire problem here, but I will show you the answer:

"Dennis claimed that he was knocked down with only one punch. But if this were true, both his cheeks would not have been bruised unless a very large fist hit him right in the middle of his face. But since the picture shows that Dennis's nose was unharmed, he had to be lying. Dennis soon admitted that he had faked the robbery and stolen the money himself."

ESPIONAGE by Deborah Bachrach, Lucent Books, San Diego, CA, ISBN 1-56006-134-0. Spying from a historical perspective is presented for young readers, grades 5 through 8. Traces the history of spying and the issues it raises for present and future generations.

TOP SECRET
ISBN 0-8075-8027-9.

TOP SECRET Codes to Crack by Burton Albert, Jr., published by Albert Whitman & company, Niles, IL. A basic book on the art of cryptology, some stuff that's so simple, it would probably be very hard to crack frankly, for instance:

"Switch Ditcher"

"To ditch those with an itch to sniff out a secret, try this twist on a letter switch. If a word has two, three, or four letters, switch only the first two letters:"

"GO EAT A BEE'S WING"
"OG AET A EBE'S IWNG"

"If a word stretches five letters or farther, flip-flop the first two and the last two letters:"

"I PREFER HONEY MYSELF"
"I RPEFRE OHNYE YMSEFL"

"*HINT*: This key works best with words that have no more than six or seven letters. Also, the word strings can be made to look mighty mysterious with big, bold letters snipped from newspapers, magazines, and other products of printing machines."

SECRET CODES by Falcon Travis, Hodder & Stoughton Publishers, Mill Rd., Dunton Gree, Sevenoaks, Kent TN13 2YD. Another book designed to allow young cryptographers to exchange secret messages, while also teaching them about the makeup of codes, code grills, symbols, one time pads, invisible inks and special code words.

Includes a section on codes and ciphers in games and contests and also shows how to break codes. A little more complete than the last entry and an interesting book in it's own right.

THE SPY CODE HANDBOOK How to make code and cipher machines to outfox your enemies by Duncan Ball & Ian Ball, CollinsAngus & Robertson Publishers Pty Limited, ISBN 0 207 17718 X. Whew!!! Now we're moving up in the world, if the Germans had had this book, the war would have lasted another 5 years.

In all seriousness, this book shows the basic design of a number of devices that have been (in more complicated forms, of course) used to automatically encode and decode messages between secret agents for years and years.

Learn how to use the triangle encoder, the code wheel, my favorite word template, the Jefferson Wheel, Playfair Mat, Notch encoding, and so on.

An interesting book that, again, will serve as a basic text on cryptology whether your are a child or old enough to put a copy of PLAYBOY in front of the book while you read it.

"The Combination Letter Template is a variation on the simpler, one-piece Letter Template. The principle of hiding the message in plain sight is the same. The message is simply scrambled and can only be read with a similar template. The advantage of the Combination version, which is made in two pieces instead of one, is that any one template can be used in 192 different ways instead of forty-eight ways. By turning one piece of the template while keeping the other piece still, you can create a whole new Letter Template."

"The Jefferson Wheel. When the third president of the United States, Thomas Jefferson, invented this very clever way of enciphering message, the cipher must have seemed unbreakable. It was so good that it was used as a military cipher, even as recently as the First World War."

"We now know that the Jefferson Wheel system is not unbreakable but it is very difficult to crack because it is a multiple-substitution cipher. This means that a given letter, for example "a", might be enciphered as "C" and the "X" and then "T" all in the same message, making it very hard to guess which letter might be which."

"Jefferson's original machine had a number of cylinders strung together on a rod. To simplify making the wheel we've flattened the cylinders out into discs but the principle is exactly the same."

WHEN ANDY'S FATHER WENT TO PRISON
ISBN 0-8075-8874-1

WHEN ANDY'S FATHER WENT TO PRISON by Martha Whitmore Hickman, Albert Whitman & Company, 5747 Howard St., Niles, IL. Several of my favorite fan letters from BOOK II HOW TO GET ANYTHING ON ANYBODY came from nice folks who said things like, "great book! Techniques really work. I just got a little carried away."

They tended to come with a prison based return address. So, if you are going to indulge yourself and ignore my warnings, this book might be a nice Christmas present for the kids.

A story about when Andy's father is sent to prison for robbery and the family moves to be near him. Andy is afraid of what the kids at his new school will think and how he solves the problem.

HOW TO LOCATE & BUG ANYONE

Once thought of as only seen in James Bond type movies, ES has moved into the general populace with a bang. No longer the exotic fare of spy books, electronic assisted intelligence collection is actually very common.

How hard is it to purchase room bugs, telephone taps, long distance parabolic microphones, video cameras hidden in briefcases, car antennas, plants, power transformers and rocks (!)? {Knox Security}.

An interested party can:

- Go to your neighborhood Surveillance Supplier for automatic telephone conversation recording interfaces, miniature wireless mics (room bugs), miniature recorders, tapes and all the ancillary materials associated with stage one surveillance.

    You know, good old Radio Shack...

    For those of you hooked on the idea of justice, you'll be gratified to know that after three books highlighting Tandy Corporation as the most extensive supplier of low end surveillance equipment in the world, they have finally canceled my credit card.

    I prefer to think of this as pure coincidence; in fact, I fervently believe they should not only offer my readers a small discount, but me, say a minor commission on surveillance products, after all I've done for them.

    Well anyway, tell 'em Lee sent you...

- Visit one of the many "spy shops" and shop in person.
- Place a mail order for any manner of spy goods from one or more mail order companies (both in the US and abroad) who make a living supplying devices one step removed from the CIA.

- Construct an exotic intelligence gatherer from a simple "kit" or circuit available from a number of sources.
- Pay your local private detective, handyman or ex-KGB agent to procure and place such a device for you.

Electronic surveillance is the ultimate shortcut to intensive intelligence. A small transmitter clustered in-between the leaves of the rented Rhododendron at the next board of director's meeting of your main competitor (or, say Exxon oil) can produce real time data that is simply not available by any other means.

A recorder on your competitor's, your in-house manager, or your girlfriend's phone can just cut through miles and miles of bullshit...

Electronic surveillance is not an exact science, it's more of an art – a black art. In order to get the results the agent must take all factors into consideration including how and where the bug is going to be planted, how long the batteries must last, how strong the unit should be, if someone is likely to be looking for this type of activity and so on.

The key to a successful job is planning, planning and more planning. If possible test all the equipment involved in a similar environment before actually planting the unit. Will the signal penetrate the building's walls?

How far will your receiver pick up the audio? What happens if you plan to use a vehicle as a listening post and some thoughtless SOB takes the parking place you had counted on?

Then there is the question of risk, both personal and psychological, versus the potential gain. One gentleman I know who does this sort of thing for a living recently worked two "significant others" surveillance jobs.

One was an older man, quite well off, who was married to a woman quite a few years his junior. He was getting suspicious of various behaviors and had my friend tap her phone and install an infinity transmitter at the house.

The first conversation he listened to was between her and a girl friend wherein she not only confessed an affair but made jokes about the "old man" trying to have sex with her, ending the conversation with the fact that she wished he would "hurry up and die" so she could inherit and get on with her life.

The second job was for a doctor who had recently become engaged and was just looking for some supporting evidence before going through with the wedding.

He got it. The woman admitted to her old boyfriend that she was marrying strictly for the money and planned to keep up their relationship on the side.

Results?

The second guy called my friend to thank him from making the biggest mistake in his life.

The first guy had a heart attack after listening to the tape.

Some responsibility travels with these actions.

Note that most professionals charge quite a bit of money to plant a bug or tap. The primary reason is the risk involved. Traditionally if a spouse plants a bug in a domestic dispute and gets busted he/she will skate. If a pro is involved, and busted, he can probably plan on subletting his apartment for the next year...

Exactly how prevalent is the use of electronic surveillance? The largest supplier of civilian bugs and taps would probably be one FEDC (First Electronic Development Company) in Japan. They do not sell to retail customers directly, but supply both Micro Electronics and T. Satomi who not only sell direct, but distribute the units to many other companies both in the US and abroad.

I'm trying to say they are pretty good and pretty popular.

The units are very effective and quite inexpensive. FEDC uses three main frequencies for all their transmitters and accompanying receivers.

Recently I happened to be in New York City with a friend who is, among other things, a real scanner buff. We set up his car scanner on these three frequencies and cruised the city for the better part of a day.

We were able to get audio in *every borough,* often every few blocks.

Remember these units are extremely low powered and have a range of several hundred feet, yet reception was almost as easy as listening to a regular radio station...

OKAY.

Time for the big disclaimer – *most* electronic surveillance is illegal without a warrant, even the procession of devices "designed primarily for the surreptitious interception of conversations" is against the law.

I am NOT, read this slowly, pronounce every word, <u>AM NOT</u> advocating the ownership or use of illegal devices.

People DO go to jail for this...

On the other hand, in some states it is perfectly legal to record any conversation in which you take part in (without notifying the other party of such recording). In some, the owner of a business can legally record his employee's telephone calls (made from business phones), without any warning, and some states even allow the owner of house to tape all calls made by *anyone in his house with no notification necessary.*

Police departments, among other groups, are infamous for getting the goods by less than scrutible means and then producing them in court from a "highly reliable informant."

And they ain't the only ones...

An informal, but probably fairly accurate survey conducted by yours personally would indicate ES is used in the following situations (in some sort of order):

- Spousal surveillance. Right. Just hook up the $24.95 Radio Shack "Telephone Secretary" to your long play recorder and stash it in the garage, near the telephone wires and *voilà*, a concentrated version of what girlfriend/wife passes on about your personal habits to her best friends...

And/or who she's having these dilemmas assuaged by. NOTE, Lee's second law of personal constructs states "nobody says nice stuff about their significant other on the phone."

For some reason it doesn't seem to be allowed.

So be prepared to hear the worst if you resort to this method of information collecting, and take the time to compare it to a recording of you and you best friend discussing the high points of the monogamous system.

Well, look at that...

- The big number two would have be business intelligence, not always as conducted by an outside party. Competitors, inside people coveting your next promotion, a private secretary who likes to amuse her friends over the after dinner joint, about what a geek you are, your boss (or employer) who is worried about the upcoming union vote, salary cutback, or just wants to see who is goofing off or spreading stories in the executive's toilet (has happened, sometimes legally).
- Private detectives doing their thing.
- Professional business spies; sorry, I mean professional competitor intelligence people.
- Illegal law enforcement surveillance.
- Real spies. Yes, even though we send out invitations to the North Koreans, Iraq, Iran and Russia for each and every White House cocktail party, there seems to be a lot of still-employed spies lurking around trying to prove their worth.
- Hobbyists. No I'm not kidding. This concept may be the next hula-hoop, spying on your neighbors and friends for the pure entertainment value of the act. I recently did an audio piece for a major "network show" about the interesting stuff that can be scooped from the ether with a scanner or near-field detector and the right antenna.

Besides the obvious cellular phones, you got your wireless units that can be inter-cepted a mile or two away with a long antenna, not to mention those cute little baby-sitter transmitters that people never turn off even if the baby is no longer in the bedroom, CB's, two-ways, backstage security at the hot rock concert, the Feebs, the local narks busting your neighbor (you know, the one with the new Mercedes). "Private channels" between TV reporters and the newsrooms, cops, etc., and manyother interesting entities of the airways.

Remember that these choices represent only *passive surveillance* possibilities, nobody is forcing them to talk or has actually planted a surreptitious listening device.

These are the freebies...Imagine the possibilities if you put actually some effort into the eavesdropping effort.

Legal law enforcement surveillance. Approximately 1,000 warrants are issued in an average year for court ordered ES. All fall under strict guidelines as to length of the effort, who can be recorded, and when and if the parties have to be arrested or notified of the surveillance.

1,000 a year? Makes you wonder how AID, HDS, and other major law enforcement surveillance suppliers can not only make a living, but keep their 100+ employees off unemployment, doesn't it?

Well, the point of this dissertation is that electronic surveillance is very productive, very accessible and very cost efficient.

It's also quite easy to do...

Now these pages are not designed to make you a summa cum expert in the fine art of audio surveillance, this just would not be fair to those who of us are not Johnny-Come-Lately's in the spy biz.

The first, and definitely way-paving book to bring the fine art of electronic spying and other esoteric arts to the general public would have to be THE BIG BROTHER GAME, Scott French, Lyle Stuart Publishing. ISBN 0-8184-0241-5.

Scott took the then-virgin science of audio surveillance with covert entry techniques and other "black" sciences and made them accessible to Mom and Pop Public.

The book was outlawed in several countries (selling for as much as $200 "street value" as the DEA would say, in England). It earned a number of dubious honors and got Scott the chance to have some down to earth, no holds barred, talks with the FBI, who were less than enthused with his selection of topics.

It also has been used by every bloody intelligence agency from the KGB to Mother's Against Drunk Drivers.

Okay, the last part's a lie, but the part about the KGB is true as is the CIA, Howard Hughes and many other rogues.

A bit out of date, but still the book that broke it open.

I would like to think that my very own follow-ups, HOW TO GET ANYTHING ON ANYBODY and BOOK II HOW TO GET ANYTHING ON ANYBODY have moved the Olympic spying torch in the right direction.

To my way of thinking, the ultimate compliment came when a gentleman from one of the country's largest private detective firms was called in front of the US senate to show how he turned up "forbidden" evidence" on whistle blowers on the Alaskan pipeline project including their private phone call information, hidden addresses, letter covers and so on.

In response he quietly held up a copy of BOOK II HOW TO GET ANYTHING ON ANYBODY...

You can't buy that kind of testimonial.

Disneyland, I'm going to Disneyland...

Short side of a long tale, I'm not going back over the how-to's and where-for's of electronic surveillance simply to take up room in this book.

Look at the first two in order to understand what has come before.

In the WHOLE SPY CATALOG I'm going to concentrate of what's new, what works, how to get the correct tools and how to implement them to best effect.

I am, of course, assuming you have a legal reason for knowing these things.

If you are not 100% proof positive – contact a good lawyer.

Let's look at electronic surveillance from the bottom up; what do you need, how's the best way to get it?

NUTS AND BOLTS

How big is the electronic surveillance game? To what extremes has the hunt for audio taken mankind? How common is it? How difficult is it?

Let's start, as the Rabbit told Alice "at the beginning, go to the middle and stop when we reach the end".

For the most part, the equipment and techniques I'm including are unclassified, and usually available. ES operates on Reaganomics – the trickle down theory is always in effect. First the big guys, the CIA, DIA, NSA and so on, get the goodies and then as they are replaced by even newer, better designed units, the technology trickles down into law enforcement and then into the general marketplace.

Or, at least that's the way it used to happen. Neat things like the first infinity transmitters, first scrambled bugs, burst transmitters and other high tech gear were rumored in the early sixties, and then available through a few law enforcement only suppliers like the George Cake Company and KEL.

The FBI has closed its research facility at Black Lick Road, Newington, VA and now has a 400,000 square foot four floor, (two above ground – two below) research facility at Quantico that employs some 700 people from meteorologists to electronic engineers, to keep as much technology in-house as humanly possible.

They have first access to military and other agency toys. They also immediately purchase anything new on the open market, test it and then duplicate it if they like it.

The NSA even has its own chip making plant.

Today the business is, as they say on wall street, market driven. Although, still not on a par with the technology employed by the three letter agencies, very sophisticated gear often appears first on the "civilian" marketplace because that's *where the customers are.*

Of course, there are some limitations imposed on this type of technology, but a number of ways exist to bypass many of these restrictions as we'll see in a few minutes.

How exotic does electronic surveillance actually get? You might want to look at US Patent # 3,952,583 reprinted in part here. Yes, it's a real patent for reproducing ambient audio from tree bark.

SUMMARY OF THE INVENTION

The subject invention provides a novel method and apparatus for the covert surveillance of distant conversations, movements of people, movements of vehicles, and the like. This is accomplished by the remote detection of vibrations of a diffuse surface of which some examples are windows, window shades, door panels, walls and trees.

The remote detection is accomplished by the employment of coherent radiation. A beam of coherent radiation is projected onto the diffuse surface to be monitored. The diffuse surface is composed of randomly distributed points. The beam of coherent radiation is scattered by these points. This results in a time-varying intensity distribution, which is dependent on the vibration frequency of the diffuse surface. The time-varying intensity distribution is detected by a photodector and converted into time-varying electrical currents. These currents are used to activate a loudspeaker for audible display or an oscilloscope for visual display. In addition, these currents can be used to activate an alarm or a similar device.

It is an object of the subject invention to provide a method and apparatus for the remote detection of vibrations of diffuse surfaces.

It is a further object to employ both visible and invisible wavelengths of coherent radiation in a method and apparatus to carry out the remote detection process.

Rumor has it that this concept was offered to a number of US military intelligence agencies.

I don't know if they ever actually used it...

I can tell you that Converse Technology, Inc., a publicly traded firm (NASDAQ), known for the design and manufacture of several telephone/communications related products has recently marketed a product known as AUDIODISK.

AUDIODISK is a multiple channel, digital multimedia recording system designed for intelligence gathering and surveillance applications.

AUDIODISK is probably a bit over-built for most of my readers; each system has the capacity of recording something like 93,000 conversations at once...

Are they selling? Well Converse was happy to recently announce the receipt of two orders totaling $35 Million.

Now, who do you suppose would want to monitor thousands and thousands and thousands of "private conversations"?

A large chunk of the AUDIODISK business comes from foreign governments.

Some also seems to come from the US...

It's a fairly well-known fact that The National Security Agency has, for years, monitored each and every overseas phone call, FAX or telex. Such monitoring is done in real time by computers and artificial intelligence programs that search, in many languages, for key words or phrases.

If they hear a bad word, the conversation is recorded and electronically flagged.

NSA denies they do this on internal calls, but with the installation of fiber optic cables, microwave and satellite links, *it would certainly be possible.*

NSA owns the largest and fastest computers in the world.

Period.

They are also the largest employer of any single security agency.

HOW TO LOCATE AND RECORD ANYBODY...

Although the thrust of electronic surveillance over the last few years has been towards video set-ups, audio, almost unnoticed, has also made some great leaps forward. In this section I'm going to concentrate on improvements and new concepts in the exciting world of audio surveillance.

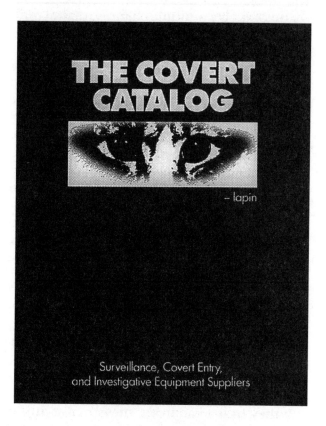

THE COVERT CATALOG
ISBN1-880231-14-X

I will be mentioning a number of specific products and suppliers, for a complete listing I suggest THE COVERT CATALOG from Intelligence Incorporated ($34.95). The CC actually started life as a section of this book.

The concept was to show sample pages from manufacturers and suppliers of audio surveillance, video systems, cameras, transmitters, covert entry gear, lock picks, spy schools, expositions, training materials, body armor, spy shops, electronic tracking systems and so on.

I wanted to provide a picture of who actually makes what, when to buy from the Original Equipment Manufacturer and when to go to a distributor or dealer, as well as how to get the best prices by shopping directly at the source.

When the concept grew from a single chapter to 220 pages, I decided to package it as a separate book. I tried to include every legit supplier I could from giant law-enforcement only houses to the Japanese company that really makes half the gear advertised by mail order suppliers and shops.

THE COVERT CATALOG is printed electronically, in fairly short, fairly expensive runs in order to keep it as current as possible.

The only other "catalog of catalogs" I could locate in or near this field is THE UNDERGROUND DATABASE.

This work is much wider in scope, listing suppliers for cable TV boxes, hobby materials and so on. The listings are much less detailed and seem to have been pulled primarily from ads in *Soldier Of Fortune* type magazines.

Many of the suppliers are duplicated in several different categories.

RECORDERS

The heart of any audio surveillance job, whether trying for room or telephone conversation is the recorder that actually collects the sound.

Recorders come in a variety of shapes and sizes equipped for many different types of audio collection and reproduction.

One feature found in many surveillance oriented recorders is the ability to record for a length of time exceeding that of the tape used. Most small recorders utilize cassettes as the recording medium.

At "normal" speed the amount of recording time on one side of any cassette is going to be somewhere between 1/2 and hour to a full hour. The longer the tape is, the thinner it will be physically.

Thin tapes tend to jam and/or break more easily in low end recorders than do their thicker (shorter) counterparts. They are also subject to "bleed through", a phenomenon in which the magnetic field from one side of the tape affects the recorded image on the other side, especially when stored for a length of time.

Tape that has bled through is very difficult to listen to as it has the "echo" of the other audio image superimposed on the original material.

This means that most of the tapes you will use can record a maximum of 45 minutes or perhaps on full hour before requiring a turn over.

One exception to this rule are the cassettes sold by Executive Protection Products in Napa, California. They offer special, longer play cassettes hand loaded for extended recording times.

The simplest solution to limited recording times is to slow the recording speed of the recorder (and playback unit, if separate) down to a fraction of its rated speed. This has the same effect as lengthening the tape itself.

Like every good thing in life there are some trade-off's – the first one being that as tape speed decreases fidelity drops off sharply. Music masters are recorded at the highest speed available, usually 30 inches per second, so each segment (or note) of audio is exposed to more tape.

With each subsequent speed reduction the same audio must be captured on significantly less tape.

As the tape speed drops, certain frequencies also "fall off".

The tape also may suffer from increased physical misalignment causing an increase in both wow and flutter.

While you should not plan on recording music on any slow-speed recorder, it is still important to maintain an acceptable signal to noise ratio, as well as, good enough fidelity to understand the audio.

This is particularly important in surveillance applications where the original audio may be located in less than recording studio conditions. While there are a number of things the operator can do to help guarantee the quality of the recording when setting up the recorder, and some fairly sophisticated noise reduction systems that can improve recorded tapes, nothing in the world can recover audio that *isn't on the tape.*

Many lower priced "surveillance" recorders slow the tape speed by simply increasing the size of the capstan "doughnut" and, in fact, I've actually seen some examples where a rubber band was glued around the wheel, or electrician's tape wrapped around it.

All of these solutions are unacceptable, uneven wear on the doctored doughnut will soon cause major variations in the tape speed to the point where it may become impossible to play back a tape recorded earlier on the same machine.

Such cheap approaches do nothing to compensate for the various audio deficiencies that also crop up.

There are a couple of ways to reliably control the speed of a recorder:
- Replace the speed control chip in electronically managed units
- Replace a *gear* in the capstan drive

The units also should incorporate a frequency compensation circuit that will over accentuate the high frequencies when recording. Some top line units also increase the strength of the bias signal in order to saturate the tape.

Under most circumstances I do not advise the purchase of any unit that does not meet these criteria.

The only exception would be when it is necessary to trade off size for fidelity. If a recorder is to be hidden in a very small package, or secreted on someone's body, it may become necessary to use a sub-miniature, micro cassette based recorder.

The good news is that most of these units offer the option of recording at half speed to increase the recording time. The bad news is that it is virtually impossible to add much in the way of additional circuitry to compensate for any loss in fidelity because the units simply do not leave any extra room in their case to hold additional boards.

It is possible to slow these miniature recorders down using the same methods as with their larger cousins, but I don't advise taking it to the extremes because the smaller tape is already carrying the same sound with about half the area.

A micro-cassette recorder line that has proved itself in law enforcement applications is the PEARLCODER models offered by Olympus. These units can be purchased at any better electronics store.

Most law enforcement types do not seem happy with the Olympus L-400 due to a high motor noise component.

The very, very best sub-miniature recorder is undoubtedly the JBR made by the leader in film and video recorders, Nagra. The JBR was designed to the specifications of an FBI agent and named after him.

The unit scarifies a few amenities, such as the ability to rewind the tape or play it back without separate units, for size, but it is crystal controlled, reel-to-reel and offers perfect sound capture and reproduction.

It is also several thousand dollars and sold only to law enforcement...

The closest civilian counterpart is probably the RN-36 by Panasonic. This unit also houses the playback amplifier in a separate case. The tiny recorder snaps in and out of the housing for recording and playback.

The RN-36 is micro-cassette based and offers good sound at a price about $2800 less than the Nagra. The problem is in locating them – they work so well law enforcement agencies scarf them up.

A few people do modify the 36 for longer record time but it is difficult to get anywhere over 2 hours on a 90 minute tape.

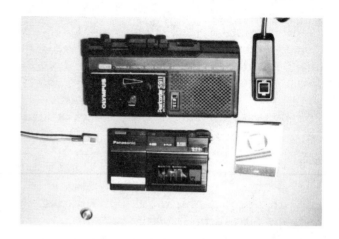

The RN-36 and the Olympus PEARLCORDER.

Small, "throw-away" recorders that work as well, or some people think *better than* either Radio Shack or Olympus are available from, well, K-Mart.

These small K-Mart GE units, that are really made by Panasonic are great for quick and dirty jobs and they are about as cheap as you are going to get.

A few other features are optional in surveillance units that you may or may not worry about:

• Does the unit make an audible "click" ("crick" on the Japanese units) when the tape ends and the unit shuts off? This can be embarrassing in certain situations.

• Is the VOX (voice activated relay) that will automatically turn the recorder on and off with the presence of sound (to save batteries and tape) included in the unit or must it be added? Is the VOX fully adjustable or is it simply switched on and off? How fast does the VOX activate and deactivate? Slow units, or those that switch off too rapidly produce a very annoying "whirp" with every segment of audio during playback.

Note that *all* VOX's are pretty much shunned by law enforcement folk, especially on a government level. Because of their nature you will always miss a tiny portion of the conversation and a single mistake can toss the tape right out of a courtroom.

Record several different sections of audio, at different levels and then listen to the playback to see if it is acceptable.

- Will the unit record directly from a phone line or will it require an external drop out relay to record phone conversations? If this connection is internal, test it to see the degree of hum on low level recordings.

- Is the unit mono or stereo? For 99% of all applications a monaural recorder is fine, and may even be preferable because there will be only one microphone (or receiver) in use and twice as much tape is available for the actual recording.

In some court level recording situations a stereo recording can provide more realistic and listen able audio. This is particularly true when the recording is to be accomplished with several people present. The stereo feature helps eliminate the "cocktail party effect" where the voices blur together into one unintelligible mass.

Marantz stereo recorders are a traditional solution to this problem when extreme miniaturization is not an issue and now Radio Shack makes an inexpensive "Marantz type" stereo handheld recorder, the 141205, for about 80 dollars.

These are great for briefcase applications, intelligence kits, anywhere a high quality recording is necessary.

The other major consideration is a bit more subjective – do you need a professional unit or can you get by with an "amateur" version?

The difference is in both the original recorder, as well as, in the modifications. Most pro units are "battleship" grade, i.e., larger and built much more solidly. A professional unit should offer a choice of battery or AC power, have a large internal speaker, at least one earphone jack (often more than one), provisions for an external microphone and a heavy duty motor/drive.

These units are by their nature larger than their non-professional cousins, but if size is not a mitigating factor they will last longer and player better.

A good example of a professional, slowed speed recorder with all the bells and whistles is made by OMNICRON. Their recorders are not made for surveillance per se, but for logging – that is the automatic recording of on-going audio, such as the dispatcher in a police station.

The units run at slow speeds, some offer more than one channel of recording at the same time. The fidelity is good and the unit was *made* to run at its operating speed.

They are also fairly expensive.

Intelligence Incorporated offers the a professionally modified EIKI recorder that offers many of the same features at a more reasonable price including record times of up to 20 hours on a single tape.

Even with special circuitry it is just not possible to recover the same quality of audio as it is with a standard speed recorder.

Extended play, smaller cassette recorders that seem to be correctly modified and compensated and without the usual "surveillance" markup of several hundred percent are sold by both II and VEC Electronics.

A recorder can be used for stand alone surveillance; one can simply turn the unit on, adjust the VOX to the correct level and stash it under the couch, or behind Aunt Mildred's portrait.

Such an attempt is pretty five and dime and the result is going to be right up Mr. Woolworth's alley.

At least, *at least*, try to establish where the center of the conversation is going to take place and attempt a placement that will be not only in the vicinity, but offer an unobstructed path to the audio.

Avoid insides of filing cabinets or the bottom of wastepaper baskets because the tunnel effect can create a strange, "hollow" ambiance that does not help keep the target audio up front and clean.

Remember that, unlike our ears, recorders are not selective – they record incoming sound at the same level without discriminating between wanted and unwanted audio. If other people (besides your targets) are talking nearby they will be also be recorded, possibly over the conversation you need.

Radios, record players and televisions are obvious sources of audio interference and should be avoided.

Uh, so are bed springs...

If used as a body wire, the recorder should be separated from the body by a piece of Moleskin or an Ace bandage. The microphone should not chafe against clothing or be positioned so the clothing will muffle the recording.

The wearer should be instructed how to stand near the sound source, not cross his or her arms, nod in agreement rather than adding unnecessary "uh-huhs", and not feel as if the recorder is in plain view of everyone in the room.

It is very important to run practice scenarios with first time wire wearers.

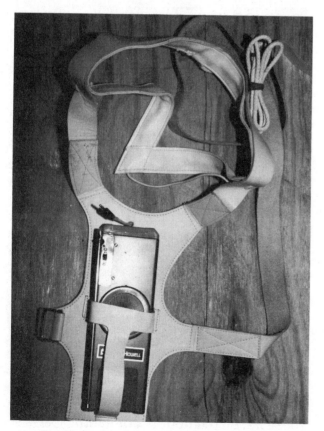

One of the very first Kel based body wire units.

A complete discussion on the placement of both recording devices and transmitters is presented in the book HANDS-ON ELECTRONIC SURVEILLANCE.

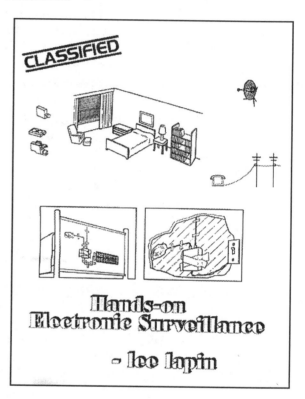

HANDS-ON ELECTRONIC SURVEILLANCE A serious look at installation procedures from body wires to bugs and taps. Pretty much the only thing like it.

The next best thing one can do to improve the quality of a recording is to use an external microphone hooked to the recorder. This set up offers a number of advantages over the stock internal microphone:

- A tiny mic element can be used which is easier to conceal and can be placed closer to the COC.
- A more sensitive microphone can be used to improve sound quality.
- The sound can be run through an external preamplifier and/or compressor. The preamp will allow for more sensitive operation, the compressor has the effect of reducing the background noise-to-audio ratio, providing a more understandable recording.

Good external microphones are available from any competent electronics or surveillance supplier. Compressors and pre-amps come from Viking electronics.

A special type of microphone that is powered by the recorder (or pre-amp) and incorporates an amplifier *with the mic element* is called a line driver. LD's can actually send sound down thousands of feet of wire with little or no loss in quality.

This is especially handy if you can incorporate telephone, intercom or alarm wires that are all ready in place.

One other recent offering of interest is a combination microphone/pre-amp that plugs directly into and sits on the microphone jack of a cassette recorder. This provides for a much better pick up range allowing the combination to be concealed in a room as a *fait accompli'* and still provide acceptable audio.

This inexpensive unit, the R E 8000A is available from Iliadis Electronics.

It works magic on most recorders, the only problem I had with the unit after testing it on several different recorders was that one unit had a little bit too much motor noise which the pre-amp boosted into an unacceptable motor boat sound.

For the most part this little 70 buck unit will greatly enhance a room recorder's pick up capability.

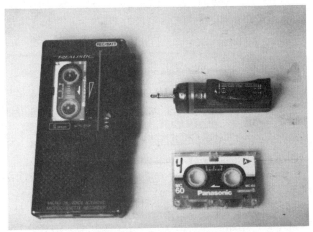

The R E 8000A actually has dual pre-amps and built-in filtering.

Another traditional use for recorders has been to place them in an object not normally associated with audio capture. Briefcases are a prime example of this particular facet.

A locked briefcase can easily be "forgotten" after an important conference, meeting or job interview.

When the embarrassed owner shows up 20 minutes later to claim his portfolio, he has a crystal clear record of what the principles discussed after the meeting.

Professional briefcases can be purchased from a number of suppliers, or a clever person can make his own by simply mounting a recorder in a case with the microphone sealed in place over a tiny hole.

It is wise to use a separate mic element and a compressor or pre-amp like the Iliadis' unit to guarantee steady sound. A switch of some sort should be employed to activate the unit at the proper time. A simple solution is a mercury switch that will activate the recorder when the case is moved to a horizontal position.

The criteria for a commercial case should include:

- A completely "buried" recorder so the case can be opened without casting suspicion.
- An extended play, VOX activated recorder.
- No visible holes in the case (some manufacturers hide the mic directly under the latch hole).
- Incorporation of a remote turn-on feature. Note that most cheaper models utilize a key chain automobile alarm transmitter for this purpose. Not a satisfactory concept, realistic range is about 25-50 feet. A couple of cases are available with an Israeli based remote that will provide several hundred feet of clearance.
- A hardened case; preferably a Haliburton type metal shell.
- Possibly a fail safe operation indicator. One supplier hides an inauspicious LED under the latch lever that can only be seen by someone looking for it...

Recorders hidden on one's person can be boosted by the use of a specialized microphone.

Defense Systems Group has pioneered the development of camouflaged body wire microphones.

They offer two models, each based on an extremely sensitive electret mic element that is connected to a miniature power supply/amplifier. One mic is hidden in a fake Monte Blanc pen, the other in a dress shirt *button*.

The pen is placed in a shirt pocket, a tiny hole is punched in the back of the material and the cord is positioned so it runs to the hidden recorder.

The button is simply incorporated into an available buttonhole and the wire placed inside the shirt and down to the recorder.

Very slick, very hard to find, makes for court level recordings.

A less expensive "boosted" pen mic is also carried by Intelligence Incorporated.

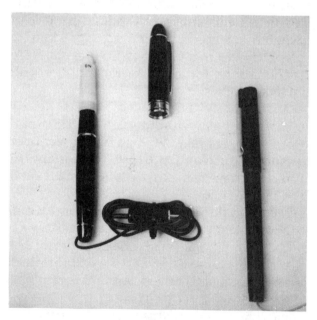

The Defense Systems faux Monte Blanc amplified pen (L) next to II's model.

SURVEILLANCE SCIENCE

In Surveillance situations, you should be aware of a number of considerations in order to obtain the highest quality product.

- The closer the microphone is to a sound source, the better the audio recording. A distance of a few inches can reduce the sound considerably.
- A microphone inserted behind a pinhole will pick up the same amount of sound as a microphone located inside the room, but at a reduced level. The microphone should be sealed securely against the barrier or wall.
- The agent should be aware of audio disturbances, especially those that may be overlooked during quiet periods, i.e. hidden water pipes, refrigerators, dishwashers, and air conditioners.
- Most of the intelligibility of speech ranges between 600 to 800 Hz and 4 to 5 KHz. If frequencies outside this range are blocked or attenuated, a large percentage of any audio disturbances will be reduced, however, intelligibility will remain.
- Room construction (windows, carpet, and brick for example) and furniture placement will effect sound pickup by softening or increasing the reflection of sound.
- Getting a preliminary survey of your target room will help in determining the most probable conversation area for best bugging.
- People with access to target areas should check out construction details, remember those air conditioners and heating ducts which might conduct sound away from the target area.
- Its easier to distinguish single conversations in a room full of talking people if you use binaural recordings.

WALLS NO WALLS

The Art Of Non-Invasive Surveillance.

Or as the FBI likes to call it, Non-Access Surveillance.

As readers of my earlier books know, for some reason I've always had a morbid fascination with listening through walls. This inclination is probably a left-over from my rocky childhood days sitting crouched in the dark basement pressing a crystal guitar pick up to the wall we shared with the Nicholson family.

The Nicholson family with three teenage daughters. Three gorgeous, teenage daughters who were just in that stage when boys were objects of desire.

The Nicholson parents both worked day jobs.

True, my grades suffered a bit at the time from a noticed lack of attention to my homework, but the experience has definitely given me an edge in my real profession, the writing of porno novels...

And wherever you are today ladies, I would like to offer my heartfelt thanks for the many wondrous hours I spent never watching daytime television. I'm probably the only person alive today (well, of any age) that has never seen a single episode of the Mickey Mouse Club or Popeye The Sailor.

An experience I still can look forward to in my senile years.

All right, enough reminiscing, the point is that listening through walls is in fact quite possible and the equipment has become a trifle more sophisticated at about the same rate my taste in women has.

The theory is still the same, you need to pick up the faint sound waves that travel both through the air and the solid structure itself then amplify them several thousand times while keeping the noise down.

The most reliable method was pioneered by a number of law enforcement suppliers in the 50's and 60's and involved special microphones that had their pickup element sealed against the outside world except for a hollow plastic tube.

The tube came in two basic garden varieties, rigid and flexible. The larger, say 1/2" diameter rigid tube was designed to be inserted in a hole in the wall, usually the hole created when an electrical outlet face plate or telephone wall box was removed.

In most apartment houses, hotel rooms and condos, contractors save money by placing these units directly across from one another. If even a tiny crack or outlet hole is open (and often if it's not), into the target room the sound will be picked up by the tube microphone.

A couple of words of caution here, never use a metal tube, and do not poke *anything* into a live electrical outlet without the necessary knowledge and precautions.

Caution note number two, just as with bugs and taps, it is illegal to use most through wall devices to overhear or record conversations without the consent of the parties involved in said conversations.

Check the laws.

On the brighter side of things you do not need access to the actual target room (often obtained through something those in the business call breaking and entering) to record the audio therein.

The tube mic that utilizes a smaller, flexible plastic tube is designed to be inserted into cracks or under doors where it accomplishes the same job as its fatter cousin

These mics are still available from several sources or you can easily construct your own version with some hobby store plastic tubing, a small mic element and some liquid plastic or fiberglass.

Remember the idea is to stop all sound from reaching the microphone except that which enters through the tube.

Once you have opened or drilled a tiny hole in the wall (exact procedure in BOOK II HOW TO GET ANYTHING ON ANYBODY), the tube should be further insulated from ambient noise by wrapping it in foam or fiberglass building insulation.

It should NOT touch any portion of the wall except at the opening.

The microphone should be connected to a moderate gain amplifier, or in some cases can be run directly into a tape recorder.

Micro and Security Electronics has refined the idea of a tube microphone with their SM-66 HI-POWER PROFESSIONAL, contact type mic (we'll get to those in a minute), amplifier and a hollow syringe type needle that, well, let's let Micro tell you what it does: "Attached needle microphone catch the raw voice through extremely narrow crack of door, window, or wall excepting the noise of surrounding on building."

I don't think I could have said it better.

The second sonic solution depends on the wall itself for audio transmission. When a person speaks the surrounding walls, windows, and even objects in the room vibrate slightly with the audio.

These vibrations can be picked up by what is known as a contact microphone. Essentially these devices utilize a piezo electric crystal that "translates" mechanical vibrations into sound.

This sound is minute and must be amplified several thousand times before it becomes audible. The contact mic should be pressed tightly against the wall, and full padded headphones should be employed to avoid feedback.

A quick trick is to use double sided Scotch type tape (made by 3M, available in office supply stores) to stick the surface of the contact mic to the wall.

Contact microphones are easily available from most surveillance suppliers and even some hobby sources like Edmund Scientific. Low end units, as you would suspect, do not usually work as well as those that cost a bit more.

The most famous contact microphone is probably the "CONCRETE MIC" offered by Cony Electronics in Japan. You can find their quaint advertising in many other catalogs offering the unit for several times the original $70 price.

And let me be the first to break the bad news to you Virginia, it does not "pick up mutual conversations though concrete block of 30 CM thickness".

On the other hand, neither does anything else on the market.

Traditionally the best contact microphones have come from German suppliers like PK Electronics or specialty houses like Kaiser Electronics and carry a price tag of $300 or $400.

Luckily for people who share my fascination with this science, the engineers at one company seem to have spent much of their childhood in dark basements also...

Iliadis features a number of units designed to hear through structures. Their basic MICRO-EAR model includes a sensitive vibration pickup that can be pressed against a wall or will magnetically leech onto anything metal, a good amplifier and Walkman type headphones.

Although the company suggests you use the product as a security monitor by attaching the contact mic to anything metal, such as a filing cabinet or a car door, the unit works on non-metallic walls better than the low end Japanese units, and just about as well as the high end German units.

Price? Ninety bucks.

For an additional ninety bucks Iliadis will throw in a crystal controlled transmitter that hooks up to the amplifier and broadcasts the sound to your scanner (48.9 MHz) several hundred feet away.

This is a bargain, trust me when I tell you this.

Iliadis has gone one step further and combined the contact mic and transmitter in a single unit. The magnetic sensor is covered by a thin rubber membrane and four AA batteries snap directly into the back.

Again, Iliadis suggests leeching it onto a file cabinet to function as an in-room sound catcher/broadcaster. This concept works quite well, thank you, but how does the combo unit work on walls, or even on an outside window?

Pretty good. Nice pickup range, especially on a metal surface, but will work on any smooth wall. Crystal controlled, very stable signal easily picked up by a scanner.

Only complaint is battery time is only a few hours, but for a quick drop, non-invasive surveillance job it does work

It is also possible to use a non-contact microphone designed to function as an "electronic stethoscope" to pick up audio that is too faint for the unaided ear. The best acoustic stethoscopes are undoubtedly those made by Kaiser Electronics.

Mr. Kaiser offers several models, one of which is designed to accentuate the ultrasonic end of the audio spectrum for the detection of mechanical devices such as bomb timers, but it works quite well in the speech frequency bands.

A couple of years ago a new approach to the problem of collecting and converting low level mechanical vibrations appeared on the industrial scene. Paper thin strips of Piezo film, a unique polymer product that acts as a transducer (microphone/speaker), temperature sensor, infrared reader and vibration sensor have been employed as accelerometers.

The feather weight metallic film picks up minute vibrations that can be amplified and presented as a display of mechanical vibrations or as *sound*.

Atochem North America 172 Big Valley Road, Folsom, CA 95630, markets Piezo film in a number of configurations including a $150 accelerometer kit that works well as a contact mic.

Security Research in England offers an accelerometer packaged as a complete contact mic system including a 35 – 95 dB gain amplifier, VOX switcher, and probe kit.

This unit is probably the ultimate toy for people who like to keep a close tab on their neighbors. Price? Ah, figure on parting with a several grand...

Contact mics can be improved by the addition of a "spike." This is nothing more than a solid, nail-like, uh, well, spike.

The spike is usually pointed at on end and designed to grip a contact mic at the other. Early spy films had wily eavesdroppers pounding the spike into the outer wall of buildings and then hooking up the earphones in order to hear every whisper in the structure.

In real life one inserts the rod portion of the device into a hole that has been drilled into, but not through, the target's wall. The spike transfers the vibrations back to the contact mic, providing a much shorter and more accurate path to the required vibrations.

Spike mics went out of vogue for a time, but are back from Audiotel, Intelligence Inc., and even Illidas who offers an odd, foot and a half long flattened strip with a wooden handle that can be "inserted into the ground in order to hear footsteps and subterranean water flows," or inserted into a wooden wall to "listen for termites." — Okay...

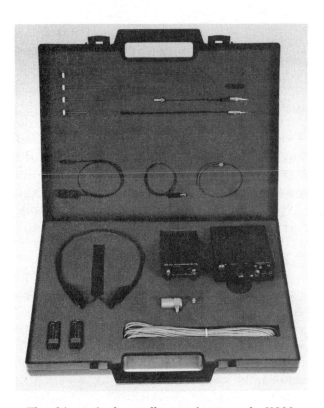

The ultimate in thru wall entertainment – the X500 Through wall listening system. includes 95dB amplifier, 4 interchangeable probes, an accelerometer, VOX, recorder output and a neat carrying case.

A look at a 1950s era spike mic.

Most spike mics now have gone back to the concept of using a needle thin "spike" that is really a tube coupled tightly onto an extremely sensitive electret mic element. Most kits offer several "spike" lengths.

The best, and most expensive unit comes from our friends across the pond at Security Research which is part of their X500·package and includes; four tube "spikes" ranging in length from a little over an inch to a bit over a foot, a microphone element that is designed to fit onto each spike and a special microphone power supply with a 95 dB gain factor, as well as, various features to insure high level recording.

They'll even throw in a long, thin drill bit for inserting said spikes through said solid object.

Figure about $1500 delivered.

Intelligence Incorporated offers a hybrid kit consisting of a high gain amplifier, two needle "spikes" and electret element along with a crystal contact element and a transparent plastic pick up that will listen, quite unnoticed, through glass!

About $600.

No drill bit...

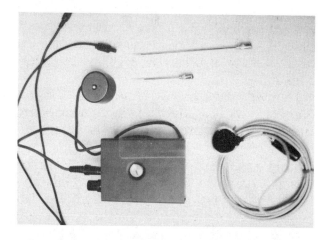

The Intelligence Inc., two spike, one contact mic, glass sensor plus high gain amp for those important conversations that take place in the next room.

Pinhole mic installed in drywall. Note it should not puncture the target surface and the LP end uses foam padding to help insulate the m element.

Other applications involving passive surveillance exist; lasers that bounce an infrared beam from the outside of a window and then reproduce the interior audio have been used by the CIA since the early 60s, and are commercially available from PK/STG Electronics ($25K).

"When access is impossible the STG laser surveillance system can be used from outside the premises. As no installation is required, you will not even need to enter a building or a room. Normal conversations within a room create minute vibrations on exterior windows which act much like the diaphragm of a microphone oscillating with sound waves."

STG goes on to advise that perfect transmitter/receiver alignment is essential so they furnish tripods and use a 500mm lens on the receiver to collect the modulated beam.

They also suggest the use of an optional IR viewer to help align the whole system.

Do these Starwars bugs work?

Sort of.

Usually. If there's not too much exterior noise or too much interior superfluous noise, and they are aimed correctly and God is on your side.

A considerably cheaper "hobbyist" version ($24,700 cheaper) can be obtained from Information Unlimited.

A medium level surveillance unit (neighborhood of $7K, I believe) can be ordered from Operative Supply in North Carolina. This particular unit uses a novel approach to laser monitoring.

I feel no qualms about explaining the theory behind this particular piece of gear because I was chatting with the owner of said Operative Supply one sunny afternoon and I said, "you know if I was going to build a surveillance laser this is how I would do it..."

After my discourse he laughed and said, "That's exactly how I do it."

Is there a moral in here? Well, maybe it's that ideas are free and synchronicity does exist.

I guess.

At any rate the "hobby" level units suffer from several inherent problems which, until now, have been expensive to solve. The most powerful lasers generally available to the generally public run about 5 thousandth's of a watt (5 milliwatts).

Most fall into the visible spectrum, as opposed to infrared.

This is not a lot of power when you are trying to bounce a tiny fraction of the light from a semi-reflecting surface such as a window pane.

Thanks to the fall of the Soviet Union, cash hungry Russians are flooding the market with cheap night vision equipment. The first generation units are so bad that many came, or come, with IR laser diodes to boost their performance. These boosters average about 1/2 a watt (500 milliwatts), enough power to make the use of a laser a viable option.

When in doubt, flood it.

The FDA has cracked down on the import of some of these units because they pose a health hazard and can blind a person if aimed directly at one's eyes, but there are a lot of them still available.

By utilizing one of these pre-made lasers and a fairly simple fiber optic or photo diode receiver (both of which are easily available), the correct receiving lens and a simple adjustable audio filter, it is possible to construct a reasonably priced unit that will allow one to sit several hundred feet from the target window, aim an invisible stream of coherent light at it and listen to the audio inside the room with no access to the target area.

It's far from perfect but has been employed by various intelligence agencies for about 20 years...

For a more exacting look at the theory and aiming procedures see BOOK II.

LONG DISTANCE PASSIVE

It is also within the realm of possibility to record sounds from a distance. The most practical device for this type of aural acquisition is the parabolic microphone. A PM employs a dish to collect and focus available sound into the waiting mouth of a mic element mounted in front of the dish at its focal point.

The industry standard is the DAN GIBSON model, made by, yes, Dan Gibson! This Canadian gentleman has been selling these mics for years to nature lovers, film makers, sports sound people (it's the thing you see pointed at the NFL receiver when he tries to convince you that "mother" is only half a word after dropping a floater).

They work well, I tested them for BOOK II and found it was possible to even capture some audio through closed windows at short distances.

Sony has entered the field with a similar model. Also made from clear plastic for somewhat unobtrusive audio gathering, their dish is smaller and designed for video camera people.

Not as sensitive as the GIBSON.

A third entry in the parabolic collection field comes from CSI. Their AUDIO TELESCOPE appears to be more sensitive than the GIBSON or SONY and is about half the price of Dan's unit.

The CSI toy has a more sensitive mic element and some additional filtering to cut down on background and wind noise.

It is also made from aluminum, a factor you might wish to consider if you plan on aiming it at your neighbor, the paranoid gun collector.

Bugs, devices that pick up and transmit local audio, usually by radio signals are more common today than ever before. Good sub miniature transmitters can be purchased off the shelf or by mail order. Some are simply circuit boards with the components mounted in plain view, some are sealed in small plastic boxes, others come disguised in calculators, lamps, pagers, baseball hats, girlfriends or other innocuous containers.

A number of changes have affected the world of audio surveillance in the recent past. Besides the laws that have been on the books since the days of President Nixon and the Watergate mess limiting the ownership and use of devices "designed primarily for the surreptitious interception of conversations" to law enforcement types, the Federal Communications Commission has also tightened the regulations surrounding the sale of non-FCC type approved transmitters.

Most small audio transmitters are not type approved due to the rather arduous and expensive process of FCC certification. Have these rules that prohibit the sale of non-accepted units made it difficult to find a good bug?

I'd suggest you pick up a copy of Popular Electronics, Nuts and Volts or any other electronic hobbyist publication, or wander down to the local spy shop for an afternoon's shopping...

For years most bug manufacturers slid their way around the legal limitations by claiming their devices were, in fact, not designed for the surreptitious interception of anything, but rather were "baby monitors" or wireless microphones that let you play Karaoke star over your FM radio.

When the non-type approval laws sprung on the scene a few units disappeared, a few companies began selling to law enforcement folk only, and some discovered a loophole that allowed the sale of non-assemble "kit" transmitters for hobbyists.

The key phrase to look for is "easy to construct" or "partial" followed by the word "kit." In the King's English this means the unit is fully constructed except for one wire, a battery clip or microphone.

Most such "kits" do not require any other electronics skill than the ability to snap in a clip-on wire.

After a short time most of the units that were removed from the new, more restrictive marketplace were put right back on it. In fact, it's now possible to purchase very sophisticated telephone transmitters (taps), which were once prosecuted as being "devices designed, etc." (it's really hard to claim you're using it to monitor the baby's phone calls), from 75 or so "spy shops" and a bunch, I'm talking a bunch here, of mail order companies.

Why? — 'Cause.

'Cause the FCC only has a few agents to enforce their laws and standards for every bloody radio and TV station in the country, and doesn't seem to have the inclination to prosecute small fry mail order dealers or attempt to part the Red Sea of new spy shops.

With some exceptions.

A certain law enforcement only manufacturer of surveillance gear *reportedly, allegedly* ratted out a whole slew of dealers that were selling non-type approved video surveillance transmitters and the Feds did send out "cease and desist" letters, but this has to be viewed as more of a marketing ploy rather than pure law enforcement for the good of the people.

At any rate, bugs are more available, better, more fun and probably more inexpensive than at any time in the past. A number of brand spanking new approaches to the art of audio monitoring have sprung up like mushrooms after a rain storm.

Yeah, yeah, so I'm mixing my metaphors, what's the problem? You guys all English teachers in another life?

Anyway, recent technology has made transmitters smaller, flatter, more accurate and in some cases, much more difficult to uncover. Again I ain't going to hover around the basics here, read the HOW-TO books, and HANDS-ON ELECTRONIC SURVEILLANCE for the techniques, THE COVERT CATALOG for a complete list of sources, and let us concentrate on the newest, the best, the cheapest, how to be a smart surveillance shopper.

One interesting trend is the availability of modular systems that utilize a single transmitter with a variety of add-on features allowing for different applications. The GEM line made by SDMS, a firm located in the UK, is a good example of this thinking.

Three basic transmitters output a signal in the 135 – 220 MHz range and are crystal controlled. Each uses narrow band FM for its output and each works a 6 –12 volt power supply.

The three models vary in power output (and resulting battery life) from 35 MW on the low power model to a healthy 275 MW on the "very high power" model.

This spread is advisable because it's normally a good procedure to use the least amount of power that will get the job done. The less power put out the less distance the unit will transmit, which in turn means there is less of a chance of someone coming across the signal accidentally (with a scanner or nearfield radio), and the more difficult it is for some who is looking for the unit to locate it.

Ancillary advantages include smaller size and longer battery life.

On the other hand, if it is not possible to locate the listening post nearby, or if the signal must penetrate thick steel or reinforced concrete walls, a higher power unit must be utilized

Each basic transmitter has an internal microphone and can be put in place, as is. Each unit is also supplied with five adapters that can change their configuration considerably.

The five standard adapters include:
1. Room adapter which accepts any power supply from 6 to 12 volts.
2. Telephone adapter converts the module into a series telephone transmitter which gets its power from the phone line.
3. Body adapter allows the transmitter to be worn as a wire with an external mic.

4. Vehicle adapter connects the module to the power supply of the vehicle.
5. Panic button converts the audio to a continuous tone when pressed.

The nice GEM folk also offer a separate "mains" adapter which allows the transmitters to operate from 110-120 volts. A good idea, although I suspect a $15 Radio Shack universal power supply would do the job cheaper.

SDMS also offers a line of similar transmitters and switches that are operated by remote control. The activator signal emanates from a command transmitter or transmitter plug-in module that fits into the matched receiver.

A remote controlled bug acts as a passive receiver, drawing very little battery current until it "hears" the activation tone. At this point it switches back to an audio transmitter. This configuration extends battery life and allows the unit to be activated only during pertinent times.

England, or as it's known in postal circles, the UK, sports an unusual policy towards exotic surveillance gear; they make it, they advertise it, and they will sell it to anyone who resides not in England.

Keeps the riff-raff where they belong; in other countries.

If you are going to order direct from any factory on the other side of the pond a couple of rules apply, now realize I'm not, certainly not, advocating the bending or fracturing of any laws, but as a journalistic exercise this is how some people purchase surveillance gear from an overseas supplier:
• Pay extra to have it shipped via DHL, Air Express International or other private shipping company, at the very least use UPS. I personally do not utilize the postal service because I think you have a better chance of actually seeing your package, but a couple of my friends disagree with this philosophy feeling that the postal service is reliable and attracts less attention.
    The private services have a sort of deal with the customs department wherein they will

evaluate the contents of your package, and if it doesn't out and out resemble a kilo of white powder, will usually take your word as to what the exact components consist of. You simply pay them an import fee based on the declared value of the package.

• Keep the declared value under about $900. This allows the process to continue without chatting with an agent of the Customs Service. Some people actually break up their order into a series of smaller orders to facilitate this process.

Others ask the supplier to fib about the declared value.

Be careful here...

• Never, ever use words like "transmitter", or "surveillance" when explaining to the DHL people what those little black boxes do in real life.

A good choice is "electronic parts". Keep it simple and believable.

• Suggest the supplier stamp the boxes with the same non-suggestive language. Don't lie, I mean a telephone tap really is an electronic part, and God knows, you could use a bug to test your security...

• Pay for your order up-front by having your bank transfer the correct amount of money, based on the current exchange rate, directly into the supplier's account. Then FAX or call and notify them of the situation.

Cost is minimal (about $25) and having the cash in-hand seems to motivate people in this industry who are tired of seeing "requests for catalog" and no bread.

The various Japanese companies like Micro, T. Satomi and Sunmechatronics, as well as, the more reputable English firms that have been in business for years and years are very reliable. It is possible to actually send them cash money and the order will be handled in a reliable and honest fashion.

GEM units, as far as I can tell, are sold to law enforcement without question and to anyone else who has a realistic letterhead and the poise to conduct the transaction with little question.

The more common and far less expensive versions of a modular, or at least components that are designed to function as a system, are made by a couple of Japanese manufacturers.

Micro Electronics LTD offers their TX-200 a "high power" transmitter that "allows you to transmit voice over an exclusive receiver up to 1,000-1,500 meters". The 200 has a built-in mic for use as a room transmitter and comes with a tie-pin mic that allows it to function as a body wire.

Micro also offers a number of "telephone checkers"—series taps that will throw a telephone conversation some distance on the same frequencies as the 200. These taps are attached to the tip and ring (red and green) wires that lead into a phone unit, or a building, leech their power from the line itself and begin broadcasting both sides of the audio when the telephone receiver is lifted from the cradle.

Both these units can, of course, be picked up on any receiver or scanner that will receive their VHF signals. They also can be paired with small, high sensitivity, crystal controlled receivers available directly from Micro.

These receivers are actually more sensitive than most scanners or even communications receivers because they are designed to operate on 3 channels only.

The transmitters can be ordered on any of the three available frequencies, the receiver will switch back and forth allowing the operator to choose which unit he wishes to monitor at any particular time.

This concept is good if transmitters have been installed in several different rooms, or a combination of rooms and phone lines in order to have continuous coverage of a particular target.

Micro also sells the CR-120 AUTOMATIC TELEPHONE RECORDER, A combination receiver and recorder set up to automatically record any and all audio from one of their telephone taps.

This is definitely the lazy man's solution to tapping; no scanners, long play recorders or carrier interfaces to worry about. Just attach the tap, put the receiver/recorder within range, activate it and come by occasionally to change tapes and batteries.

These same units are also labeled RUBY and sold by Ruby Electronics (a division of Security Research) in England and by VEC Electronics in America.

Both these sources offer fairly reasonable prices. The same units are also sold by many shops and mail order catalogs with a 100%-1200% mark-up tagged on.

On the other hand, if you order from an American source there is no customs to worry about or other red tape to cut through.

A word of warning here, some very small suppliers act only as drop shippers, i.e., they do not stock many products, but simply pass your order on to the real supplier after taking their cut.

Not good.

Try to stay with large, trustworthy dealers who keep the items in stock.

Intelligence kits, i.e., complete with some combination of transmitters, receivers, filters, taps, recorders are also available for any job you can dream up. AID packages them for lazy law enforcement types that do everything from detect intruders to bug a complete building.

A number of private suppliers offer less expensive versions.

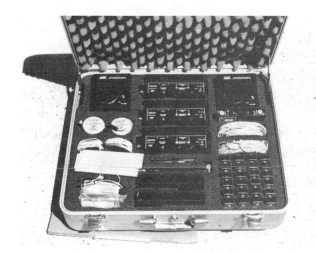

A modern, $8000, AID kit.

THINNER, SMALLER, BETTER

Surface mount and C-MOS semi-conductors and chips now allow the existence of fairly stable and reasonably powered transmitters in a number of different configurations. Wafer transmitters, very thin circuits that utilize surface mounted components and are powered by a flat button cell are now available in several unusual configurations.

If you are a cop or government agent I suggest you look at the DST-100 a digital, stereo transmitter that offers very high quality audio (especially when teamed with its own DSR-100 receiver), including background noise reduction, individual speaker enhancement and interference cancellation obtained through the use of spatial processing.

From JBR Technology (boy there's a familiar name) 6964 Conservation Drive, Springfield, VA 22153, this tiny, flat unit is concealed in baseball caps, pagers, sun visors, radar detectors, plants, beer cans (now that's low) or pieces of wood.

Plan on mortgaging your first born for the unit.

LEA checks in with their own baseball cap transmitter for a bit over $1000 (note the photo) but I'd be just a tad nervous about buying a couple pounds of any controlled substance from someone who still thinks the Raiders play for Oakland...

A 1950's era , pre-tape recorder, "intelligence kit" that captured audio on a belt.

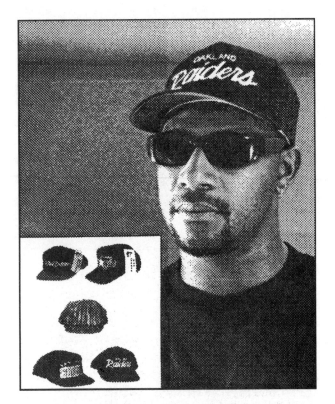

Another choice would be from Schnell Electronics, in Chanute Kansas. They produce several credit card sized transmitters. These units are small enough to actually plant them on a suspect without his knowledge by slipping them into a jacket pocket or purse.

Schnell sells their COVERT line of audio transmitters only to law enforcement. They will, however, be happy to sell FCC type approved, credit card sized tone transmitters that can be used with a directional receiver to follow a suspect package.

Various Schnell units can be configured to start transmitting only when movement is detected (placed under a car fender or in a briefcase). Some units can be rigged to provide a first and second alert capability. For example: a briefcase can be wired to signal you when it has been removed from it's resting place while a second signal tells you it has been opened.

Also can be used as a panic button to call in the cavalry.

A similar surface mount "alarm" type transmitter can be configured to produce a signal

when a tiny pin is removed. Conversely it can be transmitted when the pin is inserted, or it is possible to produce a continuous tone in one condition and a broken tone in the other.

These units are highly favored by people like the DEA because they are small enough to be stashed inside the "walls" of a padded mail bag or Federal Express type pouch.

The pin is installed so that it is removed when the package is opened.

This solves a sticky legal problem – if someone mails you drugs or other illegal items, you really haven't established possession as long as the container remains sealed.

However, once you open it the contents officially become yours...

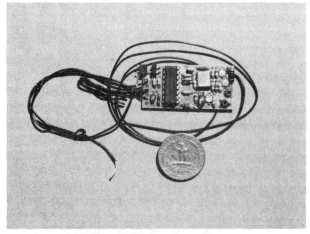

A civilian make-or-break signaling transmitter.

Civilians can also go back to our old friends at Micro Electronics, Japan's answer to K-Mart, and pick up a couple of CD-500/s, "card sized, extremely thin type transmitter. Easy operate at any time, any where, not aware anybody."

You know, if each of us bought just one unit from these guys they could probably hire someone who speaks both Japanese and English to write up their sales brochures...

Crystal controlled, about the size of a credit card, and sporting a 30 hour battery life, these units transmit in the area of 360 MHz which give them the advantage of a reasonable transmission range with a two inch internal antenna. With my ACE scanner I could grab the signal on a continuous basis at ranges varying from 200 - 700 feet depending on intervening conditions, antennas, God's will and so on.

Priced about $250 direct, these are very adaptable transmitters, the battery is a wafer type, placed internally so the units retain their integrity.

The CD-500 can also be also ordered hidden inside a miniature calculator.

Makes a great gift for your favorite executive, fits in the wife's purse...

Micro also offers a crystal controlled ball point pen transmitter ($200) that both writes and reaches out and touches someone. Those wacky copywriters at Micro call this unit, "Most interested camouflaged transmitter in the World."

I will admit they are a great way to review that conversation you and the CEO of IBM had after the eight shots of Tequila at TGIF's, or simply eliminate misunderstandings in a verbal agreement.

Micro Electronics' CD-500 naked and hidden in a calculator (actual size). Doesn't look all that threatening, does it?

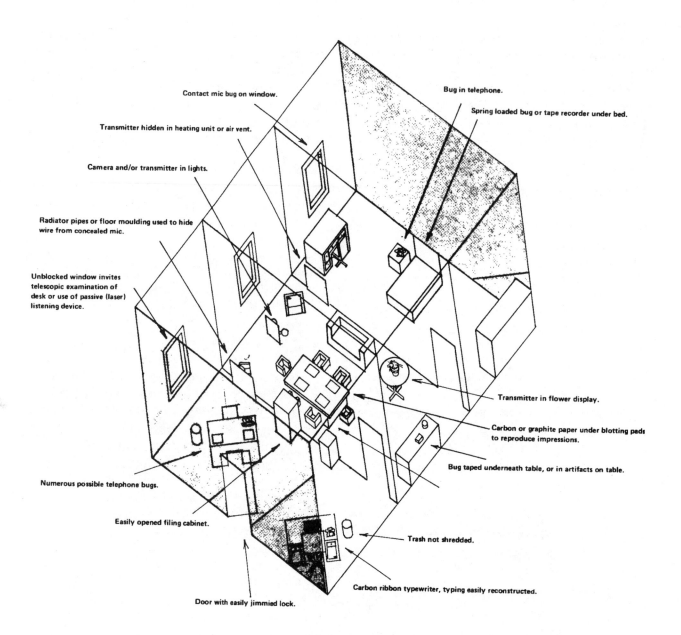

Contact mic bug on window.

Bug in telephone.

Transmitter hidden in heating unit or air vent.

Spring loaded bug or tape recorder under bed.

Camera and/or transmitter in lights.

Radiator pipes or floor moulding used to hide wire from concealed mic.

Unblocked window invites telescopic examination of desk or use of passive (laser) listening device.

Transmitter in flower display.

Carbon or graphite paper under blotting pads to reproduce impressions.

Bug taped underneath table, or in artifacts on table.

Numerous possible telephone bugs.

Easily opened filing cabinet.

Trash not shredded.

Carbon ribbon typewriter, typing easily reconstructed.

Door with easily jimmied lock.

INFINITY

One of the most interesting concepts to invade the science of surreptitious audio interception is the infinity transmitter. Invented in the early 60s, these small "black boxes" were placed inside a telephone where they sat, dormant until the operator dialed the phone from any direct dial phone in the world, and blew a small harmonica (really) into the mouthpiece of his telephone.

The resulting tone caused the buried infinity transmitter to stop the target phone from ringing and then began to send all of the room audio down the line to the waiting eavesdropper.

If anyone else called they got a busy signal, if the suspect picked up his phone it immediately disconnected, automatically going back to the dial tone.

Infinities were made obsolete when AT&T changed over to electronic switching, cutting off the audio path for the activation tone.

But, clever electronic engineers who missed the concept of being able to dial in on private conversations, thought about the problem and came up with a number of solutions.

Shomer-Tec was one of the first "civilian" companies to offer a new and improved infinity transmitter that "stored" the ring signal for a few seconds while listening for a touch-tone sequence that would activate its interior microphone.

They improved on the design by allowing several external microphones to be hidden anywhere down the line that could be activated by changing the code.

Sherwood Communications also provides a touch-tone activated infinity unit that can be used with four external microphones, switching between them on command.

Quite inexpensive.

Then came along a strange little company, appropriately called Listen Electronics. Listen has taken the infinity concept from the Jurassic era into the 21st century.

Listen packages their toys in a number of clever housings:

- THE ROOM SURVEILLANCE TELEPHONE is a common push-button phone with a built-in infinity. Plug the phone in at the location you wish to monitor. Call, punch in the code and, "clearly listen to all conversations around the unit."

  Between $130-$175 depending on which phone you need.
- CODED ROOM AND TELEPHONE MONITOR works as a room monitor and a telephone tap. The unit automatically switches back and forth if the telephone is used. Requires two lines. About $300.
- DIALER TAP. Another lazy agent device. Install it, connect the target line and a spare phone line and it will *call you* every time the target phone is used, letting you, or your recorder listen to the call.
- REMOTE CONTROL TELEPHONE RECORDER. Picture a recorder that automatically tapes all incoming our outgoing calls. Not too hard, right? Now picture it combined with your personal answering machine that will let you call in and replay all "messages," fast forward, rewind, tell you when the calls were made. Now make it also able to record and replay all room conversations in the vicinity under the same circumstances...

  Not bad for $500.

Listen also features slave monitors and automatic answering devices built into wall jacks and telephones.

Another method of bugging a room does not involve radio transmission but actually send room audio over the electrical wiring in a building or between houses.

Known as carrier current transmission this form of eavesdropping has a number of unique advantages over radio bugs:

- They can be installed directly in a wall socket or an appliance which plugs into a wall socket for a permanent installation.
- Carrier current units do not require batteries and are always on.
- They are very difficult to find and not likely to be accidentally overheard.

A couple of suppliers sell CC units, but most are simply "wireless intercoms" sold for about $100+ at the McDonalds of surveillance equipment – Radio Shack. The transmitter blocks the AC from the audio components and then places a low level, low frequency RF signal on the wire pair.

This signal will travel several hundred feet, through the wires, where it is picked up by the matching receiver.

The one limitation is that the signal will not cross over a power company transformer unless it has been specially "strapped."

The Radio Shack 12-649 tunes SW, TV, VHF, AM, FM with a directional antenna. It is very sensitive and acts as an ideal companion for many bugs and taps.

Your Friendly Neighborhood...

Even though they've dropped a few items of interest, good 'ol Radio Shack still carries quite a bit of stock that can be used directly for, or converted into surveillance gear.

Some things you might wish to put into your trousseau would include:

1. Drop out recorders ("telephone secretaries") that auto start recorders when a phone is lifted from its cradle. The cheaper version ($19.95 as of this writing) is a series unit that only works on one line, the more expensive, is a parallel version that works on all extensions.
2. An $11.95 amplifier that will bring low level audio up to line level for recording or transmitting purposes.
3. Numerous small recorders including the stereo model already mentioned.
4. Inexpensive handheld video monitors and "Watchman-like" video receivers.
5. The 12-649 a very sensitive receiver which covers most surveillance bands and features a directional antenna for locating and/or receiving small signals. Under $100!
6. Carrier current "intercoms."
7. Tools, wiring (including 4 wire telephone cable is which exactly what the phone company uses), connectors, coax, meters, frequency counters, batteries, wireless micro phones, video gear and other ancillary equipment of interest.

Here's a look at what federal agents are taught to bring along to any surreptitious surveillance job (besides the actual equipment to be planted). Maybe you'd want to put together a similar kit for those unexpected side trips.

TOOLS	SUPPLIES
Butane soldering iron	Bungee cords
Drywall saw	Double sided tape
Drills (include):	Drywall compound (spackle)
DC rechargeable	Drywall tape
Electric AC	Duct tape
Hand	Electrical tape
PC board drill	Foam material
Drills (metal cutting):	Hooks
Masonry	Lag bolts
Star	Machine bolts with nut and washers
Twist	Modeling tape
Drills (Wood bits)	Nails
Ear Syringe	Plaster
Exacto knife kit	Plumbing Strap
Flashlight	Putty
Hacksaw	Screws (sizes 1/4-20)
Hammer	Sheet metal screws
Inspection mirror	Sponge rubber
Keyhole saw	
Linoleum knife	
Magnetic retriever	
Mechanical retriever	
Portable vacuum cleaner	
Razor knife	
Regular vacuum cleaner	
Sailmakers awl	
Scissors	
Shaped scraper tools	
Sheet metal shears	
Stud finder	
Spinal needle	
Wood Chisels	
Wood Saw	

TELEPHONE TAPS

Up 'til now we've dealt with bugs, i.e., devices that record or transmit room conversations. This type of spying is ideal for some applications ranging from the bedroom to the boardroom, while other situations lend themselves to the interception of telephone conversation.

Telephones are ideal surveillance targets – they distill information by virtue of their design, provide a number accessible tie-in points for an interloper and their circuit arrangement serves to activate eavesdropping equipment.

The simplest form of telephone tapping is to attach a tape recorder across the red and green wires of a normal telephone circuit. The recorder can be isolated by a simple transformer or even a resistor and capacitor to pass the audio while blocking the line and ringing voltage from the recorder.

In this case, the recorder's VOX is adjusted so it begins recording when conversation is present.

A slightly more elegant solution is to utilize a drop out relay that senses the change in voltage when a telephone receiver is lifted from the hook. This voltage drop clicks in a relay that closes the remote start jack in the recorder and allows the recording of the audio until the receiver is replaced on the hook.

Drop-outs come in both series and parallel configurations, the former works on one telephone unit only, the latter, if attached on the master line, will activate when any unit in the building is utilized.

These devices are inexpensive, and available from legitimate telephone equipment suppliers including Radio Shack, where they are usually referred to as telephone secretaries or automatic phone recorders, as well as from many spy suppliers. It's also possible to purchase an extended play recorder with built-in dropouts.

Some units work better than others. Some drop-outs may introduce hum when coupled with a recorder, especially a recorder that is AC powered. Some may provide less than adequate audio levels and some may offer less that

10,000 ohms impedance, making them easier to locate with a simple countermeasure search.

The most exotic, and probably the best dropout I've have used is called "THE MOTHER", as in "the mother of all dropouts." This unit is powered from a battery and coupled to the telephone line *optically*.

This unit has absolutely no hum because there is no shared electricity and the audio is crystal clear as it is fed into an LED, turned into light, amplified and converted back into sound by an optic receiver.

Available from Intelligence Incorporated, about $80.

Most dropouts work only on the standard Bell four wire phone. Offices that utilize electronic phone systems, usually based on six wires, are not generally adaptable to stock dropouts.

Custom Interface Devices markets a version of a dropout which will activate on multi-line phone systems.

Recorder based phone taps are normally placed inside the house, or nearby locations such as a garage where the drop wire runs from the telco bunch to the protector block on the outside the building.

Disadvantages of this system include the necessity of the eavesdropper to expose himself when replacing the tape and/or batteries and the size of the units themselves.

The obvious solution to most of these problems is the use of a transmitter (tap) to broadcast both sides of the conversation to a waiting receiver. Like dropouts, taps come in two basic varieties, series and parallel.

SERIES TAPS

- Are installed by cutting one side of the wire pair and draw their power from the phone line itself.
- Work only when the phone is in use.
- Use the telephone line as an antenna.
- Have their power limited by the amount of current they can draw without tripping the phone company equipment.
- Are easier to locate and defeat than are parallels.

- Should be placed on the line after all the target telephones merge into one path.

Series units are often placed inside the outside protector block where they are quickly hidden by unclipping a single wire and adding the tap. They also can be placed further down the wire, at B boxes (telephone connector boxes where the target pair appears) or inside rubber installation boots on poles.

PARALLEL, OR BRIDGING TAPS

- Use a battery for their power. This means they can have almost unlimited power. It also means someone has to change the battery occasionally.
- Normally use a separate antenna.
- Are more difficult to locate.
- Can be installed anywhere in the loop and will broadcast all conversation on any unit in the system.
- Install almost instantly as they are simply clipped across the tip and ring wires.
- Parallel taps can be installed several blocks from the phone at a B box or multiple.

Both types of taps can be easily purchased from a number of suppliers including hobbyist magazines, spy shops and many of the companies listed here and in THE COVERT CATALOG.

More exotic taps can be accomplished by such tricks as "splits," where a pro recombines the wires in a 25 pair distribution cable and then lifts the audio out at a distant re-cross point. This system, in effect, induces cross talk in the line and is very difficult to locate.

Long play recorders and cascaded battery packs have been buried in metal cases near underground distribution cables. A drop out relay connects the recorder to the target line and the eavesdropper simply digs the unit up every week or so to collect the conversations and replace the batteries.

A number of courses are available in counter surveillance and few in electronic surveillance, although most of these latter are limited to enforcement folk. Most of these are listed in THE COVERT CATALOG.

On the other hand it takes no great skill to successfully tap almost any phone with available equipment. Tiny taps from various Japanese suppliers can be installed directly in the instrument itself, in a wall box, in the outside protector box or at a connector box in the basement of an apartment house or inside the telephone room of a business.

The correct line can be located by dialing the target's number and running a wetted finger down the row of contacts (trust me on this, you'll feel the ringing line) or by the judicious use of a telephone lineman's handset.

When one decides to tap a telephone several variables must be considered; budget, access, length of time the tap will need to be active, recovery of the audio and who will be looking for traces of the installation being a few of the more important.

It is possible to tap just about any telephone in the world. Perhaps the hotline (which is actually a teletype I believe) between the White House and the Kremlin may have been one of the more difficult challenges, but I'll bet there were at least "agency" ears in place...

If you are willing to spend the money, I have a nice little brochure produced by some folks involved with the federal government that explains, in detail, how to tap a particular phone by picking off its signal as its being broadcast between cities via microwave.

Of course, this particular procedure requires a bit of ground work, the purchase of a rather large and rather expensive microwave dish, renting a barn (?) in the microwave path in which to house your new equipment and, well, if I get enough reader mail from people that really want to try this, I'll waste about 6 pages in detailed explanation.

For the moment let's concentrate on more likely approaches.

For the most part professionals tap as far from the actual phone as they can. This is done for several reasons, including the fact that there is usually less risk involved in violating an appearance point than breaking into a home or office.

It is also much more difficult to find a distant tap and the chance of accidental discovery is probably less.

On the other hand a simple drop-out recorder stashed in a closet or garage can be installed in a hurry and may work just fine for a limited time, or even for a longer period, if the target harbors no suspicions and stays out of your closet...

On the other hand if you are half way serious about installing or finding taps, you should know a few basic facts about how the phone company is put together.

Any subscriber loop may have a number of different cable types and appearance points along its length. Large, underground main feeder cables usually leave the central office to serve urban areas, as these cables get further from the central office they may be spliced onto aerial or buried branch feeder cables.

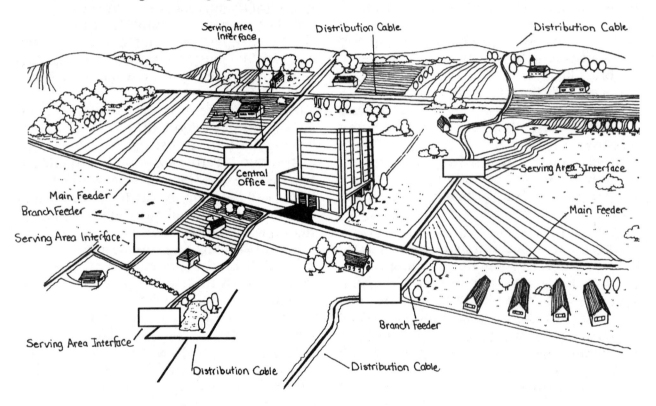

The term "cable" usually refers to a bundle of 6-3000 wire pairs enclosed within a single covering. The pairs involved will usually be twisted and heavier cables may have steel suspension strands included to add strength.

All modern telephone wiring utilizes what is known as PIC (polyethylene insulated conductors) with ten colors of insulation available. PIC actually helps our cause by the use of readily accessed terminals which contain all pairs within a distribution cable, thus adding numerous points to which a single telephone can be tapped.

Some of the places the cable may be exposed:
• subscriber distribution areas
• cable junctions
• where buried and aerial cable meet
• cable loading points
• cable reel splice points
• repeater points
• outside protection boxes
• aerial boots
• pedestals

The use of PIC cables in aerial situations has eliminated the necessity of pressurized or sealed boxes, replacing them with the convenient rubber boot which can be easily peeled back to expose the terminals.

Feeder cables are then divided into distribution cables to serve a particular neighborhood. Eventually each customer is connected by a drop or service wire.

The further from the central office the fewer pairs that will be included in each cable.

In aerial systems the drop wire is usually connected to an aerial distribution cable consisting of 25 pairs, when it meets the branch feeder cable it will go through another terminal consisting of 200 pairs (in 8 groups), several blocks later it will connect to a main feeder cable consisting of 600 pairs (24 groups).

In aerial set-ups the main feeder will often be pressurized to keep out moisture. These cables normally have a pressure drop alarm on them which makes them not as convenient for most eavesdropping applications.

Aerial boots and connect boxes are not pressurized or locked. It is fairly common for good agents to climb a pole and visually trace the distribution cable's entrance, and either note the color coding of the cable for further consideration, or stash a small transmitter at this location.

The correct pair can be visually traced, tracked by using a small tone generator, or by using a slide rule color chart available from telephone equipment suppliers to the various other feeder/main cable connections.

It's also possible to place a lineman's handset across the terminals in any box, or onto the wire pair and dial the three digit ring back number for the area which will automatically readout the phone number.

It's also possible to dial the number from an adjoining line and look for the 90-volt ringing current, or in-places which have caller ID, dial a confederate and have him read back the number.

I do not advocate the climbing of telephone poles by the uninitiated, most also have power lines adjacent to them which can put bad end on an otherwise good day.

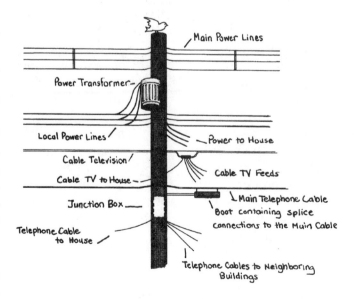

Most newer installations are done under ground to avoid those unsightly overhead wires. Underground wiring is actually one of two varieties:

1. Buried wiring consist of one of two types of cabling: buried cable is placed directly in the ground with no conduit or ducts and is very open to unauthorized "penetrations." Buried cables tend to run from B boxes to subscribers houses, as well as, branch feeders and trunk/toll cables.

   Buried wiring is spliced in manholes (a no-no, bad gases, alarms) buried splice pits, conduit boxes and splice pits. These connect points are usually buried in a very shallow fashion and covered lightly with soil.

2. Underground cable is housed in a fixed conduit structure which is harder to penetrate. It is spliced in manholes or conduit boxes.

The good news is that all underground wiring makes above ground appearances in easy to access boxes and pedestals. These cross connect points can be opened with simple tools (i.e., socket wrenches). Walk around any neighborhood that uses buried wiring and you will spot both the large cross connect boxes, which contain several 66 blocks, or their like and small pedestals which branch off to certain sections of the neighborhood.

If you want to be real clever, you can find long distance truck/toll cables by following the well kept up, right of way and the frequent signs warning of the cable's presence and asking you to call a certain number before digging in the vicinity.

Buried wiring has several different types of appearances, including a pedestal housing with a ready access count, a PH with a fixed count, in-line direct (buried) and below ground in a concrete housing.

The pedestal is placed above ground on a pole or stake where the cables enter the bottom of the housing and are looped through or spliced. A ready access type has a specific group of 25 or fifty pairs pre-assigned to the local subscribers.

Fixed count pedestals has 6 or 12 pairs terminated that serve specific houses.

Below ground closures are pretty much the same units except that the top of the enclosure is kept level with the ground line. This type of box has a lid that removes easily for servicing the enclosed terminals.

Cross connect terminals are large boxes with several terminal boards in them that are used to:

• Terminate unequal cable pairs, i.e., where the number of feeder pairs is not equal to the number of distribution pairs. This leaves open, unused pairs that, oh, heck, you might think of a reason for using.

• Improve the ration of cable fills on cables that are about to overflow.

• Remove multiples and dead bridges and allow the splicing of cable pairs between loading coils.

To make a long story short, these nice, open boxes, have appearance points for not only every phone in the neighboring locale (where they connect the subscribers to the distribution cables), but some that occur quite a distance away. These can be found by the various trace methods I've outlined, or by the use of a distribution map that your friendly telco repairman has access to...

Subscriber Loop

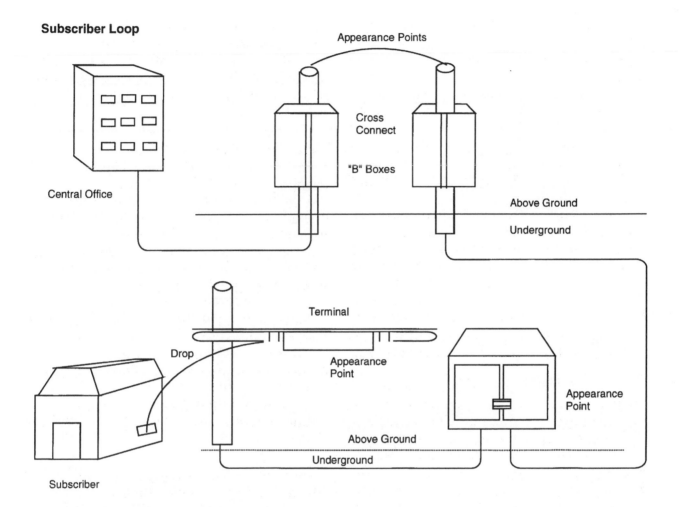

In small towns, or older installations, it is possible to have a situation where a building is large enough to justify wiring an entire complement into the building, making the interface between the feeder cable and distribution plant a direct run, otherwise, the cable will appear in a nearby cross connect ("B box") or two.

The feeder cables enter the box from the back, the top 1/3 loops over the top, the bottom 2/3 of the feeder wires wrap around the bottom of the box.

Most eavesdroppers do not simply hide a tap or recorder at an appearance point or B box – instead it is much safer to attach an unused wire pair or even add your own pair (using the correct color coded wire, usually left in a box or can be purchased from telco suppliers) as an "extension" phone or bridge.

This pair can then be tapped a bit further down the line where normal telco installation people will not be looking.

Most appearances, either in cross connect boxes or in phone rooms inside of office buildings, use a standard type of connecting terminal. This terminal can be used to terminate the wire (end it there or loop it through, connecting it to other pairs or letting it continue its journey back tot he central office.)

Wires are set into the terminal by using a special tool IT IS NOT WISE TO ATTEMPT THIS MODIFICATION WITHOUT THE TOOL. One blade of the 714B (or Siemon S66BT) tool automatically strips away the insulation from the pair, the other sets it into the terminal.

This $15 tool *should* be a part of your kit.

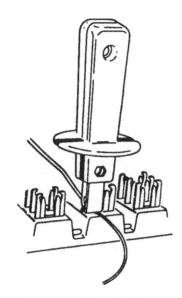

Connecting block terminals and 714b tool.

To summarize: a tap can be installed on the back of a 66 block or cross connect block, and the nice telco people *may* not find it when they go to add a new subscriber.

Or you can add your own "extension" by bridging to the target's terminals with an unused pair (no dial tone) or by adding your own "new" pair and running the wires down the cable for some distance before installing the tap.

The drop wire or buried service wire that is utilized to connect a customer to his distribution cable is a favorite place for taps. Most of these entities consist of 2-4 insulated wires in a common plastic covering.

The wires are arranged in pairs and the pairs are usually twisted together (hence the term "twisted pair") If two pairs are in the wire they are normally twisted together to form a "twisted quad."

The red and green wires are the tip and ring of the target phone and where most taps will be placed. The yellow and black wires can also be used for infinities, slaves, hot wiring, or a variety of other bugs that require unused wiring to conduct their business.

If the target's drop wire is completely exposed and your feel nervous about running an "extension" from it to a box or other enclosure which will house your tap, check out the small protector block which connects the drop wire to the inside phone wiring. This small box has an easily removed cover and will contain screw on connections (plus a couple of fuses) and is a very nice place for a small tap.

If you have access to the inside of the premises you will discover many taps including a very pleasant slave from Listen Electronics will fit into the inside wall boxes where the actual telephone connects to the wiring.

A current favorite of law enforcement and higher level agents is to use a two piece carrier current tap or bug stashed in the wall box. The unit, designed by a Mr. Brady and sold by various AID type suppliers fits a rubber covered transmitter directly into the box.

The resulting signal is picked off the phone line hundreds of feet away by a special, low frequency receiver.

This is a very difficult to locate unit because no one expects to see a carrier current signal on a phone line. It can be picked up by carrier current detectors, as well as, by physical inspection.

Brady carrier current phone line bug. Note how the transmitter fits exactly into a telco box.

This section excepts the very newest installations which utilize fiber optic cable.

Fiber optics can be taped, but the necessary expertise and lack of available equipment makes it outside the scope of this publication.

BEST BUGS FOR THE BUCKS

Here's a purely subjective list, in no particular order, of what I consider to be the best deals in the great electronic marketplace in the sky. A few things you need to decide before filling out the wish list are:

- What band do you want the unit to transmit on? Cheaper units often utilize the FM broadcast band. This approach has a couple of things to recommend it; availability of receivers, the ability to "snuggle" your tiny transmitter next to a normal radio station (please don't use one that features "easy listening" or "light rock," it offends the mental picture I have of my readers) where it is difficult for a countermeasures person to locate it, and finally the availability of the units themselves. FM "wireless microphones" can be purchased from many sources.

  The broadcast band has a number of things going against it; the availability of receivers means that your little program may be a lot more public than you planned on, especially if the unit is to remain in place for any length of time, the presence of "real" radio stations can make it difficult to keep the receiver locked on to your tiny signal, and the fact that it's, well, amateurish...

  Good bugs will transmit above or, in some cases, below the broadcast bands. In the old days most fell into the public service frequencies as receivers were plentiful. In fact, most policemen already came equipped with said receivers.

  With the increasing use of scanners and communications receivers this limitation has pretty much been abandoned for life in the less crowded frequencies.

- Should the unit be tunable, i.e., free running, or should it be crystal controlled? Free running units can be tuned, a handy feature if your first choice of frequency has been taken by some selfish son of a bitch with a license...

  They also have a bad habit of drifting off frequency with changes in temperature, battery voltage or the presence of people or

metal objects. In short, they drift, making it unwise to use an unmanned listening post. A further negative factor is that units with an oscillator tend to put out additional signals on harmonics, doubles and quadruples of the original frequency. These harmonics make the unit easier to locate and may end up on a channel that is already being monitored by someone else.

  Crystal controlled units are locked on a particular frequency and cannot be easily changed (a few units allow for the replacement of the crystal in the field) and make for a stable operating platform.

  If the frequency is in use near listening post, a clever operator will have another unit or two on hand set to other frequencies.

- Power supply. Most transmitters, by their nature, tend to be located in places that one does not wish to visit on a periodic basis. A bug or tap is only as good as it's battery supply.

  It is possible to cascade batteries together for a longer operation period, but this takes away from the idea that the unit should be small enough to hide in unlikely places. Do you need higher power, longer life or would it be better to use a unit that operates from the building's AC wiring.

  This raises an interesting point – always, *always* use fresh batteries for each operation. For most apps, or ops, depending on your outlook, lithium batteries are well worth their extra cost as they outlast any other types.

  A second choice would be <u>industrial alkaline</u> cells. These can be found in electrical supply shops and industrial hardware stores and have considerably more energy on tap than do their commercial cousins.
  Don't use mercury cells unless the units spec sheets call for them.

- Distance required. This is going to be a function of both output power and antenna length. The lower the frequency, the longer antenna that is required to transmit the signal properly. Units that come hidden in ball point pens, calculators, ashtrays and so on generally do not transmit as effectively as do units that incorporate a separate, longer antenna.

- Size and disguise. Do you need a transmitter hidden in a Wandering Jew or can you live with a four inch square plastic box (that may still require an external battery)? Price and transmission strength are at stake here.

With that criteria in mind let's look at my top choices:

1. The little crystal controlled taps and bugs made by Micro Electronics (Japan). Available in 3 different UHF channels the units can be received on a scanner or matching two or three channel (switchable) receiver.

   About $120 per, receivers in a couple of models, starting about $150, a bit more for the CZ-10 receiver, but worth the extra $25 because "The sound is very clear without noise, thanks for Hi-sensitivity."

   Sold for hundreds of dollars by half the spy shops in the world.

2. The crystal controlled transmitters and taps offered by T. Satomi and Co. (Japan) and sold by Sunmechatronics and Ruby (Lorraine Electronics) and the other half the spy shops in the world.

   These units are fairly stable, well made and average about $100-$125 per transmitter and $225-$250 for the matched receivers.

   In Japan, of course, a bit more by the time they are purchased from a US supplier.

3. Anything from Listen Electronics.

4. The "credit card" transmitters sold in or out of calculators by Micro, also crystal controlled on the same channels as their other units.

5. The MA-100 telephone tap built inside a stock dual modular telephone adapter from Seymor Radix. True, it's not crystal controlled, and it does live in the FM broadcast band, but it's also a "snap together" kit that

can be instantly installed by any fool and costs a whopping $24.95!

Oh, yes, they also charge $1.00 for shipping and give a dealer discount...

6. The WP-6 from Aegis Research. Another "easy to assemble" unit that lives inside a 6 socket electrical plug extender. Operating from 110 volts this bug offers a number of unusual advantages including a fully adjustable audio gain control so you can set it for the ambient audio conditions, a built-in filter that emphasizes the speech frequencies, direct FM Varactor circuitry (gives nice clean sound) a DC controlled oscillator and internal voltage regulation which minimizes any drifting.

   Price? Well, let's just say it's sold to dealers for about a hundred and a half, so figure the appropriate markup and how friendly you are with a dealer...

The Aegis plug-in-and-forget-wall socket/transmitter. Similar models available from AID for the law enforcement community.

7. The VT-75 (look it's another "easy to assemble" kit!) from Deco Electronics. A single chip at the heart of this tiny unit coupled with an electret mic element and FET front end allow very sensitive audio pick up and a two stage buffer amplifier and stable oscillator gives quite stable operation from the bottom of the FM band to about 10 MHz above it.

This nice touch means you can put it in the broadcast band or go above it using a scanner or detuned FM receiver for private listening.

The VT-75 is also novel because it can, by the addition of two resistors, work as a telephone tap!

Power it by a button cell and it's one of the tiniest units around; boost the signal with a longer antenna and nine volt battery, and that will double or triple the effective range. About $50...

8. Xandi Electronics offers several super tiny room and telephone transmitters. A couple are smaller than a dime...

A clever consumer can buy them in the form of plans only, a circuit board and parts or as a, YES!, easy to assemble kit!

Broadcast band, non-crystal, but at $30-$60 who's gonna complain?

9. Cony Electronics (Japan) takes a licking and is keeps on ticking. Or, maybe, still crazy after all these years.

Cony makes non-kit, tiny, teensy, transmitters that use button cells to transmit local audio over the FM band, series and parallel phone taps and the infamous "concrete mic."

Their stuff works, it's easy to install, and at an average of about thirty bucks per bug they can be installed in any number of casual locations, you know, friends, relations, neighbors, anybody who ah, well, you might be curious about but don't want to invest a $400 bug in...

Cony has been the primary supplier of $30 units that sell for $300 in spy shops, and $39.95 in catalogs for the last ten years and they're still out there doing their thing.

Makes you proud to be Japanese, don't it?

10. VX-100 from Deco – a *crystal* controlled surface mount module that puts out a full 100 milliwatts of room audio on 140 MHz. Custom frequencies available.

This unit puts out crystal clear audio which can really, honestly be picked up at a distance of 1/4 to 1/2 mile after going through a wall or two with a non-directional antenna and average scanner. Increase the length of the transmitting antenna, add a directional at the receiver end and/or more sensitive receiver and it's a dynamite deal for about $80.

Powered by a 9-volt battery you need only solder three wires and you're in business. Small enough to be stashed in a variety of containers.

Take my advice and buy a couple before the Feds decide "easy assemble kits" are not.

11. Suma designs subcarrier or narrow band units. Real, not that easy to assemble kits; these units provide the sophistication of government level surveillance equipment at a fraction of the cost.

BEST BUGS NO MATTER WHAT THE BUCKS

1. GEM line of modular transmitters.
2. JBR STEREO transmitter.
3. Any scrambled unit from various suppliers including Micro and PK in Germany.
4. One or more of LEA's cute hidden body wires/bugs like the one hidden in a wrist watch or, my personal favorite, the surface mount transmitter in a baseball cap.
5. Narrow band and (optional) scrambled transmitters from Security Research. The bandwidth makes them difficult to receive by accident, scrambling adds that last bit of security.
6. A spread spectrum unit.
7. A frequency hopper, if I could find one...
8. An infrared transmitter (if the conditions allow for it) from PK or STG.

LISTENING POSTS

The second, and no less important, component of an audio surveillance operation is the place where the intelligence is received and usually recorded. The FBI, DEA and others with Big Bucks like to establish LP's in an apartment or building near the target room.

This allows for simplicity in reception and often gives a visual edge to the surveillance.

The rest of the world, people like us, tend to use more mundane settings for our listening pleasure. An LP can be established in an automobile (hopefully in the trunk) and parked near the transmission site, in an object such as a briefcase or cabinet, or even on a person who is then placed near the transmission site.

The LP normally consists of an antenna, receiver and recorder. The receiver, at least in civilian operations is usually a scanner (not bad, but not as sensitive as the next two choices), a dedicated, crystal controlled receiver on the same frequency as the transmitter (T. Satomi, Micro, Ruby, etc.) or a high end communications receiver.

The last choice is usually one made by someone like ICOM. These all band receivers are very sensitive and very stable and allow for a number of adjustments to bandwidth and frequency that fine tune any reception.

The output of the receiver is usually fed into a recorder, often an extended play model. This output can be controlled by the VOX setting on the recorder if it works with a line input or can be regulated by a device specifically designed to activate the recorder when audio is present and then shut if off after a specified number of silent seconds.

The poor man's listening post.

I've tried two of these devices, one made by Capri Electronics and the other, called the NITELOGGER, available through various electronic and scanner magazines. They work very well and allow completely unattended recording.

Of course, any of these methods depends on the fact that you have carefully selected a clear frequency for your job. If you place the unit at night and a mobile radio that belongs to the local pizza company actives during the day you will be somewhat disappointed with the results.

The best way to stage any operation is to set up all your equipment, with the same type of batteries you will be using on the job and let it run for 24 hours. This will "burn in" the components (most electronic failures occur in the first few hours of operation), allow you to plan your battery replacement intervals and provide a check on the frequency you plan to use.

This test should be done in the same physical area that you expect the job to transpire in.

Possibly the very most important, and surely most often overlooked component in an LP, is the antenna. If you use a rubber duck, dipole, or whip antenna you can improve the sensitivity by cutting, or extending it tot he correct length for the frequency involved.

This will provide satisfactory, non-directional, reception.

A smart eavesdropper modifies this by employing a directional antenna aimed at the transmitter. The more directional an antenna becomes, the higher the gain factor. A good directional antenna may be the *single most important improvement* you can make to your audio surveillance system.

Most directional antennas are yagi's – a central element with a number of horizontally mounted reflecting elements, all cut to reflect the target frequency. Most common outdoor TV antennas are yagi antennas.

These units are very directional and can increase your effective range by a factor of 2-5 times!

The antenna must be designed to work in the frequency band you wish to monitor. They can be purchased from companies like Antenna

Specialists, Grove Electronics or through electronic or ham radio suppliers.

Martronics will custom make a yagi antenna with the number of reflecting elements you wish and cut to the exact frequency you are going to operate on. Their custom jobs are actually about the same price, or even cheaper than over the counter yagi's.

An exotic helical coil antenna from Martronics. A good antenna can be the most important part of a listening post.

It's possible to be real, real clever and use a directional antenna on both the transmitter and the receiver (more common in video surveillance), but you have to judge the amount of notice a four foot long TV-style antenna growing from a briefcase or a potted plant is going to cause before installing this improvement.

Intelligence Support Group Ltd., sells a PATH LOSS CALCULATOR MODEL 28SND which allows the agent to solve complicated path loss problems and to determine whether a transmitter is powerful enough to transmit back to a listening post.

Device is user friendly but a bit pricey for casual jobs and designed primarily for government level installations where a test run might compromise the mission.

REPEATERS

What if you simply cannot get a listening post within range of the transmitter? Or perhaps you could place one but it would be un-

wise to visit it on a periodic basis to change batteries and tapes?

It is possible to use a low powered transmitter that will send a signal to a receiver or scanner, then have that signal interfaced with a much higher powered transmitter (usually a walkie-talkie) in order to change frequencies and project the signal much further.

The interface device is known as a repeater. It intercepts the audio from the receiver, turns the higher powered transmitter on, and rebroadcasts the new signal to a distant receiver.

This set up allows for the use of a very low powered (and hard to find) bug or tap at the target and the remote placement of the actual listening post.

If a VHF or ham band transceiver is used as the repeater transmitter it should have an external power supply, either bundled batteries or a car adapter as the new, 1-5 watt transmitter will only last for a few hours on its internal batteries.

This is an elegant solution to a perplexing problem but it does have a drawback or two. The repeated signal is so powerful that the chance some scanner operator, FCC person, or other bothersome type will discover it is quite high.

If the audio is, ah, how to say this? *Interesting,* say a conversation between two high power executives, or, or, say two consenting adults, you know it will not remain a secret for very long.

Repeaters should be used for short periods of time only or the signal should be scrambled to discourage unwanted eavesdroppers.

As opposed to wanted eavesdroppers.

Two methods exist to scramble the signal; feed the original audio into a walkie-talkie with a scrambled output, or scramble the bug's transmission.

Very nice, law enforcement level repeaters are sold by SWS Security. Very nice non-law enforcement level repeaters are sold by Electron Processing, Inc., for about *$50!*

Both units are designed to work with a scanner or dedicated receiver and a walkie-talkie.

For those of you with more money then time, or have a fear of wires, complete briefcase based repeater systems with various bells and whistles (like programmable receivers and/or transmitters, recorder outputs, etc.) are available from Telemobile Inc., and Surveillance Technology Group among others.

Most of these units are going to be aimed, or restricted to, law enforcement and the price of the Haliburton briefcase is more than the cost of an EPI repeater.

HOW TO LOCATE AND TAP ANYONE'S TELEPHONE

Tapping 101 – a hard and fast course in the art of telephone eavesdropping. Best ways, quickest ways, methods that require inside access, techniques that do not...

Easiest

1. Replace the actual instrument with a pre-tapped model. Looks the same from the outside, only an expert would spot the inside modifications. Listen Electronics (among others) will supply the phone you need with the required features in the color you want.
2. Replace the wall box with a pre-tapped unit, or add a modified two way modular jack. Quick, not likely to be noticed, over-the-counter units.
3. Stash a tap (or bug) in the phone itself. Loosen the two screws on the bottom, and add anything from a Cony, Deco, Sheffield, Micro, unit across any points where the tip and ring appear on the "network."
4. Unscrew the mouthpiece, clip on a mini tap and slide it up into the handset where it's almost impossible to see.
5. Replace the telephone's microphone "button" with a drop-in that contains a transmitter. Twenty second installation, still available from a number of overseas suppliers.
6. Follow the wiring throughout the house or apartment and connect a drop out relay and recorder across the lines. Look for a place where it will not be noticed such as an attic, garage, etc.

A modified carbon button drop-in transmitter. Note the soldered ring and thicker construction than a normal phone mic.

Be real cute and put the recorder in a sealed box that says, "Specific Bell (or whatever your local company calls itself) Equipment – Do Not Disturb Under Penalty Of Law."
7. Unscrew the outside protector or junction box and add a tap inside. No internal access required.
8. Climb the local pole if an aerial system is in use (and you have a flair for the dramatic), locate the correct pair in the rubber boot or terminals in the distribution box, place unit there.
9. If your telco uses an underground system go to the local distribution box, identify the connectors, pull the connect boards forward and attach tap on the back of the board. Most boxes are not locked and can be opened with a "can wrench" or socket set and most have a coil of the correct color coded wire in the box for "new installations."
10. Same as above, but use a $20 punch down tool to cross connect the target's wire pair to one that goes to your listening post or transmitter. Hard to find unless someone has a "map" and is looking for abnormalities. Tools available from legit telco equipment suppliers and from surveillance suppliers.

Most phone company personnel wouldn't recognize a tap if they found one in their breakfast cereal, and most do not particularly care what is on the line, just so the customer is a happy camper.

11. Be really slick and bribe, damn, that's such a harsh word, "befriend" a local lineman to tell you where the next appearances of the target line appear before they hit the central office.

12. Be really, really slick and buy the nice phone guy lunch while he leaves the cable map of the line with you for a few minutes. This paper follows the outside cable from the terminal to the central office and shows all poles and terminals in between, where each cable stops, the number of wires in the cable where the cable "appears" at various locations and so on.

This map is kept available for personnel who need to assign new wires to new numbers and, although, not usually left in distribution boxes, is available to most installers and repair personnel.

Some professionals, cops, PI's and the like, "employ" telco personnel on a part-time basis in order to secure access to these records.

Note that most phone companies warn their people that they will be immediately fired for providing records to "unauthorized" people.

Note that most phone companies pay very badly.

There are a number of very high level (and very rare) taps that flood the telephone instrument with microwaves or use "keep alive" diodes to pick up room conversation, split and re-split the line in the distribution cable and so on.

Your odds of being exposed to these are slight, UNLESS you are the CEO of a company that has just spent 50 million bucks on a research project that your competition would love to have a quick look at.

The other side of the coin, is, of course, that you are the CEO of a more informal company that has just imported 50 million dollars of research material; say stashed in a shipment of Colombian Pineapples...

Then you got to worry about not only the above attacks but law enforcement favorites like loop extenders and slaves. These toys "extend" a phone line, usually from the central office, but sometimes from a connect block, to the listening post.

13. If you want to utilize one of these ideas (say you have a listening post in the same apartment building as the target), talk to Listen Electronics or other suppliers of slaves and bridges.

BUSINESS PHONES

A slightly different kettle of fish, this one. Electronic phone systems that use more than 4 wires require a different approach. If the business uses an internal phone system, that is, one that has its own "central office" or PBX (or VSCBX – Very Small Computer Branch Exchange), it is known as "key system" and handles many of the tasks that would-be otherwise the responsibility of the phone company's central office, such as providing dial tone and switching calls.

These private phone companies offer some unique opportunities for surveillance.

1. Many of these systems offer a feature called "supervision" which allows a manager to silently bridge across any internal line by dialing a preset code. Most buyers never alter this code which can be broken. The first sequence to try is the serial number of the unit itself.

2. Most of these systems have a line code that can be accessed by dialing from the outside and using the supervisory function to listen to any conversation taking place. On ROLM systems this is typically line number 399.

No log is kept of this access.

3. It is possible to go into the equipment itself and switch out the line card with one that has built-in bridges or taps.

4. Bridges can easily be accomplished at the expander card where the lines are connected

together. If a jumper is put in place your phone will ring every time the target line does.

5. Install a relay to override the lockout at the PBX that will put any line on the modem automatically.

6. Use the built-in monitor feature that many of these systems have to listen to room audio. This is a separate line on most systems, look for clues in the manual like "intercom functions."

7. By design most electronic systems are hard to tap because they select outgoing trunks at random – the target places a call and the unit simply chooses a free line to patch the call onto.

    Some systems allow the "supervisor" to program which line will be chosen for certain outgoing calls. This allows for remote tapping.

8. It is also possible to run a wire from the target's line to a certain outgoing line which makes tapping a viable option.

9. Commercial systems, whether they are privately owned or use the phone company's equipment, normally lead to a frame room in the building where the inside lines are connected to the outgoing trunks. These rooms have a couple of interesting features; they are usually unlocked, and the helpful telco people often mark the line destinations on the walls.

    Frame rooms usually consist of a number of terminal blocks called 66 blocks. These can be recognized by their knife blade terminal clops that crush the insulation of any wire pushed into them with a special tool known as an impact tool.

    66 blocks are where the cross connecting, the mating of the various wires, takes place. If the clips on a 66 block all face the same direction, it is known as a parallel block and all the terminals are connected by a metal bus.

    If three (of the six) terminals in a row face one direction and three face the other it is a "split block." Most frame rooms also have

one or more connecting blocks where each clip is separate from its neighbor. The connecting block(s) actually connects the outside feeder cable to the inside 66 blocks.

    The frame room normally handles the connects for an entire building, sub-frame rooms or individual 66 blocks distribute the signals to each floor.

    These are ideal places for some types of taps. It is usually *not* a grade A idea to put a little black box on the front of a pair of terminals because the telco people who frequent this room will, quite naturally, be curious about its presence.

    One the other hand, the backs of the 66 blocks rarely come under examination, and the clips themselves are ideal places to run the correct colored wire (usually a roll is left behind in the room) to another set of terminals, which are attached to a wire leading to a slave unit, transmitter, or recorder.

11. Electro mechanical systems, an older version of a private phone system use a Key System Unit (KSU) that interfaces between the phones and the telco cabling in order to control the functions of the various phone instruments including; assigning incoming calls to the correct lines, providing busy signals, hold functions and "in-use" lights.

    The KSU is usually located within a couple of hundred feet of the telephones. It contains a power supply, KSU card, interrupter, frame assembly, etc.

    This is an ideal location to place a tap because this is where individual lines are connected to the outside world. KSU's normally run to a 66 block for the actual phone connects.

12. Frame rooms, KSU's, PBX's and phones are connected by wires which are typically run above dropped ceilings (ever push those little white tiles up to see what lives above your head?) or through subfloors.

    Great, great places to attach, stash, or bridge.

13. The best way to trace lines from a particular instrument, be it the only one in a house or one of 600 in an office building, is to place

a small tone generator on the line and then follow it with the induction amplifier that comes bundled with the generator.

Cheap and effective; this arrangement will show which clip or wire in a cable bundle is your target line, AS LONG AS YOU CAN GET WITHIN A FEW INCHES OF IT.

An even slicker approach is to use an RF generator and receiver (Jensen Tools) for your search. After the transmitter is hooked to the phone, or connector, the receiver will follow the signal from several feet away *even if the wires are buried*.

With this system you can pick and choose a convenient attack point that is available to you, but difficult for the other side to find.

A final suggestion is that if you are going to be involved in this sort of endeavor you purchase a nice leather tool belt, a lineman's handset, impact tool, strippers, etc. from a telco supplier, make a "Specific Bell" ID card (how many people know what the real thing looks like?) chew gum, work slowly and generally adopt a "Hey! I work for a monopoly. You want me to fix this or not? Don't matter to me pal," attitude.

In most areas, ex-phone company employees have set up shops to install interior wiring, which the real phone company no longer does (or charges an arm and a leg for). These friendly retired field personnel can often be hired for a few hours of instruction/consultation if you are unclear about local color codes and wiring schemes.

To recap here you need to attach a recorder or transmitter across the pair of wires that carry the audio, usually the red and green set. This can be accomplished at the phone, in the wall block, at the outside protector block, on the drop cable, in the junction box, at a 66 block in a frame room, at an "appearance" where the same lines reappear in a secondary junction box some distance from the primary box, in the telephone company's central office or frame room, or any point along the line itself.

Lines can be traced manually using their color code or by following the tone produced by a tone generator you have installed near the phone. A lineman's handset can be used to temporarily intercept the audio at a junction box or other terminal to verify the correct line.

A proper surveillance installation takes into account how long the unit must remain in-place, undetected, who is likely to look for it (and with what) as well as the ease with which the information can be recovered without endangering the eavesdropper.

The very easiest method is to simply strip the insulation from the audio pair and hook up a VOX controlled recorder which will turn on and record whenever the line is in use. The recorder must be isolated from the 90 volt ringing voltage (or a unique dish known as Stouffer's fried recorder will suddenly occur) by a transformer or a capacitor. The quickest, safest, method is to spend $25 with Iliadis for a pre-wired isolation cable that is meant to be plugged into one of their amplifiers, but can also be inserted directly into a recorder.

They offer two connectors, one that ends in alligator clips, one in a standard plug in telephone jack.

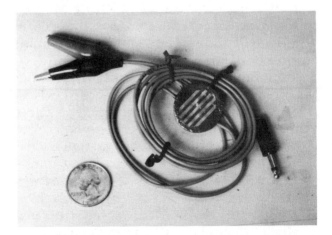

$25 and your recorder is matched to the phone line.

The next step is to use a drop out relay which accomplishes the same thing by sensing the change in voltage when a phone is in use.

There are methods to defeat suspected drop outs and VOX based recordings. There are also fairly clear cut methods for discovering any tap effort. As one would suspect, it is usually a trade off between the amount of money invested and the level of tapping involved.

A component phone sweeper, or even someone who spends the time to learn the system and is equipped with some tools can find most taps.

Is there a tap that cannot be found?

Sort of...

Security Research has taken an old theory and updated it into a unit known as the TCI-01 TELEPHONE INTERCEPT. This device takes into account that a very small electrical field surrounds any wire carrying electricity. If that field can be intercepted and amplified it is possible to listen or record the audio without ever making physical or electrical connections to the wires themselves.

This means that *absolutely no* change is made in the line's characteristics, the tap leaves no footprints to follow.

This type of attack is also one of the very simplest to install because no wires need to be stripped, nothing needs to be unconnected, one simply clamps the sensor around the target wires.

If this is such a hot idea why isn't it in widespread use?

Actually it has been used in the past by law enforcement types in an interception unit called a Kel kit (made by Bell and Howell). In the Kel coils of wire are wrapped around a spring loaded clothes pin which is then clamped onto the target wires.

The primary problem is one of noise. Any amplifier automatically increases available noise, (usually 60 cycle hum from nearby AC circuits) at the same rate as it does the target audio. In many cases the audio level is just too small and the noise floor too high.

Security Research's unit utilizes a slightly different approach by sensing the change in capacitance of the wire pair. It also incorporates a notch filter for 50/60 cycle hum and a variable filter for noise in general.

To use the unit, the eavesdropper simply places the spring loaded clip onto the outside of one of the line pair allowing the other wire to touch the other side of the clip. No stripping, easy, one step installation.

Then, using the units, speaker or headphones, our hero adjusts the clip for maximum audio. Next step is to adjust the filtering for the clearest audio.

At this point a switch can be flipped to turn off the external amplifier in order to save the battery. The TCI-01 has a built-in VOX that will control any recorder with a remote mic jack.

How well does it work?

Ah, good. You do have to open the out PIC layer of the cable in order to insert the spring loaded clip between the actual tip and ring (red and green) wires, but the hum is minimal, the installation instant, and it works.

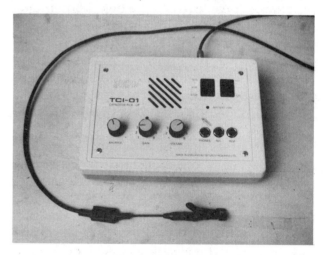

The TC-01 passive tap.

DIALED NUMBER RECORDERS

One important piece of information in telephone surveillance is whom was called. It is sometimes possible to ascertain this by playing back the beginning of the phone call into an inexpensive DTMF detector which will translate the tones into visual representations of the numbers dialed.

This works if, and only if, the recorder starts and gets up to speed in time to record all the tones and if the recorder is good enough to reproduce them correctly. Many extended play machines are not this accurate.

Another solution is to install a device which automatically translates the dialing tones and records or prints out the number. These units, known as dialed number recorders or pen registers, used to be a favorite of law enforcement folks because they did not require a warrant to install.

Simply stated DNR's did not violate the callers privacy because they did not intercept the audio.

In recent years courts have ruled that a warrant IS required, so the popularity of DNR's has drifted a bit. Most professional systems, such as those made by Racom and Bartec also have the capability of recording the audio, a feature early, non-warrant models did not concern themselves with.

For years the best, cheap DNR was made by Radio Shack. For about $100 this call auditor printed out the target number the time of the call and it's duration.

RS has stopped making this wonderful toy, but similar models are still available from a number of spy suppliers for about $300.

The best law enforcement DNR's are made by Bartec and come in a number of various configurations – some record audio when told to, some will not. Some take many lines, some do not.

Some. You get the idea.

The only problem with a DNR is that most law enforcement (I'm sorry guys, but this is true,) do not report it in-place until they get enough goodies for a warrant. Many conversations are recorded by simply flipping on the audio switch which should not be utilized it that particular situation.

The most complete and probably best line of LE DNR's is made by Racom.

NEW AND GOOD

Several unusual pieces of surveillance gear have made recent appearances in the marketplace or have been found by countermeasures people.

Racom DNR that will also record audio if necessary.

X BAND

A number of companies, including Innotek Inc., 605 Landsford, Fort Wayne, IN 46825, advertise X-band transmitters for the "long range testing of radar detectors." These inexpensive units (about $40) are really being sold as kind of a joke — guy in fancy new Ferrari passes your Hyundai at 143 MPH on the freeway?

You simply pull out the old radar tester and zap him with a blast of 10.525 GHz microwaves that immediately causes his radar detector to scream with pain.

He slams on brakes, skids sideways and you wave gaily as you pass him in the slow lane.

A interesting idea as far as it goes, but if you read the small print in the ad you'll see the company will sell you "application notes for FM modulation" for a couple of bucks extra.

Apply application notes and you are now the proud owner of a device which will transmit room audio in a tightly controlled beam over a distance of a thousand feet or so.

At a frequency that no countermeasures receiver will ever see...

So what good is a transmitter, no matter how fancy, that broadcasts in a band you can't receive?

Wander down to the local library, or talk to that ham radio operator that lives down the street (you know the one who messes up your TV reception every time he talks to his pals in Tonga), and ask to borrow the February 91 copy of the magazine, *73 Amateur Radio Today.*

Flip it open to page 10, and peruse the article entitled Radar Detector to Microwave Receiver Conversion for precise details on how to modify your little radar detector to receive audio from the above transmitter.

The author, one should note, claims receiving ranges measured in *miles.*

Or spring for a top level spectrum analyzer that will demodulate signals in the 10 GHz range and skip the soldering.

To rephrase this; one can buy a $40 "bug" that will transmit on a frequency that is not only virgin, but beyond the reach of almost every piece of countermeasure gear. It will send the room audio in a tight beam that can't be detected even with the correct gear, unless you are virtually in its path, for long distances.

This threat was brought to my attention in a well detailed report from Murray Associates – Counterespionage Consultants to Business & Government, Clinton, NJ.

Mr. Murray has this unusual habit of actually buying, or constructing the latest surveillance gear and then testing it for effectiveness and ways to find and/or defeat it.

Another example of modifying an inexpensive unit not designed for surveillance applications can be accomplished by the use of a LASER BROADCASTER available from a number of electronic hobby suppliers for under $200. Read NUTS AND VOLTS.

This unit consists of a 5 mW laser diode modulated by an audio input and a separate fiber optic based receiver.

The idea is to use a small crystal microphone or Sony Walkman to modulate the beam and then recreate the audio some distance away.

It works, the problem is that the input expects a fairly strong signal and will not pick up room audio.

The solution to this minor dilemma is to take our little preamplifier from Ilidias corporation (the one we used earlier to hot rod a tape recorder), and plug it directly into the laser transmitter module. It will then pick up all room audio allowing the beam to be modulated by it.

Granted the laser is a visible one, there is a bright red dot involved, but an infrared filter could be easily placed over the diode or the diode itself could be replaced with an IR model.

Glass will attenuate the beam's power somewhat, but it will still go a respectable distance and this is something that does not show up as a threat on most counter measures gear.

Homemade instant laser bug.

BURST BUG

Sort of... The idea behind this unit is not new; the German Navy communicated with their U-Boats during WW II by taping the message on a special recorder and then sending it out in a "burst" of several seconds duration.

The received "condensed" message was then played back on a recorder that stretched out the audio so it could be understood.

The idea was to limit the surface exposure of the U-boat and hide it from anti-sub patrols.

It didn't work because of advanced triangulation techniques developed by the British, but that's not particularly germane to our story.

A couple of English firms, are marketing a unique "black box" based, loosely, one might add, on this technique. The ULTIMATE INFINITY RECEIVER monitors the output of one or more transmitters, usually telephone taps from a convenient listening post within the transmission range.

Its sister unit does the same thing with room conversation.

The boxes have an inboard long term recording system. When activated they function as unmanned listening posts, recording the incoming audio. Then the eavesdropper calls the UIR from any telephone, anyplace in the world, presses the right buttons and the system plays the cassette back at very high speed directly into your specially matched recorder. That will slow the entire mess down and allow real time monitoring.

Cute. Cuts down on those nagging long distance phone bills and let's you keep in touch.

I also should point out real burst bugs that "inhale" audio, store it up digitally and then periodically broadcast it to a waiting receiver are, indeed available.

But not to you and me.

Or at least not to me, if you happen be a field agent for the CIA, DIA, 4-H Club, you may be able to enjoy the advantages of a BB.

OTHER HIGH LEVEL BUGS

Would include those that operate in a spread spectrum mode. Two different manifestations come under this heading; frequency hoppers and true spread spectrum.

The first system uses a special chip that changes the frequency of a transmission many times a second, putting out a tiny bit of audio at each change. Taken individually the pieces sound like nothing more than bits of static.

A matching chip in the receiver switches frequency at exactly the same rate allowing for uninterrupted reception. Communications hopping transceivers from UHF base stations to walkie talkies are available and in use by many agencies including the CIA and the FBI since it is nearly impossible to eavesdrop on this technique.

Transceivers that hop are available, although only legally to people with badges of one sort of another, making the bugs are a bit harder to find.

True spread spectrum technology dissipates the transmission over a very wide portion of the spectrum. This leaves very little power in any conventional band and makes the signal very hard to find, much less demodulate, without a special receiver.

SS units were also a no-no as far as the FCC was concerned, until 1985, when the technology was deregulated. It is now legal to employ SS technology in both one way and two way communications, license free on three bands: 902-928 MHz, 2400-2483.5 MHz and 5725-5850 MHz, as long as the output power is under 1 watt.

Spread spectrum transmitters usually convert the audio to a digital format and then spread it in a predefined method. The receiver must be in-sync with the transmitter in order to hear it.

The negative aspects of this concept include the fact that, because the signal is spread out, more power is required to achieve the same distance as a conventional width transmission.

A number of these units are available as we speak; Amdel Racing Electronics has a 1 watt unit that can be used for covert communications or surveillance. The unit is, of course, larger than the tiny 35 milliwatt bugs we are used to and consumes more power, but it is a fairly secure means of broadcasting.

Brandi Press offers books, plans, circuits and suppliers for both spread spec and frequency hopping units. They have been in the biz, designing units for the government for a number of years and will consider custom work.

Tele-Movil sells ready-to-be planted SS units of varying power hidden in briefcases and other who-would-suspect (?) objects.

Tactical Communications (Tacticom) in Dunkirk, Maryland, has been in business for 30 years designing specialized communications gear including; both direct sequence spread spectrum and frequency hopping gear.

They specialize in fast turnaround designs of communications equipment in various packages including briefcases. In 1992 they turned the plans and publishing portion of the business over to Brandi Press.

Another gentleman of Italian descent, who I am vaguely acquainted with, decided his particular organization needed some high level bugs that would not be easily found by countermeasures people hired by the other side, or even the FBI.

He bought 10 of the new spread spectrum wireless phones on the market and took each of them apart, getting rid of earphones and other extraneous pieces.

My friend ended up choosing the AT&T unit as the best for this conversion. With just some minor knowledge of electronics and a few simple tools you now have a excellent, filtered, spread spectrum unit with rechargeable batteries and an AC powered receiver all ready to go.

Unisys Corporation markets spread spectrum chips for use in various types of transmitters and receivers. They sell complete units to the Department of Defense, but "because of both a corporate commitment towards pursuit of more commercial markets and the emergence of spread spectrum technology in commercial applications Unisys is making the PA-100 technology publicly available."

They will also help design particular applications.

And finally a couple of new, inexpensive, great bugs have come onto the marketplace.

SUMA Designs, an English firm has just released an amazing line-up of extremely high level bugs. A number of these units are sold by Intelligence Incorporated. Please note these are not FCC type accepted and as such can only be sold legally in the US as a kit.

These are not "easy-to-assemble" or "partial" kits – they are real kits which must be assembled,

adjusted and tested by someone who knows what they are doing. Manufacturers do not take assembled kits back because the builder cannot seem to get them up and running...

So what do you do if your electronics engineering skills are a trifle rusty?

1. Find an electronics assembly shop in the yellow pages and have them put it together and test it. Usually located in larger cities.
2. Find a radio/TV repair person who seems to know what he is doing and pay him to assemble.
3. Go to your local college, junior college or trade school that teaches a class in electronics. Ask the teacher to recommend a good student for some assembly work...

The SUMA kits include:

The SCRX Subcarrier Room Transmitter. Room audio is coupled to an ultrasonic carrier which is then transmitted to a special receiver that demodulates the carrier. Normal receivers will hear absolutely no sound on this frequency.

The SCRX can be adjusted to broadcast in the 100-120 MHz band with a true output of 20 milliwatts, good enough for several hundred feet, maybe a quarter of a mile. Powered by a 9-volt alkaline battery, life is 25 hours of continuous running.

The SCLX does the same thing for a telephone line. Same specs, but no battery required, it leeches directly from the nice folks at the telephone company.

SCDM Subcarrier Audio Demodulator receives audio from the earphone jack of your receiver, filters out the ultrasonic carrier and amplifies the audio while demodulating it from the carrier.

The result is fed to an amplifier which will drive a pair of head phones. Requires a 9 to 12-volt power supply.

The QTX180 is a crystal controlled narrow band room transmitter. Narrow band units condense the audio down to a small portion of the usual carrier, providing excellent security. They can be monitored by the matching receiver module or by a scanner or surveillance receiver that has an adjustable bandwidth control.

They cannot be heard by traditional wide band receivers.

This particular unit puts out 15 milliwatts and will go about 30 hours on a 9 volt battery.

They also offer narrow band telephone transmitters in both series and parallel configurations.

One of my personal favorites is their RCTX system which consists of a transmitter with an onboard remote controlled receiver. The unit stays in a dormant mode until the operator presses the remote control which turns the unit on for a 2 minute period.

If you wish to keep listening, keep pressing.

The unit can be activated from a distance of about 200 meters. This unit is pleasant because it conserves the battery until needed *and can be shut down during a countermeasures sweep.*

Another neat unit, at least in theory, as I've never actually used one is offered by Sipe Electronics, POB 2371, 4150 Krefeld 1 Germany.

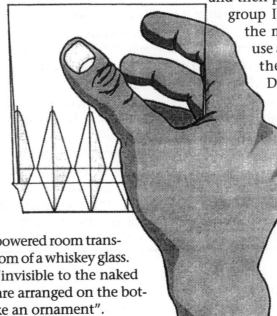

Their SIPE MT is a solar powered room transmitter hidden in the bottom of a whiskey glass. The tiny transmitter is "invisible to the naked eye" and the solar cells are arranged on the bottom of the glass "just like an ornament".

The transmitter turns itself off automatically when the glass is turned upside down.

Great for those little diplomatic get togethers, ey?

Not sure if glass is dishwasher safe.

FAX INTERCEPTION

Although considered "safe" by people who should know better, FAX machines are also subject to electronic eavesdropping.

When two FAX's communicate they begin the exchange with a series of protocol hand shake signals that establish the parameters of the conversation, including the baud rate, type of machines involved, etc.

This handshake must be completed before the transmission of data begins. Additional signals, such as end-of-page and end-of-transmission, are also necessary for a successful mission.

Some FAX machines will not work if they sense something on the line that does not return the handshake, some can be programmed to accept calls only from a list of "OK" numbers, therefore, a FAX interceptor must be able to overcome these minor problems.

One method is to record the data stream by a direct connection digital tape recorder (DAT), and then play back through a modified group III FAX in order to print out the message. It is also possible to use a tap transmitter to broadcast the digital signal to a remote DAT and do the same thing.

Professional FAX intercept devices (which do not require a handshake and do not appear to the sending FAX) are available from a number of sources. The FAXMATE from Tech Support Systems is one of the lesser expensive FAX "grabbers" on the market.

Like most lower end units it is a modified FAX modem and works with an IBM PC. The FAXMATE is sold both to law enforcement and private security, to "stop unauthorized FAX use, stop industrial espionage" and so on. It also "monitors all incoming and outgoing faxes."

Other dedicated (usually law enforcement only) FAX intercept devices can be purchased from STG, among others.

HDS offers law enforcement cards that insert directly into an IBM PC and will demodulate both FAX and modem data. They also package the card with a portable 386 computer including a gas plasma screen and printer.

The DFS-SYSTEM ONE can be hooked across any subscriber loop and will record and demodulate any incoming FAX or computer messages.

HDS also offers a series of products under the heading of the PLMS 300 SERIES which can be configured to grab all incoming phone and voice mail messages, FAX and modem data, and can include a dialed number recorder, as well as, a dial-up slave transmitter.

For those times when you really don't want to miss a message.

Not cheap, but HDS will rent out their intercept cards on a monthly basis.

Aeromaritime (Germany) sells a sophisticated intercept system as does El-Tec International.

A new modified FAX intercept modem called the FAXSNIFF is also on the market in the $2000 price range.

Bargain FAX Interception

There is one other method that can be used for very dollar-effective FAX monitoring. This unit is not designed as a tap, or as anything surreptitious, but rather as a luxury for the busy business man. It's known as a BOOMERANG and is made by Tanji Designs. It sells for about $300 from various Sharper Image type suppliers (even the United Airlines in-flight sales catalog now offers it)...

The BOOMERANG is designed to be plugged into the facsimile line ahead of the machine itself. It sits on the wire transparently waiting for incoming messages. When a FAX comes in the BOOMERANG digitally records it in its RAM before passing it onto the machine.

The unit can store 60 pages of material. It can be programmed to direct dial any other FAX machine and pass the data on at a certain time, or you can call in from a remote FAX and pick up "your" messages.

The unit does require AC power but is small enough to fit conveniently out of sight in many areas and does not look like a tap if found. In fact, one could probably attach it in plain sight, next to the target FAX with a note on company stationary that said something like, "line noise filter – do not remove."

Or it could be super-glued directly onto the rear of the machine in question and would probably never be noticed, or if it were, it would simply be considered a part of the system.

The BOOMERANG FAX recorder.

Most FAX compromises don't involve fancy equipment, they happen at the receiving end where unauthorized personnel physically access the incoming message.

This can be eliminated by locking the FAX in a secure area and denying access to all but those with a need to know.

A more, well, spy-like answer is to buy a FAX machine from several companies that feature models with a built-in paper shredders so messages can be passed into the great beyond after they are read (remember Mission Impossible? "This tape will self destruct in five seconds"), and one model even "prints the message in invisible ink that must be treated before the message becomes visible."

It is also very possible to scramble FAX messages to discourage unwanted interception. Because the transmitted date is already in digital form it is actually simpler to scramble than are voice messages.

A number of companies offer FAX scramblers, one of the best is probably the FAX SCRAMBLER I by Metme corporation. This unit offers two levels of security on both in-coming and outgoing faxes.

It is not a public key system but operates from a 6 digit (1 million try out combinations) security code entered by the user that can be changed at any time. The codes must match before the unit will allow transmission, then it encrypts the data.

It is portable and compatible with group II and III FAX machines.

Cycomm also offers stand alone FAX scramblers which use both DES and proprietary algorithms to protect communications, and a new unit from Sweden is available from VEC Electronics.

STU III FAX scrambling is also available for those who deal with classified government contractors or are really, really worried about their messages falling into the wrong hands.

Talk to Motorola.

PAGER INTERCEPTION ON A BUDGET

Paging intercept systems have been available for several years. Most will track a particular pager by its cap code or the number one dials to activate the unit. The systems automatically record all messages to the target pager, usually phone numbers but they will also grab alphabetical message groups if the paging system is so equipped.

These systems are designed for law enforcement and average $2,000 – $4,000.

The nice folks at Universal Radio, Inc., 6330 Americana Pkwy., Reynoldsburg, OH 43068, have produced a tricky unit known as the UNIVERSAL M-400.

Said tricky unit, is a universal decoder; hook it up to a receiver and it will automatically decode DTMF (touch tones), FAX (graphics only, not text), ASCII, Baudot, (aircraft addressing and reporting systems), CTCSS tones (used to "hide" private conversations) and, get this, both POCSAG and GOLAY.

Now, of course, you realize that these are the two standard paging formats in use today. Ac-

tivate the M-400 and it will begin displaying (and remembering) every page it "sees."

Note that it cannot be set to only grab one code, and that it only works on the format it's set to receive; *BUT* you can output to a computer and/or printer and use its search functions to select the pages of interest and, if you want to cover all bases, you could use two UNIVERSALS, one set to GOLAY, one to POCSAG...

This decoder costs $400.

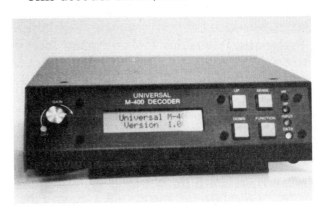

Universal Radio decoder.

BOOKS

For some odd reason the field of electronic surveillance doesn't draw as many writers as, say, the romance field.

I dunno why...

There have been some landmark publications, many of which we've already covered or out of print. The very first big seller was done, if memory holds true, in the early 60's and was entitled THE ELECTRONIC INVASION. Out of print and out of date, at the time it was a real eye opener.

THE BIG BROTHER GAME, (French), HOW TO GET ANYTHING ON ANYBODY (me) still around, still useful, both available from Intelligence Inc.

Mick Tyner has done a couple, the best being THE SPOOK BOOK.

Hal Lipset, probably the most famous real life private detective ever (and one of the best) finally put many of his experiences together in a book entitled THE GOOD DETECTIVE, formerly THE BUG IN THE MARTINI OLIVE, POCKET BOOKS, ISBN 0-671-88672-X . Hal's stuff is worth reading for the concepts and cleverness alone.

My favorite story, I might add, told to me by the man in person, was when he had to meet a major crime figure in a steam bath. No clothes.

The guy wasn't too excited about the prospect of a recording being made.

Both men were naked. Hal got it anyway.

Where?

A specially designed transmitter in a hollowed out bar of soap...

What legends are made of.

TELEPHONE EAVESDROPPING AND DETECTION, Taylor-Hill Publishing by two college instructors in the art of telephone surveillance and counter surveillance, is undoubtedly the best work ever published on the fine art of telephone based eavesdropping.

SURVEILLANCE FUN

This is probably the best deal in the book – I mean there's just not a reason to not send for this, if you'll excuse the double negative.

Mentor Publications, POB 1549-L, Asbury Park, NJ 07712, a publisher of books of interest to our kind of folks has put together a "BLACK BAG" TRIVIA QUIZ on IBM PC discs.

This is not a "what is a bug?" amateur program but a quite sophisticated, multi-choice test on all aspects of surveillance, entry techniques, and how-to spy stuff.

100 questions. I took it at the request of a very professional friend who grudgingly admitted I came within a point of his score (and I swear I hit one entry key incorrectly) and saw the scores of other professionals who landed 30 points below us...

Fun, entertaining, makes you think about what's really what. Besides you can embarrass your know-it-all friends.

Cost? A dollar for a 5.25 disk, two bucks for a 3.5. MS-DOS only...

Okay now for the old self plug – I would really suggest you get a copy of BOOK II HOW TO GET ANYTHING ON ANYBODY, if you don't already own one and especially if you find this particular book in the least interesting. They are not replacements, but rather companions.

THE COVERT CATALOG and HANDS-ON ELECTRONIC SURVEILLANCE, same thing, what he said.

Also see chapter on books.

This entire field of non-invasive, "black" surveillance still intrigues me and as soon as I return from my six year trip around the world I have been promising myself, when I got this book done, I plan on testing everything from accelerometers to lasers on video...

NEWEST BITS AND PIECES FROM THE WORLD OF ELECTRONIC SURVEILLANCE

KGB surveillance devices are now on the market!

Really! You can order a catalog for the measly sum of one US dollar (sent airmail) from a nice gentleman named Anastasios POB 19063, Athens 11710 Greece.

He is reputed to have "great" Eastern bloc contacts and offers an interesting selection of gear, including a laser listener...

There are a number of new conferences, courses and shows in the security/surveillance field. Jim Ross' SURVEILLANCE EXPO remains the only dedicated surveillance show open to the public, but a number of other security/weapons/surveillance events have and are appearing.

Not to be redundant but please check THE COVERT CATALOG for the latest details.

A couple of things I will note here is that NITIA (National Technical Investigators) has regional chapters and regional shows. If you are a cop or cop type, you might want to join and attend their offerings.

Don't waste your time if you have no law enforcement connection and just think it would be cool to see what the guys in white hats are using. You won't get in. They do background checks.

LEIU (Law Enforcement Intelligence Unit) is now hosting very difficult to attend shows where the real heavies display their goodies, as well as training seminars in such delicate topics as Organized Crime Check Cashing Schemes, Crimes Related to the Casino industry, various surveillance courses and certificates.

They even have a raffle, and no, I don't know what the prizes are.

Again don't bother these folks unless you gotta badge.

A real badge...

AID ("the world's largest manufacturer of surveillance devices") is expanding their courses to now include:

- Basic and advanced electronic surveillance
- Basic and advanced video surveillance
- B & A telephone intercepts, covert entry update workshop
- Tactical electronic operations
- Advanced neutralization of locking devices (oh, yes, very nice...)
- And many more.

They have an 800# if you think you might qualify.

Jarvis Institute in Tulsa, Oklahoma still offers the best courses I've ever attended in surveillance, counter surveillance, telephone tapping, B & E and so on.

Some (ah, not telephone tapping or B & E) courses are open to the non-badged public.

Other Books include TECHNIQUES IN COUNTER SURVEILLANCE The Fine Art of Bug Extermination by Peter Lieg Eco-Tec, 110 pages. A good, hands-on technical book that crosses with hands-on countermeasures, but also covers other items and areas of interest including IR sniffers, sub-carrier demodulation, some circuits, some new concepts.

HOW TO BUILD A BUG PROOF ROOM Angus Glas, Paladin Press. Okay, say you're expecting the Russian Ambassador to dinner and he's requested a secure room to discuss your future with the Eastern Bloc economic plans, or, or maybe you are the nephew of the head of a major Colombian drug cartel and you need a place to talk to customers.

This book is for you.

Actually technically correct, it would apply to major corporations with the need for audio security. Combine it with a few of my techniques, a line protector or two, and the bad guys are going to have to knock on the door and pretend to be building inspectors to get any goods.

HOW DO REAL SPIES COMMUNICATE WITHOUT COMING UNDER SURVEILLANCE?

On July 19, 1977, patent number 4,037,159 was issued to one Albert Martin. This patent disclosed a brand new idea for audio communications known as the CHIRP system. It utilized a transmitter that sent out successive signals that sound like, well, chirps.

Each burst signal starts at different initial frequencies but has the same frequency-time slope. The bursts are made according to a predetermined pseudo random program that is known at the receiving station.

These broadcasts are considered quite jam and interception proof. They can be bounced off satellites, the ionosphere or even meteor showers. Some stations send out timed CHIRP bursts simply to find the best method of propagation at any given moment.

CHIRPS can handle diversity radio, codes, and frequency hopping encryption. In addition, CHIRPS emulate many other natural phenomenon including the burst of static when a piece of electrical machinery is switched on, intermittent medical equipment and other RF emitters.

CHIRPS are used by all major powers who spy on each other.

This next section is for my customers from foreign intelligence agencies and "embassies." Please, just skip over it if that description doesn't apply to you.

Thank you for your help in this matter.

Hey guys, the US has just installed TOP SECRET equipment that is software driven and whose purpose in life is to instantly analyze all CHIRP type signals, automatically eliminating any that are generated by natural phenomenon or non-communication equipment.

Said unit will also slope decode any remaining communication signals.

Sorry about that diversion, but I figure I owe something to every reader...

BOOK II HOW TO GET ANYTHING ON ANYBODY
ELECTRONIC SURVEILLANCE TO DATABANK CRACKING

• AUDIO SURVEILLANCE. Who, what, why and most importantly, how...Equipment used, government and professional tricks of the trade, including unconventional, hard-to-find, bugs.
• ACOUSTIC ANALYSIS AND HARDWIRING. Playing a hard room–Tradecraft for audio intelligence gathering. Photos and operation notes on the super secret CIA fine wire kit.
• ACCESSIBLE HIGH LEVEL BUGS AND TAPS. The hottest items available; operating tips, sources and suggestions. How the government does it, what they pay, who they buy from. Best bugs on a budget-side by side tests of the true performers + four pages of the best, trickiest, slickest, most unusual and true blue bargains in all types of electronic surveillance equipment. Cheap units you can buy that no one will find! Long distance bugging, reach out and touch someone from a distance; updates on passive LASER and microwave systems.
• THROUGH WALLS. A guided tour by two FBI instructors in the art of seeing and hearing through solid walls. • INTELLIGENCE KITS. A brief history of law enforcement and sexy spy kits from plastic belt recorders and early KELS to photos of the latest audio and video monitoring systems, PLUS do-it-yourself systems for every surveillance occasion. • THE PHONE COMPANY. Not sold in any stores–a quick course in telco systems, cabling, cross connects, drop outs, VOX's and lineman's tricks. How professionals tap any phone system, including: How to tap a phone with no equipment!
• OBTAINING CONFIDENTIAL PHONE COM-
PANY INFORMATION. Trace, track, and obtain inside telco data including unlisted, unpublished phone numbers. Answering machine and voice mail cracking techniques.
• CELLULAR TELEPHONE OPERATIONS AND INTERCEPTS. • VIDEO SURVEILLANCE. True tricks of the trade! • NIGHT VISION. Infrared and starlight • HOW TO TAIL ANYONE ANYWHERE. Foot/auto tailing tactics plus an in depth look at how the major electronic systems (Adcock, Doppler, etc.) function.
• SURVEILLANCE PHOTOGRAPHY. High speed, low light, hidden camera and document copying. New films, new cameras, new tricks for candid surveillance photography.
• COMPUTER CRACKING. The hacker's handbag; tricks for defeating or bypassing passwords on any system. Van Eck freaking – A brand new, ready made, inexpensive unit that will read any computer from hundreds of feet away. • INFORMATION TRACKING. Thousands of new databases hold personal, financial and "private" information on literally everyone (and every business) in the US, now they can be accessed by anyone! Trace, track and dig out SS numbers, addresses, phone numbers, credit histories, motor vehicle records, real property, marriage, death, divorce, legal info as well as forwarding addresses, and newspaper morgue records. Build a complete dossier on anyone from the comfort of your living room. "I'm really not supposed to be telling you this, but our instructors use BOOK II as an instruction manual at Quantico." — An active FBI agent

SAVE $10!

Cut out this page (no xeroxes) and send it (no credit cards) to Intelligence Incorporated and they will send you a copy of BOOK II for $24.95 plus $5.00 s and h. California residents add 8% sales tax. 2228 S. El Camino Real, San Mateo, CA 94403.

HOW TO LOCATE & TAP ANY TELEPHONE

Alexander Graham Bell's invention has proven to be quite possibly the most important single piece of intelligence-gathering paraphernalia ever conceived. Not only can we access HUMINT, databases, our controllers, the competition, help when necessary and make those all-important dinner reservations at Tavern On The Green, many use the telephone to steal.

Telephones distill information, making them a natural focal point for both overt and covert gathering.

Let's get down to brass tacks—no spy worth his salt uses a cellular phone. Come on, the days of picking up chicks in Washington bars by whispering what passed for coded conversations into your shirt pocket, cellulars have long since fallen into the void of the passé'.

Besides (as we'll see in a moment) cellulars are far from secure and a bother when you suddenly find yourself on a hillside in Tanzania too far from the nearest cell.

Today's well equipped spy, world traveler, or phoneaphobic uses the suitcase based Magnavox Magnaphone. Weighing in at a mere 50 pounds the Magnaphone can travel as airline luggage (don't worry about the customs folks in Zaire, just slip 'em a few bucks) and "It's as easy-to operate as a telephone."

The Magnaphone will automatically locate the best satellite for your location (which can include such probable locations as the sides of Mount Everest or the Sahara desert) and puts your call through. Works in the rain, features auto redial, the umbrella antenna folds for easy storage, built-in telex, and it's fax capable. Dial your number, push a button and the best INMARSAT (a communication satellite positioned in a geo-stationary orbit) is chosen automatically and your call is placed just like you were in a phone booth in a major city in the U.S..

Well, actually, if you've tried to use a phone booth in a major city lately, you may well find that the "surprisingly affordable" Magnaphone is the real way to, as Magnavox puts it, "just say hello to your loved ones."

Bet it would attract a bit of attention in a singles bar too...

The marvelous MAGNAPHONE

WIRELESS AND CELLULAR

Okay, let's get back into the easy and fun stuff. If you think about it, wireless (cordless) phones and cellular phones are not really phones: they're radios. This means anyone with the correct receiver can listen in on any wireless or cellular conversation.

How? Cordless phones are the easiest, as they operate on a limited number of frequencies which are received by almost all scanners. You simply program a scanner bank to run through the frequencies until you find one or more calls you wish to listen in on.

By the way, this is perfectly legal in most states because the federal courts have ruled you "have no expectation of privacy on a cordless phone". However a couple of states, notably California, have instituted laws which prohibit the interception of any electronically transmitted conversation.

It will be interesting to see how these laws stand up the first time the notion of public airways is tested in court.

Cordless phones have a limited range of several hundred feet but this can be increased substantially by using a scanner, which has more sensitive electronics than does the typical phone.

Furthermore you can purchase special antennas tuned to the cordless bands to boost the reception range. If you wish to listen to a specific phone located in a specific area, you can use a directional gain antenna allowing you to "point" at the building under consideration from a fair distance.

"Long wire" 49 MHz antennas available from Cellular Security Group claim cordless reception at a range of 1-3 miles from the target phone.

Program your scanner and take a nice Sunday drive through a suburban neighborhood and you will be quite surprised at the intimate conversations taking place. Of course you can also try this with the receiver of your cordless phone and you may pick up some calls, but the lack of sophistication of this approach offends my sense of play to a great degree.

CORDLESS PHONE FREQUENCIES		
CHANNEL	BASE FREQUENCY	HANDSET FREQUENCY
1	46.610	49.670
2	46.630	49.845
3	46.670	49.860
4	46.710	49.770
5	46.730	49.875
6	46.770	49.890
7	46.830	49.930
8	46.870	49.930
9	46.930	49.990
10	46.970	49.970

The base will repeat both sides of most wireless phones...

CELLULAR PHONES

Cellular phones are rapidly replacing soap operas as a source of good clean smut—plus you often actually know the actors and actresses. Please note it is illegal to eavesdrop on cellular phones (at least at this is written) but believe me that doesn't stop many potential listeners.

Cellulars are a bit harder to track because they "hand off" to different frequencies as the person moves about. There is a system detailed in Bill Cheek's book SCANNER MODIFICATION HANDBOOK, (from CDB), and reprinted in BOOK II of HOW TO GET ANYTHING ON ANYBODY to program a scanner to follow cellular hand-offs without missing much of the conversation.

I sat with a detective on a hill overlooking a major city and followed a drug dealer's conversations with this system for the better part of an hour without missing anything of great importance.

Cellular reception range can be increased by the use of a specially designed cellular ground plane antenna that maximizes the reception of the 800 MHz band in which cellular phones transmit, as well as a choke which also maximizes reception in this area of the spectrum.

A new high gain cellular antenna which is pointed at the phone in question and provides a chunk of gain (15 dB) is offered by Electron Processing Inc., POB 68, Cedar, MI 49621. This antenna can be hooked up to a frequency counter or Optoelectronics preselector or directly to a scanner in order to single out a certain phone and follow it from a distance.

EPI also features a nice selection of preamplified scanner antennas.

The ultimate expression in cellular eavesdropping went on for a number of years as our satellites picked up cellular calls from the Kremlin and high Soviet party officials talking on their car phones from deep space, before the Russians caught on to the process.

TUNE IN ON TELEPHONE CALLS, Tom Kneitel, available from CRB Research ($12.95 plus shipping) is an invaluable tool for anyone desiring to drop in on telephone calls.

The new edition covers the brand new 900 MHz cordless bands, hundreds of HF frequencies bands for high seas telephone listening, air/ground airline frequencies and so on. The most complete work in this field.

Some scanner manufacturers have excluded the cellular bands from their units: SCANNER MODIFICATION HANDBOOK, Bill Cheek, also from CRB, gives detailed instructions for simple un-modifications to allow these units to pick up cellulars. GRE also sells a converter that will also allow

un-cellular scanners to receive the 800–900 MHz band.

What do you hear on cellular conversations? Well, if you're following one particular person you are going to get a lot of private and probably confidential information.

Loose, random scanning?

In one afternoon I listened to several nice young ladies at our local escort/massage service call in as they got to their job sites (gave the addresses) and then give a blow by blow report of the session afterwards. One guy called his office, talked to his secretary, called his wife to tell her he was going to work late at the office, and then called his mistress to set up the evening's entertainment in some detail.

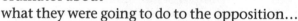

Later came a call from a local politician in a hotly contested race talking to his dirty tricks coordinator about what they were going to do to the opposition...

Need to follow a single cellular phone, record every call placed or received by that particular user? A little harder, but still possible, Tech Support Systems 1203 Normandy Way, Santa Clara, CA 95050, will sell you a $3,000 Cellmate —a modified cellular phone, recorder, auto turn-on device that fits in a briefcase and simply acts as an extension phone to the number you are interested in.

As long as your CELLMATE is within the range of the phone or the cell it is using, it will turn on and automatically record every call, in or out, made with the target phone.

CELLULAR INTERCEPTION
—LATEST DEVELOPMENTS

Cellular interception technology has made some leaps and bounds lately. Curtis Electro Devices, 4345 Pacific St., Rocklin, CA 95677, is marketing a device named CELLPHONE.

The stock CELLPHONE is a hand-held instrument that has a range of about two miles in which it will read out any cellular phone number, called number and *Electronic Serial Number* of any targeted phone. It will also produce the audio for your edification and follow the call thru hand-offs, as well as auto-store the last 99 calls with time and date.

As this is written the unit will not track or lock onto one particular number, but rather will pick up the strongest signal in both local channels (wireline and non-wireline) and then supplies the information.

It can be used with a gain antenna (BNC connector) to isolate one direction (but not necessarily one signal) and is used by law enforcement people for stakeouts. The usual method is simply to park down the street from the target phone and aim the antenna at the target.

If another phone comes between the target and the CELLPHONE (and the unit is not currently tracking the target) it will pick up the new signal.

If the unit receives directly from the portable phone you may get only the target's side of the conversation (as with a scanner). If you track the cell you'll get both. This minor annoyance can be cleared up by coupling this unit to a standard (non-surveillance model) CELLLPHONE in order to guarantee reception of both sides.

Still, this is not a modified cellular phone, but a monitor engineered to do one thing and do it very well; track cellular phones and provide readouts of the numerical data. The cost is under $2,000 and it's the best thing around for that money or a lot more...

As I mentioned, the CELLPHONE also provides a readout of the ESN. This is a major advantage in legal applications and, uh, major, *major* advantage in illegal apps, because, of course, if you have an active phone number and a valid ESN and access to the equipment necessary to burn the EPROM in a cellular phone, you will never have to pay those annoying little phone bills at the end of each month. Curtis will sell to law enforcement folk only...

CIVILIAN COUNTERPARTS

Electronic Countermeasures Inc. 65-31 Ave SW., Calgary, Alberta Canada T2S 2Y7, has ingeniously combined an IBM PC based software program with a direct (wired) interface for many all band (ICOM, for instance) radios.

In order to monitor calls you tune the radio to the control channel of your nearest cell (built into the software package) and let it read there. You can focus on any call within the cell and the computer will issue automatic GoTo commands to follow the call thru each hand-off. This means you will get the entire conversation with no drop outs or frantic channel searching.

This is ideal for mobile surveillance but you can also use the program as a "one search" by programming in a certain phone number which forces the system to ignore all other calls and focus only on your desired target. You must be in the same cell as your target or in an adjacent cell but tuned to the control channel of the cell the target is in for this to work.

It takes a couple of days of cruising to plot the rough outlines of each cell in a certain city by using the S meter of your receiver, or, of course, you can talk a friendly phone person into giving you a cell map, simplifying your job considerably.

You can even petition the FCC for local cell maps but this requires the use of rented researchers and is a slow and at best, tenuous process.

Once you have the conversation you need not be in the same cell, all hand-offs will be auto followed.

Price? Around $500, information packet $3.00. Not bad.

Custom Computer Services, POB 11191, Milwaukee, WI 532311, offers the Yankee counterpart to ECI. Dubbed the Digital Data Interpreter Test Set, this product also consists of PC based software and a "kit" for direct radio interfacing.

The range of commands seems to be greater; one can monitor any specific control frequency and watch as numbers are dialed and received,

power change requests are given and acted upon and GoTo hand-off commands are implemented.

Particular phone numbers can be programmed in and spurious data "filtered" out while the computer records each call's time in, time out, number called, etc.

Priced at a very reasonable $330 plus the possibility of an interface kit ($8-$18 depending on the radio). These units appear to be a real answer to the problem of cellular interception.

Neither of the above systems will provide the ESN of the target phone.

A third alternative is to actually modify a cellular phone to receive any number you want it to by paying some nice electronics technician who has more child support than morals to change the electronic serial numbers of your phone to do the same thing, or do it yourself by using the techniques described in one of these two books:

CELLULAR TELEPHONE HACKERS' GUIDEBOOK, Dynaspek, Inc., POB 564, Westmont, IL 60559, $49.95. This is a *serious* book that shows step-by-step instructions for reprogramming 250 models of cellular telephones. This allows someone with a bit of electronic knowledge and some basic equipment to  reprogram the electronic serial numbers and other necessary features to change the phone number of the phone to any number desired.

Text, graphics and circuits show exactly how to manipulate cellular phones. This is not bedside material and you will need some electronic smarts to utilize the steps, but it is a very exacting, technical look at violating the integrity of most cellular phones.

Many cellular phones can be "taught" to act as a receiver picking up all phone calls in the area. Usually this procedure is accomplished from the keyboard with no internal programming necessary.

A number of the cellular hacking books show the programming procedure for each particular model phone.

TWO GOOD SOURCES FOR "CELLULAR TELEPHONE EXPERIMENTER'S KITS" ARE:

Network Wizards
POB 343
Menlo Park, CA 94026

Disc based programming data, cables and connectors.

California Grapevine Communications
25082 Luna Bonita Dr
Laguna Hills, CA 95653

Hundreds of programming templates for various cellular instruments.

These books bring us to another area spies need to be concerned with: how do you place calls that cannot be traced? One can't be calling the Russian Embassy, or even your private inside telephone guy and leave tracks. One way is to modify a cellular phone so it uses a different number every time it is accessed, making tracking (and unfortunately billing) impossible. This aspect benefits spies and others who worry about those federal and police departments that love to use their $25,000 phone monitors to record all calls to or from a certain number.

Remember, your information is priceless. Don't let it become compromised. Many phone companies have separate buildings or rooms where the authorities can simply plug in the goodies and start tracking. And all long distance and some local records can always be called up after the fact by those with warrants or by those with a little pull with a phone man...

Of course, if you use an (illegal) continuously self-modifying phone, do send your payment in to the phone company anonymously. Neither this book nor my personal philosophy suggests that you cheat anyone.

Thank you for your help in this matter.

BOOK BARGAIN

The best cellular "phone book" is probably CELLULAR & CORDLESS PHREAKING published by John Williams of Consumertronics. This manual explains how cellular phones are programmed, which models lend themselves to "modifications" and how such modifications are accomplished.

Unlike many of the other available books on this subject, Consumrertronic's offering is jammed with hands-on information. No large white borders, big type, double spacing, half pages, courses in basic electronics or other padding.

It's a bargain at $69.95, remember most of these books started out selling in the several hundred dollar range.

Another source book is PHONE PIRATES by Ian Angus, Telemanagement Press, 8 Old Kingston Road, Ajax, Ontario, Canada L1T 2Z7 $55.00. Written for corporate types, the aim of this work is to prevent toll theft of all kinds. The book includes some decent chapters on various scams, ID, cellular and PBX time stealing, shoulder surfing, and various studies of toll fraud victims.

A few information sources listed and several "profiles" of bad guys who are involved with this field.

I should point out the first profile is of John Williams, whose products I highly recommend...

A basic book for security managers who haven't ever really had any exposure to the concept of free calling.

One way in which cloned cellulars make money for their owners is through Cell Sells, or Cell Shops. These are temporary offices operated, often out of a hotel room in an ethnic area of a major city (New York and Los Angeles currently lead the list) where people can come and make calls to anywhere in the world for a flat rate of $10-$30.

The calls are, of course, made on an illegally cloned phone.

The cellular companies are starting to crack down on hackers – new security measures are coming into play (primarily computers searching for phones that "roam" too often or bill to numbers outside the area, calling pattern analysis to locate cell shops and direction finders for clones that operate at the same time the originals do) and some arrests have been made.

Possible upcoming security measures to fight number hacking include encrypting the phone number and EIN number when cellular goes digital and taking "digital fingerprints" of each legitimate phone (every transmitter registers a unique RF fingerprint which can be recorded) and requiring a match before the call is placed.

Of course, hacker technology is also moving forward at a spectacular pace. While researching this chapter I was offered a phone with a built-in scanner/EIN decoder and the ability to reprogram its own numbers.

Every time the instrument makes a call it searches out an active number that is not in use at the moment and automatically sets itself up as a clone of that phone.

This means each and every call is made on a different, active, number.

A bit difficult to trace...

$2500 from your friendly neighborhood clone supplier.

HOW PREVALENT IS CELLULAR HACKING?

The California Highway Patrol recently finished its installation of solar power cellular phones along some of California's more rural roads. The phones are set up so the only call possible is directly to the Patrol operator in order to summon help or report an accident.

However the phones still contain a phone number and EIN...

In the first routine audit, conducted a few months after the phones became active, some 25,000+ minutes of unauthorized calls had been billed to the help phones by hackers who cracked the numbers and programmed clones.

AND NOW FOR SOMETHING COMPLETELY DIFFERENT...

Another approach to wireless eavesdropping is to use a nearfield or proximity receiver. These are not scanners. They do not look through hundreds of programmed frequencies for a signal; instead, they use their electronic dampening to select only signals that emanate from the area near you.

This means these receivers will pick up bugs, body wires, telephone taps and walkie talkies carried by cops, agents, fire department personnel, newspaper and TV crews. (Hey, I've been there! If there is a media crew in the country that lacks one of these, BUY ONE NOW.) You always want to see what the other guys are doing.

In addition, the proximity receiver will pick up "confidential" conversation between security guards at political events, rock concerts, Secret Service agents, the hiway patrol officer when he calls in to find your heinous crimes and *all wireless phone conversations and cellular phone conversations in the area.*

These receivers sell in the $10,000 range.

Until now. Optoectronics has developed a device called the INTERCEPTOR that automatically locks onto nearby signals.

It works quite well, the major limitation being one of range, but the price is right at less than $400.

Add $150 for the cellular filter/booster and suddenly you can just sit there with your "Walkman" plugged into your ear and listen to every cellular conversation in the area.

Add about eight hundred more and you get the ultimate pre-selector amplifier that increases the range tenfold (by limiting and amplifying the frequency range you are interested in).

Couple this set up to a gain, directional antenna and you have a new toy that will virtually de-bug a room, alert you to a hidden transmitter, zero in on all wireless/cellular phone calls and two way conversations in a certain area.

For a look at the actual operation, ranges and operating methods of most of the above wireless/cellular phone interception methods look at BLACK SURVEILLANCE, a video tape ($69.95) available from Intelligence Incorporated.

It takes a bit of practice and is not perfect for working from a moving vehicle as you pick up snatches of conversation from vehicles going in the other direction, but for tailing a cellular, two way or CB user, it's ideal, and it really shines for stationary surveillance applications.

Two days after I received our INTERCEPTOR I was driving in traffic and trying to listen to the various signals that came and went as the car passed into different signal areas.

Some jerk-off in a Rover with Rhino guards tailgated me the entire way! (Do you remember the last time a loose rhino tried to ram a Rover in downtown San Francisco?) Two or three feet behind my bumper, he seemed oblivious to the rest of the world as he talked on his nifty cellular and alternately slammed on his brakes to avoid hitting me and then accelerated suddenly to make up the four feet the braking cost him.

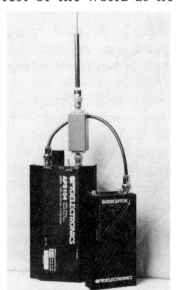

The interceptor and aps-104—one of the best methods for following a nearby cellular

Finally, we got to a stop light and he pulled up next to me. He was arguing with tearful girl-friend about the "relationship" They finally decided to have dinner at a local restaurant in order "to sort things out."

She, "I'll meet you at 7, it's on fifth, off Harrison right?"

He, "Uh, no, I think it's actually on Harrison."

I tapped on my window and motioned for him to roll his window down. "Actually it's on third, right off the freeway. Don't order the pasta and by the way, Diane's a hell of a lady."

The reaction was right out of a Daffy Duck cartoon; he started to wave and say thank you and then it sank in...

He was still at the light with his hand out the window, pointing at me when I turned...

I like the INTERCEPTOR. No tuning, no hassle, no paranoia, (do you suppose those cops in the next car are talking about us?)...

Coupled with a Martronics gain antenna you can track anyone...

C Two Plus Technology, 3174 Mobile Highway, Montgomery, AL 36108, will take a cellular phone and add the capability to operate on the same phone number as your primary unit.

This means you can have two phones on the same number without paying your friendly cellular company for two lines. They do not deactivate the signaling portion of the phone so you CANNOT operate both phones at once (or use one as a clone for surveillance purposes), but will do everything else for a moderate fee.

The field is constantly changing and there are so many questions one might wish to pose to a certified phone engineer, or hacker. How to reach the experts?

The new PHOENIX PROJECT bulletin board offers an on-line program with down -loadable files, real time interactive conferences with cellular experts and a "CB simulator" (like on CompuServe) where you can log on with an alias and ask whomever, whatever.

This is just a part of this exciting board, and at the time of this writing they will sign you up as a subscriber for a mere $25. Add $20 more and you get THE COMPLETE GUIDE TO NOKIA, TANDY, AND RADIO SHACK HARDWARE in the deal.

A book which "tells you everything you ever wanted to know about these phones."

At any rate this is a real hands-on book with photos of the exact circuits in question, how to service them and where substitutes are obtainable.

Phoenix Rising Communications, 3422 W. Hammer Lane, Suite 110, Stockton, CA 95219.

CALLER ID

Many states have allowed their respective telephone companies to offer a number of services including what is popularly known as caller ID. This system sends a series of tones down the line before the phone is answered that will display (on a $50 black box) the phone number and/or name of the calling party before you answer the phone.

The idea is cute: you don't answer phone calls you don't want to answer you know who called and didn't leave a message (by comparing your answering machine hang ups with your ID box print out), stops prank calls (assuming people are really stupid enough to make crank calls from their home phone and they wonder why the jails are over crowded), but the truth is a bit more convoluted.

Computers are in place to automatically record your incoming number and name and compare it to an address to place you on every mailing or call out list you can imagine, and I feel it quite frankly violates your right to privacy by leaps and bounds.

It's also a wonderful way to make the phone company money by charging for the service, and, in some areas, charging for blocking the service. Damn knows those AT&T people need more money...

A few states, California being one, have decided caller ID *does* violate your privacy and have refused to allow it. This means you will not be able to ID calls from these areas, box or no box.

For those of you who think I'm exaggerating about the commercial privacy invasion features of caller ID I would point out a company called Allied Electronic Services, Inc., POB 819, Stonybrook Rd., Lebanon, NH 03766. who will lease you their Omni Comm 400, the only caller ID system currently available that instantly cross matches the incoming call to give you the caller's number, and then, by some quick computer footwork, the caller's name and address *before* you pick up the phone.

Of course this information can be automatically recorded into your computer for future use and you will be happy to know they are about to offer a new feature called On Screen Street Mapping...

For some time rumors have existed that the signals are there on all phone lines, legal or not, and one simply needed the right "black box" to use this secret system. This simply is not true; it only takes fairly simple equipment to look for the tones and they just aren't there.

When you call certain pre-selected systems such as 411 or 911 is in effect in most areas. Another system will automatically display the incoming calling number and address so emergency crews can respond to these calls. This is known as ANI.

ANI is not caller ID.

Now suppose you live in an ID OK state and really don't want the company you are calling to complain about the shoddy product they sent you, or a real estate agent to ask a simple question and don't look forward to a thousand return calls about the advantages to moving to Three Mile Island, to have your number before the call even takes place.

This latter feature is especially important if you are skip tracing, running down a criminal, or trying to locate someone who is difficult to locate. Or even just don't want to leave a record of any outgoing (or incoming!) call, for whatever reason.

Several choices here: call from a phone booth, of course, you can't leave a return number and it's a bit of a hassle. Spend $300 for an interesting idea known as a LOGOS BOX. This small unit hooks up to your phone line and simply blocks out the ID tones as well as forwards the call to any number you choose, so you still get to make or receive calls without revealing your real number or location.

Primarily designed so cops and agents don't have to reveal their home or department numbers to snitches or agents-in-place, it has many other possibilities as well.

All American Associates, DCE, 907 Ware St., Vienna, VA 22180, does the LOGOS BOX.

Several services offer 900 numbers wherein you call their number, they dial out and for $2.00 a minute leave behind a reverse track record that goes only to this weird 900 # corporation. There is no way to match the incoming and the outgoing records.

To access a "new" dial tone call 1-900-STOPPER ($2.00 a minute), 1-900-RUN WELL will do the same thing for international calls ($5.00 a minute). There is NO way AT&T, the FCC or the FBI can associate your call to any out-going call. The called party simply gets a call from an AT&T WATS line.

If you want to receive calls without the caller knowing your number, or even where in the world you are, (a blind drop technique used by spies for years, now available to the general public) call 1-800-VOICE 99, pick a 4 digit extension number and then tell the system the secret number where you want your calls transferred.

Then have people call you on 1-800-STOPPER and punch in your four digit extension. The caller will, of course be charged the 900 rate but he ain't going to know anything about you.

Carry it a step further and the same company will give you a free blind drop where callers leave messages and you pick them up at your convenience. This service runs at $2.00 per minute on both leaving and picking up calls..

Free info at 1-800-STOPPER.

If the idea of 900 calls on your phone bill appalls you, they also accept credit cards.

Another method to avoid CNI and toll records of sensitive calls is to use a phone debit card. Long in use in European countries ,these cards are now sold in the US.

One simply purchases a card with a certain amount of "time" attached to it. When a call is placed the user dials a toll free number and punches in the access code. The call is then placed on the company's line rather than the subscriber's.

The cards automatically deduct the time used and warn the user when only one minute remains. The cards bill a flat rate for calls in the US and another for international calls. By shopping around it is possible to actually beat the rate of collect or phone charged-to-the-card calls.

Debit cards are available from Western Union, AT&T, Amerivox, Global Telecommunication Solutions, and the Time Machine, Inc. Most are listed with 800 directory assistance.

You can also use a calling card from a booth. Ask the operator to assist you in making the call (which, as of now, does not show up on caller ID) or go thru 0-700 numbers where possible, or use a series of call forwarding tricks, all which do cost extra money.

A very well-researched booklet entitled PRINCIPLES OF CALLER ID is available from International MicroPower Corporation, 65 Palm Dr., Camarillo, CA 93010, that takes the reader on a very complete trip down the theory and operation of caller ID. They also sell some of the very cheapest ID boxes available including computer caller ID interfaces.

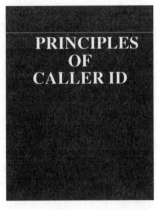

PRINCIPLES OF CALLER ID

Finally, some telcos offer a blocking service wherein the caller pushes a preset code (line *7) and the caller ID tones are blocked. A pleasant touch but, as one might suspect with the altruistic nature of phone companies, they will add an oh-sominor charge each time this service is accessed. The active nature of this defense means you can easily forget to utilize it or that anyone else calling from your phone will not be aware of the trick.

A permanent caller ID blocker that refuses to pass the tones on *any* call is available from Intelligence Incorporated.

REVERSE TRICKING

So you need to find someone who has an unlisted number or is using a mail drop with no number or a voice drop? Here's how you do it – most people don't realize that every time they call an 800 number the called party will, of course, receive the number the call was placed from when they get their phone bill as they have to pay for the call.

Some phone companies offer a 900 number, where, for about $2.00, one can get an instant readout of the number and or name of the last incoming call. If your telco isn't quite that hip yet, or you want some real wizardry on your side, contact Tel-Scan, 2641 N. Taft, Loveland, CO 80538.

For a small fee they will rent you one of their 800 numbers, which is answered ambiguously, or if you rent the whole line, answered anyway you wish it to be answered. Now you write a letter to the person you are searching for, or his best friend/family and simply say, "Jones and Smith Attorneys at Law need to talk to John about the 3 million dollars left to him by his great uncle on his mother's side...

Or "Congratulations! our records show your last lottery ticket," or, "yes, it's true, we drew your name from the win-a-new-Mustang contest we ran last week and we need to know if you want the burgundy or natural leather interior..."

Just call us at 1-800-555-1212...

Some detectives will send a simple, hand written note to the target's last address or friends saying, "urgent, call me. Jack"

Who could resist?

Ten minutes after the incoming call Tel Scan hands over a phone number on the target. This works in all 50 states on listed and unlisted numbers and is not affected by caller ID blockers. It requires no hardware and can be set up immediately. Tel Scan will even rent you a voice mail box to store incoming calls and the accompanying information.

Not bad, huh? You might want to think about this next time you get a call informing you of old aunt Sally's sudden demise and deep fondness for you...

Spies as well as other, perfectly legitimate people, often wish to place a call without leaving tracks. The simplest selection is to make it from a phone booth.

In the good old days it was accomplished with a device known as a blue box. The blue box emitted tones that instructed the actual phone company equipment to do whatever you wanted it to – say go through this satellite, route me through China, then New

Mexico and finally to the President's private number.

This is no joke, it has happened more times than the Secret Service would care to admit. It's also good for bookies who don't want calls traced (nor to have to pay for them), organized crime and so on.

Without going into intimate detail here the blue box is pretty well gone from the U.S. phone scene because of system changes, but it is still available and usable in Europe. In fact, in the Netherlands, where phone phreaking (hacking) is not completely illegal you can buy a software based "box" that does many things including blue boxing and demon dialing (a system of searching out people's WATS lines or computer modems and cracking them) for $250.

The DEMON DIALER is $250 money order only, from Hack Tic, Postbus 22953, 1100 DL, Amsterdam, Netherlands.

Red boxing, a method of making free phone calls from public phones in the U.S., is still alive and well, (remember, this is important if you don't want to make sensitive calls from your home number – I am NOT advocating cheating the phone company in any way). Red boxes duplicate the sound the telco computer hears when you drop quarters into the little slot on the public phone.

How hard is it to find a red box? Well, not as hard as you might think: you simply buy a Radio Shack auto dialer and replace the crystal (simple instructions that come with the new crystal) and the next sound you, or the phone company hears, will be the correct tone of non-existent money dropping into a existing slot...

Hey, spies sometimes do things we folks with high moral standards wouldn't dream of, but always for a higher purpose. Now imagine how obvious you would be if you had to carry 500 quarters in your pocket..

Some replacement crystals are sold—for legitimate reasons only—by Electronic Design Systems, 144 West Eagle Road, Suite 103, Havertown, PA 19083.

UNLISTED

Is it possible to get an unlisted number? Sometimes.

If a person has foolishly filled it in on something he shouldn't have: an application for a loan, or an apartment rental or warranty card, a good database tracker may come up with the number.

There are also various tricks detailed in BOOK II HOW TO GET ANYTHING ON ANYBODY which will often work if you have the chutzpah to deal with the phone company. Many PI's can sweet talk a number from a relative (who may not even know it's unlisted).

In some areas it is possible to tell an operator that the call you want to make to Robert Redford is an emergency, you're a nurse, his grandchild has just been, etc. The operator will not give out the number but will sometimes dial it while you are still on the line. If you record the tones and feed them through a simple device known as a DTMF detector (see the Surveillance section) you will get a readout of the number in question.

The best and the only real newsletter on phone phreaking, unlisted numbers, boxes, breaking into systems and computer hacking is a slick mag edited by one Emmanuel Goldstein, called 2600 (2600 cycles was a key tone for controlling phone company computers in the days of Captain Crunch and the Phone Phreaks).

You *must* send in your $18 for a year's subscription to this magazine (POB 752, Middle Island, NY 11953) if you haven't already done so. 2600 owes its roots to legendary rags like TAP, but 2600 is the NewsWeek of system hacking, both computer and phone and they publish updates on "inside" telephone numbers that can be used to get unlisted numbers, or talk to employees at the company office party.

2600 is published in New York as it is the only state that has refused to crack down (and believe me there has been some pressure from the various phone companies) on this type of information availability.

PRIVACY

Don't want to be recognized by the person you are calling, or to have incoming callers tag you? TRANSITION 2000 is a telephone that allows you to adjust the pitch of your voice up or down. You can sound like a secretary or a mob crusher pretty convincingly. Although at either end of the spectrum the upper and lower registers start to sound a bit metallic and phony, the mid ranges will let you call your friends and say terrible things about them with little fear of retribution.

Call up and leave conflicting messages on someone's voice mail from different people.

Made by Questech, Suite 238, 4951-B E. Adamo Dr., Tampa, FL 33605. They also offer a stick-on changer that will work on any existing phone. GUESS WHO 2001 attaches to any existing phone (except cordless and Trimline) and works with multi-line systems. $69.95 plus $5.00 s/h from Questech or Shomer-Tec.

TRANSITION 2000 voice changing telephone

Several companies have recognized the problem of wireless phone security and we are just now starting to see some solutions being marketed. The first encrypted cordless phone was made by Sharp and sold only in Japan. Now GTE makes the PHONEMATE 2910 which features encrypted communications between the handset and the base, as does a company called VTECH.

And now, believe it or not, Radio Shack will sell you an encrypted cordless phone, the DOUFONE ET-499 for $159.95. All these units make it much more difficult for the scanner or nearfield receiver user to eavesdrop on your calls. Although it will take some time to determine how effective the scrambling is (several companies sell unscramblers for simple systems), this is a step in the right direction.

An even better idea is to go to the nice folks at Escort and, for a $300 outlay, purchase a DIGITAL SPREAD SPECTRUM cordless phone. This spreads the signal over a wide bandwidth (digitally) that makes it almost impossible to pick up on a scanner or interceptor type receiver. It is also on the new 900 MHz band which provides up to a half mile range from the base to the handset.

Obviously the new 900 phones that are not scrambled are even easier to pick up surreptitiously because of their extended range. Code-A-Phone, Box 5656, Portland, OR 97228, sells a non-scrambled 900 MHz "interference free" phone with a claimed 1/2 mile range.

CELLULAR PRIVACY

A bit bristlier of a hedgehog that one – cellulars are gradually going digital (so more units can share the same channel) which will make interceptions much more difficult. But at the moment your choices are limited to a couple of companies that will sell you a set of scramblers. You put one scrambler on your phone and the other must be installed at the wireless company's equipment so it can unscramble the call before completing the landline section of the call. (Unless you have just one other cellular you need privacy on, leave out the phone company altogether).

CYCOMM, 6665 SW Hampton, Portland, OR 97223, offer "affordable" voice scramblers for cellular phones. Their products can go cellular to cellular or directly through the MTSO rack (at the cellular phone company's equipment room) in a completely transparent mode by automatically sensing their own equipment and then either de- scrambling the call at the point where it goes land line. If the other end of the voice path is equipped with a CYCOMM SCRAMBLER the entire conversation transpires in the scrambled mode.

CYCOMM'S units are true scramblers utilizing a split band inversion technique to divide and mix the audio, as do most low end scramblers, but they combine it with a rolling code, semi-public key that makes eavesdropping pretty near impossible.

Unless, of course, you work for the NSA.

CYCOMM also offers a really hip, unique service – you buy one scrambler for your land-locked or cellular phone and then route your calls through their 800 number that is equipped with a matching unit.

This means, for the first time in history, you can call someone who does not have a scrambler and know the first, and most exposed leg of the audio journey is protected.

Small set up fee, $25 monthly minimum and $0.95 a minute (including all long distance charges within the US) to protect those sensitive conversations.

Their products are really pretty inexpensive, averaging about $550 for a cellular unit and $950 for its land line cousin. They can also be used to secure voice mail and fax transmissions.

Bell Atlantic Mobile Systems is providing STU III privacy service to customers in the Washington, D.C. area and one would expect to see this occur in other parts of the country.

TOLL FRAUD AND TELABUSE, published by Telecommunications Advisors, 1 S. Columbia St., #500, Portland, OR 97258, is a huge, two volume set by a number of "experts in the field" which talks about how hackers violate privately-owned PBX's, Voice Mail and call diverters to steal phone time, andhow to reduce your overall telecommunications expenses.

It appears to be basically the good guys explaining how the bad guys (who, of course, read the other books in this section) slide and sleaze by. This is aimed at the Blue Crosses and Fortune 500's of the world in order to explain the potiential problems or evaluate security.

Good guides for legal prosecution, where your company's risks lie. About $300.

REGULAR PHONE PRIVACY

A form of user-configured personal privacy can be had by installing a device that "pre-screens" your calls and if the caller doesn't punch in a security code you have provided, your phone will never ring. Good for losing junk calls, making sure that old boyfriend gets the idea, letting you nap unless it's really an important call.

Basically the LINEMINDER answers the phone BEFORE the first ring and says, "What's the haps, pal? Enter your security code now."

If no code or an incorrect code is entered the call is terminated before caller ID can grab the line. Not bad. I should also point out that both LINEMINDER and LOGOS do not let potential burglars or other drop ins get your address and know you're not home, nor do they pass on those irritating mechanical sales machines, ex-wives, snoops, etc. LM Communications, 997 Senate Dr., Centerville, OH, 45459, offers the LINEMINDER, about $90.

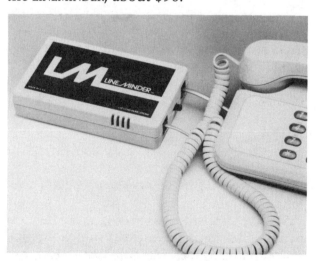

LINEMINDER call screener

Allied Electronic Services, POB 819, Stonybrook Rd., Lebanon, NH 03766, offers an incoming caller ID service that grabs the call (in applicable states), compares it to a national directory displaying the caller's name, phone number and address on the first ring, and if it's a prior caller, his past history. About $100 per phone line.

800 AND 900 NUMBERS

In 1967 Bell Telephone introduced the idea of the 800 receiver-pays phone calls. Since that time many changes have occurred in the 800 system including the spread to other carriers and the introduction of the 900 EVERYBODY pays system.

NATIONAL 800/900 TELE-PHONE SERVICE CODE BOOK, Kenneth Sperry from CRB Research is the first book to "open" some of the secrets of these systems.

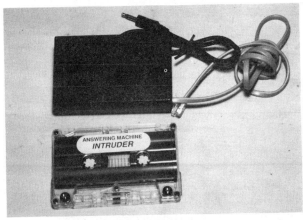

ANSWERING MACHINES AND VOICE MAIL

People will leave all sorts of valuable information on any type of voice mail box or answering machine without a second thought. Not a good idea...

Answering machines are the worst, Most are protected by a three digit security code and then a simple menu which allows the caller to listen to the messages, erase them, change the outgoing message and, in some machines even turn on a microphone which allows the caller to listen to the room audio remotely.

Consumertonics sells a nice little report that shows how to use a Radio Shack auto dialer to crack the possible 999 codes in the least possible time by trying certain sequences and combinations.

Shomer-Tec has a nifty device that is near magic – dubbed the ANSWERING MACHINE IN-TRUDER, this toy will, when coupled with a cassette recorder, crack the code of any 1 to 3 digit

protected machine within a couple of minutes. Shomer-Tec is even nice enough to provide you with helpful tips about the manipulation codes for most popular machines.

You know, in case you're out in the field, maybe in a hostile country somewhere, and gosh darn, the strain of beating the local counterspies has made you forget your answering machine remote code. Not for spying on other people's messages, leaving erroneous outgoing announcements or general snooping.

Voice mail boxes are harder to crack as they usually utilize four, sometimes even five digits and will kick you off after a few bad tries, requiring a recall(s). Still, with patience and a good old RS $25 dialer, you can usually crack these machines as well.

As a matter of fact, this device has raised so many questions about answering machine security that you can now buy a device which will protect your machine from cracking by hanging up after the third incorrect attempt.

It's also, ah, sold by Shomer-Tec...

THE ANSWERING MACHINE INTRUDER

Demon dialing programs or the NETHERLANDS RAINBOW BOX will also help crack numerical passwords. A number of books and newsletters offer suggestions: always start with 1234, 4321, four multiples of any number; check out the default passwords for the type of answering machine (if you know what type it is, or try each set); try birthdays and addresses of owners. Good spies will bug the

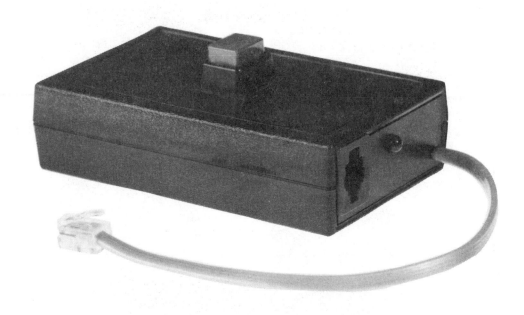

The HOLD INVADER

target's phone, or record the wireless/cellular transmission wherein the subject calls his voice mail, and then run the tones (or play back the user's voice if necessary) to decode the security numbers.

If the target has a cellular phone I flat out guarantee you can monitor him for a day or two and he WILL call in from his cellular to check his voice mail, punching in those DTMF codes that are oh, so easy to decode...

These techniques and tricks are a real boon to anyone collecting data on a subject or target company, or just for lonely people who don't get enough messages of their own...

Just kidding here! Talk to your lawyer, but it is, in most cases, illegal to access other people's messages.

There are a couple of brand new products on the market that probably rightfully should

be in the surveillance section, but I love them so much that I'm sliding them in here.

The first is a lovely device, available from Shomer-Tec, called the HOLD INVADER that really isn't electronic surveillance. Think of it as sort of a bargaining tool...

Suppose you're in the middle of this intense deal to buy a container full of Russian night scopes, right off the ship, and you're only, well, say a few thousand apart and the negotiating process is starting to break down.

You say, "Look, let's take a second. Let me talk to my financial guy here and you two discuss this deal, 'cause I think it's our final offer. I'll just put us on hold for a couple of minutes."

Then you reach down and hit the button in the middle of the HOLD INVADER which immediately turns off your microphone and ampli-

The X-PHONE

fies the incoming sound 20 times so you can hear the conversation going on in the other room quite clearly, thank you.

Think when you "take the phone off hold" and resume the conversation you may have gotten just a bit of an edge on the deal?

It's a great edge manufacturer, yours for a hundred dollar bill...

Infinity transmitters have been around for years (devices that let you call into a modified phone and listen in on all the room audio – covered in BOOK II HOW TO GET ANYTHING ON ANYBODY) but how about this: a telephone that looks and works like a normal phone until you flip a little switch.

Now your nice little innocent phone waits until it hears a noise in the immediate area and then calls you automatically and automatically sends room audio down the line. Kind of a lazy man's infinity transmitter.

It can be used legitimately as a burglar alarm, alerting you to any sudden activity in a space that should unoccupied, or, of course, it could be placed in a conference room or bedroom.

Hey, I ain't advocating this, and it most cases it could be illegal. Talk to a good attorney before you give it as a gift to your next girlfriend.

Available from Shomer-Tec or Intelligence Incorporated.

The phone is available mail order from or in stock at places like The Sharper Image. If you don't need a new phone get the Guess Who? Which contains the same electronics but plugs into your existing phone (except on cordless and handset dialing phones), and allows you do it to it.

Fun and useful.

Antenna Specialists Co, 30500 Industrial Parkway, Cleveland, OH 44139, offers the MICRO CHOKE which gives pinpoint response at the 800 cellular level, a yagi style 800 MHz 12 dB gain antenna as well as a unique corner reflector that houses a "normal" cellular antenna between two folded metal wings that claims the same gain as other mobile and stationary antennas.

Any good 800 gain antenna will let you target a certain phone, greatly extend your reception range, and even let you skip over local cells to focus in on the cell that is currently active for your target, show frequencies on GoTo's (when hooked to a counter) and generally act as the best eighty-five bucks you ever shelled out.

Electron Processing, Inc., POB 68, Cedar, MI 49621, carries a nice selection of amplified scanner antennas as well as a wonderful device called the CELLBEAM which is a very directional cellular yagi-type directional antenna with a 15 dB gain factor.

One of the very best antenna sources is Martronics, 4820 Deer Creek Way Paso Robles, CA 93446. They make custom antennas for all applications as well as a cellular yagi directional antenna which comes with a mast a base plate.

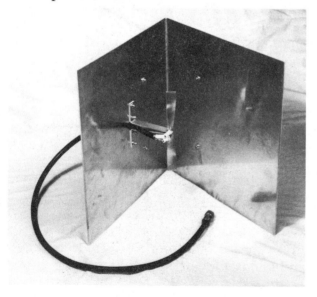

Martronics' high gain CORNER REFLECTOR

The antenna can quickly be aimed and anchored in position for cellular tracking by simply driving one wheel of a car onto the base plate.

Martronics also makes a very directional, high gain corner reflector antenna for a more discreet form of cellular monitoring.

COUNTER INTELLIGENCE (TELEPHONE)

The upswing in telephone and fax tapping has necessitated the development of answer generation of countermeasures. In order to decide what is correct for your particular situation you first must establish a threat level.

Who wants what you have?

If it's a jealous "significant other" or in-house business rival the chances of eliminating the threat are pretty good.

If it's the FBI, CIA, or even the local cops, odds are pretty bad...

Local phone surveillance is usually accomplished with some variation of an automatic recorder starter (as sold by every spy shop in the world as well as Radio Shack), VOX triggered recorder or a transmitter that sends the audio a few hundred feet to a waiting receiver/recorder.

Law enforcement (authorized) taps tend to be installed at the local phone company, making them quite hard to ferret out without a "friendly" lineman.

Operative Supply POB 2343 Atlantic Beach, NC 28512 is one of the country's first "spy shops" and, unlike many of their Johnny-come-lately cousins, design and manufacture some of their own gear.

They have just come out with a cellular interception unit based on the same modified Panasonic phone as is the CELLMATE. OP's CELL-TELL has a number of additional things going for it, including a considerably cheaper price tag.

CELL-TELL will monitor either the wireline or non-wireline system in a given area, ID the phone number, the active channel, decode DTMF tones, target up to 10 different mobile numbers (both in-and-out calls) track hand-offs from one cell to the next, and automatically record the calls.

Unfortunately, limited to law enforcement only, this unit may be one of the most user friendly cellular interception systems available.

They also offer something known as the MOUSE TRAP the worlds smallest cellular interception system. Based on a modified flip phone, it can also scan or target up to ten different numbers, display the DTMF tones, channels and so on.

Can be secreted in a vest pocket, briefcase or just left in its charger to automatically keep the target under surveilance. Add to this cellular auto recorders...

Pretty cool.
Catalog $19.95.

HOW TO LOCATE AND VIOLATE ANY COMPUTER

PASSWORD CRACKING

When Bolivian government forces seized WordPerfect files from a suspected terrorist group, the terrorists did not expect that their secrets would become known to government forces.

They had encrypted their files using WordPerfect's password file lock. But using WPPASS, a password-cracking software, US officials gained access to the files.

"The US government and my country team, in particular, thank you for your critical assistance," said Robert S. Gelbard, US ambassador to Bolivia, in a letter to Eric Thompson, president of Access Data Recovery Service of Orem, Utah. Access Data's WWPASS package enabled US officials to crack the passwords.

These programs work with text files generated by specific programs, including WordPerfect, Lotus Development Corporation's 1-2-3 and Microsoft Corporation's Excel.

The password-cracking programs do not decode an encrypted file and convert it to plain text. Instead, they attempt to figure out the password used to encrypt the file. Although these programs refer to their file-locking schemes as "password protection" systems, what they actually do is use a user-selected password as the encryption/decryption key.

WPPASS, which works with many versions of WordPerfect, analyzes password protected files using statistical analysis of the frequency of letters used in words contained in the file.

Access databases its password-cracking program works breaks passwords based on the normal frequency of letters occurring in English words and sentences.

The programs have even proven useful for other languages.

Multilingual capabilities: in English, German and French, the letter "E" is the most often used. To decode a block of text, one could find the most common letter, assume it was substituted for "E", and proceed down the list of single letters and pairs of letters according to their normal rate of occurrence.

Although Italian, Spanish and Portuguese differ in terms of which individual letters are most common, enough similarities exist to let the password-cracking software produce a useful analysis in many cases.

I tested WPP'S products and was pleasantly surprised. Although a number of different levels of penetration are offered, I found the simplest approach worked almost every time. My first try was against an encrypted WordPerfect file.

49 seconds later I had the "lost" password...

B-Safe Industries sells cracking software that works on Lotus 1-2-3, Microsoft Excel, Paradox, WordPerfect, and Novell Network to "military and law enforcement agencies" only.

They also sell a program called MICRO-LAW which encrypts entire floppy disks at one time (not file by file as many others do). This program has been tested and gotten good reviews, it works only on floppies, not hard disks, but the encryption is based on a method developed by them and as the nice folks at Micro Law say, "don't forget your password because even we can not unlock the disk once it's encrypted."

These same programs are available through a number of other law enforcement oriented suppliers.

Don't forget the utility programs like HYPERZAP and SUPERZAP which go around the password to recover data from each sector of a disk.

TEMPEST

The most novel method of violating a computer is, without a doubt, the method invented by one Dr. Van Eck, a Dutch scientist a number of years ago. The good Doctor has achieved some level of international fame with his concept of reading a computer screen remotely.

What he did was design a receiver that would pick up the RF signals generated by the electron beam that "paints' the CRT screen on any computer. With a directional antenna Doc Van Eck sat in a van several blocks from target computers and recorded everything the operator was typing. He then published a book of plans showing how he did it.

After the book had been sold internationally by a number of companies, Van Eck came out and admitted he included some errors in his schematics "on purpose." Stating, in his defense, that he was, after all, not in the business of showing people how to eavesdrop on computers.

A few years later British television replicated the experiment for a broadcast.

This entire process became known as Tempest.

Since that time a number of manufacturers have come out with Tempest proof monitors and CPU's. The government has actually adhered to an anti-Tempest standard for a number of years.

The problem seems to be that nobody is sure how well this procedure actually works. There is some speculation that Tempest equipment makers may have, ah, how to put this?

Overstated the dangers in order to sell more equipment, you know, like the various anti-virus program designers that seem to always be finding a new virus that you desperately need protection from...

In fact, some counter measures folks have gone on record stating that the Van Eck idea is the best science fiction since Star Wars.

What is the truth of the matter?

I can tell you I have seen a nice man from some agency or another aim a directional antenna at pipes and air ducts leading from a computer room and pull up the screens being typed on his equipment.

I can also tell you I have a video tape (and still photos) showing a commercially available Van Eck unit working as advertised. This unit is designed by John Williams of Consumertronics.

He has done major mods on the first generation units he offered a few years back and now sells a completed unit for $4,000 (plus $80 shipping). I can tell you that a certain, very close-by government just ordered a major supply from John.

I am including a photo. If you find you are still a doubter, the entire video tape can be ordered from John for $69.

Range is about 1 KM under perfect conditions, at least 100 meters through closed windows, trees and practical antenna considerations. The unit comes with a nominal antenna to show that it actually works, however Mr. Williams advises the use of a TV fringe area yagi in order to isolate the signal of interest.

Note this is not something you just set up and turn on – the radiated signal from the monitor is weak and may be in competition with nearby noise sources. A number of interrelated adjustments may be necessary to receive the signal on a constant basis.

It's a little like trying to watch Milton Berle in the 1950's with a Phillips black and white television and a set of early rabbit ears.

You adjust this, you turn the antenna, a little aluminum foil here, someone holding the antenna there.

Well, you get the idea.

But it does work. You can't pull anything out of RAM but you can video tape a computer screen form a distance of 100 meters to 1 KM and that's pretty amazing.

Anti-Tempest monitors are available from Candes Systems, Inc., Box F Mainland, PA 19451, and a complete line of non-Tempest gear, including laser printers and FAX machines is offered by Mitek, Systems, Inc., 6225 Nancy Ridge Drive, San Diego, CA 92121.

A look at the Consumertronics computer cracker.

VIDEO SURVEILLANCE

Video surveillance is now becoming the industry standard for surveillance. While some systems include a facility for audio transmission as well, most are pure video.

In any sort of crime documentation, from selling drugs to spousal cheating, video is usually the more important component.

The drop in price and availability of video gear, from what was around a few years ago, is quite astounding.

Video can be used through walls, ceilings, from briefcases, from inside an article of clothing, at long distances, for a short period of time, for days at a time, with or without wires and with or without human operation.

In fact, the many video recorders that are designed to work

A Watec surveillance camera with 'normal' front lens.

with some sort of alarm – an infrared (PIR) switch, the opening or closing of mechanical contact, change in light level or motion in part of the viewed area allow video systems to act as completely unmanned stakeouts.

The first part of any video system is the camera. The camera captures the signal. Solid state cameras, those using chips, instead of tubes are pretty much the standard for video cameras now. In fact, prices have fallen considerably and quality has gone up from the first chip units due to mass production.

One of the best brands of miniature surveillance-oriented cameras is the Watec line. They sell many, many units to the government and can afford to keep the quality on a very high level.

When the first Watec came on the market in 1991, about 1 out of 10 didn't function up to spec. They immediately recalled those and sent them back to Japan for repair or replacement. The defect rate now runs about 1 out of 1,000.

The company existed prior to 1991, as an OEM manufacturer. They made cameras for other companies before deciding to enter the America & world markets. The head of Watec America is Dr. C. L. Liu, formerly a vice-president of a world-wide, giant electronic corporation and is very well respected in Japan.

Watecs tend to be the choice of almost all government agencies and research facilities. The only complaint I sometimes hear about the Watec camera is that it is too small.

Traditionally we have thought of surveillance, both overt and covert, being conducted with bigger cameras. However, smaller units offer a number of advantages, including the fact that they can be concealed almost anywhere including on a person.

The average life of a CCD chip camera is well over five years and, unless they're dropped or abused, or you put the wrong voltage on them they're virtually indestructible.

Watec has a team of engineers there that constantly strive to improve the product. The main components are from the best Japanese manufacturers, from connectors to screws and the chips are top level. Watec offers a power-over-coax model, which is a favorite of many surveillance folk because it eliminates the need for running extra power cords or trying to find power at the camera site.

Although Watec only claims a range of 500 feet with the power over coax camera, I have first hand experience with it working fine up to 800 feet away.

The second type of miniature video surveillance cameras are board cameras. Constructed directly on a circuit board these units offer a number of advantages and a few disadvantages, as well.

Price is very low due to the lack of a case and they can be secreted in a number of different containers. Board cameras vary in price according to their resolution, size and lens.

Most come with a fixed lens, others use a C-mount to allow for different lenses for different applications.

Chinon is one of the largest manufacturers of board cameras and right now they offer several models that are ideal for covert work. They don't sell direct but can be purchased through a number of dealers.

Some of the disadvantages of board cameras include the fact that most do not come with power or video out cables and the user must do a bit of soldering. They are also a bit prone to shorting out from body sweat (if used as a body worn camera) or if any exposed contacts touch metal.

If you plan to use a board camera without a particular stash place in mind I suggest you play a bit extra for the dealer to pre-wire it and, if possible, mount it in a concealment of some sort.

All these cameras, board or packaged, can be powered from battery packs or AC adapters and it's a good idea to have a selection on hand for different situations which may arise.

The second component of major importance is the lens. The lens is what turns the image into something that the CCD can transmit to the recording/viewing media. There is a series of lenses that are manufactured exclusively for the Watec cameras due to their wide popularity.

These require you to remove the lens mounting ring with 1/16 inch hex wrench.

The amount of light gathering ability of any lens is referred to as the f-stop. The lower the f-stop, the more light that will pass through the lens.

Pinhole lenses require higher f-stops than do normal lenses due to their construction. In a pinhole any rating near 2 is considered very good.

The iris controls the amount of light, depth of field and so on. Most surveillance cameras now, either board units or Watec type packages utilize an automatic iris which electronically limits the amount of incoming light for optimum image gathering.

When you use an auto iris camera it's best to focus it in less than bright sunlight. That way it will stay in focus when if light gets brighter.

You will also need to figure the field of view of any camera (this depends on several factors such as lens length and chip size) and pre-focus the unit for the area under surveillance. Auto focus is never used in professional surveillance applications. In fact, it's never used in professional or broadcast video operations either.

Some high tech cameras feature a 3 position, auto-electronic shutter which focuses as an auto iris.

Lenses which have a feature known as backlight compensation are also useful in situations when you're looking at a scene, say in a store and you have bright light coming in through a window.

This less-than-ideal situation will cause the auto iris to not function and the backlight compensator will improve your viewing to a great degree.

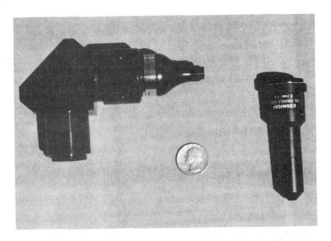

A right angle and straight pinhole lens for miniature cameras.

A ready made pinhole lens mounting platform for use with drop ceilings ·(ceiling tiles). Greatly simplifies installation, guarantees correct picture.

On one end of the lens scale we have pinholes. Pinhole lenses are designed to take an image through an extremely small opening. Some can utilize a hole about twice the size of the period at the end of this sentence. This makes for a variety of applications including being stashed in briefcases, viewing through button holes, through walls, and one of the most popular applications, above a "dropped" ceiling (the type found in most office buildings).

In fact, you can purchase a custom made dropped ceiling mount consisting of a flat steel plate and bracket which automatically positions a pinhole lens above and through these "tile" ceilings with a minimum of effort and set up time.

B.E. Myers and Sherwood both stock auto cutting kits which include a template, drill guide, hole saw, depth control and clamp-on mount for cutting and mounting a pinhole through drywall for between room viewing.

Both of these accessories will simplify your time-on-target, as well as, insure against minor errors like cutting a three inch hole in the subject's side of the wall...

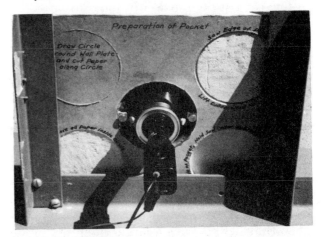

A look at the Sherwood kit that guides you through dry wall cutting and then mounting of a Watec based pinhole system. Trust me, there's not many things more embarrassing than sawing completely through the connecting wall at an inappropriate time....

Pinholes come in a wide variety of configurations including different focal lengths, right angles, different physical lengths and so on. They have become known to the general public because of the various FBI stings (why do senators hand over money to a man with a briefcase?) and their use on various "reality based" TV shows, where they are smuggled into unscrupulous plastic surgeons' offices, unscrupulous repair person's offices, unscrupulous welfare cheat's living rooms and scrupulous dope dealer's abodes.

Pinholes have long been a favorite of various government agencies who rent an office or hotel room next to the bad guys, and then drill a hole, often using a drill guide, almost through the dividing wall.

The final 1/4 inch is then pierced by a dentist drill or other tiny sharp instrument. The pinhole lens is then secured against this hole. Note that most pinhole lenses are constructed so a small portion of the lens case actually protrudes through the hole.

A couple of tricks to help this procedure come off without a hitch:

- If possible always mount the lens above eye level. Most people do not look up.
- If possible mount the lens near a light that will cause unwanted viewer's eyes to "shut down" before they see the lens.
- If the lens is brought through a dropped tile ceiling or white wall use liquid paper to "white out" the tip of the lens tube.
- A little bit of talcum powder and charcoal in an air sprayer creates instant dust. You mix it right in and use a special wire and it's not likely to be noticed.

Pinhole lenses, by nature, have a higher f-stop than lenses with a larger opening. However, the cameras that are generally used for surveillance have excellent light-gathering capabilities. Sherwood Communications offers some of the finest surveillance lenses I've seen.

One economical method to equip your group with a series of pinhole lenses for almost every occasion is the 10 in 1 Pinhole kit available for VMI, Sherwood and others.

Ten pinhole lenses can be assembled from the KPT811X Convertible Pinhole Kit, (although they share components so only one lens can be used at any given time) which consists of: Straight: 8, 11, 16, 22 mm; Right Angle: 8, 11, 16, 22 mm; a clamp-on Sprinkler head and an 11 and 22 mm. The lenses are specifically designed for television cameras where minimum exposure of front elements is of primary importance.

The semi-wide angle lens, (8 mm) all the way through the narrow field 22 mm lens, allow for a number of flexible installations. The Sprinkler head allows for effective covert surveillance of critical areas.

10 in 1 Kit is packaged in a convenient storage box to hold lenses not being used. It is designed to be used with any "C" Mount 2/3 or 1/2 inch CCD camera. These lenses are a fast F.2 - 2.3 aperture, with adjustable manual iris, and are self-aligning.

I'm not sure I'd say this kit is a good as 10 dedicated lenses, but for the money it provides a wide degree of flexibility.

Lenses, and/or cameras, can be ordered stashed in sprinkler heads, car radio antennas, plants, rocks (rocks?!), TV's, Teddy Bears or electric company transformers (Knox Corporation – designed to sit innocently outside a person's window and record what goes on through the looking glass).

Thank you Lewis Carroll.

Sits on a *telephone pole* outside your window, sees and records everything...

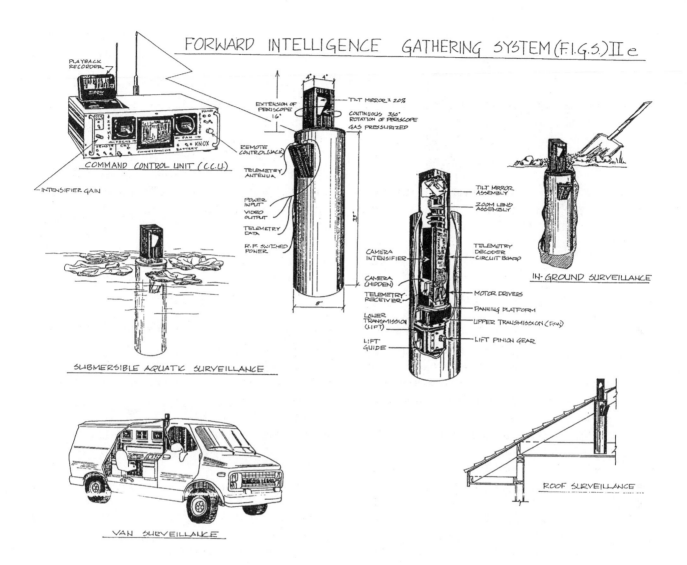

FORWARD INTELLIGENCE GATHERING SYSTEM (F.I.G.S.) II e

Knox Engineering has designed a wondrous video surveillance device that can be buried as a telephone pedestal, mounted on a roof or even placed into a phony electric company transformer. For suppliers of these and more exotic combinations see both THE COVERT CATALOG and BOOK II HOW TO GET ANYTHING ON ANYBODY.

A tiny board camera hidden in perfect view – in an electric pencil sharpener. Always plugged in, rarely used, left in plain view on the desk. See if you can find the tiny hole for the board camera's pinhole lens... Buy it this way or take out your trusty screwdriver and make it up.

The other end of the lens scale are telephotos. One unit of note is Sherwood's stakeout zoom lens. It's a manual zoom, manual focus photo iris lens, which means you zoom it in, focus it up, and let the iris of the camera take over.

Sherwood also carries very special accessories, such as an adapter that allows almost any SLR camera lens to be used (i.e., Olympus, Nikon, Pentax, Minolta) with a video camera.

A major advantage of small CCD cameras that most people are not aware of, is the fact that the size of the chip format affects the relative focal length of the lens. This means a lens, designed to go onto a 1 inch format is optically "lengthened" by using it on a smaller format camera.

Now the formula for using it with 1/2 inch format camera, which most CCD cameras are at the present time, (although there's a trend towards 1/3) is 5.4 to 1, so if you have a 500 mm lens, you have an effective focal range of 2700 mm.

Sherwood also stocks a low priced, high quality, 100 - 500 mm zoom lens, which has proven to be a favorite of narcotic squads and intelligence units. The lens is 12 inch long and weighs 3 and 1/4 pounds and when coupled with a 1/2 inch format Watec camera will read a license plate from a 1/4 mile away...

Think I'm kidding about the use of small video camera for surveillance work? Note the above Watec 1/2 inch coupled to the "narc special" lens. The camera is so small and light it needs no steadying – the lens is screwed onto a regular camera tripod. Next photo I shot with my SLR 120 mm semi-telephoto lens of a sign in a parking lot about a quarter of a mile away. I have thoughtfully circled the sign so you have some idea of what we are looking at. I could read the sign on the monitor like I was two feet from it...

The size of the lens is compensated by the fact that it has a mounting stud on the bottom allowing it to be mounted on a tripod. This takes the strain off of the camera, as well as, the lens itself. It also stops vibrations which are amplified on long lenses.

One piece of very inexpensive gear that will prove to be of value to anyone who works with surveillance video is a field of view wheel. This small plastic calculator allows you to align the focal length of the lens with the correct CCD target size and will then produce both the vertical and horizontal dimensions of the image that will be captured.

MIXED FORMAT CONVERSION FORMULAS

1" lens with 2/3" camera	Focal Length x 1.43
1" lens with 1/2" camera	Focal Length x 2.00
1" lens with 1/3" camera	Focal Length x 2.94
2/3" lens with 1/2" camera	Focal Length x 1.37
2/3" lens with 1/3" camera	Focal Length x 1.81
1/2" lens with 1/3" camera	Focal Length x 1.33

GBC Corporation 315 Hudson Street, New York, NY 10013, is a major supplier of surveillance video gear. They have developed a computer program that calculates the exact lens and field-of-view information to allow for quick set-up of any format video camera format including 1/3", 1/2", 2/3", 1" or any custom format you input.

This $20 program shows lens focal length and field-of-view in degrees, feet and meters allowing almost instantaneous, short time-on-target camera placement.

LENS TERMINOLOGY

Focal Length – The distance from the optical center of a lens to the front of video pickup device (tube and chip cameras). Focal length is measured in millimeters, and is often engraved on the front ring of the lens.

- The longer the focal length, the narrower is the field-of-view.
- The shorter the focal length, the wider is the field-of-view.
- As the focal length increases, the viewing angle decreases and is magnified, making objects appear closer and larger.
- A lens with a focal length similar in proportion to that seen with the eye is referred to as a "normal" lens (25 mm for 1" format, 12 mm for 1/2" format, 16 mm for 2/3" format).
- A lens with a greater than normal focal length is referred to as a "telephoto" lens.
- A lens with a smaller than normal focal length is referred to as a "wide angle" lens.
- A lens which has a variable focal length is called a "zoom" lens.

Iris – The amount of light transmitted through a lens is controlled by an adjustable diaphragm, or iris, located in the lens barrel. The opening is referred to as the aperture, and the size of the aperture is controlled by rotating the aperture control ring on the lens barrel.

F-Stop – In lenses with adjustable irises, the maximum iris opening is expressed as a ratio: focal length of the lens/maximum diameter of aperture. This maximum iris, the f-number, is engraved on the front ring of the lens. The f-number refers to the amount of light that passes through a lens. With a "fast" f-number (a low number like f1.2), the lens is capable of gathering more light and producing higher quality pictures. With a "slower" f-number, such as f1.8, the lens gathers relatively less light. Due to their construction, pinhole lenses require more light and slower f-stop.

Focus – Most lenses can be adjusted to focus on objects at varying distances from the lens. Some lenses are fixed-focus types, meaning that all objects farther away than some specified distance will be in focus. In most applications, adjustable-focus lenses are more useful than fixed-focus lenses. The focusing ring will be inscribed with a scale in both feet and meters.

Zoom – With a zoom lens the focus length can be changed while the object being viewed remains in focus. Thus, a zoom lens, used in telephoto mode, can bring distant objects into clear view and, used in wide angle mode, can clearly view the scene as a whole.

The next item in a surveillance arsenal is video recorder. Another factor to consider when choosing a surveillance camera is the resolution it is capable of. In cameras, the resolution factor is measured by lines.

With a video camera you get some sort of visual image at 120, which was about what the old tube cameras would produce. CCD's go all the way up to 700.

However, a 700 line camera is fairly expensive and will be wasted if you are recording the image on a video recorder. Good video recorders capture 240-300 lines in color, 350 in black and white.

One of the hottest recorders out there is the Sanyo SRT 500, which will get full 24-hours of video and audio at the 24-hour speed on a T160 tape. It's good enough to have been approved for use by a tough customer: the casino industry.

The 24-hour recording time is accomplished by recording 20 frames of video per second instead of 30. The result is almost indistinguishable to the naked eye.

Most recorders use 110 volts, however, you can get many in a 12 volt configuration for vehicular use. Most video recorders are VHS when used for surveillance. However, there are 8 mm decks. If you are going to be recording audio with video, it is only available in the 2, 12 or 24 hour mode and usually requires some kind of amplification circuit to capture clean audio at these speeds.

One exception is the GYYR machine that records the audio in a zig-zag fashion on the tape and will actually record *about 10 days* of real-time audio on one tape.

There are recorders to fill every purpose. Besides real-time, you have time lapse units that capture days of action. A time-lapse tape can be played back in a normal speed machine to get a fast forward effect until something of interest is found at which time it is put back in the original recorder for viewing.

Gyyr's TLC1824 time-lapse recorder provides 24 hours of 400 line resolution video on a single tape.

Sony makes an 8 mm recorder that is the smallest on the market known as the EVO-220. It so small, about the size of your hand, that it is actually suitable for body-worn use.

The unit can be ordered with an alarm recording adapter, which will provides a quasi time-lapse mode; i.e., you can have it tape 30 seconds of video every 10 minutes. It also has a sleep mode which leaves the recorder dead until it's triggered by something, (usually a set of contacts on a door or drawer or a passive infrared motion detector), and a timer function mode.

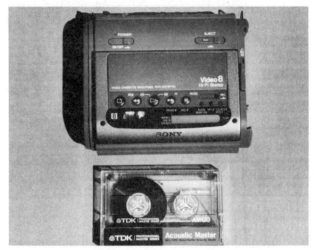

The Sony EVO-220, currently the smallest VCR in the world. Can be triggered by many situations, hidden on the body.

I saw the results of this unit after being used to document non-humane killing of stray animals in a county in North Carolina.

The system they used consisted of a color camera, a stake-out zoom lens, a battery pack, and the VCR with equipped with a timer. The investigators got the "humane" workers who were saving time and money by simply killing the animals with bricks and wire loops.

The operators were trying to hide from the investigators by changing the killing times.

The video equipment was hidden in different cars every day to prevent the investigators from being made.

The alarm recording adapter, can be set it so when it is triggered it turns on and then it turns itself off after a specific time, awaiting the next trigger.

A plethora of monitors are on the market and every surveillance fan should possess at least one to make sure the system is set-up correctly the first time.

One of the most common set-up monitors, the Sony EI/CCIR. Also look at Radio Shack stuff.

Video motion detectors are featured that allow you to leave your system either dormant or in slow recording and have it go into real-time once it gets a trigger. To use this type of unit, you bracket the area you are interested in on the screen, set the sensitivity and when anything comes into the target area the system starts up.

Another interesting device is known as an eclipser, this "enhancer" comes into play when you're doing a video. Say you're taping a crack buy or an illicit meeting, cars pull up, and their headlights tend to whack out a normal auto-iris lens, or you're doing a scene with a bright porch light behind the participants, the eclipser can be adjusted to "knock out" the light source and provide good video.

It's best to use an eclipser during the shooting, although some units will also work to some degree on recorded tape.

Another handy unit is a splitter. This device allows the operator to accept the inputs for up to four cameras, show the pictures on a single monitor and record it on a single recorder.

I've recently seen a quarter quad splitter successfully used in a situation where there was time card fraud at a manufacturing company. They had one camera aimed at the time clock and the other aimed at the recreation area and recorded people in the recreation area while someone else was punching their time cards.

There is also a digi-splitter which allows you to put two non-sync cameras together without external synchronization and record both on a single tape.

Getting the signal from A to B, is usually accomplished by cable – primarily RG59. Or, in some cases, via fiber optics. Various systems are available depending on how you want to go and what your dollar is, from several manufacturers. Sherwood features pre-made batches of cables in various lengths.

Video adapter kits are handy for everybody and special cables are available such as a 1/16 inch thick mini-coax which can be easily disguised.

Zip cord, SPHS, is great stuff. It looks just like an electrical cord and is a favorite of various government intelligence agencies. You can run zip cord well over 500 feet – probably close to 1,000 feet, but it ain't cheap.

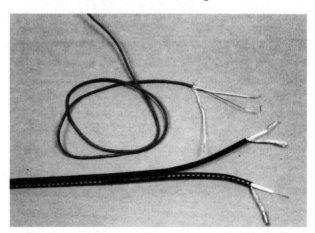

Two coax and power carrying cords that will pass as power cords.

Fiber optic cable utilizes a tiny transmitter and receiver which converts the video signal into light (and back into a signal a the receiver). The advantages to fiber optic cable is that it's innocuous (looks like spaghetti), does not suffer from electrical interference, can be run next to or across power lines, through water, in rough weather and really doesn't need to be cut or measured – simply buy a reel of cable that is long enough for the job, string it and leave the rest on the spool. The signal loss is so small, distance is not much of a factor.

It is also possible to send video images over normal telephone line – even that which must be processed and hassled by telephone company equipment. In the past this concept was, to say the least, very limited in scope.

Usually a still frame was taken and then slowly broken into digital signals which could be passed down a phone line, much as would be a FAX or modem signal. The processing speed so limited the technique that only a few frames a minute could be passed along with any degree of clarity.

New chips, in particular one known as the SUPERSCAN have changed the face of video-by-phone by speeding up the refresh rates, as well as, the clarity of the image.

The system(s) require a transmitter to change the image signals and bandwidth to something the telco can handle, and a receiver to reproduce the procedure.

Most are designed for portability and the prices have fallen dramatically. A good video-by-phone system will allow the operator to dial up a remote video camera, sit back and watch the action from the comfort of his living room.

Systems worth of note are made by NIT 5410 Newport Drive, Suite 23, Rolling Meadows, IL 60008, and Telesite USA 97 Taylor Dr., Closter, NJ 07624.

The other option is wireless transmission. the FCC opened the 900 MHz band for unlicensed, low-power video transmission. These units can be purchased from video suppliers for "amplified" prices or directly from consumer outlets under names like The Rabbit and Genie, among others.

The TeleSite system in action.

Regardless of published claims, they have a realistic range of about 75 – 100 feet. Most require 110 volt power and the receiver puts out only a modulated signal that will play back on a regular TV or VCR on channel 3 or 4.

Their transmitters accept a signal from a camcorder or video camera.

A couple of companies, Martronics and SuperCircuits offer high gain, yagi style receiving antennas that will boost the range of these inexpensive devices to several hundred feet.

The FCC has also opened up the 2400 (2.4 Gigahertz band), license free, for use with type-improved transmitters. The truth of the matter, anything that is type accepted is going to be limited in range. The FCC, also known as Uncle Charley, does have a responsibility to make sure that everything you can buy is going to produce a minimum of interference.

Fortunately or unfortunately whatever the case may be, this is basically a garbage band. It has clutter and signals do not propagate well at that frequency. The stuff's fairly expensive. A kit, that you're lucky to get 1,000 feet with, is well over $2,000. A true technician can hide wire. It doesn't take a lot of practice.

The next step is to purchase non-type accepted units from a number of dealers. These are sold "to law enforcement only, or for use outside the US". Most are crystal (or SAW) controlled for extreme stability and can be ordered on a number of channels or on non-TV frequencies that require a receiver (or converted TV) to bring them over to a frequency that can be viewed on a TV monitor.

The units that work directly on an existing channel are, of course, less expensive and will do for short jobs, but there is a risk of getting a higher rating for your little TV show that you want if someone tunes across the channels.

Many of these units are built in 1/2 to 1 watt configurations. A good 1 watt transmitter, with a sensitive receiver and gain antenna, can do a couple of miles in a line of sight application.

The higher the power the lower the battery life. A normal 1/2 watt will do about four hours on a body-wearable sized battery pack. More in a briefcase sized pack.

Some of these units are sold in "easy-to-assemble" kit form, some in actual kits, some fully assembled. I will hazard a guess at this point that we will soon see an FCC crack-down on the assembled and easy-to versions...

If more power is needed you can run the transmitter signal through a linear amplifier available from sources like SuperCircuits. These units can boost the power anywhere from a few watts to a hundred or so.

Their use is not legal in most situations.

Finally, ham radio operators are allowed to transmit TV on certain frequencies and high power transmitters are relatively inexpensive from ham radio outlets or through magazines like *QST* and *73*.

Let me give you a piece of advice here, if you run a high-powered ham unit for a surveillance operation in a metropolitan area, some ham *will* see it and will probably call it to the attention of the local FCC.

They're fine for use out of the country and fine for use in extremely remote areas. However, if there is a ham repeater in your community, there's a ham ATV (amateur television operator) who likes to watch the bands these units operate on.

The opposite end of the inexpensive kits would probably be the units made by HDS (Household Data Services – just purchased by Westinghouse). HDS, a law-enforcement only supplier, located in Reston, Virginia.

HDS offers 5 different "series" of video systems starting at one watt and ending at ten. They operate in the L and S bands (2450 – 2483 MHz) which have been approved for use by state and local law enforcement.

The units can also be ordered in the UHF band for use by the feds.

HDS units have an optional audio sub carrier (or two) that allows for the transmission of both audio and video, a feature most wireless video transmitters do not include. They will configure the system for you in a number of ways including with 9, 9.5 or 14 dBi gain antennas coupled to their own receiver.

HDS are professionally made and professionally priced...

Wireless video reception in the both 900 and 2400 MHz band can be improved by using fancy receive antennas. The units are rigged so you can't modify the transmitting antenna. Optional antennas are available in the yagi configuration. Proper placement is very important and getting good video transmission is much harder than audio transmission. It borders on being a black art. As a friend says, "it will go this far if everything's perfect and you have a strong wind blowing the signal."

Wireless is always a tempting way to go since no cabling is involved and it's pretty easy to set up, but many good surveillance folk I know, even those that can do it legally, prefer the less technical solution of hardwiring.

Also, the non-use of RF means you get discovered less. RF signals pop up on a bug detector as a buzz. Any countermeasures guy worth his salt will investigate.

A commercial version of a combination camera/transmitter, this working model is from Watec and is a gem, don't plan on buying it unless Watec see its way clear to try and get it FCC type approved, but this is exactly how wireless video should look and work. Note the clamp-on magnetic mount.

Most video cameras are also rated as to their light gathering ability measured in lux. While this does provide some sort of guide to the ability of the camera to produce an image with very little light, there really is no industry standard and many lux ratings are, uh, a often bit exaggerated.

Natural Light Levels:	
Conditions	**LUX**
Direct Sunlight	100,000+
Full Daylight	10,000+
Overcast Daylight	1,000
Dusk	100
Twilight	10
Deep Twilight	1
Full Moon	.1
Quarter Moon	.01
Moonless Night (Star Light)	.001
Overcast and Moonless	.001

The above figures are approximations.

One solution to this dilemma is to use an IR illuminator. There are several on the market that are designed to flood an area with infrared light in the correct frequency range for video pick up.

A good IR source will be totally invisible to the naked eye, yet produce a clear video image. The "magic" filters that fit over 100,000 candle power handheld spotlights usually leave a "red eye" that can be picked out by the naked eye.

Sherwood markets a small, square illuminator that can be ceiling mounted and uses 64 IR diodes to produce enough infrared light to illuminate a good sized room but remain completely invisible to the naked eye.

Another inexpensive item that belongs in any spook's kit is an RF modulator. This unit will allow you to use an existing TV in your listening post, hotel room or your home to play back the signals from a camera or VCR.

This means you don't have to haul a monitor around with you.

Remember, home TV's do not have the capacity to accept direct video.

The thing is whatever works, works. In some cases – you know a room is going to be used for an illegal transaction. Say a doctor is using a room to seduce a patient. You can just throw something up because his mind is on a part of the female anatomy and not his walls.

Successful cases have been done quick with an almost obvious system hidden under a paper bag during a drug meet. The nark eyes the drug seller and they concentrate on not trusting each other. Their faces are on each other and they're concentration is on each other. The human eye tends to gravitate to the biggest object in the room.

Plenty of people have been busted by camcorders. A cardboard box on a shelf works great. Visual surveillance limited only by your imagination.

Camcorders come in both professional surveillance and consumer models. In this particular case what you see is not necessarily what you get.

Sony made the first surveillance camcorder with interchangeable lenses. It was rated at two lux and you could even put a night vision module on it. Then they went and "improved" it. They removed the eye piece and made it four lux instead of two.

Both models are discontinued. On the used market they're worth just as much as when they were new. They're built like tanks.

Canon made a camcorder designed for surveillance, known as the L1, followed by the L2. Sounded great, interchangeable lenses. However, it used a mount that was supposedly going to become industry standard, but nobody followed them.

You can put Canon EO lenses on it or you can buy and adapter from dedicated video suppliers that will allow FD Canon lenses to fit it.

The Canon units have a very good low light capability and feature a 2,000 mm lens attachment (expensive) that can hook up to a 2X doubler for surveillance that goes the distance.

Cost is another factor, the Sony units, as one investigator/reader puts it, "require a departmental budget behind you. For the Canon, however, I only had to force my wife into prostitution to pay for it."

The price difference is due, in part, to the fact that Sony lists their unit as a professional unit, while Canon calls theirs a high end consumer device.

This raises the interesting question of why your average camcorder user needs a 2,000 mm lens, but that's another story...

It is also possible to use a low-end consumer camcorder as a surveillance system by adding a few options. Sherwood carries both a pinhole lens, as well as, a tele-zoom lens which will fit on a consumer camcorder. An 8 mm pinhole lens converter with a 37 mm mounting thread allows you to add step-up rings to fit any camera.

The tele-zoom lens allows you to get excellent telephoto without vignetting, or edge distortion. When using the tele-zoom lens, you focus your camera on infinity and then use the zoom and focus feature of the lens. If you have a 6 to 48 zoom lens, this mod will turn it into a 196 mm lens.

The other weak point of a consumer camcorder is the microphone. An inexpensive "bionic ear" type reflector or a more expensive shotgun replacement mic will give about 6 times the pick-up distance. These add-ons turn an under $1,000 camcorder into a potent surveillance unit.

Step up rings, zoom lens, parabolic ear, and maybe an extended tape, turn a low-end consumer camcorder into a piece of serious surveillance gear. And you thought you didn't have a budget for video surveillance.

At the moment the best real low end unit is probably the RCA Pro 8008. Despite being inexpensive it's made by Hitachi and it kicks ass. Almost anything in the RCA line, both VHS and 8 mm, works well.

The Pro 8008 will probably soon be replaced by something else. Watch the ads in your local paper and buy from an electronic chain store to save a couple of hundred bucks.

Try for a low f-stop and a built-in mic jack.

You might also consider such add-ons as extended length battery packs, tripods, lights, carrying cases (both hard and soft), fanny packs that hold the equipment, special video mounts car mounts, 110 volt inverters and wireless mics.

Now you can go covert with existing equipment. Remember pinhole lenses invert the image. In CCTV this can be cured by turning the camera upside down. However most camcorders do not respond well to this inversion. The exceptions are models made by Hitachi and sold under the following brands: VHS: Hitachi, J.C. Penney, Memorex, Minolta, Mitsubishi, Pentax, RCA, Realistic (Radio Shack), Samsung, Sears, Technica and Vivitar. 8 mm: Hitachi, Minolta, Pentax and RCA. These models allow the unit to operate upside down with correct view on playback.

Other camcorders can be used without inverting the camcorder; however, the monitor must be turned upside down to secure normal playback.

BODY WORN VIDEO

In the past, on-the-body video cameras had to be disguised as a button, tie clasp or emblem. There are now a series of disguised cameras which are virtually impossible to detect. The camera lens is so small it actually shoots through the fabric. Most come with a low light, wide angle, auto-iris camera, custom harness with miniature cable and will run about 5 hours on a four AA battery pack.

These units are compatible with the Sony EVO-220 video recorder or body wire video transmitters.

PHOTOGRAPHING VIDEO IMAGES

It's very possible you may wish to take still photos of a recorded video image. Here's how: Move in close to the television or monitor screen with your camera, if your TV screen is small, use a close-up lens to get a larger image. With a camera that has a built-in exposure meter, fill the viewfinder with the TV image so that the meter measures only the TV screen. If your camera is too far away from the TV screen, the exposure meter will measure too much of the dark area surrounding the image, resulting in overexposure.

Set the camera on a tripod, if available, set the shutter speed at 1/30 second or slower to avoid dark diagonal lines in the photo and get a uniform exposure. If your camera has an automatic aperture setting, set on automatic. If not, take a meter reading with the shutter on 1/30 or slower and set the aperture. Since the TV and monitor screens vary, bracket your exposure at least three times.

VIDEO ENHANCEMENT

It is possible to greatly increase the quality of a video image by choosing a particular frame, or frames, isolating them, digitizing, scaling and then manipulating certain elements of the image including color/field, brightness, contrast and image composition.

The chosen images can then be printed directly into hard copy photographs.

Although the idea behind this process was to provide graphics for multi-media events, speeches and special effects, many cops and attorneys have discovered the advantages they can provide in identifying suspects and during the process of litigation.

One company, in particular, is known for their entry into the legal enhancement field – MAI2 11 Spruce Hill Road, Armonk, NY 10504.

It will be interesting the first time a clever defense attorney gets up in front of a court of law and shows how digital tape (surveillance, up to this point, is analog) can literally be made to show anything with no proof of alternation.

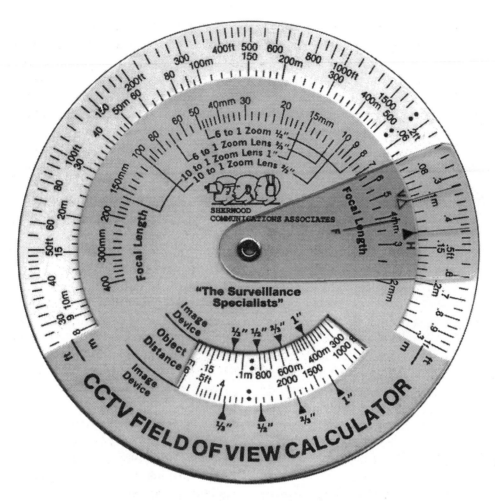

The FOV calculator. A very useful piece of gear.

Above: One of the smallest board cameras available. Courtesy of Chinnon Corp.

NEW VIDEO

I've just tested the first prototype of a new wireless video system that left me very impressed. Designed by a well known surveillance engineer, these SAW controlled, surface mounted component units provide rock steady video/and or audio. They come packaged in custom designed aluminum cases that provide a steady alignment platform unlike some of their counterparts.

The VI 900 is available with a 1/3 CCD 380+ line board, automatic iris camera already installed, or just as a transmitter. In either configuration it operates in the 900 MHz spectrum providing a healthy 150 milliwatt output.

The enclosed camera/transmitter is one of the smallest I've seen (2" x 2" x 1.25") and operates on any regulated 12 volt source, either a transformer or battery pack.

The receiver will demodulate the audio subcarrier, features a field strength meter for best alignment and accepts any antenna with a BNC connector. The output can be routed to any video monitor. The unit can also be custom ordered on a UHF channel with no receiver required.

I personally employed the unit in an ideal situation (line-of-sight, no hills, no steel walls) and pulled a strong signal at 1.8 miles!

With a 1/4 wave non-directional antenna.

Less than optimum conditions will, of course, decrease the range, a directional antenna would increase it significantly.

The camera/transmitter comes ready to go for about $1200, less for the x-mitter alone, more with various additions.

Law enforcement direct ordering, anyone else must sign an affidavit as to the legalities of his purposes. It is not FCC approved for the general population.

Intelligence incorporated.

The VI 900 stand alone transmitter.

A great video combo: the VI 900 with matching receiver.

B & E

It is an unfortunate fact of life that spies occasionally have to enter a building without the express permission of the residents. Said entry may be for the purpose of investigation, recognizance, or to plant a bug or video camera.

Unlike our cousins on SWAT teams who have the unwarranted pleasure to kick in doors at their leisure, or even common, street level burglars who live by the smash-and-grab philosophy, a good spy needs to slip in with a minimum of notice and then slide back out without leaving any evidence of his passing.

Easier said then done.

Unlike many books, entry techniques, especially lock picking, tends to come off better in the movie version.

It is possible to pick many locks, often in a few seconds, with the proper equipment and a bit of skill.

The first and still one of the most useful entry aids is the video B AND E, A TO Z available from Paladin Press. This two hour marathon teaches the uninitiated how locks work, basic picking techniques, slipping, raking, safe cracking and other things everybody should have a grasp of.

Think of it as the Boy Scout Handbook for the 90s.

However, things have changed in the 10 years since B AND E was conceived. It's now possible to open many, many doors, locks and other contrived devices with a minimum of hassle and a maximum of smarts.

Fer instance – the "electronic" lock pick was invented by a close personal friend of mine some 20 odd years ago. At the time "John Smith" was a small town police chief and locksmith.

He wanted a simple, in-the-field method to open pin tumbler locks (the most common locks in the world) with no damage and little commotion. He took what was, at the time, one of the most successful quick-pick methods, the Lockaid pick gun and refined the concept.

The pick gun works by inserting a thin needle "pick" into the shear line of a pine tumbler and then suddenly bouncing the top pins away from the bottom pins.

This action frees the tumblers for a split second so the cylinder can be turned with a tension wrench, opening the lock. The pick gun depends on a number of variables being not-so-variable at the correct time including spring tension, position, force and so on.

Note the inserted key splitting the tumblers at the shear line.

John took the same needle pick and coupled it to an electric motor which drives an eccentric cam that bounces and re-bounces the tumblers against each other several times a second, creating a series of opening windows.His first effort, THE COBRA, was a bit crude, consisting of a separate belt mounted battery pack cabled to the actual pick.

But, man, oh man did it open the eyes of the unbelievers.

Since the original design HPC has copied the concept by taking a Black and Decker electric screwdriver and replacing the front end with a bounce pick. Thousands of the HPC ELECTRIC PICK GUNS were sold in a direct mail promotion to every locksmith in the country.

They work okay, but the conversion creates a beast that is neither man nor animal. Several Chinese firms have also copied the concept and are sold through spy shops, but these plastic knock-off's just don't make it as well in the real world.

Meanwhile, back at the ranch, John completely revamped the COBRA, stepping up the voltage, employing a more powerful motor, removable/rechargeable battery packs, specially designed picks, a Halogen lamp to illuminate the keyhole, rubber grips and variable tension controls.

The COBRA III+ is machined from aircraft grade aluminum.

Does it work?

Hot damn, does it work!

Intelligence Incorporated offers a video, SUPERPICKING that graphically demonstrates how locks work (using a plastic see-though lock cylinder) and how to pick them open with a variety of tools.

At one point, both the inventor of the electronic lock pick (the mysterious "Mr. Smith") and the California lock picking champion (yes, there is a lock picking contest, watch for it on ESPN) use the COBRA III+ to attack 20 some unmodified, pin tumbler locks including Schlages, Kwicksets, and a variety of other common locks.

The average time to open each lock varies from 3-20 seconds with the COBRA...

This tricky device really does let those spies who failed high school wood shop quickly and quietly open most locks just like the big boys.

And, in fact, many police and intelligence agencies use the COBRA for those times when they have misplaced their keys...

The COBRA III+ available from Intelligence Incorporated, $499.

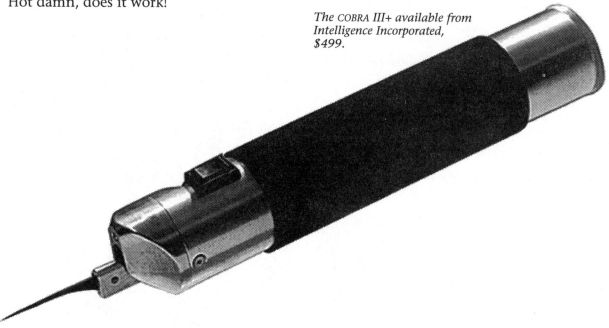

One of the most amazing entry tools to ever hit the market is the child of another friend of mine (hey, what can I say I hang out with interesting people). Bob spent twenty years as an engineer with various armed forces and agencies before going into the locksmithing biz.

He became quite well-known for conducting seminars to teach professionals master keying and general lock tricks. Bob decided there had to be a way to open most doors *even those protected by super high security Medico type locks* without too much hassle and without destroying the lock.

After several years of experimentation he finalized the design on a device known as the Mule Tool. This creature, or rather, system, consists of a number of pieces of rolled steel, bent in particular shapes, some plastic string, a tab or two, a pad of special gripping material and a wedge.

What can the Mule Tool do?

- Open normal key-in-knob cylinder locks as found on most doors, *regardless of the type of lock involved.*
- Open deadbolt locks, again without regard to the creed or color of the lock involved as long as it does not use a key on the inside of the door to open the lock
- Pop open panic bars from the outside of the door
- Defeat in-floor door blocking bars in a couple of seconds
- *Re-lock deadbolts from the inside* after the agent leaves the vicinity

The Mule Tool system works by sliding underneath any door with a tiny bit of clearance between the door and the ground, reaching up, "grabbing" the knob, or deadbolt latch, from the inside and then turning it to open the door from the inside.

The first time I went to see a demonstration of this unit it was because a mutual friend told me Bob had invented a "lock pick that will open any lock in the world."

I tried to explain to him why this was flat out impossible, some locks are high security,

some have no pins, some have side bars, some...

"No, no, it really does. I've seen it. Here call this guy."

So, I show up at a rather well known hotel where Bob is about to demonstrate the Mule Tool to the head of security. The man is upset.

"Damn, I wanted to use my office but I locked the keys inside and it's a steel door with a Medico lock. We can't get in until my assistant comes on duty with some spare keys."

Bob laughed, took this strange looking thing out of his bag, knelt in front of the door and in 30 seconds we were inside the office.

"I'll buy that thing," I said.

"No you won't, I was here first." And the security manager bought the Mule Tool and placed an order for three more.

Since then, the tool has sold to a number of hotel managers (ideal for opening doors when he guest has lost the last key, or worse yet, doesn't answer his door), police, locksmiths and intelligence agents.

The Mule Tool runs $220 for a standard system that will work on locks installed at the usual heights, or $400 for a full kit that will work on non-standard locks as well.

A demo tape showing the Mule Tool in it's full glory, will set you back a mere $20 (refundable with purchase) from Intelligence Inc.

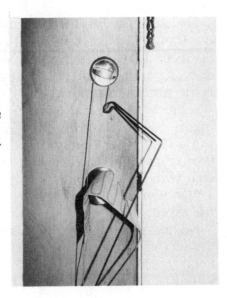

The Mule Tool geared to open a deadbolt, key in knob and chain.

HOW ABOUT THIS SCENARIO:

James Bond walks towards the target embassy building, knowing that dozens of denizens inside with baited breath and Black Talon loaded Uzi's wait for him to pick the lock on the front door and walk foolishly into their trap.

James, whistling "God Save The Queen," quietly, walks completely around the building, stopping at the servants garage, reaches in his pocket and surreptitiously presses a black button on a black box.

A few seconds later the door swings quietly open and James slips inside...

Automatic garage door openers work on two basic frequencies. Each individual door is protected by a digital code, allowing thousands of openers to be placed in a housing development with no cross opening problems.

The AGO is a sub-miniature computer that sequences through 12 code combinations each second on all the popular frequencies.

What does this mean?

When I first tested the AGO I walked my dog down the streets of a local yuppie, high rent condo project. In a matter of seconds garage doors started popping open like flowers after a rainstorm.

I walked faster as to not be completely obvious (range is about 75 feet so it normally takes 30 seconds to 1+ minute to open the target door, if you move out of range before the code is hit, nothing happens.)

A block later I came upon two women talking in the middle of the street. One was holding a Great Dane or some other obnoxious breed that immediately decided to have a long chat with my Malamute.

"Do you mind if they play for a second?" she asked.

No, no problem. I unobtrusively switched the AGO off and put it in the pocket of my windbreaker while the two animals went through the ritual of sniff each other's bodily orifices.

"How cute. They like each other." She turned to look at a garage door that suddenly popped open two condos down the street.

"That's strange. I know nobody's home there."

"Planes." I said, recovering well. "Sometimes planes flying overhead cause a door to open like that."

Both women shook their heads in understanding.

The second door began opening.

They both looked at me.

"UFO's maybe. I've read about that sort of thing in the *Enquirer.*"

They looked back at the dogs and the door nearest our little gathering began its slow ascent.

"My God!" The dog owner grabbed her heart. "That's my house! Nobody's home. What the hell is going on here?"

I not quite as unobtrusively began rummaging around in my pocket for the misplaced on-off switch.

"Damned if I know, but my dog and I are going somewhere safer!" I pulled on the leash and took off for better places.

The AGO will activate about 99% of all automatic garage openers in US in less than two minutes. This unit is used by SWAT teams and others as an alternative to the kicking in of doors, often at some risk to kickers, but it can also be used to replace a misplaced garage transmitter.

With the AGO it is possible to actually see the digital readout of the code when the door opens and then program a replacement opener.

Is this the future of unexpected entry? Go in not with a bang but with a digital whimper?

Well the unit does save a lot of wear and tear on both the equipment and the spy in the proper circumstances..

$299, Intelligence Incorporated.

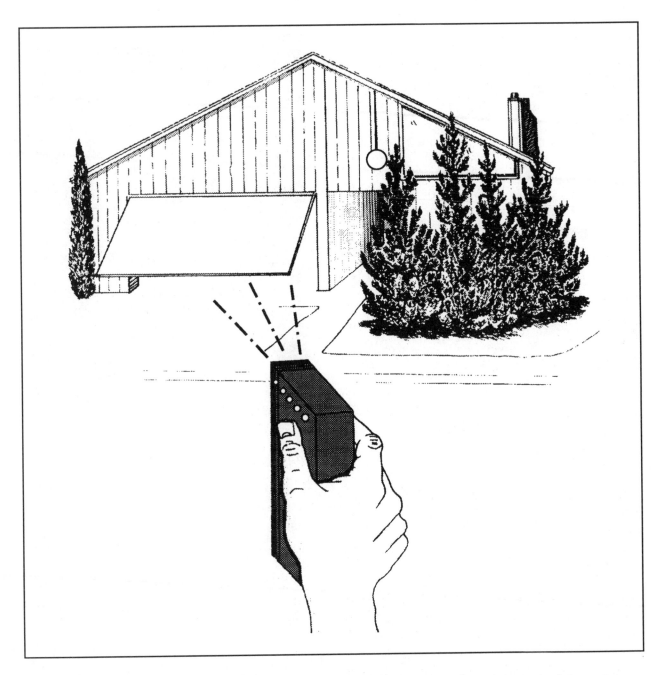

The AGO is a sub-miniature computer that sequences through 12 code combinations each second on all the popular frequencies.

AUTOMOBILE OPENING

The usual number of suspects still produce the usual number of auto opening tools – wires, Slim Jim's, peg legs, flexible grabbers and so on. Intelligence, Incorporated offers a single alternative to many of these kits.

The MASTER Z TOOL is designed to effectively open almost all vehicles that are valuable to Slim-Jim type, door lock mechanism attacks. The system utilizes a single tool and a thick play-by-play manual that shows how to apply the Z TOOL at the correct angle and correct depth for nearly every popular recent vintage model.

Probably the best and easiest to use all-around car opener for the spy who needs to occasionally violate the sanctity of a bad guy's pet transportation.

After thinking it over I've also got to mention that the device you seen advertised on TV by "police chiefs" known as THE CLUB which locks your steering wheel, making the car, well, just this side of impossible to steal?

Disc wafer locks, about 30 seconds to a practiced pick person.

You're not practiced? In that case, HPC makes a $30 device that pops the lock open in seconds, even in the hand of an amateur.

I know, maybe this shouldn't be mentioned, but Kraco, the OEM supplier of THE CLUB guarantees to pay your insurance deductible (up to $500) if the a car "protected" by THE CLUB is stolen?

Took a friend of mine 2 1/2 years to get them to cough up the check...

Buyer beware.

SURREPTITIOUS ENTRY Willis George, Paladin Press this book is a historical classic detailing exactly how Mr. George learned how to burglarize, lock pick and safecrack under the US Treasury department to work among alcohol and drug smugglers in Cuba.

He went on to become a to agent for Naval Intelligence in WW II breaking into Nazi offices and gathering intelligence.

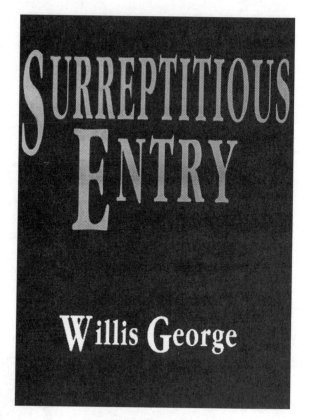

SURREPTITIIOUS ENTRY
ISBN 0-87364-562-6

He joined the OSS and was appointed chief instructor of surreptitious entry techniques (what a great job title), eventually heading his own lock picking and safecracking team wartime Europe.

I do not recommend this book simply because it is an exciting read, although it certainly is, but because the field has not changed that much. The tricks and techniques Mr. George developed and used are virtually the same way the Feds (and other, less legal organizations) do it to this very day.

NIGHT VISION

NEW STUFF

Night vision has come a far distance since the first practical infrared "scopes" were used in WW II. The most significant breakthrough would have to be the invention of passive, light amplifying tubes that worked on light in much the same manner as vacuum tubes worked on electricity.

These units, pressed into service in Viet Nam, actually amplified weak moonlight, or even starlight to produce a monochrome image of the scene being viewed.

Early Starlight scopes were considered classified – so much so that in some cases Special Forces were instructed to bring the 'scope back instead of a comrade if things went from bad to worse.

Even early civilian models bore super-glued warning stickers informing the owners that it was a felony to take the unit outside of the United States.

Second generation units made the theory into reality; allowing determined viewers to actually see in medium starlight conditions, or with an infrared booster, in total darkness.

Rather than repeat myself I would suggest you read the section in BOOK II HOW TO GET ANYTHING ON ANYBODY on the theory and operation of night vision devices.

Thus warned, let's look at what's new and good in this exciting field.

Starlight type tubes are rated in terms of photo cathode sensitivity. This is the tube's ability to see in faint light. Once the light falls to a certain level (say a cloud comes over the sky) weaker tubes will suddenly lose their ability to see.

This sensitivity rating is given in micro amps per lumen. Think of this measurement as energy produced per "piece" of light. The higher the rating, the more sensitive the tube.

A ROUGH GUIDE IS:

- 2nd generation 240 micro amps per lumen
- 2nd generation plus 325-425 micro amps per lumen
- 2nd generation "super" 400-525 mapl

Second generation tubes were the first practical units. First gen scopes such as the AN/PVS Viet Nam models were certainly better than nothing, but their gain was low, they were bulky and a bit fragile.

If first generation units are pictured as vacuum tubes, seconds are transistors.

Each subsequent development improved the scope's low light capabilities as well as adding resolution and tube life.

Each tube improvement also raised the price of the finished units.

- 2nd generation plus (also known as 2 1/2 generation) added 20% to the cost of the average scope
- 2nd generation super is about double the cost of a plus

These stages were important in several respects, but to paraphrase our friends in the computer industry, should be considered an "upgrade."

None were radical enough to be considered a new generation.

And now, turn the card over, Vanna, we have generation *3* scopes being adapted as a NATO standard and available on the general market.

Third gen tubes use a gallium arsenide photo cathode to produce an incredible 1200 micro amps per lumen, or 4 times the sensitivity of a 2nd generation plus; 3 times a super.

An added enhancement of this technology is a 400% increase in tube life.

As one would expect, 3rd gen units cost more than their second cousins, but not as much as they could. Specifically, most 3 units run about 25% over 2 supers.

The new generation also offers a bonus in near infrared sensitivity. Older tubes "saw" only far IR, that is, wavelengths in the "normal" infrared spectrum. Near IR can be thought of as a minor variation in the temperature of the viewed object.

This feature is quite useful when viewing, or shooting, a live object...

If you are considering the purchase of a night vision device, decide what actual applications will come into play. Do you need to connect to a camera, either still or video? Is size a consideration? Should the front lens (read magnification) be changeable? Do you need a unit that will mount on a rifle? Are you going to boost with a separate laser?

And, of course, how much do you plan on spending...

Bear in mind that only a few companies in the States make light amplifying tubes, Litton is probably the primary supplier, ITT, Varo and Intevac EOS being the other choices. A number of secondary firms implement the tubes in various formats, but the basic tube, the heart of any system, will be pretty much the same.

Litton Electron Devices 1215 S. 52nd st, Tempe, AZ 85218 will send you a nice, free catalog of their products and PR sheets showing how they are applied, as well as a list of dealers. They do not sell finished units on a direct basis.

A couple of their new offerings include a single eye, monocular goggle. Why is this important?

Because anyone who has ever used fixed focus night vision goggles can attest to the problem of trying to switch viewing distances suddenly; say you are flying a helicopter, watching the landscape and you get a sudden urge to see the instrument panel...

Can be done with practice, but it is disorienting. The single eye "goggle" gives the operator "the best of both worlds", allowing him to set the scope for the normal distance and use his naked eye for close-up viewing.

Litton also is now offering a variety of *underwater*, starlight type scopes. Hey, it gets dark down there.

BE Meters, 17525 NE Ct., Redound, WA 98052, will sell you neat stuff including night vision goggles, rifle scopes, pocket scopes, camera scopes, modular systems, laser enhancers, digitally stabilized camcorders with 3rd generation scopes attached and a host of goodies to accessorize your new night scope.

Or, how about a radar interfaced low light recording system that turns on automatically and tapes any vehicle exceeding the speed limit (MPH displayed on the tape) and the subsequent chat with the nice officer.

Sheesh...

At any rate, they are not cheap, but nobody is, and their line is one of the most complete around.

NVEC, or Night Vision Equipment Company, POB 266, Emmaus, PA 18049 is another major player in the starlight game.

Aspect Technology, 900 E. Plano Pkwy., Plano, TX 75074 checks in with a very affordable (well, for night scopes I mean) line of gear which includes a couple of gen 3 scopes for less than $4,000.

This is K-Mart pricing, kids, trust me.

STANO Components, POB 2048, Carson City, NE 89702, has long been an inexpensive supplier of military surplus scopes and now compliments their line with weapon systems, pocket scopes, binoculars and special purpose units.

Other nifty stuff?

You can now purchase Starlight-type scopes in underwater configurations (built into a face mask or on a camera), enhanced low light video cameras that still grab an image in near darkness (VMI, Electrophysics), or even a zero light video periscope that uses an IR enhanced (active) system mounted on an extendible pole to allow "discreet, clear video observation" around corners or over walls and obstacles in complete darkness.

Litton Electron Devices will send you a nice, free catalog of their products and PR sheets showing how they are applied, as well as a list of dealers.

NIGHT VISION GOGGLE
AN/PVS-5B GEN II
M912A GEN II
M915A GEN II PLUS

SUBMERSIBLE WEAPONS SIGHT
M921

MONOCULAR
M982 GEN II PLUS
M983 GEN III
M982D (underwater)
M983D (underwater)

AVIATORS NIGHT VISION SYSTEM
AN/AVS-6 GEN III
M927 GEN II PLUS
M929 GEN III

LONG RANGE WEAPONS SIGHT
M937XR GEN II PLUS
M938XR GEN III

POCKETSCOPE (3X)
M942 GEN II PLUS
M944 GEN III

POCKETSCOPE (1X)
M942 GEN II PLUS
M944 GEN III

AN/PVS-7A GEN
M972 GEN II PLUS
M973 GEN III
M972D (underwater)
M973D (underwater)

BINOCULAR (4X)
M975 GEN II PLUS
M976 GEN III

POCKETSCOPE
M911A GEN II PLUS

BINOCULAR (3X)
M977 GEN II PLUS
M978 GEN III

MEDIUM RANGE WEAPONS SIGHT
M937A GEN II PLUS
M938A GEN III

WEAPONS SIGHT
M845 MK II GEN II PLUS

NV TEST EQUIPMENT
ASSESSOR
ETS-85L

EYE SAFE LASER AIMER
AN/PAQ-4A
IRAD-350ES

INFRARED POINTING DEVICE
IRPD ranges to 8,000 meters

NV TEST EQUIPMENT
Nitrogen Fly-Away Purge Kit

INFRARED LASER AIMER
IRAD ranges to 8,000 meters

NV TEST EQUIPMENT
Purge Kit Device

IMAGE INTENSIFIERS
18 MM & 25 MM GEN II, GEN II PLUS
GEN III. and 1.06 micron image
intensifier tubes

INFRARED MARKER KIT
IRM-K for landing and drop zones

Litton Electron Devices
1215 S. 52nd st,
Tempe, AZ 85218

NEWER STUFF

I have little doubt the future holds generation 3 plus, 3 super, 3 extra-new-and-super and finally gen 4 and 5 scopes that will be able to count the hairs on Charles Barkley's head in complete darkness, but in one sense the future is already here.

Thermal viewers, or thermal imagers are viewers that "see" near IR; or heat. These units interpret minute differences in temperature rather than light.

Near IR viewers have been used in military applications for some time, often as tank or large gun sites. They have not really made it into the consumer market because most thermal imagers require an extensive cooling system to keep their sensing elements at a very low temperature.

Some early thermal sites employed a volatile coolant like liquid nitrogen in order to keep the unit's temperature in the 77K region. Newer models make use of a Stirling-Vacuum arrangement to achieve the same results electronically.

Thermal imaging has a number of advantages over other types of night vision devices:

- Completely passive, no active radiation that might give the location away
- They quickly locate anything, living, mechanical, or natural that produces heat
- The effective range is usually much greater than a starlight scope
- TI's will also pick up residual heat showing where a person, or vehicle has *been*

Thermal units establish the background temperature of an area, null it out and then display the scene by temperature gradients.

HOW GOOD ARE THERMAL VIEWERS?

Recently I had the opportunity to spend a night with the INS border patrol. We were patrolling the infamous "Smuggler's Gulch" area between San Diego and Tiajuana. The night was a covered starlight condition.

I brought my starlight scope along to get some photos of the officers in action. Part way through what was turning into a particularly busy night I asked "my" agent how we were being dispatched to hot spots several miles apart with amazing accuracy.

"Well, I'm really not supposed to show this, but since you know a little bit about night vision..."

We drove to the top of a hill about two miles away. Two agents were operating a high tech surveillance van with a monochrome TV monitor and what appeared to be a large intensifier unit mounted on the end of a 15 foot extendible stalk that "grew" from the top of the van.

I sat behind the agents and watched 5 illegals sneak through a patch of dense ground cover. The dispatcher guided an INS jeep to the spot and the on-site agents called in on their radios.

"Ah, dispatch we can't see anybody. It's pretty thick in here."

"Okay," one of the agents inside the van responded, "lead agent raise your arm." On the screen one of the tiny figures raised his arm. "Right. The suspects are approximately 5 meters in front of you at your two o'clock. There are five of them and they are all lying on the ground."

The agents walked directly to the spot and made the arrest.

I got out of the van and tried to see the target area. "How far away are they?"

The operator looked at a range guide on the monitor and said, "just about 2 miles."

I put my starlight scope to my eye and could make out the van, about 50 meters away, but nothing else.

About 2 miles...

The business end of the INS thermal viewer

Their scope as seen through my scope

A daylight look at a profesional thermal viewer

Thermal viewing gear is now available on the general market. Mitsubishi Electric, 5665/5757 Plaza Drive, Cypress, CA 90630, offers a wonderful unit about the size of a professional video camera.

The output is displayed on a monitor or can be taped directly from the viewer.

How much? Well, let me just point out that you get one year's service free. A service contract for the second year is $9,000.

A smaller, handheld viewer is available from Agema Infrared Systems, 550 County Ave, Secaucus, NJ 07094. The THERMOVISION 210 is a direct (no monitor) viewer about the size of a large 35 mm camera designed for covert security and law enforcement applications.

The effective range is about 1500 feet in total darkness. The unit is used by border patrols and law enforcement for both exterior and interior search and seize missions. Besides providing a picture of the scene it will show cool spots (or hot spots) on vehicles or other large objects. This feature allows for finding hidden compartments in vehicles or hidden hitchhikers.

Price? $10-$20K.

If I had to make a guess, based on a few, ah, rumors that have drifted my way, I'd want to invest in the company that perfects the best *thermal* weapon scope in the near future because I do believe NATO is about to drop the third generation rifle scopes and buy a couple of million thermal scopes for the next Desert Storm...

The only problem with this is that it is difficult to tell friend from foe thru a thermal viewer. Shoot 'em all, let-God-sort-them-out thinking...

A thermal image through the THERMOVISION 1000

FoV can be switched instantly and zoomed

POOR MAN'S THERMAL UNIT

So perhaps you haven't got 5 figures, I don't know, maybe the recession is a problem, is there a thermal viewer in your future?

Maybe. Or I should say, sort of, kinda...

Game Finder Inc. ,POB 658, Huntsville AL 35804, sells a unit called, oddly enough, THE GAME FINDER. This is not a viewer but a handheld (or wrist mounted) near IR detector that will sense temperature changes of less than one degree.

The original concept was to allow hunters to track down wounded game after losing the blood trail. An LED bar graph readout alerts the user to hot spots in the environment. THE GAME FINDER will "see" through heavy brush or even smoke.

The unit can be used as a motion detector by holding it stationary, pointed at the area in question. If a person or animal walks into the target zone the indicators will flash on and off.

Range varies depending on the size and temperature of the target as well as on-site conditions, but a good operator will be able to pick out a large deer, or human at several hundred yards in wooded cover.

Since its introduction the unit has been used to find and track game, locate unconscious victims in a smoke filled room, avoid ambushes, track down escaped convicts hiding in the woods and a variety of other applications.

Rescue crews have utilized THE GAME FINDER to find victims thrown from a vehicle at a crash site. In fact, it can even locate still-warm body parts that may have become carelessly separated from their owner.

Under $300.

STARLIGHT OVER RUSSIA

The second major development in the see-in-the-dark-game has been the sudden introduction of relatively inexpensive Russian made units into the world marketplace. The sheer numbers of the units being offered is staggering and the claims and specifications differ widely for the same units.

If you are going to consider the purchase of a Russian night vision scope you need to realize a number of things.

Let me back the story up for a moment here: soon after the collapse of the Soviet Union I got a call from a reporter buddy who was stationed in Moscow.

"You got any interest in Russian Starlight scopes?" He asked.

"Sure, why?"

"'Cause they are selling on the street and in flea markets for about $100 a scope."

Great, I figured I'd corner the market and make a fortune...

To make a long story somewhat shorter, I spent about two months calling everybody from the U.S. Customs (who would not, at that time, authorize the entry of any Russian military gear) to the State Department, various Russian embassies, American night vision engineers at Litton, engineers at a Russian night vision factory, and so on.

During the course of my investigation I finally met several Russian engineers who had just moved to the West and was able to piece together most of the story. I figured importing just a couple of hundred units would probably pay my phone bill for the past two months.

That, of course, is when the restrictions were lifted and every bloody mom and pop store in the U.S. began advertising Russian night scopes...

When you are examining the plethora of Russian scopes bear in mind:

1. All the light amplifying tubes are made at one of three factories, none of which actually assemble the final products. About 30 different factories make the final gear. The

two major producers are Baigish and Rostov. They produce the majority of the devices now on the market. The units were all produced for the military (the Russian government did not encourage civilian ownership of night scopes for some odd reason) and are "military grade."

In the U.S. we call this "battleship grade." Simply stated, they tend to be heavier and bulkier than their American counterparts.

2. The Russians started with first generation units of two different types. The single stage scope is modeled after, and not quite as good as our Viet Nam era first gen units.

That is to say, you need very strong moonlight for the unit to work at all, *not starlight.*

Single stage first gen translates as very low light amplification, short battery life, small diameter tubes and poor resolution.

The Russians later "improved" the first gen units by using a three stage cascade system like the American PVS-2 and PVS-3. Several units on the market are of this variety including the Baigish 5P, Rostov NS-2, 8P, 8B and 3B.

While these are a step up from the single stage units they still suffer from first generation setbacks.

Many of these first scopes were "improved" by adding a diode infrared laser to the optional handle of the scopes. The laser is a full 1/2 watt IR unit that spreads from a thin dot to a wide beam and allows the user to read license plates etc., in the dark.

This does help, but far from makes the first generation units usable except in limited circumstances.

The laser is so powerful it has been outlawed by the FDA for safety reasons. Even though the beam is invisible to the naked eye it is strong enough to burn an iris if aimed directly into someone's face.

Some of these units are still floating around. There are also IR illuminators (not lasers) on the market which *are* deemed safe by the FDA.

I do not recommend any 1st generation unit for professional use, such as law enforcement, EXCEPT for applications like sweeping a warehouse before sending in SWAT teams (with the laser, not without).

3. Russian second generation units are as much as an improvement over the previous units as were our first second gen units over the standard ANVPS Vietnam type scopes.

Russian made H-10 a second generation "work horse"

I tested a second generation H 10, a full military spec unit that features changeable ocular and rear lenses, against my personal American made 2nd generation scope. The Russian unit is heavier, does not offer the same flexibility in front end lens selection (mine uses standard camera lenses) and is a bit more difficult to attach to a still or video camera.

I also found the target to be rougher than my Litton-made tube; i.e., the resolution is a bit poorer. Small black dots (target flaws) are noticeable in the Russian unit, virtually none in my unit.

On the up side *it was at least as bright if not brighter* than my scope. The light amplification factor seemed to be a touch higher and the price (retail) of $1500 is just less than half the cost of my scope.

There are indications, as the competition heats up, that this price will fall even further, making this scope a great deal.

The optional laser handle will fit onto this scope for extreme conditions but it is a pretty good all-around Starlight scope as-is.

4. The Russians made several single tube, double eye units like the B7A and B6. These units have a visor-like eyepiece that covers both your eyes (but is not a true binocular) and good front end optics.

The B6 uses a bigger and better (25mm) LAT than the B7 (18 mm).

The "visor" units are not designed for camera work, just for general surveillance and will not accept the laser handle.

5. Most Russian rifle scopes suffer from several problems when compared to their American counterparts: although the first gen units are actually smaller and lighter than their American rivals (they use a single stage and a 18 mm LAT instead of the US 25 mm or 40 mm) they do not produce the same image. Most Russian rifle scopes on the market (including those with a built-in laser) are first generation units.

When it comes to 2nd gen rifle scopes the Russians have caught up somewhat and both country's offerings are about the same size and weight (for instance the US PVS-4 and Russian NS-2AR).

The exception to this is the Russian PN-51 which is very bulky and can only be mounted on the side of a weapon.

Even the second gen rifle scopes tend to have a non-movable, non-illuminated recticle. This gives some sort of sight picture but will disappoint shooters used to American optics.

A "new" rifle scope, the NS2AR is on the market that bears consideration. It is a 2nd generation unit that adapts to most American scope mounts including the CAR 15, AR-16 and 1/2 inch Weaver mounts with only minor modifications. It does not have an illuminated recticle, unlike most NATO sights.

This scope comes with 3.5X magnification, but can be boosted to 4.7 with optional optics. An add-on adapter will allow the scope to be used with a camera.

Pricing is under $2,000 for a good Starlight based rifle scope.

The Baigish 5P does feature an illuminated recticle, but is a rather poor quality, 1st generation scope.

6. Russian night vision goggles are not (at this time) comparable to American units. Most are first generation, some have bulky power supplies (and may need to be carried on one's belt) and feature a dubious fit.

The most common "mistake" in night vision ads is to show the Russian PN-63 goggles, labeling them as a micro channel 2nd generation unit.

They are NOT! And they will not compare to US 2nd gen goggles...

Rumors of 2nd generation goggles are circulating, but I would want to examine any goggles before contemplating any purchase.

Because of the massive influx of these goods onto the market some dealers are, uh, how to put this delicately? Lying.

Or, more kindly, just misinformed. Bear in mind light gain and amplification factor is not only hard to measure, it is not the most important quality in a good scope. Also bear in mind:

- The Russians *never made* a 3rd generation unit. People are fibbing when they say 3rd gen units are available. The simple truth is that the Russians acquired American technology and copied it, so their selections run a bit behind. People who say Russian 2nd units are equal to American third are misinformed or, well, ah, don't buy a used car from them.
- It is comparing apples to oranges to say any Russian scope is second generation+ of even second 1/2, 'cause the units just ain't the same. In my humble observation, *the best* Russian units will fall someplace between 2nd and 2+, on most scales.

- *All* double tube and most single tube binoculars are *first generation*.
- Units with a built-in laser (as opposed to add-ons) are generally first generation.
- Some units on the market are seconds, or failed to meet military specifications.
- Russian units do *not* feature Zeiss lenses. When East Germany fell into Russian hands much of the Zeiss factory was disassembled and shipped to Russia where it was reborn as the Zenit factory. The optics produced here do not compare with the genuine article.
- Russia is a long way to go for repairs.... If you are going to buy a Russian scope I would suggest you deal with one of a couple of companies (or their dealers) that have actual Russian repair personnel on staff in the U.S.

I would also suggest you make certain the company you are dealing with offers a one year warranty, on-site, quick turn around for repairs, a return period or at least a trade-up policy and has a quantity of good units in stock.

A number of "great deals" have fallen through because the TU 154 was stalled on an airport runway waiting for avgas.

And waiting, and waiting, and waiting...

Reasonable, non-black market units usually come with an electronic flash guard, daylight filter, carrying case, and the other amenities you would expect. Be wary of those that do not.

Other suppliers that have Russian engineers or personnel and sell at both wholesale and retail levels include:

Moonlight Products, 10211 Pacific Mesa Blvd., San Diego, CA 92121; Cal Armory, 881 West San Bruno Ave, San Bruno, CA 94066, and Lifesearch International 803 Arguello St, Redwood City, CA 94061.

See THE COVERT CATALOG for a complete list of night vision suppliers.

NEW STUFF

Because the Russian manufacturers have been privatized, a couple of exciting new items are in the works. HiTek, 400 El Camino Real, Redwood City, CA 94063, a California-based importer has purchased a new plant in the ex-Soviet Union with the concept of "Americanizing" the product by combining American research with Russian labor.

They are probably the largest supplier of Russian night vision equipment in the U.S. (also available through Intelligence Incorporated), stocking the H-10 scope I tested, B7A, the new rifle scope, etc.

A couple of their first projects constructed with the American market in mind are finally available.

The Pirate Scope is a modular, 2nd generation+ 18 MM tube based system that accepts camera lenses (Pentax thread) on the front end, has a cute, legal IR illuminator that fits on the scope body, and will adapt to almost any still or video camera on the back end.

The unit is still "battleship grade," but lighter and more flexible than most Russian products.

This same tube-assembly is available from other dealers with a built-in recticle BUT I warn you that the 18 mm tube, even with a flash guard, does not accept rifle recoil well...

The Russian/American PRIATE *nightscope*

The HT-5 is a "non-military" grade unit, i.e., a bit smaller, lighter and easier to use than the Pirate; it contains a 25 mm tube, *removable weapon recticle*, the same IR diode laser and front end/rear end configurations as the Pirate.

Why the italics on "removable recticle"?

'Cause your uncle Lee went through the '60's and occasionally gets a quick glimpse of the future, and the future lady says that the U.S. is about to make any weapon oriented-night scope illegal.

If you buy a nice unit with a built-in sighting system and my version of the future comes to pass, it be illegal...

The 5 features the best 2nd generation tube available in a modular format that allows the user to configure his own system. A variety of eyepieces and camera adapters are available for the rear end; the front end comes with 2.5X magnification but can be varied with add-on optics.

The HT-5 is the wave of the future in Russian gear and is built to compare directly with American units such as the PVS-4.

HiTek is also introducing the first Russian thermal scope into the local market as we speak.

Those clever Japanese have entered the starlight market with two Fujinon scopes. Both the PS-910 II and the PS 910-C II are built around the same 2nd generation tube. The 910 fits in the palm of your hand and is the only scope (except the Litton underwater models) that is guaranteed waterproof.

The C model is not waterproof but will accept a variety of regular and zoom camera lenses on the front end.

Both units have advanced, high-gain hybrid image intensifiers, auto brightness control, LED infrared projection light source for black conditions. The systems are lightweight, compact and feature a large 8 mm exit pupil (larger than a 7x50 binocular) with adjustable diopters.

Both provide a very respectable 95 line pairs per millimeters at the surface of the projection screen and will operate for about 60 hours on two penlight cells.

The C unit can even add a times 2 lens extender in order to double the effective length of the front lens. An optional SLR and CCTV camera adapter allows use on both types of cameras.

Price on both systems is $2500 (plus $150 for the IR intensifier) making them the least expensive, non-Russian scopes on the market.

Available from a number of dealers.

The Fujinon system in both configurations

Okay, I've found an American made line of palm sized pocket scopes that are some of the very best, and very lightest I've ever used.

Built around a modular concept, the LEOPARD scope has a C-mount front end (accepts any C-mount camera lens), comes with a 1X. 2X and 3X available directly from the supplier.

The LEOPARD scope

Diopter adjustable ocular end with rubber eyepiece, threaded to accept a 49 mm step up ring for adaptation to any SLR or video camera, an optional head strap that allows the user to employ it as a one-eye goggle, optional weapons mount, optional IR laser with weapons mount (so you can wear the unit and simply aim at the little red dot – still legal) a camera relay lens and, get this, a cute little adapter which screws onto the threads on either side of the scope.

On the eyepiece end you can use it to begin the step-up process in order to adapt to a camera, on the front end it will screw onto the included lens and then physically clamp down on a rifle scope, or spotting scope, providing the flexibility of a high powered weapon's mount for about $100.

The LEOPARD is available in three configurations as of this writing:
- With a reconditioned 2nd generation tube for about $1500
- With a new 2nd gen tube for about $2500
- With a new full 3rd gen tube (4 times the power, 4 times the tube life) about $3000

Made by NAIT and sold by Intelligence Incorporated, this is one of the best scopes I have ever used, at a price that simply cannot be topped.

Operative Supply is also offering a similar pocket scope that they put together themselves. A bit more expensive, good reputation.

A super IR mini flashlight is available from Aegis Research (or thru II) that puts out the brightest beam I've tested with very little visible light. Battery life checks in at about four hours.

Great for interior scope searches or boosted night vision.

For do it-your-selfers, EPI POB 22208 San Diego, CA 92192 offers a variety of IR lenses designed to fit over various flashlights and spot lights. They claim to block 99-100% of visible light and are constructed of Polysulfone with "true infrared pigments".

They operate best in the 900-1600 nanometer range. The company also offers adapters that fit nearly every popular flashlight made.

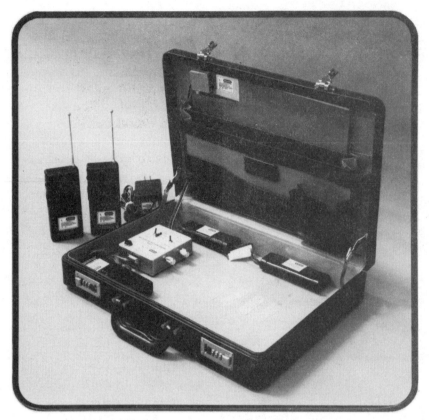

Bringing the war home – THE HUGHES RADAR UNIT

RADAR

There is one other type of "night vision" which should be of interest to surveillance folk, radar.

Man portable radar, designed for tracking objects as small as a man first appeared in the late, great, Viet Nam conflict. The units work and some have found their way into the surplus marketplace.

They are moderately expensive and not ideally suited for city environments because they range up to a mile or so from the base station.

The Hughes Missile Systems Company has introduced something called the MDR or Motion Detection Radar. This is a modular system that requires a control unit, a transmitter, one of several antennas and one or more output devices (remote amplified audio and/ or transmitters & receiver.

In the basic configuration the system runs about $2500 and can be configured for differ-

ent applications by adding optional modules. The control unit has both power and frequency controls to optimize the performance in any situation.

The eight pound unit can "see" through almost any material including brick walls and thick foliage. The range is determined by the use of either low or high powered transmitters and receivers or high gain – low gain antennas.

The standard unit will detect the movement of a person's hand at about 20 feet and a body at a couple of hundred.

The MDR can sweep buildings or hidey holes for suspects, alert the user to the presence of a moving object on the other side of a wall, act as an alarm or automatic stakeout partner.

The output is not the conventional CRT, but rather an audio tone that signals any target acquisition.

GUARDING BODIES

Body guarding, or as it has become known, executive protection, is one of the last fields where a person can actually use skills such as martial arts, shooting, evasive driving, and other renaissance arts.

Generally the same things that used to get you into trouble.

Executive protection can be either a full time position, usually protecting a corporate bigwig, or part time working for rock stars, jocks or show biz folk. It tends to pay quite well and is better than sitting at a fast food place watching those fries brown.

Body guarding is like flying – most assignments consist of hours of routine tedium, possibly interrupted by moments of sheer terror.

One advantage to this profession is that a four year degree is not usually required, or even expected. If you already possess some skills the actual techniques involved can be learned in fairly short, intensive courses.

There are several executive protection "schools" in the US. The first is:

Executive Security International, Ltd.
POB 80
Basalt, CO 81621

ESI was conceived by Bob Duggan in early 1980 when the first training programs were developed as a practical extension of his martial arts training and as one of the outgrowths of the Aspen Academy of Martial Arts. In l981, ESI was founded as a closely held Colorado Corporation and as a career school approved and regulated by the Colorado State Board of Community Colleges under the Private Occupational Education Act.

In 1989 ESI received approval for its Intelligence Gathering and Investigation Program. In 1992, ESI was approved to offer a two-year Associate of Applied Science in Criminal Justice degree program, with an Area of Emphasis in Security and Investigation. ESI also offers an 8-day Maritime and Yacht Security Program; a 7-day Hotel, Resort and Cruise Line Casino Security Program and a Personal Protection/Security Operations Program.

1991 inaugurated ESI's second decade in the business of training protection specialists and intelligence agents for public agencies, private industry, and individuals. During the fourteen years of its existence, ESI has trained hundreds of graduates for both vocational careers and avocational pursuits.

ESI is a unique institution, it's one of the few private schools in the country that offers more than 1600 hours of training in Executive Protection, Intelligence Gathering & Investigation, Resort & Gambling, Maritime and Yacht Security, and Personal Protection/Security Operations. In addition, ESI provides training programs for law enforcement agencies, property and perimeter security for estates and businesses, as well as custom designed security training for corporations.

ESI's training programs are designed so that students do not have to quit their job in order to attain their education, or take any more than is deemed necessary to the furtherance of their career. The Certificate Programs are designed as Home Study and Resident Training programs which allow students to acquire the academic components of the course material by correspondence at their own pace until they are ready to come to Aspen, Colorado to complete the practical sections of the course. Resident Training sections are modeled after military language schools. At ESI the instruction is based upon Total Immersion, High Intensity, Close Supervision, Induced Stress, Reality Simulation, Team and Individual Performance.

ASSOCIATE OF APPLIED SCIENCE DEGREE IN CRIMINAL JUSTICE

This program requires a total of 80 semester hours of college credit. 68 hours must be taken through ESI unless credit is awarded for an equivalent course taken at another accredited institution, or student successfully tests out of a course.

CERTIFIED PROTECTION SPECIALIST, CPS

This program is an integrated academic and practical training curriculum consisting of the Home Study and Resident Training in executive protection. The program has a special emphasis on training international protection specialists, civil police, and military personnel in the principles of personal protection. The career objective of this training is to prepare the ESI graduate for a professional occupation in executive and dignitary protection. Other career alternatives include executive protection chauffeur, courier services, hotel and casino security, industrial and private estate protection.

The present Advanced Executive Protection Program consists of the 450-hour Home Study and the 15-Day (150 hours) Resident Training in Aspen. The Home Study is a home correspondent lesson/test program which is structured in such a way as to allow the student to study at his own pace.

Considered as a single curriculum, the Advanced Executive Protection Program consists of an intensive 600 hours of study in the field of executive security and requires on the average a year to compete. Enrollment in the Advanced Executive Protection Program is begun with the Home Study prior to arrival for the Resident Training.

Academic components of Home Study include: Principles of Protection, Electronic Security, Pro-files of Terrorism & Violence, Bomb Search & Identification, Human Behavior & Dangerousness, First Respondent Medicine, Fundaments of Defensive Shooting, Social Relationships & Manners, and Executive Protection Driving.

ESI offers an Associate Of Applied Science Degree in Criminal Justice with an Area of Emphasis in Security and Investigation.

ESI's Home Study and Resident Training courses are approved by the Colorado Department of Higher Education, Division of Private Occupational Schools, for college credit, and are so noted in this catalog. Each course is listed with its clock hours and the corresponding semester credit hours.

EXECUTIVE PROTECTION 15-DAY PROGRAM

This program is designed to provide professional protection specialists with a wide range of skills to enter into careers in executive protection. Students who successfully complete the course will be certified by ESI and may elect to have college credit for the program. In order to achieve Rank Level 1, ESI graduates must complete the Home Study Program as well as the 15-day Resident Program.

Includes: Executive Protection Driving; Defensive Shooting Tactics; Unarmed Defensive Tactics; Bomb Search & Identification; First Respondent Medicine; Electronic Security; Human Behavior & Dangerousness; Profiles of Terrorism; and Principles of Protection. The price of the program includes all necessary equipment and ammunition.

ESI also offers a number of Certificate Programs. These programs are particularly useful to those students who may choose not to pursue a college degree, or who already have a degree but wish to upgrade their educational and training skills, or who are enrolled in a Criminal Justice program with another school but wish to enroll in an ESI program for college credit. Those individuals who enroll in an ESI Certificate Program and successfully complete it are awarded either a Certified Protection Specialist, CPS or Certified Investigation Specialist, CIS.

CERTIFICATE PROGRAMS:
- Advanced Executive Protection
- Intelligence Gathering and Investigation
- Maritime and Yacht Security
- Hotel, Resort, and Cruise Line Casino Security
- Personal Protection/Security Operations

To help employ their students, the Aspen based corporation also operates ESI Protective Services. A security firm which provides investigation and protection services. ESI Protective Services provides corporations, attorneys, public agencies, and individuals with trained and competent investigators and executive protection agents, offering a wide variety of services.

ESI has graduated about 1,500 students who work as:
- Actively working executive protection agents and protection teams
- Corporate security managers responsible for protecting their company executives
- Training managers responsible for the training of protection agents and teams
- Security and limousine companies providing executive protection services
- Executives and their families who need to know their roles in the protection function
- Police departments, the U.S. Marshals Service, and all government agencies responsible for providing protection to government employees and private individuals
- Students involved in criminal justice and private security programs
- Individuals considering a career in the executive protection field

THE SECOND SCHOOL OF NOTE IS:
Executive Protection Institute
Arcadia Manor, Route 2 Box 3645
Berryville, VA 22611

This institution is run by one Dr. Richard W. Kobetz, C.S.T. Dr. Kobetz is quite well known, some of his accomplishments include:
- Creator of the training concept of the Personal Protection Specialist (P.P.S.) which emphasizes planning and advance work to avoid confrontation
- One of the pioneers in the development of the Tactics and Negotiation Techniques (T.M.T.) response to hostage-taking, training thousands of personnel world-wide on these techniques
- Practical working experience from special agent to director of security and patrolman to Chief of Police
- Served on numerous commissions including: The U.S. Task Force on Disorders and Terrorism, the Joint Criminal Justice Standards
- Committee of the Institute of Judicial Administration, and The American Bar Association
- Retired Commanding Officer of the Chicago Police Department
- with career service in a variety of operational "street units"
- Served as a delegate to INTERPOL
- Author of ten books and dozens of chapters, articles and monographs on security and police topics

The main program offered by EPI is called **Providing Executive Protection.**

This training program offers seven (7) intensive days of over 100 hours of instruction, with a minimum of theory and an emphasis upon practical hands-on learning and realistic exercises. Each student participates in learning sophisticated, innovative skills and techniques pertaining to personal performance on protective assignments.

As Dr. Kobetz says, "All the Providing Executive Protection programs begin in Winchester, Virginia. We conduct our classes at the largest privately operated law enforcement and security training facility in the world, located in the Shenandoah Valley of Virginia, near Washington, DC. Our resources include accommodations, classrooms, driving tracks, gymnasiums, training grounds and weapons ranges at North Mountain Pines Training Center, the Executive Protection Institute, Arcadia Manor and Farms, and various public and private facilities throughout the vicinity. Lodging and training locations change frequently during the program in conjunction with practical exercises and instructional requirements for most interesting and realistic experiences throughout the three-state area.

Our program is the first and only one being offered to revolutionize the traditional "bodyguard" position to one of Personal Protection Specialist (P.P.S.). The impact upon the field has been obvious and gratifying. We are considered the premier program, because we establish the standards and continue to improve upon them. The successful completion of this course is now included within many job descriptions for protective positions. We are often imitated – but never duplicated.

Shenandoah University in Winchester, Virginia, will award ten Continuing Education Units (C.E.U. Credits) for attendance at this program upon application. In addition, three college credit hours may be applied for upon submission of a paper after successful completion of this program. Shenandoah University is a fully accredited, private school, founded in 1875 and offering a broad liberal arts program at both the undergraduate and graduate level."

EPI also offers training programs and seminars in physical security systems design, corporate aviation security, executive/VIP protection, yacht and maritime security and so on in cities from Orlando, Florida to Los Angeles, California.

Most seminars range in length from 2–7 days and are quite reasonably priced.

EPI will also provide custom designed training courses at their facilities or on-site in such areas as counter terrorism, corporate counter espionage, hostage negotiations, protective driving, shooting, security awareness, travel security, and so on.

Graduates of their programs have included practitioners with major international corporations, private families, security, law enforcement, military and government agencies, involved with the protection of:

Celebrities, corporate executives, governors, mayors, military commanders, politicians, presidents, religious leaders, royalty, US secretarial cabinet members, VIP's, witnesses, and world leaders.

THE INTERNATIONAL BODYGUARD ASSOCIATION
Rt. 3, Box 639
Brighton, TN 38011

The IBA is a professional association for persons with at least one year of experience with a federal, state or local government agency or for a private firm as a protective service specialist.

The Association is dedicated to "advancing the knowledge of the protective service agent; to maintain high standards and efforts, to promote efficiency of protective service agents and the services they perform, to aid in the establishment of effective security programs, and to emphasize a professional approach to the bodyguard function."

They publish an annual directory of members to provide an instant reference tool of who to contact the world over, offer a professional certification program, a home study course and 3 day seminars on the art of Providing Protective Services.

They also offer a book on the same subject matter.

The head of the Association has been providing personal protection for US and foreign dignitaries, military officials, celebrities, as well as physical protection for families, parties, conferences homes and offices since 1967.

He has a TOP SECRET government clearance, a Ph.D. in Criminology, M.S in Forensic Sciences and a BA. in Public Administration, has taught various college and police courses as well as special operations to SWAT teams, the army, US Navy, Coast Guard and is certified by the FBI as an instructor in various fields.

Yearly membership is $35 (plus a $10 sign-up fee). If you do not meet the minimum requirements you can join as an associate member.

PROVIDING EXECUTIVE PROTECTION
0-9628411-0-2

PROVIDING EXECUTIVE PROTECTION, Executive Protection Institute, Arcadia Manor and Farms, Berryville, VA 22611, hard cover, 280 pages and includes photographs, charts, illustrations, bibliography, professional resource list and index. A definitive text on a topic of current interest. Price is $29.00 U.S. plus $3.00 domestic postage; $6.00 per copy for Canada and Mexico; $8.00 per copy for all other countries.

Edited by Dr. Richard W. Kobetz, this book is written by the leading authorities practicing in the field. A thorough approach to the subject is developed through such chapters as: Appearance and Dress; Dining, Etiquette, and Protocol; Advance Work, Travel, and Hotel Security; Team Dynamics: Working Together, Working Smart; Defense Against Terrorist Tactics; Operational Intelligence: Profiling Your Principal; Stress and the Personal Protection Specialist; Manners and Mannerisms for the Personal Protection Specialist; Threat Assessment in Person Protection; Legal Considerations in the Use of Force; Terrorism: The Female Dimension; Advance Work, Travel, and Hotel Security; A Perspective on Personal Protection; Portable Protection Technology; Establishing a Command Post; An Introduction to Providing Protective Services; Techniques and Principles of Protections: Close Range; Emergency Medical Care; Interviewing Unwanted Visitors; Defensive Driving Techniques; An Executive's Guide to Security Construction Projects.

This book is a must for personnel involved in personal protection, those who would like to be involved and for anyone interested in how it is done for their own safety. Favorable comments on the book have been quoted from: Dr. Henry A. Kissinger, former Secretary of State and Chairman of Kissinger and Associates, Inc.; Mr. Winthrop P. Rockefeller, noted Businessman and Philanthropist; Honorable R. Roy McMurtry, Q.C., Associate Chief Justice, Ontario, and former Canadian Ambassador to Great Britain and Attorney General for the Province of Ontario; Ambassador L. Paul Bremer, III, former U.S. Ambassador-at-Large for Counter-Terrorism.

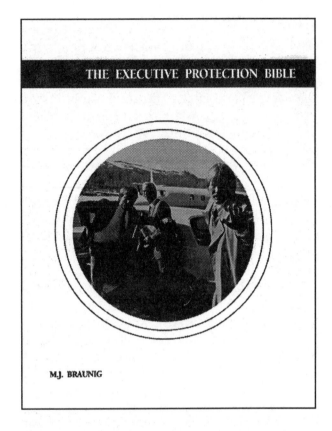

THE EXECUTIVE PROTECTION BIBLE

M.J. BRAUNIG

EXECUTIVE PROTECTION BIBLE
(Available from ESI or Intelligence Incorporated)

ESI checks in with a large format, *600 page* treatment of the field entitled, THE EXECUTIVE PROTECTION BIBLE. This extremely comprehensive work includes all aspects of guarding bodies from evasive driving to successful business management.

Chapter Titles Include:
- Executive Protection – the players and their roles
- Security Objectives – prevention of intentional and unintentional injuries
- The Threat – targeting the client
- Threat Assessment – threat modeling
- Intelligence Sources – in-house files
- Protective Details – organization responsibilities – command post – formations
- Advances – Advancing hotels, special events, routes, transportation

- Foreign Advances – passports, visas, shots, customs, logistics
- Physical Security – perimeter & interior
- Electronic Security – intrusion detection-electronic surveillance countermeasures
- Vehicle and Driving Security – convoys, evasive maneuvers, armoring
- Bombs and Bomb Incident Management – threats, searches, evacuations
- Corporate Executive Protection – protecting corporate clients – working relationships
- Protecting Executives Abroad – special problems and risks
- Crisis Management – crisis management teams
- More Crisis Management – extortion-kidnapping-hostage taking-hostage negotiations
- Crisis Survival – survival skills
- Violent Employees in the workplace –behavioral clues, screening, terminations
- Crowds, Cranks and Stalkers – celebrity and domestic stalkers - handling cranks
- Special Event Security – liability factors access control - security factors
- Women As Protectors – female agents
- Defensive Weapons – handgun features and recommendations
- Unarmed Defensive Techniques – control and weapons disarms techniques
- First Respondent Medicine for the protective agent – responses to most likely medical incidents
- Executive Protection Protocol – dress, communication, relationships
- Legal Aspects of the Agent's Job – liabilities, deadly force, negligence
- Working in the Industry – resumes, interviews, working tools

THE EXECUTIVE PROTECTION BIBLE is 600 pages of how-to, intensely applicable, up-to-date information that you can use immediately. It contains material not seen before in print (outside the US Secret Service) about the serious business of providing protection to dignitaries, celebrities, corporate executives and private individuals. It is comprehensive in covering all aspects of executive protection .

DEAD CLIENTS DON'T PAY, Leroy Thompson, Paladin Press. "Basically the BG's assignments will break down into two categories: protection of a client's physical person or protection of an area containing the client. Within these broad categories, assignments can be broken down further into protection against kidnapping, protection against assassination, protection from intruders and protection of an area."

A brief outline of a bodyguard's duties. Not nearly as detailed as the above books, too much on choosing a weapon and too little hands-on training.

DEAD CLIENTS DON'T PAY
ISBN 0-87364-287-2

HUNTING BODIES

In an allied field,
**THE NATIONAL INSTITUTE OF BAIL
ENFORCEMENT OFFICERS**
POB 6757
West Palm Beach, FL 33405

offers 2–3 days seminars in the art of bounty hunting. The courses are taught by full time "professional bail enforcement agents" and prepare graduates to get arrest contacts, network nationally, locate and arrest criminal fugitives and, of course, collect arrest fees. Specifically:

• Surveillance
• Tracking and arresting
• Cross border operations
• The business of bounty hunting
• Weapons use
• Looking for Judas
• State and federal laws
• Criminal styles of flight
• "And much more"

All graduates are certified and eligible to join the National Association of Bail Enforcement Agents.

BOUNTY HUNTER by Bob Burton and published by Paladin Press provides an overview of the bail-arrest profession along with specific views of certain professionals. It's a nice starting point for anyone interested in the field from an academic standpoint.

The author also takes great care to point out that this is simply a framework of information from which to work and one must take into account such minor details as:

Do you have the necessary skills?

Have you considered the possibility of being seriously hurt?

Do you have the capability of dealing with members of all strata of society in a positive way?

BOUNTY HUNTER ISBN 0-87364-296-1

All these factors must be taken into consideration before you open yourself to the possibility of injury, ridicule and possible legal action. The author even warns, "Don't expect to be nominated head of the Chamber of Commerce of your local city. The word 'bounty hunter' is laden with colorful and dubious associations. Hell, even your mom will wonder."

An even-handed glance at the laws, tools and tricks of the trade and some very legitimate advice for the would be fugitive chaser.

As Mr. Burton says, "best of luck and stay off the skyline."

COUNTER INTELLIGENCE

The upswing in telephone and FAX tapping has necessitated the development of answer generation of countermeasures. In order to decide what is correct for your particular situation you first must establish a threat level.

Who wants what you have?

If it's a jealous "significant other" or in-house business rival the chances of eliminating the threat are pretty good.

If it's the FBI, CIA, or even the local cops, odds are pretty bad...

Local phone surveillance is usually accomplished with some variation of an automatic recorder starter (as sold by every spy shop in the world as well as Radio Shack), VOX triggered recorder or a transmitter that sends the audio a few hundred feet to a waiting receiver/recorder.

Law enforcement (authorized) taps tend to be installed with the cooperation of the local phone company, making them quite hard to ferret out without a "friendly" lineman, although most are <u>not</u> placed at the central office, contrary to popular belief.

In fact most phone companies have become quite careful about whom they install taps for, or even give out subscriber information to. After all their revenue comes, not from the police department, but from customers and as a public utility they do have people to answer to and a number of rather unpleasant lawsuits have slid policy away from illegal or even semi-legal surveillance on their part.

Now the attitude is more, "you gotta a warrant? Okay, here's a map, you put in the stuff."

There are three major choices if you suspect you are a victim of audio intrusion:

1. Hire a competent countermeasures consultant to "sweep" your rooms and your phone lines. The key word here is "competent". This is a difficult and demanding task and the simple application of a commercial "debugging" unit will miss many taps. This is fairly expensive and only guarantees the viability of the line at the time of the search. It will not help if anything is installed five minutes later.

2. Do it yourself. It is possible, with the right guide and some basic equipment to find *most* in-place taps. Like everything else in life you get what you pay for: simple equipment finds simple taps, expensive equipment finds professional taps. The good news here is that after the initial investment you can repeat the search procedures as often as security dictates.

3. Install tap defeating equipment to monitor the line in question and provide some basic security.

Let's look at number 3 first, no $49 mail order gimmick with a red and a green light is going to show any tap other than someone lifting an extension phone. There is no such thing as free lunch.

A few units on the market do provide some protection by monitoring the line voltage (most taps affect this measurement to some degree), and balancing the line while lowering he loop voltage to the point where auto recorder starters will not be able to sense the change in voltage when a phone is lifted off hook.

Being totally honest here, as is my wont, I will tell you that it is not as easy to drop the voltage as it was in years past, before electronic switching systems became the standard.

A good balancer will still work and provide a degree of protection to any system.

Some balancers go a step further, flooding the line with static "white noise" when the phone is in use. Any tap or recorder near the target gets the cover noise.

Sounds good in theory, but any eavesdropper worth his salt knows that a simple rf choke, or audio filter will remove the masking static, leaving clear conversation behind.

White noise units are also frowned upon by the phone company as the impetuous of cleaning up the "dirty" line falls on their equipment, but there have been few actual prosecutions.

Good line balancers will decrease the range of series taps (those that depend on the telephone line for their power) to a serious degree, throw the frequency off on non-crystal controlled transmitters and generally make life tough for the average tap.

It's also a good idea to monitor line voltage, (most units have a display showing the voltage) as many taps cause a drop in voltage. Minor fluctuations are normal, but a drop of several volts indicates a problem.

A good balancer will stop most amateur, or even semi-professional recorder starters. This instantly cuts out about 75% of all tapping attempts.

The main problem lies in complacency – an inexpensive line minder does not take the place of a good search, it simply acts as a first barrier to frustrate or alert the user to a variety of tapping techniques.

Here's a tip, if you use a balancer or other tap defeating equipment *don't use it* except on sensitive calls. If you use it all the time and the eavesdroppers know you are making calls and their equipment isn't recording anything they will probably become a trifle suspicious and look for another way to penetrate your security.

UNITS

The best voltage adjuster/tap stopper I tested is the TAPOUT AUTOMATIC TAP STOPPER from Intelligence Incorporated. This unit will take the voltage as low as possible while allowing the telco equipment to function. This alone stops auto-recorder starters, and most phone-dependent line taps.

The TAPOUT also shows the line voltage, both on and off hook and loads the wire with electronic noise while the phone is *on hook*. This is perfectly legal and effectively beats infinity transmitters, X-phones, room mics (that utilize the phone line), hook switch defeats, VOX recorders and a number of other crafty tricks.

A very efficient first line of defense, well worth the money.

A higher priced, but unique defeater comes from Defense Systems Group. The CMS balances the voltage, alerts the user to any rf (from a tap/transmitter) in the area, and then does something no other unit around can claim.

The CMS amplifies the audio when the line is *on hook*. The unit can be connected to most tape recorders via the remote jack. When this is accomplished the recorder will turn on at the slightest noise and record the audio.

I tested this unit with both series and parallel taps, a lineman's handset, several infinity transmitters and a variety of other taps.

In every case the unit caught the installation by "hearing" the clicks that resulted when any of the devices were connected to the line. The recorder's tape counter was zeroed, so any positive reading meant it sensed audio and turned on.

Most eavesdroppers will make a call to make certain their tap is functioning, the catches this quite nicely. It also grabs any other audio on the line.

What would be on your line when the phone is not in use?

A good question. While testing this appliance I connected it across a neighbor's terminals, He is (or was in this case) a doctor who specialized in Medicare patients. He was also (without his knowledge) under investigation for billing fraud.

I have a nice tape of the gentlemen from the FBI setting up their taps and talking on the "dead" phone line...

No I didn't tell him. I like the FBI just fine, and no doubt they hold me in high regard, but I have this misplaced fear of hearing the words, "anything you say may be used against you in a court of law..."

Just a personal hang-up.

About 15 years ago some early countermeasure's folk marketed a telephone analyzer unit that claimed to be the best tap finder in the world. The idea was quite unique – the unit isolated the building's wiring from the incoming telco lines, sent tones and current into the in-house wiring and then compared the results to the originals.

Any difference meant a suspect wire.

The unit was priced about $15,000 and a bit ahead of the technology of the time.

SECURITYCALL POB 33194, Los Gatos, Ca, 95031 offers a $400 "wiretap detector alarm system" designed for both phone and fax lines. The SC 1100 contains a microprocessor that measures line "status" and then makes constant, real-time comparisons in order to alert the user to any change that might indicate a tap.

It accomplishes this by placing small "slaves" on each wire and periodically conducting a 5 second test to see if any one of 8 measurements (voltage, current, resistance, etc.) disagrees with the norm.

If any measurement is outside of the parameters the line should be physically checked for a tap.

Guess what? It works!

The concept is limited because the lines *must* be clean when the unit is installed or it will consider the altered readings as normal. It only works from the point where the telco lines enter the building, it does not look backwards into the phone company's wiring. This means it can miss a tap attached to the outside wiring, the pole, a B box or any remote location.

Unless, of course, you install it at an outside point.

The good news is that it works quite well, thank you, clearly indicating every tap I applied after the initial set up.

The SC was not designed specially for people in our line of work – rather it is sold to major corporations so they can legally guarantee the security of in-house information.

If a client accuses the corporation of spilling the confidential beans, they simply show the box and say, "hey, it wasn't us pal, nothing on our lines."

SECURITYCALL in-place computer.

The one across the board failing of all counter measures and telephone sweep units, even $10,000 TDRs is the fact they have trouble finding what are the most common law enforcement, government and top private spy taps; bridges, slaves and extension loops.

These devices are the stock in trade of all legally oriented surveillance manufacturers and can be installed at any appearance point all the way to the central office. This fact alone makes them nearly impossible to prove or disprove their existence.

When the cops/narcs/feds/or your ex-wife's lover, the KGB colonel, rents an apartment at the second B box of your loop and sets up anything from a simple extension phone to a slave, you just ain't gonna know it.

Until now.

An engineer has recently patented a device, the COMSEC C3 which will indicate the presence of any of these taps up to, and including, those placed at the central office.

It does this by, well, "listening" to the capacitance of the line in question every time you hang up after a call. If there is any sort of bridge or slave on the line, it too will "hang up", say 30 seconds later.

This action creates a change in the line conditions that the COMSEC will indicate.

The unit protects one line and should remain on-line at all times. Coupled with regularly scheduled sweeps or a good anti-tap unit the COMSEC will protect your phone, FAX or computer lines to a degree never before possible.

Intelligence Inc., other dealers $449.

SWEEP AND SEARCH GEAR

A number of new devices have recently appeared on the market for finding bugs and taps. I'm not going to duplicate the work done in BOOK II HOW TO GET ANYTHING ON ANYBODY, but rather cover changes since it was published.

Having said that, let me say this about that – most of the gear and all of the techniques covered therein is still available and still works. Audiotel sells updated versions of their SCNALOCK receiver, their BROOM non-linear junction detector and a new handheld bug finder.

ISA has upgraded and improved their line as has TSA and other names in the counter surveillance field. This is basically a dog eat dog world – if a surveillance or counter measures manufacturer has been in business for 10 years or more their stuff is going to do pretty much what they say it will do. This particular universe is too small for phonies and people who don't want the word to get around.

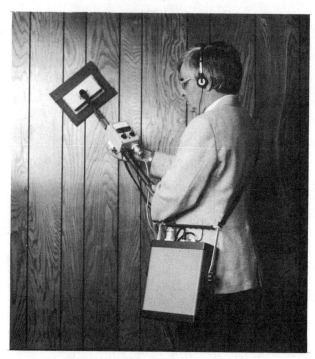

A non-linear junction detector in action.

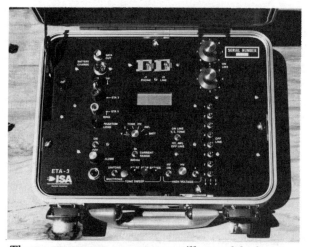

The ISA TELEPHONE ANALYZER is still one of the best ways to analyze telephone instruments.

A couple of high end bug finders have recently debuted. CSI offers a $4500 unit that consists of a special tone source, an ICOM communications receiver and a computer controller.

The tone generator is placed in the room to be swept and the computer/receiver energized.

The controller steps the ICOM through every available frequency and modulation while "listening" for the signal from its generator.

If it finds the signal it means that a transmitter is operating in the area. The unit will sweep a typical room in about 1/2 an hour.

This is a fairly foolproof concept, if coupled with complete search procedures for carrier current, IR and subcarrier devices gives a high probability of safety.

One weakness is the fact that the tone is audible which means it will alert anyone listening that something unusual is taking place in the target area. Because the device needs an exact match on the tone it will not find any bug that scrambles its signal.

What may just be the ultimate in countermeasures gear has been developed by Research Electronics Incorporated. REI has long been known for effective counter measures gear, their chief designer engineer used to be employed by our old friends at AID designing toys for the law enforcement community.

The OSCOR (OMNI SPECTRAL CORRELATOR) is a portable microcomputer controlled scanning spectral correlator that monitors audio (20 Hz – 15 KHz), RF and microwave signals (10 KHz – 3000 MHz), and infrared signals. It uses passive sound pattern matching to recognize surveillance devices.

OSCOR can be used in an auto mode where it continuously scans all bands for acoustic pattern correlation and will set off either a visual or audible alarm if it detects the presence of a surveillance device.

In non-techie terms a "fingerprint" of the area is taken and used as a reference signal that is then compared with received audio. In a typical room many passive acoustic signals such as talking, air conditioning, music, etc., exist. When OSCOR senses the same information on both the reference and received channels it automatically issues a threat alert warning.

The unit can also be operated in a manual mode where it provides a variety of functions that have previously only been possible by combining a number of expensive pieces of equipment including a spectrum analyzer, surveillance receiver, carrier current detector, telephone analyzer, chart recorder and so on.

The unit is driven by a software "key" allowing for easy system updating and will analyze and graphically correlate area, telephone or unknown wire audio showing an averaged bargraph and threat level indicator.

It will sweep through all bands in several bandwidths and refresh rates using various intermediate frequency receive sections, filters and demodulators. Basically OSCOR will find:

- FM, AM, microwave RF signals utilizing either wide or narrow bandwidths.
- Subcarrier bugs/taps
- Carrier current units using room or phone wiring
- IR or laser on-premise or off premise devices
- Tape recorders
- Audio in telephones, on telco lines or other wiring
- Basically anything putting room audio where it should not be.

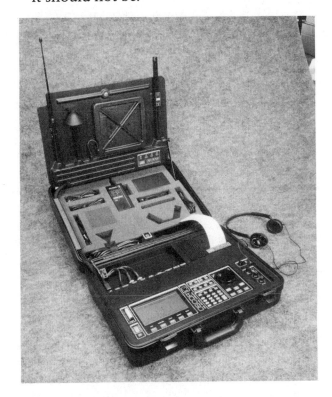

OSCOR in all its glory...

An enclosed chart recorder allows you to keep a permanent record of any signals you encounter for future comparison.

There are also plans to provide the unit with a telephone jack so it can be left in an area that needs protection in the auto mode and the operator can call in and run manual tests without revisiting the actual premises.

An amazing unit for either counter measures people who perform sweeps or for a high level of client threat protection. A bit over $12,000 from REI or Intelligence Incorporated.

On the low end of the scale we have several contestants. The first is the MODEL 262 COUNTERSURVEILLANCE DETECTION SYSTEM from Sheffield Electronics. This unit is an attempt to fill a number of sweep slots in a VLP (very low priced) unit.

The 262 will find RF transmitters ranging in frequency from 4 MHz to 2.1 GHz+, indicating them by a large meter. The sensitivity is adjustable to compensate for ambient radio signals and the unit will demodulate the signal (thru headphones) so you can check out the audio component of any suspect signal.

The 262 has a wider frequency range than most low priced units, I found the sensitivity to be better than that of many higher priced units. The designer, Mr. Arrington, has included an input so it is possible to detect subcarrier transmitters if you have an FM receiver that can have its multiplex output routed to the 262.

It also does a good job of finding low frequency carrier current bugs by simply bringing the antenna near the building's wiring.

A high gain microphone amplifier is included so you can trace audio leaks and the meter can be switched over to a volt meter mode allowing basic telephone line measurements. A nice pictorial chart of possible meter readings for various types of taps is included.

All good stuff and it sells for $695.

My complaints are that the unit does not include (at this time) a microphone to use with the amplifier, earphones (Sheffield suggest you buy from, hey, my pals at Radio Shack!) and the overall technology is fairly 1980's.

That is to say, mostly discrete components, a number of modular circuit blocks tied together, (it uses three batteries, one of which expires faster than the other two because they power different circuits).

Yeah, I know, everybody is a critic. The unit does work and is priced at about the same level as were early one transistor field strength meters that couldn't find a bug with both hands.

You _will_ see this unit at double the price in a number of catalogs – Sheffield will not discount to dealers (again to keep the price as low as possible) so anyone who wants to sell it has to add 50-100% markup to make a profit.

The SHEFFIELD 262.

Seek Electronics has taken many of the concepts that went into REI's CPM 600, one of the best, if not the best, lower priced counter measures units around for the last few years and brought them into the next decade with a brand spanking new unit (I've just tested the first prototype) called the CSR-1.

A quick exam of the circuitry shows a definite improvement over the front end RF section used in the 600 giving the CSR-1 an immediate advantage in upper frequency detection and probably in sensitivity. Seek claims 3 GHz, as the magic figure. I'm not a doubter, but did not have the equipment to actually verify the number.

This unit will also detect infrared incoming (laser readers) or outgoing (IR bugs) and does a fine job on carrier current units using a special probe which simply has to be brought near an electrical outlet or other wiring to demodulate the burried carrier current signal.

The engineer who designed the unit tried it against carrier current telephone (such as the ever popular Brady units) and discovered they are set on frequencies so low that most carrier current detectors will not find them.

He promptly redesigned the unit so it would go low enough to find these signals.

A bar graph for signal strength, sensitivity adjustment, headphones/speaker for demodulating, make the CSR-1 definitely one of the best, if not the best, lower priced pieces of counter measures equipment around.

Seek does not sell retail, Intelligence Inc. stocks the CSR-1 as will a number of other dealers in the near future.

Note that the Seek unit as well as many other RF detectors will not find sub-carrier transmitters because they used a phase locked loop and are not tunable.

On the other hand there are damn few SC bugs out there (unless, of course you people all go out and buy the ones I'm... Never mind.)

The CSR-1 comes complete with all ancillary probes, headphones and so on, unlike many units that start cheap and then demand that you buy one of these and two those to make everything work like God intended it to.

Possibly the best low-priced counter measures unit available. A bargain at about $1300 from Intelligence Inc.

Aegis Research, a counter measures firm run by a couple of electronics engineers who have put in a number of dues-years designing things I like.

And you should.

They have two items of note for this chapter – the PROSWEEP Counter Surveillance System and the PASS Personal Counter Surveillance Monitor.

Both these units are very compact, almost belying their effectiveness. Constructed in heavy duty aluminum alloy housing both units utilize the latest in microstipline circuitry and surface mounted components.

The PASS is a pocket sized CS monitor designed to guard against bugs, body wires, video transmitters and pulsed tracking transmitters. It is fully self-contained and designed for non-technical person operation.

An LED readout gives signal strength and a vibrator allows you to stash the unit in your pocket (well, a big pocket, maybe a fanny pack). It will detect AM, FM and a number of unusually modulated transmitters. Earphones allow the confirmation of strange signals.

No "personal monitor" will successfully compete against a full blown spectrum analyzer or $5,000 surveillance receiver, but if you have ever wondered if that nice man you met at the sports bar who now seems to be overly interested in your tax return is wearing a body wire...

This is the most realistic, nicest unit of its type I've had the privilege of testing...

The PROSWEEP is a handheld counter surveillance system intended for both "personal and professional" sweep applications. Like the SEEK and the REI it employs a "wand" type probe antenna for wide band RF detection.

The PS gives the operator a sweep mode for those afternoon quickie searches, a demodulator let's you hear the audio, signal strength is shown by both audio and visual indicators and the basic, quite inexpensive, I might add, PROSWEEP can be expanded to grab IR signals, VLF carrier current devices or audio.

Top end is 2.5 GHz, 40 dB RF gain factor.

No cheap plastic cases, solid connectors and controls, latest electronics. Good stuff, well made, does what it says it will.

Consider your threat level, is it better to have a $1,000 bug detector that will find *most* transmitters and can be used as often as needed, or should you take the grand and spend it on two professional sweeps to cover both corporate board meetings that year?

If you are considering the purchase of sweep equipment and you have the chance to test before buying first start with a cordless telephone as a "bug". If it can't find what is a veritable power house of RF, how is it going to find a tiny, 8 milliwatt bug?

Next try it on a low power Micro/Cony/Ruby/ bug and see at what range detection actually transpires.

Ideally you would then take a signal generator and test range against frequency, building up to the top end of the spectrum.

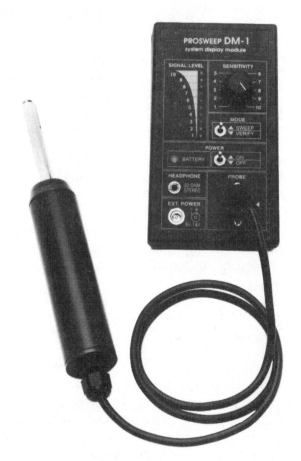

Ageis Research's fine units.

No signal generator? Aegis Research sells a 1.6 GHz signal source that is a handy way to test both equipment and people who tell you they can find secret stealers for rather large amounts of money...

Note the judicious use of the word "if" in the above suggestion. Most dealers do not allow the return of counter measures equipment after purchase (or, for that matter, surveillance equipment) because many customers feel the need to use the goodies only once.

WRITTEN MATERIALS

HANDS-ON COUNTERMEASURES, Lee Lapin, Intelligence Incorporated. $24.95 ($5.00 shipping and handling per order). One of my favorite writers, this is Lee hard and fast manual for law enforcement personnel government agencies and those civilians with a legitimate use for state-of-the-art electronic eavesdropping methods.

A stand-alone guide for conducting your own countermeasure sweeps, installing the best preventative measures. Step-by-step instructions for analyzing telephone wiring and equipment with simple tools (a VOM) or going the whole route with TDR's and professional analyzers.

Beginner or pro this manual will act as a repeat reference guide and instruction manual.

TELEPHONE EAVESDROPPING AND DETECTION. Taylor Hill Publishing Company, POB 1815, Houston TX 77404 or Intelligence Incorporated. Suppose you took one of the only college instructors in the fine art of telephone surveillance and stopping same, put him with an electronics engineer co-writer and several ancillary tech types – you know, VP's from Bell Tel, lineman, countermeasures folk, and your average ruffian.

A thick, hard cover book complete with wiring diagrams, line measurements, how to isolate any type of tap (with or without a friend in the phone company), remove it, lie to it or zap it off the face of the earth.

Yeah I know it's expensive but this book stands alone.

LOW TECH COUNTER SURVEILLANCE MEASURES

Like most things in life, the amount of real security you have depends heavily on how much money you wish to spend to insure same.

However, also like many things in life, there are some shortcuts that depend on smarts instead of dollars. Let's look at some...

We all like to get involved with "my scrambler is bigger than your scrambler" discussions when considering information protection or brag about the Maxwell Smart "quiet room" we are just about to build in the center of the living room, but I would estimate 80% of surveillance or information attacks are launched at a level that really does NOT require heavy capital expenditure to defeat.

In fact a rather mundane mixture of common sense and creativity, two qualities you all possess or you wouldn't be reading this sterling publication, can effectively minimize any risk factor.

Here are some simple tips to lower your compromise cholesterol:

1. Remember cellular phones can and are intercepted by scanner buffs and snoops all the time (pretty funny when the couple that kidnapped and killed the Exxon official a while ago set up the meet with the FBI on a cellular so they couldn't "be tapped or followed", maybe they'll get this book in prison...).

DON'T say sensitive stuff on a cellular. If you have to, invest in a scrambler that can be installed at the switch and on your mobile unit. Call your local wireline and non-wireline company to see if they are cooperating in this program.

Buy (or lease) one Cycomm scrambler and use one of the pay-by-the-minute scramble sources I've listed.

2. Wireless phones can be easily and legally monitored at distances of a half mile by anyone with a $65 receiver and a gain antenna. There are several 900 MHz scrambled wireless phones available at this time, think about investing in one.

3. Fax messages can be intercepted by experts (or anyone with $ and a nose for news) BUT most faxes are compromised at the receiving end because they are located in an unsecured area where other employees or visitors can see the hard copy.

Secure your fax in a safe location, hopefully under lock and key. If this is not possible at least one company makes a fax that prints out "invisible" messages until they are treated by the intended receiver.

4. Landline telephones are compromised very easily, thank you, by $25 Radio Shack drop out recorders. Make occasional physical searches on your line, and at least do minimal VOM line characteristic recordings. Tap your own line with an auto-start tape recorder to see if suspicious noises and calls appear after hours that would indicate someone was installing and testing a phone tap.

Use pay phones for important calls BUT not the one nearest to your house or place of business. They can be, and are, tapped just as easily as are private phones. For incoming calls use call forwarding from a buried phone (at a mail drop, answering service or friend's house) or a call diverter to call you at another location.

Change your location often and/or scramble the second part of the call that actually comes down your line from the diverter.

Use a 0-700 # which you can instantly route to any number you wish. Change locations often or route it to a forwarder/scrambler combination before the final leg to your wire.

By the way, 0-700 numbers also defeat incoming caller ID traces and do not leave a record on the callers bill of your actual number or location.

6. Defeat out-going caller ID by using a Logos box ($300+) that uses three way calling to avoid sending out the identifying tones, call from a phone booth, the Stealth anti-ID device or use one of the 900 number, $2.00 a minute, private services.

7. Many answering machines can be defeated by a single touch tone, even top end models use a 3 digit guard that can be hacked in a few minutes. Use voice mail with a 5+ digit security code or rent a voice mail (look in the yellow pages) from a commercial service.

Don't use your real name, give the number and code out only to appropriate people and use the service as a message drop.

Remember there is a brand new device on the market that, for a minor outlay (in this case about $120 worth of minor outlay) will crack any answering machine using a 1-3 digit coding system.

8. Beat mail covers by using a drop NOT IN YOUR NAME, do not file change of address cards.

9. Beat mail interception by using a simple book code; you and other party agree on the same–same book (don't use the Bible, or the latest New York Times Best Seller or Patriot Games or anything else as obvious) then simply use a page and word count to pinpoint the words in your message.

Completely random, cannot be cracked without the book key; and yes I suppose a hundred Crays all cracking at once could find the book, but if you're in that much trouble take this book back to the library immediately and forget my name.

10. Reach over and unplug your phone when you are having a sensitive conversation in the room to kill most infinity transmitters. Run masking noise, preferably human voices or random sounds in the human speech frequency range (not running water or music) on top of and over your in-house conversations.

11. AND, OF COURSE THE ULTIMATE SECRET THAT WORKS DAMN NEAR EVERY TIME: KEEP YOUR BIG MOUTH SHUT...

SCRAMBLING

Scrambling, or as it is properly known, encryption, is used to make any communication unintelligible to anyone except the intended listener. It can be applied to phone conversations, FAX, computer or even video.

No encryption method is completely unbreakable, with the possible exception of the chips made by NSA, in their own 91 million dollar chip plant located in a windowless building on the NSA grounds (speculation was that they wanted to build chips that the FBI couldn't decode), or the high level STU III phones offered by Motorola.

Although the latter may be open to NSA cracking, no one seems to be sure.

The "common" high level encryption technique is to turn everything into a digital format and then use DES (digital Encryption Standard) to scramble and unscramble it.

The DES algorithm is quite secure, although a couple of articles have recently been published in code newsletters about the theory and practice of breaking DES (see the section on Newsletters).

It is also a given fact that the government, although they deny it, can break the DES method. The tip off came when the Feds, in the form of the NSA, asked IBM to shorten the algorithm by a couple of digits, which IBM promptly did.

Taking up to much time on those nice Cray super computers guys? Had to make it a bit easier? Cut down on overtime?

First level DES encrypted telephones are sold to the public (trade name SECTEL) by Motorola through their dealer network. This point to point, public key system is secure enough for all but really secret data. Contractors who deal with the federal government on classified mat-

ters are allowed to go up one level in the STU III hierarchy and government agencies get the top level.

Most low end scramblers use frequency inversion, where the available bandwidth is split into one or more frequency bands which are then interchanged. This works only on very low security communications, as it is fairly simple to switch the frequency bands around until you find the original combination.

Books (including DESCRAMBLER SCHEMATICS REVEALED, $10 from Electroman Box 24474, New Orleans, LA 70184) show exactly how to build units that will break these simple encryption schemes.

A number of hobbyist suppliers sell both frequency inversion scramblers and unscramblers. In fact, one can often take a frequency inversion scrambler and change the codes until it "breaks" a target transmission.

There is one type of frequency scrambling that does work. This is known as variable split inversion this technique reshuffles a number of frequency bands around several times per second, according to a user selected code. Quite difficult for anyone but the Feds to intercept.

Cycomm corporation manufactures a number of these units designed to work with both cellular and land line telephones. They currently support about 40 models of cellular phones and the units can be used in various configurations:

- End to end, with a unit on each cellular.
- Cellular to landline with a unit at each end.
- Cellular to MTSO rack at the cellular phone company. This method encrypts every transmission from your phone to the "central office" so it cannot be monitored with cellular phone readers or scanners.
- PBX and normal two wire phones.

- Or you can buy one unit and dial up their 800 phone line to use the equipment at Cycomm's office to decrypt the call and place the outgoing portion on their lines.

They have just come out with a new unit, the HPU 350, which works with Microtek's pocket FLIP PHONE. This is the most popular phone in the world as of this writing. The Cycomm requires no modification to the phone.

The unit has three user selectable levels of security; normal, medium which shifts the frequencies once every 512 milliseconds, or high with shifts occurring every 128 milliseconds.

There is some trade off in quality of transmission at the higher shift frequencies.

Priced in the $700 neighborhood, these scramblers are good for most personal and business calls where you are not concerned with the possibility of heavy, government-type, cracking.

A new type of scrambler is coming onto the market – this is a simple digital unit that uses new chips made by at least one American and one Japanese supplier to perform a one chip analog-to-digital conversion. These chips are employed in the newer 900 MHz cordless phones.

The scrambler simply uses the chip to turns a voice into a series of digits, and then provides an 8-way DIP switch so you can reverse each of the 8 bits outputted from the converter chip.

This provides a user selected code with 64 choices. Once these chips become widespread it is going to be fairly simple to take the same chip, add a dip switch and run a scrambled conversation through the unit, 64 times if necessary, to break the code.

I'd be a little careful about considering these units for any sort of high security application. There is also some speech degradation present, in the unit I tested the call sounded like the speaker had a couple of marbles in his mouth, however, the conversation was intelligible.

The next big move in encryption is going to be the government "suggested" CLIPPER CHIP.

The idea here is to provide privacy on all communications.

Privacy, that is, except for one little fact they don't like to mention…

President Clinton is currently touting the use of a data-encryption standard using an embedded chip in every piece of communication equipment. This dates back to when Congress passed the Computer Security Act of 1987, in response to database and electronic criminal activity. It charged the National Institute of Standards and Technology with the task of creating a national standard for encryption. Unable to devise a process that passed all the tests, the institute turned to the National Security Agency for technical help. Together, the two agencies created the CLIPPER CHIP system.

On April 16, 1993, the Clinton administration revealed the CLIPPER plan. Soon thereafter, a letter landed on the President's desk. Signed by officials of 25 heavyweights in the telecommunications industry – people from Digital Privacy and Security Working Group, Apple Computer, AT&T, Digital Equipment, Hewlett-Packard, IBM, MCI Telecommunications and other companies – complaining about the whole concept.

"While we recognize the importance of authorized national security and law enforcement needs," the letter said, "we believe that there are fundamental privacy and other constitutional rights that must be taken into account when any domestic surveillance scheme is proposed."

The flaw in the CLIPPER plan, you see, is that the National Security Agency would have the power to eavesdrop, since it would control the codes. The agency wants to build in a "trap door" to allow easy monitoring whatever it, or anyone it deems worthy. And if a code were to be broken, stolen or replicated – which the company officials said would almost certainly happen – it could be sold on the black market and used to destroy the entire security system.

The physical chip, was designed by a California-based defense electronics contractor, Mykotronx, which received a classified formula from the National Security Agency (NSA). The company sells chips to the Pentagon and NASA and takes pride in its tamper-resistant features. Even with an electron microscope, no one has yet been able to divine the chip's secrets.

CLIPPER'S algorithm, Skipjack, is a public/private key system much like RSA. Each public key is based on large prime factors and a complex calculation that includes the private key.

Part, or most of the code scheme "lives" in the chip itself.

The CLIPPER chip Washington decided on is an improved version of its aging Data Encryption Standard (DES), which protects sensitive information in everything from crop reports to automatic tellers. Compared with DES, Skipjack's algorithm has twice as many rounds of scrambling and a considerably longer key number (with which the message data is interwoven). There are 72 quadrillion different keys with DES; Skipjack would require an illicit eavesdropper to test 16 million times that many before deciphering a scrambled call.

Except of course, for the "back door" NSA wants left open.

Skipjack has two 40-bit decoder keys that developers of products with encryption are required to place in escrow with two government agencies. These agencies could then be authorized to hand the keys over to law enforcement agencies, if they could show probable cause that someone is committing a crime.

Uncle Sam assures us this is the best-ever data security system and that we have nothing to worry about from government snooping, which just wouldn't happen.

A phone that can't be tapped is every cop's nightmare because anyone from drug traffickers to terrorists would be able to scheme and plot without being overheard, so the NSA has already said they would provide the codes to the FBI and various law enforcement bodies as needed.

As one writer said, "Would you hand over a spare set of house keys to your local police to help them fight crime, trusting that they would never enter your home without good reason?"

Welcome to the CLIPPER chip.

Still, outside observers are hardly convinced that the new chip is secure. Unlike all published encryption formulas, including DES, Skipjack is secret and is being evaluated only by academics with security clearances. Programmers suspect that the NSA has left itself one method to decipher Skipjack's messages – and that hackers or criminals will discover another.

The argument has validity. Cryptography journals publish key codes all the time. Clever computer hackers will hack away relentlessly. However, the argument which I like best is simply that is that secrecy in computer systems just doesn't work anymore.

Too much information is already out.

The better alternative is to use what Motorola already does, a complete Public Key Cryptography system. Invented in 1976, by mathematician Whitfield Diffie and his colleagues at Stanford University, the system combines publicly available decoding algorithms (i.e., the keys) with private digital signatures, creating a very simple, secure and virtually unbreakable system, well except, again by the NSA, but it does make them work for it.

Computer and telecommunications interests overwhelmingly favor the Public Key system. But law enforcement and national security officials are opposed – precisely because it's so difficult to penetrate. Wiretapping and eavesdropping becomes suddenly much more difficult.

Right now the critical privacy protection laws are the Electronic Communications Privacy Act and the Foreign Intelligence Surveillance Act, which, together with several presidential directives, are the core of legal protection for individuals above and beyond the Constitution itself. But the acts are full of legal loopholes to take care of emergencies and national security problems.

Read what you will here.

In fact, the first presidential directive came from Gerald Ford, when he sought domestic surveillance of dissidents and drug users through none other than the National Security Agency.

Marc Rotenberg, Washington director of Computer Professionals for Social Responsibility, a public-interest group that has collected more than 50,000 signatures on an anti-Clipper petition, says, the government has admitted the system could be easily breached by NSA, which wouldn't need a warrant if it made the request under the shroud of national security.

People argue that the chip makes desktop surveillance too easy! According to the group, Responsibility, your government eavesdropped on 1.35 million conversations in 1991, and made 3,000 arrests as a result of court-authorized intercepts.

A healthy number.

Beyond the "limited" access to CLIPPER decryption keys, lies the fact is that ordinary people will be responsible for safeguarding them. And ordinary people can be bribed and/or do stupid things...

All of which has led to the rather unusual speech by FBI Director Louis Freech, saying that Americans should be "willing to give up some of their freedoms to become more secure."

Okay...

The CLIPPER chip has been proposed as a voluntary standard. But once the Internal Revenue Service, the Pentagon and other agencies order tens of thousands of CLIPPER phones, it will be impossible to do business with the government using any other equipment.

Another White House proposal would require that all future telecommunications systems – everything from phones to online services – be "wiretap friendly," says Jerry Berman, executive director of the Electronic Frontier Foundation.

Of course they aren't necessarily talking about friendly to you and me – just friendly.

At least one phone manufacturer and one customer – AT&T and the federal government have already said they will use the chip. NIST is also exploring ways to make the technology available through telephone companies. You may soon be able to add scrambling to your monthly bill as easily as you can voice mail.

The government expects that by requiring CLIPPER chips in every piece of communications equipment it buys, they will become the standard. There is also talk about barring data that is not encrypted by the CLIPPER from any national information superhighway, further assuring its acceptance.

Face it, before too long, technology will catch up with the CLIPPER chip. Prime-factor requirements grow as processor technology advances, the mips required to break an algorithm increase at a far faster pace than for encoding and decoding. That which takes a special processor today will be done on a PC CPU tomorrow.

If a scheme doesn't have to be carved in silicon, other algorithms become more attractive. Unless the government outlaws other cryptographic schemes, CLIPPER may not become as widely accepted as hoped.

Finally, all those other cryptographic schemes add to the problem of easy interception because any of them can be *run right on top of CLIPPER*. Even if the chip becomes widespread, sophisticated folk will simply add one or more other encryption programs on top, negating the "easy eavesdropping" concept.

RECORDING ENHANCEMENT AND SCRAMBLING

It is possible to enhance the audio from a bug or tap through a number of methods. While it can be done in real time, it is much wiser to record the incoming signal as-is and then work on the tape at your leisure.

This can be accomplished by specialists like Kevin Murray, or by the FBI who had/has the world's best audio lab.

It was also possible to take the tape to a recording studio and have the sound engineer put it through the paces.

Said paces usually include the use of active and passive filters, notches, parametric equalizers and specialized recording devices such as a harmonizer which can shift registers up or down an octave or so.

All these options are still viable but *extraneous*. The advent of PC based digital processing systems which work in conjunction with your own computer will perform audio magic that even the FBI couldn't claim ten years ago.

And do it for a few hundred dollars.

These hardware/software devices will let the operator construct various "filters" strictly by the use of computer code. This allows you to optimize custom filters for any audio mode.

The better programs show the audio on screen, sometimes in a 3-D configuration. The operator can then shape the sound, create filters, visually select and eliminate unwanted noise or other interfering audio and optimize the target signal.

This works like a draw or CAD-CAM program, wherein the mouse can select certain frequencies or "frames" of audio and individually process them for maximum effect.

These programs are evolving rapidly enough that I'm not going to list them separately, but suggest you go to your friendly newsstand or bookstore and pick up copies of amateur radio magazines (*73, QST*) , as well as, any musician oriented or recording engineering magazines like *Mix* and read the ads and the reviews.

There is also a new product from Best Products and IBM M-Wave division which does some just amazing stuff with regard to digital signal process.

RECORDING ENHANCEMENT AND SOME SCRAMBLING

It is possible to enhance the audio from a bug or tap through a number of methods. While it can be done in real time, it is much wiser to record the incoming signal as-is and then work on the tape at your leisure.

This can be accomplished by specialists like Kevin Murray, or by the FBI who had/has the world's best audio lab.

It was also possible to take the tape to a recording studio and have the sound engineer put it through the paces.

Said paces usually include the use of active and passive filters, notches, parametric equalizers and specialized recording devices such as a harmonizer which can shift registers up or down an octave or so.

All these options are still viable but *extraneous*. The advent of PC based digital processing systems which work in conjunction with your own computer will perform audio magic that even the FBI couldn't claim ten years ago.

And do it for a few hundred dollars.

These hardware/software devices will let the operator construct various "filters" strictly by the use of computer code. This allows you to optimize custom filters for any audio mode.

The better programs show the audio on screen, sometimes in a 3-D configuration. The operator can then shape the sound, create filters, visually select and eliminate unwanted noise or other interfering audio and optimize the target signal.

This works like a draw or CAD-CAM program, wherein the mouse can select certain frequencies or "frames" of audio and individually process them for maximum effect.

These programs are evolving rapidly enough that I'm not going to list them separately, but suggest you go to your friendly newsstand or bookstore and pick up copies of amateur radio magazines (*73, QST*), as well as, any musician oriented or recording engineering magazines like *Mix* and read the ads and the reviews.

A breakthrough, perhaps an epiphany, is happening even as we speak. At least two companies, Best Data Products in Chatsworth, California and Spectrum Products are marketing new, software driven real time telephone line signal processors.

Both use what is known as M-Wave technology from IBM to act as an answering machine, FAX modem, voice identification unit, and so on. They also have the capability to digitally process the signal to clean up the phone lines.

Both PC boards offer 16 bit processing, high sample rates and data compression.

Guess what?

It is possible to take the toolbox tools, teach your computer to break the audio into a large number of bands and then write your own algorithm to scramble them in any way you want.

Provide the end user with the same program and you've just created a scrambling program that will drive anyone trying to break it into a frenzy. No single key, user changeable on all parameters.

Run it alone or on top of a "normal" scrambler and, unless you'rehaving a casual conversation with the head of security in Iraq, ain't nobody going to spend the time and effort to break it.

Please note, as one of the design the engineers involved told me, "This is not what the program is currently designed for. You will have to do some DSP programming with our tool kit, or have someone do it for you. It does not come out of the box as a scrambler." Still...

PRIVATE DETECTIVES

This entire book has been devoted to techniques, tricks and equipment used by people who want to find out information. Basically, of course, this is what a private detective does, the difference is that a "real" PI has a nice little piece of paper from the state that he resides in, that basically says that he is allowed to hang around on sidewalks watching little girls near schoolhouses, without being arrested.

Okay, that may be a bit harsh.

Licensed PI's can legally do a number of things you and I can't. Specifically, this includes pretexting, or as we say in the business lying, investigating other people that we have no direct connection with, parking in standing only zones for over 10 minutes and free tickets to the Laker's games.

In all seriousness, private investigation is a pretty good business because it can be run with low overhead, in fact, many PI's run their businesses out of their homes. The bad news it that it's not nearly as lucrative as it used to be, no fault-divorce laws have put a major dent in the pocket book of America's private investigation community. It's true that many "significant others" still want some sort of proof of instability before they will file, but it is no longer required by law. As much as I hate to see two people sit down together in a civilized fashion and discuss ending the relationship, those damn politicians have made it possible.

Private investigators operating in many other fields as well, including, insurance cases, worker's compensation cases, retail theft, internal company (or store) theft, background checking and so on...It's just the field is not quite as open as in those good ol' days when every sixteen year old was running off to Haight Ashbury, and every frantic parent was calling a PI to find them or a PI to divorce the no good SOB father, who's influence it was because of, that they ran off in the first place.

If you have the urge to become a licensed PI, or an unlicensed PI, or just want to know how to take advantage of many of the same resources, this chapter is for you. Let's begin with the education factor – private investigation is not on the curriculum of many colleges, hence one has to do a bit of searching to find legitimate courses.

Investigative Training Institute, POB 3379, Annapolis, MD 21403. ITI gives seminars which are taught by state police investigators and detective agency owners in criminal justice professions. They offer a two level seminar schedule which is designed to help you pass the Maryland PI exam, which definitely applicable to other exams as well. Some of the program material includes:

- The Maryland and Virginia Private Detective Laws and Regulations
- Public Information Sources
  - Their locations throughout the Baltimore/Washington Area
  - The Freedom of Information Act
  - The Privacy Act
- Criminalistics
  - Fingerprint evidence
  - Ballistics and tool mark evident
  - Shoe and tire print examination
  - Hair and fiber evidence
  - Blood and body fluid analysis
  - Polygraph examination
  - The psychological stress evaluator
  - DNA fingerprinting

- Pretexts
- Interviews and Interrogation
  - Recorded statements
  - Written statements
  - Constitutional precautions

The step two program moves onward by including:
- Behavior
  - Body language
  - Personal space
  - Eye contact
  - Verbal and non-verbal cues
- Basic Interviewing Techniques
  - Multi-suspect interviews
  - Elimination of suspects
  - Identification of deceptive behavior
  - Preparation for interrogation
  - Constitutional considerations
- Interrogation
  - Profile of the interrogator
  - Interrogation setting
  - Structured technique
  - Fielding denials
  - Obtaining confession
  - Securing specific details and written confessions
- Advanced 35mm Photographic Techniques
  - Special film
  - Night vision application
  - Close-up photography
- Video Surveillance Applications
  - Discussion of available formats
  - Covert use
  - Low light
  - Time lapse

The seminars are extremely inexpensive, assuming your are in or can get to Maryland, averaging about $50 per session with discount rates for multiple attendants.

ISS Seminars, Investigative Support Services 29415 Avenida La Paz #1, Cathedral City, CA 92234.

Dear Mr. Lapin,

My organization is in the business of providing preparation to private investigators who are preparing to take the California license examination. I offer an eight hour seminar a week before the test. So far there has been no one who has taken the seminar who has not passed the test. In the fall we will be offering additional classes.

I wish you great success in your endeavor.
Very truly yours,

Diane Evans
Director

ISS prepares people to pass the California PI exam, no small feat. One should point out that, up to this point, they have had no one that has gone through their course fail the exam. Again, this aimed toward a specific state, but certainly would not be a bad idea if you were trying to pass another states exam.

"The licensing test has been made more difficult, yet the state officials continue to decline to provide or recommend any study material or lists or reference books."

"The tests were increased to 150 questions (the test taking time remained at 2 hours.) According to the state those questions were taken from a pool of over 500."

"A prospective licensee may never have worked in a particular field and may never intend to work in that field, but must answer questions from all categories."

"Civil and criminal law, interviewing, report writing and note taking principle, surveillance, document research, undercover procedures and techniques, worker's comp, subrosa are just a few of the areas covered. Not many investigators have worked in all those fields."

"ISS Seminars has researched prepared material and has formulated a comprehensive review for the state licensing test."

"A question/answer format is used to present the material."

"The practice questions have been designed to illustrate and teach the various basic principles in a variety of areas. This Q & A method helps to establish the student's "need to know." If an answer is incorrect or unknown then the correct answer will be more memorable."

United States Academy of Private Investigation, A Division of Probe, Inc., POB 2133, Beverly Hills, CA 90213. A home study course for private investigators that consists of 4 training manuals and 20 lesson plans. All assignments, examinations and so on, are graded by examiners at Probe. Upon graduation, you receive a diploma and a letter of recommendation. An inexpensive course coming in at about 150 bucks, if you pay for it in one fell swoop.

The United States Academy of Private Investigation studies include:

Section One:
- The Court System
  - Civil & Criminal
- Investigative "Overt" Operations
- Rules of Evidence
  - Identification
  - Handling & Marking
  - Storing and Safekeeping
- Surveillance & Stakeouts
- Statements & Confessions
- Investigation Specialties

Section Two:
- Report Procedures
- Informant Reporting
- Investigation Reports

Section Three:
- Undercover "Covert" Operations
- Undercover Report Writing
- Investigation Techniques
- Store Detective Services

Section Four:
- Starting Your Detective Agency
- Client Development

- Client Proposal Letters
- Agency Operation Forms
- Investigation & Surveillance Aids

Lion Investigation Academy, A Division of American Detective Agency, 434 Clearfield St., Freemanburg, PA 18017. Lion was founded more than 14 years ago, with the idea of educating those about to enter the private investigation and security fields. They earned a pretty good reputation, especially for a home study school. You will find many people in the field who have studied with Lion.

A couple of options are open, the first one is the fact that "The Lion Investigation Academy is authorized by the Pennsylvania Department of Education to award the Associate in Specialized Technology (AST) degree in Private Investigation. This is a career degree with maximum concentration in Private Investigations. This program has been designed to provide an opportunity for men and women to acquire the skills necessary to qualify for career positions and earn a degree. The requirements call for the completion of at least 60 credits.

When you think you've mastered the lessons, you are then obligated to take a test, this is how it's done:

Procedure: When the student approaches the completion of studies in a given semester, the Academy will request that the student submit the name, mailing address, telephone number and profession of a willing proctor. The Academy will accept high school or college administrators, faculty member, guidance counselors, members of the clergy, attorneys, members of the judiciary, or others of comparable professional status as proctors. A relative of the student is not acceptable under any circumstances.

Each course runs about $100 and the curricula includes:

CURRICULA:

Associate in Specialized Technology (AST) Degree in Private Investigations.

Completion of this four semester program qualifies a graduate for an AST degree in Private Investigations.

Semester I

Inv. 100 Introduction to Private
              Investigations
Inv. 101 Surveillance and Stake Out
Sec. 200 Applied Security I
Inv. 102 Interrogation and
              Investigative Procedures
Rel. 300 Introduction to Psychology

TOTAL CREDITS: 15
TOTAL CLOCK HOURS: 390
Proctored Final Examination

Semester II

Inv. 103 Investigations I
Sec. 201 Specialized Services
Inv. 104 Civil Investigations
Rel. 301 Communications
Rel. 302 Introduction to Sociology
TOTAL CREDITS: 15
TOTAL CLOCK HOURS: 360
Proctored Final Examination

Semester III

Inv. 105 Plaintiff and Defense
              Investigations
Inv. 106 Investigations II
Sec. 202 Applied Security II
Sec. 203 Industrial and Preventive
              Security
Rel. 303 Psychology
TOTAL CREDITS: 15
TOTAL CLOCK HOURS: 420
Proctored Final Examination

Semester IV

Inv. 107 Undercover Investigations
Inv. 108 Investigative Court Procedures
Sec. 204 Applied Security III
Inv. 109 Investigations III
Rel. 304 Sociology
TOTAL CREDITS: 15
TOTAL CLOCK HOURS: 390
Proctored Final Examination

The courses appear to be well thought out; their instructors and consultants are names in the field.

You have six years to complete the studes and still receive your degree.

Lion also offers a quicker diploma program in basic private investigation training.

The course is set up on 4 parts; 5 lessons per part, a total of 20 lessons. After each part (5 lessons), there will be a 35 question test. There must be a passing grade of 75% on the 35 question test. If the student should fail the test, he will be allowed to retake the test 3 times. The final exam consists of 60 questions and the student must attain a passing grade of 85%. The test questions are a combination of true-false, multiple choice, and narrative.

The entire course is in four part making a total of 20 lessons. There is a test after each part and a final exam.

The entire course cost is $400 plus a $25 non-refundable registration fee.

FINDING A PI

Something called the ION NETWORK has been set up by a couple of PI's to make it easy, for clients or potential clients, to find legitimate investigators in all parts of the world. This done is primarily through a resource line.

"THE RESOURCE LINE is a service offered nationwide to clients, at no cost, who need to identify and contact an appropriate investigator in an area where they don't already know one. R/L personnel determine the client's criteria, pull up names and information about all investigators who might qualify from our database of over 5000 investigators, and start making phone calls.

When contact is made with an investigator who meets the client's criteria and is available, they are asked to call the client. If hired, the investigator is asked to pay a referral fee of 20% when they are paid. No membership is required to receive RESOURCE LINE referrals. The client and investigator are asked to rate each other after the case is concluded. This information becomes part of our database. Slow pay and unreasonable clients need to be identified as well as investigators who don't perform professionally."

"The PRL (Public Records Liaison) Network consists of designated investigators and/or public records researchers, with fast access to the 4000 county seats and state capitols nationwide who will handle index searches for high volume clients for such items as judgments, liens, criminal convictions, etc. for fixed fees. A FAX may be used for PRL reporting. E-mail (Electronic mail using a computer and modem) reporting will cost $3 more per request. Proposed payments will be $20 by FAX, $23 by E-mail. Most requests will be for two or more searches.

ION, Investigators anywhere RESOURCE LINE, 2111 E. Baseline, Suite F7, Tempe, AZ 85283.

- There is no charge to the caller, no membership fee, and no directory to buy.
- By matching your needs with all of the investigators in the area or with the required specialties, your chances of having the best person for the job are improved. ION has collected information including experience, specialties, association memberships, and references on nearly 6,000 investigative agencies worldwide. Information is updated continuously in our computer.
- Competency ratings provided by clients become part of the RESOURCE LINE database.
- The RESOURCE LINE save you time, frustration, telephone costs and risk.

How to use the RESOURCE LINE:

Call 1-800-338-3463 and tell us what you need, where you need it, the qualifications of the investigator you want, and other pertinent information.

They publish a newsletter called IONIQUE which give various tips and news about the investigative business, for instance:

State Hunting License Records

"State hunting and fishing license information can be a good information tool. Currently, thirty-one states maintain central repositories of fishing and/or hunting license records which may be accessed by the public in some manner. Although a number of these record repositories are in boxes in the basement, more and more are becoming computerized.

The US Fish and Wildlife Service is implementing a Migratory Bird Harvest Information Program which will change the database procedures of many state hunting license agencies. Under this program (which will help biologists better manager the nation's migratory bird populations), hunters will provide their names and addresses when buying state licenses for hunting migratory birds. Each state must then provide these names and addresses to the Service. California, Missouri, and South Dakota are already participating in a pilot program. Additional states will be phased in, starting in 1994, at the rate of about 1 million hunters a year.

States that do not currently maintain a database or central record repository of hunting license information must do so by 1998.

The Service's policy indicates all records of hunters' names and addresses will be deleted after their surveys, and no permanent record will be maintained by the Service. However, this requirement would not apply to the individual state entities, and the possible release of these records for investigative or search purposes will depend on each state's sunshine laws."

ION also puts on a conference every year, covered in the newsletter, where you can mix and mingle with some of the best private investigators around. As well as, see what exhibitors and trainers have to offer.

The ION subscription rate to become involved with all of the this is $200 per year.

NEWSLETTERS

INTEC Investigative Technology, PO Drawer 429, Magnolia, MS 39652. INSIDE SECRETS NEWSLETTER published by Mike Enlow, a gentleman you'll be well acquainted with by the time you are through with this chapter, publishes a newsletter aimed specifically at private investigators and researchers. Mr. Enlow, himself, is a legal investigator who has had his share of the limelight by investigating a number of notorious cases including senators and other heavy hitters.

Mr. Enlow likes to call himself the millionaire's PI, drives a new Mercedes, writes books, gives seminars, and generally seems to know what he's talking about. His newsletter is a compilation of electronic surveillance tips, new laws, how to conduct a physical search, pretest tips, how to get a statement from a witness who refuses to cooperate (no rubber hose involved), as well as, listing various information sources.

For instance this entry on school records:

"School records can provide loads of information on any given subject. All right. How do you get school records? Good question. School records are not easily accessible. However, all things are possible. The first thing you do is check the yearbooks where your target attended college and determine the year they graduated. Then write to the college and request a copy of "your" diploma!

Once you have that, go with "your" diploma to the school requesting copies of "your" transcripts. With a copy of "your" diploma in hand, you will increase your credibility 1000%! You will usually gain cooperation from school personnel to obtain copies of "your" records and transcripts."

Mr. Enlow also runs a information brokering service for PI's or person's of good repute (i.e., my readers). And, in fact, will make you a deal where you can join his FAX accessible information service and get his newsletter, if you mention my name, for a one-time, low price.

Not sold in many stores.

There are a couple of other newsletters, we've already mentioned IONIQUE, and if you look in the newsletters section of this book, you will see a number of newsletters that would be interest to private detectives, including THE EAGLE.

SOFTWARE

There are a number of software programs designed to help private detectives run their firms, you know, billing, reporting to clients, keeping reports and so on. I'm not going to cover these, they are a little too general and you can most certainly find them listed in any of the various association newsletters. What I am going to cover is a rather unique and new program called WATSON.

WATSON is not necessarily designed for private investigators, but rather is an easy-to-use but powerful analysis application. Its unique combination of database tools, analytical functions and automatic chart drawing, help organize, analyze and present investigative information. WATSON works with the analyst through an entire project; analyzing data quickly and efficiently, and systematically working through otherwise impossible tasks.

WATSON enables the analyst to carry out investigative work in a number of ways: for example, graphical charts allow the investigator to view the information in a logical format. If the data changes, WATSON immediately updates the charts, exposing vital new links.

Imagine the following scenario. A small group of people manages to open over 180 bank accounts in a period of just eight months. They use more than 80 aliases and almost 30 different addresses. Stolen money is deposited in the accounts and transferred between them, making it difficult to trace the numerous transactions from start to finish.

Using WATSON's customized data entry forms, details of accounts, names and addresses can be quickly and easily entered into the database manually.

Next, WATSON graphically represents the links between each account, the name of the person and the address when the account was opened. Once WATSON has established a common link, accurate inferences are drawn about who used certain aliases.

More penetrating analysis allows WATSON to display sequentially when cash transactions occur and amounts passing between accounts. Without WATSON, the process of finding and illustrating links would be laborious and time-consuming. WATSON draws even a complicated chart in significantly less time than if it was drawn manually, and automatically updates charts as information changes.

WATSON specializes in managing vast amounts of data that are otherwise almost impossible to handle. For example, telephone analysis used to investigate a widespread network of criminal activity. Normal surveillance procedures are augmented by investigating the telephone activity between the individuals considered central to the investigation. The inquiry may involve over 1,500 telephones and 7,500 calls between them.

WATSON shows the simple links between telephone numbers, and the information associated with the calls between target phones – date, time, duration. WATSON then explores they calling activity among all the phones associated, either directly or indirectly, with the target phones. And at the end of the investigation, the analyst can print charts that clearly indicate the telephone links between the suspects, in a format that is both easily understood and suitable for presentation as evidence.

This rather unusual software program organizes the chaos of raw data gathered during your investigation, whether be by a PI or a cop, and puts into link and event charts which help the analyst systematically work through possible solutions and then draw his conclusions. When new information comes available, WATSON, of course, updates everything involved with that particular thread.

WATSON is developed in England and can be purchased from a number of places, including Harlequin Inc., One Cambridge Center, Cambridge, MA 02142.

BOOKS

A number of books exist which will tell you about being a private detective, a few that will explain how to be a profitable private detective, two that will tell you how to have fun with private detective stuff, and a couple that will actually tell you how to become a private detective. Let's start with the latter.

OBTAINING YOUR PRIVATE INVESTIGATOR'S LICENSE
ISBN 0-87364-390-9

OBTAINING YOUR PRIVATE INVESTIGATOR'S LI-CENSE, Paladin Press, by Orion Agency Inc. Not exactly *Gone With the Wind,* this book this strictly a compilation of what each state requires from somebody who wants to become a PI, as well as, the fees involved and what they're allowed to carry after passing the test ("private investigators may not carry metallic badges, guards may carry approved metal badge or cloth insignia. – Arkansas").

Maybe slightly outdated by this point, copyrighted in 1985, BUT it still provides some tips on test taking and what to expect later. Below is an example taken from this book (page 18)

ALABAMA

Address:	License Commission Courthouse 109 Government Mobile, AL 36602
Age:	18
Experience Required:	None. All that is required for licensing as PI in Alabama is payment of license fees.
Insurance Requirements:	None. Liability insurance is strongly suggested.
Fees:	Detective agency: $151. The business, not the individual, is licensed here.
Collections:	$151
Other Licensing:	For watch guard and watch-dog, no license is required.
Firearms:	Regulations for firearms are dealt with through sheriff's department in local areas.
Note:	Information related here is for state/county. The License Commission advises that some larger metropolitan area do regulate PI's. No examination.

REQUIREMENTS TO BECOME A P.I. IN THE 50 STATES AND ELSEWHERE ISBN 0-9630621-1-5

REQUIREMENTS TO BECOME A P.I. IN THE 50 STATES AND ELSEWHERE by Joseph J. Culligan, Hallmark Press, Inc., 1337 N.W. 155th Drive, North Miami, FL 33169. Written and compiled by Joseph Culligan, a fairly well-known PI, who has authored other books in this field. This reference manual is considerably more complete than the previous guide.

The exact forms for applying for licenses, as well as, bonding and a number of the rules governing PI's in each state are reprinted. Again, don't be expect to be entertained by the writing, these are simply forms that are reprinted in full.

The book does tell you exactly what you need to become what in each state, plus Canada.

State of California general qualifications for licensure:

"Each person listed on the application (owner, partner, corporate officer, qualified manager) is required to meet certain general qualification regarding fitness for licensure. The person who will be in active charge of the business is referred to as the qualified manager or qualified certificate holder. Each company license must have one person designated as the qualified manager, and that person must meet the general license qualification as well as more specific qualifications regarding age, experience and examination. The qualified manager may be an owner, partner, corporate officer or any other person meeting the requirements for qualified manager."

"If a denial of licensure is based on a crime or act of the applicant, the crime or act must be substantially related to the qualifications, functions or duties of the business or profession for which the application is made. A criminal history check is made on all applicants. The director may deny a license if any person listed on the application as owner, partner, corporate officer or qualified manager has done any of the things listed below:"

- been convicted of a crime. any conviction of any crime or plea of nolo contender even if the conviction was dismissed under Penal Code section 1203.4 must be disclosed on the application;
- committed any act involving dishonesty, fraud or deceit with the intent to substantially benefit himself or injure another;
- committed any act which, if done by a licensee of the business or profession in question, would be grounds for suspension or revocation of license;
- knowingly made a false statement of fact required to be revealed on the license application;
- failed to renew a license while it was under suspension or has a license which is under suspension;
- been refused a license or had a license revoked, or been an officer, partner or manager of any person/business that has been refused a license or had a license revoked by the bureau;
- while unlicensed, committed, or aided and abetted the commission of, any act for which said license is required. For alarm company applicants only: license will not be issued unless at least one year has passed since the date of the conviction.

"Other provisions may apply depending on the type of license. Evidence of rehabilitation may be submitted with the application with the application for consideration by the bureau."

This book also includes addresses where prospective PI's can write to obtain complete licensing requirement packages and other relevant information.

Well done.

THE PROCESS OF INVESTIGATION
ISBN 0-409-95018-1

THE PROCESS OF INVESTIGATION Concepts & Strategies for the Security Professional by Charles A. Sennewald, Butterworth Publishers, 80 Montvale Ave., Stoneham, MA 02180. THE PROCESS OF INVESTIGATION is a list of concepts and strategies for the security professional, be he, private investigator, a security guard, or in-house security manager. The book, although copyrighted in 1981, still contains a host of relevant data, as well as, step by step instruc-

tions for taking care of the business that private eyes take care of.

Remember, pal, it ain't all glamour here, we're talkin' payin' the bills. How do you pay the bills? Well, one of the things you do is hire out to stores, or chains to find thieves, boosters, and employee thefts. Let's take a look at how Mr. Sennewald thinks people steal from stores. I say the list is pretty good...

- Put merchandise on beneath one's outer garments and wear the stolen items out concealed. A lot of swimwear and intimate apparel is stolen this way.
- Place soft, folded items such as sweaters under the coat and armpit.
- Push items off a counter so they fall into a waiting shopping bag.
- Place articles in the bag of a previous purchase.
- Carry into the store empty bags of the same or other stores and fill these bags with items while the shoplifter is shielded behind piles or racks of merchandise or in the privacy of a fitting room.
- Hand merchandise to children who accompany you and let the children carry it out.
- Wear special "boosting" coats that have hooks sewn on the inside to accommodate soft goods that are quickly placed there.
- Wear special "boosting" coats that have modified lining that makes the whole coat a huge pocket.
- Carry booster boxes into the store. Such boxes appear to be ready to mail, wrapped and string-tied, or they may be disguised as fancy gift boxes. They are empty and have a false or trapdoor, or the bottom or side may be fitted with a spring-type hinge. Push the good in and the false side gives way; withdraw the hand and the side snaps back to its original position.
- Wear special "booster" bloomers, similar to old-fashioned ladies' underwear that comes down just above the knee. The legs of the garment are tied, or strong elastic is used so that stolen merchandise will not slip out. Stolen goods are pushed down the front of

the bloomers, or an accomplice can push good down the back.

- Hide stolen items in the crotch area. Even items as bulky as a fur coat or several men's suits folded up can be hidden in this way between the thighs of a woman wearing a long, full skirt or dress, who simply walks out of the store after concealing the items. Even typewriters have been removed in this fashion.

- Switch price tags. A garment's $50.00 price tag is replaced by a $25.00 tag from another item, and the more expensive article is then purchased at the lower price. Similar switching is often done with boxed items. For example, four cubes of margarine are removed from the package and replaced with four cubes of pure butter, which is then purchased at the price of the margarine.

- Pick up merchandise and immediately take it to a clerk, demanding your money back.

- Run into the store, grab items and run out to a waiting car, catching everyone by surprise (if you are noticed at all).

PI SCHOOL
ISBN 0-87364-637-1

The next logical step in your educational process would be PI SCHOOL HOW TO BECOME A PRIVATE DETECTIVE by Wayne Harrison, Paladin Press.

Although the table of contents is interesting, including such things as surveillance, interrogations, obtaining false IDs, how to open locks, video tape and so on. You have to be slightly suspicious because this fairly small format book only has 100 pages and, I mean, come on guys, look how many pages are in this book, ya know... On the other hand, there are a few things that are of use, for instance, his technique of pretext, roping:

"Position yourself in an area of the subject's residence. Carry a small scoop and a services of jars or test tubes. If the subject comes out of the house to find out what you are doing, tell him your are collecting soil samples for a chemical lab interested in what type of minerals might be available for a production plant that is considering locating there (brick manufacturing always seems believable)."

"If you present your pretext well, the subject may even let you take "soil samples" on his land, hoping you will find something he can sell at a profit. And, if you are a good investigator, you could rope the subject and find out what he does for a living and what his hobbies are; you may even observe him working around the house."

Copyrighted in 1991, this is sort of a borrow-a-bit from this book, borrow-a-bit from that book – book.

BE YOUR OWN DICK PRIVATE INVESTIGATING MADE EASY by John Q. Newman, Loompanics Unlimited ISBN 1-55950-083-2. Well, at least the title of this book is original, although the book itself runs the usual 110 pages, much of which is devoted to addresses of DMVs and rather long worksheets, there are a few useful tips on conducting background investigations and who has what.

Active Investigations—"The active investigation proceeds in a totally different manner than the passive background investigation. This concept became very popular in Great Britain years ago. It is called "positive vetting."

"An active background investigation pursued to its furthest ends should be able to reveal every significant event in a person's life, from their birth to the present. In effect, this is what active investigations of the highest order attempt to do. This also exposes the inherent weakness of the passive investigation. The passive investigator relies upon databases that will only contain information on the exceptional citizen. The other tool the active background investigation utilizes is time-line techniques. With these techniques, a chart can be plotted that shows a person's movement through each phase of his life. A person who passes such an investigation can be said to have few secrets left."

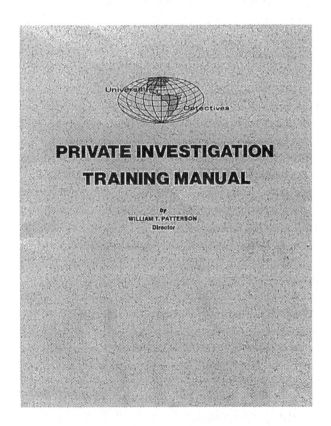

PRIVATE INVESTIGATION TRAINING MANUAL
ISBN 0-87364-161-2

PRIVATE INVESTIGATION TRAINING MANUAL by William T. Patterson – Director of Universal Detectives, Paladin Press.

"It is understood that no course or book on this vast subject could possibly cover all its aspects. We have compiled the manual with the main intent of teaching essentials only. Unlike other courses and books, we have eliminated long, descriptive material and tried to condense as much as possible in the shortest time possible. In this way it is easier for you to study, review and digest all the information given."

"When possible we have made lists in outline form for easy reference and memorization. Our manual is full of diagrams, photos, check lists and outlines designed to hasten and aid you in becoming an investigator."

The above is correct, it is difficult to cover everything you need to know, in a 152 page book, so there is some validity in the idea of including various forms and reports.

On the other hand, of course, same various forms and reports take up pages and pages that the writer doesn't have to worry about filling with his own clever verbiage.

Again, much of the more hands on material concerns things like catching shop lifters and theft prevention.

Theft Prevention—"There are a multitude of ways in which businesses and individuals can prevent thefts and in your capacity as investigator it will behoove you to acquaint yourself with them so that you may advise your clients about these possible preventative measures."

"For instance, store owners can prevent much shoplifting by installing large mirrors or closed circuit TV cameras in various places in their stores. In addition, guards placed at the entrances have a psychological effect which helps in reducing thefts."

"It is self-evident that car prowlers may be prevented by keeping cars locked. Above all, the ignition key should never be left in the ignition switch. Such measures will prevent amateur car thieves but there is little that can be done to stop the real professional. In any event articles of value which might tempt a car thief should be locked out of sight in the car trunk. In some cases auto alarms have proved effective."

"To prevent purse snatching a purse should always be held securely in the hand. Shoulder strap bags are most vulnerable to pickpockets. Men should never carry their wallets in accessible pockets and extra cash should always be in travel checks."

"New means of theft prevention are constantly being initiated and the investigator will do well to keep abreast of them."

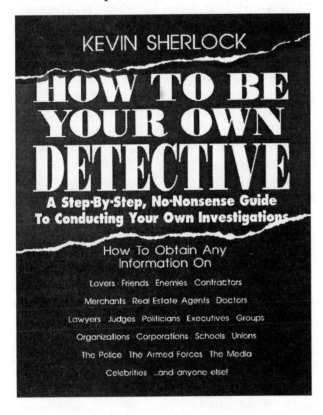

HOW TO BE YOUR OWN DETECTIVE
ISBN 0-918751-27-6

HOW TO BE YOUR OWN DETECTIVE by Kevin Sherlock (At least the guy's got the right last name), J. Flores Publications, POB 830131, Miami, FL 33283-0131. A step upward in the world of private investigations. A 240 page, 8 1/2 x 11 format, small print book, this crams in a sure-bit more on the how-to and where-fore's of investigating, than do many of the quickie *make great money, meet interesting people,* books do.

Mr. Sherlock, who actually works as an investigator, goes over a number of case histories, their problems and their solutions. Some of the nomenclature is terms a good PI should be familiar with.

"You can see if there are any mortgages or loans involving the property by checking the grantor and grantee books in the county recorder's office under the present owner's name and under the name of people who previously owned the land. If loans or mortgages exist, or if there is proof they have been paid off and the money lender has released his claim on the property, the instrument column of the record will show them and refer you to the books and pages where the loan documents are. You can then review the loan paperwork in the loan books (mortgage books, certificate of release books, or similar records) to see what loans were made for the property and whether the alleged owner has paid off the loans."

"The "military" applications here are obvious. You can get information on your target's possibly shady financial dealings, his business partners, and his possible crookedness on a number of fronts. Maybe he gets sweetheart loans at low rates if he's a borrower. Maybe he forces buyers to do business with his banking buddies. Maybe he's overextended, or maybe he's using the same piece of property as collateral in more than one deal. Maybe loan rescheduling or late payments are proof he's in some financial trouble. Maybe he's making loans or getting loans that smell funny. Maybe he's calling in loans or manipulating them in some other way to make money illegally or unethically. Maybe there's conflict of interest. Maybe buddies of his are involved in the provisions of loans."

This book even includes an IBM 5 1/4 disk with much of the material from the book on it. HOW TO BE YOUR OWN DETECTIVE does serve as a good entry or reminder on how to deal with a number of subjects including:
• Personal data such as Social Security numbers, addresses, phone numbers, birth,

death, marriage, and divorce information and personal dirt.

- Criminal and legal information.
- Labor, environmental, and health code violators.
- Coroner, medical and professional malpractice records.
- Lawsuits and other legal entanglements.
- Real estate, zoning, planning, and land use records.
- Individual and corporate tax records.
- Corporation, industry, and finance information.
- How to track white-collar criminals and sex offenders.
- School taxing, spending, and quality of education records.
- Political finances and politicians' personal finances.
- Government taxing and spending.

DARKNESS TO LIGHT IS YOUR SPOUSE CHEATING ON YOU – YOU HAVE A RIGHT TO KNOW by Michael E. Enlow – Legal Investigator, Enlow Publications, Suite #275, 1456 Second Ave., New York, NY 10021. DARKNESS TO LIGHT—kind of a convoluted title—is copyrighted in 1990 by Michael Enlow, who does investigations, writes books, runs an information brokering business and so on. I've got nothing against wanting to know if your spouse is cheating on you, I admit that some of the things that Mike covers are valid items one might not think of otherwise, however, Mike apparently decided that this book could be expanded, hence the publication, PRIVATE INVESTIGATION MADE SIMPLE—INSIDE SECRETS OF THE MASTER by Michael Enlow, Enlow Publications. Copyrighted in 1993, this is a large format, hands-on, how-to book that is a basic guide to being your own lawyer, skip tracing, alarms, false IDs, shoplifting intervention and various little tricks are taken from Mike's newsletter. As well as, a number of actual cases that Mike was involved with and how he solved them.

HOW TO MAKE $100,000 A YEAR AS A PRIVATE INVESTIGATOR by Edmund J. Pankau, Paladin Press ISBN 0-87364-720-3. Mr. Pankau is a well-known PI who specializes in financial investigations and has gone from being a freelance investigator to owning a agency that has a payroll in excess of $1,000,000 a year. Instead of focusing on qualifications for a license or surveillance techniques, this manual concentrates on how to find the jobs, how to get them going, how to act like a professional and how to make money in your chosen profession.

As I thumb through Ed's book, I notice we both seem to think the same experts are worth recommending (Sue Rugge, George Theodore and so on) and that we also crossover in recommending various databases, newsletters, journals and magazines.

Ed has a good reputation and apparently has made quite a bit of money in this field. This book is new and should be read by anybody who is seriously considering working as a PI.

"You don't know how to get this phone bill? It's real easy! Just call the hotel the next week after your subject leaves and ask for the audit or bookkeeping department with this little white lie. "Hello, this is Bobby Johnson with the Audit Department of Intergalactic Industries. Our salesman, Mr. Smith, was in your hotel last week and made a number of long distance calls on his bill. He didn't itemize these in his expense account, and I need to get those numbers for verification that they were business related."

"They'll give them to you every time. By having the information listed above, you will soon have a much better idea of the movement patterns and the people whom your subject is likely to see if you lose contact in traffic or have to break off surveillance because the subject is "starting to wag his tail." The first time I had to follow someone, my supervisor just told me to go out there and follow him to see where he was going.

Or how about this example:

"After teaching a seminar session for the account executives of Prentice Hall On-line in San Francisco, we all went to dinner at the "killer" restaurant that had the best pasta that ever hit my mouth. OF course, we washed this down with a goodly amount of wine and came back to our hotel with more than just a little bit of a buzz on. I successfully negotiated the lobby, rode up on the elevator to the eleventh floor, and then drew a total blank. I knew that this was my floor, but I had no idea of my room number. I fished my plastic card key out of my pocket (all hotels are now going to these access cards because they can be reprogrammed daily, for each new customer, without having to rekey the hotel rooms), and saw that there was no room number on the key."

"Feeling slightly stupid, I picked up the house phone and called the operator to ask what room I was in. My voice was a little slurred, it was almost midnight, and I explained to the night operator that I didn't want to fumble abound on the floor, trying my key in five other people's rooms before getting lucky or getting punched out by some big dude who thought I was trying to burglarize his room. Amazingly, the sweet voice on the other end of the phone told me I was in Room 1158 as she laughed at my little situation."

"As soon as I snapped to what she'd done, I sobered up in a heartbeat with a realization that I had just figured out a new way to find out a target's hotel rooms. Since that time, I've tried this little game in every hotel from Seattle to St. Louis and found that it works almost every time. Just sound a little sheepish, slightly tipsy, and do it late at night when people would expect you to be drunk and it works almost every time."

From here we get into slightly more specific of the PI field, for instance:

A PRIVATE EYE'S GUIDE TO COLLECTING A BAD DEBT by Fay Faron, Zero to Sixty Pubco, 123 Townsend Street, Suite 220, San Francisco, CA 94107. I'm not going to spend too much time raving about Fay's book, for two reasons: 1) I've already raved about it in another section, and 2) the fact that Fay has actually spiffed the book up and turned it into TAKE THE MONEY & STRUT! A Private Investigator's Guide to Collecting a Bad Debt, Zero to Sixty Pubco., 123

Townsend Street, Suite 220, San Francisco, CA 94107. Fay is clever, cute, intelligent and licensed. A combination you don't often find in women (O.K., O.K. or in guys, either). Her books are summations of her years of experience in the fields of process serving and private investigation. Fay is actually getting famous as I write this, she now runs her own information broker agency (Locate Central) and writes a column syndicated by one of the largest syndicators in the United States.

Enough said.

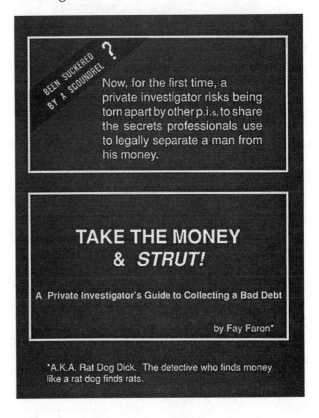

TAKE THE MONEY & STRUT!

WHEN IN DOUBT CHECK HIM OUT
ISBN 0-9630621-2-3

Or how about WHEN IN DOUBT CHECK HIM OUT A Woman's Survival Guide For The 90's by Joseph J. Culligan, Hallmark Press, Incorporated. Mr. Culligan is a member of the National Association of Investigative Specialist and was actually elected to their hall of fame. I grant you it's not exactly the football hall of fame, but we each have our aspirations. Although this book pretends to be for women to check out guys, as you can imagine most of the sources; DMV, birth, marriage, social security, etc. records really are not gender specific.

There's nothing wrong this with this book and in fact, it has some good sources and approaches, the only complaint, which is not as much of a complaint as a comment, is that of course, many of the sources are duplicated in the book you are reading at this present time. They are only so many places to find marriage records or find DMV addresses.

There a few sources I haven't seen in other books such as the following:

"You may order the accident report from the jurisdiction that is noted on the driving record. The following list of state police agencies is in-cluded in this chapter since the state will usually have a copy of every accident involving damage and injuries. If the jurisdiction on the accident report is unclear, the state police will be able to either provide you a copy of the accident report or will evaluate the accident location from the information on the driving record and advise you exactly where to make your inquiry so you will be able to pull all the files."

STATE POLICE AGENCIES

ALABAMA
Alabama Department of Public Safety
Suite of Alabama
Post Office Box 1511
Montgomery, Alabama 36192
ALASKA
Department of Public Safety
State of Alaska
Post Office Box N
Juneau, Alaska 99811
ARIZONA
Department of Public Safety
State of Arizona
2102 West Encanto Boulevard
Phoenix, Arizona 85005
CONNECTICUT
State Police Department
State of Connecticut
294 Colony Street
Meriden, Connecticut 06450
DELAWARE
Delaware State Police Department
State of Delaware
Post Office Box 430
Dover, Delaware 19903
DISTRICT OF COLUMBIA
Department of Public Safety
District of Columbia
Post Office Box 1606
Washington, DC 20013
And so on...

Perhaps Mr. Culligan called that book A Woman's Survival Guide For The 90's because he planned to sell another other book, YOU, TOO, CAN FIND ANYBODY, Hallmark Press, Inc.

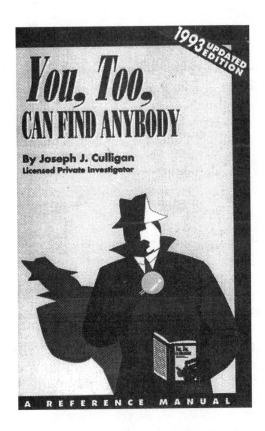

YOU, TOO, CAN FIND ANYBODY
ISBN 0-9630621-0-7

FIND THEM FAST, FIND THEM NOW
ISBN 0-8065-1080-3

Sort of a nice way to use the same information in two books – after all why waste all that good stuff about getting birth certificates on just women?

Basically, a list of DMV offices, child support enforcement divisions of the IRS, bankruptcy record offices, how to contact the Peace Corp and read a voter's registration card. $19.95.

YOU, TOO, CAN FIND ANYBODY by Joseph J. Culligan, called "Stunningly Complete" – P.I. Magazine, this VHS tape pretty much brings to mind the question of why waste all that nice material on two books, when you can have two books and one video tape that show how to order birth, death, marriage and divorce records from every state?

Somewhat along the same lines would be FIND THEM FAST, FIND THEM NOW Private Investigators Share Their Secrets For Finding Missing Persons by Frederick Charles Hoyer, Jr. and John D. McCann, Citadel Press. Large format, 86 pages, large print, lots of lists, generally lists of clerks (jeez, I wonder if you know to find a city clerk by now?) and good advice like look in a WHO'S WHO directory...

I don't know, how many trees do you think died for this book?

Teen Runaways—"I believe that the main reason teenagers run away from home is due to their rebellion against their parents. School officials, the police, and even public property are often targets of their anxieties."

Well, at least you'll get some good philosophy out of this book, if nothing else...

PRIVATE EYES
ISBN 0-8065-1182-6

PRIVATE EYES The Role of the Private Investigator in American marriage, Business and Industry. By Sam Brown and Gini Graham Scott, Citadel Press Book, Published by Carol Publishing Group. Not a "hands-on" book, this is sort of "hey, it's pretty boring doing insurance and personal injury stakeouts, but somebody's got to do it," work. There a some good tips in it about what agencies have what information, or how to follow-up and pyramid on a particular piece data. The book itself is primarily a biography of a number of investigators and technicians that have done some interesting investigations.

I would hope paragraphs like the following:

"So how did they locate these bugs? Was the equipment different than that for locating phone taps?"

"Very definitely; much different," Cameron explained, and this time he pulled out a medium-sized black box, and the size of a reel to reel tape recorder, with several knobs and buttons on it. "It's called a bug detector," he continued. "And basically what you do is place it in a room, and it produces a tone which can pick up any form of electronic transmission. So if the bug is transmitting anything, the detector will pick this up."

Would seem a bit basic to you folks by now. If not, and you still think:

"Well, I think the most important and the easiest thing to do is having a post office box. So I use that instead of my address. Secondly, when I apply for credit anywhere, I use that. This helps, because this information becomes a matter of public record, and under certain circumstances anyone can reach it. Say if you're in litigation, the other party can contact the DMV for this information or subpoena your credit records. And even if you move, if your old address is on record, it can be used to track you down. For instance, if I have an old address, I can contact the neighbors, and a neighbor might know where you've gone."

Is really hip, inside information that hasn't been presented before, this book's for you!

Alright, now we go for a crossover, you know something that could be a hit in rock and roll, but still turn on country music fans? Well I guess that kinda describes the books by Greg Hauser. Like, SO YA WANNA BE A PRIVATE INVESTIGATOR, HUH, BINKY? Greg has been a successful private investigator for 25 years, has contributed a number of "hands-on" books aimed towards the PI or, at least, the investigative business. His "Binky" book is more a report on how to set up a private investigative office, how to conduct and just as importantly document various type of field and in-house investigations, a quick summation of what records are kept where, new organizations you might want to join, and a number of full page case records you can actually rip out, xerox and use to build data on just about anybody.

This book is a nice beginners text and sells for $29.99 plus $2.50 for shipping and handling.

Mr. Hauser, has also written an additional of selection of "books" which are actually more like reports, that is, they are stapled together with one color paper covers, on how to conduct a professional workman's compensation investigation, how to conduct a criminal defense investigation, how conduct lounge evaluations, and how to conduct liability investigations.

One book, in particular, called DETECTIVE AGENCY FORMS is intended for specific use in the investigative field and covers the majority of assignments you would into. Contents include:

- Assignment Sheet
- Checklist
- Log Sheet
- Reports:
  - information
  - surveillance
- Case Log Sheet
- F.O.I.A.:
  - Police departments
  - Workers' compensation departments
  - Court requests (F.O.I.A.)
- P.O. Box
- Proof of Service
- Contracts
- Weekly Financial Report
- Employee Regulations
- Insurance Questionnaire

Besides the forms themselves, Greg explains what an assignment sheet is and what it should compose of, why a checklist is valuable, how to make contracts for Proof of Service, and other legal situations that may come up in an investigator's career.

WORKERS' COMPENSATION FRAUD details how to conduct an investigation and how to fill out the reports as to appear professional and please your client.

THE PRETEXT MANUAL goes into the fine art of pretexting, something you should know a about if you've come this far. Some of the pretexts are fairly common ones used by most detectives, some are rather unusual and would work for specific assignments. Remember, it only takes one good pretext to "win" a case.

"Taxicab Pretext. This pretext is used to learn the destination of where a taxicab has dropped the subject off. It will be crucial for the investigator to have the taxicab's company name and vehicle ID number. The investigator contacts the taxicab company and states that you are a pharmacist. Your clerk just gave the subject inadvertently the wrong prescription. Advise the taxicab company that upon discovering the error, you immediately ran out of your store to notify the customer but unfortunately the customer had already departed in taxicab #_____. Next the investigator should ask the taxicab company to give the address and location of where the customer was dropped off so you could immediately notify them of the error before the customer takes the wrong medication."

So you're working a daytime job, watching those fries turn brown at McDonalds and you're not sure you're cut out to be a detective? Consider the case of Charles A. Siringo and you'll feel better. Mr. Siringo was a cowboy for years, before he decided to become a storekeeper in the thriving metropolis of Caldwell, Kansas. When a blind phrenologist measured his head and told him he was "cut out" for detective work.

Immediately, Mr. Siringo joined the Pinkerton Detective Agency.

This was in 1886.

A COWBOY DETECTIVE, A True Story of Twenty-two Years with a World-Famous Detective Agency by Charles A. Siringo, University of Nebraska Press and printed by First Bison Book, 1988; Reprinted from 1912 edition, published by the W.B. Conkey Company, Chicago ISBN 0-8032-4198-4 and ISBN 0-8032-9189-2.

For the next 22 years he roamed the west as an undercover operative using more pretexts and guises than Sherlock Holmes, to bring the bad guys to justice. He survived the labor riots at Coeur d'Alene, Idaho, in 1892, caught moonshiners in the Appalachians and chased Butch Cassidy all over the place. His record earned him a little place in the heart of the heads of the Pinkerton organization. Nevertheless, the Pinkertons, ever since his criticism, went to court to block publication of this book. After two years of litigation, the book was published in 1912, and its still a kick today.

This book should have been subtitled Real Cases Wthout Databases, as Mr. Siringo and his trusty horse pulled off some of the better investigative coups in the history of private detective work. A fun read, even more so because it's true.

"A supply of whiskey was taken along, and my life was made miserable keeping the men from fighting. To prevent McChesney from killing some one, I slipped the cartridges out of his pistol without letting him know it. Soon after this, McChesney and one of the "boys" got into a fuss while riding along, and McChesney pulled his pistol and began snapping it at the fellow, who pulled his loaded pistol and would have killed McChesney if I hadn't shoved my cocked revolver into his face just in time. I made him ride on ahead while I keep McChesney behind with me. We arrived at Keeline ranch before night, and were a hungry, sleepy crowd."

Man, this is detective work before they invented the VCR.

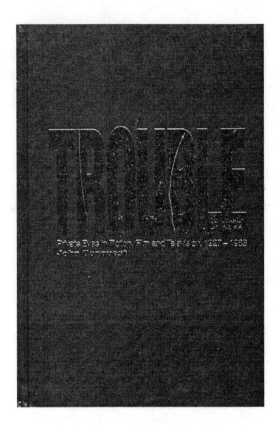

TROUBLE IS THEIR BUSINESS
ISBN 0-8240-5947-6

Speaking of VCR's, TROUBLE IS THEIR BUSINESS Private Eyes in Fiction, Film and Television by John Conquest, Garland Publishing, Inc., New York & London. Will help fill those long, empty nights while you are studying for the old PI exam by showing you what to tune in on the movie channel, or harass your video store into stocking.

McQUAY, Mike—"A cyperpunk pioneer, combining hard-boiled style with futuristic technology and advanced social decay. Mathew Swain lives in an unnamed South-Central Texas city whose Old Town is a quarantined mutant ghetto on the site of a nuclear power station meltdown. In 2083, virtually every public service has broken down, the rich live in armored fortresses and, with bodies usually collected by Meat Wagons and immediately atomized, the police charge in advance to investigate crimes. The series, dedicated to Chandler, is wryly witty, exciting tough-guy stuff."

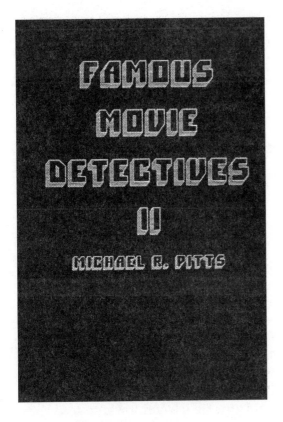

FAMOUS MOVIE DETECTIVES II
ISBN 0-8108-2345-4

Furthermore, speaking of movies, how 'bout FAMOUS MOVIE DETECTIVES II by Michael R. Pitts, The Scarecrow Press, Inc., Metuchen, NJ & London $47.50. Film detectives continue to be among the most popular movie heroes and heroines today. FAMOUS MOVIE DETECTIVES II provides a look at the celluloid careers of more than three dozen of these sleuths, including Arsene Lupin, Hercule Poirot, Mike Hammer, Miss Jane Marple, Perry Mason, Philip Marlowe, The Shadow, Sherlock Holmes and The Whistler. It also includes a number of screen gumshoes with brief movie careers, like C. Auguste Dupin, Father Brown, Kitty O'Day, Lew Archer, Lord Peter Wimsey, Thatcher Colt, Tony Rome, and Travis McGee, as well as, such TV detectives as Frank Cannon and Kojak.

Each chapter highlights a different detective, covering the character's films, the performers who played him or her, the character's image in other media (stage, radio, television, record-

ings, etc.), plus a detailed filmography and a bibliography of the fictional works about each detective. Illustrated with scores of photographs, this book includes additions and corrections to the base volume, FAMOUS MOVIE DETECTIVES.

"In a obvious attempt to create box office interest in a husband-and-wife sleuthing team, à la Nick and Nora Charles in the Thin Man features.

Columbia Pictures purchased the screen rights to the characters of Bill and Sally Reardon from William Collison's magazine stories and cast Joan Blondell as Sally and Melvyn Douglas as her husband in THERE'S ALWAYS A WOMAN. Blondell had previously been very good as the amateur detective nurse in MISS PINKERTON ('32). In this outing she is the wife of a private eye who is down on his luck, and as a result takes back his old job with the district attorney. When a society woman (Mary Astor) is murdered, Sally decides to aid Bill in investigating the case, and her hair-brained schemes get him into a great deal of hot water with his boss until Sally, by accident, ends up solving the case. *Variety* noted, "All the elements of first-rate cinema entertainment are present." Highlights of the feature included a very funny sequence where Sally get the third degree from the police, and the scene where Bill and Sally get tipsy. An interesting footnote to the film is that future screen siren Rita Hayworth was assigned an important supporting role, that of Sally's pal in the D.A.'s office, but most of her scenes were deleted upon the release of the picture. Apparently Hayworth was not available for the sequel, so her part was basically dropped. In 1939 Joan Blondell, Melvyn Douglas, and director Alexander Hall were reteamed for another comedy-mystery, THE AMAZING MR. WILLIAMS.

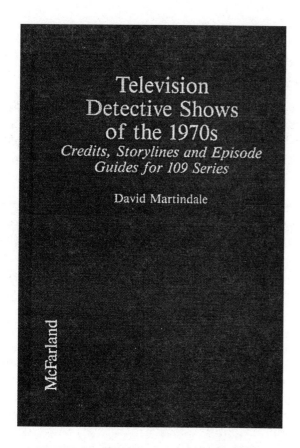

TELEVISION DETECTIVE SHOWS OF THE 1970S
ISBN 0-89950-557-0

TELEVISION DETECTIVE SHOWS OF THE 1970S Credits, Storylines and Episode Guides for 109 series by David Martindale, McFarland & Company, Inc., Publishers, Box 611, Jefferson, NC 28640.. I like books who's titles sum up what they do, on the other hand I've always liked TV shows who's theme song tells you the entire plot of the show "Lassie, Lassie, come home and save Johnny who has fallen in the stream, we'll all get together and have a nice birthday party, you get to blow out the candles and we'll all be happy – 26 minutes from now."

This title certainly falls into that category. Settle those arguments, win Trivial Pursuit or just peruse the TV guide with a practiced eye. A typical entry reads as follows:

"THE SNOOP SISTERS"
NBC. 90 minutes. On the air: Dec. 19, 1973. Off: Aug. 20, 1974. Broadcast history: Dec. 1973, Wednesday, 8:30–10:00 p.m. Eastern: Jan. 1974–Aug. 1974, Tuesday, 8:30-10 p.m. 4 episodes, preceded by 1 made-for-TV movie.
Cast: Ernesta Snoop (played by Helen Hayes), Gwendolyn Snoop (Mildred Natwick), Lieutenant Steve Ostrowski (Bert Convy), Barney (Lou Antonio). *Executive producer:* Leonard B. Stern, *Producer:* Tony Barrett. *Directors:* David Friedkin, Leonard J. Horn, Boris Sagal, Leonard B. Stern. *Writers:* Leonard B. Stern, Hugh Wheeler.
Production company: Universal Television

"Their names said it all: Ernsta and Gwendolyn Snoop, the Snoop Sisters, had a habit of sticking their noses where they didn't belong. Only you couldn't convince the old girls they weren't wanted. As they saw it, murder was their business. They were spinster mystery writers who felt perfectly at home with a body in the drawing room, be it fiction or the genuine article. And with a police lieutenant nephew who worked the homicide beat, real corpses sometimes outnumbered the imagined ones. Lieutenant Ostrowski tried his damnedest to keep his aunts out of trouble – even going so far as to hire Barney, an ex-con, to serve as their chauffeur-bodyguard – but our sibling Miss Marples refused to cooperate. This game of murder was just too much fun to be missed. And, besides, they always caught their killer."

"*The Snoop Sisters* was one of four rotating elements in the 1973-73 version of *The Wednesday Mystery Movies*, which shortly after its debut became *The Tuesday Mystery Movies*. Other segments were *Bancek*, *Tenafjy* and *Faraday and Company*."

NEW AND MISCELLANEOUS

Next, things that came in too late, or that I didn't find until it was too late to include them in the proper chapter.

1. There is now a service that uses satellites to track cellular phones. One would assume they use the area query feature to have the target phone respond a couple of times to get an exact fix on the person or vehicle carrying the phone.

Remember, you do not have to be using the phone in order for it to respond to an electronic "question" from the local cellular company, and three watts is enough for a satellite to track using direction antennas.

The service is open available only to government agents at this point.

2. A brand new device that uses GPS, Global Positioning Satellites to track a vehicle or package is on the market. Developed by Intelligence Support Group in cahoots with a "black" engineering section of a well-known electronics and chip manufacturer, the unit, at the present time is a trifle large for covert work – about the size of a cigar box, but it will no doubt shrink in subsequent models.

It seems logical to take a GPS unit, place the sensing receiver on a target vehicle, and then couple it to a transmitter in order to broadcast back the coordinates of the unit to it's own display unit.

The fly in the ointment here is that the transmitter would have to be so high powered, operating in either a continuous or occasional burst mode that it would not be FCC legal. It would also use a fair bit of power for continuous updating.

ISG has beaten this problem in a most clever fashion, their unit 'talks" to the host PC in your office or following vehicle by using the cellular phone network. The operator simply places a call and "asks" the unit where it is at the moment.

Great idea, I hope to show it in action on a video tape.

3. Brand new newsletter. I mean I ain't seen a copy yet 'cause it's not out. But, the publishers assure me, via a slick mailer, that it soon will be. Entitled SPECTRUM and available from Matrix Communications POB 16893, West Palm Beach, FL 33409, for $30 a year, it promises to be "a unique newsletter going above and beyond what similar publications only dare dream of attempting."

Okay...

Dealing with all aspects of electronic communication each issue will target a specific area of the spectrum – from DC to light. They also promise a full disclosure (little play on the competition here?) giving the reader previously "restricted" or "privileged" information on frequency allocations, equipment modifications, hacking secrets and "MORE!"

4. Reverse Engineering. I love this concept, it's so, so Japanese. See, if you have a particular piece of gear that you like, hell maybe you'd want to build a couple more just like it. You can send it to Bomarc Services POB 113, Casper, WY 82602.

They will tear it apart and provide you with a schematic which could then be used to build, or service your unit. They also offer a number of stock plans, many of which fall into the security/surveillance fields, which they have already "studied," including various bugs, taps, trackers, call guards and so on.

They will also arrange to buy or trade for interesting equipment.

5. IALEIA (INTERNATIONAL ASSOCIATION OF LAW ENFORCEMENT INTELLIGENCE ANALYSTS) is a group of, well, of people dedicated to the propagation of law enforcement and intelligence analysis.

Their literature includes committees on private security, training and accreditation. They will take on associate and corporate members.

Joining this organization will provide you with such benefits as the 3 times a year newsletter INTELSCOPE MAGAZINE which "sharpens the analyst's wits and analytical abilities" as well as a twice-yearly journal composed by fellow analysts consisting of techniques and procedures to enhance the craft. Contact them at POB 52-2924 Miami, FL 33152.

6. The SOFTWARE DETECTIVES at 800-667-6503, will attempt to find any software in the world. They search over 60,000 titles and average about $50 per search or $125 including product literature and a demo disk.

7. IRSC, covered elsewhere, is now also offering a 3 year, regularly updated, post office forwarding information database with instant response.

F I N I S H

And for those of you whom this book has totally depressed – you no longer feel a drive to go on living in a society where your life probably is an open book – the alternatives seem few and grim – I would like to offer a couple of final suggestions...

UNINHABITED OCEAN ISLANDS from Loompanics is an exact guide to the last vestiges of our society that have yet to see what a shopping center mall looks like. Longitude, latitude, a fairly thorough description of each island in question, what amenities it offers (like water, we're not talking paved roads here) who owns it and whether you can take up residence there.

Some are actually large, tropical, fairly inviting places like my favorite, Palmyra, which actually has its own airport from WWII, probably not real serviceable, a scenic bay, a nice history (including a famous murder case), coconuts, seagulls and beaches.

Oh yeah, and occasional entertainment, as the Russians operate a missile test firing range near the island.

Palmyra is owned by a Hawaiian family who never actually used it and have traditionally allowed anyone who wanted to sail there, to take up temporary residence,.

Then the US government decided it would make a perfect dumping ground for nuclear waste and tried to buy it, the owners swore they would sell cheap rather then see a great island turned into a 30,000 ton wasteland, so you could check it out, maybe make a deal with the owners...

Neighbors? The nearest neighbors, as well as the nearest grocery store, are 400 miles upwind on another island. Still.

Or, as a final solution I offer you membership in the COMMITTEE FOR IMMEDIATE NUCLEAR WAR, 2001 SW 9th Terrace Ft. Lauderdale, FL 33324. An organization that promotes global nuclear war as a solution to such problems as "boredom, soap operas and peddlers on 14th Street." They also support political candidates who promote immediate nuclear war and conduct seminars on the "beneficial effects of global nuclear war."

good hunting — lee

INDEX